Contents

How to use this guide

The **Map of principal sights** assists you in planning your visit by locating the city's major monuments and neighbourhoods, whilst the overleaf map *(p 7-9)* helps you discover lesser-known or off-beat sights, street markets, speciality shops...

The **Introduction** provides background information on history and the arts.

The **Paris at leisure** section offers an insider's look at Paris – its neighbourhoods, cafés, shops, entertainment venues and recreational facilities.

The main **Sights** section is divided into 43 chapters *(see alphabetical listing above)* that describe a neighbourhood or a key monument along with its surroundings; detailed area maps complement the texts. Cross references to the **Michelin plan of Paris (No. 11)** are given for each chapter heading. Brief descriptions of St-Denis, Versailles and Disneyland are also provided *(for complete descriptions of these and other excursions around Paris, consult the* Green Guide to Flanders, Picardy and the Paris Region *and the* Green Guide to Disneyland Paris*)*.

The clock symbol ☉ placed after sight names refers to the admission times and charges section in the **Practical information** section, where you will also find a wealth of travel tips, useful addresses as well as a calendar of events and a glossary of French terms.

The **Metro map** is found at the end of the guide for easy reference.

Bon voyage!

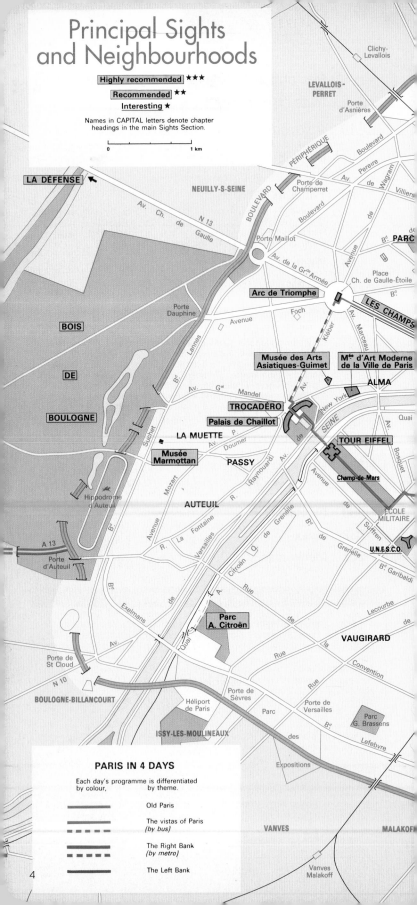

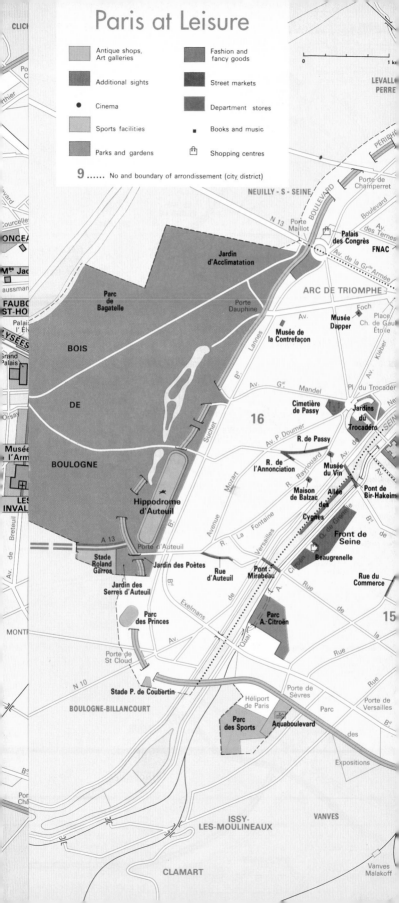

Paris at Leisure

Antique shops, Art galleries

Additional sights

Cinema

Sports facilities

Parks and gardens

Fashion and fancy goods

Street markets

Department stores

Books and music

Shopping centres

9 ...... No and boundary of arrondissement (city district)

0   1 km

LEVALL
PERRE

CLICK

Po
C

rthier

Courcelle

ONCEA

Mée Jac

aussman

FAUBO
ST-HO

Palai
l'Él

YSÉES

Grand
Palais

Orsay

Musée
l'Arm

LES
INVAL

Breteuil

Av. de

MONT

NEUILLY - S - SEINE

N 13   Porte
Maillot

Palais
des Congrès

FNAC

Av. de la Gr⁴ᵉ Armée

ARC DE TRIOMPHE

Jardin
d'Acclimatation

Parc
de
Bagatelle

Porte
Dauphine

BOIS

DE

BOULOGNE

Hippodrome
d'Auteuil

A 13

Porte d'Auteuil

Stade
Roland
Garros

Jardin des Poètes

Jardin des
Serres d'Auteuil

Parc
des Princes

Porte de
St Cloud

N 10

Stade P. de Coubertin

BOULOGNE-BILLANCOURT

Foch

Av.

Ch. de Gaul
Étoile

Place

Kléber

Musée
Dapper

Av.

Av.
des Ternes

Boulevard

PERIPH

Porte de
Champerret

Lannes

B⁴

Musée de
la Contrefaçon

Av.   G⁴ᵘ   Mandel

Suchet

16

Cimetière
de Passy

Av. P. Doumer

R. de Passy

R. de
l'Annonciation

R. Raynouard

Maison
de Balzac

Mozart

Avenue

La Fontaine

R.

Versailles

B⁴

Pl. du Trocadéro

Jardins
du
Trocadéro

SEIN

Musée
du Vin

Pont de
Bir-Hakeim

Allée
des
Cygnes

Cl. de Grenelle

Front de
Seine

Beaugrenelle

Rue
d'Auteuil

Pont
Mirabeau

B⁴

Exelmans

de

Quai

A

Rue
du Commerce

15

Rue

Parc
A.-Citroën

Av.

de

Rue

Héliport
de Paris

Porte de
Sèvres

Parc

Porte de
Versailles

B⁴

Parc
des Sports

Aquaboulevard

des

Exposition

B⁴

Por
Ch

ISSY-
LES-MOULINEAUX

VANVES

CLAMART

Vanves
Malakoff

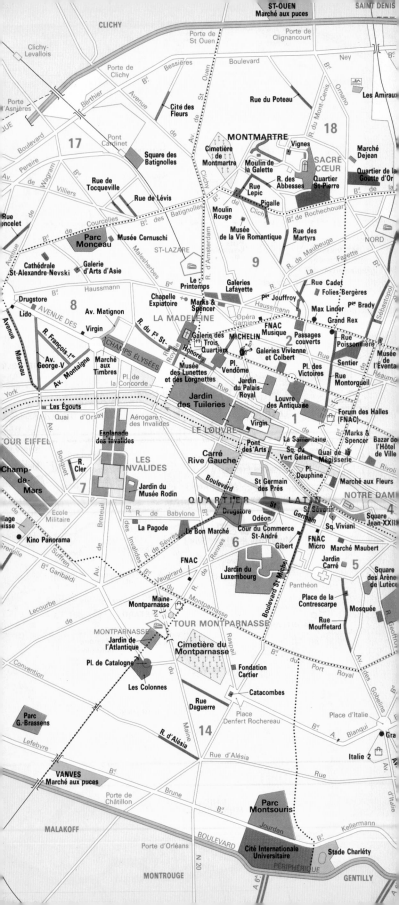

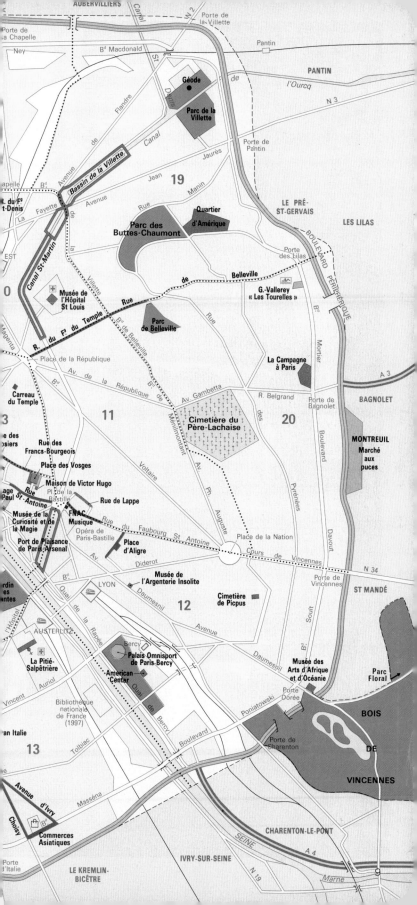

Introduction

History

Gallo-Roman period

3C BC	The Parisii settle on the Ile de la Cité.
52 BC	Labienus, Caesar's lieutenant, defeats the Gauls, under Camulogenes, who set fire to Ile de la Cité before fleeing.
1C AD	The Gallo-Romans build the city of Lutetia.
c 250	The martyrdom of St Denis, first Bishop of the city.
280	Lutetia destroyed by the Barbarians.
360	Julian the Apostate, prefect of the Gauls, is proclaimed by his soldiers Emperor of Rome when in the Cité. Lutetia becomes Paris.

Early Middle Ages

451	St Geneviève turns Attila away from Paris.
508	Clovis makes Paris his capital and settles in the Cité.
8C	Charlemagne makes Aix-la-Chapelle (Aachen) his foremost city. Paris, abandoned, declines.
885	Paris, besieged by the Normans for the fifth time, is defended by Count Eudes who is elected King of France in 888.

The Capetians

Early 12C	Abelard first studies, then teaches, in Paris. Suger, Abbot of St-Denis and minister under Louis VI and Louis VII, rebuilds the abbey.
1163	Maurice of Sully undertakes the construction of Notre-Dame.
1180-1223	Philippe Auguste erects a wall around Paris and builds the Louvre.
1215	Foundation of the University of Paris.
1226-1270	Reign of Louis IX: Pierre of Montreuil builds the Sainte-Chapelle, works on Notre-Dame and St-Denis. The king dispenses justice at Vincennes.
1253	Foundation of a college by Sorbon, later known as the Sorbonne.
1260	The dean of the Merchants' Guild becomes Provost of Paris.
1307	Philip the Fair dissolves the Order of the Knights Templar.

The Valois

1337	Beginning of the Hundred Years War. The death of Philip the Fair and his three sons ('the cursed kings') resulted in a problem of succession: Philip the Fair's nephew, Philip de Valois, preferred by the French barons over his grandson, Edward II, King of England. The following century marked by battles between the English and the French who laid claim to the French Crown, between the Armagnacs, supporters of the family of Orléans, and the Burgundians, supporters of the dukes of Burgundy.
1358	Uprising under Étienne Marcel. The monarchy moves to the Marais and the Louvre.
1364-1380	Charles V builds the Bastille and a new wall around Paris.
1407	Duke Louis of Orleans is assassinated on the orders of John the Fearless.
1408-1420	Fighting between the Armagnacs and the Burgundians. Paris handed over to the English.
1429	Charles VII besieges Paris in vain; Joan of Arc is wounded at the St-Honoré gate.
1430	Henry VI of England is crowned King of France in Notre-Dame.
1437	Charles VII recaptures Paris.
1469	The first French printing works opens in the Sorbonne.
1530	François I founds the Collège de France.
1534	Ignatius Loyola founds the Society of Jesus in Montmartre.
1559	Henri II is fatally wounded in a tourney.
1572	St Bartholomew's Day Massacre.
1578-1604	Construction of the Pont Neuf.
1588	The Catholic League turns against Henri III who is forced to flee Paris, after the Day of the Barricades (12 May).
1589	Paris is invested by Henri III and Henri of Navarre. The former is assassinated at St-Cloud.

The Bourbons

1594	Henri IV converts to Catholicism; Paris opens her gates to him.
1605	Creation of the place des Vosges.
14 May 1610	Henri IV is mortally wounded by Ravaillac.
1615-1625	Marie de' Medici has the Luxembourg Palace built.
1622	Paris becomes an episcopal see.
1627-1664	Development of the Ile St-Louis.

The marriage of Marie de' Medici to Henri IV (detail) by Rubens

1635	Richelieu founds the Académie Française.
1648-1653	Paris disturbed by the Fronde.
1661	Mazarin founds the College of Four Nations, the future Institut de France.
1667	Colbert establishes the Observatoire and restructures the Gobelins Tapestry Works.
17C	Construction of Versailles; development of the Marais.
Late 17C	Erection of the Louvre Colonnade and the Invalides.
Early 18C	Construction of the place Vendôme and development of the Faubourg-St-Germain.
1717-1720	John Law's Bank.
1722	Institution of the first Fire Brigade.
1727-1732	End of the Jansenist crisis; the St Medard "Convulsionnaires".
c 1760	Louis XV has the École Militaire, the Panthéon and the place de la Concorde constructed.
1783	First balloon 'flights' by Pilâtre de Rozier, and Charles and Robert.
1783	Treaty of Versailles: independance of 13 American States.
1784-1791	Erection of the Farmers General Wall including the gateways and tollhouses by Ledoux.

Bust of Louis XIV by Bernini

The Revolution and the First Empire

14 July 1789	Taking of the Bastille.
17 July 1789	Louis XVI at the Hôtel de Ville: adoption of the tricolour.
14 July 1790	Festival of Federation.
20 June 1792	The mob invades the Tuileries.
10 Aug. 1792	Taking of the Tuileries and the fall of the monarchy.
2-4 Sept. 1792	September Massacres.
21 Sept. 1792	Proclamation of the Republic.
21 Jan. 1793	Execution of Louis XVI.
1793	Opening of the Louvre Museum and the institution of the National Natural History Museum.
1793-1794	The Terror.
8 June 1794	Festival of the Supreme Being.
5 Oct. 1795	Royalist uprising suppressed by Napoleon.
9-10 Nov. 1799	Fall of the Directory.
1800	Bonaparte creates the offices of Prefect of the Seine and of the Police.
2 Dec. 1804	Napoleon's coronation at Notre-Dame.
1806-1814	Napoleon continues construction of the Louvre and erects the Arc de Triomphe and Vendôme Column. Stay at Malmaison.
31 March 1814	The Allies occupy Paris.

The Restoration

1815	Waterloo. Restoration of the Bourbons.
1821-1825	Construction of the Ourcq, St-Denis and St-Martin Canals.
1830	Fall of Charles X; flight to the Palace of Holyroodhouse.
1832	A cholera epidemic kills 19 000 Parisians.
1837	The first French railway line links Paris with St-Germain.
1840	Return of Napoleon's ashes from St Helena.
1841-1845	Construction of the Thiers fortifications.
February 1848	Fall of Louis-Philippe; proclamation of the Second Republic.

Victor Hugo

From 1848 to 1870

June 1848	The suppression of the national workshops creates disturbances in the Faubourg-St-Antoine.
1852-1870	Gigantic town planning undertakings by Baron Haussmann: the Halles, railway stations, Buttes-Chaumont, Bois de Boulogne and Vincennes, the Opéra, the sewers, completion of the Louvre, laying of the boulevards through the old quarters. Paris is divided into 20 *arrondissements*.
1855-1867	World Exhibitions.
4 Sept. 1870	The Third Republic is proclaimed at the Hôtel de Ville.

Baron Haussmann

The Third Republic

Winter 1870-1871	Paris is besieged by the Prussians and capitulates. Napoleon III goes into exile in England.
March-May 1871	The Paris Commune is finally suppressed by the Men of Versailles during the Bloody Week (21-28 May); fire, destruction (Tuileries, Old Auditor General's Office, Hôtel de Ville, Vendôme Column) and massacres.
1885	State funeral of Victor Hugo.
1889	World Exhibition at the foot of the new Eiffel Tower.
1892	First multi-storey building constructed of reinforced concrete.
1900	First *métro* line in operation between Maillot and Vincennes. The Grand and Petit Palais are built. Cubism is born at the Bateau-Lavoir. The Sacré-Cœur Basilica is erected on the Butte Montmartre.
1914-1918	Paris under threat of German attack is saved by the Battle of the Marne. A shell hits the Church of St-Gervais-St-Protais.
1920	Interment of the Unknown Soldier.
1927	Inauguration of Monet's *Nymphéas* series at the Orangerie.
February 1934	Riots around the Chamber of Deputies.
June 1940	Paris is bombed then occupied by the Germans. Hostages and resistance fighters detained at Mont Valérien (Suresnes).
19-25 Aug. 1944	Liberation of Paris.
1950	Opening of the downstream port of Gennevilliers.

The Fifth Republic

1958-1963	Construction of the UNESCO HQs, CNIT, and ORTF/Maison de Radio-France buildings.
1965	Paris region Town and Development Plan published.
May 1968	Strikes and demonstrations: Nanterre, Latin Quarter, the Boulevards, the Champs-Élysées.
1969	Transfer of the wholesale markets from the Halles to Rungis.
1970	Réseau Express Régional (RER) in operation to complement the Metro system. Thirteen autonomous universities created in the Paris Region.
1973	Completion of the boulevard Périphérique (ring road) and Montparnasse Tower.
February 1974	Opening of the Palais des Congrès.
25 March 1977	The first election of a mayor of Paris (J Chirac), 11 predecessors between 1789 and 1871 having been appointed rather than elected.
1977	Inauguration of the Centre George Pompidou.
May-June 1980	Official visit of Pope John Paul II.
1986	Inauguration of the Orsay Museum.
1989	The opening of the Louvre Pyramid, Grande Arche at la Défense and Opéra-Bastille overlap with bicentenary celebrations.
1995	Jacques Chirac is elected president
1996	Bibliothèque Nationale opens at Tolbiac.

Urban growth

The capital's site was carved out of the limestone and Tertiary sands by the Seine which flowed at a level of 35m – 100ft, above its present course.

The Gallo-Roman Wall: ◆ – The Parisii, taking advantage of the *Pax romana*, emerged from Lutetia, built by the Gauls and defended by the river and surrounding swamps, to settle along the Left Bank of the river. The Barbarians later forced them to retreat to the Cité (*c*276). On the island, they built houses, fortifications and a rampart wall to defend themselves against future invasions.

The Philippe Auguste Wall: ◆ – Between the 6C and 10C, the swamps were drained and cultivated, monasteries founded and a river harbour established near the place de Grève. Between 1180 and 1210 Philippe Auguste ordered that a massive wall be built, reinforced upstream by a chain barrage across the river and downstream by the Louvre Fortress and Nesle Tower.

The Charles V Rampart: ◆ – The Town, which was on the Right Bank (as opposed to the University on the Left Bank, and the Cité), prospered as roads were built connecting it with Montmartre, St-Denis, the Knights Templar Commandery and the castle at Vincennes. By the end of the 14C, Charles V had erected new fortifications, supported in the east by the Bastille. The ramparts enclosed a Paris of just under 440ha – 1 3/4sq miles and counting 150 000 inhabitants.

The Louis XIII Wall: ◆ – Throughout the 16C, the Wars of Religion and the siege by Henri of Navarre maintained a threat on the city, forcing Charles IX and Louis XIII to extend the 14C wall westwards to include the Louvre Palace.

The Farmers General Wall: ◆ – The monarchy moved to Versailles as Paris encroached upon the surrounding countryside, its population 500 000 strong. The Invalides, Observatory, Salpêtrière, St-Denis and St-Martin Gates were erected; new city confines were required, calling for a new wall (1784-1791) complete with 57 **toll-houses** to be designed by Ledoux.

The Thiers Fortifications: ◆ – During the Revolution many of the larger estates were broken up but little was built. Under the Empire, Paris faced problems of overcrowding and supply. The Restoration encouraged great industrial developments and social change: gas lighting was installed in the streets, and the railway allowed for growth and economic development in outlying villages (Austerlitz, Montrouge, Vaugirard, Passy, Montmartre, Belleville). Thiers determined the capital's perimeter with another wall (1841-45), reinforced at a cannon-ball's distance by 16 bastions, the official city confines from 1859. Subsequently, twenty *arrondissements* were created in the 7 800ha – 30sq miles, as Haussmann began his transformation of the city (Population – 1846: 1 050 000; 1866: 1 800 000).

The present limits: ◆ – The forts remained intact (Mont Valérien, Romainville, Ivry, Bagneux...), but the walls, after serving in the city's defence in 1871, were razed by the Third Republic in 1919. Between 1925 and 1930 the confines of the city are re-defined to include the Bois de Boulogne and Bois de Vincennes, but not extending elsewhere beyond a narrow circular belt to give an overall surface area of 10 540ha – 40 3/4sq miles, for a population, in 1945, of 2 700 000.

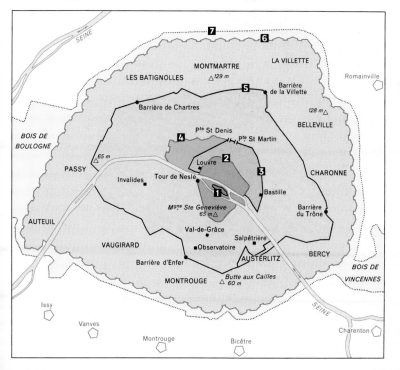

Art

ABC OF ARCHITECTURE

To assist readers unfamiliar with the terminology employed in architecture, we describe below the most commonly used terms, which we hope will make their visits to ecclesiastical, military and civil buildings more interesting.

Ecclesiastical architecture

illustration I ▶

Ground plan: The more usual Catholic form is based on the outline of a cross with the two arms of the cross forming the transept: ① Porch – ② Narthex – ③ Side aisles (sometimes double) – ④ Bay (transverse section of the nave between 2 pillars) – ⑤ Side chapel (often predates the church) – ⑥ Transept crossing – ⑦ Arms of the transept, sometimes with a side doorway – ⑧ Chancel, nearly always facing east towards Jerusalem; the chancel often vast in size was reserved for the monks in abbatial churches – ⑨ High altar – ⑩ Ambulatory: in pilgrimage churches the aisles were extended round the chancel, forming the ambulatory, to allow the faithful to file past the relics – ⑪ Radiating or apsidal chapel – ⑫ Axial chapel. In churches which are not dedicated to the Virgin this chapel, in the main axis of the building, is often consecrated to the Virgin (Lady Chapel) – ⑬ Transept chapel.

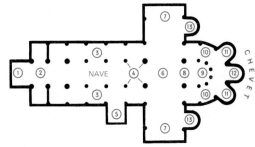

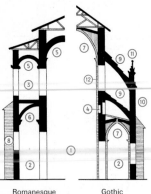

◀ illustration II

Cross-section: ① Nave – ② Aisle – ③ Tribune or gallery – ④ Triforium – ⑤ Barrel vault – ⑥ Half-barrel vault – ⑦ Pointed vault – ⑧ Buttress – ⑨ Flying buttress – ⑩ Pier of a flying buttress – ⑪ Pinnacle – ⑫ Clerestory window.

Romanesque   Gothic

◀ illustration III

Gothic cathedral: ① Porch – ② Gallery – ③ Rose window – ④ Belfry (sometimes with a spire) – ⑤ Gargoyle acting as a waterspout for the roof gutter – ⑥ Buttress – ⑦ Pier of a flying buttress (abutment) – ⑧ Flight or span of flying buttress – ⑨ Double-course flying buttress – ⑩ Pinnacle – ⑪ Side chapel – ⑫ Radiating or apsidal chapel – ⑬ Clerestory windows – ⑭ Side doorway – ⑮ Gable – ⑯ Pinnacle – ⑰ Spire over the transept crossing.

◀ illustration IV

Groined vaulting:
① Main arch –
② Groin –
③ Transverse arch.

illustration V ▶

Oven vault: termination of a barrel vaulted nave.

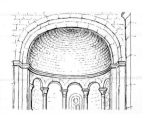

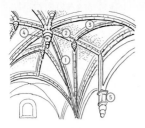

illustration VI
Lierne and tierceron vaulting: ① Diagonal – ② Lierne – ③ Tierceron – ④ Pendant – ⑤ Corbel.

illustration VII
Quadripartite vaulting: ① Diagonal – ② Transverse – ③ Stringer – ④ Flying buttress – ⑤ Keystone.

▼ illustration VIII

Doorway: ① Archivolt. Depending on the architectural style of the building this can be rounded, pointed, basket-handled, ogee or even adorned by a gable – ② Arching, coving (with string courses, mouldings, carvings or adorned with statues). Recessed arches or orders form the archivolt – ③ Tympanum – ④ Lintel – ⑤ Archshafts – ⑥ Embrasures. Arch shafts, splaying sometimes adorned with statues or columns – ⑦ Pier (often adorned by a statue) – ⑧ Hinges and other ironwork.

illustration IX ▶
Arches and pillars: ① Ribs or ribbed vaulting – ② Abacus – ③ Capital – ④ Shaft – ⑤ Base – ⑥ Engaged column – ⑦ Pier – ⑧ Lintel – ⑨ Discharging or relieving arch – ⑩ Frieze.

Military architecture

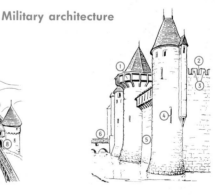

illustration X
Fortified enclosure: ① Hoarding (projecting timber gallery) – ② Machicolations (corbelled crenellations) – ③ Barbican – ④ Keep or donjon – ⑤ Covered watchpath – ⑥ Curtain wall – ⑦ Outer curtain wall – ⑧ Postern.

illustration XI
Towers and curtain walls: ① Hoarding – ② Crenellations – ③ Merlon – ④ Loophole or arrow slit – ⑤ Curtain wall – ⑥ Bridge or drawbridge.

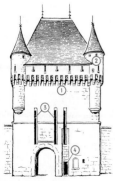

◀ illustration XII
Fortified gatehouse:
① Machicolations – ② Watch turrets or bartizan – ③ Slots for the arms of the drawbridge – ④ Postern.

illustration XIII ▶
Star fortress: ① Entrance – ② Drawbridge – ③ Glacis – ④ Ravelin or half-moon – ⑤ Moat – ⑥ Bastion – ⑦ Watch turret – ⑧ Town – ⑨ Assembly area.

17

ART AND ARCHITECTURAL TERMS USED IN THE GUIDE

Acanthus: broad-leaf plant inspiring Classical motif applied to capitals and friezes.

Aisle: *see illustration I.*

Altarpiece or **retable**: *see illustration XVIII.*

Ambulatory: *see illustration I.*

Apsidal or **radiating chapel**: *see illustration I.*

Archivolt: *see illustration VIII.*

Axial or **Lady Chapel**: *see illustration I.*

Baldaquin: canopy over an altar, often supported by twisted or 'barley-sugar' columns as at St Peter's in Rome.

Baluster: upright member supporting handrail or balustrade.

Barrel or **tunnel vaulting**: *see illustration II.*

Basket arch: depressed arch common to late-medieval and Renaissance architecture.

Bay: *see illustration I.*

illustration XVIII
Altar with retable or altarpiece:
① Retable or altarpiece –
② Predella – ③ Crowning piece –
④ Altar-table –
⑤ Altar front

Bishop's throne: Gothic chair with a high back.

Blind arcading: sequences of arches, sometimes intersecting, applied to a blank wall for decorative effect.

Boss: decorated keystone at junction of ribs.

Buttress: *see illustrations II and III.*

Capital: *see illustration IX.*

Caryatid/Atlas: female/male figure used as a column to support frieze or balcony; *see illustration XVI.*

Chevet: Rounded east end of a church with radiating chapels for the cult of saints; *see illustration I.*

Clerestory: section of structural elevation with windows; *see illustrations II and III.*

Coffered ceiling: vault or ceiling decorated with sunken panels as found in Classical Antiquity (Pantheon in Rome).

Corbel: *see illustration VI.*

Cradle vaulting: *see illustration II.*

Crypt: underground sanctuary or chapel below main body of church.

Curtain wall: *see illustration XI.*

Depressed arch: flattened semicircular arch sometimes called a basket arch.

Diagonal arch: *see illustrations VI and VII.*

Dome: *see illustrations XIV and XV.*

Exedra: niche, usually semicircular, with a bench around the wall.

Ex-Voto: object or memento dedicated to a patron saint in thanks (for marriage, birth of a child) or in memory of a dead loved one (drowned sailor, lost soldier).

Faience: tin-or lead-glazed (white) earthenware, overglazed with colour.

Festoon or garland: decorative feature of a painted or sculpted panel.

Flamboyant: latest phase (15C) of French Gothic architecture; name taken from the undulating (flame-like) lines of the window tracery.

Flame ornament: flaming urn or vase decoration used in Classical art.

Flèche: small slender wooden spire sometimes covered in lead, over transept crossing – feature of French Gothic style; *see illustration III.*

Fluting: column or pilaster ornamented with vertical shallow grooving.

Flying buttress: stone arch directing lateral thrust from main wall to external pier developed in Gothic architecture. A pinnacle increases structural stability.

Foliated scrolls: sculptural or painted decoration of stylised foliage, often in a frieze.

Folly: ornamental building constructed as a feature in a landscaped garden or park with no functional purpose. Fashionable during the 18C, they reflected a taste in revival architecture ('Classical' temples, 'Gothic' arbours, 'Chinese' pagodas).

Fresco: mural painting applied to wet plaster.

Gable: triangular part of an end wall carrying a sloping roof; the term is also applied to the steeply pitched ornamental pediments of Gothic architecture; *see illustration III.*

◀ illustration XIV
Dome on squinches:
① Octagonal dome –
② Squinch – ③ Arches of transept crossing

illustration XV ▶
Dome on pendentives:
① Circular dome –
② Pendentive – ③ Arches of transept crossing

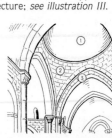

Gallery: *see illustrations II and III.*

Gargoyle: *see illustration III.*

Groined vaulting: *see illustration IV.*

High relief: deeply cut or carved surface.

Hypocaust: an underground furnace to heat the water for the baths or rooms of a house.

Keep or **donjon**: *see illustration X.*

Keystone: *see illustration VII.*

Lierne: short rib connecting two main ribs in Gothic vaulting; *see illustration VI.*

Lintel: *see illustrations VIII and IX.*

Lombard arcades: decorative blind arcading composed of small arches and intervening pilaster strips; typical of Romanesque architecture in Lombardy and assimilated into Gothic.

Low relief: bas-relief shallow carving applied to a surface.

Machicolations: *see illustrations X and XII.*

Moat: ditch dug around fortified building for defensive purposes.

Modillion: small console supporting a cornice.

Mullion: a vertical section dividing window area.

Nave: *see illustration I.*

Niello: blackened surface applied to engraved silver.

Organ: *see illustration XVI.*

Oven vaulting: half-dome of apse; *see illustration V.*

Overhang or **jetty**: overhanging upper storey.

Ovolo moulding: egg-shaped frieze decoration in Classical entablature.

Peristyle: a range of columns surrounding or on the façade of a building.

Pier: *see illustrations II and III.*

Pietà: Italian term designating the Virgin Mary mourning the dead Christ across her knees.

Pilaster: engaged rectangular column.

Pinnacle: *see illustrations II and III.*

Porch: *see illustrations I and III.*

Portico: a Classical colonnaded space in front of a façade or in an interior courtyard.

Postern: *see illustrations X and XII.*

Predella: painted horizontal panel suspended from central section of an altarpiece.

Quadripartite or **four-part vaulting**: *see illustration VII.*

Recessed tomb: niche accommodating gravestone or tomb.

Reliquary: ornately fashioned container of a sacred relic (bones, fragment of the Holy Cross, thorn from the Crown of Thorns).

Roodscreen: open screen, often richly painted or carved, separating areas reserved for clergy (chancel) and laity (nave).

Rose or **wheel window**: *see illustration III.*

Rustication: large blocks of masonry often separated by deep joints and given bold textures (rock-faced, diamond-pointed...); commonly employed during the Renaissance.

Spire: *see illustration III.*

Splay: a slope, applied usually to the sides of a door or a window; *see illustration VIII.*

Stalls: *see illustration XVII.*

Stucco: mixture of powdered marble, plaster and strong glue; carved or moulded into relief ornamentation.

Tracery: intersecting stone rib-work of windows articulating panels of glass (usually Gothic).

Transept: *see illustration I.*

Transverse arch: *see illustration VII.*

Triforium: passageway below clerestory (Romanesque); *see illustration II.*

Triptych: three-part altarpiece comprising a central panel with hinged wings.

Voussoir: wedge-shaped masonry forming an arch or a vault.

Watch-path or **wall walk**: *see illustration X.*

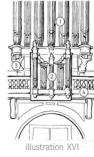

illustration XVI

Organ:
① Great organ case –
② Little organ case –
③ Caryatids – ④ Loft

illustration XVII

Stalls: ① High back –
② Elbow rest –
③ Cheek-piece –
④ Misericord

illustration XIX ▶

Renaissance ornament:
① Shell – ② Vase – ③ Follage –
④ Dragon – ⑤ Nude child –
⑥ Cherub – ⑦ Cornucopia –
⑧ Satyr

ARCHITECTURE

Little Gallo-Roman building survives in Paris. A few cradle-vaulted arches still stand in the Roman baths at the Hôtel de Cluny, but what remains of the Lutetia arena has been so heavily restored as to be of little archeological interest.

Romanesque – This style, known in England as Norman, is better represented elsewhere in France than in Paris. Isolated elements include the chancel columns and belfry-porch at St-Germain-des-Prés, the apse of St-Martin-des-Champs, and the odd capital in St-Pierre-de-Montmartre and St-Aignan Chapel.

Gothic – The Paris region (Ile de France) is the cradle of Gothic architecture, born from a need for large-scale churches as tall and as light as possible. Its development evolved from the use of the ogive or pointed arch and the groin vault (St-Germain-des-Prés chancel), whose thrust and weight were contained by side aisles and external buttressing (St-Julien-le-Pauvre apse). The solid piers in time were whittled down to elegant and decorative flying buttresses.

Early Gothic (12C) – Notre-Dame Cathedral best shows the transition of building technique and style from the 12C to early 14C: the vast chancel, slightly projecting transept and the dark triforium gallery are typical of early Gothic. Naturalistic organic decoration based upon plants indigenous to the Paris basin adorn the capitals. Limited amounts of light permeate small narrow windows in the nave, later incorporating small round windows or oculi at the transept crossing.

High or Rayonnant Gothic (13C-14C) – During the reign of Louis IX, structural engineering reached new heights, notably with Pierre of Montreuil. Huge expanses of glass replaced solid masonry, allowing a profusion of light to flood the soaring internal space. Slender piers support the vault, reinforced externally by unobtrusive buttressing or flying buttresses (the St-Martin-des-Champs refectory). Altogether, the new structural design broadened opportunities for stained glass.
The chevet of Notre-Dame, Sainte-Chapelle and the Royal Chapel at Vincennes together epitomise the noblest expression of **High Gothic**. It is this style, in particular, that was assimilated in England at Canterbury and London (St Stephen's, Westminster). The outbreak of the Hundred Years War (1337-1453) between the Burgundians and the Armagnacs, combined with more local unrest provoked by Étienne Marcel, stunted the development of civil architecture which continued to be defensive and sombre, almost feudal in style (the Bastille and Men at Arms Hall in the Conciergerie).

Late or Flamboyant Gothic (15C) – The Gothic style continued into the 15C tending towards a proliferation of exaggerated decoration for its own sake: an excess of liernes and tiercerons articulate vaulting (St Merri transept, St-Germain-l'Auxerrois porch); window tracery evolves into playful flame motifs; the triforium is eliminated making way for the ever taller clerestory; piers run the full height of the elevation, exploding into ribs unbroken by capitals (St-Séverin ambulatory); eventually exaggeratedly decorative vault bosses hang from the roof (St-Étienne-du-Mont).
The Tour St-Jacques and the Billettes cloister are examples of the style applied to buildings other than churches, being built at the same time as the Hôtel de Sens and Hôtel de Cluny. In domestic architecture, however, defensive features – turrets, crenellations, wicket gates – are transformed into decorative features trimmed with richly sculpted elements, balustrades, mullioned dormer windows – as in the early châteaux of the Loire.

The Renaissance – War with Italy led to a familiarity with and taste for the Antique and its profane decoration. Ogive vaults were replaced by cradle or coffered roofs (St-Nicolas-des-Champs); rounded arches (St-Eustache) are supported by fluted columns crowned with Ionic or Corinthian capitals (St-Médard).
The roodscreen at St-Étienne-du-Mont is the finest complete example of Renaissance design, which elsewhere includes mythological and profane motifs (St-Gervais stalls).
Pierre Lescot introduced from Italy the continuous façade broken by projecting bays with semicircular pediments (Cour Carrée in the Louvre, Hôtel Lamoignon). Statues nestle in niches between fluted pilasters; cornice and frieze articulate floor levels and doorways, while inside, ceilings are frequently coffered (Henri II staircase in the Clock Pavilion of the Louvre).

Classical architecture – At the end of the Wars of Religion (1562-1589), the inspiration of the Antique increased as the king reasserted his power.
17C and 18C ecclesiastical buildings were modelled on Classical prototypes, designed with columns, pediments, statues and cupolas reminiscent of the churches of Rome.
Paris' skyline, peppered with domes, owes much to the Jesuit style of the Counter-Reformation. The rounded profiles of St-Joseph-des-Carmes, the Sorbonne, Val-de-Grâce, St-Paul-St-Louis represent the way this favourite of Roman Baroque elements was assimilated by the architects of Louis XIV and XV – Hardouin-Mansart (Invalides, St Roch), Libéral-Bruant (Salpêtrière), Le Vau (St-Louis-en-l'Ile), Soufflot (Panthéon).
Civil buildings were modelled on Versailles, shaped by Classical symmetry and line. The purest Louis XIII style is typified by the alternate use of brick and stone (place des Vosges, place Dauphine); Salomon de Brosse blends French and Italian features (Luxembourg Palace) while Mansart, Androuet Du Cerceau, Delamair and Le Muet evolved in the Marais, a distinctive design for the Parisian town house or *hôtel*.

More grandiose projects in the Classical style were fashioned by Perrault (Louvre Colonnade), Le Vau (Institut de France) and Gabriel (place de la Concorde, École Militaire) between 1650 and 1750. Later, under Louis XVI, taste moved towards the more elegant simplicity of the Antique (Palais de la Légion d'Honneur) as epitomised by Ledoux (Farmers General Wall toll-houses), many of whose architectural projects were never built.

Second Empire and innovation – The Empire and Restoration is not marked by any significant architectural achievements: the Madeleine, the Arc de Triomphe and the Arc de Triomphe du Carrousel are mere pastiches of the Antique. With the Second Empire, however, Paris was irrevocably altered by Baron Haussmann's massive urban planning programme and the new application of cast iron in construction. The technique of cladding metallic sub-structures was refined by Baltard (St Augustin, Pavillon Baltard at Nogent-sur-Marne), Labrouste (Bibliothèque Ste-Geneviève), and Hittorff (Gare du Nord); a celebration of the new building method is epitomised in Gustave Eiffel's Tower.

The Opéra-Garnier is perhaps the finest stone edifice of the period which is otherwise less preoccupied with monumental than with residential building developments. For the first time, architects collaborated with structural engineers to design ever more economical and functional designs using industrially manufactured, therefore cheaper, materials (cast iron, plate-glass, artificial stone) and improved building methods. Whilst the Grand and Petit Palais, Pont Alexandre-III and Sacré-Cœur are backward-looking in inspiration, the théâtre des Champs-Elysées (Frères Perret), Palais de Chaillot and Palais de Tokyo, fashioned in reinforced concrete, look forwards to the modern age.

Contemporary developments – Since 1945, under the influence of Le Corbusier (Fondation, Cité Universitaire), architectural design has undergone a fundamental reappraisal. The result is a wide variety of form (Maison Radio-France), style (UNESCO) and line (CNIT). The most recent modern trend is for glass and aluminium clad buildings (Tours GAN and Manhattan, Centre Georges Pompidou, Institut du Monde Arabe), visually so distinctive from those in pre-stressed concrete (Palais des Congrès, Tour Montparnasse).

Current projects fall within the wider context of town planning, with new buildings designed as a part of a large scheme integral to the renovation of an area (Maine-Montparnasse, Les Halles, La Villette) or to the creation of a whole new space (La Défense, Tolbiac). Among the most recent developments are the Opéra-Bastille, the Finance Ministry in Bercy, Cité de la Musique at La Villette, the Grande Arche at La Défense, the Bibliothèque Nationale at Tolbiac.

La Défense

Modern buildings to look out for

Forum des Halles, Centre Georges-Pompidou, Cité des Sciences et de l'Industrie and the nearby Cité de la Musique (la VILLETTE), Institut du Monde Arabe, Opéra Bastille, Pyramide du Louvre, the CNIT and the Grande Arche (la DEFENSE), Palais Omnisports, Ministère des Finances, American Center at Bercy and the Bibliothèque de France in Tolbiac (BERCY), La Fondation Cartier near the place Denfert-Rochereau (MONTPARNASSE), and the plastic reflective forms of Le Ponant apartment block built on the site of the old Citroën car factory (VAUGIRARD).

SCULPTURE

The Gallo-Roman pillar of the Paris boatmen now at the Musée Cluny (see LATIN QUARTER) is the capital's oldest sculpture. Low reliefs and statues carved 1 000 years later by skilled anonymous craftsmen for Notre-Dame and other churches also tell their own story.

Over a period of three centuries following the Renaissance, the monarchy endowed Paris with many sumptuous religious and civil monuments sculpted by the greatest craftsmen: Jean Goujon (Fontaine des Innocents), Germain Pilon (St-Paul-St-Louis), Girardon (Richelieu's tomb), Coysevox (Tuileries Gardens), Coustou (The Marly Horses), Robert Le Lorrain (Hôtel de Rohan), Bouchardon (Fontaine des Quatre Saisons), Pigalle (St-Sulpice). It was not, however, until the mid and late 19C that Paris became gradually transformed into an open air sculptural museum with parks, gardens, squares and street corners populated with figures by Carpeaux (Observatory Fountain) and Rude (Marshal Ney, the Marseillaise), by Rodin (Balzac, Victor Hugo), Dalou (Place de la Nation), Bourdelle (Palais de Tokyo, Théâtre des Champs-Élysées), Maillol (Jardins des Tuileries) and Landowski (Ste-Geneviève on Pont de la Tournelle). Hector Guimard epitomised the style of 1900 in his famous wrought-iron métro entrances as Calder's mobile (see les INVALIDES – UNESCO), Louis Leygue, Agam (La Défense) and Arman's (St-Lazare Station) sculptures symbolise the work of the 20C abstractionists now appearing in parks and in new urban schemes.

PAINTING

An idea of medieval Paris may be gleaned from miniature painting and engravings. The first signed topographical representations of Paris appear as background vignettes in the Very Rich Hours of the Duc de Berry by the **Limbourg brothers** and **Jean Fouquet**'s Book of Hours painted for Étienne Chevalier.

Almost completely ignored during the Wars of Religion, the first detailed landscape paintings appear during the reigns of Henri IV and Louis XIII, prompted perhaps by Dutch painters who painted the banks of the Seine, the Pont Neuf and the sleepy countryside around the Invalides and the Observatory. As engravings became popular, J-B Raguenet, Hubert Robert, Antoine de Machy, later Bouhot and Georges Michel, and finally Méryon with his deeply toned water-colours, developed a pre-Romantic style which bridges the 17C to the late 19C, when the Impressionists emerged and made Paris the world art centre.

Corot, who painted the Paris quaysides and Ville d'Avray a few miles away, was followed by **Jongkind**, Lépine, **Monet** (St-Germain-l'Auxerrois, Gare St-Lazare), **Renoir** (Moulin de la Galette, Moulin Rouge), **Sisley** (Ile St-Louis, Auteuil Viaduct) and **Pissarro** (The Pont Neuf) who depicted light effects in the capital at all hours and in all seasons. The list continues with **Seurat** (The Eiffel Tower), **Gauguin** (The Seine by the Pont d'Iéna), **Cézanne** and **Van Gogh** (Montmartre scenes) and **Vuillard** who painted the peace of Paris squares and gardens in a more poetic vein; each celebrates his personal vision of Paris.

Toulouse-Lautrec portrayed a totally different view of Paris life by sketching cabaret artists before and behind the footlights with wit and intimacy; André Gill, Forain, Willette and Poulbot portrayed not Paris but the Parisian, whether a music-hall artist, politician, pierrot or street urchin.

During the first decades of the 20C, Paris was the international epicentre of art, attracting foreign artists (Picasso, Modigliani, Chagall, Soutine) to the Paris School and providing inspiration to all; the Bateau-Lavoir (see MONTMARTRE) and la Ruche (see VAUGIRARD) hummed with talk about art, theory and expression.

Among those completely devoted to painting the Paris city-scapes and social scenes were Marquet, who enjoyed a panoramic view of the city from his window, and **Maurice Utrillo** who painted the unfashionable areas, the grey skies and his beloved Montmartre. More modern depictions of Paris rendered familiar through reproductions are by Yves Brayer and Bernard Buffet.

PHOTOGRAPHY

The pride and love Parisians have for Paris have also inspired her photographers: when the invention of photography was presented to the Institut de France on 7 January 1839, it was done with daguerréotypes of Paris. When these same images were exhibited in Vienna with much success, they were praised for their minute detail, down to a broken window pane or a missing roof tile. The real Paris had been truly captured for posterity. The first social historians include **Louis-Jacques Mandé Daguerre**, **Henri Le Secq**, **Charles Nègre** and **Félix Nadar** who produced some of the finest portraits of the 19C by perpetuating such personalities as Baudelaire, Balzac, Gustave Doré and Gérard de Nerval, while **Charles Marville** documented the urban landscape before the radical changes implemented by Haussmann. Since then, Paris has often been caught unawares by famous photographers both in colour and black-and-white. Favourite images steeped in nostalgia recall the Paris of days gone by; they provide a valuable pictorial record of everyday life and of the social upheavals that changed the city's atmosphere. **Eugène Atget**, one of the fathers of modern photography, snapped at the streets and tradesmen in a Paris that no longer exists (cabbies, street singers, rag merchants, lace sellers, etc).

The coal merchant by Robert Doisneau

In more recent times, **Edouard Boubat**, **Izis**, **Brassaï** (known as the "Toulouse-Lautrec of the camera lens") and **Marcel Bovis** were concerned with immortalising the magic of Paris at Night; **Jacques-Henri Lartigue** recorded the Roaring Twenties; **Cartier-Bresson**, the archetypal globe-trotter and founder-member of the Magnum agency, caught views of Paris that resemble water-colours (*Ile de la Cité*); **Albert Monier** was one of the first to turn his atmospheric images into postcards that sold in their millions (*Autumn morning on the quai d'Anjou*); **Willy Ronis** succeeded in capturing for posterity scenes from the village of Belleville-Ménilmontant, which has now changed beyond all recognition; **Robert Doisneau** specialised in mischievous shots allied to the poetic musing of Prévert, imbibed with tenderness. Together they contribute to the visual catalogue of the passage of time and its changing faces.

MUSIC

Yesterday – Music, in France as elsewhere, consistently developed under the patronage of the Church: by the end of the 12C a school of polyphony had been established in Notre-Dame, expressing in harmony the deep religious faith of the period. This was interrupted by the Hundred Years War (1337-1453). It was not until the reign of François I that the art flourished once more, boosted by the institution of a national musical printing works. Narrative ballads written by **Janequin**, Italian Renaissance-style madrigals and courtly songs accompanied on the lute became popular.

In 1571, the poet **Baïf** founded the Academy for Music and Poetry to re-establish interaction between musical composition and the Pléiades known for their respect for Classical verse-form and poetic rhyme. "That most noble and gallant art" developed naturally at the royal court, first at the Louvre and later at Versailles, where sovereigns, their consorts and companions disported themselves in masques, ballets, allegorical dances, recitals, opera and comedy. The Académie Royale de Musique (1672), dominated in every genre by Lulli, attained new heights in choral music at Notre-Dame (with Campra), St-Gervais and the Sainte-Chapelle (with the **Couperins**), St-Paul-St-Louis (**Charpentier**) and Notre-Dame-des-Victoires (**Lulli**).

The Regency saw the birth of comic opera at the fairs of St-Germain and St-Laurent, and the revival of symphonic works and grand opera by **Rameau** (1683-1764), despite hostility from the Encyclopedists. This was the so-called War of the Buffoons in which Rameau's main protagonists were Diderot (*Le neveu de Rameau*) and J-J Rousseau (*Le Devin de Village*).

Not long after, the young **Mozart** passed through Paris; **Gluck**, Parisian by adoption, had his mature operas performed: *Orpheus and Eurydice, Iphigenia in Aulis* and *Alcestis* (1774-1779).

Composition, since the Revolution, has centred round the Conservatoire National, founded in 1795. It harboured the young Romantic school including Cherubini, Auber and the young **Berlioz** who wrote his *Symphonie Fantastique* in 1830; these were followed by **César Franck**, Massenet, **Fauré**. Paris became the international musical capital, drawing the Italians **Rossini** and Donizetti, the Polish **Chopin**, the Hungarian **Liszt** and the Germans **Wagner** and **Offenbach** to come and stay, often for years.

From 1870 **Bizet**, **Saint-Saëns**, Charpentier and Dukas, Parisians by birth or adoption, invigorated the interpretation of symphony and opera, d'Indy founded the Schola Cantorum *(see* PORT-ROYAL*)* and **Debussy** and **Ravel** co-operated with **Diaghilev**'s Russian Ballet. In 1918 came the Group of Six (Honegger, Tailleferre, Auric, Milhaud, Poulenc, Durey) and the rival Arcueil School with **Satie** and Sauguet.

Since 1920 – Paris continued to nurture new musical expression. The "ondes Martenot", the Jeune-France Group, Schaeffer who created "concrete sounds", Henry, **Boulez**, Xénakis and **Messiaen**, all have made an individual contribution to the musical scene. The continual draw of major foreign musicians to Paris led to the institution of the 'Paris School' in 1951. Since 1972, the Autumn Festival has assisted composers with the staging of avant-garde compositions (Xénakis' *Polytope II*). Last but not least, with the French National Orchestra, Radio France's new philharmonic orchestra and the Ensemble Intercontemporain, Paris has remained

Musician at the harpsichord by Duplessis

true to its age-old musical tradition of performing intrepid, innovative works at high-quality concert venues.

High points at the **Garnier Opéra** (inaugurated in 1875) have come under the directorships of J Rouché (1915-1945) and Rolf Liebermann (since 1973); since 1989, however, the main venue for lyrical and orchestral works has been the new **Opéra-Bastille** designed by Carlos Ott.

The **Théâtre des Champs-Elysées** is another interesting concert hall upholding since 1913, its tradition for innovation in musical composition and interpretation as intended by its founder G Astruc. It was this vision that facilitated the collaboration of such figures as Cocteau, Picasso, Diaghilev and Chanel and provoked great subsequent reactions in the fields of painting, sculpture and fashion.

The **Théâtre du Châtelet** was the former home of operetta (1928-1970); now renamed the Théâtre Musical de Paris, it continues to stage prestigious concerts and opera.

Music has been further sustained by the building of the **Cité de la Musique** at La Villette. This complex, designed by the young French architect Portzamparc, accommodates the Conservatoire National Supérieur de Musique, a musical instrument museum, the National Institute for Music Teaching, and a concert hall.

The main centre for truly contemporary music, however, is the **IRCAM** (Institut de Recherche et de Coordination Acoustique et Musicale), one of the affiliations of the Centre Pompidou. Encouraged by P Boulez, IRCAM pioneers work to international acclaim using sophisticated electronic technology, sound processors and computerised sound studios or "anechoid chambers".

LITERATURE

Middle Ages and Renaissance – The richest early French literature to survive is in the tradition of the troubadours in the Langue d'Oc; Paris itself earned its literary significance only in the 13C when the University was founded, the only one in Northern France for some time, and the Parisian dialect was adopted as the language of the court. Low life on the streets is depicted at this time in epic poems and mystery plays, whilst individual personalities and mundane business are the subjects of poems by Rutebœuf and **Villon** (15C). Despite his sharp criticism of Paris, **Rabelais** sent Gargantua and Pantagruel to the Sorbonne, and was himself to live and die in the Marais (d 1553). As the city evolved into the kingdom's capital, it attracted eminent men, inspiring a devotion in many equal to that harboured for their native soil: **Montaigne**, Guillaume Budé – founder of the Collège de France, **Ronsard** and the **Pléiade** poets, Agrippa d'Aubigné – witness to the religious conflicts which engulfed Paris and the rest of the country at the end of the 16C.

The 17C and 18C – As the city succumbed alternately to embellishment under Henri IV and Louis XIII and to disruption with the Fronde during Louis XIV's minority, writers, intellectuals, wits and lesser mortals developed what was to be a uniquely French cultural phenomenon, the cultivated philosophic conversation of the *salons*, first at the Hôtel de Rambouillet (17C) and later at the houses of the Marquise de Lambert, Madame du Deffand, Madame Geoffrin (18C).

In contrast to the open exploration and discussion of ideas in the *salons*, the Académie Française, founded by **Richelieu** in 1635, sought to exert a restraining influence on all branches of literature; Saint-Amand meanwhile wrote satire, Boileau burlesque and Madame de Sévigné her *Letters* on daily life.

In the 18C, Louis XV and Louis XVI showed little interest in literature. Society resorted to *salons* and cafés (Procope, La Régence) for exchange and debate. **Marivaux** and **Beaumarchais** (*Barber of Seville* and *Marriage of Figaro*) tinged their light comedies about Paris society and lifestyle with irony, while that precursor of Romanticism, **Jean-Jacques Rousseau** (1712-1778), born in the provinces, expressed his disdain for the place so full "of noise, of smoke and of mud"! Others concerned with the dichotomy between ethics and society include l'**Abbé Prévost** (*Manon Lescaut*), Restif de la Bretonne (*Nights of Paris*) the **Marquis de Sade** and **Choderlos de Laclos** (*Dangerous Liaisons*). It is **Voltaire** (1694-1778), master social critic, historian, novelist (*Candide*), essayist, letter-writer, diarist, dramatist and Humanist philosopher, who perhaps epitomises the best of 18C writing in Paris, ironic and witty with a light touch and perfect turn of phrase.

It is also important to acknowledge Paris' international intellectual influence during the Age of Reason, its ambassadors being **d'Alembert** and **Diderot**, who secured subscriptions to their 28-volume Encyclopedia from Catherine the Great of Russia among others.

The 19C and 20C – Paris' proudest novelists **Hugo** and **Balzac** came from the provinces. Both, in *Les Misérables* and *La Comédie Humaine* respectively, portrayed the city as a character with a personality of its own subject to moods, sickness, in the role of monster and marvel. Dwarfed by these two giants, **Dumas the Younger**, **Musset**, the song-writer Béranger, Eugène Sue (*Mysteries of Paris*), Murger (*Scenes of Bohemian Life*), **Nerval** pale into the background. Contrasts in humour and reflections on life's contradictions are explored against the back-drop of Haussmann's upheavals in verse by **Baudelaire**, the Parnassian and Symbolist poets, and in the emerging social-history, realist novel by **Émile Zola** (*Les Rougon-Macquart*).

Old Montmartre lives on in the songs of Bruant (1851-1925), the novels of Carco (1886-1958) and Marcel Aymé (1902-1967), Montparnasse in the poems of **Max Jacob** (1876-1944) and Léon-Paul Fargue (1876-1947). While others, **Colette** and **Cocteau**, **Simenon**, Montherlant, Louise de Vilmorin, **Aragon**, Prévert, Sacha Guitry, **Éluard**, **Sartre**, Simone de Beauvoir, **Beckett** merely celebrate their muse in more general terms.

ASSOCIATION WITH THE BRITISH

Many an Englishman has harboured a secret admiration for Paris – if it were not for the Parisians, as has the Parisian for Britain but for the British!

The geographical proximity of the two nations has never been so close as today: London is a mere three hours by train from Paris, closer to the French capital even than Marseille. But in the realms of politics, the instinct for self-preservation maintains a certain distance commonly known as the **Entente Cordiale**, a relationship that has been reiterated through history with many treaties – 1763 terminating the Seven Years War, 1814 and 1815 ending the Napoleonic era, 1856 sealing the alliance at the end of the Crimean War, 1904-1910 commercial treaties which concluded in the Entente Cordiale, 1919 the Treaty of Versailles.

Since the 17C, Paris has been a major attraction for British travellers: artists on their way to Italy (Charles Dickens, John Ruskin), 'gentlemen' on the Grand Tour (Lord Byron), public figures from persecution at home (Oscar Wilde, Duke and Duchess of Windsor) or impoverished journalists (W M Thackeray) and students (Orwell).

By the mid 19C, Thomas Cook was organising group 'package' holidays, since, as he stated in Cook's Excursionist and Advertiser of 15 May 1863, "*We would have every class of British subjects visit Paris, that they may emulate its excellencies, and shun the vices and errors which detract from the glory of the French capital. In matters of taste and courtesy we have much to learn from Parisians...*"

Observation of what Lawrence Durrell has called "*the national characteristics... are the restless metaphysical curiosity, the tenderness of good living and the passionate individualism. This is the invisible constant in a place with which the ordinary tourist can get in touch just by sitting quite quietly over a glass of wine in a Paris bistrot*".

AMERICANS IN PARIS

The world's quintessential expatriate city, Paris has long held a special fascination for Americans. Offering an incomparable urban setting, a rich cultural legacy and a deep-rooted respect for artistic pursuits and individual freedom, the French capital has provided a stimulating environment for successive waves of celebrated American émigrés.

18C-19C – Franco-American ties developed out of shared conflict with the British and a steadfast commitment to Revolutionary ideals. Francophiles **Benjamin Franklin** and **Thomas Jefferson**, sent to France as official emissaries of the new republic, contributed to establishing early political, cultural and scientific links between the two countries.

Throughout the 19C Paris reigned as the cultural capital of the Western world and as such attracted numerous American artists including Whistler, Eakins and Impressionist Mary Cassat. Many of America's leading architects – notably Richard Morris Hunt, Henry Hobson Richardson and Louis Sullivan – studied at the world-renowned **École des Beaux-Arts**, the supreme arbiter of neo-Classical 19C architectural trends.

"**where the twentieth century was**" – Referring to the city's pivotal role in the birth and development of modern literary and artistic movements, **Gertrude Stein** (*see* PERE-LACHAISE) asserted "Paris is where the twentieth century was."

Like two other prominent life-long expatriates – Natalie Clifford Barney and **Sylvia Beach** – Gertrude Stein was lured by the city's stimulating environment, which allowed a degree of artistic and sexual freedom unthinkable in early-20C America. Beach's **Shakespeare and Company** bookshop and the celebrated literary salons of Stein and Barney became important meeting places for the city's intelligentsia.

American expatriate life in Paris reached its heyday in the 1920s. World War I was over, the exchange rate was favourable and Paris was the place to be. During that historic decade, the Left Bank was home to an astounding number of literary personalities: Ezra Pound, F Scott-Fitzgerald, Sherwood Anderson, Ford Madox-Ford and **Ernest Hemingway**, whose life and work is more intimately linked to Paris than that of any other American writer. This foremost "Lost Generation" novelist brilliantly captured the unbridled expatriate experience as played out in the legendary cafés, night spots and streets of Montparnasse and the Latin Quarter T(*he Sun Also Rises* and *A Moveable Feast*). The period's unprecedented literary production gave rise to a proliferation of avant-garde expatriate reviews (*Little Review, transitions*) and publishers (Black Sun Press, Black Manikin Press and Hours Press founded by Nancy Cunard). The first uncensored edition of James Joyce's masterpiece *Ulysses* was published in France in 1922 by Sylvia Beach.

Simultaneously Paris played host to an international colony of prodigious artists including Picasso, Chagall, Modigliani, and Americans **Man Ray** and **Alexander Calder**. Among the expatriate performing artists were dancer **Isadora Duncan** and Revue Nègre star **Josephine Baker** (*see* ALMA), who cherished the racial equality and the international fame offered by France. The dizzying Paris scene was astutely observed by Janet Flanner who, under the pseudonym Genêt, authored the "Letter from Paris" column in *The New Yorker* from 1925 to 1975.

The 1930s were marked by the presence of **Henry Miller**. Like Hemingway, Miller came to Paris to become a writer and chose a Paris setting for his first novel. The quasi-autobiographical *Tropic of Cancer* (1934), banned in the US until the 1960s, explicitly depicts a seedy Paris well off the beaten expatriate trail. During his Paris years, Miller met his American protector, muse and lover, Anaïs Nin.

Post-WW II to Present – Expatriate life in Paris was interrupted by the outbreak of World War II: most of the American writers of the 1920s and 30s had gone home or moved on to safer havens, while the international art scene had been partially transplanted to New York. The cosy Left Bank institution, Shakespeare and Company, closed its doors in 1941 after 20 years of existence. During the late 1950s and 1960s, a new American-run bookstore and lending library opened in the Latin Quarter (*see* Les QUAIS). This picturesque haunt (named Shakespeare and Company following Sylvia Beach's death in 1962) was frequented by Beat Generation writers Ginsberg and Burroughs as well as by many of the newly arrived black writers. Lured by France's deep-rooted reputation as a nation fostering a non-racist cultural climate (symbolised by the immense fame of black author Alexandre Dumas), a wave of black writers and musicians

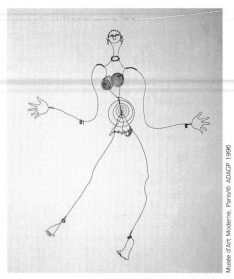

Josephine Baker by Calder, 1926

Musée d'Art Moderne, Paris/© ADAGP 1996

went abroad while McCarthyism was sweeping the US. The most influential member of this group was acclaimed writer and intellectual **Richard Wright** (*Native Son*), whose self-imposed Paris exile began in 1947 and lasted until his death in 1960. Fellow-expatriate black American writers included Chester Himes, William Gardner Smith and James Baldwin (*Another Country, Giovanni's Room*).

Although Paris' heyday as an avant-garde expatriate haven is long over, the City of Lights continues to beckon Americans. For an idea of the range of activities and events organised for and by today's expatriate community, consult the monthly newspaper, *The Paris Free Voice (available in English-language haunts throughout the city).*

This guide is sprinkled with references to famous Americans in Paris. See page 61 and consult the index under the person's name.

26

Paris today

Paris' centrifugal attraction dates from the First Empire; since then it has developed, pell-mell, as the pivot of France's political, administrative, economic and cultural life. A century after Baron Haussmann's large-scale urban re-planning, a strategy was implemented in 1960 aimed at resolving the capital's physical problems.

Local government – Since March 1977, the **Mairie de Paris** has had an elected mayor, chosen by the 163 councillors who make up the municipal council; municipal elections are held every six years. With the exception of the police force, headed by a *préfet*, the mayor has the same status and powers of mayors of other municipalities.

The municipal authority works closely with the primary units of Paris local government, the town halls of the 20 *arrondissements* responsible for local problems. Paris being both a commune and a *département*, its Council sits as a municipal authority and a general or departmental council.

The city's coat of arms features the boat motif from the armorial bearings of the watermen's guild whose members were appointed by Louis IX in 1260 to administer the township. In the 16C the device was complemented by the motto *Fluctuat nec mergitur* (she is buffeted by the waves but does not sink).

Seal of the Watermen's Guild (1210)

The **Ile-de-France** Region comprises eight *departements* (Paris, Seine-et-Marne, Yvelines, Essonne, Hauts-de-Seine, Seine-St-Denis, Val-de-Marne and Val-d'Oise), each with its own prefecture, covering a total area of 12 011km^2 – 4 637sq miles with a total population of 10 073 053 (Paris: 105km^2 – 40sq miles; 2 176 243).

Metamorphosis – Paris' historic, architectural and archeological treasures have been safeguarded by the enlightened policy of André Malraux and his followers who instituted a programme of cleaning, restoration, and revitalisation of whole areas such as the Marais and preservation of archeological finds. Meanwhile, structural engineers and planners wrestle with today's problems – traffic and transport (ring road, express-way, RER), supply (Rungis, Garonor), cultural centres (G Pompidou Centre), sports facilities (Bercy), commercial property development (La Défense, Front de Seine, Maine-Montparnasse) and urban renewal (Place d'Italie, Belleville, Bercy); the emphasis being on the preservation and restoration of the historic heritage.

Major cultural projects include the Cités des Sciences et de l'Industrie and de la Musique at La Villette, the Musée d'Orsay, the Grand Louvre project, the new Opéra-Bastille, the Grande Arche at la Défense and the Bibliothèque National at Tolbiac.

The transfer of the wholesale markets from the Halles to Rungis, the explosion of the University into 13 autonomous universities, the decentralisation of the Higher Schools of learning, have contributed in relieving congestion at the centre. Modern hospitals, both public and private, have been erected. Green spaces (La Villette, André Citroën) have been created, aged parks and gardens refurbished...

Population – Paris, which has over 2 million inhabitants, is one of the most densely populated cities in the world. The inner-city population is slightly in decline although figures show the constant influx from the provinces or abroad, to sustain minority concentrations in particular neighbourhoods: Jews (Marais), White Russians (Montparnasse), Spaniards (Passy), North Africans (Clignancourt, La Villette, Aubervilliers), Oriental Asians (13th *Arr.*).

The true Parisian, however, remains easily identifiable among the cosmopolitan crowd: hurried, tense, protesting, frivolous, quick-witted, ever ready to poke fun or play on words – epitomised by the cabaret singer, the market stallholder, or the barman.

Paris quarters – Some quarters retain their traditional association with a medieval trade or guild, thereby preserving something of the atmosphere of past centuries: seed merchants on quai de la Mégisserie; publishing and bookshops in the Odéon area; cabinet-makers in the rue du Faubourg-St-Antoine; bric-à-brac and second-hand clothes in the Temple and Sentier quarters; antique dealers in rues Bonaparte and la Boëtie; art galleries in avenue Matignon and rue du Faubourg-St-Honoré; *haute couture* houses in rue du Faubourg-St-Honoré, avenue Montaigne and rue François-Ier; luxury goods in the Opéra quarter; stringed instrument makers in rue de Rome; porcelain, crystal and glassware in rue de Paradis; jewellers in rue de la Paix and place Vendôme. Meanwhile government offices line rue de Grenelle and congregate around the Trocadéro; financial institutions around Bourse, Opéra, Champs-Élysées, La Défense; students collect around their faculties in the Latin quarter: all are knitted together amongst schools, workshops, warehouses and small shops which, with the many large undertakings, make up Paris' infinitely varied economy.

27

Montmartre, la place du Tertre

Paris
at leisure

Shopping

Department stores

The large department stores provide the ideal solution to anyone pressed for time: open from Monday to Saturday, stocking most of the famous brands (fashion, perfume, leather goods), on-hand duty-free service for overseas visitors, in-store refreshment facilities (restaurant, cafeteria).

Bazar de l'Hôtel de Ville (BHV) *52 rue de Rivoli;* Ⓜ *Hôtel-de-Ville* – Wednesday late-night opening to 10pm. **Au Bon Marché** and its food hall, **La Grande Epicerie de Paris** *rue de Sèvres;* Ⓜ *Sèvres-Babylone.* **Galeries Lafayette-Haussmann** *40 boulevard Haussmann;* Ⓜ *Chaussée-d'Antin* – 8th floor panoramic restaurant. Thursday late-night opening to 9pm. **Marks & Spencer** *35 boulevard Haussmann;* Ⓜ *Havre-Caumartin* and *88 rue de Rivoli;* Ⓜ *Châtelet.* **Au Printemps Haussmann** *64 boulevard Haussmann;* Ⓜ *Havre-Caumartin* – Thursday late-night opening to 10pm. **La Samaritaine** *19 rue de la Monnaie;* Ⓜ *Pont-Neuf* – Thursday late-night opening to 10pm. **Les Trois Quartiers** *23 boulevard de la Madeleine;* Ⓜ *Madeleine.*

Fancy Goods

Paris enjoys an international reputation beyond compare for clothes design, *haute couture* and fashion accessories (jewellery, perfume, leather goods and silk scarves), on the cat-walk and in exclusive shops.

Parfumerie Caron

Fashion labels and perfumers – **Céline:** *avenue Montaigne.* **Cerruti 1881:** *rue Royale.* **Chanel:** *rue Cambon; avenue Montaigne.* **Christian Dior:** *avenue Montaigne.* **Christian Lacroix:** *avenue Montaigne, place St-Sulpice.* **Courrèges:** *rue du Faubourg-St-Honoré.* **Daniel Hechter:** *boulevard St-Germain.* **Jean-Paul Gaultier:** *Galerie Vivienne.* **Francesco Smalto:** *rue François 1er.* **Givenchy:** *avenue George V.* **Grès:** *rue du Faubourg-St-Honoré.* **Gucci:** *rue du Faubourg-St-Honoré.* **Guerlain:** *66 avenue des Champs-Élysées, place Vendome, rue de Sèvres, rue Bonaparte, rue Tronchet.* **Guy Laroche:** *rue du Faubourg-St-Honoré; avenue Montaigne.* **Hanae Mori:** *avenue Montaigne.* **Hermes:** *rue du Faubourg-St-Honoré.* **Hiroko Koshino:** *rue du Faubourg-St-Honoré.* **Issey Miyake:** *place des Vosges.* **Jean-Louis Scherrer:** *avenue Montaigne.* **Karl Lagerfield:** *rue du Faubourg-St-Honoré.* **Kenzo:** *place des Victoires.* **Lanvin:** *rue du Faubourg-St-Honoré.* **Louis Ferraud:** *rue du Faubourg-St-Honoré.* **Nina Ricci:** *avenue Montaigne.* **Paco Rabanne:** *rue du Cherche-Midi.* **Per Spook:** *avenue George V.* **Pierre Balmain:** *rue François 1er.* **Ralph Lauren:** *avenue de la Grande Armée.* **Shisheido:** *Galerie des Valois – Palais Royal.* **Sonya Rykiel:** *boulevard St-Germain.* **Torrente:** *Rond-point des Champs-Élysées.* **Ted Lapidus:** *rue François 1er.* **Ungaro:** *avenue Montaigne.* **Versace:** *rue du Faubourg-St-Honoré.* **Yves St-Laurent:** *rue du Faubourg-St-Honoré; avenue Marceau.* **Yves St-Laurent – Rive Gauche:** *place Saint-Sulpice.*

Jewellers and Goldsmiths – **Boucheron:** *place Vendôme.* **Cartier:** *rue de la Paix.* **Chaumet:** *place Vendôme.* **Fred:** *rue Royale.* **Mauboussin:** *place Vendôme.* **Mellerio:** *rue de la Paix.* **Poiray:** *rue de la Paix.* **Alexandre Reza:** *place Vendôme.* **Van Cleef & Arpels:** *place Vendôme.* **Buccelatti:** *place Vendôme.*

Luggage and leather goods – **Céline**: *rue Cambon*. **La Bagagerie**: *rue du Faubourg-St-Honoré*. **Didier Lamarthe**: *rue du Faubourg-St-Honoré*. **Goyard**: *rue St-Honoré*. **Hermès**: *rue du Faubourg-St-Honoré*. **Lancel**: *place de l'Opéra*. **Morabito**: *place Vendôme*. **Louis Vuitton**: *avenue Montaigne*.

Crystal and china – **Baccarat**: *place de la Madeleine*; *rue de Paradis*. **Bernardaud**; *rue Royale*; *rue de Paradis*. **Christofle**: *rue Royale*. **Cristallerie St-Louis**: *rue Royale*; *rue de Paradis*. **Lalique**: *rue Royale*; *Carrousel du Louvre*. **D.Porthaud**: *avenue Matignon*. **Villeroy & Boch**: *rue Royale*.

Home interiors – **Besson**: *rue Bonaparte*. **Manuel Canovas**: *place de Fürstenberg*. **Pierre Frey**: *place de Fürstenberg*. **Yves Halard**: *boulevard St-Germain*. **Nobilis**: *rue Bonaparte*.

Florists – **Lachaume**: *rue Royale* – see street markets below.

Shopping centres

Down the Champs-Élysées: **Galerie Élysée Rond-Point**, **Galerie Élysée 26**; **Galerie du Claridge**; **Galerie Arcades du Lido**; **Galerie des Champs-Élysées** Ⓜ *George V et Franklin-Roosevelt*. **Carrousel du Louvre** Ⓜ *Louvre-Rivoli* – with direct access to the Louvre, includes a *Virgin Megastore*. **Centre commercial Maine-Montparnasse** Ⓜ *Montparnasse-Bienvenüe*. **Centre commercial Italie II** Ⓜ *Place d'Italie*. **Les Boutiques de Paris** *Palais des Congrès*; Ⓜ *Porte Maillot*. **Forum des Halles** *1-7 rue Pierre-Lescot*; Ⓜ/RER: *Châtelet-Les-Halles*. **Les Trois Quartiers** *23 boulevard de la Madeleine*; Ⓜ *Madeleine*. **Centre Beaugrenelle** *rue Linois*; Ⓜ *Charles-Michels*. **Les Quatre Temps** *Parvis de la Défense*; Ⓜ/RER: *La Défense*.

Arcades

The majority of these period arcades were built in the early 19C ensuring their survival and success by accommodating retailers of quality goods that quickly won favour with fashionable Society. Nowadays, they provide a picturesque context for unusual, often old-fashioned, shops.

Galerie Vivienne – *4 rue des Petits-Champs*; Ⓜ *Bourse*. Built in 1823, this is one of the busiest arcades in Paris. Light floods through the glass roof. Notice the half-moon windows on the mezzanine, and the mosaics designed by the Italian artist Facchina who worked on the decoration of a number of the capital's buildings. There are old bookshops (nos 45 and 46, the Petit Siroux bookshop established in 1826), haberdashers selling fabrics, and a tearoom (A Priori Thé at no 35).

Galerie Colbert – *6 rue Vivienne*; Ⓜ *Bourse*. Opened in 1826 and now renovated, this arcade runs into the Galerie Vivienne and is part of the Bibliothèque Nationale which organises exhibitions, conferences and debates here. The auditorium beneath the rotunda is used for concerts.

Passage Choiseul – *23 rue St-Augustin*; Ⓜ *Quatre-Septembre*. This arcade, which is less lavish than the ones described above, first opened to the public in 1827. It contains several printers, clothes and costume jewellery shops running along the rear of the Bouffes-Parisiens theatre.

This arcade was immortalised by the writer, Louis-Ferdinand Céline, who lived here as a child and gave a fairly cutting description of it in his work *Mort à Crédit* (*Death on the Instalment Plan*).

Ph. Gajic/MICHELIN

Galerie Véro-Dodat

Passage des Panoramas – *11 boulevard Montmartre*; Ⓜ *Rue-Montmartre*. This was the first real arcade to be built in Paris and was described by Zola in his novel, *Nana*. It consists of several galleries housing boutiques, phone-card dealers, philatelists and printers.

Passage Jouffroy – *10 boulevard Montmartre*; Ⓜ *Rue-Montmartre*. Situated just next door to the Musée Grévin, this was the first arcade in the city to be heated. It now contains a second-hand bookshop among a variety of retail businesses, some selling oriental items (one serves Turkish coffee, cakes and pastries).

Galerie Véro-Dodat – *19 rue Jean-Jacques Rousseau*; Ⓜ *Palais-Royal*. Opened in 1826, this arcade undoubtedly boasts the finest interior decoration. High-quality shops with windows encased in brass surrounds have been rebuilt in the original style, their windows full of old-fashioned charm like the old toy shop (Robert Capia), the Gauguin bookshop or the violin maker's at no 17.

Passage Verdeau – *6 rue de la Grange-Batelière*; Ⓜ *Richelieu-Drouot, Rue Montmartre*. This arcade extends beyond the Passage Jouffroy, not far from the Hôtel Drouot and stocks antiques and old books (La France ancienne); **Roland Buret** boasts a vast collection of back-numbered comics.

Passage du Grand-Cerf – *145 rue Saint-Denis*; Ⓜ *Etienne-Marcel*. This arcade was built between 1825 and 1835 on the site of the Grand-Cerf hostelry; it has recently been restored. Paved in marble, it boasts an elegant and very high glass roof, wrought-iron walkways, and wood-framed shop windows. The shops are all modern.

Passage Brady – *18 rue du Faubourg-Saint-Denis*; Ⓜ *Strasbourg-Saint-Denis*. Scents and perfumes of India waft through this arcade which houses a good number of restaurants and food shops.

Antique and art dealers

The art trade in the late 19C was limited to just a few galleries located principally on the Right Bank. Today, antique dealers, art galleries and specialist bookshops are to be found on both banks, organising prestigious fairs and exhibitions that attract growing numbers of collectors and interested amateurs. Most generally open after 10.30am and close at lunchtime (midday – 2pm).

Right Bank: **Louvre des Antiquaires** Ⓥ – *2 place du Palais-Royal*; Ⓜ *Palais-Royal*. Three floors of stands and dealers, covering 10 000 m² – 107 600sq ft, specialise in everything from Antiquity to modern day. **Triangle Rive Droite** – *Avenue Matignon, rue du Faubourg-St-Honoré, rue de Miromesnil, rue de Penthièvre, rue La Boétie*; Ⓜ *Miromesnil*. At the start of each new season, dealers collectively organise an open day with exhibitions of new work. **Village St-Paul** – *Rue St-Paul*; Ⓜ *Saint-Paul* (*see main text under* le MARAIS). **Hôtel Drouot** – *9 rue Drouot*; Ⓜ *Richelieu-Drouot*. Important auctions attract large crowds. **Beaubourg** – *Rue Chapon, rue Quincampoix, rue de la Verrerie*; Ⓜ *Rambuteau, Hôtel-de-Ville*. **Bastille** – *Rue de Charonne, rue de Lappe, rue Keller*; Ⓜ *Bastille*. Galleries display works by some of the big names in international contemporary art.

Left Bank: **Carré Rive Gauche** – *Rue du Bac, rue de Beaune, rue de Lille, rue des Saints-Pères, rue de l'Université, rue de Verneuil and quai Voltaire*; Ⓜ *Rue-du-Bac/RER: Musée-d'Orsay*. Each year during the *Cinq jours de l'objet extraordinaire*, over 100 antique dealers and art galleries display the best of their collections (ceramics, tapestries and rugs, paintings, earthenware and pewter, antique furniture). **Village Suisse** Ⓥ, *78 avenue de Suffren*; Ⓜ *La Motte-Picquet* is a conglomeration of 150 antique and bric-à-brac shops. **Boulevard St-Germain** – Ⓜ *Rue-du-Bac*. **Rue Bonaparte** and **rue de Seine** – Ⓜ *Saint-Germain-des-Prés*. Numerous galleries displaying extraordinary artistic creations (Art-Déco, modern sculpture, paintings), dealers in original engravings, prints and old books populate these streets.

Rue Jacques-Callot, between rue de Seine and rue Mazarine is another well-known collector's paradise.

The **Biennial International Antiques Fair** held in early autumn is a particularly important venue for connoisseurs and collectors from all over the world.

Books and music

Note: a bookshop is a '*librairie*' in French, a library is a '*bibliothèque*'.

The **FNAC** hypermarket chain stock an impressive range of books, maps and comics, records and tapes, film and photographic equipment and processing services: browsers welcome: each outlet varies slightly in emphasis: **Étoile** – *26-30 avenue des Ternes*; Ⓜ *Ternes*. ☎ 01 44 09 18 00. **Montparnasse** – *136 rue de Rennes*; Ⓜ *St-Placide, Montparnasse-Bienvenüe*. ☎ 01 49 54 30 00. **Forum des Halles** – *Metro/RER: Châtelet-les-Halles*. ☎ 01 40 41 40 00. Music and video only: **Italiens** – *24 boulevard des Italiens*; Ⓜ *Richelieu-Drouot*. ☎ 01 48 01 02 03. **Bastille** – *4 place de la Bastille*; Ⓜ *Bastille*. ☎ 01 43 42 04 04. For computer hardware, software and peripherals: **FNAC Micro** – *71 boulevard Saint-Germain*; Ⓜ *Cluny-Sorbonne*. ☎ 01 44 41 31 50. **Virgin Megastore** – *52-60, avenue des Champs-Élysées*; Ⓜ *George V*. ☎ 01 40 74 06 48 and *Carrousel du Louvre*; Ⓜ *Palais-Royal*. **Joseph Gibert** – *5 place St-Michel*; Ⓜ/RER: *Saint-Michel*. ☎ 01 43 54 57 32, other outlets in the square specialise in academic publications and at *26-30 boulevard St-Michel*; Ⓜ *Cluny-Sorbonne*. ☎ 01 43 25 70 07.

Specialists – **Galignani** *224 rue de Rivoli*, one of the oldest bookshops in Paris, stocks English and French books. **La Hune** and **L'Ecume des Pages** *Boulevard St-Germain*, near the *Deux-Magots*, stay open until midnight. The heart of the publishing world is Odéon where new and second-hand editions bookshops proliferate, often with a thematic specialisation. **Monte-Cristo** *Rue de l'Odéon* stocks collections of adventure fiction by Jules Verne. **Le Moniteur** *Place de l'Odéon* specialises in architecture and urban development. In *rue Bonaparte* **Le Coupe-Papier** concentrates on theatre and cinema; **La Licorne** on historical reference books and **La Porte Etroite** on painting and architecture. **Maritime Outremer** *rue Jacob* deals in every aspect of the sea and sailing. In *rue St-Sulpice*, **Claude Buffet** and **Jean-Claude Vrain** deal in old books, **La Chambre Claire** in international photography. Along the river, besides the *bouquinistes*, **Honoré Champion** and **Arenthon** deal in historical documents and prints.

Museum bookshops – Among the best are the **Librairie des musées** *10 rue de l'Abbaye;* Ⓜ *Saint-Germain-des-Prés*, the **Librairie des Galeries nationales du Grand Palais**, the **Librairie du Musée d'Orsay**, the **Librairie du Musée du Louvre** specialising in Art from its origins to 1845 (*for addresses see museum listing in main text*). The **Virgin Megastore** complements these books on contemporary art and modern literature. The **Librairie du Musée Carnavalet** and the well-stocked **Librairie du Patrimoine** (Heritage Bookshop) *Hôtel de Sully, 62 rue du Faubourg-St-Antoine;* Ⓜ *St-Paul* are good for literature about Paris.

Foreign Language – **W.H. Smith** – *248 rue de Rivoli* (English); **Brentano's** – *37 avenue de l'Opéra* (American); **Village Voice** – *6 rue Princesse*; **Shakespeare and Co** *37 rue de la Bûcherie* is an idiosyncratic place packed with romantic literature which welcomes browsers; **Marissal Bücher** *42 rue Rambuteau*, and **Calligramme** *8 rue de la Collégiale*, invite visitors to discover literature and culture from across the Rhine; the **Tour de Babel** *10 rue du Roi-de-Sicile*, in the heart of the Marais, specialises in Italian literature. **Librairie Polonaise** *123 boulevard St-Germain* and **Libella** *12 rue St-Louis-en-l'Ile* stock books in Polish.

Shakespeare and Co.

Gourmet treats

Delicatessens – **Fauchon** – *26 place de la Madeleine*. **Hédiard** – *21 place de la Madeleine*. **Comptoir de la Tour d'Argent** – *2 rue du Cardinal-Lemoine*. **Pétrossian** – *18 boulevard de la Tour-Maubourg* (caviare).

Bread – For crispy country-style *baguettes* and special breads baked with olives, nuts or dried fruit seek out **Lionel Poilâne** *8 rue du Cherche-Midi* and *87 rue Brancion* (try the apple pastries!). **René St-Ouen** – *111 boulevard Haussmann*. **Michel Moisan** – *114 rue de Patay*. **Ganachaud** – *150 rue de Ménilmontant*.

Cakes and pastries, ice-cream, chocolates – Even those who can resist the temptation of cakes and pastries should not hesitate to stop off for afternoon tea in one of the tearooms, with their delicious, mouth-watering array of macaroons, chocolate cakes, mocha biscuits, puff pastries, fruit tarts, strawberry gateaux and nougatine ices: **Berthillon** – *31 rue St-Louis-en-l'Ile* (founded in 1954). **Paul Bugat** *5 boulevard Beaumarchais*. **Carette** – *4 place du Trocadéro*. **Carton** – *6 rue de Buci*. **Dalloyau** – *99-101 rue du Faubourg-St-Honoré*. **Duc de Praslin** – *44 avenue Montaigne*. **Ladurée** – *16 rue Royale*. **Lenôtre** – *44 rue d'Auteuil*. **La Maison du Chocolat** – *56 rue Pierre-Charron*. **Gérard Mulot** – *76 rue de Seine*. **Peltier** – *66 rue de Sèvres*. **Stohrer** – *51 rue Montorgueil*.

Cheese – **Androuet** – *41 rue d'Amsterdam*. **La Ferme St-Hubert** – *21 rue Vignon* (restaurant-cheese shop). **Barthélémy** – *51 rue de Grenelle*. **La Maison du Fromage** – *62 rue de Sèvres*. **La Ferme St-Aubin** – *76 rue St-Louis-en-l'Ile*.

Street markets

Food – An important supplier of fresh produce to the Parisian house wife and gastro-nome is the local market; colourful stalls manned by provincial types provide an ideal opportunity to enjoy the sights, sounds and smells of Paris city limit.

Venues: **place Monge** Wednesday, Friday and Sunday; **boulevard Raspail** Tuesday and Friday, Sunday for organic produce; **avenue de Saxe** Thursday and Saturday; **boulevard Richard-Lenoir** (Ⓜ *Bastille* and *Oberkampf*) Thursday and Sunday; **rue** and **place d'Aligre** daily except Monday since 1778; **boulevard Blanqui** Thursday and Sunday; **boulevard Edgar-Quinet** Wednesday and Sunday; **rue de la Convention** Tuesday, Thursday and Sunday; **avenue du Président-Wilson** Wednesday and Saturday (meat and embroidered linen!); **place de Joinville** near la Villette, Thursday and Sunday; **place des Fêtes** Tuesday, Friday and Sunday; **boulevard de Belleville** Thursday and Sunday; **place de la Réunion** Thursday and Sunday; **rue Montorgueil** daily except Saturday; **rue Mouffetard** daily except Monday; **rues de Buci et de Seine** Tuesday to Saturday; **rue des Martyrs** daily except Monday; **rue du Faubourg-du-Temple; rues Poncelet, de Tocqueville; rue Lepic** and **rue des Abbesses; rue Daguerre; rue St-Charles** and **rue du Commerce; rues de Passy** et **de l'Annonciation**. Note: Some street-markets operate all day, but will close at midday on Sunday – temporary markets usually operate mornings only.

Aligre market

Clothes and leathers – **Carreau du Temple** – Ⓜ *Temple, République*. Mornings, daily except Monday.

Fabrics – **Saint-Pierre Market** – *Montmartre, below the Sacré-Cœur;* Ⓜ *Anvers*. Monday to Saturday.

Live animals and birds – **Quai de la Mégisserie** – Ⓜ *Pont-Neuf* or *Châtelet*. **Place Louis-Lépine** – Ⓜ *Cité*. Sunday.

Flowers – **Place Louis-Lépine** – Ⓜ *Cité*. Tuesday to Saturday. **Place de la Madeleine** – Ⓜ *Madeleine*. Daily except Monday. **Place des Ternes** – Ⓜ *Ternes*. Daily except Monday, closed Sunday afternoons.

Antiquarian and Second-hand Books – **Parc Georges-Brassens** – *rue Brancion entrance;* Ⓜ *Porte-de-Vanves*. Saturday and Sunday.

Stamps – *Avenue Marigny, junction of avenue de Marigny and avenue Gabriel;* Ⓜ*Champs-Élysées-Clemenceau* open Thursday, Saturday, Sunday and public holidays.

In 1887, a stamp dealer named Octave Weber arranged to meet collectors every Thursday on avenue Marigny: soon, specialists were drawn from the Tuileries and the Luxembourg Gardens. Today, traders sell postcards and phone-cards.

Flea Markets – The 'Puces' for short, operate at **Porte de Vanves** – Ⓜ *Porte-de-Vanves*. Saturday and Sunday; **Porte de Clignancourt** – Ⓜ *Porte-de-Clignancourt*. Saturday, Sunday and Monday; **Porte de Montreuil** – Ⓜ *Porte-de-Montreuil*. Saturday, Sunday and Monday.

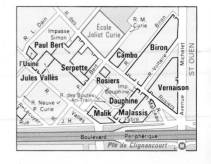

TRADITIONAL SHOP-FRONTS

LE MILLE PATES

A. Éli

E. Baret

LE BISTRO DE LA GARE
montparnasse

E. Baret

E. Baret

Guilloï/MICHELIN

PAPETERIE · MAROQUINERIE
A FRANÇOIS Iᵉʳ
334 · B. BIBERON & FILS · 334

E. Baret

Entertainment

The full programme of shows and films is published every Wednesday in the **Officiel des Spectacles** and **Une semaine de Paris-Pariscope** which includes an English-language version, *Time Out*, and in the monthly brochure, *Paris Sélection*, published by the Tourist Office ☎ 01 47 20 94 94 for recorded information, Minitel: 3615 CAPITALE.

The big green **Colonnes Morris** were designed in the 19C by a theatre bill printer and continue to publicise events in the capital.

THEATRE

The Paris region has more than 100 theatres, some of them national, some grant-aided, others privately-owned. Most of them lie within the **Opéra** and **Montparnasse** districts and along the **Boulevards**; most enjoy a long-standing reputation. The popular theatres perpetuate a tradition that is typically Parisian but the general public is currently showing a taste for other types of theatre.

Reduced-price tickets are obtainable for shows being staged the same evening, from three kiosks: – the **west promenade beside the Madeleine Church** from 12.30pm to 8pm (or 4pm on Sundays), except Mondays, Ⓜ *Madeleine*; in the **salle des échanges** in the station (Ⓜ*/RER: Châtelet-Les-Halles*) from 12.30pm to 7.30pm, except Sundays, Mondays and bank holidays; opposite the **gare Montparnasse** (Ⓜ *Montparnasse-Bienvenüe*). For further information, use the Minitel: dial 3615 and key in **THEA** or phone the theatres direct.

Morris Column

J. Sierpinski/SCOPE

National Theatre

Comédie-Française-Salle Richelieu – *1 place Colette*; Ⓜ *Palais-Royal*. Founded in 1680 by Louis XIV, its repertory is traditionally taken from the French classics, but foreign authors and modern works are not totally excluded.

Théâtre du Vieux-Colombier – *21 rue du Vieux-Colombier*; Ⓜ *St-Sulpice*. This is the Comédie-Française' experimental theatre and, as such, promotes contemporary works. It was here, on 22 May 1944, that Jean-Paul Sartre's *Huis Clos (In Camera)* was first staged.

Odéon-Théâtre de l'Europe – *1 place de l'Odéon*; Ⓜ *Odéon /RER: Luxembourg*. Jean-Louis Barrault staged Ionesco's *Rhinoceros* here and, later, Samuel Beckett's *Waiting for Godot*. The Odéon is the "Community Centre of European Theatre" and is now independent of the Comédie-Française. Foreign companies stage productions in their own languages.

Popular Theatre

Théâtre Antoine-Simone-Berrlau – *14 boulevard de Strasbourg*; Ⓜ *Château d'Eau*. Formerly known as the Théâtre-Libre, it has staged a number of major works including *Poil de Carotte* by Jules Renard in 1900, *Les Mains Sales (The Red Gloves)* by Jean-Paul Sartre in 1948, *Cat on a Hot Tin Roof* by Tennessee Williams, *A View from the Bridge* by Arthur Miller, and *Ciascuno a suo Modo (Each in His Own Way)* by Pirandello.

The **Théâtre de l'Athénée-Louis-Jouvet** *4 square de l'Opéra-Louis-Jouvet*; Ⓜ *Opéra, Havre-Caumartin*, was inaugurated at the end of the 19C. Jean Cocteau's *Ondine* was first performed here in 1939, as was Jean Giraudoux' *The Madwoman of Chaillot* in 1945. **Louis Jouvet** died here in 1961, having been taken ill during a rehearsal for Graham Greene's *The Power and the Glory*.

Théâtre des Bouffes-Parisiens – *4 rue Monsigny*; Ⓜ *Quatre-Septembre*. Stages nothing but comedy.

Théâtre Dejazet – *41 boulevard du Temple*; Ⓜ *République*. This small, Italian-style theatre was built on what was once known as the "boulevard of crime" because of the murder mysteries which were staged here in the 19C *(see* REPUBLIQUE*)*. Murals depict Parisian life in those days.

Théâtre Edouard VII-Sacha-Guitry – *10 place Edouard VII;* Ⓜ *Opéra*. One of the greatest of all the popular theatres. From 1920 to 1930, Sacha Guitry staged his most famous plays here. The theatre has a tradition of staging Anglo-Saxon plays (*A Streetcar Named Desire* was performed here, for the first time in France, in 1949).

Théâtre des Mathurins – *36 rue des Mathurins;* Ⓜ *Havre-Caumartin*. The Pitoeff Theatre Company was formed here in 1927 and gave performances of Ibsen's *The Doll's House*, Anouilh's *Traveller without Luggage* and *Antigone*.

Fringe (contemporary writers, avant-garde theatre etc)

Théâtre de l'Atelier *43 rue d'Orsel;* Ⓜ *Anvers* introduced Parisian audiences to Pirandello.
Cartoucherie-Théâtre de l'Aquarium – *route de Champ-de-Manœuvre;* Ⓜ *Château-de-Vincennes and free bus service or bus no 112 to the Cartoucherie stop.* **Théâtre de l'Epée de Bois**, **Théâtre du Soleil**, **Théâtre de la Tempête**.

The **Théâtre du Soleil** was formed in 1964 by a small group of university students under the direction of **Ariane Mnouchkine**. After years of struggle, success came with a staging of *1789* allowing the company to settle in a dilapidated cartridge factory in Vincennes (1970). Productions were directed according to traditional fairground shows, with different plots being performed simultaneously on four platforms around which the audience could wander. Inspiration is drawn from Shakespeare, the Greek tragedies, Japanese and Indian theatre, and set against a mixture of historical periods, cultures and genres; the close relationship between stage and audience and the heightened sense of movement quickly appealed to an international public. In *Le Retour des Erinyes*, Mnouchkine addressed more contemporary issues, namely the contamination of hemophiliacs with the AIDS virus, in a story that unfurls like a Classical myth.

Comédie des Champs-Élysées – *15 avenue Montaigne;* Ⓜ *Alma-Marceau*. Works by Jean Giraudoux that were performed here include *Siegfried* in 1928 and *Amphytrion* in 1929 (with Michel Simon); these were followed by Jean Cocteau's *The Infernal Machine*. The **Studio des Champs-Élysées** is an experimental theatre in which Marguerite Duras' *Musica* was staged in 1965.

Essaïon de Paris – *6 rue Pierre-au-Lard;* Ⓜ *Hôtel-de-Ville*. This tiny theatre set in medieval cellars serves as a crucible for new ideas and previously-unknown works by living authors writing in French. Vaçlav Havel gave his first play here. There is a reading every Saturday afternoon.

Théâtre de la Huchette – *23 rue de la Huchette;* Ⓜ *St-Michel*. Since 1957, Ionesco's **La Cantatrice Chauve** *(The Bald Primadonna)* has been staged in this theatre; it has always met with the same success.

Le Lucernaire *53 rue Notre-Dame-des-Champs;* Ⓜ *Notre-Dame-des-Champs*, specialises in experimental works and is one of the most informal theatre venues in Paris. It has two theatres (six plays are staged here every evening), three cinemas, an art gallery, a bookshop specialising in works relating to the theatre and cinema, and a restaurant.

Théâtre Mogador – *25 rue Mogador;* Ⓜ *Trinité*. Since 1940, this theatre has staged *Cyrano de Bergerac*, *The Baker's Wife*, and more than 30 operettas including *Violettes impériales*.

Théâtre de Poche-Montparnasse – *75 boulevard du Montparnasse;* Ⓜ *Montparnasse-Bienvenüe* – The theatre became famous for its productions of work by Marguerite Duras, the mimes of Marcel Marceau and Eugène Ionesco's *The Lesson*.

Théâtre du Rond-Point – *2bis avenue Franklin-Roosevelt;* Ⓜ *Franklin-D.-Roosevelt*. This building was formerly the Panorama, then the Ice Palace. Since 1981, it has been a theatre; it was originally directed by Jean-Louis Barrault.

Théâtre de la Ville – *2 place du Châtelet;* Ⓜ *Châtelet*. Formerly known as the Théâtre Sarah-Bernhardt. Since 1968, it has been a powerhouse of popular culture (drama, music, dance).

CAFÉ-THÉATRES, CHANSONNIERS AND CABARETS

A number of now-famous film stars made their debut in the café-theatres of Paris. **Au Bec Fin** *6 rue Thérèse;* Ⓜ *Pyramides* was where Raymond Devos had a number of successes and Dominique Lavanant and Pierre Palmade launched their careers; **Le Café de la Gare** *41 rue du Temple;* Ⓜ *Hôtel-de-Ville* was set up by Coluche and Romain Bouteille and had Miou-Miou and Patrick Dewaere among its cast; **Le Double Fond** *1 place du Marché-Ste-Catherine;* Ⓜ *St-Paul*. True to its name (literally "The Double Bottom"), this theatre is renowned for its magicians and illusionists.

The 'chansonniers' are typically French entertainers, setting comic or satirical sketches to music. The most popular include: **Le Caveau de la République** *1 boulevard St-Martin;* Ⓜ *République* which was established in 1901, and became the forerunner of the café-theatres. Its first stars came from *Le Chat Noir*, the famous cabaret in Montmartre; since then, it has witnessed the rise of countless singers and songwriters. The satirical posters advertising the shows are famous in their own right; **La Vieille Grille** *1 rue du Puits-de-l'Ermite;* Ⓜ *Place-Monge* and **Les Deux Anes** *100 boulevard de Clichy;* Ⓜ *Blanche*.

What the French call a '*cabaret*' is an informal bar where musical or satirical live entertainment is performed; perhaps the two best-known are **Le Lapin Agile** *22 rue des Saules;* Ⓜ *Lamarck-Caulaincourt*, and **Don Camillo** *10 rue des Saints-Pères;* Ⓜ *St-Germain-des-Prés*. What English speakers tend to think of as 'cabaret' includes highly polished musical floor-shows put on by carefully choreographed dance-troupes in dazzling – sometimes skimpy – attire.

Crazy-Horse – *12 avenue George-V;* Ⓜ *George-V, Alma-Marceau*. One of the finest of all the Parisian floor-shows, with shapely dancers dressed in sparkling costumes.

Folies-Bergère – *32 rue Richer;* Ⓜ *Cadet, Rue-Montmartre*. The theatre has an Art Deco façade. Many famous people have strolled along the gallery described by Maupassant, including Loïe Fuller and Yvette Guilbert, Maurice Chevalier, Yvonne Printemps and Mistinguett, Josephine Baker and Charles Trenet.

Lido – *116 avenue des Champs-Élysées;* Ⓜ *George-V*. This is undoubtedly the most international of the glitzy Parisian shows with the feathers and sequins of the famous Bluebell Girls filling the stage for every number.

Moulin-Rouge – *place Blanche;* Ⓜ *Blanche*. The Moulin-Rouge was opened in 1889; Toulouse-Lautrec was a regular visitor. Among its legendary stars were La Goulue, Mistinguett, Maurice Chevalier and Josephine Baker. It now puts on dinner-shows with sequin-studded dancers doing the French cancan.

CIRCUS

The gold-lettered name of the **Cirque d'Hiver** still features as part of the famous pink and red façade in rue Amelot (11th *arr.*) but most circuses now perform on the outskirts of Paris.

Musée des Arts Forains ⊙ *50 rue de l'Église;* Ⓜ *Félix-Fauré* collects together a number of merry-go-rounds from a forgotten era. Carved animals and beasts from Bohemia and England gave way to crude representations of cars, planes and eventually rockets; as technology evolved the fads of the funfair kept track. Still, charm and nostalgia pervade the atmosphere of this draughty warehouse full of the magic that has enchanted children since before the advent of cinema and television.

MUSIC

Opera and Ballet

The **Opéra-Bastille** *place de la Bastille;* Ⓜ *Bastille* was inaugurated on 17 March 1990 with a new production of Hector Berlioz' *The Trojans*; The **Opéra-Garnier** *place de l'Opéra;* Ⓜ *Opéra* now specialises in ballet; historic performances at the **Châtelet-Théâtre Musical de Paris** *place du Châtelet;* Ⓜ *Châtelet* include those by Diaghilev's Ballets Russes, Caruso, Gustav Mahler conducting his own *Second Symphony* (1910), Nijinsky's ill-received interpretation of Debussy's ballet *L'après-midi d'un faune*.

J. Moatti/EXPLORER

Ballet by Roland Petit

Classical

Besides the large concert halls, churches, museums and even river barges, provide Paris with varied concert venues for leading international soloists and orchestras.

Salle Gaveau – *45 rue La Boétie;* Ⓜ *Miromesnil*. Lamoureux and Pasdeloup concerts were held here and the greatest virtuosi of all time have played here. On 2 February 1927, the famous violinist Yehudi Menuhin, then aged just 11, performed Lalo's *Spanish Symphony*. The Paris audience was bowled over by his playing.

Salle Pleyel – *252 rue du Faubourg-St-Honoré;* Ⓜ *Ternes*. Pleyel was an Austrian composer and a famous piano-maker; to verify the quality of his instruments, he organised concerts by the most acclaimed musicians of his day. In 1830, Frédéric Chopin played at the inauguration of the first salle Pleyel, then in the rue Cadet. Since then, the Orchestre Symphonique de Paris, the most eminent conductors and outstanding soloists (Fyodor Chaliapin, Arthur Rubinstein, R Casadesus, Pablo Casals etc) have given dazzling performances here. The hall was renovated in 1981 and is acknowledged to have fine acoustics. It can be adapted to suit all types of instrumental ensembles.

Opéra-Comique – *5 rue Favart;* Ⓜ *Richelieu-Drouot*. Other halls include the **Théâtre des Champs-Élysées** *15 avenue Montaigne;* Ⓜ *Alma-Marceau* (home of the French national orchestra), the **Maison de Radio France** *116 avenue du Président Kennedy;* Ⓜ *Passy*, and the **Auditorium St-Germain** *4 rue Félibien;* Ⓜ *Mabillon*.

Concerts and organ recitals are often arranged in **Notre-Dame**, the **Sainte-Chapelle**, the **Madeleine**, **St-Eustache**, **St-Germain-des-Prés**, **St-Gervais**, **St-Julien-le-Pauvre**, **St-Louis-en-l'Ile**, and the **Cognac-Jay Museum**.

Pop, Rock, Folk and Funk

Olympia – *28 boulevard des Capucines;* Ⓜ *Opéra.* This large venue has hosted an eclectic range of concerts by French and international stars.

Casino de Paris – *15 rue de Clichy;* Ⓜ *Trinité.* Mistinguett starred in the review *En douce* (1923). Maurice Chevalier and Josephine Baker both triumphed here. These days, stars include Véronique Sanson, Liane Foly, Eddy Mitchell and Laurent Voulzy.

Palais des Congrès – Ⓜ *Porte Maillot.* Artists have included Charles Trenet, Léo Ferré, Charles Aznavour, Shirley MacLaine, Liza Minnelli, Frank Sinatra, Maurice Béjart's dance company, Beijing Opera Ballet and the St-Petersburg Kirov.

Le Zénith – *Parc de la Villette, 211 avenue Jean-Jaurès;* Ⓜ *Porte-de-Pantin.*

Palais-Omnisports de Paris-Bercy – *8 boulevard de Bercy;* Ⓜ *Bercy* (sport, opera, pop concerts).

La Cigale – *128 boulevard de Rochechouart;* Ⓜ *Pigalle.* La Cigale opened during the Edwardian era as a variety hall with names such as Mistinguett, Maurice Chevalier and Arletty before being turned into a cinema. In 1987, under the impetus of the Rita Mis-ouko group, it was redecorated by Philippe Starck and now attracts avant-garde bands and international stars.

Le Bataclan – *50 boulevard Voltaire;* Ⓜ *République.*

Jazz

Clubs, cellars and night-clubs ensure that nights are hot in the Latin Quarter, along the Champs-Élysées, in Montmartre and around Montparnasse. The best-known jazz venues are:

Le Baiser Salé – *58 rue des Lombards;* Ⓜ *Châtelet* ☎ 01 42 33 37 71.

Les Bouchons – *19 rue des Halles;* Ⓜ *Châtelet* ☎ 01 42 33 28 73.

Au Duc des Lombards – *42 rue des Lombards;* Ⓜ *Châtelet* ☎ 01 42 33 22 88.

Le Petit Opportun – *15 rue des Lavandières-Ste-Opportune;* Ⓜ *Châtelet* ☎ 01 42 36 01 36.

Le Sunset – *60 rue des Lombards;* Ⓜ *Châtelet* ☎ 01 40 26 46 60.

La Cave de la Huchette – *5 rue de la Huchette;* Ⓜ/*RER: Saint-Michel* ☎ 01 43 26 65 05.

Chez Félix – *23 rue Mouffetard* ☎ 01 47 07 68 78.

Le Petit Journal Saint-Michel – *71 boulevard St-Michel;* Ⓜ/*RER: Luxembourg* ☎ 01 43 26 28 59.

Les Trois Maillets – *56 rue Galande;* Ⓜ/*RER: Saint-Michel* ☎ 01 43 25 96 86 or 01 43 54 00 79.

Le Latitude Jazz Club – *7-11 rue St-Benoît;* Ⓜ *Saint-Germain-des-Prés* ☎ 01 42 61 53 53.

Le Montana – *28 rue St-Benoît;* Ⓜ *Saint-Germain-des-Prés* ☎ 01 44 39 71 00.

Le New Morning – *7-9 rue des Petites-Écuries;* Ⓜ *Château-d'Eau* ☎ 01 45 23 51 41.

Le Petit Journal Montparnasse – *13 rue du Commandant-Mouchotte;* Ⓜ *Montparnasse, Gaîté* ☎ 01 43 21 56 70.

Au Clairon des Chasseurs – *3 place du Tertre;* Ⓜ *Abbesse* ☎ 01 42 62 40 08.

As the evening draws to a close, it is not unusual for musicians in the audience to get up on stage with the band and "have a jam session".

CINEMA

On 28 December 1895 the Lumière brothers organised the first-ever public showing of the cinematograph in the Indian Lounge of the Grand Café on the boulevard des Capucines. Since then, Paris has been ever faithful in her love for the big screen and continues to be entranced by the 7th Art. There are more than 400 cinemas in the French capital.

Le Rex Cinema

A. Ei/MICHELIN

Panoramic screens: **Gaumont Kinopanorama** *60 avenue de la Motte-Picquet*; Ⓜ *Motte-Picquet*; **Grand Rex** *1 boulevard Poissonnière*; Ⓜ *Bonne-Nouvelle*; or recently-opened, **Grand Ecran Italie** *30 place d'Italie*; Ⓜ *Place d'Italie*. **Spherical screens** include the **Géode** at La Villette and the **Dôme Imax** at La Défense.

Worth checking out: **La Pagode** *57 bis rue Babylone*; Ⓜ *St-François-Xavier* – The unusual Japanese-style complex was built in the gardens of a large mansion house for his new wife by Alexandre Marcel, in 1896. The **Saint-Lambert** (15th *arr.*) is a paradise for children of all ages with its quasi-permanent programme of animation and cartoons. The **Entrepôt** (14th *arr.*) is a 3-screen-arts-centre where people meet for a film, browse in the bookshop or eat in the restaurant. In the Latin Quarter (5th *arr.*), the **Accatone** selects programmes by subject-matter or theme, the **Racine** and **Studio des Ursulines** screen films by young directors, while **Action Écoles** and **Action Rive Gauche** specialise in Hollywood classics. The **Reflet Médicis** and **Reflet Logos** (like their bookshop, the **Ciné-Reflet**) are classified as "research" cinemas screening all-time greats. Many more specialise in experimental film and avant-garde productions.

The **Cinémathèque** in the Palais de Chaillot is another attraction for film-buffs, as are the **Salle Garance** at the Centre Georges-Pompidou showing seasons of films. There is also the **Vidéothèque de Paris** situated within the Forum des Halles (place Carrée, access via the Porte du Jour, Porte St-Eustace, or Porte du Pont-Neuf) where all the films, whether documentaries or fiction, bear some reference to Paris.

Films about Paris

Hôtel du Nord (1938) directed by Marcel Carné – This film contains the famous line spoken by Arletty, "Atmosphere, atmosphere, do I look like I' ve got atmosphere?" The Hôtel du Nord still exists, near the Canal St-Martin whose bridges and locks are inseparably linked to the film, although it was, in fact, shot on a studio set.

Les Enfants du Paradis (*Children of Paradise*, 1943-1945) directed by Marcel Carné – Arletty/Garance, Jean-Louis Barrault/Baptiste, Frédéric Lemaître/Pierre Brasseur, Maria Casarès, dialogue by Prévert...this film is one of cinema's all-time classics.

Gigi (1948) directed by Claude Dolbert – This period movie is full of local colour. The story of a young girl, brought up by her aunt, is married off to a rake. Not to be confused with the musical version.

Zazie dans le métro (*Zazie on the Underground*, 1959) directed by Louis Malle – A burlesque comedy which is a screen adaptation of an idea by Raymond Queneau.

A bout de souffle (*Breathless*, 1959) – A light touch on the camera and natural settings. **Jean-Luc Godard**'s film laid down the basic principles of the **New Wave**.

Les 400 coups (*The 400 Blows*, 1959) directed by François Truffaut – A lively spontaneous Parisian lad, Antoine Doinel, ends up in a borstal-type institution. The unforgettable shots of the streets of Paris are reminiscent of the photographic art of Doisneau.

Charade (1962) directed by Stanley Donen – Audrey Hepburn is chased through Paris by a gang of ruffians and helped by Cary Grant. Is he or is he not interested in the missing 250 000 dollars?

Last Tango in Paris (1972) – Bernardo Bertolucci directs this fateful story of obsessive love in Paris. Stars include Marlon Brando and Maria Schneider.

Le locataire (*The Tenant*, 1976) directed by Roman Polanski – A lonely young man falls victim to a conspiracy in an apartment block full of hostile neighbours.

Le dernier Métro (*The Last Metro*, 1980) directed by François Truffaut – The oppressive atmosphere of Paris during the German Occupation.

La passante de Sans-Souci (1981) directed by Jacques Rouffio – A moving performance by Romy Schneider in her last film. Having fled to Paris (Hôtel George V then Pigalle) to escape Nazi killers, she is finally caught.

Diva (1981) directed by Beneix – Paris serves as a refined context for two very different themes. A beautiful black opera singer gets indirectly entangled with the harsh and violent underworld.

Subway (1985) directed by Luc Besson – This was filmed like a video clip, with musical backing by Eric Serra. The leading actors (Isabelle Adjani and Christophe Lambert) express their love in the labyrinthine world of the Paris Metro.

Les amants du Pont-Neuf (1991) directed by Léo Carax – The décors are artificial and heighten the unreal atmosphere of the life led by two young homeless lovers in the middle of the Pont-Neuf while work is being carried out on the bridge.

Insider's Paris

To become acquainted with the elusive quality of Paris, there is no better way than to take to the streets on foot. After dark, each neighbourhood boasts its own charismatic haunts a few of which are listed here. Remember, however, that the metro system begins to shut down after midnight!

Paris owes some of its charm to its many cafés, of which there are 12 000 in the city: stretched along the boulevards with tables spilling onto the street, haunted by the *literati* true to the spirit of the "Left Bank", or merely hosting locals from the neighbourhood. The most popular time of day is after work before dinner and a night out (5 to 7pm).

After dark, the quest for the best night-spot is a delicate issue. The discerning Parisian tends to be discreet in his choice of venue, relying on word of mouth for being at the right place at the right time, exclusive to all but the initiated and dedicated night-owls. With changes in trend the 'hottest' venues move from les Halles to the Marais, Bastille or Montmartre to the Temple area, Charonne, Belleville or Butte-aux-Cailles: once the smart set moves on, life goes back to what it was before.

Pubs – The conviviality of our Irish and British neighbours has acclimatised very well to life in Paris, attracting to places steeped in rustic charm an open-minded clientele of all ages who share an extrovert sense of humour. There is the **Cave Montpensier** (1st *arr.*), **Flann O' Brien** (1st *arr.*), **James' Ulysses Bar** (1st *arr.*), **Irish Pub** (2nd *arr.*), **Kitty O' Shea** (2nd *arr.*), **Quiet Man** (3rd *arr.*), **Connoly's Corner** (5th *arr.*), **Finnegan's Wake** (5th *arr.*), **Le Requin Chagrin** (5th *arr.*), and the **James Joyce Pub** (17th *arr.*).

Other purveyors of fine beers include **Le Sous-Bock** (1st *arr.*), **Baragouin** (2nd *arr.*), the **Pub St-Germain** (6th *arr.*), the **Taverne de Nesle** (6th *arr.*) and the **Falstaff** (14th *arr.*).

Bistros – The term "*bistro*" was coined from the Cossack word meaning "Quickly!" shouted with their drink orders by the men who remained after the occupation of Paris after the fall of Napoleon I. These days, "bistros" vary greatly in style, ranging from a small informal café to restaurants offering the most sophisticated *cuisine*.

Places of historical interest – Set in contexts with historic associations, memories of important events or people, these places continue to be typically Parisian. Many have lost their authenticity and original décors may have changed, but they still attract nostalgic visitors in search of a suggestion of that painter, writer, poet, philosopher or adventurer's passing. Along the boulevard St-Germain are **Les Deux Magots**, **Le Flore**, the **Brasserie Lipp**, and **Le Procope**. Montparnasse boasts **Le Sélect**, **Le Dôme**, **La Coupole**, **La Rotonde** and **La Clôserie des Lilas**. The Opéra district includes **Harry's New York Bar** and the **Café de la Paix**. **Fouquet's** stands on the Champs-Élysées and **Bofinger** near Bastille.

Design – Famous architects and designers have had a hand in designing certain cafés, giving these immediate appeal. Among the most popular are **Café Marly** and **Café Richelieu** within the Louvre complex, the **Café Beaubourg** (alongside the Centre Pompidou) and **Iguane** (11th *arr.*).

Students – Visitors, foreign students attending the Sorbonne and young *au-pairs* congregate at weekends in the Latin quarter and around the St-Germain area, at **Le Piano Vache**, **Le Violon Dingue**, **Polly Magoo**, **Le Cloître**, **Le Saint** (5th *arr.*), **Chez Georges** and **Le Dix** (6th *arr.*), to **La Scala** (1st *arr.*), **La Locomotive** (18th *arr.*), or in the Marais district **Au Petit Fer-à-Cheval**, **Pick-Clops** (4th *arr.*), Montparnasse and Blanche **Le Dépanneur**, **Moloko** (9th *arr.*), the Opéra district **Hard-Rock Café** (9th *arr.*), the Halles **Baragouin**, **Le Café Noir**, **Le Rex-Club** (2nd *arr.*) or on the Butte-aux-Cailles **La Folie-en-Tête** (13th *arr.*).

Tex-Mex – Spare ribs, burgers and Mexican or Texan cuisine and drinks (tequila, margarita) are popular among night-owls at **La Perla** (4th *arr.*) and **Mustang Café** (14th *arr.*). A taste of **Spain** and its *tapas* can be found in the rue de Lappe (11th *arr.*) and on the Butte-aux-Cailles (13th *arr.*).

Afro-Caribbean – *See ETHNIC ENCLAVES below.*

Latin America – Amateur bands perform in the cellar of the *Café-Corail* (2nd *arr.*).

Jazz – *La Paillote* and the *Birdland* (6th *arr.*) are famous for their extensive record collections (*see jazz listing above*). The *Café de la Plage* (11th *arr.*) and *Folie-en-Tête* (13th *arr.*) both host live music.

Rock-blues – The *Café-Corail Concert* has live bands, as does *L'Utopia* (14th *arr.*).

Paris on the internet

Bars offering public access to the internet are proliferating in Paris – do check on the cost of connection which seems to vary considerably.

Le Web Bar *32 rue Picardie* in le Marais open to 2am – **Café Orbital** *rue du 4 Septembre* near la Bourse – **Cybercafé** *Cité-Ciné* at les Halles – **Net Coffee** *27 rue Lacépède* in the Latin quarter begins closing down at 10pm – **Virgin Café** *Virgin Megastore Champs-Élysées* – **Bistrot Internet** *Galerie Lafayette* – **La Tête dans les Nuages** *5 boulevard des Italiens* – **High-tech** *66 boulevard Montparnasse* – **World Net Café** *Cinéma UGC, Cité les Halles*.

BY NEIGHBOURHOOD

Districts are listed alphabetically – refer to Principal Sights map on page 4-6.

Bastille and Faubourg-St-Antoine

The opening of the **Opéra Bastille** has brought lustre to the run-down working-class district occupied largely by migrants from the Auvergne and Aveyron regions. Furniture and clothes shops abound alongside contemporary art galleries and artists' studios in the labyrinth of little streets. It has become fashionable to mingle with the less fortunate in Paris' 'down-town' known as the "Bastoche". With its numerous brasseries, in particular **Bofinger** which was established in 1864, place de la Bastille has become the mandatory stop-off point between the Marais and rue de Charonne, rue de la Roquette, rue de Lappe, rue St-Sabin and rue Keller, where restaurants, cafés, beer cellars, wine bars and dance halls proliferate. Tequila, claret or Valdepenas may be quaffed with "*tapas*" or dinner may be preferred overlooking yachts moored in the **marina**.

Le Balajo – *9 rue de Lappe;* Ⓜ *Bastille.* The main action happens on Monday and Thursday nights, when an air of nostalgia is solicited by an eclectic programme of hits from the 1950s, 60s and 70s. Open Monday, Thursday to Saturday 11pm – dawn.

Le Bar Sans Nom – *49 rue de Lappe;* Ⓜ *Bastille.* Torch-style lighting and walls covered in plants give a homely feel to a bar that serves really good fresh fruit juices. Open daily 8pm – 2am.

Le Bistrot du Peintre – *116 avenue Ledru-Rollin;* Ⓜ *Ledru-Rollin.* Windows are reflected in mirrors framed in great carved Art Nouveau wooden frames. Fine bar.

Café de l'Industrie – *16 rue St-Sabin;* Ⓜ *St-Sabin, Bastille.* This is a classic local venue with a quiet colonial-style back room. Rue St-Sabin is just off the tourist track through rue de Lappe. Open Sunday to Friday 11am – 2am.

Café de la Plage – *59 rue de Charonne;* Ⓜ *Ledru-Rollin.* Tinged with urban Bohemia, the laid-back atmosphere that pervades the bar is inspired by live jazz (basement) or jam sessions by one or two amateur musicians. Open daily 1pm – 2am.

La Chapelle des Lombards – *19 rue de Lappe;* Ⓜ *Bastille.* West Indian, Latin-American and African music disco for all tropical rhythm fans. Open Monday to Saturday 8pm – dawn.

Iguana – *15 rue de la Roquette;* Ⓜ *Bastille.* A mini *Café Beaubourg* overlooking the major crossroads at rue de la Roquette and rue de Lappe. Open daily 9am – 4am.

L'Entrepôt – *14 rue de Charonne Bastille;* Ⓜ *Ledru-Rollin.* Enticing décor with one wall advertising *Ripolin* paint and another shoe polish, masked by fake bricks. Mexican specialities. Open daily 7pm – 2am.

Pause-Café – *41 rue de Charonne;* Ⓜ *Ledru-Rollin.* Quiet, traditional café with a stylish U-shaped bar set in the centre of the high-ceilinged room suffused with light from low hanging lamps. A good place to get away from it all. Open Tuesday to Saturday 9am – 1am.

E. Baret

Place de la Bastille from the Arsenal Marina

Batignolles-Ternes

The village of Les Batignolles, which was made famous by Verlaine and Mallarmé, marks the boundary between the working-class commercial neighbourhood of the 17th *arrondissement* and its residential sector. Large numbers of shops line rue des Moines and rue des Batignolles off the delightful **place du Docteur-Lobligeois** dominated by the distinctive white columns of the church of Ste-Marie-des-Batignolles. Further east, beyond avenue de Clichy is the **Cité des Fleurs** (rue Cardinet), one of the finest town houses in Paris.

West of Les Batignolles, on the other side of the railway tracks, the main attractions are the shops in rue Lévis and rue de Tocqueville, place and avenue des Ternes (with the best FNAC store) and rue Poncelet.

L'Endroit – *67 place du Docteur-Félix-Lobligeois;* M *Rome.* This designer bar with its sophisticated lighting overlooks a picturesque square in the heart of Les Batignolles village. Open Monday to Saturday midday – 2am.

James Joyce Pub – *71 boulevard Gouvion-St-Cyr;* M *Porte-Maillot.* The bar is crammed every evening with revellers of all ages, from all walks of life. The stained-glass windows depict Dublin's main landmarks. Open daily midday – 1am (1.30am Friday, Saturday).

La Main Jaune – *place de la Porte-Champerret; Metro/RER: Pereire-Porte-de-Champerret.* The teenage roller-disco venue made famous by the film *La Boum*, where dancing is done on skates (for the most talented at least). The décor designed by Philippe Starck multiplies the mirror effects and emphasises the place's maze-like depth. Open Wednesday and weekends 2.30pm – 7pm; Friday, Saturday and eve of holidays 10pm – dawn.

Street scene in Belleville

Belleville-Ménilmontant

Like Montmartre, the Belleville and Ménilmontant neighbourhoods nestling on a hillside were annexed by Paris during the last century. The urban redevelopment launched by Haussmann brought large numbers of working-class people to the area; these have been followed by thousands of immigrant Jews, Russians, Poles, North Africans, Turks, Yugoslavs, Pakistanis, and lately Asians. Most of the exotic restaurants are concentrated in **rue de Belleville**.

The district is slowly being rebuilt in concrete, with new buildings standing alongside the old houses of rue Ramponneau, rue des Envierges and rue des Cascades. To the north lies the rugged, picturesque **Parc Buttes-Chaumont** with the "**quartier d'Amérique**", built on former quarries from which gypsum was once exported to the United States beyond. Between rue David-d'Anger and rue Mousaïa is an unusual group of suburban houses.

Le Baratin – *3 rue Jouye-Rouve;* M *Belleville, Pyrénées.* One of "the" main addresses in Belleville, a short walk from the park and Chinese restaurants, this wine bar is popular with locals and artists. Open Tuesday to Sunday midday (5pm weekends) – 2am.

Bistro-Cave des Envierges – *11 rue des Envierges;* M *Pyrénées.* The landlord claims his establishment to be "The temple of wine" – an excuse for his annual search for good vintages. Open midday – midnight (8pm weekends).

Champs-Élysées

A recent face-lift has reinstated the avenue's identity as the place in which to be seen browsing in the arcades or the **Virgin Megastore**, loitering in a café or going to see a newly released film. By day as by night, tourists mingle with visitors to the capital to dine out in a neighbouring street, enjoy one of the spectacular revues at the *Lido* and *Crazy Horse* or while away the hours until dawn at a famous club.

Café de Paris – *93 avenue des Champs-Élysées*; Ⓜ *George-V*. The street café is especially pleasant in summer; the back room is modelled on an English gentlemen's club, with red moleskin seats and under-stated formality.

Fouquet's – *99 avenue des Champs-Élysées*; Ⓜ *George-V*. This listed building is home to one of the last famous Champs-Élysées street cafés, popular with show-biz personalities; actors nominated for the César awards come here to celebrate. Open daily 8.30am – 2am.

Gobelins – Butte-aux-Cailles – Tolbiac

Like all the *buttes* or hills in Paris, Butte-aux-Cailles has its own distinctive character. Village streets (rue Samson, rue des Cinq-Diamants, rue de la Butte-aux-Cailles) are thronged with locals and inhabitants of the high-rise development at Glacière and place d'Italie. The 13th *arr.*, an old working-class district under permanent redevelopment, is acquiring a more frenetic, exotic quality with the encroachment of Chinatown.

La Folle en Tête – *33 rue de la Butte-aux-Cailles*; Ⓜ *Place-d'Italie, Corvisart*. Musical instruments decorate this pleasant bar conducive to reading, chess, drawing, chatting among friends or listening to musicians. The clientele is young. Open Monday to Saturday 10am – 2am.

Papagallo – *25 rue des Cinq-Diamants*; Ⓜ *Corvisart*. A large bar which serves *tapas*; gets very busy at weekends. Open 6pm – 2am.

Grands Boulevards and Opéra

This district basked in fame from the 19C through to the 1950s, providing prestigious locations for the head quarters of major banks (Crédit Lyonnais, BNP, Société Générale). Little of its original charm subsists today, home now to the expensive luxury and fashion boutiques around La Madeleine and Opéra.

The Boulevards are busy throughout the day, drawing shoppers to the **Printemps**, **Galeries Lafayette** and **Marks & Spencer**, who might break for a drink on the terrace of the famous **Café de la Paix** before going on to the cinema, preferably to the **Grand Rex** or **Max Linder**. At the end of the day, people meet in one of the brasseries for a bite maybe before a performance at the **Opéra**, the **Folies-Bergère** or **Olympia** to hear a favourite singer.

Bar Romain – *6 rue Caumartin*; Ⓜ *Opéra, Madeleine*. The woodwork, furniture and paintings recreate the atmosphere of decadent Rome. An elegant, friendly establishment conveniently near *Olympia*. Open daily midday – 2am.

Café de la Paix – *12 boulevard des Capucines*; Ⓜ *Opéra*. Strategically located on the capital's busiest crossroads, one of the greatest achievements of Haussmann's town planning programme, this café has featured in society circles since it opened in 1862; it latterly attracted numerous stars including Maurice Chevalier, Josephine Baker, Mistinguett and Serge Lifar, to name but a few. Open daily 10am – 1.30am, (11am – 2am bar).

Café Vogue – *50 rue de la Chaussée-d'Antin*; Ⓜ *Chaussée-d'Antin*. The huge premises with its lofty glazed roof accommodates a corner café, dance floor and restaurant, and Piano bar. Student Happy Hour on Wednesday evenings. Open Tuesday to Saturday 10pm – dawn.

Le Corail Café-Concert – *140 rue Montmartre*; Ⓜ *Rue Montmartre*. Live music in the basement: Brazilian at weekends, rock and blues on Wednesdays and Thursdays. Open Tuesday to Sunday around the clock.

Hard-Rock Café – *14 boulevard Montmartre*; Ⓜ *Richelieu-Drouot*. Like its sister outlets world wide, this shrine to the music cult displays clothes from the wardrobes of Madonna (bra-top), Prince (jacket), Michael Jackson (trousers) and Maurice Chevalier (straw boater). Standard Hard-Rock fare. Open daily 11.30am – 2am.

Harry's New York Bar – *5 rue Daunou*; Ⓜ *Opéra*. Where else could Americans *rendez vous* in Paris over a serious "Bloody Mary" or "Blue Lagoon"? Open daily 10.30am – 4am.

Kitty O' Shea – *10 rue des Capucines*; Ⓜ *Madeleine, Opéra*. A lively, friendly pub for home-sick Dubliners, panelled in wood from Ireland, it often plays Irish music. Open daily until 1.30am.

Rex-Club – *5 boulevard Poissonnière*; Ⓜ *Bonne-Nouvelle*. A large clinical space, sparsely lit by bright lights projected onto the bar and stage, hosts an eclectic programme of live music playing mainly techno-trance, (storm on Fridays). Open 11pm – dawn; closed throughout August.

Les Halles – Beaubourg

Much of the erstwhile atmosphere of the "belly of Paris" went when Baltard's pavilions were removed. The Forum des Halles tunnels its way below ground like a rabbit-warren between the rotunda of the Bourse du Commerce and the brightly-coloured tubes of the Centre Georges-Pompidou. Renovation of the area has opened up the space around the Church of **St Eustache** which is now floodlit and the Stravinski Fountain is a popular place to watch the world go by.

The "navel of Paris" nevertheless continues to bustle with people of all kinds converging upon the shops, sometimes from the provinces, drawing buskers, mime artists, and eccentrics of every possible kind. During the day, the main crowds collect in the Forum, thronging the **place des Innocents**, rue Pierre-Lescot and the narrow streets lying perpendicular to it (rue des Prêcheurs, rue de la Grande-Truanderie) which are lined with shops selling jewellery, Art Nouveau bric-à-brac, and records; **rue St-Denis** is full of shoe shops and boutiques; **rue du Jour**, of women's fashions. At night, the crowds move away to the east, between the Church of St-Merri and the Fountain of the Innocents (rue des Lombards).

Banana Café – *13 rue de la Ferronnerie;* Ⓜ *Les Halles.* This 'hip' café is often very crowded with live gigs in the basement. Open daily 11pm – dawn.

Le Baragouin – *17 rue Tiquetonne;* Ⓜ *Les Halles, Etienne-Marcel.* This bar attracts much of its clientele from Brittany, happy to share a beer with fellow Bretons at a long central table in the vaulted back room. Open daily 5pm – 2am (7pm – 1am Sunday).

Le Bistrot d'Eustache – *37 rue Berner;* Ⓜ *Louvre-Rivoli.* This bar, opposite the gardens so desolate after dark, has a good following particularly Thursday, Friday and Saturday nights. Open daily to 2am.

Café Beaubourg – *100 rue St-Martin;* Ⓜ *Châtelet, Hôtel-de-Ville.* A designer café with interiors by Christian de Portzamparc, it has a spacious, comfortable terrace stretching along the side of the Centre Georges-Pompidou. Noticeably frequented by 'beautiful people'. On wet days, it's good to take refuge inside by the window between rows of shelves filled with magazines, and enjoy a hot chocolate! Open daily 8am – 1am (2am Friday and Saturday).

Le Café Noir – *65 rue Montmartre;* Ⓜ *Etienne-Marcel.* This café particularly appeals to the young. Sixties music. Open 3pm – 2am.

Le Comptoir – *14 rue Vauvilliers;* Ⓜ *Louvre-Rivoli, Châtelet.* Large L-shaped bar serving *tapas.* Open midday – 2am.

Flann O' Brien – *6 rue Bailleul;* Ⓜ *Châtelet, Louvre-Rivoli.* On the evening of St Patrick's Day (17 March), the bar is crowded to celebrate the spirit of the Emerald Isle. The walls are covered in traditional Irish green. Open daily 4pm – 2am, live performance from 10pm.

Irish Pub – *55 rue Montmartre;* Ⓜ *Etienne-Marcel.* A genuine Irish pub imbued with atmosphere, complete with beams and a large wheel on the wall. Open daily 4pm – 2.30am.

Le Petit Marcel – *65 rue Rambuteau;* Ⓜ *Rambuteau.* A pocket-sized bistro with a crowd of regular customers, situated between Les Halles and Beaubourg. Attractive old-fashioned décor. Open daily 7pm – 2am.

Stravinski Fountain

Quigley's Point – *5 rue du Jour;* Ⓜ *Les Halles.* Quiet atmosphere and quality décor (counter, wainscoting, upholstered seats, portraits of writers carefully hung round the walls). Busiest during the daytime. Open daily 10am – 2am.

Le Sous-Bock – *49 rue St-Honoré;* Ⓜ *Châtelet.* This bar boasts an extensive choice of beer (400 kinds) and dart board. Open daily 11am – 5am.

Ile Saint-Louis

Its aristocratic 17C residences provided inspiration for Baudelaire who stayed in the Hôtel Lauzun. A stroll along the river banks or quaysides on the island is one of the most romantic walks in Paris.

Berthillon – *31 rue St-Louis-en-l'Ile;* Ⓜ *Pont-Marie.* This is the most famous ice-cream maker in Paris, famous for smooth, creamy ices and delicious sorbets. Open 10am – 8pm Wednesday to Sunday for take-away ice creams; 1pm – 8pm Wednesday to Friday, 2pm – 8pm Saturday, Sunday for eating-in. Closed throughout the summer.

Le Flore en l'Ile – *42 quai d'Orléans;* Ⓜ *Pont-Marie.* Tea room and restaurant. Superb view over the apse of Notre-Dame. Open daily 10am – 1am.

Latin Quarter

The student quarter boasts many avant-garde and experimental cinemas drawing people from all walks of life like a magnet. The **Boul' Mich** (boulevard St-Michel) is a colourful succession of boutiques, cafés, sandwich and kebab bars, of pizzerias with garish signs. Crowds loiter around the *fontaine St-Michel.* The **rue St-André-des-Arts**, now rather touristy, leads to the Odéon district with its many cinemas (go through the picturesque **Cour du Commerce St-André** along the rear of *Le Procope*). The statue of Danton is another traditional meeting place. The rue de l'Odéon is famous for its bookshops; rue Monsieur-le-Prince is lined with exotic restaurants and is home to a very old Parisian bistro (*Polidor*); rue de l'École-de-Médecine is wellknown for its Viennese cake-shop.

The narrow pedestrianised streets on the east side of the boulevard St-Michel, around rue de la Huchette, are packed with gaudy Greek restaurants catering almost exclusively to tourists. One big attraction must be the **Studio Galande** *42 rue Galande* where the cult movie The Rocky Horror Picture Show has been running for 18 years!

Fontaine Saint-Michel

A quieter atmosphere pervades place Maubert and **rue Dante** where all the specialist strip-cartoon dealers have their shops. Back towards the Panthéon, rue de la Montagne-Ste-Geneviève and rue Laplace are popular student haunts. The rue Mouffetard ("la Mouffe") leads to the charming **place de la Contrescarpe** and the St-Médard district which is famous for its market. These are some of the most picturesque places in the whole of Paris.

Le Bateau Ivre – *40 rue Descartes;* Ⓜ *Place-Monge.* A small bar which has borrowed from Rimbaud's poetry a name for a cocktail and for a painting hung up near the ceiling. Open daily 4pm – 2am.

Le Cloître – *19 rue St-Jacques;* Ⓜ*/RER: St-Michel (exit Notre-Dame).* A pleasant bar papered with posters popular with people of all ages. Open daily 3pm – 2am.

Connoly's Corner – *12 rue de Mirbel;* Ⓜ *Censier-Duabenton.* Set back from the rue Mouffetard, this is a very friendly pub where ties hang like trophies. Open daily 4pm – 1am; live music Saturday from 5pm.

Finnegan's Wake – *9 rue des Boulangers;* Ⓜ *Jussieu, Cardinal-Lemoine.* This peaceful establishment is one of the real Irish pubs in Paris. Open daily 8am (4pm weekends) – midnight.

La Fourmi Ailée – *8 rue du Fouarre;* M *St-Michel, Maubert-Mutualité*. Step into a book-shop and find yourself in a serene tea shop; a good place to stop at just round the corner from Notre-Dame. Open Wednesday to Monday midday – 6.30pm.

Le Piano Vache – *8 rue Laplace;* M *Maubert-Mutualité*. All three bars with their timber beams are usually populated with students. When really busy, the back room fills with thick cigarette smoke. Open daily midday – 2am.

Polly Magoo – *11 rue St-Jacques;* M *St-Michel (exit Notre-Dame)*. A Sixties atmosphere pervades this rather Bohemian bar. Open daily midday – 4am.

Le Requin Chagrin – *10 rue Mouffetard;* M *Place-Monge*. One of the most discreet bars in the district. Open daily 3pm – 2am.

La Restauration Viennoise – *8 rue de l'École-de-Médecine;* M *Odéon*. Students from the Latin Quarter are particularly familiar with the mouth-watering cakes and pastries sold here, having all sat at one of the tables of this establishment at some time or another. Open weekdays 9am – 1915; closed throughout the summer.

Le Saint – *7 rue St-Séverin;* M *Cluny-Sorbonne/RER: St-Michel*. A good student disco in a long vaulted 13C cellar: a "must" for any nocturnal visit to the Latin Quarter. Open Tuesday to Sunday 11pm – dawn.

Le Violon Dingue – *45 rue de la Montagne-Ste-Geneviève;* M *Maubert-Mutualité*. This is the place to be when the American "Superbowl" final is being broadcast! Open daily 6pm – 2am.

Le Marais

This old district was saved from destruction by the novelist-cum-Arts Minister André Malraux. It accommodates both a well-established Jewish community in the **rue des Rosiers** and a younger gay set. "Trendy" bars have flourished (junction of rue Vieille-du-Temple and Sainte-Croix-de-la-Bretonnerie) and off-beat fashion designers operate from around the **rue des Francs-Bourgeois**. More traditional shops survive by the Blancs-Manteaux market, in and around the rue St-Antoine. The delightful **place du Marché-Ste-Catherine** is surrounded by cafés. At the end of the gardens in the Hôtel de Sully, a narrow passageway leads beneath arcades to the **place des Vosges** lined with boutiques, antique shops and art galleries. The north end of the Marais is quieter, with a large number of museums. Further north still is the **Temple** district, the mecca for tailored leather. It also includes a few of the best-known Parisian nightclubs.

Au Petit Fer-à-Cheval – *30 rue Vieille-du-Temple;* M *St-Paul, Hôtel-de-Ville*. A wonderful little bistro. Note the chandelier and the engraved glass partition separating off the back room. Open daily 9am (11am Saturday and Sunday) – 2am.

Café Martini – *11 rue du Pas-de-la-Mule;* M *Chemin-Vert*. A chic, sophisticated café that blends into the artistic atmosphere of the nearby place des Vosges. Open daily 8am – 2am.

L'Ebouillanté – *6 rue des Barres;* M *Pont-Marie, Hôtel-de-Ville*. This is the tiniest tea-room in the capital (room on first floor) located in a street behind the Church of St Ger-vais and St Protais. A step back in time, the scene is straight out of a cloak-and-dagger film. Tea is served with cakes, salads, and 'bricks' (delicate Moroccan-style deep-fried filled pastries). Open midday – 9pm.

Les Enfants Gâtés – *43 rue des Francs-Bourgeois;* M *St-Paul*. The walls are hung with bill-posters and photographs of actors. An ideal place to break from hours of shopping in a vast armchair, to play a game of chess or backgammon, or to browse through the paper. Open daily midday – 7pm.

Le Loir dans la Théière – *3 rue des Rosiers;* M *St-Paul*. A tearoom decorated in a relaxing shade of pale green. Open daily midday – 7pm (closed in August).

Mariage Frères – *30 rue du Bourg-Tibourg;* M *Hôtel-de-Ville*. Full of charm, this shop stocks over 400 varieties of tea and a wide range of tea-related articles and accessories. The tearoom serves excellent cakes and, of course, a full choice of teas. Don't miss the small **museum** on the upper floor, strongly scented, containing a display of unusual tea-pots: dromedaries, "toppling" pots and Art Deco enamelware, caddies, labels and tea chests. Open daily midday – 7pm.

Le Piano-Zinc – *49 rue des Blancs-Manteaux;* M *Rambuteau*. Laughter, smiles, good fun and raucous singing pervade all three floors of this hassle-free establishment in "Gay Paree". Open 6pm – 2am.

Le Pick-Clops – *corner of the rue Vieille-du-Temple and the rue du Roi-de-Sicile;* M *Hôtel-de-Ville, St-Paul*. A funky bar with pink fluorescent neon lighting.

Quiet Man – *5 rue des Haudriettes;* M *Rambuteau*. A small Irish pub (basement room). Mind the darts! Open daily 4pm – 2am.

La Tartine – *24 rue de Rivoli;* M *Hôtel-de-Ville, St-Paul*. A truly Parisian bistro. Open Thursday to Monday.

Le Zinc – *4 rue Caron;* M *St-Paul*. Located at the entrance to the place du Marché-Ste-Catherine, the *Zinc* is popular with bull-fighting fans (numerous posters). Open daily 11am – 2am (8.30am – 6pm Sunday)

Opus Café – *167 quai Valmy;* M *Louis-Blanc, Colonel Fabien*. A vast loft-like space near the Canal St-Martin. Open Monday to Saturday 8pm – 3am.

Montmartre-Pigalle

In the late 19C, shortly after the village was incorporated into the city of Paris, a journalist wrote: "The local bars have closed, the lilac trees have been cut, the hedges replaced by stone walls and the gardens divided into building plots. However, of all the suburbs, Montmartre has its own special brand of charm, a varied and complex charm that is a combination of good and bad things". Many faces of Montmartre still exist today, glimpsed occasionally in what remains of the old provincial village.

Between **place Clichy**, one of the most crowded squares in the capital with its large number of restaurants and cinemas clustered around the unmistakable *Wepler* brasserie, and **place Pigalle**, the streets are populated with concert venues, theatres, nightclubs and sex shops. Beyond place Pigalle and its immediate vicinity animated by many different types of people, lie boulevard de Rochechouart, the Tati store and the picturesque, cosmopolitan Barbès district.

At the foot of square Willette, the extraordinarily busy **St-Pierre Market** provides an opportunity to find fabrics and clothing at rock-bottom prices. On the other side of the boulevard, the **Goutte-d'Or** district proffers Arab and African fabrics, wholesale food shops, hardware, luggage and jewellery shops.

Below boulevard Montmartre, the 9th *arrondissement* encompasses the predominantly residential area known to some as la Nouvelle Athènes (*see main text under* SAINT-LAZARE). This includes **place St-Georges**, a popular meeting place for night-owls when the atmosphere of the Romantic spirit may be evoked through its middle-class 19C streets.

Au Virage Lepic – *61 rue Lepic*; Ⓜ *Blanche*. A small informal Montmartre bistro as good for a drink as for a meal. Open Wednesday to Monday until 2am, closed throughout the summer.

Paris Centre Studio – *54a rue de Clichy*; Ⓜ *Place-de-Clichy*. Part of a dance school, a large room with parquet floor and mirrored walls enables experienced dancers to practise their steps. Iodine sprays reoxygenate the air and make it more invigorating. Sessions at 8.30pm, 10.30pm, 00.30am, 2.30am (weekends).

Le Dépanneur – *27 rue Fontaine*; Ⓜ *Blanche*. The first bar to have earned a name for itself in the district is famed for its tequila. Open around the clock.

La Locomotive – *90 boulevard de Clichy*; Ⓜ *Blanche*. The Loco is a safe bet, just round the corner from the Moulin-Rouge. It attracts large numbers of tourists and young people. Live music every Tuesday and Friday. Open Tuesday to Sunday 11pm – dawn.

Le Moloko – *26 rue Fontaine*; Ⓜ *Blanche*. The busiest bar on the block with dancing on the ground floor, soft lighting and comfy armchairs in which to collapse upstairs. Open daily 2pm – 6am.

Le Pigalle – *99 boulevard de Clichy*; Ⓜ *Pigalle*. Large brasserie opposite the *Folie's*, the 1950s décor in orange, yellow and black is listed as being of special historic interest! Open 8am – 5am.

Le Sancerre – *35 rue des Abbesses*; Ⓜ *Abbesses*. One of the most famous addresses in Montmartre, by day or by night. Open 7am – 2am.

Montparnasse-Alésia

At the turn of the century, this rural district was favoured by the artists of the Paris School; between the two World Wars its bars were frequented by the "lost generation" of American writers; today, it is dominated by the huge **Maine-Montparnasse complex** and its skyscraper.

The streets of Montparnasse are busy day-in-day-out. Rue de Rennes is an artery for traffic and shoppers between St-Germain and Montparnasse; rue de la Gaîté is lined with theatres and peep shows; rue Montparnasse and rue d'Odessa accommodate endless *crêperies* selling pancakes and fried snacks to travellers coming through the Gare Montparnasse, the terminus for trains arriving from Western France and Brittany. Rue du Maine has several good restaurants. Along the boulevard oyster-serving brasseries, famous cafés and multi-screen cinemas cater continuously for the crowds. Beyond the cemetery, however, a quiet neighbourhood thrives in rue Daguerre (towards Denfert-Rochereau), rue Didot, rue Raymond-Losserand (towards Pernety) and avenue du Général-Leclerc.

La Clôserie des Lilas – *171 boulevard du Montparnasse*; Ⓜ *Vavin*. This bar with its cosy atmosphere was once frequented by a number of great figures from the early 20C world of art and literature (Breton, Hemingway): their names live on, through the copper plates on some of the tables. Open daily 11am – 2am.

In the early 1920s noted American poet Ezra Pound lived with his wife Dorothy at no 70bis rue Notre-Dame-des-Champs above a working sawmill. In their modestly appointed apartment, Pound began writing his lifetime work, the *Cantos*.

Le Dôme – *108 boulevard du Montparnasse*; Ⓜ *Vavin*. This was another favourite haunt for American tourists in the 1920s and the post-war years. Open Tuesday to Sunday midday – 3pm, 7pm – 00.45am.

Le Sélect – *99 boulevard du Montparnasse;* Ⓜ *Vavin.* The bar was immediately successful when it opened in 1924. In contrast to the large neighbouring brasseries, the café has managed to retain its quiet, intimate atmosphere. Open daily 8.30am – 12.30pm.

La Coupole – *102 boulevard du Montparnasse;* Ⓜ *Vavin.* The bar, which was refurbished throughout in 1988, is still one of Paris' major night-time venues, where a lively crowd dine late into the evening. Open daily 7.30am – 2am.

La Rotonde – *105 boulevard du Montparnasse;* Ⓜ *Vavin.* Foujita, Derain, Modigliani, Vlaminck and Van Dongen once met here to discuss their hopes and expectations. Open daily 8am – 2am.

Le Falstaff – *42 rue Montparnasse;* Ⓜ *Montparnasse-Bienvenüe.* A much-loved beer bar in a street packed with pancake houses. Jovial atmosphere. Open daily midday – 4.30am.

Mustang Café – *84 rue Montparnasse;* Ⓜ *Montparnasse-Bienvenüe.* Bar and Tex-Mex food opposite the *Falstaff.* Open daily 9am – 5am.

Le Rosebud – *11bis rue Delambre;* Ⓜ *Vavin.* Suits and ties are not out of place in this rather smarter bar decorated with posters of Mistinguett. Open daily until 2am.

Le Troupeau – *11 rue Francis-de-Pressensé;* ⓂPernety. A small bar and a cellar with just enough room for two musicians; frequented by locals; cheap drinks. Open daily 7pm – 2am.

L'Utopia – *79 rue de l'Ouest;* Ⓜ *Pernety.* Situated in a somewhat run-down part of town, this venue has good live rock and blues music. Open Tuesday to Saturday 10.30pm – 3am (dawn Friday, Saturday)

Palais-Royal – Saint-Roch

The **Palais-Royal** gardens are among the finest in Paris. Treat yourself to an ice cream in the *Muscade* tearoom at the far end, or to window-shopping along the gallery for lead soldiers, medals or antiques. Note the old-fashioned feel. Pause by the sophisticated window display in the *Salons du Palais-Royal Shiseido,* the old bookshops, or the delightful little toy shop in the Beaujolais arcade on the corner with one of the passages leading into the street of the same name. Saunter along the street from **place des Victoires**, a mecca of high fashion (*Kenzo*), towards **avenue de l'Opéra** past the countless little restaurants, costume-jewellery or interior design shops, and a Japanese delicatessen (*Kioko*).

Angelina – *226 rue de Rivoli;* Ⓜ *Tuileries.* The classic, elegant tearoom overlooking the Tuileries Gardens, well-known for its cakes and its epicurean (and very rich) chocolate, "*L'Africain*". Open daily 9.30am – 7pm.

Cave Montpensier – *15 rue Montpensier;* Ⓜ *Palais-Royal.* A chain of small vaulted rooms that serves good beer 'British-style'. Open daily 4pm – 1am.

La Scala – *188bis rue de Rivoli;* Ⓜ *Palais-Royal.* Three storeys of dance floor, bars, laser shows and a giant screen attract a very young clientele. Open daily 10.30pm – 6am.

Saint-Germain-des-Prés

The oldest belltower in Paris, across the square from the terrace of the *Deux Magots,* keeps watch over a district that ceaselessly hums with activity. The intellectual ferment of the golden days of the 1950s with the "cellar rats" and the Existentialists may have gone but the charm lives on. The ambience is sustained by famous cafés and brasseries on the **boulevard St-Germain**, jazz clubs in the rue St-Benoît and rue Jacob, pubs in the rue Guisarde, rue Bernard-Palissy and rue des Canettes, and the late-opening bookshops peppered about. Up-market designer shops, antique and art galleries lend a decidedly "Left Bank" elegance to the old streets, picturesque crossroads and tiny squares such as the **place de Fürstenberg**. The main focus of the bustle is the **carrefour de Buci** with its street market, basic stores and fine '*traiteurs*' or gourmet delicatessens.

Brasserie Lipp – *151 boulevard St-Germain;* Ⓜ *St-Germain-des-Prés.* This brasserie, opened in 1880, has always been a meeting place for writers and politicians. Hemingway wrote much of his novel *A Farewell to Arms* here. Open daily until 1am.

Café de Flore – *172 boulevard St-Germain;* Ⓜ *St-Germain-des-Prés.* This café opened in the mid 19C, but came into its own later frequented by writers like Apollinaire, Breton, Sartre, Simone de Beauvoir, Camus, Jacques Prévert who spent entire days here. Open daily 7am – 1am.

Now... a chance to sample some of the aspects of Paris described in the **Michelin Green Guide,** *and more besides, in Michelin's brand new "***Vidéo Découverte: Paris***". Fifty minutes of sights and sounds evoke the exciting and romantic atmosphere of this dream city. But better hide your credit cards... you'll be heading for the travel agent's once* **Michelin** *has shown you what Paris has to offer!*

Les Deux Magots

Les Deux Magots – *6 place St-Germain-des-Prés;* M *St-Germain-des-Prés.* Like its neighbour, the *Café de Flore*, this establishment has been frequented by the intellectual élite since the end of last century; its literary prize, instituted in 1933, is awarded annually in January. Open daily 7.30am – 1.30am.

Le Procope – *13 rue de l'Ancienne-Comédie;* M *Odéon.* This cafe, founded in 1664, was one of the main centres of literary talent during the era of La Fontaine and Voltaire, later of Daudet, Oscar Wilde and Verlaine, whose portrait of him asleep at a table in the café adorns one wall. Open daily midday – 1am.

La Rhumerie martiniquaise – *166 boulevard St-Germain;* M *St-Germain-des-Prés.* Opened in 1932, this is the place to enjoy rum, of course, in every possible form (Planters, coconut etc.). Open daily 9am – 2am.

Birdland Club – *20 rue Princesse;* M *Mabillon.* In summer, the door opens out onto the street surrounded by drinking dens and restaurants like another room in a rambling club. This is one of the hot spots for good jazz. Open daily 6.30pm (10.30pm Sunday) – dawn.

Chez Georges – *11 rue des Canettes;* M *St-Germain-des-Prés.* This is one of the cheaper places in the neighbourhood; its interior is fairly low key with *rétro* posters. Open daily Tuesday to Saturday 6.30pm – 2am.

Dix – *10 rue de l'Odéon;* M *Odéon.* A hang-out favoured by students, decorated with Belle-Époque theatre posters. In the basement, mirrors have replaced the pipes in the magnificent organ made in the north of France in 1901. Open daily 6pm – 2am.

La Paillote – *45 rue Monsieur-le-Prince;* M *Odéon /RER: Luxembourg.* Small tables and alcoves with garden swings allow customers to rock to the music! The disc-jockey has some 2,000 jazz records from which to play personal requests. Open 9pm – dawn.

La Palette – *43 rue de Seine;* M *Odéon.* One of St-Germain's best-loved bistros with a delightful terrace and a fun collection of artists' palettes and paintings. Open Monday to Saturday 8am – 2am; closed throughout August.

Pub St-Germain – *17 rue de l'Ancienne-Comédie;* M *Odéon.* This beer-drinker's paradise stocks 450 different beers from all over the world. Kitsch décor on two floors above ground and two below. Open around the clock.

La Taverne de Nesle – *32 rue Dauphine;* M *Odéon.* A genuine beer hall serving a broad range of international brands. Open daily 8pm – 4am (5am Saturday, Sunday).

Exotic delicacies!

Try the contrasting blends of sweet and savoury, crunchy and smooth, colour and flavour of Vietnamese cooking: **Bhan Cuan** – steamed minced beef packages wrapped in rice leaves and served with mint; **Bo Bun** – cold noodles, minced beef, stir-fried vegetables and crushed peanuts; **Phô** – beef soup with rice noodles and bean-sprouts flavoured with mint and coriander leaves!

Couscous is a traditional dish from North Africa and consists of gently rolled and steamed semolina moistened with a rich stew of vegetables, chicken or lamb, flavoured with saffron, cinnamon, cumin and fresh mint and coriander...

ETHNIC ENCLAVES

Paris is a cosmopolitan city with a large number of ethnic communities: Caribbean, African, Slav, Far-Eastern, Latin-American, Jewish, Indian, Pakistani... Some have taken over entire neighbourhoods, in many cases under extreme living-conditions. Off the well-trodden tourist track, people come here to shop, to eat an exotic meal, to search for a specific music recording, piece of fabric or out-of-the-ordinary purchase. Scores of restaurants, grocers and delicatessens offer cooked delights from across the world. Hop into the metro for a gastronomic trip around the world!

Afro-Caribbean

African and West Indian communities tend to be segregated by nationality and trade, sometimes, if constrained by society these become ghettos in run-down neighbourhoods (18th *arr.* or along the north side of the Paris ring road). It was from this social context that **zouk** music (a combination of African and West Indian musical rhythms) evolved during the early 1980s with *Kassav;* that Radio Nova (on 101.5 FM) fashioned the concept of "world sono" which finally took off under the English name of "**World Music**".

Zouk: **La Cinquième dimension** *Shopping mall Montreuil-sous-Bois* (*in the suburbs*) is the mecca of *zouk* at weekends.

Black Cinema: **Images d'ailleurs** – *21 rue de la Clef* is the first and only cinema club to specialise in showing black culture films.

Books and Music: **L'Harmattan** – *16 rue des Écoles* and **Présence africaine** *25bis rue des Écoles.* M *Maubert-Mutualité, Cardinal-Lemoine.* For 'tropical' music, the **FNAC Forum** has a broader selection than other FNAC stores.

Art: **Musée des Arts d'Afrique et d'Océanie** – *293 avenue Dausmesnil;* M *Porte Dorée.* Permanent collection and contemporary exhibitions *(see* BOIS DE VINCENNES*).* The **Musée Dapper** *50 avenue Victor Hugo;* M *Victor-Hugo* is a tiny, intimate museum that organises bi-annual exhibitions of exquisite African artefacts, painting, textiles, carvings... accompanied by excellent catalogues. The **Musée de l'Homme** *Palais de Chaillot;* M *Trocadéro* (Museum of Mankind) houses an important permanent ethnological collection. ☎ 01 47 04 62 10.
Dealers specialising in African artefacts are grouped around Bastille (rue Keller) and St-Germain-des-Prés, including: **Argiles**, *16 rue Guénégaud*; **Galerie Majestic** *27 rue Guénégaud*; **Galerie de Monbrisson** *2 rue des Beaux-Arts*; **Mazarine** *52 J-P Laprugne, 52 rue Mazarine.* For printed fabrics sold by weight, try **Chez Toto** *50 rue Polonceau.*

Special shops: Most exotic food-stores are run by Orientals. **Izrael** *30 rue François-Miron* (this is the best-known grocery store in Paris and it is stacked high with goods, like Ali Baba's cave); **Le Village Africain** *2bis rue de l'Arbalète* (dried fish and meat from Africa and Brazil); **Aux Cinq Continents** *75 rue de la Roquette* (delightful store that has been in existence for 60 years); **Au Jardin Créole** *18 rue d'Aligre* (Caribbean goodies only a few yards from the famous market); **Marché Dejean** *rue Dejean, between the rue des Poissonniers and rue du Poulet* (fish, meat and fresh or ready-prepared African specialities sold by women from their market stalls – Saturday mornings only); **Spécialités antillaises** *14-16 boulevard de Belleville* (Caribbean ingredients).

North African and Middle Eastern

Many writers and journalists have made Paris their home, keeping abreast of both their indigenous culture and that of their adopted land; Tahar Ben Jelloun, the comedian Smaïn, the singer Cheb Khaled, and dramatists Moussa Lebkiri or Fatima Gallaire are all an integral part of the Parisian cultural scene.
The Metro line linking Nation to Porte-Dauphine (no 2) crosses several important concentrations of Mediterranean culture: **Barbès** and **Goutte d'Or** (18th *arr.*), **Belleville** (19th and 20th *arr.*). The **Strasbourg-St-Denis** district between the rue de Hauteville and the passage Brady is predominantly Turkish (with public steam baths).

La Grande Mosquée – *1-2 place du Puits-de-l'Ermite* has been used for countless films. Mint tea is served in the Moorish café next door *(see* JUSSIEU*);* the Hammam is next door.

Raï

This repetitive music from the working-class districts of Oran combines *fado* with *blues.* It has literally taken over Paris. The singer-poets are all "**cheb**" (ie "young people") such as Cheb Khaled, the undisputed King of Raï, Cheb Kader, or Cheb Mami. Amongst the most popular is **New Raï** *26 rue de la Montagne Ste-Geneviève.* **Le Petit Lappe** *20 rue de Lappe* plays all the latest music from the Capital of Raï, Marseille.

Art and culture: The **Institut du Monde arabe** *1 rue des Fossés-St-Bernard*; Ⓜ *Jussieu* has a particularly useful library and reference section; other facilities include interesting temporary exhibitions, and an expensive roof-terrace restaurant with an excellent view. **Musée des Arts d'Afrique et d'Océanie** *293 avenue Dausmesnil*; Ⓜ *Porte Dorée* – Permanent collection and contemporary exhibitions *(see* BOIS DE VINCENNES*)*.

Books – **Avicenne** *25 rue de Jussieu* (the best Arabic bookshop); **Ozgül** *19 rue de l'Echiquier* (Turkish books); **Asfar** *177 rue Jeanne d'Arc* (latest of the Oriental bookshops stocks a wide range of Arabic and North African literature).

Theatre – **Roseau Théâtre** *12 rue du Renard*; **Théâtre de l'Arcane** *168 rue St-Maur*; **Théâtre du Lierre** *22 rue du Chevaleret*.

Markets: **Marché d'Aligre** *place de l'Aligre* (largest of all the Arab markets; daily except Mondays); **Marché de Belleville** (Tuesday and Friday mornings); **Marché de Barbès** (Wednesday and Saturday); **La Ville de Mogador** *16 rue du Vieux-Colombier*; **Le Bosphore** *5 rue d'Enghien*.

Chinese

Until 1975, the predominant waves of immigrants came from Southern China; the latter-day arrivals come from post-war homelands in Indo-China, Malaysia and the Philippines. Although not as famous as the Chinatowns of New York or San Francisco, the 13th *arr.* (between avenue d'Ivry, avenue de Choisy and rue de Tolbiac) is disconcertingly 'foreign', lined with 150 restaurants and shops piled high with exotic produce each, differentiated by vividly-coloured signage. This urban district scarred by hapless modern multi-storey construction has succeeded in making a name for itself in tourist guidebooks. The Chinese population, the largest concentration in Europe, is particularly busy around the Chinese New Year (end of January – beginning of February). Considerable commercial activity animates the area around the shopping centre at the foot of "Les Olympiades", a residential complex surrounded by a labyrinth of shops and restaurants filled with the colours and scents of the Orient (access from the flight of steps in the avenue d'Ivry).

In **Belleville**, there is a smaller group of Asian restaurants (including the huge **Nioulaville** *32 rue de l'Orillon*) and stores.

A plaque on the wall of 13 rue Maurice-Denis (12th *arr.*) pays homage to the 120 000 Chinese who came to France during the First World War, 3 000 of whom decided to stay in Paris at the end of the war, forming the first Chinese community near the Gare de Lyon.

Books: **Le Phénix** *72 boulevard de Sébastopol* (generalist books on the Far East with specialist section on China and Japan) and **You Feng** *45 rue Monsieur-le-Prince* (largest specialist bookshop on China).

Art: Paris is home to a number of pre-eminent collections of Oriental art amongst which the **Musée des Arts asiatiques-Guimet** *6 place d'Iéna* and its annexe **Hôtel Heidelbach-Guimet** *15 avenue d'Iéna* (the 'Louvre' of Asian art from the Caucasus to Japan – *see* ALMA); the **Musée Cernuschi** *7 avenue Velasquez* (Chinese antiques – *see* PARC MONCEAU) and the **Musée Kwok-On**.

Musée Kwok-On

The extensive collection of theatrical costumes, musical instruments, Chinese puppets of various kinds provides an ample source for exquisite temporary exhibitions. Named after Mr Kwok-On, a Hong Kong citizen, the collection is presently installed at 57 rue du Théâtre; Ⓜ Charles-Michels.Scheduled reopening 1997. For details, call 01 45 75 85 75 or check local press.

Shops: **Tang Frères** *48 avenue d'Ivry* and at *168 avenue de Choisy*; **Paris Store** *44 avenue d'Ivry* and at *12 boulevard de la Villette*; **Ban Heng Store-Europasie** *15 avenue de Choisy*; **Mandarin du marché** *33 rue de Torcy*; **Hang Seng Heng** *18 rue de l'Odéon*; **Odimex** *17 rue de l'Odéon* (porcelain and ceramics); **Compagnie Française d'Orient et de Chine** *167 boulevard St-Germain*. It is also worth checking out the **rue du Temple**, as far as the rue Rambuteau. **Phu-Xuan** *8 rue Monsieur-le-Prince* specialises in Chinese herbs and medicaments.

Indian and Pakistani sub-continent

Most immigrants from the Indian sub-continent are not actually Indian but Pakistani, Tamuls from Northern Sri Lanka or recently-arrived Bangladeshis. "India" in Paris runs along the rue St-Denis (between the Gare du Nord and Porte de la Chapelle, around rue Jarry, passage Brady, and place du Caire). There are numerous food shops and restaurants in rue Gérando at the foot of the Sacré-Cœur, and beside the Lycée Jacques-Decours (Ⓜ Anvers).

Art and Culture: **Centre Culturel Mandapa** *6 rue Wurtz* – The art-centre stages some one hundred or more Indian plays, dance shows and music concerts every year. **Maison des cultures du monde** *101 boulevard Raspail* – Traditional Indian, Pakistani and Bangladeshi music, dance and theatre are performed at this venue.

Books: Librairie de l'Inde *20 rue Descartes*. The **Musée Guimet** *(see above)* bookshop has an excellent section on India, its civilisations, the arts from the Gandhâra ("Greco-Buddhist" art from Pakistan and Afghanistan) and from throughout the Far East.

Food shops: **Shah et Cie** *33 rue Notre-Dame-de-Lorette* (the oldest Indian grocery store in Paris); **Mourougane** *71 passage Brady* (import of Pakistani specialities).

Japanese

The Japanese community (businessmen, employees of Japanese firms, students and artists) is concentrated in the area around the **Opéra** and **rue Ste-Anne** where opportunities abound to taste *sashimi, sushi* and *tempura*.

Art: The **Musée Guimet** and its annexe, **Hôtel Heidelbach-Guimet**, houses a rich collection of Buddhas and Bodhisattvas brought back to France by Emile Guimet; the **Musée Kwok-On** *(see above)*; **Musée d'Ennery** *59 avenue Foch* (finest collection of *netsuke* in the world, laid out in a remarkable oriental décor). The **Musée départemental Albert-Kahn** *14 rue du Port, 92100 Boulogne-Billancourt* (*see Michelin Green Guide FLANDERS, PICARDY AND THE PARIS REGION*) is also a "must", with its Japanese garden, tea house and collection of autochrome plates.

Fashion: Japanese designers have acquired an international reputation. Most of their boutiques are located around the place des Victoires and in the St-Germain-des-Prés district: **Kenzo** *3 place des Victoires, 16-17 boulevard Raspail,* and *18 avenue George-V*; **Comme des garçons** *40-42 rue Étienne-Marcel*; **Yohji Yamamoto** *47 rue Étienne-Marcel* and at *69 rue des Saint-Pères*; **Issey Miyake** *201 boulevard St-Germain, 17 boulevard Raspail, 3 place des Vosges*; **Zucca** *34 rue Saint-Sulpice*; **Irié** *8 rue du Pré-aux-Clerc*.

Books: **Junju** *262 rue St-Honoré* and **Tokyo-Do** *4 rue Ste-Anne* (for all the Japanese newspapers or a selection from thousands of *bunko* (paperbacks) and *mangas* (comic books); **L'Harmattan** *(see under "Afro-Caribbean")* and **L'Asiathèque** *(see "Chinese")* also have books on Japan.

Food stores: **Kioko** *46 rue des Petits-Champs* (brimming with multi-coloured bags of cocktail snacks, sauces, sake and frozen raw fish).

Jewish connections

Historically, the Jewish quarter was the **Marais** (4th *arr.*), a community that was decimated during the German Occupation but whose numbers have swelled again with the arrival of North African immigrants; these have settled in the **Sentier** (2nd *arr.*) and Belleville (19th *arr.*), more particularly in the suburbs. Nowadays, one half of all Jews in France live on the outskirts of Paris.

Culture: Synagogues: Liberal Synagogue, *24 Rue Copernic* ☏ 01 47 04 37 27. Great Synagogue, *44 Rue de la Victoire* ☏ 01 42 85 71 09 or *17 Rue St-Georges* (9th *arr.*) ☏ 01 40 82 26 26. The **Musée d'art juif** presently at 42 rue des Saules, in Montmartre, is soon to be transferred to Hotel de St Aignan, 41 rue du Temple, in the Marais. The collection centres around North African religious articles, models and casts and includes paintings by Chagall, Lipschitz, Mané-Katz and Benn.

In the Middle Ages, there were two main synagogues in rue de la Cité and rue de la Tâcherie (behind the Hôtel de Ville). By the 18C numbers had grown with settlers from Alsace and Lorraine moving to the Réamur Sébastopol area, especially around Hôtel du Chariot d'Or in rue de Turbigo. Confidence was high when all Jews were granted French nationality during the Revolution. Haussmann included two synagogues in his plans for urban development: rue de la Victoire founded in 1874 and rue des Tornelles founded in 1876. This was built with an iron substructure that was manufactured in Normandy, most probably under the auspices of Gustav Eiffel! The façade of the synagogue at 8 rue Pavée was designed by Guimard.

Important memorials: **La Rafle du Vélodrome d'hiver** – bronze by Walter Spitzer; **Mémorial du Martyr Juif Inconnu** *rue G L'Asnier*, and at Père-Lachaise Cemetery **Monument à la mémoire des déportés de Buna, Monowitz, Auschwitz III** by Tim.

Bakeries-Cake shops – Mouth-watering enticing specialities such as apple and cinnamon strudels line the windows of **Sacha Finkelsztajn** *27 rue des Rosiers* and *24 rue des Ecouffes* or of **Murciano** *14 rue des Rosiers*. For specialist delicacies there is **Dukat Penzer** *24 rue des Rosiers* and **Klapish Frères** *1 rue des Hospitalières-Saint-Gervais*.

For a good view of the city:
Arc de Triomphe (Platform)
Montparnasse (Tower)
Notre-Dame (Towers)
Basilique du Sacré-Cœur (Dome)
Eiffel Tower (3rd platform)
Georges Pompidou Centre (5th floor)
Consult the PARIS AT LEISURE for additional viewpoints.

Sport

The principle sports venues host international competitive events, league matches and even pop concerts.

The **Palais Omnisports de Paris-Bercy** (POPB) hosts the Paris Motocross, ice spectaculars, the World Indoor Funboard Championships, the Paris Trialmaster, the Martial Arts Festival, a Six-Day Paris Cycling Event and a Tennis open tournament. Judo and athletics championships are held at the **Pierre-de-Coubertin Stadium** (16th *arr.*).

Palais omnisports de Paris-Bercy

The New Charléty Stadium – Charléty is one of a new generation of stadia with a less aggressive architectural design than that of the Parc des Princes that blends harmoniously into the urban environment. It comprises extensive facilities: a 20 000-seater stadium, a multi-purpose hall, training grounds, eight tennis courts, gardens, the headquarters of the Paris Université Club (the famous PUC founded by students in 1906), the French Sports Federation and offices designed to house the Ministry of Youth and Sport.

Tennis – **Roland-Garros** the famous venue for the French International Tennis Tournament is on the edge of the Bois de Boulogne.

Horses racing – Courses at **Longchamp** and **Auteuil** on the periphery of the Bois de Boulogne, and at **Vincennes**.

Football and rugby – The **Parc des Princes** on the southern edge of Bois de Boulogne hosts the majority of international matches. It also has a small sports museum (*see main text under* BOIS DE BOULOGNE).

Water sports – The main pools are **Les Amiraux** (18th *arr.*), a listed building, and the **piscine G.-Vallerey** – **"Les Tourelles"** (20th *arr.*) where many records have been broken.

Aquaboulevard (15th *arr.*), nicknamed "Paris Beach", comprises a sports, fitness, recreation and water park complex.

Piscine Deligny

The former 'plage du Tout-Paris' consisted of a stretch of the Seine reserved for swimming. Instituted by a swimming teacher in 1801 alongside the public showers and laundry boats (*bateaux-lavoirs*), facilities were improved in 1937 with sophisticated filtering systems. It was here that Louis-Philippe and George Sand, amongst others, learnt to swim; it served Parisians until 5.20am on 8 July 1993 when it sank. Moves are afoot to restore the Piscine Deligny to working order.

A different perspective over Paris

Paris is built on a series of hills, her undulating streets affording plenty of views over the densely packed zinc rooftops. Broad panoramic views open up as one climbs the hill to Montmartre (from the esplanade in front of the Sacré-Cœur or from the place E. Goudeau) in Belleville or Ménilmontant, and as you come down from the Butte-aux-Cailles (avenue des Gobelins from the place d'Italie), the Montagne-Ste-Geneviève (rue Soufflot), the hills of Passy (place du Trocadéro) or the modern complex of building "Mont-Parnasse" (place des Cinq Martyrs-du-Lycée-Buffon). The historic city centre is ringed by tall modern buildings at the Porte d'Italie, the Porte de Crimée, Maine-Montparnasse and the Fronts de Seine lining the river, the Bibliothèque de France (Tolbiac), or La Défense leading westwards out of the city.

BIRD'S-EYE VIEW

See admission times and charges for an indication of the opening times of the main tourist venues.

Tour Montparnasse ☉ – Ⓜ *Montparnasse-Bienvenüe*. Arguably the best view in Paris because the tower stands on the southern edge of the historic city halfway between the Eiffel Tower and the Gare d'Austerlitz, The Val-de-Grâce Hospital, St-Sulpice and the Palais du Luxembourg seen from this height are reduced to toy-town proportions. At night, the view over the Champ-de-Mars, the Eiffel Tower and, in the distance, the towers of La Défense, the Montparnasse Cemetery reduced to a dark patch, is unforgettable.

Eiffel Tower – Ⓜ *Bir-Hakeim/RER: Champ-de-Mars-Tour-Eiffel*. This is the view of all panoramic views but it makes many of the main city sights look like something out of Gulliver's Travels. Mist and pollution haze may restrict the view; the best air quality is immediately after a heavy downpour when the sun shines through the clear air. From the top of the Tower, the city suburbs can be seen to extend to green fields in the surrounding countryside.

Arc de Triomphe – Ⓜ*/RER: Charles-de-Gaulle-Etoile*. From the platform at the top of the arch, one can but admire Baron Haussmann for implementing his ambitious street planning: the "Triumphant Way" acts like a great axis from the Louvre to La Défense whilst the other ten avenues fan out from the Étoile.

Tower of Notre-Dame – Ⓜ *Cité*. Undoubtedly this is the oldest, most romantic view of Paris from between the medieval chimeras, punctuated by the dome of the Panthéon, the bell-tower of the Church of St-Etienne-du-Mont, Beaubourg and the succession of bridges over the Seine; an overview of the filigree flèche and cathedral nave are unforgettable.

Chimeras of Notre-Dame

J. Bottin

Centre Georges-Pompidou – Ⓜ*/RER: Châtelet-les-Halles*. The view skims across the rooftops of the best-known buildings such as Notre-Dame with the Panthéon in the background, the Church of St-Merri nearby, the Tour St-Jacques, the buildings of the Louvre, the impressive bulk of St-Eustache, and the dome on the Bourse du Commerce in Les Halles. This is a wonderful view at night.

Dome of the Sacré-Cœur – Ⓜ *Anvers, Abbesses*. Along with the Eiffel Tower, this is the other main viewing point from which to survey the city, the historic centre and the working-class residential 18th *arr.* stretching out at the foot of the basilica, the urban districts to the north and east of Paris as far as the suburbs of St-Denis.

Belleville Park – Ⓜ *Belleville, Pyrénées*. Like Montmartre, Belleville lives in a world of its own. It is an old working-class district with a blend of different cultures; from here, the view of Paris has its own special charm. An observation platform has been built at the top of the park, at the end of the rue Piat.

No2 La Samaritaine ☉ – *19 rue de la Monnaie*; Ⓜ *Louvre-Rivoli*. The terrace provides the prime view of the spires on Ile de la Cité, not forgetting Perrault's colonnade at the Louvre, the Pont-Neuf and the Institut de France. A viewing table has been set up to help visitors pick out the main sights.

Le Printemps – *64 boulevard Haussmann;* Ⓜ *Havre-Caumartin /RER: Auber.* The terrace of this large store provides a superb view of the belltower on the Ste Trinité below Montmartre and the Sacré-Cœur, and of La Madeleine.

The Panthéon – Ⓜ *Cardinal-Lemoine.* The Latin quarter and the Left Bank can be seen between the magnificent colonnade around the drum of the dome.

Institut du Monde Arabe – Ⓜ *Jussieu.* The view stretches from the roof terrace over the east end of Notre-Dame, the Ile de la Cité, and the Ile St-Louis.

Hôtel Concorde-Lafayette – Ⓜ *Porte-Maillot /RER Neuilly-Porte-Maillot-Palais-des-Congrès.* The view from the Panoramic bar extends over La Défense and the Bois de Boulogne.

The Great Arch at La Défense – Ⓜ *Grande Arche de la Défense /RER La Défense.* From one of the external transparent lifts or the rooftop, there is an unrivalled view of this business quarter – nicknamed the 21st *arr.* – built at the end of the "Triumphant Way".

There are a number of restaurants that combine the pleasures of good food with a view over Paris: consult **Paris et Environs – Hôtels et Restaurants** in the **Michelin Red Guide to France**. For sightseeing by helicopter – *see* PRACTICAL INFORMATION.

Parlez-vous anglais?

If your French is rusty or non-existent, where can you turn for current information about what's on in Paris?

The weekly *Pariscope* guide, offering comprehensive listings of the city's myriad cultural happenings, includes a "Paris in English" section *(available wherever newspapers are sold)*. The monthly newspaper *The Paris Free Voice* features general-interest articles and reviews written from the expatriate point of view and contains listings of the month's cultural events. It is available at various English-American haunts throughout the city (bookstores, cafés, restaurants – see our listings in the PARIS AT LEISURE section).

ALONG THE RIVER

Much of the summer romance of a lazy glide down river has disappeared but a boat trip can offer an enjoyable respite from sight-seeing on foot, affording unusual views of the city along the banks of the Seine. The larger **bateaux-mouches** serving dinner tend to cruise more gently; all are fitted with powerful lights (whose quality varies from one boat to another) which make for a memorable, mesmerising experience of the city. *For details of boat companies and embarkation points, see* PRACTICAL INFORMATION.

The Bridges

Many of the capital's 35 bridges are great feats of structural engineering and add to the architectural heritage of the city. From several the open view is imbued with timelessness and serenity, notably early in the morning or at sunset when light seems to throw the buildings into soft focus.

Pont Mirabeau – View of the Front de Seine development and the Eiffel Tower. The central archway is a work of sheer technical genius. The bridge is the title of a poem by Apollinaire, written when he was in love with the painter Marie Laurencin:

> "*Sous le pont Mirabeau coule la Seine*
> *Et nos amours*
> *Faut-il qu'il m'en souvienne*
> *La joie venait toujours après la peine...*"

Pont Bir-Hakeim – Metro line 6 (between Nation and Charles-de-Gaulle-Etoile) crosses the river affording a magnificent view of the Eiffel Tower – particularly at night. Running between apartment blocks high above street level fleetingly providing an oblique view into private apartments reminiscent of some of Monet's Impressionist painting, this indeed provides an alternative view of the city.

Pont Alexandre III – Gilded, winged horses rearing up at each corner frame a superb view of the Invalides.

Pont Concorde – The vast panoramic view of the urban landscape has recently been included in UNESCO's "World Heritage" list. From the bridge, the magnificent layout of place de la Concorde may be admired, presided over by the distinctive white outline of the Sacré-Cœur on the skyline, the glass roof of the Grand-Palais breaking out above the sweet chestnut trees on the Cours-la-Reine, the Chaillot Palace, and the Eiffel Tower. Full circle and the eye is drawn along the Tuileries Gardens to the Ile de la Cité flanked by the banks of the Seine.

Pont Royal – The Great Gallery of the Louvre facing the quai Voltaire and the Orsay Museum, upstream, there is a superb view of the Ile de la Cité from the corner of the bridge and the quai des Tuileries.

Pont des Arts – This bridge gives a romantic view of the heart of Paris, the square du Vert-Galant and its willow trees, the Pont-Neuf, the houses concealing place Dauphine on Ile de la Cité, and pointing skywards, the *flèche* of the Sainte-Chapelle and the towers of Notre-Dame.

Pont-Neuf

Pont-Neuf – From here one overlooks the square du Vert-Galant and the most elegant side of the Louvre, the Pont des Arts and the Institut de France. In 1985 this landmark was splendidly "wrapped" is 40 000m² (430 000sq ft) of saffron-coloured nylon canvas by contemporary artist, Christo.

Pont au Change – To the south is the Conciergerie; to the north, the theatres on the place du Châtelet. To the west are the Pont-Neuf and Eiffel Tower.

Pont St-Louis – Linking Notre-Dame with the Ile St-Louis, it is strategically placed to catch good views of the Hôtel de Ville and the dome of the Panthéon.

Pont de l'Archevêché – From the south-west corner, you can enjoy 'the' classic view of Notre-Dame, with its nave and famous flying buttresses.

Pont de la Tournelle – Superb view of the apse of Notre-Dame and the Ile St-Louis.

The Quais

Right Bank – Car drivers will appreciate the Georges-Pompidou express-way from the Pont du Garigliano to the Pont d'Austerlitz, taking them through Paris from west to east along the banks of the river. From it, you can recognise the capital's many bridges and its most famous monuments.

On foot along the quai du Louvre, quai de la Mégisserie and quai de Gesvres, there are a large number of *bouquinistes* who open for business late in the morning and sell second-hand books, post cards and engravings.

From the quai de l'Hôtel-de-Ville and the quai des Célestins, there are some attractive views of the old houses on the Ile St-Louis.

Notre-Dame from île St-Louis

Around the Ile St-Louis – For a delightful saunter through historic Paris skirt the Ile St-Louis along the quai du Bourbon and quai d'Anjou past fine 17C mansions. Ice-cream enthusiasts might linger in the rue Saint-Louis-en-l'Ile to taste the delights of the most renowned ice cream makers in Paris, **Berthillon**. From the quai de Béthune and the quai d'Orléans, the view over the east end of Notre-Dame is at its best in the early morning or late in the day when the coaches have left the quai de l'Archevêché.

Left Bank – *Bouquinistes* line this side of the Seine, between the Pont du Carrousel and the Pont de la Tournelle.

After a stop on the Pont des Arts to browse through the stalls on the quai de Conti under the watchful eye of Condorcet, go down to the quayside, away from the noise and bustle of the street to contemplate the timeless views of the square du Vert-Galant, the Pont-Neuf and the towers of Notre-Dame.

Leave the banks of the Seine at the quai St-Michel and wander through the narrow rue St-Séverin, rue Xavier-Privas, rue du Chat-qui-Perche, rue de la Bûcherie, and back to the square, a popular meeting point for young people in the Latin Quarter. Seek out the somewhat ramshackle Shakespeare & Company bookshop, the famous haunt of young, impoverished English-speaking writers in the 1920s steeped in a poetic nostalgia all its own.

From the Pont au Double, go back down onto the riverside walk (Batobus embarkation point) to admire the south side of Notre-Dame and the delightful Square Jean-XXIII where great swathes of ivy cascade down the walls.

Around the Arsenal Basin – With its terraced tiers of greenery, pontoons equipped with small floating gangways and moorings for a myriad of sailing boats, the Arsenal Marina in Paris comes somewhat as a surprise in the heart of a large city especially when glimpsed from the Bastille metro.

Along the St-Martin Canal – Film fans will find it hard to imagine the background and atmosphere that was made famous by Marcel Carné's film, *Hôtel du Nord*, but the superb metal footbridges spanning the canal, the boats passing through the locks, and the presence of a few anglers fishing from the banks give the place a distinctive charm.

PARIS BY NIGHT

The city is floodlit throughout the year from nightfall (between 5.15pm and 9.20pm) and midnight Sundays to Fridays and to 1am on Saturdays, the eve of bank holidays and during the summer months. The fountains are turned off from 1 January to 1 April to safeguard against frost.

At dusk, the best-loved sights are dramatically floodlit, imbuing the city with a splendour and glamour that are absent during the day. Contours of building, fountain and sculpture are picked out by an interplay of highlight and deep shadow exaggerating line, gesture, texture and crisply defined detail. At Christmas, the city sparkles and glistens with sequins of brightness, the Champs-Élysées, avenue Montaigne, rue Royale or boulevard Haussmann take on a fairytale quality with trees and shop windows decked in seasonal lights. Meanwhile, in the back alleys and older districts of the city, street lights suffuse the buildings and blindfolded shop-windows with a strange stillness.

On foot or by car, the main sights line the **banks of the Seine**: the **place de la Concorde** with its two fountains; the **Champs-Élysées** climbing up to the **Arc de Triomphe**; the **Cour Napoléon** and **Pei's Pyramid** which, together with the majestic walls of the Louvre are reflected in the rippling waters of the passive fountains; the place André-Malraux and the arcades fronting the **Comédie-Française**; the area around the abbey of **Saint-Germain-des-Prés** although not as white as the limestone of the **Sacré-Cœur**, takes on a paler hue beneath the lights; the **Invalides** with its striking gilded dome; **Notre-Dame** which is even more impressive when the floodlights of the river boats pick out the exquisite detail of its sculpted façade, and the **Esplanade du Palais de Chaillot** from which there is a wonderful view of the Champ-de-Mars and the École Militaire, while fountains play below in the **Trocadéro** Gardens. On the other bank of the Seine, a pause must be made beneath the **Eiffel Tower** to glance up at the latticed ironwork, monumental and yet so delicate.

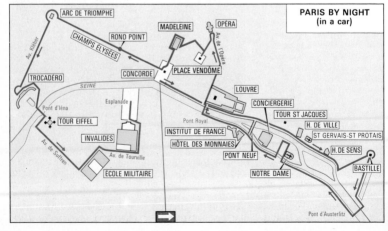

Les Invalides and place de la Concorde, from rue Royale

PARKS AND GARDENS

Over the past decade, Paris has evolved into a city of trees and flowers, boasting almost 400 parks, public and private gardens, little squares, and, of course, its two vast stretches of woodland (Bois de Boulogne and Bois de Vincennes – 846 and 995 hectares respectively) where lakes and waterfalls complement fountains and ponds.

A new style of urban landscape gardening has been developed integrating water, stone, glass and varieties of plants that appeal to all the senses: sight, sound, touch, smell... These are places in which to stroll, relax, play, feed the birds, break for lunch and a gossip or merely to enjoy a bit of peace and quiet with a good book.

Some of the gardens are used for concerts, flower arranging demonstrations, classic car-meets as well as providing an all-year-round setting for classical or avant-garde sculpture (for information, ☎ 01 42 76 50 00, or contact the local town hall). Amongst the best are:

Bagatelle for its irises and rose garden; the botanic gardens and greenhouses of the **Jardin des Plantes** (Ⓜ *Jussieu*); the **Parc Montsouris** (Ⓜ *Cité Universitaire*) and the square des Batignolles (Ⓜ *Brochant*) with their English-style gardens; the most picturesque of the landscaped parks is the **Buttes-Chaumont** (Ⓜ *Buttes-Chaumont*); the elegant **Palais-Royal** Gardens as a haven of peace in the very heart of Paris (Ⓜ *Palais-Royal*); the intimate Unesco Japanese Gardens (Ⓜ *Cambronne*); the **Jardin Atlantique** on a concrete slab suspended above the railway tracks of Montparnasse Station (Ⓜ *Montparnasse-Bienvenüe*); the cherry trees in the gardens of the university halls of residence (Ⓜ *Cité Universitaire*).

The **Luxembourg Gardens** are frequented by courting couples and pick-nickers on a summer's evering; it is where students from the Latin Quarter come to bask in the sunshine and children enjoy an hour or two in the playgrounds; the gardens round the **Rodin Museum** (Ⓜ *Varenne*) amongst the sculpture set out along the straight pathways (spectacular view of the Invalides dome); **Monceau** where the wrought-iron gates open onto a collection of statues of Musset, Maupassant, Chopin and countless other man-made features (Ⓜ *Monceau*); the botanical **Auteuil** Greenhouses and, just next to them, the Poets' Garden containing memorials engraved with the most famous lines written by French poets (Ⓜ *Porte d'Auteuil*); the **Parc André-Citroën** amongst the new, sophisticated gardens complete with hi-tech glass-houses (Ⓜ *Javel*); the **Parc Georges-Brassens** with its grassy slopes, vineyard and beehives in the heart of a quiet urban district (Ⓜ *Porte de Vanves*); and the **Parc de la Villette**, which is the largest park in Paris, punctuated with futurist buildings (Ⓜ *Porte de la Villette/Porte de Pantin*).

New gardens continue to be planned at the **Parc de Bercy**, the **Promenade du boulevard Richard-Lenoir**, while restoration of the **Tuileries Gardens** continues.

For organised guided tours of the Parisian parks and gardens see PRACTICAL INFORMATION Section.

Parc Monceau

OTHER CURIOSITIES

Walking through the various districts of the city, the eye may be caught by a sculpted stone façade, an intricately wrought balcony, traditional architecture reflected in a new mirror-plated window – this is a place full of striking contrasts and unusual sights.

Philip Augustus' City Wall – *Rue des Jardins-Saint-Paul*; Ⓜ *Saint-Paul*. The rusticated stonework of the city wall built during the reign of Philip Augustus, and the remains of two of its towers, contrast with the Classical profile of the Church of St-Paul-St-Louis. Other sections of the wall can be seen at 3 rue Clovis, in the inner courtyard at 62 rue du Cardinal-Lemoine, or at 47 rue Descartes (beyond the carriage entrance and past the half-timbered inner archway; Ⓜ *Cardinal-Lemoine*).

Pagoda – Rue de Babylone

Palais-Royal – The striated columns designed by Daniel Buren stand out against the Classical buildings of the Palais-Royal, fuelling the controversy about juxtaposing ancient with modern.

St-Alexander Newsky Russian Orthodox Cathedral – *12 rue Daru*; Ⓜ *Ternes, Courcelles*. Its golden onion domes, hallmarks of the Russian Empire, are somewhat disconcerting when glimpsed from boulevard de Courcelles and rue Pierre-le-Grand.

Pagodas – One is home to an Asian art gallery with red ochre walls (*place du Pérou, 17th arr*; Ⓜ *Courcelles*); the other, nestling amid trees and shrubs at 57 rue de Babylone, is a cinema and tearoom (Ⓜ *St-François-Xavier*). Both evoke images of the Far East, reminiscent of the taste in fashion for things Oriental at the turn of the century.

Montmartre Vineyard – *Rue Saint-Vincent*; Ⓜ *Lamarck-Caulaincourt*. Gamay and Pinot Noir grapes are harvested annually in mid October, a cause for much local celebration.

Sundials

Paris boasts 109 sundials!

The oldest are located at the Hôtel de Ville, in the Tuileries Gardens, and at the church of St Gervais (twin dials). One of the most splendid is set at the far end of the main courtyard in the Sorbonne. The most modern one is surely the fibre-optic solar clock in the form of a calibrated wave in the Jardin des Halles. The most cynical is at the Laënnec Hospital, inscribed with: "Alas! The hour that you are looking at may be the hour of your death."

Artists' studios and homes of famous people – Historical private houses are cluttered with memorabilia and steeped in memories, places where the spirit of their former occupier lingers: Honoré de Balzac, Henri Bouchard, Antoine Bourdelle, Georges Clemenceau, Eugène Delacroix, Gustave Eiffel, Victor Hugo, Gustave Moreau, Louis Pasteur, Ary Scheffer, Ossip Zadkine– *see* INDEX *at the back of the guide for listing in Sights Section.*

Commemorative plaques – Numerous commemorative plaques adorn the fronts of Parisian houses and apartment blocks. They stand as reminders of famous or forgotten writers, musicians, painters, politicians and momentous events providing the hawk-eyed passer-by with a snippet of history, animating the neighbourhood with eminent personalities. Some plaques of particular interest to English-speaking visitors:

74 rue du Cardinal-Lemoine (5th *arr.*) – The first of **Ernest Hemingway's** many Paris addresses (*see* LATIN QUARTER).

Hôtel d'York, 56 rue Jacob (6th *arr.*) – The signing of the Treaty of Paris by which England recognized the Independence of the United States took place in this building on 3 September 1783. The Crown was represented by David Hartley and Richard Oswald. Benjamin Franklin, John Jay and John Adams signed on behalf of the fledgling US Government.

19 rue de Tournon (6th *arr.*) – Scottish-born hero of the American Revolution (*"I have not yet begun to fight"*) John Paul Jones resided in a small apartment in this building during the last two years of his life (1747-1792). He died here a destitute and disappointed man.

14 rue Monsieur-le-Prince (6th *arr.*) – Black American writer **Richard Wright** and his family lived in this apartment block from 1948 to 1959 (*see* LUXEMBOURG – Odéon).

27 rue de Fleurus (6th *arr.*) – In the courtyard pavilion of this building lived American expatriates **Gertrude Stein** and Alice B Toklas from 1903 to 1937. Stein's modern art collection and literary salon have become legendary (*see* PERE-LACHAISE).

13 rue des Beaux-Arts (6th *arr.*) – On 30 November 1900 celebrated Irish writer and wit **Oscar Wilde** died in a modest room of the Hôtel d'Alsace that formerly occupied the building.

53 rue de Varenne (7th *arr.*) – American novelist **Edith Wharton** *(The Age of Innocence)* lived and entertained in this elegant residence from 1908 to 1918.

Hôtel de Coislin, 4 place de la Concorde (8th *arr.*) – On 6 February 1778 representatives from France and America (Benjamin Franklin) met in this grand building to sign the Treaties of Friendship, Commerce and Alliance. France thus became the first nation to recognize the United States as an independent country.

Corner of Rue Raynouard and Rue Singer (16th *arr.*) – On this site formerly stood the Hôtel de Valentinois where Benjamin Franklin's lived from 1777 to 1785, during his mission as American emissary to the French court.

Further reading

Reference

Paris – John Russell *(Thames & Hudson)*
The French – Theodore Zeldin *(Collins)*
The Crazy Years (Paris in the Twenties) – William Wiser *(Thames and Hudson)*
Americans in Paris – Brian Morton *(Quill)*
Women of the Left Bank, Paris 1900-1940 – Shari Benstock *(University of Texas Press)*
The French Revolution – Christopher Hibbert *(Penguin)*
Paris Art Guide – Fiona Dunlop *(A & C Black)*
Access in Paris (Disabled Tourists' Guide) – *Obtainable from Access Project (PHSP), 39 Bradley Gardens, London W13 8HE*
Le Guide – Paris Bus with text in English – lists all bus routes.

Biographical

A Moveable Feast – Ernest Hemingway *(Granada Paperbacks)*
Down and Out in Paris and London – George Orwell
The Sun King – Nancy Mitford *(Hamish Hamilton)*
A Place of Greater Safety – Hilary Mantel *(Penguin)*
Sartori in Paris – Jack Kerouac *(Paladin)*
The Autobiography of Alice B.Toklas – Gertrude Stein *(Penguin)*

Fiction

A Tale of Two Cities – Charles Dickens
The Scarlet Pimpernel – Baroness Orczy
The Old Wives' Tale (the 1870-71 siege) – Arnold Bennett
Peter Abelard – Helen Waddell
A Narrow Street – Eliot Paul
Tropic of Cancer – Henry Miller *(HarperCollins)*
Perfume – The Story of a Murderer – Patrick Suskind *(King Penguin)*
Flowers for Mrs Harris; Love of Seven Dolls – Paul Gallico *(Penguin)*

Keep us informed!

Send us your comments and suggestions

MICHELIN TYRE
Public Company Limited
Tourism Department – The Edward Hyde Building –
38 Clarendon Road – WATFORD –
Herts WD1 1SX

What to find where
(see INDEX for the page number)

Art

Antiquities: Louvre; Musée Cluny; Musée de l'Homme; Arènes de Lutèce.

Painting: Louvre; Musée d'Orsay; Musée National d'Art Moderne, Centre Georges Pompidou; Château de Versailles; Musée d'Art Moderne de la Ville de Paris (Palais de Tokyo); Musée Carnavalet; Musée Picasso; Musée Marmottan; Musée Maillol; Musée du Petit Palais; Musée Gustave Moreau; Musée Eugène Delacroix; Musée Henner; Musée Hébert; Musée de l'Orangerie; Musée Montmartre; Musée de l'Art Naïf Alain-Fourny.

Sculpture: Louvre; Notre-Dame de Paris; Musée d'Orsay; Cathédrale de Saint-Denis; Musée des Monuments Français; Musée Rodin; Musée Maillol; Musée Bourdelle; Musée Bouchard; Musée Zadkine; Espace Dalí; Fontaine Stravinski; Jardins des Tuileries.

Literature: Maison de Balzac; Musée de la Vie Romantique; Musée Adam-Mickiewicz.

Furniture: Louvre; Musée Cluny; Musée des Arts Décoratifs; Musée Cognacq-Jay; Musée Jacquemart-André; Musée Nissim de Camondo; Hôtel de Soubise; Faubourg-Saint-Antoine; Mobilier National (Gobelins).

Tapestries: Louvre; Musée Cluny; Musée Nissim de Camondo; Manufacture des Gobelins.

Silver, Glass and China: Château de Vincennes; Musée du Baccarat; Musée Bouilhet-Christofle; Petit Musée de l'Argenterie Insolite.

Fashion: Musée des Arts Décoratifs; Musée de la Mode et du Costume; Faubourg-Saint-Honoré; Musée des Lunettes et des Lorgnettes; Musée de l'Éventail; Musée Fragonnard; Musée de la Contrefaçon.

Music: Musée de l'Opéra-Garnier, Cité de la Musique.

Ethnic: Musée Guimet; Musée de l'Homme; Musée de l'Art d'Afrique et d'Océanie; Musée Cernuschi; Institut du Monde Arabe; Musée Dapper; Musée Arménien; Musée d'Ennery; Musée Kwok-On; Centre Bouddhiqe du Bois de Vincennes; Musée de l'Art Juif.

Science

Natural History: Musée de l'Histoire Naturelle, Jardins des Plantes.

Anthropology: Musée de l'Homme.

Astronomy: Palais de la Découverte; Musée des Arts et Métiers; l'Observatoire.

Medicine: Hôpital Militaire du Val-de-Grâce; la Salpêtrière; Musée de l'Assistance Publique; Institut Pasteur; Musée des Moulages de Hôpital Saint-Louis.

Mineralogy: École Supérieure des Mines; Musée de la Minéralogie; Galerie de Minéralogie.

Technology: Cité des Sciences et de l'Industrie; Palais de la Découverte; Musée des Arts et Métiers; Musée Marie-Curie.

Radio and Television: Eiffel Tower; Maison Radio-France; Belleville; Notre-Dame-de-Bonne-Nouvelle.

Miscellaneous

Cemeteries: Père-Lachaise; Montmartre; Montparnasse; Picpus; Passy.

Coins and Medals: Louvre, Musée de l'Ordre de la Libération; Hôtel des Monnaies; Bibliothèque Nationale de France.

Freemasonry: Musée du Grand-Orient.

Locks: Musée Bricard.

Magic: Musée de la Curiosité et de la Magie.

Maritime: Musée de la Marine.

Military: Musée de l'Armée; Musée de l'Ordre de la Libération; Musée de la Légion d'Honneur. **Philately**: Musée de la Poste; Théâtre Marigny.

Police: Musée de la Préfecture de Police.

Sport: Parc des Princes; Longchamp; Roland-Garros.

Tobacco: Musée-Galerie de la SEITA

Waxworks: Musée Grévin; Espace Grévin.

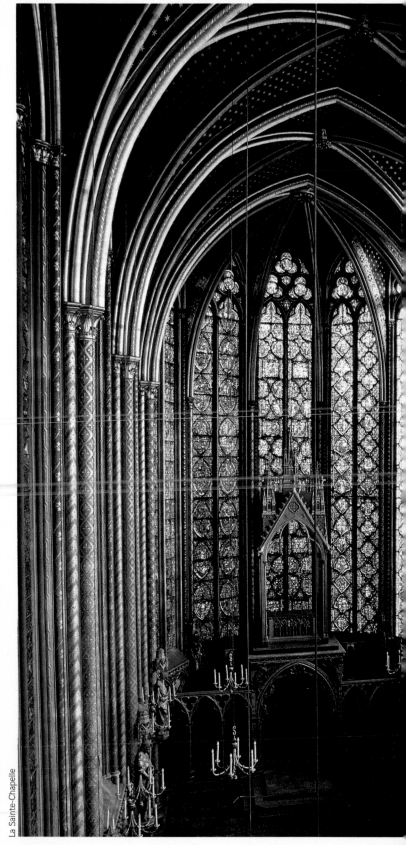

Sights

ALMA

Michelin plan 11 – folds 16, 17, 28 and 29: G 8, G 9 – H 8
Ⓜ *Alma-Marceau. Buses: 42, 63, 72, 80, 92*

The area around the **place de l'Alma** is one of the most luxurious quarters of Paris where elegant residences nestle amongst couturiers and perfumers at the heart of the refined world of fashion. The square and bridge, created in the time of Napoleon III, are named after the first Franco-British victory of the Crimean War (1854).

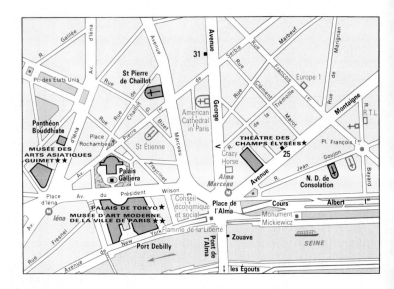

Pont de l'Alma – The original bridge, slowly undermined by the Seine, was replaced in 1972 by an asymmetrical steel structure with a 110m – 361ft span. Only the **Zouave** (upstream by the single pile) remains of the four Second Empire soldier statues which decorated the old bridge; he serves as a high water marker and is much loved by Parisians – once in January 1910, the water reached his chin.

Port Debilly – *Quai de la Seine*. It was here, formerly known as 'Les Bonhommes', that Robert Fulton an American engineer launched on 9 August 1803 his 'chariot driven by fire', a prototype steam-boat. Unimpressed, Napoleon dismissed the potential of this invention which might otherwise have changed the outcome of his intention to invade England...

★Palais de Tokyo – *11 avenue du Président Wilson*. The Palais de Tokyo was built for the 1937 World Exhibition, replacing the Savonnerie Tapestry Works. The two wings linked by a portico, over look a series of terraces, which are adorned by figurative low-reliefs and statues by Bourdelle *(see MONTPARNASSE)*, including his **France★** *(in the centre)*.
The **west wing** is to house a museum dedicated to the Seventh Art: Film and the Moving Image, and the Cinéma Henri Langlois.

★★Musée d'Art Moderne de la Ville de Paris ⊙ – The collection illustrates the main trends in avant-garde 20C art: **Fauve** works by Matisse and Derain, are characterised by simplified form and bright colour; Picasso and Braque, the leading exponents of **Cubism**, experiment with fractured forms, geometrical lines and textures subsequently influencing Delaunay, Léger, Gromaire and Ozenfant, while Rouault, Utrillo and Suzanne Valadon (Utrillo's mother) developed their own individual style of figurative and landscape painting; the **Paris School** stimulated by foreign artists who settled in Paris at the turn of the century (Modigliani, Soutine, Foujita, Chagall); the main movements evolving at the time of the First World War include **Surrealism** and **Abstraction**. Abstract art dismisses figurative representation in favour of the interplay of line and colour (Kandinsky, Fautrier, Helion, Arp, Magnelli, Domela); Surrealism introduces an often humorous, dreamlike interpretation to the real world drawn from the subconscious.
Dufy's **Fée Électricité★** *(The Good Fairy Electricity)*, the biggest picture in the world comprising 250 panels (600m² – 6 095sq ft), represents the civilisation of Man from the times of the ancient Greek philosophers to the modern scientists who evolved this excitingly new form of energy. Other large-scale works include *La Danse* by Matisse and decorations by Delaunay.
The museum displays works illustrating the trends and techniques of contemporary art. The experimental centre (ARC) presents innovations in the fields of plastic art, music and poetry.

Palais du Conseil Économique et Social – *Place d'Iena*. This building in reinforced concrete was designed by Auguste Perret (1936). Above the doorway 11 mosaic panels by Martial Raysse represent Origin and Hope, the first three prime factors (1, 2, 3), the most basic geometric shapes (triangle, circle and square), and the three values Liberty, Equality and Fraternity. In the forecourt, the bronze figures *Sol et Colombe*, consists of a man facing the world with the baton of Justice and the sphere of Knowledge in his hands with a woman pointing to the mosaic frieze as if towards the Future.

★★**Musée National des Arts Asiatiques Guimet** Ⓥ – *6 place d'Iéna*. This museum, founded by Émile Guimet, a successful 19C industrialist from Lyon, contains superb Oriental works of art, collected in the main to form a 'National Museum of Religions'. The ground floor is dedicated to the Far East: Khmer art (Cambodia), is well represented by intricately carved temple pediments and a series of **heads of Buddha**, typically stylised with eyes half-closed and a meditative smile. The seated Shiva with ten arms is an example of central Vietnamese art.

The Lamaist section includes a remarkable collection of Tibetan and Nepalese banners *(thanka)* as well as ceremonial objects and gilded bronzes; of the latter the most noteworthy is the graceful **dancing Dakini**.

The first floor shows the evolution of Indian art from the 3C BC to the 19C. There are the carved low reliefs from Northern India and the Hindu sculpture and bronzes from the southeast; one of the most notable is the beautiful **Cosmic Dance by Shiva**. The art of both Pakistan (represented here by the famous Bodhisattva from Shabaz-Garhi) and Afghanistan (the Begrâm treasure: sculptured ivories of Indian origin and Hellenistic plasters) are of special interest. The Chinese collection includes ceremonial bronze objects, jade and lacquer ware, Buddhist sculpture and funerary statuettes.

On the second floor are the exceptional displays of **Chinese ceramics** from the Calmann and Grandidier collections (18C *"famille rose"*) and the series of Buddhist banners (8C-11C) discovered in a cave of Dunhuang; jewels from Korea include a funerary crown; artefacts from Japan include dance masks *(gigaku)* and the "Portuguese Screen" (16C) depicting the arrival of a Portuguese ship in Japanese waters.

Buddhist Pantheon Ⓥ – *Hôtel Heidelbach, 19 avenue d'Iéna*. This annexe is essentially dedicated to Japanese Buddhism showing categories of "venerated beings" according to their progress along the path to Immortality and Enlightenment: Buddhas (the Enlightened One) and the bodhisattvas (Buddhas-to-be), or helpers along the sacred journey. Starting on the first floor, 33 Buddhist figures from China stylistically drawn from ancient Indian Buddhist sculpture show a transitional Chinese stage before the cult was diffused in Japan. The main galleries (first and ground floors) recreate Émile Guimet's original conception of a Buddhist pantheon from Japan. The **Mandala of the Lotus Sutra** consists of 23 statues: two Buddhas flank the tablet of homage of the sutra (sacred text) accompanied by other attendants. Amida, the Buddha of the Western Pure Land is portrayed in a typical seated position on a lotus pedestal; he is flanked by the bodhisattvas Kannon and Seishi descending on clouds to welcome the deceased into paradise or the "Pure Land". The rare 13C bronze statue alongside is of the bodhisattva Seishi. In the next room Kannon, the popular bodhisattva of compassion and mercy, is shown in a variety of forms. Many of the sculptures date from the Edo period (1615-1865) collected in 1876 by Guimet during a five-month visit to Japan; others are from the Louvre Oriental collection.

The other important display on the ground floor is a unique replica of the **Mandala of the Toji Temple** in Kyoto (AD 839). Conceived as an aid to meditation this grouping of Buddhist deities shows Buddha encircled by five secondary bodhisattvas, the guardian kings of the cardinal points, the warlike kings of wisdom and other attendants. At the rear there is an intimate Japanese garden, haven of peace and greenery, as intended by Guimet in his original designs.

Palais Galliera – *10 avenue Pierre-Ier-de-Serbie*. The Duchess of Galliera, wife of the Italian financier and philanthropist, had this building built (1878-1888) in the Italian Renaissance style. The mansion houses a museum dedicated to fashion and costume.

Musée de la Mode et du Costume Ⓥ – Selective exhibitions (bi-annually) drawn from a vast collection of almost 12 000 complete outfits and an additional 60 000 articles present men's, women's and children's fashion and dress from 1735 to the present day.

Gershwin in Paris

During a 1928 visit to Paris, George Gershwin found inspiration in the sights and sounds of the city for his celebrated composition *An American in Paris*. The work was featured in Vincent Minnelli's 1951 classic film of the same name. In the composer's own words:

This new piece, really a rhapsodic ballet, is written very freely and is the most modern music I've yet attempted... My purpose here is to portray the impression of an American visitor in Paris, as he strolls about the city, and listens to various street noises and absorbs the French atmosphere.

Église St-Pierre-de-Chaillot – *35 avenue Marceau.* The church was rebuilt in the neo-Romanesque style in 1937. Overlooking its façade, on which the life of St Peter has been carved by Bouchard *(see* AUTEUIL*),* is a 65m – 213ft high belfry.

Avenue George-V – This street is famous for its grand **Hotel George V** at no 31 frequented by the smart and famous jet-set, and media people meeting over a working breakfast; the neo-Gothic American Cathedral in Paris which was consecrated at the same time as the Statue of Liberty *(see* AUTEUIL*)* was unveiled in New York Harbor (1886); the **Crazy-Horse** music-hall at no 12, with its renowned programme of choreographed topless stage shows.

Avenue Montaigne – Formerly known as allée des Veuves (Widows' Alley) this disreputable area's main attraction was the Mabille Dance Hall. This closed in 1870. Today this street exudes wealth and chic, lined with elegant buildings accommodating banks, art galleries, exclusive luxury boutiques: Cartier, Versace, Pierre Balmain, Ted Lapidus, Gustave Jaunet, Rochas, Carven, Nina Ricci, Céline, Christian Dior, Lacroix, Thierry Mugler...

★**Théâtre des Champs-Élysées** – *13 avenue Montaigne.* The theatre, designed by the Perret brothers, is one of the first major monuments built in reinforced concrete (1912). The façade sculptures designed by Antoine Bourdelle *(see* MONTPARNASSE – Musée Bourdelle) depict: *Apollo Meditating, His Attendant Muses* in high relief and, on the ground floor, above the side doors, the allegories of *Sculpture* and *Architecture, Music, Tragedy, Comedy* and *Dance.* The main auditorium, with its ceiling decorated by **Maurice Denis**, is one of the finest in Paris.

It was here that Igor Stravinski first directed his *Rite of Spring* (1913), scandalising the audience with its musical and choreographic audacity; it caused such a furore that the composer had to flee from the auditorium. Since then, the Champs-Élysées Theatre has welcomed many great stars from the world of music and dance: Richard Strauss, Paganini, Diaghilev with his Ballets Russes; Jean Cocteau who produced *Les Mariées de la Tour Eiffel* in 1921; the Swedish Ballet Company who performed *The Creation of the World* in 1924 to a musical score by Darius Milhaud, a libretto by Blaise Cendrars, in costumes by Fernand Léger; in 1925, the *Negro Review* introduced Josephine Baker dancing half-naked to a Charleston and rhythms played on the saxophone by Sidney Bechet; Rudolf Nureyev starred in *Beauty and the Beast* with the Grand Ballet du Marquis de Cuevas in 1960; and six years later, Roland Petit's Ballet Company created *L'éloge de la folie* in a décor by Niki de Saint-Phalle and Tinguely.

An African Muse

Paris was taken by storm when **La Revue Nègre** launched Joséphine Baker with a new, improvised musical sound which was Jazz. Visually exciting, sensual and original, its impact cannot be underestimated.

Another important consideration affecting the liberalised attitudes of the day was wider travel to the French colonies in West Africa and the Antilles: powerful primitive sculpture and art was exhibited at the Musée de l'Homme *(see* TROCADÉRO*)* fascinating the young artists Picasso, Brancusi, Modigliani...

Hôtel Plaza-Athénée – *25 avenue Montaigne.* The hotel frequented by government ministers, royalty and diplomats was founded in 1867 and rebuilt in 1911.

At 22 **rue Bayard** is the Radio-Télé-Luxembourg (RTL) station – note the façade of the building decorated by Vasarely. Opposite is the Scottish Kirk.

Église Notre-Dame-de-Consolation – *23 rue Jean-Goujon.* A fire at a charity bazaar in 1897 killed 117 people on the site on which this memorial chapel, now the Italian church, designed by Guilbert, was erected (1901).

Cours Albert 1er – The statue by Bourdelle *(see* MONTPARNASSE*)* in the gardens parallel to the river shows the Polish poet and patriot, Mickiewicz (1798-1855). At no 40, note the fine René Lalique façade.

Les Égouts ⊙ – *On the left bank. Entrance at corner of quai d'Orsay and pont de l'Alma.* The Paris sewer system was initially the giant undertaking of the engineer Belgrand at the time of Napoleon III. 2 100km – 1 305 miles of underground tunnels, some passing under the Seine, channel sewerage towards Achères, Europe's largest biological purification station or to treatment plants on the outskirts of Paris (Pierrelaye and Triel).

The tour of part of the sewer system includes an overflow outlet, sand-filtering basins, a secondary conduit, holding and regulatory reservoirs. The larger mains also contain pipes for drinking and industrial water, telephone and telegraph cables. Explanatory panels in the Belgrand Gallery explain the historical development and workings of the Paris sewer system (water supply, purification and evacuation).

AUTEUIL

During the Second Empire, Auteuil became part of the City of Paris, but it was only at the turn of the century that the last vineyards disappeared. It still enjoys a village atmosphere; its streets named after famous composers and writers recall the era of Salon society. Many of the houses of this desirable residential area have retained good-sized gardens.

On the midstream island, the Allée des Cygnes *(see PASSY)*, below the pont de Grenelle, is a smaller version of Frédéric-Auguste Bartholdi's **Statue of Liberty**, which stands at the entrance to New York harbour *(see Michelin Green-Guide: NEW YORK)*. It was donated by the American colony in Paris in 1885 and placed on this spot four years later at the time of the 1889 Universal Exhibition.

Over the river is the modern development known as the **Front de Seine★**. An area, bordered by avenue Émile-Zola, rue du Docteur-Finlay and the embankment is the crucible for one of Paris' largest inner-city urban renewal projects. Architectural innovation in the form of several generations of high-rise buildings was given free rein in the 20 years between 1967 and 1986. The modern tower blocks have been designed to a variety of profile and finish; high-rise residential blocks are integrated with office towers, public buildings and a shopping centre, **Beaugrenelle**. A vast concrete podium, above the road network, ensures a traffic-free zone which is given over to spacious gardens and children's playgrounds.

Statue of Liberty

Ph. Gajic/MICHELIN

★Maison de Radio-France ☉ – *116 avenue du Président-Kennedy*. One concentric building 500m – 547yds in circumference and a tower 68m – 223ft tall, covering in all 2ha – 5 acres, go to make up Radio-France House. It was designed and erected by Henri Bernard in 1963 and until 1975 housed the Paris offices of the French Broadcasting Service. It is here in the 60 studios and the main auditorium (studio 104) that the programmes of national radio are produced.

A museum traces the evolution of communication and the development of transmitters and receivers from the 1793 Chappe telegraph and crystal sets to the latest transistors. The research carried out by scientists such as Maxwell, Hertz, Branly, Popov, Marconi and Lee de Forest (inventor of the three-electrode tube) into soundwave broadcast brought about the invention of the wireless. There are also experimental television sets and the reconstruction of a recording studio.

Rue La Fontaine – The street takes its name from the spring which supplied the village of Auteuil. Here, as in rue Agar, there are several buildings by Hector Guimard *(see MONTMARTRE – Place des Abbesses)*, the famous *Art Nouveau* architect. His best-known block of flats, **Castel Béranger**, is at no 14. No **60** also designed by Guimard was built in 1911.

Follow avenue du Poincaré to place Rodin, the setting for Rodin's allegory *The Age of Bronze (l'Age d'Airain)*, greatly admired for its precision at the Salon of 1874.

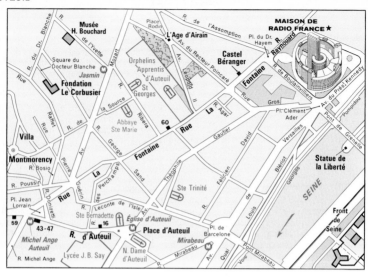

AUTEUIL

Ⓜ *Église-d'Auteuil, Michel-Ange-d'Auteuil. Buses: 22, 52, 62*

Place d'Auteuil – The Church of Notre-Dame (1880) is a Romano-Byzantine pastiche. The obelisk opposite the Ste-Bernadette Chapel is the last remaining tomb from the one-time cemetery. The monument commemorates the chancellor Aguesseau and his wife (1753).

Rue d'Auteuil – At no 11bis the 17C château is now occupied by a school. Admire at no **16** the main front of the Hôtel de Puscher; no **43-47** is an 18C mansion. The modern building at no **59** marks the site of a literary salon of a certain Madame Helvétius, who was better known as "Notre-Dame d'Auteuil". The salon was frequented by philosophers and writers in the period from 1762 to 1800, including the Americans Thomas Jefferson, Benjamin Franklin and John Adams.

The exclusive **villa Montmorency** was laid out on the site of the park of the former Hôtel de Montmorency, once owned by the Comtesse de Boufflers, mistress of the Prince de Conti and fervent admirer of Rousseau.

Fondation Le Corbusier ⊙ – *8-10 square du Dr Blanche*. Two buildings, namely villas La Roche and Jeanneret, dating from 1923, serve as a documentation centre for the work of the famous architect Charles Edouard Jeanneret, known as Le Corbusier (1887-1965). Villa La Roche houses a permanent exhibition, a library and photographic collection.

Musée Bouchard ⊙ – *25 rue de l'Yvette*. The work by the sculptor Henri Bouchard (1875-1960) varies from medals and statuettes to imposing memorials. Stone and bronze were his favourite materials. The studio display includes the plaster cast of *Apollo*, the monumental bronze in front of Chaillot Palace *(see* TROCADÉRO*)*, and the materials used in the creation of low reliefs, in particular those of the Church of St-Pierre-de-Chaillot *(see* ALMA*)*.

Rue Mallet-Stevens – *Off rue du Dr Blanche*. Private road of 'modern' houses by a Modernist contemporary of Le Corbusier, now pleasantly shaded by huge trees. The avant-garde geometric designs and interplay of cubist blocks with plain, flat surfaces – despite having been altered – still appear classically modern.

BASTILLE ★

Michelin plan 11 – fold 33 – 34 and 45 – 46: J 17, K 17 – 19

The vast crossroads, scene of the historic events of 1789, is dominated by the July Column. Today, the square remains a symbolic rallying point for demonstrations, marches and public celebrations as well as an informal meeting place for the young and trendy on a Friday night.

PLACE DE LA BASTILLE

Ⓜ *Bastille. Buses: 20, 29, 65, 69, 76, 86, 87, 91*

The Bastille *prison* – Whilst Charles V lived at the Hôtel St-Paul *(see* le MARAIS*)*, he felt it necessary to have a fortified residence built in case of danger. The first stone of the Chastel St-Antoine – renamed la Bastille after the run-down, marshy area around – was laid in 1370. Construction lasted until 1382, and depended upon forced labour recruited by press-gang from passers-by. Its history is, however, far

> '*The crowds in the streets, the lights in the shops and balconies, the elegance, variety, and beauty of their decorations, the number of the theatres, the brilliant cafés with their windows thrown up high and their vivacious groups at little tables on the pavement, the light and glitter of the houses turned as it were inside out, soon convince me that it is no dream; that I am in Paris...*'
>
> Charles Dickens.

from heroic: besieged seven times in periods of civil strife, it surrendered six times. An interesting episode occurred in 1652 when the Grande Mademoiselle Louis XIV's cousin, opened the St-Antoine gate to Condé's Fronde army who then turned against the royal guards. Renowned prisoners incarcerated here included the enigmatic Man in the Iron Mask, Bassompière, Mirabeau and Voltaire, usually detained under the notorious *lettre de cachet*. In 1784 these royal warrants were abolished: the Bastille was cleared leaving merely 32 Swiss guards and 82 invalid soldiers under the governor's command.

The taking of the Bastille – On 12 July 1789 trouble broke out: the popular Finance minister, Necker, was dismissed by the king; the Stock Exchange was closed as a militant crowd rallied. On the 14th, the mob marched first to the Invalides to capture arms, then on to the Arsenal and the Bastille. By late afternoon the Bastille had been seized and the prisoners – only seven in number, including a madman – were symbolically freed. The fortress was immediately demolished, 83 of its stones being carved into replicas and sent as dire reminders of the evil of despotism to the provinces. The following year there was dancing on the site.

The square – Paving stones mark out the ground plan of the former Bastille. The appearance of the square was modified first by the opening of the rue de Lyon in 1847, subsequently by that of boulevard Henri-IV in 1866 and the building of a railway station in 1859.

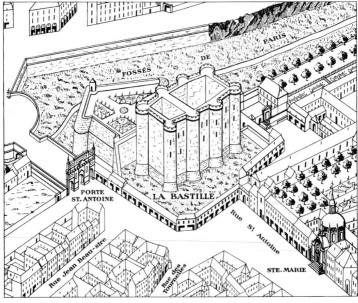

La Bastille in 1734

Colonne de Juillet – A bronze column 52m – 171ft high, crowned by the figure of Liberty (built between 1831 and 1840), stands in memory of Parisians killed during the uprisings of July 1830 and 1848. Many of those buried in a crypt beneath the column have their names on the shaft of the column.

★**Opéra de Paris-Bastille** ⊙ – On the site of the former station demolished in 1984 now rises a massive mirror-glass building often likened to a ship, designed by the Uruguayborn Canadian, Carlos Ott. The curvilinear, utilitarian design accommodates a 2 700-seat auditorium with several revolving stages for quick scene changes, workshops and rehearsal rooms.

Colonne de Juillet

The opera was officially opened by President Mitterrand on Bastille Day 1989 to commemorate the Bicentenary of the French Revolution. *Les Troyens* by Berlioz directed by Myung-Whun Chung, its inaugural production, took place on 17 March 1990.

Boulevard Richard-Lenoir – Built by Haussmann in 1859, this broad street extends north from the main square, spanning the St-Martin Canal *(see* RÉPUBLIQUE*)* from l'Arsenal almost to place de la République. It owes its name to two French industrialists François Richard and Joseph Lenoir who introduced a cotton spinning machine to France under Napoleon.

Rue de Lappe – The area was traditionally famous for its dance halls and specialist shops selling produce from the Auvergne. The neighbourhood now hums with artists and contemporary art galleries, with open-days held when studios, workshops and galleries are open to the public *(see Press for details)*.

L'ARSENAL *entrance: 1 rue de Sully.* Ⓜ *Sully Morland. Buses: 86, 87*

From 1352 this area was dominated by a Celestine (Benedictine) community. Proximity to the royal residences such as the Hôtels St-Paul and des Tournelles *(see* le MARAIS*)* ensured its patronage: the monastic church accumulated great riches and works of art, accommodating several very fine royal tombs, many of which are now in the Louvre, the Church of St-Denis or at Versailles.

In 1512, despite strong resistance from the Celestines, the city requisitioned the riverside stretch of land to set up a cannon foundry. Henri II purloined the workshops and founded a royal arsenal: seven mills were built, producing gunpowder amongst other things. Destroyed in a famous explosion (1563) that was heard as far afield as Melun to the south, the arsenal was rebuilt by Philibert Delorme before being taken over by Sully, Grand Master of Artillery, as his residence. Under Louis XIII the cannon works were discontinued and the production of gunpowder was transferred to the Salpêtrière *(see* JUSSIEU*)*.

Fouquet's trial – In 1631 Richelieu transformed the Arsenal into a special criminal court. It was here that Fouquet, Louis XIV's finance minister was tried over a period of three years for embezzlement – Colbert energetically packed the magistrate's court, but the final sentence (1664) was disappointing. Dissatisfied with the call for banishment, Louis XIV changed Fouquet's sentence to life imprisonment and banished the chief magistrate to his estate.

The Poisoners' Court – Following the execution in 1676 of the Marquise de Brinvilliers *(see* LATIN QUARTER – Maubert*)*, who poisoned her father and two brothers, murder by poison became extremely popular in the capital. A certain La Voisin, who later was condemned to burn at the stake, masterminded the dealings in lethal potions commonly known as "inheritance powder". In the face of a growing scandal the Arsenal court became the Poisoners' court in 1680.

The Library ⊙ – *20 boulevard Henri IV.* The library, created in 1757 and accommodated in what remained of the Arsenal building, was opened to the public in 1797. In the 19C it became the early meeting place of the Romantics: Lamartine, Hugo, Vigny, Musset, Dumas and the Parnassian Poets (Gautier, de Banville, de

Lisle, Heredia). The library possesses more than a million and a half volumes, 15 000 MSS, 120 000 prints and a large collection on the history of the theatre, which belongs to the Bibliothèque Nationale.

Access may be had to the manuscript room, the 18C Salon de Musique decorated with grisaille panels depicting Bouchardon's Fontaine des Quatre Saisons *(see FAUBOURG-ST-GERMAIN – Sèvres-Babylone)* in rue de Grenelle, and the 17C La Meilleraye apartments painted by a follower of Simon Vouet.

Along boulevard Morland one should note the cannon and mortar of the roof-top balustrade, recalling the original function of the building.

The statue of Arthur Rimbaud, the 19C Bohemian poet in the square is by Ipousteguy.

The barracks, **Caserne des Célestins**, (1892) stand on the site of the monastery gardens.

★**Pavillon de l'Arsenal** ☉ – *21 boulevard Morland*. This late-19C iron and glass building accommodates an exhibition centre presenting the architecture and urban development of the capital from the earliest city walls to important contemporary projects (Bercy, La Défense and La Villette). A model of the city locates the various parks and open spaces, new development areas and public services.

Square Henri-Galli – *at the end of the pont de Sully*. Enclosed here are stones from the original Bastille buildings recovered during work on the metro. In the Middle Ages the area between the Hôtel Fieubet and the Arsenal Library was occupied by a Celestine monastery – now a barracks; while beyond, between the boulevard Morland and the Seine, was **Louviers Island** which served as practice ground for crossbowmen and later as a wood depot. It was joined to the mainland in 1843.

FAUBOURG-ST-ANTOINE

Ⓜ *Bastille, Ledru-Rollin, Faidherbe-Chaligny. Buses: 46, 86*

The old densely populated streets of the Faubourg-St-Antoine have been the centre of the cabinet-making industry for centuries. The neighbourhood grew up round the fortified Royal Abbey of St Antony, founded in 1198. Water was brought by canal from the Seine and defence was provided by artillery men under the authority of the Mother Superior – nicknamed 'la dame du Faubourg'. In the 12C, pigs were allowed to roam freely in the streets of Paris up to the time when the son of Louis le Gros was thrown from his horse frightened by a charging porker. Despite imposed regulations, however, convent swine, identified by a bell, maintained their freedom, thereby continuing to uphold the Order's privilege honouring St Antony's companion *(see* BOIS DE VINCENNES*)*.

Louis XI further added to the abbey's privileges by giving it power to dispense justice locally and allowing the craftsmen in the vicinity to work outside the es-

Musée de l'argenterie insolite

tablished powerful and highly restrictive guilds. From 1657, the cabinet-makers of St-Antoine were thus licensed to design their own furniture rather than having to replicate pieces from the royal workshops, to employ exotic woods such as mahogany and ebony instead of being bound to oak, and to develop the decorative use of bronze and marquetry.

At 31 rue de Montreuil, **Réveillon** pioneered the production of painted wallpapers. Soon his workshop employed 400 people. Crowded conditions provoked social unrest that erupted into violence on 28 April 1789, forcing the industrialist to flee. In the workshop courtyard on 19 October 1783 **Pilâtre de Rozier** *(see* la MUETTE*)* made the first 'lift off' in a paper balloon inflated with hot air, while tethered by a cable.

Incorporated guilds were abolished at the time of the Revolution. In the face of mechanisation and labour-saving industrial processes, traditional multi-skilled craftsmen had to evolve specialised trades to survive. Small workshops abounded, but still in June 1848 when the national workshops were disbanded, the unemployed rallied to build numerous barricades in protest, leading to further violence in the Faubourg.

Some of the great ébénistes

Associated with the Louis XV and Louis XVI style are the following:

André Boulle (1642-1732): furniture supplier to the court, the most distinctive feature is the exquisite quality of brass and tortoiseshell inlay. His "style" enjoyed a revival during the Second Empire.

Charles Cressent (1685-1768): his bureaux and commodes are perhaps the most elegant of the Louis XIV style, embellished with curvilinear ornamental ormolu (gilded bronze) mounts.

B.V.R.B.: this was the trademark of the Bernard Van Risen Burghs, a famous family of Parisian cabinet-makers. The 2nd in line was responsible for incorporating porcelain plaques into his delicate occasional furniture inlaid with various materials (wood, metal, mother-of-pearl).

Jean-François Oeben (1720-1763): the master of Riesener and Leleu, marks the transition between the Louis XV and Louis XVI styles. His intricate geometric marquetry and furniture with hidden mechanisms are particularly famous.

Roger Lacroix (1728-1799): Flemish in origin, his real name was Roger Vandercruse and often signed pieces R.V.L.C.; after making tables and *secrétaires*, he turned his hand to curved chests of drawers and *escritoires*; patrons included Louis XV, Mme du Barry and the Duc d'Orléans.

Jean-François Leleu (1729-1807): the master of the Louis XVI style at its most grandiose, rich in ormolu *appliqués* to complement overall design.

Martin Carlin (*c* 1730-1785): he made a speciality of furniture incorporating lacquered panels and porcelain plaques.

Jean Riesener (1734-1806): 30 workshops and retail outlets on the rue St-Honoré. He was one of the innovators of the Louis XVI style and highly successful. His mahogany chests of drawers and *bureaux* with bronze mounts are distinctively sober in form and line.

Léonard Boudin (1735-1804): one of the Faubourg's free independent craftsmen. A master of marquetry (floral motifs) specialising in furniture with secret compartments.

Georges Jacob (1739-1814): established near the porte St-Martin, he dominates furniture design between Louis XVI and 1er Empire. Renowned for his armchairs, he is credited with the invention of the *fauteuil à la reine*.

Adam Welsweiler (1744-1820): he created slender furniture with finely stamped bronze or japanned (Japanese-style lacquer) panels.

Rue du Faubourg-St-Antoine – The street is lined with furniture shops and the area around honeycombed with courtyards and arcades, often with picturesque names (Le Bel-Air, l'Étoile d'Or, les Trois-Frères, l'Ours, la Bonne-Graine...)

The passage de la Boule Blanche at no 50 opens onto the entrance of the **Quinze Vingts Hospital** *(see below)* at no 28 rue de Charenton. St Louis founded the hospital for 300 (15 x 20) destitute blind people near the Louvre. It was later transferred to these 18C buildings which formerly served as barracks, erected by Robert de Cotte.

Fontaine Trogneux *on the corner with rue de Charonne* is an attractive fountain from 1710.

Passage de la Main-d'Or – *133 rue du Faubourg-St-Antoine.* Typical of the old quarter, this arcade comes out onto rue de Charonne.

Carrefour rue Crozatier – Opposite no 151 rue Faubourg-St-Antoine, a barricade was erected in protest against the dissolution of the Assembly and Napoleon III's coup d'état in December 1851.

Hôpital St-Antoine – *184 rue du Faubourg-St-Antoine.* St Antony's Hospital occupies the site of the old abbey which gave the quarter its name. Adjoining the 18C buildings is a modern building (1965), by the architect Wogenscky. *Closed to the public.*

Église Ste-Marguerite ☉ – *36 rue St-Bernard.* Built in the 17C and enlarged in the 18C, the interior is disparate in style; the low basket-arch vaulted nave contrasts with the tall and bright chancel. The marble *pietà* (1705) behind the high altar is by Girardon, a fragment of a tomb intended for his wife; to the left of the chancel, the chapel dedicated to the Damned Souls has unusual *trompe l'œil* grisaille frescoes (1765) by Brunetti. Both transept chapels contain large 18C canvases depicting St-Vincent-de-Paul *(see* FAUBOURG-ST-GERMAIN – Sèvre-Babylone*)* which originally came from the Maison St-Lazare *(see* GRANDS BOULEVARDS – Faubourg-Poissonnière*)*.

The small disused cemetery is presumed to be where Louis XVII was buried at his death in the Temple prison in 1795 *(see* RÉPUBLIQUE*)*.

Place d'Aligre – A daily market is held here *(mornings only)* for vegetables, cheap clothes and bric-à-brac.

Viaduc des Arts – *avenue Daumesnil*. This stone and pink brick viaduct used to carry the old suburban railway from the Bastille. Recently restored, its 60 vaulted archways accommodate a wide variety of businesses – silver- and goldsmiths, cabinet-makers, fine art and sculpture restorers, designers of contemporary furniture, wrought-ironwork, interiors and soft-furnishings etc. Above along the viaduct, the railway has been transformed into a walk-way with trees, gardens and shaded arbours, running all the way to the Bois de Vincennes.

Musée de l'Argenterie Insolite ⊙ – *109 avenue Daumesnil*. The museum installed in one of the vaulted units named 'Plasait, orfèvre' (goldsmiths). This interesting collection of unusual silver consists of small objects from an era of outmoded refinement – fish-bone removers, leg-of-mutton holders, tongue scratchers, a "pomander" (dried perfume ball worn on a chain or at the waist), a small portable chamber pot called a "Bourdaloue", a combined knife and fork for those with but one arm, a miser's salt-cellar from Holland, a telescopic fork, a series of "egotists" (chocolate pots for one person) and a cigar service. The English are evidently the great specialists in tea utensils. The collection is organised around several themes: dining, travelling, hunting, fashion, perfume, and the toilet, evoking a bygone way of life. A tour of the workshop concludes that of the museum.

NATION Ⓜ *Nation. Buses 56, 86, 351*

Place de la Nation – This was originally named the Throne Square in honour of the state entry made by Louis XIV and his bride, the Infanta Maria-Theresa, on 26 August 1660, when a throne was erected at which the King received due homage from the City of Paris. It was renamed place du Trône-Renversé (the Overturned Throne) by the Convention in 1794, when a guillotine was erected there, and it was here that the throne of Louis-Philippe was ceremoniously burnt in July 1848. It was given its present name on 14 July 1880, the first anniversary celebrations of the Revolution. It had been Napoleon's original intention to extend the 'Triumphal Way' *(see* CHAMPS-ÉLYSÉES*)* from the Arc de Triomphe to place de la Nation, but this was not to be.

★**Le Triomphe de la République** – *at the centre of the square*. **Dalou** (1838-1902), recently returned from England, took 20 years to perfect the composition of his monumental bronze group, 11m – 36ft high and 38 tonnes in weight. Originally intended for place de la République, the sculpture seems out of proportion with its context. An allegory of the Republic borne by a chariot drawn by lions, is flanked by Work and Justice. Peace, perhaps the best-rendered figure is slightly set back.

The two columns on either side of avenue du Trône and the pair of toll booths were designed by Ledoux *(see* INTRODUCTION*)*. The columns were subsequently topped with statues of Philippe Auguste and St Louis.

Cimetière Picpus ⊙ – *35 rue de Picpus*. In 1794 the guillotine on the place de la Nation fell on the heads of 1 306 people, including André Chénier and 16 Carmelite nuns, whose bodies were thrown into two communal graves. The ground, known as le champ des Martyrs, was later enclosed by a wall and an adjoining cemetery opened in which relatives of those guillotined on the square could be buried. Many names recall the families of the French Aristocracy (la Fayette, Rohan, Beauharnais...) At the far end of the cemetery the Martyrs' Field can be seen through a gate.

Église St-Esprit ⊙ – *186 avenue Daumesnil*. This church is impressive by its sheer size. Built and designed between the two World Wars, it demonstrates a 1930s transitional style where reinforced concrete is still moulded to traditional neo-Gothic or neo-Byzantine forms. Inside, Maurice Denis' fresco in the apse depicts Pentecost and the Holy Sacraments below.

Every year
*the **Michelin Red Guide France** gives the addresses*
and telephone numbers
of main car dealers, tyre specialists,
and garages which do general repairs and offer a 24-hour
breakdown service...
It is well worth buying the current edition.

BELLEVILLE ★

Built on the highest hill in Paris after Montmartre (128m – 420ft), Belleville owes part of its charm to the unexpectedly steep paths and winding streets. Despite the mushrooming of modern buildings, Belleville has, on the whole, kept its traditional atmosphere, its quiet streets and their secluded life, vacant lots and little snatches of greenery. The main streets, however, are full of popular ethnic restaurants (Chinese, Vietnamese).

A very old village – Once the country retreat of the Merovingian kings, then the property of several abbeys and priories, the hill and particularly the ancient hamlet of Ménilmontant were, for a long time, inhabited only by quarry workers and a handful of wine growers. In the 18C, it became known as Belleville, probably a corruption of "belle vue" or "beautiful view", becoming a commune in 1789.

Today, its territory is delimited by Buttes-Chaumont, Père-Lachaise and the outer boulevards.

Until the Restoration, open-air dance floors and cheap restaurants abounded at the foot of the hill, attracting crowds of Parisian strollers, particularly during the famous "Descente de la Courtille" on Shrove Tuesday, when an immense procession of carriages, led by Lord Arsouille, hurtled down rue de Belleville: when drivers and passengers would try to outdo each other in the extravagance of their fancy dress... while hurling crude abuse at one another. In 1860, the village, whose population had grown at an increasing pace, was annexed to Paris and allocated between the 19th and 20th *arrondissements*.

On 19th December 1915, Giovanna Gassion was born to abject poverty on the steps of 72 rue de Belleville. She later sang in the streets, before becoming a radio, gramophone and music-hall success in 1935 under the name of **Édith Piaf**. Beloved for the instinctive but deeply moving inflexions of her voice, she came to embody the spirit of France (*La vie en rose, Les cloches*).

Another famous figure to come from this neighbourhood was **Maurice Chevalier** (1888-1974), film star, entertainer and *chansonnier*; he paired with Jeanne Mistinguett at the Folies Bergères (1909) and sang at the Casino de Paris between the wars. Before attaining fame on Broadway in black-tie and boater, he was known at home for songs that were rooted in Belleville: *Ma pomme, Prosper* and *Marche de Ménilmontant*.

★**Parc de Belleville** – Passage Julien-Lacroix, with its stone steps, is the main thoroughfare through this 4.5ha – 11 acre park on Belleville Hill. The differences in ground level have been used to create tiered gardens, with cascades and waterfalls. The belvedere provides a magnificent **view★★** of Paris.

Rue des Cascades, winding and paved, is amongst the quaintest in the neighbourhood.

The **Regard St-Martin** *opposite rue de Savies* is one of four buildings of its kind constructed in Belleville to channel the supply of water which is routed down to the capital by means of underground aqueducts. The building belonged to the St-Martin-des-Champs Priory. Of the two chased coats of arms, only that on the left still shows the traces of a knight on horseback, perhaps Saint Martin. The Latin inscription records work carried out in 1633 and 1722.

Passage de la Duée – One of the narrowest streets in Paris (1m – 1 yd).

Rue du Télégraphe – At no 40, on the site of the property once owned by a National Convention member, Pelletier de St-Fargeau, **Claude Chappe** (1763-1805) conducted his first experiments on the telegraph in 1793.

Mur des Otages – *53 rue du Borrégo*. In a courtyard near the Notre-Dame-des-Otages church, built in 1936, can be seen a fragment of the wall in front of which 49 hostages (priests, nuns, Paris civilian guards) from Grande-Roquette prison were shot by the *communards* on 26 May 1871.

Passage des Soupirs – Picturesque street.

Asile des Petits Orphelins – *119 rue de Ménilmontant*. At the side of the courtyard stands an 18C mansion, its triangular pediment resting on four Ionic columns. The orphanage was established here in 1832 for the children of cholera victims.

Cité du Labyrinthe comprises a series of courtyards between rue de Ménilmontant and rue des Panoyaux.

'The last time I saw Paris, her heart was warm and gay,
I heard the laughter of her heart in every street café.'
OSCAR HAMMERSTEIN – The Last Time I saw Paris

BERCY

As part of an ambitious re-development project for the eastern section of the capital, a 50ha – 123 acre site including the Bercy neighbourhood is rapidly taking shape. New offices for the Ministry of Finance, residential buildings and the creation of a 13ha – 32 acre riverside park between the sports complex and the refurbished wine warehouses are complete. The Ministry of Finance, transferred from the traditional Rivoli wing of the Louvre, is accommodated in a massive modern structure straddling the embankment expressway, sitting perpendicular to the river, with a foothold in the water.

New archeological excavations conducted on the site have produced proof that people were living on the banks of the Seine during the Neolithic era (4 500 BC). Numerous objects have been found, made of bone, deer antler, stone and clay, not to mention the extraordinary discovery of three perfectly preserved oak-wood dug-out canoes.

A. Ei/MICHELIN

Ministry of Finance

Palais omnisports de Paris-Bercy – On the eastern side of the capital, this new sports complex was built to stage international indoor sporting events. From the outside the appearance is somewhat surprising with grass-covered walls sloping away at 45 degrees. The glass roof is sheathed with a network of girders. The end product was a collaboration between the architects Andrault, Parat and Guvan.

Sport takes first place, with facilities catering to 22 different activities, but the centre's versatility is such that it can stage a variety of entertainments from opera, theatre and ballet to rock concerts. In addition to the adaptable main arena there are two multi-purpose halls and two warming-up or rehearsal halls.

In the square to the east of the stadium is an unusual fountain with a deep gully, the "Canyon Eaustrate" by Gérard Singer recalls geological formations in the North-American continent.

Bibliothèque Nationale France – Tolbiac

Over the river from Bercy, the most ambitious of François Mitterand's '*grands travaux*' (alongside la Grande Arche at la Défense, and Pei's pyramid at the Louvre) stands as the ultimate monument to the former President's 14 years in power. Four tower blocks – in the shape of open books – punctuate the corners of a wooded space, planted with mature trees from Fontainebleau. Wood also plays a part on the inside of the starkly clinical glass structure: as a complex system of shutters control levels of light, so the symbolism (forests, wood, paper, books) designed by Dominique Perrault, is consistent. The complex is due to replace the library functions of the old Bibliothèque Nationale (*see* PALAIS-ROYAL) in 1997.

American Center – *51 rue de Bercy*. This building (1994), just beyond the Hotel Ibis, is faced with a soft-coloured stone hewn from the limestone quarries of St Maximin.

The entrance, facing onto the park, breaks out of line with the rest of the rectilinear mass. Defined by the architect as "a ballerina pulling up her skirts and inviting in the people", the centre was intended to bring together a symphony of cultures, far from Hollywood stereotypes – cinema, theatre, music and dance, as well as exhibitions and lectures. It also provides accommodation for up to 20 artists and performers. The interior consists of a series of stone volumes and glazed spaces, warm colours enhanced by natural light, designed "to make people feel at ease". A vibrant presence on Paris' international cultural scene since the 1930s, the American Center was forced to cease its activities in early 1996 owing to financial difficulties.

The American Center designed by Frank Gehry has earned him the Pritzker Prize. It is the second project undertaken in France by the Californian, the other being at Disneyland Paris.

'No city has been so fortunate in its special historians as Paris. It is a consequence of the intense love which Frenchmen have towards their great capital... Paris is emphatically the centre of light, intelligence, society and refined life...'

Herman Merivale (17C)

BOIS DE BOULOGNE★★

Michelin plan 11: folds 61 – 62
Michelin plan 11 – folds 14 – 16: E 4, E 6, F 5 - F 7
Ⓜ *les Sablons* – Buses: *43, 52, 63, 73, 82, PC*

This vast park of 846ha – 2 100 acres is cut by wide shaded roads (speed restriction), tracks for pedestrians, horses and cyclists; boating is allowed on the Lower Lake. There are lakes, waterfalls, gardens, lawns and woodland, two racecourses, cafés and restaurants for the enjoyment of the public. Race meetings at Longchamp and Auteuil attract large numbers of racegoers and roads tend to be busy. The best time for a pleasant stroll is on weekdays, in the morning. There are two waymarked paths: the round tour (red and yellow) and the short one (yellow and blue).

A royal forest – In Merovingian times the forest was hunted for bear, deer, wolves and wild boar; in 1308 local woodmen went on pilgrimage to Notre Dame at Boulogne-sur-Mer and, on their return, built a church on the lines of that on the Channel coast with funds provided by Philip the Fair, dedicating it to Our Lady of Boulogne the Lesser.

As the royal forest had become a refuge for bandits, in 1556 Henri II enclosed it with a wall pierced by eight gates; the most important being the Porte Maillot and Porte de la Muette.

In the 17C Colbert adapts it for hunting with a crisscross of straight rides marked at junction points with crosses, like the Croix Catelan. This layout has been preserved at Meudon and St-Germain. Louis XIV opened the wood to the public as a place for country walks, but its reputation soon left a lot to be desired! Judging from a contemporary chronicle, 'marriages from the Bois de Boulogne do not get brought before the Right Reverend.' It was not until the Regency that it became fashionable with High Society and great houses were built: Neuilly, La Muette, Bagatelle, la Folie St James and Ranelagh.

Decline – During the Revolution the forest provided refuge to those on the run, the destitute and poachers. In 1815, the English and Russian armies set up camp in the forest devastating a great section. In the replanting, oaks have been replaced by horse chestnuts, acacias, sycamores and maples.

The wood today – When Napoleon III gave the forest to the capital in 1852, Haussmann demolished the surrounding wall, landscaped the area after Hyde Park creating winding paths, ornamental lakes and ponds, and built the Longchamp racecourse, restaurants, kiosks and pavilions. 1854 saw the opening of the Avenue de l'Impératrice (now the Avenue Foch); the wood became the fashionable place to take the air. The Auteuil racecourse, famous for its jumps, was built after 1870. The construction of the ring road round Paris and of the Parc des Princes stadium, together with other planning decisions have caused some disruption but the wood is once again the capital's main recreation area.

'I will not describe the Bois de Boulogne. I cannot do it. It is simply a beautiful, cultivated, endless, wonderful wilderness. It is an enchanting place.'

Mark Twain.

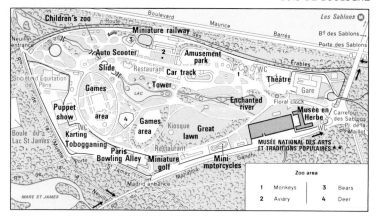

Within the park

★Jardin d'Acclimatation ⊙ – This park, primarily arranged as a children's amusement park (with enchanted river and miniature railway), includes a small zoo with a pets' corner, a typical Norman farm and an aviary. The **Musée en Herbe** ⊙ is an art-museum-cum-workshop designed for youngsters.

Duke and Duchess of Windsor

The house located along the route du Champ-d'Entrainement, 16th *arr.*, has long belonged to the City of Paris who frequently leased it to famous figures. It was leased to General de Gaulle during his provisional presidency between 1944 and 1945 and to the Duke & Duchess of Windsor from 1953 until their respective deaths. In 1986 it was contracted to Mr Mohamed Al-Fayed who has not only restored the house but recovered many of the paintings and pieces of furniture dispersed at Wallace Simpson's death.

Institutions to have benefited from the Windsor estate include the Louvre (paintings by George Stubbs) and the Pasteur Institute (jewellery collection sold to fund research into AIDS)

★★Musée National des Arts et Traditions Populaires ⊙ – *6 avenue du Mahatma-Gandhi.* Ⓜ *les Sablons – Bus 73.* Two galleries give a glimpse of day-to-day life in pre-industrial France.

The **Cultural Gallery** *(ground floor)* evokes man's environment, the technical progress made by man to enable him to exploit natural resources and the institutions he created for community living.

The **Study Gallery** *(basement)* has displays on agriculture, husbandry, domestic life, crafts, local beliefs and customs, games, music and local folklore. An audio-visual show and slides complement the displays.

★★Parc de Bagatelle ⊙ – *Route de Sèvres-à-Neuilly. Bus: 43 (from the north) or 244 (from the south).* The first house to be built on the site was in 1720; it fell into ruin and in 1775 the Count of Artois – future Charles X – bought it, waging a bet with his sister-in-law, Marie-Antoinette, that he would have a house designed and built, complete with its landscaped garden, within three months. He won.

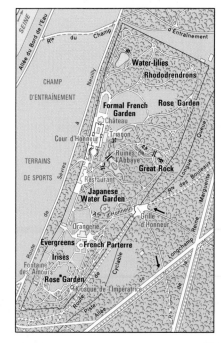

In 1806 it was acquired by Napoleon, having survived the Revolution and contemplating making it a palace for the King of Rome. At the Restoration it reverted to the Duc de Berry before coming into the possession of the Hertford family. The third and fourth marquesses and the latter's son, Sir Richard Wallace, accumulated a large collection of 17C and 18C French paintings, furniture and objets d'art.

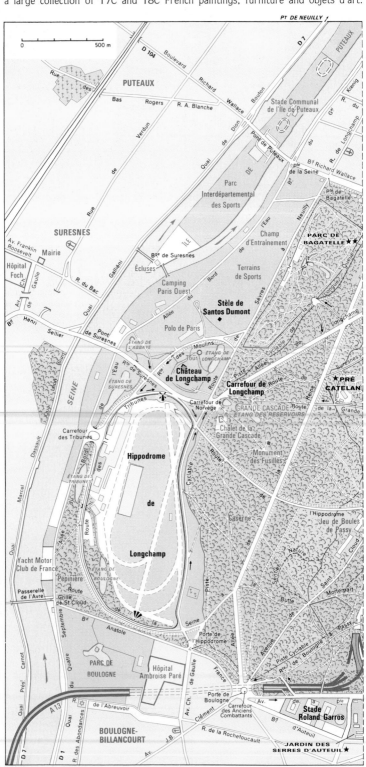

Daumesnil's refusals
the governor, General
Wagram, retorted "I'll
At the end of the Hund
came a second refusa
Louis XVIII.
In 1830 Daumesnil wa
ministers imprisoned
that before surrender

The military establis
into the Paris defence
reinforced with massiv
On 24 August 1944
26 resistance fighters
and damaging the Kin

Restoration – The
Viollet-le-Duc. Repair
has only recently been
the 17C, the moat arc
and the pavilions rest
royal houses of Franc

Tour of the ex

A walk round the ou
moat provides a good
by the impressive **kee**
military architecture.

★★Le donjon de Vincen
The 52m – 170f
tower, quartered b
rets, with a spur
north for latrines, a
room and a small o
was originally crowne
crenellated battlemer
machicolations.
The keep proper was
sed by a fortified wa
separate moat. The
the stone wall was
ced to protect again
ping (breaching defe
undermining a wall)
turrets defended t
ners. At sky level, a
sentry path, comple
battlements, and ma
tions with gun emb
below, ran right ro
inner tower.

La tour du Bois a
Colonne du Duc d'E
– The arcades of th
sical Vincennes
overlooking the for
closing the perime
on the south side, c
view as you reach t
teau *esplanade*. T
Tower in the mid
reduced by Le Vau
17C when he tran
the gate into a stat
From the bridge ove
right, the column m
cuted by firing squa
body was exhumed

La cours des Maré
1931 on the site of
towers along the eas

The art collection was transferred to London where, since 1897, it has been on view as the Wallace Collection, Hertford House. Bagatelle was sold to the City of Paris in 1905. Bagatelle is well known for its beautiful garden, particularly its walled iris garden *(May)*, roses *(June to October)* and water lilies *(August)*. Exhibitions of paintings and sculpture are held *(May to October)* in the Trianon and Orangery.

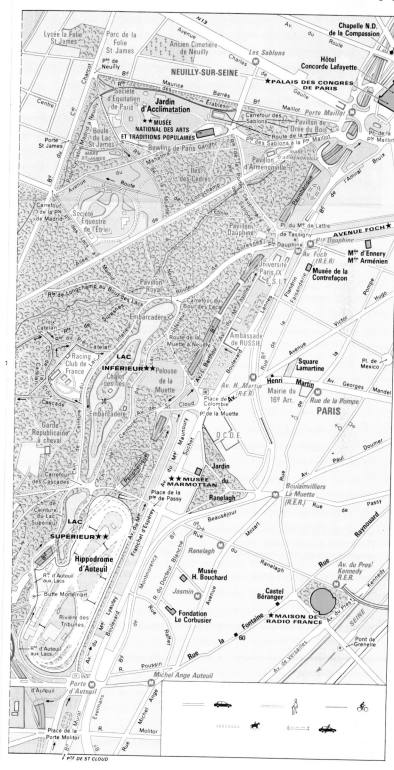

B

Vincennes – a fortress
lake-scattered wood,
to discover and enjoy

★★CHATEAU M

This "medieval Ve
keep and a majest

The manorhouse
Abbey; in the 12C
Louis IX added a H
mals, preferring,
out ceremony.

The fortified ch
John the Good
the château de
at Nogent. C
imagined a 'roya
To this end he
his favourite nol
build themselves
within the huge
but to no avail
it was not un
reign of Louis X
the nobility
to live in the king
dow.

The classical cha
Mazarin, app
governor of Vi
in 1652, had sy
cal royal pa
designed and bu
Vau to frame th
courtyard which
south over the
In 1660, one ye
the pavilions'
tion, the youn
XIV spent his
moon in the
Pavilion.

The prison
the beginning
16C to 1784, t
no longer favo
a royal resider
used as a stat
to incarcerate
ers of the Le
Jansenism,
Fronde, as well
tine lords and
at the Bastille.
Cardinal de Re
and Mirabeau.

The porcelain
factory when
and began to
A company w
often decorate
transferred to
THE PARIS R

The arsenal –
The towers w
cannon, the ra
prison.

Tour of the interior

★**La tour du Village** – This massive tower 42m – 138ft high, which also survived the 19C alterations, served as the governor's residence in the Middle Ages. It was a good place from which to survey the entrance and supervise the defences of the fortress.

Although the statues which graced the exterior have disappeared, some defensive features are still visible: slits for the drawbridge chains, groove of the portcullis, loopholes. Within the wall, on the left, is a hunt **museum** ⊙ housing documents, paintings and mementoes.

To the left of the paved alleyway is the site of St Louis' manor house (tablet on small building which has 17C foundations).

Chapelle Royale – The Royal Chapel, modelled on the Sainte-Chapelle (see ILE DE LA CITÉ) and begun by Charles V in the 14C in place of the one built by St Louis, was completed only in the 16C in the reign of Henri II. The building, apart from the windows and some decoration, is pure Gothic; the façade with its beautiful stone rose windows is Flamboyant.

The interior consists of a single elegant aisle with highly decorative consoles and a frieze running beneath the windows which, in the chancel, are filled with unusually coloured mid-16C **stained glass★** featuring scenes from the Apocalypse.

The Duc d'Enghien's tomb is in the north chapel.

★★**Le donjon** – The fortified wall, after the removal of the appended extensions, is protected by a barbican which guarded the drawbridge. The keep is in the centre of a courtyard. There is a small **museum** (audio-visual presentation) retracing its history. Each of the keep's floors, save the topmost, consists of a main vaulted

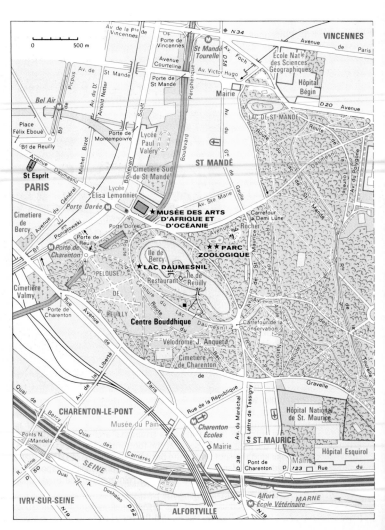

chamber resting on a central pillar with four small dependent rooms in the turrets serving as waiting room, confessional, oratory, wardrobe, treasury... These were later converted into prison cells (graffiti on the walls).

Ground floor – This served as the kitchens. In the great south hall there is a well 17m – 56ft deep and a gate which was that of the Temple Tower *(see* RÉPUBLIQUE*)* brought here after the demolition of the prison in which Louis XVI and his family were held.

First floor – A gangway provided direct access from the barbican to the first floor. The main room originally served as a royal reception room hung with tapestries. It was here that Charles V received the Holy Roman Emperor with great pomp, and where Fouquet was imprisoned (*see* BASTILLE-L'Arsenal), whereas Mirabeau was imprisoned for three years in one of the towers where he wrote a scathing condemnation of royal warrants.

Second floor – A wide spiral staircase leads to what was once the royal bedchamber. Henri V of England, Charles VI's son-in-law, died of dysentery in this room in 1422, as did Charles IX in 1574 aged 24.

★**Classical Vincennes** – The main courtyard (Cour Royale) is once more closed to the north by a portico, as Le Vau intended, and is framed by the two royal pavilions. Anne of Austria and Louis XIV's brother lived in the pavillon de la Reine, where the governor, Daumesnil, died of cholera in 1832; the last royal occupant was the Duke of Montpensier, Louis Philippe's youngest son.

Mazarin died in the pavillon du Roi in 1661 while awaiting the completion of his apartment in the Queen's Pavilion.

On the ground floor there is the **musée de la Symbolique militaire** ⓥ displaying 8 500 army insignia from 1920 to the present day.

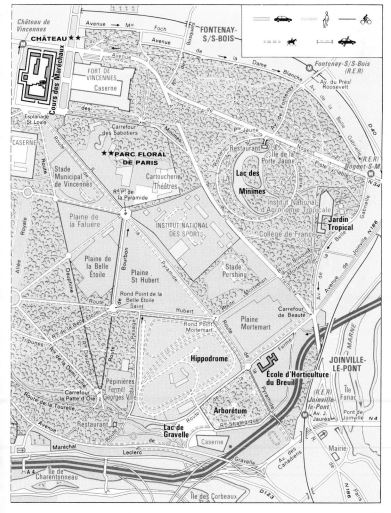

★★PARK

M *Porte de Charenton, St-Mandé-Tourelle. RER: Fontenay-sous-Bois, Joinville-le-Pont*

The bois de Vincennes with its natural attractions, its famous zoo and beautiful flower garden, is a popular recreation area. In addition to facilities for sport there are two waymarked paths: red for the complete tour, and yellow and blue for a shorter one.

The Royal Forest – Philippe Auguste enclosed the wood as a royal hunt with a wall 12km – 7 miles long and stocked it with game. **Charles V** built the small Beauté Château within it on a low hill overlooking the Marne.

In the 17C it became a fashionable place in which to go walking. Strollers gained access to the wood through six gates piercing the wall. The Pyramid monument commemorates the plantations which were carried out in Louis XV's reign.

A military firing range was opened in 1798, the first of a series of enclaves in the forest made exclusively for military and sporting purposes.

The forest in modern times – Napoleon III ceded the estate at Vincennes – excluding the château and military installations – in 1860 to the City of Paris to be made into an English-style park, on the lines of London's Hyde Park. Haussmann created the Gravelle Lake with water diverted from the River Marne which, in turn, feeds the lakes and rivers throughout the wood. The National Sports Institute dominated by a modern covered stadium offers training facilities for athletics and swimming.

Foire du Trône or foire aux Pains d'épice ⓥ – The thousand-year-old Throne or Gingerbread Fair *(see* ST-GERMAIN-DES-PRÉS*)* is held each spring *(Palm Sunday to Easter)* on the Reuilly Lawn near Lake Daumesnil. The fair recalls a concession obtained in 957 by the monks of St Antony's Abbey to sell a piglet-shaped rye, honey and aniseed bread in memory of their saint during Holy Week. The followers of St Antony used to ring bells to call the faithful, bells thus came to be hung around the necks of domestic animals to protect them. St Antony's attribute, a small pig, is always portrayed with a bell.

This colourful funfair is the capital's principal one.

Foire du Trône, Vincennes

★★**Parc Floral de Paris** ⓥ – *Route de la Pyramide.* M *Château de Vincennes.* The garden, landscaped by D Collin in 1969, extends over 30ha – 75 acres and includes hundreds of species. The Vallée des Fleurs is delightful all year round. The pavilions tucked away amid pine trees around the lake, together with the Hall de la Pinède, house exhibitions and shows (photographs, dance, posters and horticulture). Alleys lined with modern sculpture (Giacometti, Calder) lead to the children's adventure playground. The Dahlia garden from Sceaux, south of Paris, has been recreated near the Pyramid *(in flower September-October)*. The water garden with its water-lilies and lotus is at its best from July to September. There are also a Four Seasons Garden, and gardens growing medicinal plants *(best seen from May to October)*, irises *(May)* and bamboo. Flower shows are held throughout the year: Orchids *(early March)*, tulips *(from April)*, rhododendrons and azalea *(from May)*.

Lac des Minimes – *RER: Fontenay-sous-Bois.* The lake, named after a monastery on the same site which formed an enclave in the royal forest, includes three islands, of which one, the Porte Jaune, is accessible across a bridge.

Jardin tropical – *Avenue de la Belle-Gabrielle. RER: Nogent-sur-Marne.* The garden, in which stand the Institute of Tropical Agronomic Research and the Tropical Forestry Centre *(no 45bis)*, has a Chinese gate by the main entrance. On the far side of the garden, a Temple to the Memory of the Indo-Chinese killed in the 1914-1918 War was destroyed by fire in 1984. The avenue of trees is inspired by the famous one at Angkor Watt.

École de Breuil ⓥ – *Route de la Ferme. RER: Joinville-le-Pont.* This school specialises in horticulture and landscape design; it has beautiful gardens. The arboretum *(entrance: Route de la Pyramide)* extends over 12ha – 30 acres and includes 2 000 trees of 80 different species.

Hippodrome – *RER: Joinville-le-Pont.* The main racing events are listed in the Calendar of Events *(see PRACTICAL INFORMATION).* Evening race meetings are also held.
On the other side of route de la Ferme is **lac de Gravelle** dotted with water-lilies.

Centre Bouddhique ⓥ – *40bis route de ceinture du Lac Daumesnil.* South of Lake Daumesnil is the Buddhist Temple of Paris housed in one of the 1931 Colonial Exhibition buildings. The new roof with 180 000 tiles carved with an axe out of a chestnut tree is noteworthy. Inside is a monumental gilded statue of Buddha (9m – 30ft).

★**Lac Daumesnil** ⓥ – This is a popular focal point for walkers and boaters alike.

★★**Le parc zoologique de Vincennes** ⓥ – *Avenue Daumesnil.* Ⓜ *Porte Dorée.* 550 mammals and 700 birds of some 200 different species live in natural surroundings close to their familiar habitat. At the centre is an artificial rock 72m – 236ft high inhabited by wild mountain sheep.

★**Musée des Arts d'Afrique et d'Océanie** ⓥ – *293 avenue Daumesnil.* Ⓜ *Porte Dorée.* The façade of the building, erected for a Colonial Exhibition in 1931, is decorated with a great sculptured frieze illustrating the contributions made by the overseas territories to France.
The ground floor and the right side of the main hall are devoted to Oceanian art including: a large collection of bark paintings (Australia), masks (New Guinea), strange funerary figures with shrunken mummified heads and sculptures carved from tree-fern roots. On the left side of the hall are exhibited examples of Black African art; Life is symbolised by animals often with human features (Banda and Molo masks) and Death in an evocation of tribal ancestors (Kota wood and copper figures from Gabon). On the first floor are dance masks, ceremonial masks (Mali, Ivory Coast), gold pendant masks (Ivory Coast, Ghana), and magical statues (Congo).
On the second floor, the North African **Maghreb** countries are represented by fine **jewellery★**, ceramics, embroidered belts from Fez, Algerian headdresses, Tunisian pottery, carved furniture inlaid with mother-of-pearl and ivory, and woollen carpets. In the basement there are a tropical **aquarium★** and two terrariums.

Salon Paul Raynaud, former Ministry for the Colonies

CHAMPS-ÉLYSÉES★★★

Michelin plan 11 – folds 16 and 17, 29 and 30: F 7 – G 11

The Paris vista extending down the Champs-Élysées from the Arc de Triomphe, silhouetted against the sky, known the world over, is known to Parisians as the Voie Triomphale or Triumphal Way.

★★★L'ARC DE TRIOMPHE

Ⓜ *Charles-de-Gaulle-Étoile. Buses: 22, 30, 31, 52, 73, 92*

The arch and the **place Charles-de-Gaulle★★★** which surrounds it, together form one of Paris' most famous landmarks. Twelve avenues radiate from the arch which explains why it is also called place de l'Étoile (*étoile* = star).

The arch commemorates Napoleon's victories, evoking at the same time imperial glory and the fate of the Unknown Soldier, whose tomb lies beneath. A Remembrance ceremony is held there on 11 November.

Arc de Triomphe – *La Marseillaise*

Historical notes – Napoleon's original intention was for a triumphal way to extend from the Arc de Triomphe, past Le Louvre, place de la Bastille to place de la Nation. By the end of the 18C the square was already star-shaped despite having only five roads leading from it. At the centre was a semicircular lawn.

1806: Napoleon commissioned the construction of a giant arch in honour of the French fighting services. Chalgrin was appointed architect. It took two years to lay the foundations.

1810: With the Empress Marie-Louise due to make her triumphal entry along the Champs-Élysées and the arch only a few feet above ground, Chalgrin had to erect a dummy arch of painted canvas mounted on scaffolding, to preserve appearances.

1832-1836: Construction, abandoned during the Restoration, was completed under Louis-Philippe.

1840: The chariot bearing the Emperor's body passed beneath the arch.

1854: Haussmann redesigned the square, creating a further seven radiating avenues, while Hittorff planned the uniform façades which surround it.

1885: Victor Hugo's body lay in state for a night beneath the arch, draped in crepe, before being transported in a pauper's hearse to the Panthéon.

1919: On 14 July victorious Allied armies, led by the marshals, marched in procession.

1920: 11 November, an unknown soldier killed in the Great War was laid to rest.

1923: 11 November, the Flame of Remembrance was kindled.

1944: 26 August, Paris, liberated from German occupation, acclaimed General de Gaulle.

The arch – The arch's proportions and the relative scale of the sculpted reliefs are best appreciated from a distance.

Chalgrin's undertaking, inspired by Antiquity, is truly colossal, measuring 50m high by 45m wide – 164ft x 148ft, with massive high reliefs.

Rude was commissioned to carve the four main panels. Unfortunately, Etex and Cortot managed to influence President Thiers enough to steal work for three of the four groups – Rude's is the only inspired one. Pradier's Fames, four trumpet-blowing figures abut the main arches. A frieze bustling with hundreds of figures, each 2m – 6ft tall encircles the arch; in the entablature above, a line of shields bear the names of the great victories of the Revolution and the Empire.

Facing the Champs-Élysées: 1) *The Departure of the Volunteers in 1792*, commonly called **La Marseillaise**★★, Rude's sublime masterpiece represents the Nation leading her people to defend their independence. 2) *General Marceau's funeral.* 3) *The Triumph of 1810* (by Cortot) celebrating the Treaty of Vienna. 4) *The Battle of Aboukir.*

Facing Avenue de Wagram: 5) *The Battle of Austerlitz.*

Facing Avenue de la Grande-Armée: 6) *Resistance* (by Etex). 7) *The Passage of the Bridge of Arcola.* 8) *Peace* (by Etex). 9) *The Capture of Alexandria.*

Facing Avenue Kléber: 10) *The Battle of Jemmapes.*

Returning to the Champs-Élysées once more, take the underpass to the Arch platform, from the right pavement. Beneath the monument, the Unknown Soldier rests under a plain slab; the flame of remembrance is rekindled each evening at 6.30pm. Lesser battles are engraved on the arch's inner walls together with the names of 558 generals – the names of those who died in the field are underlined.

The Arch platform ⊙ – From here there is an excellent **view**★★★ of the capital: in the foreground the 12 avenues radiating from the square: you are halfway between the Louvre and La Défense, at the top of the Champs-Élysées.

Assembled in a small museum are mementoes of its construction and the celebratory and funerary ceremonies it has hosted. A documentary recalls the monument's moments of glory.

★★★CHAMPS-ÉLYSÉES

Ⓜ *Charles-de-Gaulle-Étoile, George V, Franklin D Roosevelt, Champs-Élysées-Clemenceau, Concorde. Bus: 73 runs the full length*

The avenue – The most famous thoroughfare in Paris is at once an avenue with a spectaclar view, a place of entertainment and a street of smart luxury shops.

Origin – In the time of Henri IV this area consisted of fields and marshland; in 1616 Marie de' Medici created the Cours-la-Reine, a long avenue which extended from the Tuileries along the Seine as far as the present Alma Square. The tree-lined route, in time, became the most fashionable carriage ride.

In 1667 Le Nôtre lengthened the Tuileries vista by planting trees in rows on the plain known as the Grand Cours. In 1709 the peaceful arbour was renamed the Elysian Fields – Champs-Élysées. In 1724 the Duke of Antin, Director of the Royal Gardens, extended the avenue to the heights of Chaillot – the present Étoile; his successor, the Marquis of Marigny, prolonged it in 1772 to the Neuilly Bridge. Two years later Soufflot lessened the road gradient by reducing the hill by more than 5m – 16ft; the surplus rubble was dumped, producing the still-apparent rise in the rue Balzac.

The height of fashion – By the end of the 18C the Champs-Élysées were still a wild, deserted and unexceptional area: only six private mansions had been built thereabouts. Of these, the Hôtel Massa was later transported stone by stone and re-erected near the Observatory *(see* LUXEMBOURG*)*. The Allies, who occupied Paris in 1814, installed themselves in the green heart of the capital: the English and the Prussians camped in the Tuileries Gardens and place de la Concorde, the Russians beneath the trees on the Champs-Élysées. The consequential damage took two years to clean up.

The avenue, by 1828 in the City's care, was embellished by fountains, footpaths and gaslighting. During the time of the Second Empire it became a favourite meeting place and hence a popular haunt of social gossips who, sitting on either side of the thoroughfare, watched out for society '*beaux*' out with their escorts, on horseback or in tilburies and broughams, eight abreast in a cloud of dust. Café orchestras (the Alcazar rebuilt by Hittorff in 1840), restaurants, panoramas, circuses attracted the crowds, swelled by the gentry out at race meetings at Longchamp or the great world exhibitions (1844, 1855, 1867, 1900...). In the gallant neighbourhood of the allée des Veuves, now avenue Montaigne *(see* ALMA*)*, crowds gathered at the bal Mabille up until 1870. By the light of 3 000 gaslights Olivier Metra conducted polkas and mazurkas with gay abandon, and nearby, in the jardin d'Hiver, the musician Sax used to play his new instrument, the saxophone.

The heart of the nation – Today the avenue has lost much of its aristocratic dignity, none of its brightness and little of its appeal. On 14 July, military processions with bands playing draw immense crowds. At times of great patriotic fervour (as for the Tour de France), the triumphal avenue continues to be the spontaneous rallying point for the people of Paris: at the Liberation (26 August 1944), the demonstrations of 30 May 1968, the silent march in honour of General de Gaulle (12 November 1970).

Between the Arc de Triomphe and the Rond-Point

Ⓜ *Charles-de-Gaulle-Étoile, George V, Franklin D Roosevelt. Bus 73*

This section is the second widest thoroughfare in Paris, it measures 71m – 233ft overall. (Avenue Foch: 120m – 394ft).

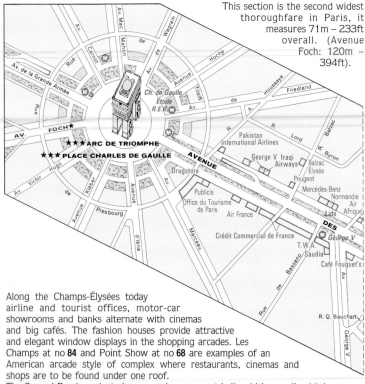

Along the Champs-Élysées today airline and tourist offices, motor-car showrooms and banks alternate with cinemas and big cafés. The fashion houses provide attractive and elegant window displays in the shopping arcades. Les Champs at no **84** and Point Show at no **68** are examples of an American arcade style of complex where restaurants, cinemas and shops are to be found under one roof.

The Second Empire private houses and amusement halls which once lined it have vanished, so the avenue appears without historical memories. The only exception is no **25**, a mansion built by La Païva, a Polish adventuress, whose house was famous for dinners attended by the Goncourt brothers and the philosophers Renan and Taine, and for its probably unique onyx staircase. **Le Colisée**, an amphitheatre built in 1770 to hold an audience of 40 000, has left its name to a street, a café and a cinema.

Le Rond-Point – *(Buses: 24, 32, 42, 49, 73, 80, 83, 93)*. Designed by Le Nôtre, Second Empire town houses contrast with modern shops. Good views.

Between the Rond-Point and place de la Concorde

★The gardens – This section is landscaped with trees and bordered with avenues of grand old horse-chestnuts dotted with occasional pavilions and the odd, small children's merry-go-round.

Impressionist artist Mary Cassat lived at 10 rue Marignan from 1887 until her death in 1926.

Avenue Gabriel – Shaded gardens on the northern side, running parallel to the Champs-Élysées, stretch along the back of smart mansions lining the Faubourg-St-Honoré: the Elysée Palace (fine wrought-iron gate with gilded cockerel), the British Embassy, the Interallied Union Circle, the United States Embassy (in the former home of the gastronome Grimod de la Reynière).

Avenue Marigny – The **Théâtre Marigny** was designed by Garnier in 1853, and used almost exclusively by Jacques Offenbach from 1855 to amuse the Parisian public with his operettas. On Thursdays, Saturdays and Sundays a stamp market is held next to the theatre. The monument on the corner with avenue Marigny is to the leader of the Resistance, Jean Moulin: the five steles bear heads with anguished expressions symbolising Pain and Suffering.

Place Clemenceau – In the square stands a bronze statue of the statesman Clemenceau, *The Father of Victory*, by François Cogné (1932).
The former Panorama, later a skating-rink, is now the Théâtre du Rond-Point, home to the Renaud-Barrault Theatre Company.

Avenue Winston-Churchill – From the centre of the avenue there is a good **view★★** towards the Invalides.
The two great halls, the **Petit** and **Grand Palais**, were built for the 1900 World Exhibition: Girault's stone, steel and glass architecture and Third Republic exterior decoration have always solicited criticism as well as admiration.

★Petit Palais – Perhaps the most enduring quality of this institution is the magnificence of the major temporary exhibitions it holds and their excellent, scholarly catalogues that come to serve as important reference books. The **Musée du Petit Palais** ⊙ owns and displays the Dutuit (antiques, medieval and Renaissance art objects, paintings, drawings, books, enamels, porcelain) and Tuck (18C furniture and objets d'art) bequests, alongside the city of Paris' collection of 19C paintings (Ingres, Delacroix, Courbet, Dalou, Barbizon School, Impressionists). The south gallery displays large historical and religious canvases (Gustave Doré) and the north gallery contains works by Carpeaux.

The museum provides a good opportunity to review the various artistic currents that evolved out of the Academic tradition, institutionalised by the Beaux Arts School and the Salons, towards Realism and individual expression.

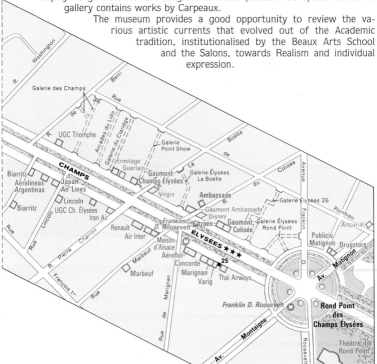

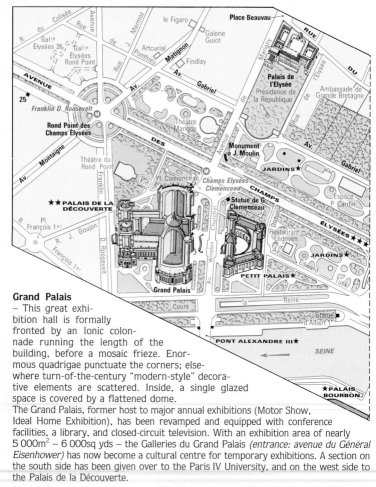

Grand Palais

– This great exhibition hall is formally fronted by an Ionic colonnade running the length of the building, before a mosaic frieze. Enormous quadrigae punctuate the corners; elsewhere turn-of-the-century "modern-style" decorative elements are scattered. Inside, a single glazed space is covered by a flattened dome.

The Grand Palais, former host to major annual exhibitions (Motor Show, Ideal Home Exhibition), has been revamped and equipped with conference facilities, a library, and closed-circuit television. With an exhibition area of nearly 5 000m^2 – 6 000sq yds – the Galleries du Grand Palais *(entrance: avenue du Général Eisenhower)* has now become a cultural centre for temporary exhibitions. A section on the south side has been given over to the Paris IV University, and on the west side to the Palais de la Découverte.

★★Palais de la Découverte ⓥ

– *avenue Franklin-D-Roosevelt.* This museum, founded by a physicist in 1937 and dedicated to scientific discovery, is a centre both for higher scientific study and for popular enlightenment. Diagrams, lectures and demonstrations, experiments, documentary films and temporary exhibitions illustrate scientific invention and innovation.

The domed **planetarium★** presents a clear and fascinating introduction to the heavens including the course of the planets in the solar system.

Grand Palais – Detail (quadriga)

A. Éti/MICHELIN

★**Pont Alexandre III** – This bridge was built for the 1900 World Exhibition and is an example of the popular steel architecture and ornate style of the period. The armorial bearings of Russia and France evoke the memory of Alexander III, father of Nicholas II of Russia who laid the foundation stone. It has a splendid single-span, surbased arch; it affords a fine view of the Invalides.

Restaurant Ledoyen – In Louis XVI's time this was a modest country inn where passers-by stopped to drink fresh milk drawn from the cows grazing outside.

L'espace Pierre Cardin – Formerly the Théâtre des Ambassadeurs, this is now a venue for exhibitions, concerts, theatre and dance shows.

★★★PLACE DE LA CONCORDE Ⓜ *Concorde. Buses: 24, 42, 52, 72, 73, 84, 94*

Everything about this square – site, size, general elegance – is impressive.
Paris aldermen, wanting to find favour with Louis XV, commissioned Bouchardon to sculpt an equestrian statue of 'Le Bien-Aimé' (the beloved) as he was known, and organised a competition to find an architect for the square. Servandoni, Soufflot, Gabriel amongst others submitted plans. Gabriel's designs for an octagon bordered by a dry moat and balustrade won. Eight massive paired pedestals intended to carry sculptures were to mark the oblique corners.

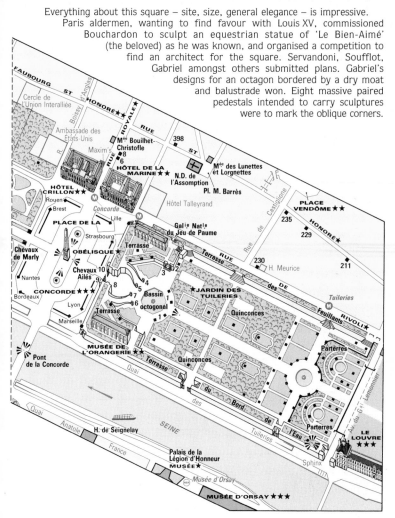

Twin edifices with fine colonnades were to be constructed to flank the opening of the rue Royale. Work began in 1755 and continued until 1775. In 1770, during fireworks to celebrate the marriage of the Dauphin – future Louis XVI and Marie-Antoinette, the crowd panicked and 133 people were crushed to death in the moat.

In 1792 the royal statue was toppled and place Louis XV became place de la Révolution. On Sunday 21 January 1793 a guillotine was erected in the northwest corner (near where the Brest statue now stands) for the execution of Louis XVI. On 13 May, the "nation's razor", now installed near the grille to the Tuileries, began to claim a further 1 343 victims including Marie-Antoinette, Mme du Barry, Charlotte Corday, the Girondins, Danton and his friends, Mme Roland, Robespierre and his confederates... The last heads rolled in 1795. The Directory, hopeful of a better future, renamed the blood-soaked area place de la Concorde.

★**Obelisk** – Under Louis-Philippe, the square's decoration was completed by the architect Hittorff. Wary of having a central statue that might become politically contentious, the king opted for the obelisk which comes from the ruins of the temple at Luxor. It was given to Charles X in 1829 by Mohammed Ali, Viceroy of Egypt, seeking support from the French. It reached Paris four years later, however, in the reign of Louis-Philippe.

The monument in pink granite, 3 300 years old, is covered in hieroglyphics; it is 23m – 75ft tall – and weighs more than 220 tons. The base depicts the apparatus and stratagems used in its transport and erection on the square. Cleopatra's Needle in London, offered by the same ruler to Queen Victoria, comes from Heliopolis and is 2m – 6ft 6 in shorter.

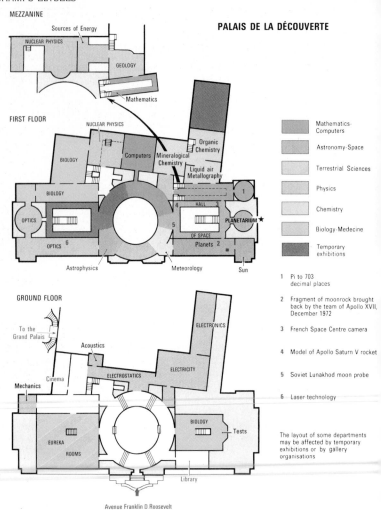

MEZZANINE

Sources of Energy

NUCLEAR PHYSICS

GEOLOGY

Mathematics

PALAIS DE LA DÉCOUVERTE

FIRST FLOOR

NUCLEAR PHYSICS

Organic Chemistry

BIOLOGY

Computers | Mineralogical Chemistry

Liquid air Metallography

BIOLOGY

1

OPTICS

4 | HALL

5 | PLANETARIUM ★

OF SPACE

OPTICS | 6

Planets | 2

Astrophysics | Meteorology | Sun

Mathematics-Computers

Astronomy-Space

Terrestrial Sciences

Physics

Chemistry

Biology-Medecine

Temporary exhibitions

1 Pi to 703 decimal places

2 Fragment of moonrock brought back by the team of Apollo XVII, December 1972

3 French Space Centre camera

4 Model of Apollo Saturn V rocket

5 Soviet Lunakhod moon probe

6 Laser technology

GROUND FLOOR

ELECTRONICS

To the Grand Palais

Acoustics

Cinema | ELECTROSTATICS | ELECTRICITY

Mechanics

BIOLOGY

Tests

EUREKA ROOMS

The layout of some departments may be affected by temporary exhibitions or by gallery organisations

Library

Avenue Franklin D Roosevelt

Sculpture – To complete the design of the square, two fountains were added, inspired by those in St Peter's Square in Rome. The north fountain represents fluvial navigation and the south fountain maritime navigation. Eight statues representing eight French cities were commissioned for the pedestals provided by Gabriel. Cortot sculpted Brest and Rouen, Pradier Lille and Strasbourg. It was at the foot of this last figure that the poet-politician, Déroulède, rallied patriots after 1870 when the town of Strasbourg was under German rule. Lyons and Marseille are by Petitot, Bordeaux and Nantes by Caillouette.

Chevaux de Marly – Replicas now replace the two original marble groups *(Africans Mastering the Numidian Horses)*, which were commissioned from Guillaume Coustou for Marly, Louis XIV's superb château near Versailles. These were to replace Coysevox's *Winged Horses* which had been moved to the Tuileries. Following Marly's destruction during the Revolution a special trailer drawn by 16 horses brought the marbles to their present site in 1795. The originals are now in the Louvre.

★★Two mansions – Gabriel's colossal mansions on either side of the opening to rue Royale *(see* FAUBOURG-ST-HONORÉ*)* are impressive without being overbearing; the colonnades inspired by those of the Louvre are even more elegant than the original, and the mansions themselves, among the finest examples of the early Louis XVI style. The right pavilion, the **Hôtel de la Marine★★**, was until 1792 the royal store; it then became the Admiralty Office. Today it houses the Navy Headquarters. The **Hôtel Crillon★★**, across the street, was at first occupied by four noblemen. It now accommodates the French Automobile Club and a famous hotel. It was in this building on 6 February 1778 that the Treaty of Friendship and Trade between the King, Louis XVI and the 13 independent States of America was signed. Benjamin Franklin was among the signatories for the States. On the rue Royale side, a plaque in English and French commemorates this treaty by which France officially recognised the independence of the USA.

Place de la Concorde, fountain

The two mansions on their far sides from rue Royale are bordered respectively by the American Embassy *(left)* and the Hôtel Talleyrand, designed in the 18C by Chalgrin for the Duc de la Vrillière, and where the statesman and diplomat Talleyrand died in 1838.

★★★**Views** – The obelisk provides the best point from which to get a view of the Champs-Élysées, framed by the Marly Horses looking up the avenue towards the Arc de Triomphe, and by the Winged Horses of the Tuileries towards the Louvre. There are good vistas also, north to the Madeleine beyond Gabriel's pavilions, and south to the Palais-Bourbon.

Pont de la Concorde – The bridge was designed in 1787 by the civil engineer, Perronet. It was completed by 1791, the stones from the Bastille having been used in its construction so that, it was said, "the people could forever trample the ruins of the old fortress". During Louis-Philippe's reign the bridge was decorated with 12 colossal statues of famous men but the ornament was not liked and the figures were dispatched first to Versailles and subsequently dispersed to provincial towns!

LA DÉFENSE★★

Michelin plan 11: folds 65 – 66
Central Parking area: access road Défense 4 from the ring road
Ⓜ *Esplanade de la Défense,* Ⓜ*/RER: Grande Arche de la Défense. Bus 73*

The quarter gets its name from a monument commemorating the defence of Paris of 1871. The bronze statue by Barrias once occupied the main roundabout before major development got under way.

The urbanisation of the area west of Paris creating new business and residential buildings is the most ambitious town planning project ever undertaken in the Paris region. The co-ordinating body EPAD (Établissement Public pour l'Aménagement de la Défense) set up in 1958, is responsible for the management of the project which covers an area of 800ha – 1 976 acres divided into two zones.

The business sector – Divided into 11 zones, the 130ha-321 acre site falls within the **Puteaux** and **Courbevoie** districts, on an axis with the Champs-Élysées, linked with the main city by the pont de Neuilly. Its situation straddling the main route access to the N 13 and N 192 – the most congested single section of road in France – has determined its fundamental structural layout, around a vast concrete **podium**. This pedestrianised area consists of a central mall with patios and squares on different levels, dotted with modern sculpture, punctuated by looming tower-blocks reaching for the sky. The tallest rises 45 floors. Since 1964 when the Essay building first opened, 47 towers have been completed and provide office space for over 900 companies, including some of France's principal ones. Most of the smaller tower-blocks are residential with the exceptions of: Eve, Défense 2000 and Gambetta. At the foot of the business and residential towers are commercial, leisure and sports complexes. The shopping centre covering 120 000m^2 – 30 acres is the largest in Europe.

LA DÉFENSE

The park area – Beyond the business area, a 90ha – 222 acre site extends westwards in the Nanterre plain, to include offices, housing, sports facilities and a park. Wogenscky's Hauts-de-Seine **Police Headquarters** (Préfecture) and Jacques Kalisz's **School of Architecture** were both completed in 1972. At the heart of this new urban development is the 24ha – 59 acre **parc André Malraux** with its botanical garden. Many of the surrounding buildings are highly original, designed by eminent architects (Théâtre des Amandiers and the Opéra Ballet School by Christian de Portzamparc).

VISIT

The new business district of La Défense, juxtaposing traditional office space with highly experimental developments, is a truly exceptional business environment. Even outside working hours, an air of restlessness pervades the 'podium' with traffic ceaselessly thundering underground through tunnels and various windows remain lit suggesting the constant hum of communications. Many of today's better-known artists and sculptors (Miró, Moretti, Calder, César...) have been commissioned to create works for this open-air gallery. It is with these points of reference that we provide a tour of this modern, sometimes impersonal, precinct.

Parvis – *For all information refer to the* Info-Défense ☉ *in the main precinct or near Esplanade-La-Défense metro exit*. From the podium there is a fine **vista★** between the towers stretching as far as the Arc de Triomphe at the Étoile.

Grande Arche, La Défense

★★La Grande Arche ⊙ – Perhaps and of the most controversial of the "Grands Projets" instigated by President François Mitterrand, this development reaffirms the role of the French State as Patron of the Arts and design. At the western end of the podium towers the great arch known as the Tête Défense, designed by the Danish architect Otto von Spreckelsen. This gigantic open cube (106m – 348ft wide) with its pre-stressed concrete frame, faced in glass and white Carrara marble, rises sheer without expansion joints. For technical reasons it is slightly out of alignment in relation to the La Défense-Louvre axis; the 300 000 tonne weight is carried on 12 piles sunk in the below-ground area which is crisscrossed by communications systems. The cathedral of Notre-Dame with its spire could fit into the space between the walls of the arch.

Scenic lifts whisk visitors to the roof to enjoy a unique view of the Paris area from the terrace.

The south vertical wall of the arch houses government ministry offices and the north wall major French and international companies. The three-storey thick roof is occupied by the International Foundation for Human Rights.

At the roof-terrace level (1ha – 2 1/2 acres), one section provides a view of the capital and its suburbs, with its historic axis right down to the Louvre, whilst another accommodates a suite of galleries holding temporary exhibitions, arranged around patios. The marble and granite mosaic paving of the patios represents a chart of the heavens. The theme of the internal decoration of the side walls of the arch by Jean Dewasne is languages and communication, to recall the now abandoned project for an International Communications Centre.

★★Colline de la Défense ⊙ – The building's modern architecture is a perfect foil to a collection of over 100 vehicles which retraces the development of road transport on six stages from its origin to the present time.

Highlights include a Benz (reconstruction of an 1886 3-wheeler), a belt-transmission Leon Bollée, a Delage 1 (one of the first popular cars), a Voisin C11 of unequalled refinement and class, a Rolls-Royce Phantom III, a Cadillac V16 roadster and a Lamborghini Miura – Ferrari's great rival.

Numerous documents, animated sketches and objects arranged according to subject clarify and enrich nigh on a century of history.

On the first floor, in the Espace **Hauts-de-Seine** a large semicircular carousel presents the different logos of 240 car model-types. A short film (18 mins) retraces the history of this area, the cradle of the automotive industry. For it was here that 260 manufacturers set up factories from 1880 to 1950, which, until 1912, were responsible for more than one half of the world's automobile production.

Temporary exhibitions are held in the museum, on the mezzanine floor of the Espace Trintignant and in the main section of the Espace J M Fangio.

Dôme Imax ⊙ – This open glass sphere houses a cinema with a 1 000m^2 – 10 700sq ft panoramic screen, providing a viewing angle of 180°, with seats tilted at 30°. Programmes include adventure films, documentaries and features on rock bands. The Dôme's night lighting system, designed by Yann Kersalé, is linked to levels of road traffic by computer.

To the right of the Great Arch is a metal sculpture by the Japanese artist Miyawaki, consisting of 25 columns interwoven with a web of stainless-steel wire.

A little further on, in place Carpeaux, is César's *Thumb* (**1**).

★Palais de la Défense (CNIT) – The Centre for Industry and Technology, the first edifices (1958) and one of the most famous of the complex, is remarkable for its sheer size and the boldness of its architecture. Its record breaking concrete vault (200m – 65ft) in the form of an inverted shell, has only three points of support, each poised on the apex of a triangle.

The building, originally designed as a venue for major trade exhibitions, is now a conference business centre accommodating offices, auditoriums, hotel accommodation, exhibition spaces and shopping arcades.

Further on, to the left, on place de la Defense is Calder's last work, a red stabile (**2**) 15m – 49ft high. Go through an opening on the left to the Fiat Tower.

Tour Fiat – Designed by a team of French and American architects, this with the Elf Tower, is the tallest building rising 45 storeys to 178m – 584ft above the podium. Its stark form, dark, tinted windows and highly-polished granite surfaces are particularly striking at night, when it appears checkered like a giant chess-board. Unlike the other towers built with curtain walls, the Fiat tower has load-bearing walls: note also the widening of the windows near the top to avoid a tapering effect.

At the foot of the tower, *The Great Toscano* (**3**) a bronze bust by the Polish artist Mitoraj, evokes some antique giant. Pass round the tower to the left to see a sculpture (**4**) in polyester resin by Delfino inspired from the world of science-fiction.

Tour Elf – Similar in height to its neighbour the Fiat Tower, the impressive Elf building was designed by a team of French and Canadian architects. The three glass curtained towers of varying height are blue-tinted varying in intensity according to the brightness of the sky.

Return to the esplanade.

The Art Gallery 4 (**5**) presents a collection of diverse works from countries all over the world.

In the centre of the esplanade, the monumental **fountain by Agam (6)** interplays with music and floodlights at scheduled times.

Opposite the Essay building, the underground **Gallery** (**7**) holds art exhibitions. Pass in front of the "*Midday-Midnight*" Pond (**8**) where the artist Clarus has decorated a ventilation shaft to represent the trajectory of the sun and moon in a *trompe-l'œil* rocky landscape.

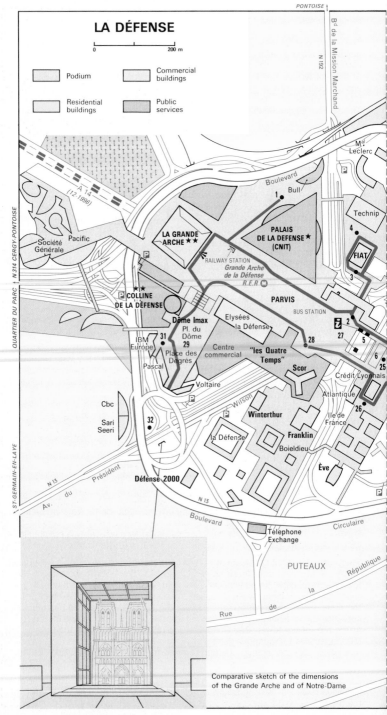

LA DÉFENSE

0   200 m

- Podium
- Residential buildings
- Commercial buildings
- Public services

Comparative sketch of the dimensions of the Grande Arche and of Notre-Dame

Place des Corolles – Defined by the Europe and American International tower-blocks, this open space is named after its copper fountain, *Corolla* (**9**), sculpted by Louis Leygue. A ceramic fresco, *The Cloud Sculptor* (**11**), by Attila adorns a low wall introducing a vivid fanciful note to this concrete environment.

Les Reflets – Philolaos' *Mechanical Bird* (**12**) adorns the terrace, as he carefully folds his immense steel wings. Beyond the Vision 80 tower, built on stilts, is the **place des Reflets** overlooked by and reflected in the shimmering **Aurore** Tower, in vibrant contrast with its neighbouring rose-coloured Manhattan Tower and the green GAN Tower. Note the allegory by Derbré of *The Earth* (**13**).

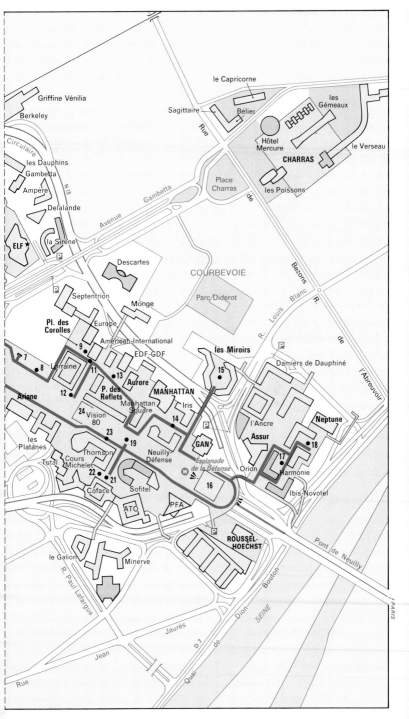

Tour Manhattan – This is one of the most original structures of the La Défense complex in terms of shape, colour and materials used. Designed as a series of curves and counter-curves, its smooth glazed façade mirrors the sky, its pure, elegant lines seeming cloaked in 'the colour of time'. As restless reflections of light and movement lend a dimension of timelessness, its smooth forms and apparent weightlessness make this building truly mesmerising.

In place de l'Iris the slender silhouette of the *Sleepwalker* (**14**) balanced on a sphere poised on the ridge of a cuboid, is by H de Miller.

Tour GAN – This green tower in the form of a Greek cross houses a group of insurance companies.

Les Miroirs – This building is by H La Fonta: the fountain (**15**) in the courtyard is enhanced by four cylindrical volumes decorated with mosaics. From the patio area there is a view of the Poissons Tower with its giant clock-barometer that gives a weather reading for the Paris region (blue – variable, green – fine, red – inclement) and marks the hours with flashing lights.

On the way note the unusual Assur Tower (UAP), shaped like a three-pronged star, designed by Pierre Dufau, and beyond the chequered layout of a residential development.

Bassin Takis (**16**) – East of the esplanade the Takis pond consists of a stretch of water on which the reflection of 49 multi-coloured flexible light-tubes of different lengths seem to play. Pause to take in the wonderful views of the arch and of Paris.

On Square Vivaldi the *Conversation Fountain* (**17**) by Busato represents two bronze figures in animated conversation.

In the place Napoleon I at the foot of the Neptune Tower, a monument shaped like the Cross of the Légion d'Honneur medal (**18**) commemorates the return of the Emperor's remains from St Helena. The imperial eagle came from the railings of the Tuileries *(see* le LOUVRE*)*.

Return to the Takis pond.

Tour Roussel-Hoechst – This attractive blue-green, steel and glass high-rise was the first to be built (1967) at La Défense.

South side – The triangular PFA Tower has sharp-angled curtain walls. The bronze low relief *Ophelia* (**19**) is by the Catalan sculptor Apel les Fenosa.

Go around the Sofitel Hotel on your left. From the terrace overlooking the square cours Michelet you can see Venet's 14m – 46ft high painted steel sculpture (**21**) and further on to the right Jakober's assemblage of welded iron resembling an American footballer's protective mask (**22**).

Further on stands a large frog-shaped fountain (**23**) with drinking water. In the square below the esplanade, 35 flower-planters (**24**) interspersed with faces and clasped hands are the work of Selinger.

The paler façade of the Ariane Tower decked in cruciform aluminium panels contrast with surrounding buildings.

By the Agam fountain, stairs (signpost) lead down to a gallery displaying Moretti's *Monster* (**25**), a sculpture featuring different textures symbolising the artist's wide-ranging experimental art forms.

A white marble sculpture "*Lady Moon*" (**26**) by Julio Silva can be seen between the Atlantique and Crédit Lyonnais Towers; further to the right rise the tapering Defense 2000 and the white elliptical outline of the Eve Tower south of the Villon quarter.

The Scor Tower in the form of a tripod partly hides the fortress-like Winthertur and Franklin Towers (the latter comprises two abutting structures) with dark-glazed façades in a severe architectural style.

Barrias' bronze group entitled "*La Défense*" (**27**) has regained its original position at the foot of the monumental Agam fountain, facing westwards from where no invader has ever come.

The Quatre Temps shopping centre comprises department stores, over 250 shops, restaurants and cinemas on two levels. The building above, Élysées-La Défense, has indoor gardens.

In front of the centre is a brightly coloured monumental sculpture (**28**) of two figures by Miró.

On the place des Degrès, the sculptor Kowalski has created *a mineral landscape* (**29**): parts of pyramids, wave of granite...

A bronze "*Icarus*" (**31**) by César stands at the foot of the elegant IBM building.

A short distance away, "*Slat*" (**32**) a sculpture by R. Serra consisting of five sheets of steel weighing 100 tons and 11m – 36ft high, has been installed at a crossroads.

'Whenever we think of the city, we do well to remember Mirabeau: 'Paris is a Sphinx; I will drag her secret from her; 'but in this neither he nor any other man has succeeded.'*

Hilaire Belloc

La Tour Eiffel

A. Ët/MICHELIN

EIFFEL TOWER ★★★

Michelin plan 11 – folds 28 – 29, 41: J 7 – J 8, K 9

These sights encompass Paris' best-loved monument straddling the gardens that once were used for military parades, and a fine example of Classical French architecture, the École Militaire.

The tower is the perfect place for a bird's eye view of the city, to pause and enjoy the thrill of just being a part of this wonderful, beautiful and historic place!

★★★EIFFEL TOWER ⓥ

Ⓜ *Bir-Hakeim/RER: Champ-de-Mars-Tour-Eiffel. Buses: 42, 69, 72, 82, 87*

The Eiffel Tower, on the quai Branly, is the capital's look-out and Paris' best-known monument. When it was erected it was the tallest construction in the world but since then, its 300m – 984ft have been topped by skyscrapers and telecommunication towers elsewhere. The addition of television transmitter aerials has increased its height by another 20.75m – 67ft to 320.75m – 1 051ft.

Historical notes – The idea for a tower came to **Gustave Eiffel** (1832-1923) as a result of his study of high metal piles and their application to viaducts. The initial project dates from 1884; between 1887 and 1889 three hundred skyjacks pieced the tower together using two and a half million rivets. Eiffel, in his enthusiasm, exclaimed "France will be the only country with a 300m flagpole!". Artists and writers, however, were appalled; the petition of the 300 was signed by Charles Garnier, architect of the Opéra, the composer Gounod, and the poets and writers François Coppée, Leconte de Lisle, Dumas the Younger, Maupassant... Despite the critics, its very boldness and novelty brought it also great acclaim. By the beginning of the new century it had become a subject for celebration by a new generation of poets (Apollinaire), dramatists (Cocteau) and painters(Pissarro, Dufy, Utrillo, Seurat, Marquet, Delaunay)... Since then its form, popularised by millions of souvenirs, is recognised the world over.

In 1909, when its planning concession expired, the tower was nearly pulled down – but saved on account of its huge antennae so vital to French radio telegraphy; from 1910 it became part of the International Time Service; by 1916 it had been made a terminal for the first radio telephone service across the Atlantic; from 1918 it was used as a transmitter for French radio and for television since 1957. The top platform accommodates a revolving light beacon (replaced in 1975 by a fixed red light) as well as a meteorological and aircraft navigation station.

The tensile masterpiece – The tower weighs of 7 000 tons, giving a deadweight of 4kg per cm^2 – 57lbs per sq inch – equal to that of a man sitting in a chair. A scale model made of steel 30cm – 11.8 inches would weigh 7 grams or 1/4oz. At each re-painting, every seven years, 50 tons of paint are used. The sway at the top in the highest winds has never been more than 12cm – 4 1/2 inches – whilst its height can vary by as much as 15cm – 6 inches – depending on the temperature.

The visitor looking upwards through the intricate filigree of pig iron, gets an overwhelming feeling of the stupendous: there are three platforms: the 1st is at 57m – 187ft; the 2nd at 115m – 377ft; the 3rd at 276m – 899ft; 1 652 steps in all to the top or lifts with specially designed brake attachments given the different angles of descent.

★★★**View** – From the 3rd platform, the view can extend 67km – 42 miles in ideal conditions, which is rare. Paris and its suburbs appear as on a giant map *(viewing tables)* – the best light is usually one hour before sunset. At level 3, Eiffel's sitting room can be seen through a window.

An audio-visual presentation *(first floor)* retells the tower's history *(20min)*. Lift machinery from 1899 can be inspected when the corresponding lift operates in the east or west corner.

Beneath Eiffel's tower, by the north pillar, there is a bust by Bourdelle of the engineer who presented the country with one of the most visited monuments in France. At night the illuminated tower has a jewel-like quality.

Nobody now questions the tower's aesthetic appeal or its utility – it has taken its place on the capital's skyline and beckons to all who come to Paris. It is often the venue for artistic and publicity stunts.

The Musées et Monuments season ticket
on sale in museums and at major tourist sights, in tourist information centres
and at the major underground (métro) ticket offices
valid for 1 day, 3 days or 5 consecutive days
provides immediate access (without paying or queuing)
to 65 of the museums and monuments in Paris and the Paris region

★CHAMP-DE-MARS

Ⓜ *Bir-Hakeim/RER: Champ-de-Mars-Tour-Eiffel. Buses: 42, 69, 72, 82, 87*

The Champ de Mars is now a vast formal garden closed at one end by the École Militaire and at the other by the Trocadéro on Chaillot Hill.

The parade ground – When Gabriel had completed the École Militaire, he replaced the surrounding market gardens, which ran down to the Seine, by a parade ground or Champ-de-Mars (Field of Mars) (1765-67). The public was first admitted in 1780.

In 1783 the physicist, Charles, launched the first hydrogen-filled rather than hot-air balloon, which came down 20 miles away near Le Bourget. Blanchard, a year later, attempted to navigate a balloon with ailerons intending to 'luncheon at La Villette'. Having ascended to 4 000m – 13 000ft he tried various manœuvres and landed at Billancourt on the far side of Paris.

The Festival of Federation – It was decided to commemorate the 14 July 1790, the first anniversary of the taking of the Bastille, by a Festival of Federation on the Champ-de-Mars. Stands were erected and mass was celebrated by Talleyrand, the Bishop of Autun, assisted by 300 priests. La Fayette, at the altar, swore an oath of loyalty to the nation and the constitution which was repeated by the listening crowd of 300 000 and, finally by Louis XVI, in the midst of general enthusiasm.

Festival of the Supreme Being – In 1794, Robespierre had the Convention decree upon a state religion that recognised the existence of a Supreme Being and the immortality of the soul. These hypotheses were solemnly affirmed on 8 June at a mammoth festival presided over by Robespierre, 'the Incorruptible' as he was known. A procession began in the Tuileries and ended on the Champs-de-Mars.

The capital's fairground – From time to time the ground has been given over to exhibitions; on 22 September 1798 the Directory commemorated the anniversary of the Republic with an Industrial Exhibition destined to replace the old Fairs of Saint-Germain *(see* ST-GERMAIN-DES-PRÉS) and Saint-Laurent *(see* GRANDS BOULEVARDS-Faubourg-Poissonnière*)* – for the first time, an incentive payment was made to exhibitors.

World exhibitions were held in 1867, 1878, 1889, 1900 and 1937 – the Eiffel Tower remaining as a souvenir of the 1889 Exhibition. In the same year, the army exchanged the ground with the City of Paris for a terrain at Issy-les-Moulineaux. The latter has now become Paris' heliport.

The gardens – The present gardens, laid out by J C Formigé, were begun in 1908 and completed in 1928. One section is landscaped 'English-style' with grottoes, arbours, cascades and small pools by the tower, whilst another part has formal French *parterres*. Wide strips on either side, along avenue de Suffren and avenue de La Bourdonnais, were sold for building and are now lined with large private houses and blocks of luxury flats.

★★ÉCOLE MILITAIRE

1 place Joffre. Ⓜ *École-Militaire. Buses: 28, 42, 49, 69, 80, 82, 87, 92*

The *ensemble*, one of the finest examples of French 18C architecture, was perfectly sited by its architect at the end of the Champ-de-Mars.

Construction – Thanks to Mme de Pompadour, Louis XV's favourite mistress, Pâris-Duverney – financier and supplier to the army – obtained permission in 1751 to found and to personally supervise the building of a Royal Military Academy where young gentlemen without means might be trained to become accomplished officers. Jacques-Ange Gabriel, architect of the Petit Trianon at Versailles and of place de la Concorde, produced grandiose plans, which the financier duly modified. The final construction, nevertheless, remains truly magnificent when one remembers that it was designed as barracks for impoverished men!

The king took no further interest in the future school, and it was only because of Beaumarchais, harp teacher to the king's daughters that any members of the royal family visited Grenelle. Money to pay for the building was later raised from a tax on playing cards and a lottery. The academy accommodated 500 students on a course lasting three years. In 1769 Louis XV laid the foundation stone for a chapel that was completed in 1772.

Its parade ground was the Champ-de-Mars.

The young cadet Bonaparte – In 1777 the Royal Academy became the Military Academy for Cadet Officers. In 1784 Bonaparte, following his studies at Brienne, was admitted on the recommendation that he would "make an excellent sailor". Aged 15 he was formally sworn-in in the Academy chapel and passed out as a lieutenant in the artillery with a report stating that he would "go far in favourable circumstances".

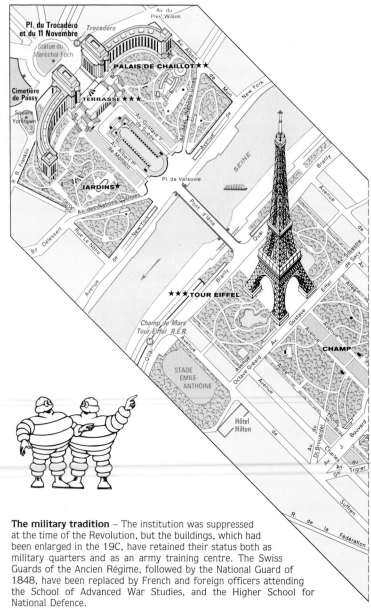

The military tradition – The institution was suppressed
at the time of the Revolution, but the buildings, which had
been enlarged in the 19C, have retained their status both as
military quarters and as an army training centre. The Swiss
Guards of the Ancien Régime, followed by the National Guard of
1848, have been replaced by French and foreign officers attending
the School of Advanced War Studies, and the Higher School for
National Defence.

Exterior – The impressive **central pavilion** which you see as you walk up from
the Champ-de-Mars, is fronted by 10 superb Corinthian columns, each two
storeys high supporting a carved pediment, with displayed trophies and allegorical
figures. A fine dome crowns the whole. Low lateral wings frame the main building.
The barracks on either side are 19C. Facing the central pavilion, is the equestrian
statue of Marshal Joffre by Real del Sarte (1939).
Walk around the academy by way of avenue de Suffren and avenue de Lowendal to
place de Fontenoy. (Lowendal commanded part of the French army, which defeated
the British and Dutch at Fontenoy in 1745.)
From the semicircular square, look across the sports ground to the **main court-
yard★**, lined on either side by beautiful porticoes with paired columns. At the back is
the central pavilion, flanked by colonnaded buildings terminating in projecting
wings.
Inside, the decoration of the chapel, the main staircase, the Marshals' Saloon and
the guardroom on the first floor is especially remarkable *(not open to the public)*.

Place de Fontenoy has entirely lost its 18C character. The huge blocks on its east
side include the Ministries of Health, Merchant Navy and Post Office; on its south
side lies the UNESCO building.

★MAISON DE L'UNESCO

7 place de Fontenay. Ⓜ *Cambronne Ségur. Buses: 49, 80*

United Nations Educational, Scientific and Cultural Organization HQ – The home of UNESCO was opened in 1958 and is the most truly international undertaking in Paris: the membership by 158 states and the construction of the buildings jointly by Breuer, Nervi and Zehrfuss, American, Italian and French architects respectively, demonstrate unique co-operation.

The buildings – The main building, in the form of a Y supported on piles, houses the secretariat (sales counters in the entrance hall with souvenirs, newspapers, periodicals, coins and stamps). A second building with fluted concrete walls and an accordion-pleat-designed roof contains the conference halls and committee rooms. The small cubic construction four storeys high beside the Japanese garden is an administrative annexe. Additional accommodation was provided in 1965, by means of two basement floors underground, lit naturally by six low-level patios and in 1970 at 1 rue Miollis and 31 rue François-Bovin.

Decoration – The decoration is also the result of international artistic cooperation. There are frescoes by the Spaniard Picasso, and the Mexican Tamayo, tiled murals by the Spanish artists, Miró and Artigas, mosaics by the French, Bazaine and Herzell, a mosaic from El Jem in Tunisia (2C), a relief by Jean Arp, tapestries by Lurçat and by the Franco-Swiss Le Corbusier, a Japanese fountain by Noguchi and an angel's head from a Nagasaki church destroyed by the atom bomb in 1945. A monumental statue, *Figure in Repose*, by Henry Moore and a black steel mobile by the American Calder, can be viewed from avenue de Suffren.

In and around the later annexes are works by the Italian Giacometti, the Spaniard Chillida, the Venezuelan Soto and the American Kelly.

The overall impression is a remarkable synthesis of mid-20C art.

FAUBOURG-ST-GERMAIN★★

Michelin plan 11 – folds 29 and 30: H 10 – J 12

Only through a half-open door will you glimpse the beautiful façades erected by Delisle-Mansart, Boffrand or other 18C architects. The Faubourg-St-Germain was originally, as its name implies, the suburb *(faubourg)* of the town which developed round the Abbey of St-Germain-des-Prés *(see* ST-GERMAIN-DES-PRÉS*)*. Until the end of the 16C the surrounding countryside was used for farming and hunting; that is all save for a strip of meadow at the river's edge finally won from the abbey by the University and named the Pré aux Clercs (Clerics' Meadow).

In the 17C Marguerite of Valois, first wife of Henri IV, took the east end of the meadow from the University as part of the grounds in which to build a vast mansion with a garden running down to the Seine. The acquisition was made so casually that the embankment came to be called the *Malacquis* (distorted to *Malaquais*) or Misappropriated Quay. On the death of Queen Marguerite in 1615 the University tried to reclaim the land but, after 20 years of legal proceedings, succeeded only in having the main street of the new quarter named rue de l'Université.

The district was at its most fashionable in the 18C. Noble lords and rich financiers built houses which gave the streets an individual character: one monumental entrance followed another, each opening onto a courtyard closed at the far end by the façade of an elegant mansion, beyond which lay a large garden.

The Revolution closed these sumptuous town houses and although they reopened their doors at the Restoration, the quarter never fully regained its status, fashionable society having migrated to the Champs-Élysées at the time of Louis-Philippe and Napoleon III.

Several mansions were pulled down when boulevard St-Germain and boulevard Raspail were opened. The finest houses remaining now belong to the state or serve as ambassadorial residences. Something of the quarter's great days can, however, still be recalled in the rues de Lille, Grenelle and Varenne.

A walk through the Faubourg from the pont de la Concorde

Ⓜ *Assemblée-Nationale. Buses: 24, 63, 72, 73, 83, 84, 94*

This area includes the buildings that house the French Government headquarters, the Assemblée nationale and several sumptuous 18C residential houses, now mainly serving official functions.

★★★**Views** – From the centre of pont de la Concorde, which was doubled in width in 1932, remarkable views stretch up river and across place de la Concorde to the Madeleine.

★**Palais Bourbon** ☉ – *Rue de l'Université/quai d'Orsay* – In 1722 the Duchess of Bourbon, daughter of Louis XIV and Mme de Montespan, acquired land on which to build a house fronting onto the rue de l'Université. By 1728 the palace and terraced gardens running down to the Seine were complete.

Twenty-eight years later Louis XV bought the property so that it could be altered to form part of the general scheme of the place de la Concorde; in 1764, however, Louis XVI sold it to the Prince of Condé who enlarged and embellished it. Finally, the adjoining **Hôtel de Lassay** was added and renamed the Petit or Little Bourbon.

Work was almost finished when the Revolution broke out. The palace was confiscated to serve as a chamber for the Council of the Five Hundred. Next it was used to house archives, before serving as accommodation for the École Polytechnique. In 1807 Napoleon commissioned Poyet to design the present façade overlooking the place de la Concorde in harmony with the Greek plan of the Madeleine church *(see* FAUBOURG-ST-HONORÉ*)*. At the Restoration the palace was returned to the Condé family, only to be bought back in 1827 and converted for use by the Legislative Assembly.

Exterior – The Antique-style façade with a portico is decorated with an allegorical pediment by Cortot (1842), statues (copies), on high, of Minerva by Houdon and Themis by Roland, and below, among other figures, those of Henri IV and Louis XIV's ministers, Sully and Colbert. The allegorical low reliefs on the wings are by Rude *(right)* and Pradier *(left)*.

Interior – Among the most impressive of the many rooms decorated with paintings and sculpture, are the lobby, with its ceiling by Horace Vernet, the Council Chamber and the **Library★★**. This is a fine room in itself added to which it is magnificently decorated with a History of Civilisation, painted by Delacroix between 1838 and 1845. Houdon's portrait busts of Voltaire and Diderot are also in the library.

Salle des Séances (Council Chamber) – *To attend a debate, apply to 33 quai d'Orsay before the session starts, or send a written request to a deputy.* Proceedings are conducted by the President of the **National Assembly** from the *bureau* formerly used for the Council of the Five Hundred *(see above)*. He faces the deputies – 577 when all are present – seated on benches arranged in a semicircle. Government members occupy the front bench below the speaker's stand (NB: the political right and left are as viewed by the president and therefore the reverse as seen from the gallery).

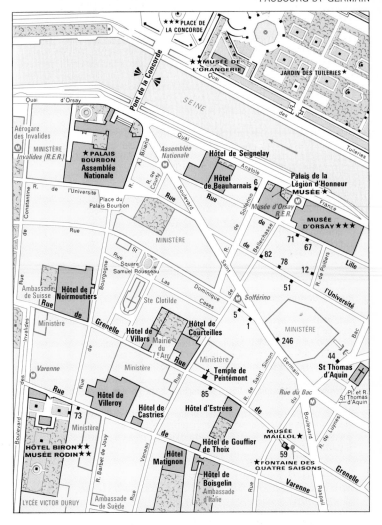

Rue de Lille – This street, named after the town of Lille, is typical of the old "noble faubourg". Nos 80 and 78 were designed by the architect Boffrand in 1714. The first, the **Hôtel de Seignelay**, occupied by the Ministry of Commerce and Tourism, was owned originally by Colbert's grandson, then by the Duke of Charost, tutor to the young Louis XV and aristocrat philanthropist who was saved from the guillotine by his own peasants. By 1839 it had passed to Marshal Lauriston, a descendant of John Law *(see HALLES-BEAUBOURG)*, the Scots financier.

The **Hôtel de Beauharnais**, next door, received its name when Napoleon's son-in-law bought it in 1803 and redecorated it sumptuously for his own and his sister Queen Hortense's use. Since 1818 the house has been the seat of first the Prussian, and later, the German diplomatic missions to France. Now restored, it is the residence of the German ambassador.

The writer Jules Romain lived at no **6** rue Solférino from 1947 to his death (1972).

Palais de la Légion d'Honneur – *2 rue de Bellechasse*. The **Hôtel de Salm** was built in 1786 for the German Prince Frederic of Salm Kyrburgh who, finding himself in straitened circumstances, organised a lottery with the property as prize to settle his debts, but the lottery was cancelled. The prince was beheaded during the Revolution. The mansion was owned by various people until it was acquired by Napoleon, who made the mansion the Palace of the Legion of Honour in 1804. It was burnt during the Commune of 1871 and rebuilt, in 1878, by the members of the Legion to the original plans. The only parts remaining of the early building are the low reliefs on the outside walls.

At the back of the palace, overlooking the river, there is a delightful semicircular pavilion in complete contrast to the severe lines of the main building. This rotunda so impressed American statesman and amateur architect Thomas Jefferson that he incorporated a modified version of it in his redesign of his Virginia estate, Monticello.

★**Musée de la Légion d'honneur et des Ordres de Chevalerie** ⊙ – The museum presents original documents, decorations, pictures, uniforms and arms illustrating the orders of chivalry and nobility of pre-Revolutionary France (the Star, St Michael, the Holy Spirit, St Louis); the creation of the Legion of Honour by Napoleon on 19 May 1802, its rapid expansion during the Empire (personal decorations of Bonaparte and his brothers, educational establishments) and its subsequent history. Further galleries show other French civil and military decorations: academic prizes, the Military Medal, Military Cross, the Cross of the Liberation *(see* les INVALIDES*)*, Order of Merit, Order of Malta.

Other buildings of note hereabouts include the Musée d'Orsay *(see* ORSAY) and in the rue de Lille at no **71** the Hôtel de Mouchy (1775), at no **67** the Hôtel du Président Duret (1706); at 12 rue de Poitiers, Hôtel de Poulpry (1700); in rue de l'Université – the main thoroughfare through the old quarter – there is no 51 the Hôtel de Soyecourt built in 1707, no 78 built in 1687 and no 82 where the poet Lamartine resided between 1837 and 1853 *(see inscription).*

> Born on a train as it crossed Siberia, **Rudolf Nureyev** defected to the West at the age of 23 to become one of the word's most famous ballet dancers. He purchased his 18C Paris residence at 23 quai Voltaire in 1978; this was to be his principal home from 1981 until his death from AIDS on 6 January 1993. He packed it with fabulous collections of 17C and 18C art, furniture and textiles which were sold in November 1995. All proceeds went to finance dance scholarships and medical research.

Rue St-Dominique – This street, which got its name from a former monastery for Dominican novices, was amongst the quarter's most interesting before a large part of it was swept away to make way for the boulevard St-Germain. No **5**, the **Hôtel de Tavannes** ⊙ has a fine round arched doorway surmounted by a scallop and crowned by a triangular pediment. It housed a literary salon in the early 19C. The artist, Gustave Doré, died in the house in 1883. Inside there is a fine stairwell with a wrought-iron balustrade. The **Hôtel de Gournay** *(no 1)* was erected in 1695.

On boulevard St-Germain but overlooking the rue St-Dominique is the Ministry of Defence which occupies a large site including the **Hôtel de Brienne**, itself consisting of two houses and a former monastery.

No **246**, boulevard St-Germain was formerly the **Hôtel de Roquelaure** (fine courtyard), the residence of the statesman Cambacérès (1753-1824) and later the seat of the Council of State. It now accommodates with no 244 the offices of the Secretary of State for Transport.

Boulevard Raspail
between rue du Bac and Sèvres-Babylone

Ⓜ *Rue-du-Bac. Buses: 63, 68, 69, 83, 84, 94*

Rue du Bac – At no 44 lived André Malraux, who in 1933 wrote '*La Condition Humaine*' which earned him the Nobel Prize for Literature.

Église St-Thomas d'Aquin – *place St-Thomas-d'Aquin.* The church, formerly the chapel of the Dominican novitiate monastery, was begun in 1682 in the Jesuit style to plans by Pierre Bullet. The façade was completed only in 1769. Inside are 17C and 18C paintings and a ceiling (apsidal chapel) painted by Lemoyne in 1723 of the Transfiguration. The sacristy has Louis XV panelling.

Rue de Grenelle – The beautiful **Fontaine des Quatre-Saisons**★ stands outside nos 59-61. Carved by Bouchardon between 1739 and 1745, this grand fountain was commissioned by Turgot, the dean of the local merchants' guild and father of Louis XVI's minister, in answer to complaints that the stately quarter was almost totally without water!
A seated figure of Paris looking down onto reclining personifications of the Rivers Seine and Marne adorn the ornate Ionic pillared fountain front. The sides are decorated with figures of the Seasons and delightful low reliefs showing cherubs performing the seasons' labours.

The stately **Hôtel Bouchardon** behind was where **Alfred de Musset**, the Romantic poet, lived from 1824 to 1839, during which time he wrote most of his plays and dramatic poetry. The house has recently been carefully restored to house a significant art museum.

The **Fondation Dina Vierny – Musée Maillol**★ ⊙ draws from the private collection of Dina Vierny, once model of Maillol and eminent art dealer. It comprises not only the paintings and sculptures of her Catalan mentor, **Aristide Maillol** (1861-1944), but those of several of his contemporaries: Bonnard, Cézanne, Degas, Duchamp, Dufy, Gauguin, Kandinski, Renoir, Rousseau, Poliakoff...

This small body of important 20C art is complemented by a contemporary Soviet collection including the 'Communal Kitchen' re-created by Ilya Kabakov. Russian by origin, Dina Vierny was instrumental in introducing Soviet artists to the European art markets during the early 1970s.

This foundation is also responsible for the donation in 1964 of 18 magnificent female nude bronze sculptures by Maillol now in the Tuileries Gardens. Two additional figures have recently been given.

At no 79 stands the great **Hôtel d'Estrées** (1713); no **85** is the **Hôtel d'Avaray** (1728), the Royal Netherlands Embassy; the **Pentémont Temple** with its Ionic cupola of 1750 was at one time a convent chapel, the nuns were replaced by the Imperial Guard and these, by the civil servants of the Ministry of War Veterans; no 110, the **Hôtel de Courteilles** (1778), dominating the street with its massive façade, is now the Ministry of Education; no 116 was built in 1709 for Marshal de Villars and considerably remodelled; no 118 is the much smaller **Hôtel de Villars**, built in 1712 and extremely elegant with twin garlanded, oval windows; no 136, the **Hôtel de Noirmoutiers** (1722), at one time the army staff headquarters was the house in which Marshal Foch died on 20 March 1929. The mansion now serves as the official residence of the *Préfet* of the Ile-de-France Region.

Rue de Varenne – The street was laid along a rabbit warren (*garenne* which evolved, in time, to Varenne) belonging to the abbey of St-Germain-des-Prés.

For Hôtel Biron★★ *and Musée Rodin*★★ – *see les INVALIDES.*

There are several attractive old houses in this street: at no **73** the great **Hôtel de Broglie** (1735); nos 80-78, the **Hôtel de Villeroy** (1724), now the Ministry of Agriculture; no 72, the large **Hôtel de Castries** (1700).

The most famous house, of course, is the **Hôtel Matignon** at no 57, built by Courtonne in 1721 but since considerably remodelled. Talleyrand, diplomat and statesman to successive regimes, owned it from 1808 to 1811, then Madame Adelaïde, sister to Louis-Philippe. Between 1884 and 1914 it housed the Austro-Hungarian Embassy, in 1935 it became the office of the President of the Council of State and in 1958 the Paris residence of the prime minister.

No 56, the **Hôtel de Gouffier de Thoix**, has a magnificent doorway orna-

> **Edith Wharton** (1862-1937), author of **The Age of Innocence**, lived at both no 53 and no 58 rue de Varenne for 13 years (1907-1920) before moving north to the Pavillon Colombe near the Montmorency Forest. At the heart of literary circles that included Morton Fullerton, Henry James, André Gide, she entertained the upper-class Faubourg society in the manner of a *belle époque* salon hostess. She is buried in the city of Versailles.

mented with a shell carving. No 47, the **Hôtel de Boisgelin** is now the Italian Embassy.

★Sèvres-Babylone

Ⓜ *Sèvres-Babylone, St-Sulpice. Buses: 39, 63, 68, 70, 83, 84, 87, 94*

This neighbourhood dotted with interesting shops is a lively residential section of Paris.

Rue de la Chaise – Hôtel Vaudreuil (*no 5*) was given by Napoleon to the Borghese family, in-laws of his sister Pauline. Next door (*no 7*) stood the convent attached to the **abbaye aux bois** where Mme Récamier held her salons between 1819 and 1849, and received the novelist Chateaubriand (living at 120 rue du Bac) daily.

Carrefour de la Croix-Rouge – This crossroads was probably the site of a pagan temple dedicated to Isis predating the abbey of St Germain. A red cross or calvary would have been installed in the 16C to rid the place of impious associations: hence the name. The present bronze Centaur statue is by César – the man who sculpted the famous figurines awarded annually to the film industry that bear his name.

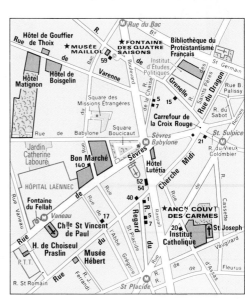

Hôtel Lutétia – *45 boulevard Raspail*. Built in 1907 by the architects Louis Boileau and Henri Tanzin, the façade decoration was sculpted by Léon Binet and **Paul Belmondo**. Inside, the décor is elegantly 'retro' with its Lalique chandelier; it was re-done by the fashion designer Sonia Rykiel and Sybille de Margerie in 1983.

Prison du Cherche-Midi – *52-54 boulevard Raspail*. The site of the former prison is marked by roughly hewn square blocks of rock. This was where Captain Dreyfus was imprisoned (1894) and charged with selling military information to the Germans; the Dreyfus affair provoked impassioned debates regarding religious prejudice and human rights that were to lead to the establishment of a 'left-wing' party (1899). Later, the prison served as an interrogation centre during the Second World War.

The Dreyfus Affair

Dreyfus was implicated on the grounds of his having similar handwriting to that of the sensitive information found in German hands. The right wing political parties called for his condemnation, the Monarchy sustained his innocence while accusing the left wing of anti-Semitic prejudice. Dreyfus was judged guilty and deported. There followed the publication of Émile Zola's letter in L'Aurore entitled *J'accuse*, which implied that the evidence had been falsified (forcing Zola into exile in England 1898-1899): the case was re-opened, the officer was found guilty a second time but given his freedom (1906). In September 1995, after 101 years, the head of the French Army's history section stated in an address to the Central Consistory of Jews that indeed 'a military conspiracy led to a conviction and a deportation – of an innocent man' thereby clearing Dreyfus of blame once and for all.

Au Bon Marché – *22 rue de Sèvres*. This department store, founded on the site of three former leprosy clinics, was the venture of Aristide Boucicault and his wife (1852). Success was achieved by several new practices we now take for granted: standardised price tagging, undercutting of competitors, offering a wide choice of quality products, maintaining stock levels, permitting a exchange of unwanted goods, discount sales and a mail-order service, prompt delivery of purchases outside Paris. Customer loyalty was encouraged by trained, courteous staff who, in turn were recompensed with free medical care and midday meals, uniforms, and facilities for evening language classes, choir practice and fencing!

Chapelle Notre-Dame-de-la-Médaille-Miraculeuse – *140 rue du Bac*. Behind the Food department is the chapel where the Virgin is said to have appeared to the novice Catherine Labouré from the convent of St-Vincent de Paul on 18 July 1830 – she was later beatified by Pius XII. This convent based at 95 rue de Sèvres is named after 'Monsieur Vincent' who dedicated his life (1585-1660) to the destitute and orphans.

Fontaine du Fellah – This unusual Egyptian-like figure dates from 1806.

Musée Hébert ⊙ – *85 rue du Cherche-Midi*. A fine 18C house accommodates a collection of the Romantic painter's work. He travelled widely in Italy, and his landscape paintings and attractive female portraits provide an insight into the tastes and social milieu of his lifetime (1817-1908).

Maison de Laënnec – *17 rue de l'Abbé-Grégoire*. René Laënnec (1781-1826) invented the stethoscope and pioneered the use of auscultation. He gives his name to the nearby hospital formerly for incurable diseases.

Hôtel de Rochambeau – *40 rue du Cherche-Midi*. Named after Rochambeau who was empowered by Louis XVI to lead an army to assist the Americans in the War of Independence against the British.

E. Barret

Fontaine du Fellah, rue de Sèvres

Quartier des Carmes M *Rennes. Buses: 48, 68, 83, 89, 94, 95, 96*

The Carmelite order originally from Mount Carmel in Palastine having been subjected to reforms by Saint Theresa of Avila became known as the Discalced Carmelites.

★**Ancien couvent des Carmes** ⓥ – *70 rue de Vaugirard.* The House of the Carmelites was founded by Marie de' Medici in 1613. In the gardens, much altered by the building of the rue d'Assas and rue de Rennes, the Carmelites cultivated the balm necessary for making their Eau des Carmes (a kind of herbal cordial drink) which provided them with substantial revenue. By the end of August 1792, during the troubled years after the Revolution, the monastery was turned into a prison; on 2 September, as the Prussians were advancing on Paris, churchmen and royalists were massacred. Subsequently, of the 700 prisoners held here, 116 were sent to the guillotine. In 1746, under the Directory, peace returned; the buildings were secured in 1797 and returned to the Carmelites.

Église St-Joseph-des-Carmes – The church was built between 1613 and 1620 and is taken to be the first example of the Jesuit style in Paris. Inside, the chapels retain Louis XIII decoration. Note the **Bernini Virgin**★ in the transept.

FAUBOURG-ST-HONORÉ – LA MADELEINE★★

Michelin plan 11 – folds 16 – 18: E 8 – E 9, F 9 – F 11

This old 'faubourg' or neighbourhood imparts a leisured elegance with its luxury shops, art galleries, antique shops and *haute couture* boutiques particularly around rue Royale and rue de l'Élysée. Its most prominent monument is la Madeleine, the church dedicated to St Mary Magdalen.

★★LA MADELEINE ⓘ

Place de la Madeleine. M *Madeleine. Buses: 24, 42, 52, 84, 94*

La Madeleine is one of Paris' most familiar landmarks, familiar to all for its distinctively striking Greek temple appearance and its convenient position at the junction of the boulevards with an artery from the place de la Concorde.

Few churches however, have had such a stormy history. It was started by one architect in 1764 on plans based on the church of St-Louis-des-Invalides *(see* les INVALIDES*)*, a second razed what had already been erected to begin a building modelled on the Panthéon *(see* LATIN QUARTER*)*; all work ceased between 1790 and 1806 as various projects were considered. Napoleon announced that on this spot should be erected a temple to the glory of the Great Army and gave the commission to Vignon. Once more the existing structure was razed and building started on the Greek temple; work proceeded slowly. In 1814 Louis XVIII confirmed that the Madeleine should indeed be a church; during the reign of Charles X it was still surrounded by waste land; in 1837 the building was nearly selected for use as Paris' first railway terminal. The church's vicissitudes ended with its consecration in 1842, although its priest was shot by the Commune in 1871.

La Madeleine

Tour – A majestic colonnade of Corinthian columns – 52 in all, each 20m – 66ft tall – encloses the church on all sides and supports a sculptured frieze. A monumental flight of steps (28) leads to the imposing peristyle giving on to place de la Madeleine and a splendid **view**★ down rue Royale, the obelisk at the heart of place de la Concorde and beyond to the Palais-Bourbon and the Invalides dome. The gigantic pediment is adorned with a sculpture by Lemaire of *The Last Judgement* and reliefs on the bronze doors represent the Ten Commandments.

The single nave church has a vestibule and an apsed chancel. In the dark vestibule note at the far end on the right a *Marriage of the Virgin* by Pradier and on the far left a *Baptism of Christ* by Rude. The nave is crowned by three domes; on the pendentives statues of the Apostles have been carved by Rude, Foyatier and Pradier. A group featuring St Mary Magdalen ascending to Heaven dominates the high altar.

In 1858, Camille Saint-Saëns was hired to play the organ. It was here that he composed some of his most remarkable pieces.

Place de la Madeleine – Next to the church is a flower-market and behind it the most famous epicure '*épiceries*' or food stores Fauchon and Hédiard.

Boulevard de la Madeleine – This busy road stretches from place de la Madeleine *(see* FAUBOURG-ST-HONORÉ*)* to place de l'Opéra *(see* OPÉRA*)* and beyond into the Grands Boulevards. Alphonsine Plessis – the famous model for Alexandre Dumas' heroine *La Dame aux Camélias* and subsequently for Violetta in Verdi's opera *La Traviata* – died at no 11.

Note on the right, the fine 1726 Hôtel du Crédit foncier de France at no 19 rue des Capucines, opposite which Stendhal collapsed with apoplexy in 1842 *(off the map)*.

★**Rue Royale** – The street runs from the Madeleine with its immense pediment raised high on its line of columns, between the two great mansions *(see* CHAMPS-ELYSEES*)* built by the architect Gabriel, to place de la Concorde, on an axis with the white mass of the Palais-Bourbon *(see* FAUBOURG-ST-GERMAIN*)*.

The famous restaurant Maxim's, at no 3, was formerly the Hôtel de Richelieu. At the end of the 18C the writer Mme de Staël lived in no **6**, and Gabriel at no **8**.

Musée Bouilhet-Christofle Ⓦ – *9 rue Royale*. Recognised goldsmiths for 150 years, their continued success has been ensured by their perfecting of electro-plating techniques. The museum displays filigree sweetmeat dishes, pieces from the service designed for Napoleon III for his château the Tuileries, an amazing tea urn dated 1873, the Art Deco service from the steamship *Normandie* and many contemporary creations.

★★RUE DU FAUBOURG-ST-HONORÉ Ⓜ *Madeleine, St-Philippe-du-Roule, Ternes. Buses: 24, 28, 32, 42, 49, 52, 80, 83, 84, 94*

Empress Eugénie, fearing bad luck, prevented there being a number 13! At **6 rue d'Anjou**, lived Marie-Joseph de La Fayette (1754-1834), the great champion of the causes of Liberty, American Independence and Franco-American alliance.

La Cour aux Antiquaires – *54 rue du Faubourg-St-Honoré*. The noble elegance of this gallery of shops, founded by Marie Laure Le Duc in 1969, is complemented by the trade in the fine and decorative arts.

Palais de l'Élysée – *55 rue du Faubourg-St-Honoré. Not open to the public*. The mansion was constructed in 1718 for the Count of Évreux. It was acquired for a short time by the Marquise de Pompadour and then by the financier Beaujon who enlarged it. During the Revolution it became a dance hall. It was lived in by Caroline Murat, Napoleon's sister, then by the Empress Josephine who redecorated it; it was here that Napoleon signed his second abdication after his defeat at Waterloo, on 22 June 1815, and that the future Napoleon III lived and planned his successful *coup d'état* of 1851. Since 1873 the Élysée Palace has been the Paris residence of France's president. The Council of Ministers meets on Wednesdays in the Murat Salon.

Place Beauvau – A fine wrought-iron gate (1836) marks the entrance to the 18C mansion built for the Prince of Beauvau, occupied by the Ministry of Home Affairs since 1861.

Avenue Matignon – This street is lined with art galleries dedicated to contemporary Fine Art: Marcel Bernheim, Guiot, Findlay, Bernheim-Jeune, Artcurial...

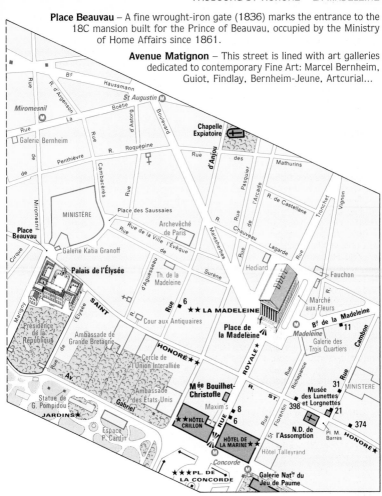

"**Maison Paul Poiret**" once occupied no 107. This couturier (1879-1944) was amongst the first 'modern' clothes designers, banning the whale-bone corset and launching a taste for strong theatrical styles and colours – Persian blues and greens, and a harsh flat orange called 'tango'. He integrated exotic features into dress design (harem-inspired *jupes-culottes*, Japanese-style kimono sleeves and long ankle-clinging hobble skirts) and may have been responsible for the revival of huge plumed hats. After World War I he employed Raoul Dufy to 'paint' his fabrics; his fashion house was the first to launch its own perfume.

Église St-Philippe-du-Roule ⊙ – *154 rue du Faubourg-St-Honoré*. The church designed by Chalgrin in imitation of a Roman basilica was erected between 1774 and 1784. The ambulatory was added around the apse in 1845. A fresco over the chancel of *The Descent from the Cross* is by Chassérieu.

★★**Musée Jacquemart-André** ⊙ – *158 boulevard Haussmann*. Ⓜ *Mirosménil*. Buses: 22, 27, 32, 43, 49, 80, 84. This elegant late-19C house contains outstanding 18C European and Italian Renaissance art.

On the ground floor the Louis XV period is vividly recalled with paintings and drawings by Boucher, Greuze, Chardin, Watteau; sculpture by Pigalle and Lemoyne, Beauvais tapestries, furniture and objets d'art. Other 17C and 18C European Schools of painting are represented by Rembrandt, Van Dyck, Canaletto, Reynolds and frescoes by Tiepolo (ceilings in rooms 4, 5, 13 and over the stairs). There are also fine 16C Limoges enamels and ceramics by Palissy.

In the Italian rooms are displayed a remarkable collection from the Florentine Quattrocento (Botticelli, Della Robbia, Donatello) and the Venetian Renaissance (Mantegna, Tintoretto, Titian). Among the most noteworthy are the Uccello's famous *St George Slaying the Dragon* and a fine bronze bust by Bernini.

Cathédrale St-Alexandre-Newsky ⊕ – *12 rue Daru.* Ⓜ *Courcelles, Ternes.* This, the Russian Orthodox Church of Paris, was erected in 1860 in the Russian neo-Byzantine style on a Greek cross plan. The main features of the exterior are gilded onion-shaped domes while the interior is decorated with frescos, gold and icons. Magnificently sung mass is celebrated in the tradition of Mother Russia.

On 12 July 1918, Pablo Picasso and Olga Khoklova were married here attended by their witnesses Max Jacob, Jean Cocteau, Guillaume Apollinaire and Serge Diaghilev.

Les GOBELINS

Michelin plan 11 – folds 44 and 56: N 15 – P 15
Ⓜ *Gobelins.* Buses: *27, 47, 83, 91*

★ **Manufacture des Gobelins** ⊕ – *42 avenue des Gobelins.* In about 1440 the dyer, Jean Gobelin, who specialised in scarlet, set up a workshop beside the river Bièvre. This continued through the generations until the reign of Henri IV when it was taken over by two Flemish craftsmen, summoned by the king (early 17C).

Colbert, charged by Louis XIV with the reorganisation of the tapestry and carpet-weaving industry, grouped the Paris and Maincy factories (at Vaux-le-Vicomte) around the Gobelins workshops thereby creating, in 1662, the Manufacture Royale des Tapis-series de la Couronne (Royal Factory of Tapestry and Carpet Weavers to the Crown). In charge, he placed the artist, Charles Le Brun. Five years later it became associated with the Manufacture Royale des Meubles (Royal Cabinet-Makers). The greatest craftsmen, including goldsmiths and gilders, thus worked side by side to decorate and furnish the sumptuous palaces of the Sun King and create a 'Louis XIV' style.

Over the past 300 years more than 5 000 tapestries have been woven at the Gobelins factory from cartoons by the greatest painters – Le Brun, Poussin, Van Loo, Mignard, Boucher, Lurçat, Picasso...

The **Savonnerie** (1604-1826) *(see* TROCADÉRO*)* and **Beauvais** (1664-1940) carpet and tapestry factories have also, over the years, been incorporated.

The factory on the avenue des Gobelins, is housed in a modern building (1914). Working methods have changed little since the 17C: warp threads are set by daylight, the colours being selected from a range of over 14 000 tones. Each weaver, working with mirrors, completes from 1 to 8m^2 – 1 to 8sq yds per year depending on the design. Its entire production goes to the state.

The four great French Tapestry workshops

Aubusson: producing hangings for the lesser 17C and 18C aristocracy and bourgeoisie; subject matter includes floral and organic compositions, animals and beasts, Classical mythology and landscapes. Rococo Chinoiseries and pastoral scenes (after Huet) are also common.

Beauvais: very finely woven often with vivid coloured silks which, unfortunately, have faded. Motifs include grotesques, Fables after La Fontaine (by Oudry), Boucher's figures from the Commedia dell'Arte, Classical mythology, Chinoiseries, and pastoral scenes (after Huet). The use of 18C designs continued into the 19C.

Felletin: coarser weave hangings with rustic subject matter.

Gobelins: sumptuous hangings often interwoven with gold. Renowned for the originality of design, series include The Seasons and Elements, The Life of the King, The Royal Residences, Louis XV at the Hunt, as well as paintings by Oudry and Boucher (Loves of the Gods). Their most influential weaver during the late 18C was Neilson, a Scot.

Hôtel de la Reine-Blanche – *4 rue Gustave-Geffroy.* This house was probably named after Philippe VI's widow, Blanche d'Evreux. According to the chronicler Juvénal des Ursins, it was here on 28 January 1393 that Charles VI was almost burnt alive at one of the many festivities organised on his physicians' orders in an attempt to cure his insanity. Dressed as a savage, his costume caught fire with near dire results! The house rebuilt in the 16C and taken over by the Gobelins in the 18C, is now a dismal-looking industrial edifice.

Mobilier National – *1 rue Berbier-du-Mets.* The building is by Auguste Perret (1935) and the two concrete hounds are by André Abbel.

A plaque on the wall of an old house opposite the Mobilier National recalls the famous 15C Gobelins dye-works.

The rue de Croulebarbe and rue Berbier-du-Mets here drive the river **Bièvre** underground. Up to the 17C the willow-bordered stream was of sparkling clear water but dyeing, tanning and bleaching soon turned it into a murky evil-smelling stream. In 1910 the stream was in-filled.

Glacière – Ice taken from the surrounding marshes during the winter was packed into wells and then covered with earth. It was this activity that gave the locality its name meaning 'ice house'.

La Butte-aux-Cailles – On 21 November 1783, having taken off from the vicinity of La Muette, the physicist **Pilâtre de Rozier** *(see* la MUETTE*)* landed his hot-air balloon on this mound, then occupied by several solitary windmills. This was the first free-flight in a hot-air balloon.

Today the district is one of surprising contrasts as badly paved streets and low-lying houses slowly give way to modern blocks of flats with new urban development encroaching upon traditional village life.

Place d'Italie – 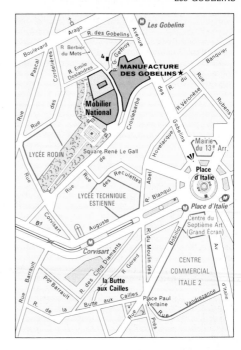 Ⓜ *Place d'Italie. Buses: 27, 47, 57, 67, 83.* The square marks the site of one of the toll-houses built by Ledoux. Today it stands on the edge of an area bristling with high-rise buildings.

From the avenue des Gobelins there is a good view of the Panthéon.

At the corner of avenue d'Italie and rue Bobillot stands the new (1992) film centre designed by the Japanese architect Kenzo Tange. This audio-visual centre attached to the Italie 2 complex, houses France's largest cinema screen.

Les GRANDS BOULEVARDS ★★

Michelin plan 11 – folds 19, 20 and 31: F 13 – F 15, G 13 – G 17

Thronged with pedestrians hurrying on business or idly window-gazing, the broad tree-lined avenues full of cars, café tables spilling out onto the pavement, inumerable cinemas, theatres and a thousand shops, a profusion of signs, advertising slogans, glowing flashing neon at night: in short the Boulevards – the atmosphere lives on.

★★THE BOULEVARDS

Ⓜ *Madeleine, Opéra, Richelieu Drouot, Rue Montmartre, Strasbourg-St Denis, République. Buses: 20, 42, 52*

The ramparts transformed – Between the Bastille and the Porte St-Denis stretched the city walls built by Charles V; between the Porte St-Denis and the present Madeleine extended ramparts built by Charles IX and Louis XIII. By 1660, the fortifications rendered obsolete by Louis XIV's victories had fallen into disrepair; these were dismantled and the ditches in-filled. The land was terraced, a broad carriageway was built to accommodate four carriages riding abreast, two side roads for pedestrian traffic were laid flanking the carriageway, and planted with double rows of trees. Triumphal arches, symbols of the Peace, replaced the fortified gates. Construction was completed in 1705.

The name 'boulevard' was coined from the military term for a terreplein (sloping bank behind a rampart used by the artillery). At first the area surrounded by open countryside remained deserted save for the odd game of *boules* by day, unsafe after dark.

The fashionable stroll – Around 1750 the boulevard became fashionable: Parisians took to cane-seated chairs in the shade to watch out for the new glazed carriages and for gentry on horseback.

At the western end of the boulevard, the nobility and the well-heeled started to build themselves fine town houses. Under the Directoire, the boulevard des Italiens, then the boulevard Montmartre, began to be frequented by members of High Society; they became known as *Boulevardiers* – an epithet for ephemeral, superficial creatures that flirted with fad and fashion.

At the eastern end, the atmosphere was quite different: theatres, dance-halls, circuses, wax-works and puppet-shows were animated by dancers, acrobats and various other entertainers; bars, restaurants, booths and barrows attracted further crowds. As local theatres at the end of the Restoration period specialised in a melodramatic repertory of death, murder, poisoning and kidnapping, the area assumed the name 'boulevard du Crime'.

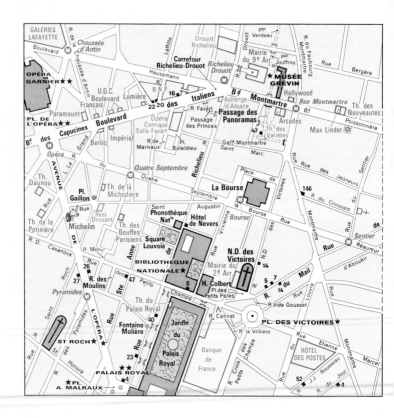

Improvements – The roads were paved in 1778 at about the same time as street lights, burning tripe oil, were installed. These were criticised for being 'garish' but lasted until gas lamps appeared in the Passage des Panoramas in 1817, and along the boulevard in 1826. The first omnibus appeared on 30 January 1828 linking the Madeleine to the Bastille. Finally, pavements were asphalted reducing the quagmire on rainy days.

The modern boulevards – Haussmann's radical urban planning transformed the area by inserting broad avenues between place de l'Opéra and place de la République. The boulevard du Crime was flattened; trend-setters mingled and were lost in the milling crowds; street-lighting, shop illumination, improved signage and changing frontages further altered the area. The attributes of fashion changed ceaselessly through the years, but the colours, the noise and the bustle are constants.

The shows – This area like that around the Opéra, boasts a number of famous theatres and night spots *(see* INTRODUCTION – Entertainment).

Boulevard des Capucines – This street takes its name from a Capuchin monastery that once stood between the present boulevard and the place Vendôme.
At no 35 lived Félix Tournachon – known as Nadar – installing his photographic studio there on 2 July 1900, in a building already dedicated to the new art by Legray and Les Bisson. Here he was to write his memoirs and complete his portrait studies of his friends and contemporaries (Rossini, Berlioz, Dumas father and son, George Sand, Baudelaire, Henri Murger...).
No 27 has a splendid façade embellished with brass and copper panels by Frantz Jourdain, maestro of the Art Nouveau decorative style. Originally intended for a *'de luxe'* branch of the Samaritaine department store *(see* les QUAIS*)*, it is now occupied by a finance house.
At no 24, between 1905 and 1956, lived Mistinguett the great heroine of the music-hall.

At no 14, on 28 December 1895, the very first motion pictures were projected to the Paris public by means of a cinematograph, a contraption invented by the Lumière brothers. These 16mm films (*Sortie d'usine, Arrivée d'un train...*) marked the birth of the Seventh art.

At no 8 boulevard des Capucines, Jacques Offenbach (1819-1880) composed his *Contes d'Hoffman*.

Boulevard des Italiens – The history of this thoroughfare is inextricably linked with that of fashion. At the time of the Directoire, the area was haunted by *Muscadins* – bow-legged and hunched fops in exaggerated garb; *Merveilleuses* dressed in high-waisted, transparent dresses in the 'style of Antiquity' or with huge extravagant Turkish-style hats. During the Restoration, these were followed by the *Gandins*, mustachioed with side-whiskers, in top hat, cravat and jacket with broad turned-down collar. Under Louis-Philippe, the *Dandys* and the *Lions* follo-wed the "fashion" from across the Channel: they began to smoke in public (1835).

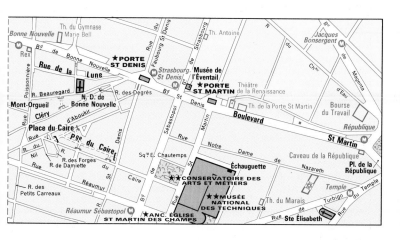

The Second Empire was a more sober age, waxed moustaches and close-cut goatee beards appeared, ladies sported crinolines and café society flourished. These included the Pavillon de Hanovre, the favourite Neapolitan ice-cream restaurant of the *Merveilleuses* – now the uninspired Palais Berlitz, at the corner of the rue Louis-le-Grand; Tortoni's at no 22; le Café Anglais; le Café de Paris; la Maison Dorée at no 20; le Café Riche formerly at no 16 and Frascati.

The Opéra-Comique – The present building stands on the site of the theatre built in 1782 by the Duke de Choiseul for the company that had recently moved out of the ruined Hôtel de Bourgogne. The troupe became known as the "Italians", hence the name of the boulevard. The name Opéra-Comique has also alluded to the **Salle Favart** where Georges Bizet's *Carmen* had its first public performance (1875), Léo Délibes' *Lakme* was staged in 1883, as were Gustave Charpentier's *Louise* in 1900 and Debussy's *Pelleas and Mélisande* which took the city by storm in 1902.

Carrefour Richelieu-Drouot – The Auberge d'Alsace stands at this crossroads, on the site of what was known, in the 17C, as the "modest and secluded" house of the poet, Regnard. Opposite, in 1796, was the famous Café Frascati which closed down when gambling was banned by Louis-Philippe.

On the north side once stood the Salle Le Peletier, which accommodated the Paris Opéra between 1821 and 1875 at the height of its success with Rossini, Auber, Halévy and Charles Gounod (*Faust*).

Hôtel des Ventes Drouot Richelieu ⊙ – *9 rue Drouot*. Reopened on 13 May 1980 the 16 auction rooms hold auctions daily at 2pm in a lively and interesting atmosphere. Rue Drouot is also the haunt of stamp-collectors.

Boulevard Montmartre – On the right at no 11 is the **Passage des Panoramas** which was opened in 1799 and leads to the Stock Exchange (la Bourse). The name comes from the two vast panoramas of capital cities and historic scenes painted and displayed in rotundas by the American, Henry Fulton, inventor of submarines and specialist in steamships. At no **47** in the arcade an engraver's shop retains its old-fashioned frontage.

At no 7 stands the **Théâtre des Variétés** built in 1807, the home of light 'vaudeville' comedy and operetta presenting the wit and gaiety of the "divine trio" of Offenbach, Meilhac and Halévy (from 1864), who staged the first performances of *La Belle Hélène, La Grande-Duchesse de Gérolstein,* and *Le Périchole,* all of which were box-office sell-outs. The rich and famous of the day, from the Tsar of Russia to the Emperor of Austria, idolised Hortense Schneider and her dressing-room was nicknamed the "Princes' Passage". Mealy sang the leading role in *Frou-Frou* here in 1900 and Feydeau's *A Flea in her Ear* had its first performance here in 1907. In 1928, it was the turn of Marcel Pagnol's *Topaze*, followed in later years by *Fanny* (1943), *Marius* (1945) and *César* (1946). Since 1991, the theatre has been managed by Jean-Paul Belmondo.

★**Musée Grévin** ⓥ – *10 boulevard Montmartre*. Grévin, a caricaturist, founded the museum in 1882. (The first waxworks were introduced to Paris in the 18C.) In addition to waxen effigies of famous politicians, artists and sports-people and re-creations of momentous historical and contemporary events in the form of tableaux, there is a hall of mirrors. Live conjuring sessions also add to the magical entertainment on offer.

★**Porte St-Denis** – 24m – 75ft high – the gate was erected at the city's expense in 1672 to celebrate Louis XIV's victorious campaigns on the Rhine when 40 strongholds were captured in less than two months. Designed by Blondel, the sculptures are by the Anguier brothers. Along the top, pyramids are decked with trophies; then, on the boulevard side, allegorical figures represent Holland *(left)* and the Rhine *(right)* with panels depicting the crossing of the Rhine; and on the faubourg side, the Fall of Mastricht.

Musée de l'Éventail ⓥ – *2 boulevard de Strasbourg*. The **Atelier Hoguet**, named after the famous fan maker, preserves the showroom used by the former **Kees** Company, one of the most prestigious of the 19C. The fan museum, annexed to the workshop, casts a nostalgic view over this refined accessory to feminine fashion, whose manufacture has primarily centred around the Strasbourg-St-Denis quarter.
Note the sumptuously carved, painted and gilded, 18C mother-of-pearl and tortoise-shell mountings. Modern fans (playing cards, pairs of scissors, leaves of a tree) are also to be admired.
Next door, the workshop is dedicated not only to restoring fans but also to supplying a demand for use in opera, theatre and cinema productions and haute couture fashion shows.

★**Porte St-Martin** – The gate was erected by the dean of the Guild of Merchants and Aldermen in 1674 to commemorate the capture of Besançon and defeat of the German, Spanish and Dutch armies. A mere 17m – 56ft high, the arch was designed by Pierre Bullet to have carvings by eminent artists who had worked at Versailles. Desjardins, Le Hongre, Marsy and Legros illustrate *(boulevard side)* the taking of Besançon, the breaking of the Triple Alliance, *(other side)* the capture of Limburg and the defeat of the Germans.

Boulevard St-Martin – This leads down to place de la République *(see* RÉPUBLIQUE*)*. The area was built up on an old rubbish dumping ground, hence the undulations and the need for laying the road at a different gradient and level from the pavements.
Two adjoining theatres stand near the gate: the Renaissance (1872) where Sarah Bernhardt played *The Lady of the Camellias*, and the Porte St-Martin which was built in 1781 to house the company from the Palais-Royal opera house which had been destroyed by fire. The first masked Opera balls were held there until it became a playhouse in 1814. Burned down during the Commune, it was rebuilt in 1873. Important performances include Coquelin the Elder, who first played the role of *Cyrano de Bergerac* years before Fernandel brought the house down with *Le Rosier de Mme Husson* and *Ignace*.

LA BOURSE 4 place de la Bourse. Ⓜ Bourse. Buses: 29, 39, 48, 67, 74, 85

The Stock Exchange ⓥ – *Best visited on a weekday during trading hours*. The main market and its square stand on the site of a Dominican convent which was secularised in 1795 and became the seat of the royalist faction responsible for the insurrection of 13 Vendémiaire *(see* PALAIS ROYAL*)* – 5 October 1795.
Paris' first exchange was John Law's bank *(see* les HALLES-BEAUBOURG*)*. When it went bankrupt, the public got to learn so much about share dealing that a public exchange was founded (1724). It was located in the palais Mazarin *(see* PALAIS-ROYAL – Bibliothèque Nationale*)*, before being transferred to the church of Notre-Dame des Victoires. Brongniart's building dates from 1808 – 1826; two wings were added between 1902 and 1907.
Today, there is much activity in the square in front of the building between 12.30pm and 2.30pm on weekdays when trading is at its busiest.
Inside, a public gallery has been created to explain the importance of the Stock Exchange in France's economy and the system of price indexing. Market trading can be watched through a glass window. Audio-visual presentations, lectures and documentary films complement the guided tours.

Le Croissant at 146 rue Montmartre is a café-restaurant much frequented by political writers and journalists. It was here that the liberal socialist and founder of *l'Humanité* newspaper, Jean Jaurès, was assassinated on 31 July 1914, on the eve of the First World War.

Place des Victoires

★PLACE DES VICTOIRES Ⓜ *Sentier. Buses: 29, 48, 67, 74*

The Square – In 1685 Marshal de la Feuillade, to curry favour with Louis XIV, commissioned a statue of the king from the sculptor, **Desjardins**. The statue, unveiled in 1686, showed the king, crowned with the laurels of victory, standing on a pedestal adorned with six low reliefs and four captives representing the vanquished Spain, Holland, Prussia and Austria. Surviving sections of the group are presently in the Louvre.

The main statue was melted down in 1792; a new figure by Desaix replaced it in 1806 only to be melted down in turn in 1815 (and reappear as Henri IV on the pont Neuf!). The present equestrian statue of the Sun King was sculpted by Bosio in 1822.

The side of the square with even numbers is the least damaged and gives some idea of the intended 17C elegance, although its harmony was impaired by the construction of rue Etienne-Marcel in 1883.

One of the façades of the **Banque de France** can be seen looking down rue Catinat, from the entrance of rue d'Aboukir. The bank at rue de la Vrillière was founded at the instigation of Napoleon in January 1800. First housed at no **4** rue d'Aboukir, it moved in 1812, to the mansion *(not open)* built in 1635 by François Mansart and remodelled by Robert de Cotte. The present building dates mostly from the 19C.

Basilique de Notre-Dame-des-Victoires – *Place des Petits-Pères.* The square occupies the site of an Augustinian monastery. The basilica (built 1629-1740) served as the Petits-Pères monastery chapel, dedicated in honour of the king's victories. It served as the Stock Exchange from 1795-1809. Inside, the wood panelling in the chancel dates from the 17C, there are seven paintings by Van Loo (*Louis XIII dedicating the church to the Virgin,* and scenes from the *Life of St Augustine*), a fine 18C organ loft and a monument to the 17C composer, Lulli *(2nd chapel on the left).* The church is famous for its annual pilgrimage to the Virgin which goes back to 1836; some 35 000 ex-votos cover the walls.

Rue du Mail – Note the conceits at no **5** a faun's mask and cornucopias adorning the doorway and at no **7** the capitals with interlaced snakes: these two 17C mansions make up the Hôtel Colbert, formerly owned by Louis XIV's minister (the grass snake is Colbert's emblem from *coluber* in Latin, *couleuvre* in French). At no **14**, the 18C Hôtel de Berthault, lived Madame Récamier.

Consult *Michelin plan of Paris* no 11, pp 182 to 189 for:
- *the area served by urban transport systems and sub-sections of each system*
- *services which run until midnight, during the night or on Sundays and public holidays*

LE SENTIER Ⓜ *Bourse, Sentier, Bonne-Nouvelle. Buses: 20, 39, 74, 85*

The Sentier quarter is the centre of the wholesale trade in fabrics and materials, trimmings, hosiery and ready-made clothes.

Passage and Place du Caire – Napoleon's victorious campaign in Egypt in 1798 aroused great enthusiasm in Paris. A taste for the Egyptian style influenced all the decorative and applied arts, architecture and fashion included. Here street names are affected by the craze, borrowed from campaigns against the Turks and the Marmalukes.

Note the Egyptian motifs applied to the house at the end of the arcade (sphinx, hieroglyphs), at the heart of the former **Cour des Miracles** (Courtyard of Miracles). This was one of a dozen or so places of refuge in Paris for miscreants on the run where, in the Middle Ages, they would congregate out of reach of the authorities.

A large courtyard, unpaved, stinking and muddy, lay hidden in a labyrinth of blind alleys, easily defensible passage ways and darkened streets. Thousands of rogues policed by their own elected leaders, occupied the area which remained off-limits to any but their own. By day pitiful lame, blind or maimed vagrants set out to beg in town only to return at nightfall; shedding their smelliest rags and wooden legs they would then indulge in the orgies described vividly by Victor Hugo in *The Hunchback of Notre-Dame*. It was this nightly apparently miraculous cure from infirmity that gave the locality its name. The neighbourhood was eventually cleared in 1667.

It was here however, that the slanderous rag *Le Père Duchesne* was printed by Hébert during the Revolution.

Le "Mont Orgueil" – The rue de Cléry, fronted by clothes shops, is the old counterscarp of the Charles V perimeter wall. In rue des Degrés stairways now cross the houses where ramparts once were. The whole quarter stands on Mont Orgueil (the proud hill), a natural mound used as a redoubt and which, in the 16C, afforded a good view or "*beau regard*" over the capital – hence the name of the street.

Where **rue de la Lune** forms a sharp angle with rue de Cléry, the poet André Chénier once lived, in a snippet of the Old Paris.

Église Notre-Dame-de-Bonne-Nouvelle ⊙ – *25 rue de la Lune.*

The Classical belfry is all that remains of the church restored by Anne of Austria – the rest of the building dates from 1823-1829. Inside numerous paintings decorate the walls. Note one by Mignard above the door in the south aisle of Anne of Austria and Henrietta-Maria, wife of Charles I of England; one at the end of the north aisle showing Henrietta of England and her three children before St Francis of Sales; an Annunciation by Lanfranco *(centre of the chancel, light-switch on the right)*, and a painting by Philippe de Champaigne *(to the right)*. In the Lady Chapel there is a fine 18C Virgin and Child attributed to Pigalle.

Treasury – *Call at the sacristy*. A small museum contains works of art including a 17C alabaster statue of St Jerome, two Descents from the Cross and an 18C silk vestment worn by the Abbot Edgeworth of Firmont who followed Louis XVI to the guillotine.

Notre-Dame-de-Bonne-Nouvelle has been adopted as the patron saint of radio and television!

★FAUBOURG POISSONNIÈRE

Ⓜ *Gare de l'Est, Poissonnière, Cadet. Buses: 30, 31, 32, 38, 39, 46, 47, 54, 56, 65*

Up until 1750, the rue Ste-Anne took its name from a chapel that stood at no 77. It became known thereafter as rue du Faubourg-Poissonnière as it was the last leg of the fish-traders' journey from the coast to the wholesale markets at les Halles.

Rue du Paradis – The street is known today for its shops of fine tableware. These are chief points of sale for the French glass, china and porcelain factories located here because of their proximity to the Gare de l'Est and the rail links with Lorraine where the industry is concentrated.

The group of buildings at nos 30-32, houses the International Tableware Centre (trade only) which represent the best-known names in porcelain and glass-making.

★**Musée Baccarat** ⊙ – *30bis rue du Paradis*. **Baccarat**, the glass-makers who have supplied royal palaces and state residences throughout the world for the last 150 years display some of their workshops' finest pieces (chandeliers, vases, perfume bottles).

Hôtel Bourrienne ⊙ – *58 rue d'Hauteville (at the back of the courtyard)*. Located at the heart of the Nouvelle-France quarter, this 18C house was owned by Fortunée Hamelin, a friend of Joséphine de Beauharnais. In 1801, crippled by debts, this famed *Merveilleuse* ceded her house to Louis-Antoine Fauvelet de Bourrienne, secretary and confidant of the First Consul. There, the witty Mme de Bourrienne established between 1813 and 1824 one of Paris' most brilliant *Salons*.

Decorated under the Empire and Restoration, the ground floor boasts a small sitting room, the dining room (furniture by Jacob and Aubusson carpet), the study, the sitting room (Savonnerie carpet, Directoire chandelier), bedroom; the **bathroom** in blue and gold reflects the sumptuous taste of the times.

Maison St-Lazare – *107 rue du Faubourg-St-Denis*. In the Middle Ages this was the capital's leper house. St Vincent of Paul *(see* FAUBOURG-ST-GERMAIN*)*, the founder of the Priests of the Mission (known today as Lazarists), died here in 1660.

At the time of the Revolutionary troubles the building became a prison and the poet André Chénier, one of its most industrious inmates, was here prior to his execution. Changed to a women's prison, it reverted to being a hospital in 1935.

Église St-Laurent ⊙ – *68 boulevard de Magenta*. The belfry is all that remains of the 12C sanctuary. The nave was rebuilt in the 15C and the church altered in the 17C (chancel sculpture and woodwork). The west front and spire date from the Napoleon III period.

The **St-Laurent Fair** was held for over 600 years on the present site of the Gare de l'Est railway station. Over a hundred stalls and booths offered their perishable foodstuffs free of tax or duty. It was on one of these makeshift stages that comic opera, a new dramatic form, was born (*c* 1720).

Église St-Vincent-de-Paul ⊙ – *place Franz-Liszt*. The church was built by the architect **Hittorff** (1824-1844) who was also responsible for the final decoration of place de la Concorde *(see* CHAMPS-ÉLYSÉES*)*. Basilical in form, the church has a columned portico and two tall towers. Inside, Flandrin's fresco runs around the nave, dividing the elevation in two. A bronze calvary by Rude stands on the high altar.

⋆**Musée du Grand Orient de France** ⊙ – *16 rue Cadet*. A large room in this modern building accommodates a collection of documents (Constitution of Anderson from 1726), badges, and portraits that encapsulate the history of this organisation, one of the main Masonic lodges of France.

Belle-époque façade

Les HALLES-BEAUBOURG★★

Michelin plan 11 – folds 31 and 32: H 14, H 15

The demolition of the City's main wholesale market has radically altered the area's character. Today, a leisure-cum-shopping centre occupies the site of the old trade halls. Crowds of all kinds are attracted to the hub of the Pompidou Centre, whilst the renovation of the decrepit Beaubourg plateau mingles zany, ultra-modern elements with medieval splendour – Stravinski fountain, St-Eustache and St-Merri.

★LE QUARTIER DES HALLES
Ⓜ/RER: Châtelet-les-Halles. Buses: 29, 38, 47, 74

The Old Halles – Paris' original central market was on the Ile de la Cité; this moved first to place de Grève (now place de l'Hôtel de Ville – *see* les QUAIS) then to Beaubourg in around 1110, before relocating to the outskirts of the city at Rungis (1969).

In 1183 under Philippe Auguste the open market was extended, permanent structures were erected and a surrounding wall built. The thenceforth king levied site and sales taxes, as an early form of VAT (Value Added Tax). Twice a week the city merchants and craftsmen were required to close their shops and conduct their business in the market where each street specialised in a trade.

By the 16C with a growing population of 300 000 in the capital, the trade in foodstuffs became of paramount importance, eventually replacing all other types of trade in the market. On the orders of Napoleon, the wine and leather markets were transferred to the Left Bank.

Until the Revolution, in the vicinity of to the nearby St-Eustache crossroads was the market pillory where dishonest traders, thieves and prostitutes were publicly exposed.

By the 19C the great market was in urgent need of reconstruction. As Rambuteau and Haussmann thrust wide avenues through the quarter (rues de Rivoli, du Pont-Neuf, du Louvre, des Halles, Étienne-Marcel), a stone pavilion was built by the architect Baltard commissioned by Louis Philippe, and being unsuitable, razed. He then designed plans for a hall of iron girders and skylight roofs, reminiscent of the Gare de l'Est, which were accepted by Napoleon III.

Ten halls in all were constructed (1854-1866) and the buildings became the model for covered markets throughout France and abroad. Two further halls were opened in 1936. The animated market scene and the rich variety of colour and smell are vividly described by Émile Zola as "the stomach of Paris" in his novel *Le Ventre de Paris* (Savage Paris). The old tradition still exists of eating onion soup, snails and pig's trotters at 5am in simple but excellent restaurants with colourful names (Le Chien qui fume, le Pied de Cochon). As the old buildings became inadequate, they were demolished and removed. One has been re-erected at Nogent-sur-Marne.

★**Forum des Halles** – An underground pedestrian concourse, lined with shops and with direct access to the metro stations, extends over 7 hectares – more than 17 acres to the east of the Commercial Exchange. At garden level, on the north and east sides, palm-shaped metal structures house public amenities (Pavillon des Arts, Maison de la Poésie...). There is a good view over the whole area from the upper terrace by the fountain.

To the west, a garden (5 hectares – 12 acres) includes pergolas along rue Berger, children's play areas, a tree-lined mall linking the semi-circular area by St-Eustache's, where a massive 70 ton stone head ("Écoute") by H de Miller stands, to the Fountain of the Innocents. The glazed galleries overlook place des Verrières; in

Forum des Halles, overview

the centre rises a pink marble sculpture by the Argentine Julio Silva, of Pygmalion: next to a unicorn, the Buddha-like figure of the Dream-Keeper presenting her twin lunar and solar faces watches over the young girl asleep created by Pygmalion. The latter is depicted stilled for eternity in his fruitless quest, while his desire is exemplified by a pig-headed man devouring the snake of temptation.

On level -4, on the Porte Lescot side, the theme of a bronze low-relief by Trémois representing a golden wall with amazing reliefs, is light travelling through the ages. On level -3 by rue de l'Arc-en-Ciel, imaginary porticoes opening onto infinity painted by Attila, form a rainbow-coloured dome. Moretti's fresco (same level, by rue des Piliers) in vivid colours evokes the evolution of man from prehistoric times (bronze human mask from Tautavel) to the age of writing including giant portraits of Victor Hugo and Louis Armstrong. On levels -2 and -1 Cueco's mosaic columns and Rieti's ceramics are decorated with wild and domestic animals.

★**Espace Grévin du Forum des Halles** ⊙ – *Level -1*. The display, in this annexe of the world-famous waxworks museum on Boulevard Montmartre (*see* Les GRANDS BOULE-VARDS), portrays the Paris of the Belle Époque (1885-1900) by means of 22 tableaux with animation and sound effects on the highlights of the capital: the opening of the Eiffel Tower, Montmartre cabarets, etc.

Additional facilities – From level -3 go through the **place Carrée** to gain access to the public auditorium, video library, photographic studio, and sports centre (swimming-pool, gymnasium, billiard room). There is also a tropical glasshouse lit by four glass pyramids.

Leave by the Porte du Louvre and cross to rue Sauval, formerly rue des Étuves (public baths had become places of ill repute by the end of the Middle Ages and were closed down under Louis XIII). From the entrance there is a fine view of the Exchange (la Bourse du Commerce) and of St-Eustache's.

La Bourse du Commerce *2 rue de Viarmes.* Ⓜ *Les Halles, Louvre-Rivoli*

The Stock-Market ⊙ – This circular building is hemmed in to the west by a semi-circle of tall porticoed mansions and to the east by gardens and the Forum. It stands on a site where for the past 800 years French history has been made. Blanche de Castille, mother of St Louis, died in the first building (Hôtel de Nesle) in 1252 on a bed of straw as a sign of humility. It then became the Hôtel de Bohème, then Hôtel d'Orléans; Louis XII lost the mansion at cribbage to his chamberlain who converted it into a convent for repentant sinners. These were dislodged in 1572 when Catherine de' Medici left the Tuileries and had a mansion, the Hôtel de la Reine, constructed by Delorme and Bullant. The building subsequently became the Hôtel de Soissons where Prince Eugene of Savoy, who served the Austrian empire and fought the infidels, was born in 1663. Under the Regency it was turned into a gambling hall, then razed in 1748. A wheat market built in Louis XVI's reign was replaced in 1889 by the present rotunda.

Abutting on the market-side wall to the south of the building is a fluted column, 30m – 98ft high, the only remaining feature of the mansion built by Bullant, which is thought to be the astrologer Ruggieri's observatory.

Inside, the vast circular hall lit by a glass dome is reserved for accredited commodity brokers.

Rue St-Honoré – This street has been, since the 12C, was one of the quarter's major thoroughfares. The site of no 96 on the corner is where the poet and comedy writer Regnard was born in 1655 and where some historians allege Molière was born in 1662. Wagner lived there in 1839.

H. Marcou/PIX

Further along, on the left, is an edifice built by Soufflot (1755). The sculptor Boizot reproduced a nymph by Jean Goujon on the façade and erected by the side of the building on the rue de l'Arbre-Sec a fountain adorned with a bronze mascaron surmounted by a marble plaque bearing France's coat of arms. This monument replaced the **Croix-du-Trahoir fountain** (Fontaine de la Croix-du-Trahoir), erected by François I, but in no way resembles it. The original stood in the middle of the road, raised on a flight of steps on which vegetables were spread for sale. To one side stood the gallows from which the street on the left took its name of the Arbre Sec or withered tree. It is also said that in 613 at these crossroads, on the orders of her enemy, Frédégonde, the old Queen Brunehaut of Austria was tied by her hair to a wild horse's tail and broken. More than a thousand years later, on 26 August 1648, the arrest of the parliamentarian, Broussel, by Anne of Austria's forces in the same spot began a street row which, by the following morning, had developed into civil conflict: the **Fronde** had begun.

Opposite, on the corner with rue Sauval, used to stand a house in which some say Molière was born in 1622 and where Regnard was born in 1655. Its replacement accommodated Wagner in 1839.

Temple de l'Oratoire ⓥ – *4 rue de l'Oratoire*. This was in the 16C the site of Gabrielle d'Estrées' house, one of Henri IV's favourites. In 1616 the Oratorian Congregation founded by Cardinal Pierre de Berulle, a secular priesthood dedicated to teaching and preaching later to rival the Jesuits, had a church built by Le Mercier (1621-1630). This became the royal chapel in the reigns of Louis XIII, Louis XIV and Louis XV. A succession of erudite and distinguished preachers such as Bossuet, Malebranche, Bourdaloue and Massillon attracted the royal family and court. The funerals of Louis XIII and his Queen, Anne of Austria, were held in the church.

When the Oratorians were suppressed at the Revolution the chapel became an arms depot. Napoleon ceded the church to the Protestants in 1811 before the seminary was re-established in 1852. The façade is 18C.

From the arches of the rue de Rivoli there is a view of the church's east end which is well preserved, and of the statue of Admiral de Coligny placed there last century. He was assassinated on the night of the St Bartholomew's massacre (24 August 1572 – *see* les QUAIS – St-Germain-de-l'Auxerrois).

Take rue Jean-Jacques Rousseau on the right where the philosopher lived at the end of his life (no **52**). On the left is the former red light street, rue du Pélican, and beyond the **Galerie Véro-Dodat**, created in 1822 by two pork butchers who installed gas lighting along it and let the shops for fabulous rents.

★★ Église St-Eustache *place du Jour*. Ⓜ *Les Halles. Buses: 29, 38, 47, 74*

Church of St-Eustache ⓥ – Gothic in plan and structure, but Renaissance in decoration, this is one of Paris' most beautiful churches. It has a long tradition of organ and choral music. Last century it hosted the first performances of works by both Berlioz and Liszt.

Construction – In 1214 a chapel dedicated to St Agnes was built on this spot. A few years later, the chapel was rededicated to St Eustache, a Roman general converted, like St Hubert, by the vision of a cross between a stag's antlers. But the Halles parish, which had become the biggest in Paris, dreamed of a church worthy of its new status. Grandiose plans were made with Notre-Dame as the model.

The foundation stone was laid in 1532. Construction was slow, however, in spite of liberal gifts and the church was not consecrated until a century later, in 1637. The original plan had been adhered to, although the west front had never been completed, when in 1754 it was decided to replace this Renaissance front by a Classical one with columns.

During the Revolution the church was renamed the Temple of Agriculture; in 1844 it was badly damaged by fire and subsequently reconstructed by Baltard.

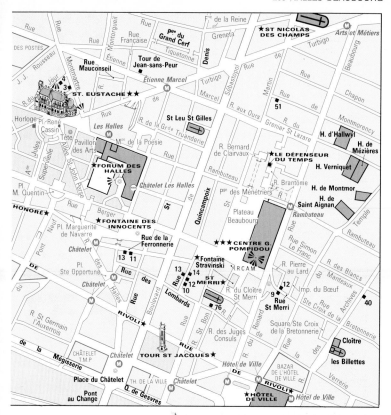

St-Eustache, so close to the Louvre and the Palais-Royal, at the centre of everything going on in the capital, and also the parish church of the Halles corporations, became a focal point of public ceremony – the baptisms of Armand du Plessis, the future Richelieu, of Jean-Baptiste Poquelin (Molière), the future Marquise de Pompadour, Louis XIV's first communion, the funerals of La Fontaine, Molière and the Revolutionary orator, Mirabeau.

The church was at one time paved with tombstones including those of Louis XIV's statesman, Colbert, Admiral de Tourville who beat the Anglo-Dutch fleets off Beachy Head in 1690 and was defeated, in turn, off La Hougue in 1692, and the composer Rameau.

Interior – St-Eustache measures 100m long, 44m wide and 34m high – 328ft x 144ft x 112ft. The church's majesty and rich decoration are striking.

The plan is that of Notre-Dame with nave and chancel encircled by double aisles and flat transepts. The vaulting above the nave, transept and chancel is Flamboyant, adorned with numerous ribs and richly carved hanging keystones.

The elevation, however, is entirely different from the cathedral's. The aisles, devoid of galleries, rise very high, the arches being so tall that between them and the clerestory windows there is space only for a small Renaissance-style gallery.

The stained-glass windows in the chancel are after cartoons by Philippe de Champaigne (1631). St Eustace appears at the centre, surrounded by the Fathers of the Church and the Apostles.

The chapels are decorated with frescoes.

1) On the door tympanum: the *Martyrdom of St Eustace* by Simon Vouet (17C).

2) *Adoration of the Magi*, a copy of a painting by Rubens.

3) Churchwarden's pew presented by the Regent, Philippe of Orleans in 1720.

4) Colourful naïve sculpture by R Mason commemorating the fruit and vegetable market's move out of Paris on 28 February 1969.

5) *Tobias and the Angel*, by Santi di Tito (16C).

6) *The Ecstasy of Mary Magdalen*, a painting by Manetti (17C).

7) *The Pilgrims at Emmaüs*, an early Rubens.

8) Colbert's tomb designed by Le Brun, Coysevox carved the statues of the minister and of Abundance; Tuby that of Fidelity (left).

9) Statue of the Virgin by Pigalle. Chapel frescoes by Thomas Couture (19C).

10) 16C statue of St John the Evangelist.

11) Bust of the composer Jean-Philippe Rameau who died in 1764.

12) Epitaph to 17C Lieutenant-General Chevert.

Exterior – Down the narrow rue du Jour, from opposite no 4, there is a good **view★** of the buttresses and upper part of the church. No 4 once belonged to Montmorency-Bouteville who was beheaded in 1628 for contravening Richelieu's ban on duelling. From no 3 rue Montmartre a blind alley leads to the beautiful north transept door.

★Transept façade – This fine Renaissance composition is flanked by twin staircase turrets ending in pinnacles. Beneath the gable point is a stag's head with a Cross between the antlers recalling St Eustace's conversion. The statues on the door shafts are modern. The pilasters, niches, mouldings, grotesques and roses are delicately fashioned.

Chevet – From the corner where the rues Montorgueil and Montmartre meet there is a view of the east end of the church with its circular Lady Chapel. The belltower's spire rising above the transept crossing was truncated in the 19C to house a signalling station.

The house of **Jean-Jacques Rousseau** is at 52 rue Jean-Jacques-Rousseau, where the great philosopher (1712-1778) lived between 1774 and 1778 and wrote his famous 'Confessions'.

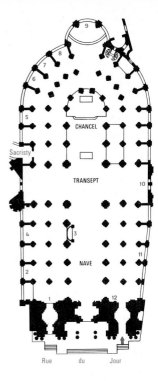

Rue Mauconseil – In 1548 a theatre was built on land belonging to the Hôtel de Bourgogne to the left of the street. The troupe excluded women players until 1634 during which time female roles were played by men in masks. Racine first presented *Mithridate* and *Iphigénie* in this theatre. In 1680 the company, by royal command, merged with that of the rue Mazarine (*see* ST-GERMAIN-DES-PRÉS).

They were replaced by a company of Italian improvisers who animated the *Commedia dell'Arte* characters Harlequin, Columbine, Isabel and Scaramouche; the latter by a clown who could still knock off his partner's hat with a high kick at the age of 83. The company was disbanded in 1697 after attacking Mme de Maintenon. The last troupe to play the theatre before it disappeared was the Comic-Opera (1716-1782).

Tour de Jean-sans-Peur – Follow rue Française (named after François I) to 20 rue Étienne-Marcel, where, in a schoolyard, stands a square machicolated tower *(closed to the public)* built by John the Fearless for his own protection in 1408 following the assassination, on his orders, of the Duke of Orléans. The tower formed part of the **Hôtel de Bourgogne**, the former Artois mansion abutting on the Philippe Auguste perimeter wall.

Rue St-Denis – The street, opened in the 17C to relieve the traffic on rue St-Martin, soon became the busiest and most prosperous in Paris. It became the main route for a king's grand entry processing with full pageantry to Notre-Dame or for royal funeral *cortèges* to lay the royal person to rest at the Abbey St-Denis (*see* EXCURSIONS – ST-DENIS).

Of the Triumphal arches, porticoes and even fountains – ideally overflowing with free wine or milk – erected to celebrate a new king, one fountain, much restored, survives from the time of Louis XI. La fontaine de la Reine or Queen's Fountain stands at no 142 (corner of rue Greneta). At no 145, the **Passage du Grand-Cerf** was built in 1825 on the site of the inn of the same name, a staging point until the Revolution.

The lower end of the street is lined with clothes shops, whilst the top end is frequented by 'ladies of the night'.

Église St-Leu-St-Gilles ⊘ – *92bis rue St-Denis*. This church, built in 1320 and remodelled several times, is dedicated to two 6C saints, Lupus (Leu in French), Bishop of Sens, and the Provençal hermit, Gilles. A new east end and north tower belfry were constructed in 1858 when the boulevard Sébastopol was laid.

Inside, the Gothic bays of the nave contrast with the vaults of the taller Classical chancel. Other items of interest include several 17C and 18C paintings, a 16C marble group by Jean Bullant of *St Anne and the Virgin*, 15C alabaster low reliefs, fragments of an altarpiece from the former Innocents' Cemetery (at the sacristy entrance) and a stone *Christ Entombed* (in the crypt).

Rue de la Grande-Truanderie – Vagabonds' Row is contemporary with the medieval Court of Miracles (*see* GRANDS BOULEVARDS – Le Sentier), which gave sanctuary to miscreants up to the 17C.

Rue de la Ferronnerie – It was while riding in this street in his carriage that Henri IV was assassinated on 14 May 1610 in front of no **11** (note the commemorative marble slab). The sign at no **13** was a crowned heart pierced by an arrow – the witnesses to the murder felt this to be an omen. His assailant, Ravaillac, was quartered on the place de Grève (*see* les QUAIS – Hôtel de Ville), 13 days later.

★**Fontaine des Innocents** – The 19C square stands on the site of the Cemetery and Church of the Holy Innocents which dated back to the 12C.

The cemetery was once encircled by a charnel house where bones from the communal graves were collected. Horrific tales about the siege of Paris (1590) are told by Henri of Navarre, of people grinding up the bones to make bread. A famous 'Dance of Death' adorned the place from the 15C to 1669, reminding all and sundry of one's ultimate fate – but instead of being a sad place, it became frequented by hawkers, public scribes and traders. In 1786, the cemetery was closed – to be replaced by a fruit and vegetable market – nigh on 2 million skeletons were transferred by night over a period of many months to the former quarries of La Tombe-Issoire, which became known as the Catacombs (*see* PORT-ROYAL).

Pierre Lescot's fountain, carved by Jean Goujon, is a Renaissance masterpiece. In 1550, it stood at the corner of rue St-Denis against a wall requiring it to have only three sides; when the cemetery was closed, it was removed to its present site and given a fourth side by Pajou (the original low reliefs are in the Louvre).

★★PLATEAU BEAUBOURG

Ⓜ *Rambuteau, /RER: Chatelet-les-Halles. Buses: 38, 47*

Beaubourg is the name of an old village included within the Philippe Auguste perimeter wall at the end of the 12C. Run-down and derelict, the old quarter was cleaned up in 1936 and subjected to major re-development in 1968. The Beaubourg plateau was to have been the site of a public library; however, in 1969, on the initiative of **Georges Pompidou** (1911-1974), the then President of France, it was decided to create a multi-purpose cultural centre.

★★★Centre Georges-Pompidou ⓥ *place Georges-Pompidou*

Note: Closed Tuesdays – Late opening from noon (10.00am weekends) to 10.00pm.

Architecture – Construction was completed in 1977. The architects **Richard Rogers** (British) and **Renzo Piano** (Italian) achieved a totally futuristic building. Innovative in conception, this gigantic parallelepiped unfolds its steel structure, glass walls and bright colours, 166m long, 60m wide and 42m high (545ft x 197ft x 138ft). Devoid of superficial decoration, this pile of metal plains like a surrealistic sculpture continues to offend certain sensibilities.

The façade appears a tangle of pipes and tubes latticed along its glass skin, giving an effect of a solid yet pliant superstructure.

Centre Georges-Pompidou

An external caterpillar-like clear tube carries the escalators upwards, diagonally across the front. The displacement of all means of access, escalators and lifts, utility shafts carrying electricity and telecommunication cabling, heating ducts, water and gas conduits to the exterior of the building leaves vast spaces (7 500m^2 – 80 722 square feet) on each floor free for exhibitions, libraries and administration services.

A gently sloping, cobbled *Piazza* extends before the centre serving as the museum's outside reception area and as an open-air theatre for street painters and mime artists, contortionists, fire-eaters and jugglers.

At the rear, the 'functional side', the colour-coded utility ducts are clearly visible (white for ventilation, blue for air-conditioning, green for water, yellow for power, red for communications).

• • • • • • • • • • • • • • • PRACTICALITIES • • • • • • • • • • • • • •

An information desk in the entrance hall supplies details relating to the services available. Tourist information ☎ 01 44 78 12 33; recorded information ☎ 01 42 77 11 12; fax 01 44 78 12 03. For detailed information see Practical Information section.

Visitors are obliged to deposit all bags, cameras and cumbersome clothing at the '*Vestiaire*' (coat-hanger symbol).

A specialised bookshop for magazines, publications, cards and posters is available on the first mezzanine level. Catalogues to current exhibitions are available at the entrance to the show.

Restaurant facilities are available on the top floor, with light refreshments, cafeteria and terrace from which there is a sensational view over Paris.

ACTIVITIES

The Centre seeks to explore the close correlation between art and daily mundane activities. This multi-purpose cultural centre at the disposal of artists, specialists and the general public offers an astonishing variety of activities and modern communication facilities to encourage curiosity and interaction.

The four main departments consist of the following:

The **Musée National d'Art Moderne / Centre de Création Industrielle (MNAM/CCI)** (Museum of Modern Art and Contemporary Industrial Design Centre) on the third and fourth floors present their extensive collections of Art, Architecture and Design from 1900 to the present day.

The **Département du Dévelopement Culturel (DDC)** (Cultural Development Department), initiated in 1992, is particularly concerned with teaching, entertainment, public speaking, political writing and documentaries.

The **Bibliothèque Publique d'Information (BPI)** (Public Information Library) consists of three storeys of library with access to French and foreign books, slides, films, periodicals, reference material, CD-ROM, micro-fiche, video, etc...

The **Institut de Recherche et Coordination Acoustique/Musique (IRCAM)** (Institute for Acoustic and Musical Research) is located on four floors underground, below the place Stravinski (*see below*). It undertakes experimentation with sound.

The **Grande Galerie** on the fifth floor accommodates temporary exhibitions. The **Salle Garance** on the ground floor holds film 'festivals' with three screenings daily ☎ 01 42 78 37 29. There are also facilities for dance and theatre, concerts (**Grande Salle**) and debates (**Petite Salle**).

Interior – On the ground floor, the *Portrait of Georges Pompidou* by Vasarély made up of white slats hangs from the ceiling, as does Soto's *Virtual Volume* in white and yellow.

★★★**Musée National d'Art Moderne** – The museum certainly ranks high amongst the most significant dedicated to modern art in the world. It traces the evolution of art from Fauvism and Cubism to the contemporary art scene. The 20C plastic arts collection was substantially enriched in 1992 with a wide range of architectural motifs and design objects. The museum space can accommodate a mere 700 to 800 works out of the 35 000 (16 000 drawings) available.

The historical collection (1905 to 1965) is held on the fourth floor. The third floor with its more flexible layout is dedicated to contemporary pieces. Outside the museum, **Constantin Brancusi**'s (1876-1957) sculpture workshop is being restored.

The growth of a museum – The exceptional collection housed by the Centre Georges-Pompidou is drawn from the Museum of Modern Art at the Palais de Tokyo (*see* l'ALMA), from bequests made by artists' families (Matisse, Chagall, Picasso, Delaunay, Brancusi, Rouault, Kupka, Henri Laurens, Magritte, Kandinski...).

A strident purchasing policy has also enabled the Centre to fill gaps in its inherited collection (Surrealism, Dada, Marcel Duchamp, 1960s American School), complemented by donations (Miró, Ernst, Chagall).

From 1900 to 1965 – 4th Floor *Throughout the galleries, notices give an outline of the main elements of each artistic movement –* To the right on entering are Matisse's *Nus de Dos*, a series of four bronze reliefs demonstrating an evolution in style between 1909 and 1930. The Graphic Art room opposite has changing displays of works on paper (prints and drawings, photographs, collages, lithographs).

Terraces – These include *Le Capricorne* by Ernst, *Une Machine* by Tinguely, a Calder *stabile* as well as works by Miró and Laurens.

South galleries – From the early 20C to post-First World War: Fauvism and Cubism.

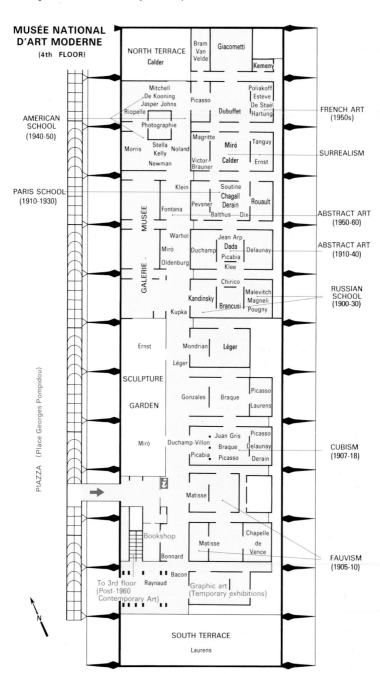

Fauvism (1905-10), a reactionary art movement (against methodical refraction of colour in Impressionism and the pastel tones of the Nabis), is characterised by simplified form and strong colour. The name '*les Fauves*', meaning wild beasts, aptly describes a directive towards Expressionism. Contour is clearly defined and colour is exploited to its ultimate decorative effect in works such as *Rue de Marly-le-Roi* by Vlaminck, *La rue pavoisée* by Dufy and *Les deux péniches* and *Le pont de Chatou* by Derain. **Matisse**, the leader of the movement, is represented by *Violiniste à la fenêtre*, *La blouse roumaine*, *Arlequin* and his distinctive gouache cut-outs or "drawing with scissors" as the artist put it (*chapel interior at Vence on the French Riviera*).

Cubism – What the Fauves were doing with colour and silhouetted form, the Cubists contradicted by translating their pictorial vision into refracted geometric planes and lines to suggest volume and texture. Cubism founded by **Braque** and **Picasso** in 1907, was to be a brief phase in their artistic development. The *Grand cheval majeur* sculpted by Duchamp-Villon (1914), *Le petit Déjeuner* by Juan Gris (1915) and *La Noce* by **Fernand Léger** (1911-12) fall into the same category.

Post 1918 – Post-Cubist works by Braque and Picasso are presented in the following two rooms, before the large room dedicated to Fernand Leger, where the figures of *La Lecture*, *Grands plongeurs noirs* and *Adieu New York* surround the *Composition aux deux perroquets*.

North galleries – Most artistic trends post-First World War to the 1960s are represented here: Abstract Expressionism, Surrealism, New Figurative Art of the Fifties and Sixties, New Realism and Pop Art.

In a rejection of figurative representation, the Abstract School wished to find expression in an interplay of colour and line. The movement pioneered in 1910 by **Kandinsky** with his *Improvisations*, is sustained by **Kupa** (*Autour d'un point* – 1911-30) and **Mondrian** (*Composition II* – 1937 and *New York City II* – 1942), whereas **Klee**'s poetic compositions never quite ostracise themselves from reality. In sculpture, **Brancusi** pursues abstraction for its own sake paring down form to its most essential, highly polished shape (*Seal*).

Born during the First World War, '**Dada**' evolved as a violent counter-reaction to what its artists saw as the course of civilisation towards its own self-destruction. They translated this debasement of values into anti-art (Arp), but retained the concept of time and movement from Futurism. As early as 1913 **Marcel Duchamp** created his 'ready-made' works of art, promoting everyday objects to the status of Art. Robert (*Manège de Cochons* – 1922) and Sonia Delaunay's (*Le Bal Bulier* – 1913) fascination with colour and movement marks the intermediate stage between the geometric Cubist style and colourist experimentation. Pevsner's spiral sculptures illustrate Constructivism.

Between 1910 and 1930, Montparnasse harboured many foreign artists who collaborated in thought to create the **Paris School** *(see* MONTPARNASSE*)*, characterised by an expression of intense feeling. Such are the realms of **Soutine**'s tormented expressionist style, **Chagall**'s world of fantasy (*Autour d'Elle*, 1945) and **Modigliani**'s decorative arabesques. On the periphery, **Rouault** explored strongly religious subjects in a strangely sombre style.

Dada inevitably lead to **Surrealism**, represented by **Salvador Dali** (*The ghostly cow*), **Magritte**, Brauner and **Miró**, who viewed painting as a means of expressing the subconscious mind. All verge on depicting the irrational and the incongruous.

During the 1950s Abstract art appealed to many French and foreign artists: some emphasized line (Hartung), others divided surfaces into large blocks of colour (Poliakoff, De Staël) or added a three-dimensional element: tar and sand (Dubuffet), or fused sculptures (Kemeny). The **Cobra** movement (1948-51) advocated spontaneous expression through the free use of bold colour and energetic brush strokes or footwork (*Planète nature*, 1960, by Kazuo Shiraga).

The last section collects together the final phases of American art post-World-War I to the 1960s (Pollock, Rothko, Noland, Newman, Serra and Stella).

From 1960 to 1990 – 3rd Floor – *access from 4th floor.* New Realism as an expression of a prosperous urban society in the 1960s incorporated objects from everyday life, piled up by Arman, compressed by César, or wrapped by Christo. In the United States, Pop Art flourished with Rauschenberg and **Andy Warhol**.

Presentations of Conceptual art (1967 onwards) are regularly changed with works from the last generation of artists interspersed with the current one. Besides the mainstay of French movements: new-realism, supporting surfaces, figurative narrative there are examples of important trends from America (Pop Art, Minimalism), Germany (Joseph Beuys) and Italy (Arte povera).

Notable permanent exhibits include Dubuffet's *Jardin d'hiver*, 1968-70 (take off your shoes).

5th floor terrace – A splendid **view★★** extends over the Paris rooftops – from right to left: Montmartre dominated by the Sacré-Cœur, St Eustache, the Eiffel Tower, Maine-Montparnasse Tower, St-Merri in the foreground with Notre-Dame behind...

The Horloge Quarter

To the north of the Georges Pompidou Centre, between rue Beaubourg and rue St-Martin, lies this recently renovated pedestrianised area brightened by attractive shops.

Le Défenseur du Temps *rue Bernard-de-Clairvaux* – This unusual brass and steel electronic clock with its Jack known as the Defender of Time was designed by Jacques Monestier. On striking the hour, this life-size figure armed with a double-edged sword and shield, confronts one of three animals symbolising the elements: a dragon (earth), a bird (air) and a crab (water). At noon, 6pm and 10pm all three attack together.

At the corner of rues Brantôme and Rambuteau stands Zadkine's *Prometheus* (*see* PORT ROYAL – Musée Zadkine) represented as having stolen fire from heaven.

The St Merri Quarter

The area to the south of the Centre around the church has always been crowded with craftsmen. In the Middle Ages drapers sold unusable cloth bequeathed to children, whilst haberdashers sold hats, bonnets, furs and perfumes, and hairdressers plied their trade to the impoverished titled and wealthy *bourgeoises*. From here, a taste for Paris fads and fashions radiated throughout Europe.

At every political insurrection the barricades went up. In June 1832, a young boy and an old man, flourishing a tricolour, were killed near the rue du Cloître-St-Merri – an event on which **Victor Hugo** based his description of the death of Gavroche in his novel *Les Misérables*. Today the quarter is adjusting to its new role as the cultural centre of contemporary art.

At the rear of the church, the **Stravinski fountain** with black and coloured mobile sculptures by Tinguely and Niki de Saint-Phalle respectively illustrating the works of the great composer (*the Rite of Spring, Firebird...*) draw the crowds.

Rue St Merri – Note nos 9 and 12 with their fine frontages, and beyond, the sordid Impasse du Bœuf, perhaps the oldest *cul-de-sac* in Paris.

For Hôtel de St Aignan etc – see le MARAIS.

★**Église St-Merri** ⊙ – Access to the church is through the St Merri presbytery (*76 rue de la Verrerie*) with a fine 18C porch.

St Merry or Medericus who died here in the 7C used to be invoked to assist in the release of captives. The former parish church of the Lombard usurers, although dating from 1520 to 1612, curiously conforms to the 15C Flamboyant Gothic style.

Outside, the west front stands directly on the narrow rue St-Martin, crowded-in with small houses and shops, much as it might have been in the Middle Ages. The Flamboyant interior remodelled under Louis XV retains good 16C stained-glass windows in the first three bays of the chancel and transept, and fine ribbed vaulting at the transept crossing.

In addition to the majestic 17C organ loft – the organ at one time played by Camille Saint-Saëns, and beautiful wood panelling by the Slodtz brothers (pulpit, sacristy and the glory at the back of the choir), the church has interesting pictures.

One bell dating from 1331, probably the oldest in Paris, survives from the medieval chapel which stood on the site of the present church.

Rue des Lombards – Its name recalls the Middle Ages when Lombard moneylenders monopolised banking transactions. The right-hand corner has remained empty since 1569 after a house on the site owned by two Huguenot merchants had been razed by decree.

Rue Quincampoix – This was where the Scots financier, John Law's "South Sea Bubble" was situated. Law founded a bank there in 1719, attracting all kinds of speculators, expanding into the neighbouring houses. The street became crowded with people making fortunes overnight – a hunchback was said to have gained 150 000 livres for the use of his back as a desk. The frenzy lasted until 1720 when the bank crashed and the speculators fled. Law's house was razed when rue Rambuteau was built.

Several old houses (*nos 10, 12, 13, 14*) survive with unusual paved courtyards, mascarons (stone masks), intricate wrought-iron balconies and nailed or carved doors.

Fountains

Canyoneastrate by Singer (BERCY), *Le Creuset du Temps* (The Melting-Pot of Time) by Shamaï Haber, a sculpture-fountain overlooked by Bofill's apartment blocks (place de Catalogne – MONTPARNASSE), and the **Fontaine Stravinski** (place Igor Stravinski – HALLES-BAUBOURG) by J. Tinguely and Niki de Saint-Phalle.

ILE DE LA CITÉ★★★

Michelin plan 11 – folds 31 and 32: from J 14 to K 16
Ⓜ Cité. RER: St Michel. Buses: 21, 38, 47, 85, 96

The Ile de la Cité is the cradle of Paris geographically at the very heart of the capital. Its history, architecture and remarkable setting make it one of the city's principal attractions; its most impressive monument is undoubtedly the Cathedral of Notre Dame, closely followed by the most exquisite Sainte Chapelle.

Lutetia – Between 250 and 200 BC Gaulish fishermen and boatmen of the Parisii tribe discovered and set up their huts on the largest island in the Seine – Lutetia was born. The township, whose Celtic name meant "boatyard on a river", was conquered by Labienus' Roman legions in 52 BC. The Gallo-Roman town prospered on shipping, so that the vessel which was later incorporated in the capital's coat of arms *(see* INTRODUCTION – History*)* is a reminder both of the shape of the island and of the way of life of its earliest inhabitants. The boatmen's existence has been confirmed by the discovery beneath Notre-Dame of one of their pagan altars *(see* LATIN QUARTER – Musée de Cluny*)*.

In 360 the Roman prefect, Julian the Apostate, was here proclaimed emperor by his legions: at the same time Lutetia was renamed after its inhabitants, shortened to Paris.

Sainte Geneviève – In 451 Attila crossed the Rhine with 700 000 men; as he reached Laon the Parisians began to flee. Geneviève, a young girl from Nanterre who had dedicated her life to God, calmed them with the assurance that the town would be saved by heavenly intervention; the Huns approached, hesitated and turned away to advance on Orléans. Parisians adopted the girl as their protector and patron.

Ten years later when the island was besieged by the Franks and suffered famine, Geneviève escaped the enemy watch, loaded boats with victuals in Champagne and returned undetected as if by miracle. She died in 512 and was buried at King Clovis' side *(see* LATIN QUARTER – Lycée Henri IV*)*.

The Count of Paris becomes King – In 885, for the fifth time in 40 years, the Normans sailed up the Seine. The Cité – the name adopted in 506 when Clovis made it his capital – was confronted by 700 ships bearing 30 000 warriors bent on pillaging Burgundy. Assault and siege proving unsuccessful, the Normans beached their boats, mounted them on logs and rolled them up-river to Paris. Eudes, Count of Paris and the leader of the resistance, was thereupon elected king.

Cathedral and Parliament – During the Middle Ages the population grew, spilling onto both banks of the river. But while the episcopal see remained under Sens (Paris did not have its own archbishop until 1622), the number of schools around the cathedral proliferated, many beconing famous throughout Europe. Among the teachers were Alexander of Paris, creator of the 12-footed *alexandrine* line in poetry. At the beginning of the 12C, the philosopher Abelard, whose moving romance with Héloïse, the niece of the canon Fulbert, began in the cloister of Notre-Dame. Chapels and convents multiplied on the island: St-Denis-du-Pas (where St Denis' martyrdom is said to have begun), St-Pierre-aux-Bœufs (whose porch is now part of St-Séverin), St-Aignan, St-Jean-le-Rond (where unwanted children were abandoned). By the close of the 13C, there were at least 22 belltowers!

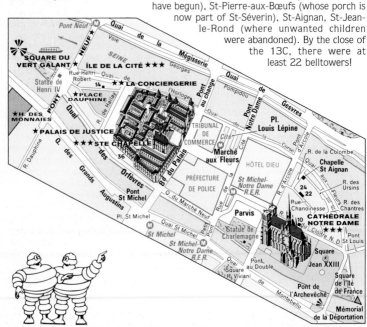

The Cité, the seat of parliament, the highest judiciary in the kingdom was, inevitably, involved in revolutions and uprisings such as that attempted in the 14C by Étienne Marcel (see les QUAIS – Hôtel de Ville) and the Fronde in the 17C. During the Terror of 1793-94 the Conciergerie prisons were crowded, while next door, the Revolutionary Tribunal continued to sit in the Law Courts, endlessly pronouncing merciless sentences.

Transformation – Under Louis-Philippe and to an even greater extent, under Napoleon III, the entire centre of the island was demolished: 25 000 people were evacuated. Enormous administrative buildings were erected: the Hôtel-Dieu, barracks (now the police prefecture), the commercial courts; the Law Courts were doubled in size; the Place du Parvis before the cathedral was quadrupled in size; the boulevard du Palais was built 10 times wider than before.

August 1944 – The Paris police barricaded themselves in the prefecture and hoisted the tricolour. For three days they held the Germans at bay until relieved by the arrival of the French Army Division under General Leclerc.

★★★NOTRE-DAME ⊙ 6 parvis Notre-Dame

The Cathedral of Our Lady, which can be seen in all its radiant glory from the parvis or square Viviani, stands in a superb setting; it has a perfection all its own, with balanced proportions and a façade in which solid and void, horizontal and vertical elements combine in total harmony. It is a magnificent religious edifice and one of the supreme masterpieces of French art.

Construction – For 2 000 years prayers have been offered from this spot: a Gallo-Roman temple, a Christian basilica, a Romanesque church preceded the present sanctuary founded by Bishop Maurice of Sully. A man of humble origin, he had become a canon at the cathedral and supervisor of the diocese by 1159 and, shortly afterwards, undertook to provide the capital with a worthy cathedral to rival the basilica built at St-Denis by Abbot Suger.
Construction began in 1163, during the reign of Louis VII. To the resources of the church and royal gifts, were added the toil and skill of the common people: stone-masons, carpenters, ironsmiths, sculptors, glaziers, moved with religious fervour, worked with ardour under Jean of Chelles and Pierre of Montreuil, architect of the Sainte-Chapelle. By about 1345 the building was complete – the original plans had not been modified in any way.

Ceremonial Occasions – Long before it was completed, Notre-Dame had become the setting for major religious and political ceremonies: St Louis entrusted it with the Crown of Thorns in 1239 pending the completion of the Sainte-Chapelle; in 1302 Philip the Fair formally opened the first States General; celebrations, thanksgivings, state funerals have followed each other down the centuries; high points in French history have been reached such as the coronation of young Henry VI of England (1430), the re-trial of Joan of Arc (1455), the crowning of Mary Stuart as Queen of France following her marriage to François II; the unusual marriage ceremony of Marguerite of Valois alone in the chancel to the Huguenot, Henri of Navarre, by the door (1572), and of Henrietta Maria by proxy to Charles I of England (1625) – although he came later to agree that "Paris is well worth a mass" and attended subsequent ceremonies inside the cathedral!
It has also been subjected to radical maltreatment: the destruction of the rood-screen by Mansart and Robert de Cotte (1699), the replacement of the medieval stained glass by plain glass (18C), the vandalism of the main doorway by Soufflot to make way for an ever more grandiose processional dais (1771)... At the Revolution, the galleries of statues were decapitated, the building became a Temple of Reason and then of the Supreme Being. All but the great bell were melted down whilst the church interior was used to store forage and food.
On 2 December 1804 the church, decked with hangings and ornaments to mask its dilapidation, received Pope Pius VII for the coronation of the Emperor (see the picture by David in the Louvre). After the anointing, however, Napoleon seized the crown from the pontiff and crowned first himself and then Josephine.

Restoration – As a result of Victor Hugo's novel The Hunchback of Notre-Dame (1831) and a general popular feeling roused by the Romantic Movement, the July Monarchy ordered in 1841 that the cathedral be restored. Entrusted to **Viollet-le-Duc** and Lassus, the 'restoration' program lasted 23 years: statuary and glass checked, extensions and appendages removed, the roof and upper sections repaired, doors and chancel restored, a flèche added and sacristy erected.

Today as before – Notre-Dame having emerged virtually unscathed from the Commune of 1871 and the Liberation of 1944, continues to participate in major historical events, happy or sad: the magnificent Te Deum of 26 August 1944 during which an assassination attempt was made on General de Gaulle, the moving Requiem Mass in his honour on 12 November 1970 and the special memorial service, arranged by the former President, François Mitterrand celebrated on 11 January 1996.

Place du Parvis – A bronze plaque in the centre of the square marks the zero point from which all road distances in France are measured.

The square was quadrupled in size as cramped surrounding buildings were cleared away by Haussmann in the 19C; it is now dominated by the grandiose façade of Notre-Dame. In the Middle Ages, when **mystery plays** were enacted before churches and cathedrals, the porch was often used to represent the door to paradise (*paradis*) – hence the evolution of the name *parvis*.

★**Crypte Archéologique** ⊙ – Excavations beneath the *parvis* have revealed traces of buildings and monuments spanning the 3C to 19C. Of particular interest are two Gallo-Roman rooms heated by hypocaust *(to the left on entering)*, fragments of the Late Roman Empire rampart, medieval cellars, and the foundations of a documented orphanage designed by Boffrand.

The west front

The overall design is majestic and perfectly balanced despite being asymmetrical; the central doorway is the largest of the three, the left gabled. This medieval conceit was to avoid monotony in design and intended to symbolise the lack of perfect order on earth.

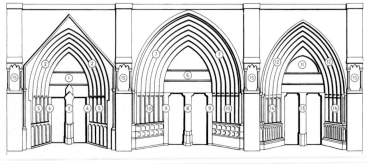

Portal de la Virgin   Portal of the Last Judgement   Portal to St Anne

The portals – In the Middle Ages the portals would have looked completely different: polychrome statues would have stood out against a gold background. Designed to be read like a Bible in stone, the scriptures and the legends of the saints are graphically retold for an illiterate congregation. Scenes tend to be read upwards, from an earthly level towards Heaven.

The six wooden door-panels have splendid wrought-iron strap-hinges. Legend has it that the side doors were worked by Satan himself to whom the locksmith, Biscornet, had forfeited his soul; the central door hinges, however, are 19C replacements as it would have been impossible for the Devil to work on those past which the Host was processed.

Portal of the Virgin *(left)* – This fine tympanum (**1**) has served as prototype to stone-masons throughout the Middle Ages. It shows the *Ark of the Covenant* flanked by three prophets who spoke of the glorious destiny of the Mother of God and three Kings from whom she is descended; above, a moving depiction of the *Death of the Virgin* with Christ and the Apostles; at the apex, the *Coronation of the Virgin* with Christ handing a sceptre to his mother who is crowned by an angel.

Consecutive bands (**2**) of bead moulding, leaves, flowers and fruit run between the ranks of angels, patriarchs, kings and prophets at the celestial court. The trumeau (stone mullion) *Virgin and Child* (**3**) is modern. Small low-relief carving representing the labours of the months and the signs of the Zodiac fill the sections on either side of the doorway (**4**).

The statues in the embrasures (**5**), were added by Viollet-le-Duc and include St Denis attended by two angels, John the Baptist and St Stephen.

Portal of the Last Judgement *(central)* – The main theme of this sculptural composition is the struggle of Good over Evil. It is far removed from its original condition: the tympanum (**6**) was breached by Soufflot in 1771 and Viollet-le-Duc has substantially restored the two lower lintels.

Above a depiction of the *Resurrection* is the *Weighing of the Souls*, in which the good are led up to Heaven by angels, the damned by demons to Hell; at the apex, a seated *Christ in Majesty* is flanked by the kneeling Virgin and St John, interceding for the lost souls.

The six archivolts (**7**) represent the celestial court. At the lowest level, Abraham receives the beautiful righteous (*left*) and demonic condemned (*right*) symbolising Heaven and Hell separated by the Word of God. The trumeau figure of Christ (**8**) is 19C, the original having been removed by Soufflot. The columnar figures of the Wise and Foolish Virgins, differentiated by open (*left*) and closed (*right*) doors to Paradise (**9**), are modern. In the embrasures (**10**), Viollet-le-Duc's Apostles stand over medallions representing the Virtues (*upper tier*) and Vices (*lower tier*).

Portal to St Anne (*south*) – The cathedral's oldest statues fill the two upper levels of the tympanum (**11**); *c*1165, they pre-date the building by some 60 years and were evidently intended for a narrower door. A rather formal *Virgin in Majesty with the Infant Christ* draws on Romanesque prototypes; she is attended by two angels and the cathedral patrons: Bishop Maurice of Sully (*standing, left*) and Louis VII (*kneeling, right*). The 12C lintel shows scenes from the Life of the Virgin, and below, from her parents, Sts Anne and Joachim (13C).

The ranks of angels, kings and patriarchs at the celestial court decorate the four tympanum archivolts (**12**). The central pier (**13**) carries a 19C slender, elongated figure of St Marcellus, the 5C Bishop of Paris who is meant to have delivered the capital from a dragon. Kings, queens and saints (**14**) frame the doorway.

Abutting the piers between portals are additional 19C statues (**15**) *(from left to right)* of St Stephen, the Church, the Synagogue (blindfolded) and St Denis.

Gallery of Kings (*above the portals*) – The 28 Kings of Judea and Israel represent the Tree of Jesse, Christ's forebears. The original figures were destroyed in 1793 by the Commune who took them for the Kings of France (*see* LATIN QUARTER – Musée Cluny); these were replaced by Viollet-le-Duc.

Notre-Dame – Interior

G. Boullay/MICHELIN

Rose window – The central great rose nearly 10m – 30ft across, is so perfectly designed that its elements have not moved in over seven centuries. From outside, it provides the standing statue of the Virgin and Child, flanked by two angels with a vast halo, the aura of Heaven.

At the same level, in the lateral bays, stand the figures of Adam (*left*) and Eve (*right*), against stone masonry separating the window lights. Together, the group (restored by Viollet-le-Duc) portrays Redemption after the Fall from Grace.

Great gallery – A superb row of delicate arches articulate the transitional tier between the main building and the base of the towers, between solid masonry and open sky. At the corners of each buttress, Viollet-le-Duc placed fantastic birds, monsters and demons, which although large, are scarcely visible at ground level, obscured by the projecting balustrade.

Towers – The twin towers soar to a height of 69m – 226ft, pierced by slender 16m – 50ft lancets. Emmanuel, the great bell in the south tower (*right*) weighs 13 tons, its clapper nearly 500kg – 9 3/4cwts. The perfect pitch of its toll (F sharp) is said to be due to the gold and silver jewels cast into the molten bronze by *Parisiennes* when the bell was restruck in the 17C.

Ascent ⊘ – Steep steps climb to a platform in the south tower providing a splendid **view★★★** of the spire and flying buttresses; the Cité and Paris beyond. Note the famous chimeras (carved wild beasts) and great bell above the great gallery. In the chapel, a museum-video retells the story of Notre-Dame *(15 min)*. This is where Quasimodo lived: the hunchback who was beguiled by the charms of Esmeralda, the gipsy dancer he kidnapped from the Cour des Miracles.

Interior

Transitional Gothic – The ordered elevation and precise overall design of the internal space is as impressive today as it must have been in the 13C. The sheer size (130m – 427ft long x 48m – 158ft wide) and soaring height (35m – 115ft) mark a turning point in the development of Gothic architecture and building techniques on a grand scale (accommodating a congregation of up to 6 500 souls). Besides the elevation, the floor plan also breaks new ground: the nave is given double aisles and the chancel a double ambulatory, separated in the middle by transepts that project only slightly from the outer aisles, thereby producing a homogenous, unified space.

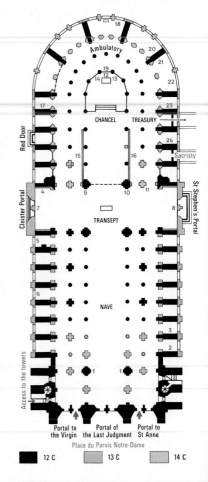

The windows – In the 13C the clerestory windows were enlarged to allow extra light to permeate the chapels across the aisles. In so doing, not only was the wall mass reduced and lightened, the gallery was lowered; the weight and thrust of the vault therefore had to be diffused across the aisles and down to solid masonry at gallery level: the problem was ingeniously resolved with the invention of the flying buttress. A section of the 12C elevation can still be seen at the transept crossing (small rose and tall lancet windows).

The medieval stained glass was replaced by clear glass inscribed with *fleur-de-lis* in the 18C and by grisaille glass in the 19C. The modern glass by Le Chevalier, installed in 1965, returned to medieval manufacturing processes and colours.

Note the massive piers (1) supporting the towers measuring 5m – 16ft across and the organ (restored in 1992) which boasts the largest number of pipes of any organ in France, accommodating up to three players at a time *(concerts: Sundays at 5.45pm)*.

Chapels – Notre-Dame is edged with a continuous ring of 37 chapels built between the buttresses in the 13C in response to demand from an increasing number of guilds and noble families; even the transepts were extended in order to maintain proportions.

In keeping with a tradition renewed in 1949, the Goldsmith's Guild of Paris endow the cathedral with a work of art annually in May. Among the most beautiful are '*mays*' by Le Brun (**2**, **3**) and Le Sueur (**4**).

On the left are the tombstones of a 15C canon (**5**), and of Cardinal Amette (**6**).

Transept – The **windows**, remarkable for their sheer size and weight, are testimony to the technical skill of the medieval masons.

The north rose (**7**) which has survived almost intact since the 13C, depicts Old Testament figures around the Virgin; in the restored south rose (**8**) Christ is surrounded by saints and angels.

At the entrance to the chancel, a statue of St Denis (**9**) by Nicolas Coustou complements the beautiful 14C **Virgin and Child** (**10**) – Our Lady of Paris, previously in the St-Aignan chapel *(see below)*. On the southwest pier is a plaque commemorating the deaths of the million or so British citizens lost in the First World War – many of whom are buried in French soil.

The nearby inscription in the pavement recalls the conversion of the 20C poet Paul Claudel (**11**).

Chancel – In front of the high altar lies Geoffrey Plantagenet, son of Henry II of England (*d* 1186). Louis XIII, childless after 23 years of marriage, dedicated France to the Virgin (1638) – a vow materialised in the redecoration of the chancel by Robert de Cotte (1708-1725). Seventy-eight original stalls remain from the embellishment, as do a *pietà* by Guillaume Coustou (**12**) with a base by Girardon, Louis XIII (**13**) by Coustou and Louis XIV (**14**) by Coysevox. It was at this time that the stone chancel screen was removed; the only remarkable 14C **low-relief** scenes to survive pertain to the Life of Christ (**15**) and His Apparitions (**16**). These were restored by Viollet-le-Duc.

Tombstones for the Bishops of Paris who are buried in the crypt, line the ambulatory (**17-24**).

Treasury ☉ – The sacristy built by Viollet-le-Duc contains manuscripts, ornaments and church plate from the 19C. The Crown of Thorns, the Holy Nail and a fragment of the True Cross are displayed on Fridays during Lent and on Good Friday in the main area of the cathedral.

Exterior

North side – A canons' cloister, now destroyed, flanked the north side giving its name to the street that replaced it.

The magnificent **Cloister Portal** was built by Jean of Chelles (*c*1250), who applied experience gained from building the Sainte-Chapelle (completed 1248) to maximise the amount of light permeating the interior. The large intricate rose perfectly integrates with the clerestory to form an unprecedentedly tall opening (18m– 58ft high), slightly larger in diameter (13m – 43ft).

Below the many-gabled carved doorway is markedly more ornate than the doors of the west front, installed 30 years before. The three-tiered tympanum illustrates events from the *Life of the Virgin* and above, from the story of Théophile selling his soul to the Devil, the subject of a popular mystery play at the time.

The fine *trumeau* figure of the **Virgin** lost its Christ Child at the Restoration.

The **Cathedral Museum** ☉ opposite, catalogues the long sequence of restoration work and the major moments in the Cathedral's history since the 17C. Pottery uncovered from under the parvis is also displayed.

The **Red Door**, built by Pierre of Montreuil was reserved for exclusive use by members of the cathedral chapter. Its tympanum illustrates the Coronation of the Virgin attended by King Louis and his Queen, Margaret of Provence; the archivolts carry scenes from the Life of St Marcel.

Seven 14C **low-reliefs** inlaid into the foundations of the chancel chapels depict the Death and Assumption of the Virgin.

South side – Beyond the 19C sacristy is the magnificent **St Stephen's** doorway, similar to the cloister door but richer in sculpture. Initiated by Jean of Chelles (1258), and completed by Pierre of Montreuil, it has a remarkable tympanum illustrating the life and stoning of St Stephen, to whom the former church that pre-dated the cathedral had been dedicated. St Stephen, St Marcel and most of the lateral figures date from the 19C.

At the base of the buttresses, eight small 13C low reliefs depict street and university scenes.

Splendid vistas of Notre-Dame and the Seine can be enjoyed from the small, verdant, south-facing John XXIII Square which is always very crowded.

Square Jean XXIII – Until the beginning of the 19C, the area between Notre-Dame and the tip of the island was crowded with houses, chapels and the Archbishop's Palace, built after Paris had been made an episcopal see in 1622, in the reign of Louis XIII (1610-1643). These were severely damaged in a riot and later razed to the ground (1831). The square opened as a formal garden with a neo-Gothic fountain in 1844.

From here can be seen a 13C section of roof which retains the original timberwork, the 90m – 295ft *flèche* reconstructed by Viollet-le-Duc who included himself among the decorative copper figures of Evangelists and Apostles!

Square de l'Ile-de-France – Napoleon III built the Cité's municipal morgue on the upstream tip of the island, attracting until 1910 those with a morbid fascination.

Mémorial de la Déportation ⊙ – A modern crypt accommodates a metal sculpture by Desserprit, funerary urns and the tomb of the Unknown Deportee from Struthof, to commemorate the suffering and loss of so much life at the Nazi camps.

The Ancien Cloître Quarter – The area extending north of Notre-Dame to the Seine belonged to the cathedral chapter. Enclosed in a wall with four gates, it was populated by the cathedral canons who each lodged their own students. Although considerably restored, the quarter is the only reminder of what the Cité looked like in the 11C and 12C when students such as Abelard, St Bonaventure and St Dominic built up the reputation of the cathedral school which was later to merge with the Sorbonne *(see* LATIN QUARTER*)*.

Rue Chanoinesse, the main thoroughfare of the former cloister, is now blighted by an annexe of the police headquarters. Nos **24** and **22** are the last two medieval canons' houses; note the stone posts in the courtyard. In **rue de la Colombe** traces of the Lutetian Gallo-Roman wall of Lutetia remain; note the curious tavern at the top of some steps. In laying rue d'Arcole, the chapel Ste-Marie was razed, where de-flowered brides could be married, sealing their vows with a ring made of straw. The **rue des Ursins** is level with the old banks of the Seine and Port St-Landry, Paris' first dock until the 12C when facilities on the Hôtel de Ville foreshore were established. At the end of the narrow street stand the last vestiges of the medieval chapel, St-Aignan, where priests celebrated mass secretly during the Revolution. At the picturesque corner with **rue des Chantres** stands a medieval mansion past which there is a fine view of Notre-Dame's skyline.

The quai aux Fleurs affords a vast panorama of St-Gervais and of the tip of the Ile St-Louis.

★★★SAINTE-CHAPELLE ⊙ *4 boulevard du Palais*

A sacred shrine – The chapel is a Gothic marvel – the deep glow of its windows one of the great joys of a visit to Paris.

Baudouin, a French nobleman who had been on the fourth Crusade before becoming Emperor of Constantinople, was forced to pledge the Crown of Thorns against a loan of money from the Venetians. Unable to meet his debts, it was left to **St Louis** (Louis IX) to redeem the payment and retrieve the Crown in 1239. In acquiring additional relics and the design of a shrine to contain them, he spent two and a half times the subsequent cost of building the Sainte-Chapelle. Only 80 years separate this exquisite jewel of Radiating Gothic from the Cathedral of Notre-Dame.

This exceptional building erected in no more than 33 months, at the behest of King Louis IX within the precincts of his private palace is attributed to **Pierre of Montreuil** (known also as Pierre of Montereau); it was consecrated in 1248. Consisting of two superimposed chambers, it conforms with private shrines elsewhere (Laon, Meaux): the upper level being used by the sovereign and his court, the lower by his household.

Originally the chapel would have stood in a courtyard, linked to St Louis' apartments by a small gallery. When the palace was remodelled in the 18C, a wing from the May Courtyard was extended up to the chapel.

Mass, when entrusted to a resident body of 12 canons and 14 chaplains, was elaborate. During the Revolution the reliquary shrine was melted down; some of the relics were saved and are now in Notre-Dame; the 17C organ played by the Couperins is now at St-Germain-l'Auxerrois *(see* les QUAIS*)*. Between 1802 and 1837 the building was used to archive judiciary papers that were stacked high against the lancet windows; restoration, when it came, was undertaken by Duban and Lassus (1841-1867).

Exterior – The impact made by the Sainte-Chapelle was immediate. Its innovative great windows (15m – 50ft high) encroached upon the wall space making it seem insubstantial, built of glass rather than masonry; its vault appeared precariously supported by the slenderest piers, not reinforced with great flying buttresses, but rather anchored in place by a sculpted gable and balustrade. This remarkably delicate feat of balance and counter-balance was so perfectly engineered that no crack has appeared in seven centuries. The *flèche* soars to 75m – 246ft. Its lead-covered wooden roof, destroyed by fire and rebuilt three times, dates from 1854. The lead angel perched on the apse roof once revolved by clockwork to show the Cross it bears to all points of the compass. Level with the fourth bay is an extension made by Louis XI to accommodate a chapel (*ground level*) and an oratory (*above*).

Interior – Access is through the **lower chapel** intended for the palace retainers. Forty columns, garishly decorated in the 19C, carry the central vault (only 7m – 23ft high and 17m – 56ft wide), contained by the external buttresses. The floor is paved with tombstones.

A spiral staircase to the left leads to the **upper chapel**, a great bejewelled glass-house lit by the faintest ray of sunlight. The **stained glass** is the oldest to survive in Paris. Of the 1 134 scenes represented over a glazed area of 618m^2 – 6 672sq ft, 720 are original. The king summoned the best master-craftsmen from work recently completed at Chartres (1240) hence their similar treatments: roundel-scenes, brilliant use of colour eclipsing simplicity of composition. The principal theme is the celebration of the Passion, as foretold by the Prophets and John the Baptist. The design of the main rose is only known from an illumination in the *Très Riches Heures du Duc de Berry* (1413-1416). The existing *Flamboyant* rose was commissioned by Charles VII and illustrates *St John's vision of the Apocalypse*.

The restorations undertaken in the mid-19C are hard to detect.

The windows should be read from left to right and from bottom to top, with the exception of nos **6, 7, 9** and **11** which read lancet by lancet.

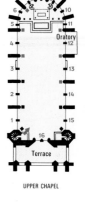

UPPER CHAPEL

1) Genesis – Adam and Eve – Noah – Jacob.

2) Exodus – Moses and Mount Sinai. 3) Exodus – The Law of Moses.

4) Deuteronomy – Joshua – Ruth and Boaz.

5) Judges – Gideon – Samson. 6) Isaiah – The Tree of Jesse.

7) St John the Evangelist – Life of the Virgin – The Childhood of Christ.

8) Christ's Passion. 9) John the Baptist – Daniel. 10) Ezekiel.

11) Jeremiah – Tobias. 12) Judith – Job. 13) Esther.

14) Kings: Samuel, David, Solomon.

15) St Helena and the True Cross – St Louis and the relics of the Passion.

16) 15C Flamboyant rose window: the Apocalypse.

The chamber is encircled by blind arcading, its capitals delicately carved with stylised vegetation; attached to each shaft is a figure of an apostle holding one of the Church's 12 crosses of consecration – the six original ones *(red on the plan)* are most expressive (others are in the Musée Cluny – *see* LATIN QUARTER). The painting is modern. Two deep recesses in the third bay were reserved for the king and his family. In the next bay, on the right, is the door to the oratory added by Louis XI: a grille enabled him to follow the service unnoticed.

The reliquary shrine would have stood at the centre of the apse on a raised platform surmounted by a wooden baldaquin. Of the two twisting staircases enclosed in the open-work turrets, the left one is original occasionally used by King Louis IX who relished opening the shrine's doors encrusted with stones, to show off his prized relics. The porch onto the terrace dates from the 19C.

★**Palais de Justice** ⊙ – To balance the power of the Church, the Ile de la Cité also accommodated the Law Courts – the pre-eminent seat of the civil and judicial authorities.

King's Palace – The stone buildings erected by the Roman governors for their administrative and military headquarters were requisitioned first by the Merovingian kings (where Clovis died) then by the early Capetian kings who fortified the palace with a keep and built a chapel in the precincts.

In the 13C Louis IX lived in the Upper Chamber (today the First Civil Court), dispensed justice in the courtyard and built the Sainte-Chapelle; Philip the Fair constructed the Conciergerie, a sumptuous palace "more beautiful than anyone in France had ever seen". The Hall of the Men-at-Arms was the largest ever built in Europe. The former Chapelle St-Michel which gave its name to the bridge and boulevard on the left bank, was razed to the ground in the 18C.

On 22 February 1358, the mob under Étienne Marcel *(see* les QUAIS – Hôtel de Ville*)* entered the apartments of the Dauphin, the future Charles V, and Regent whilst his father John the Good was being held in England. When the troubles had subsided, Charles V moved out of the palace where he had been compelled to witness the bloody slaughter of his counsellors, preferring to live at the Louvre, the Hôtel St-Paul or at Vincennes outside Paris. In the palace, he installed his Parliament.

It is interesting to note that Charles VII, Henri IV and Louis XIV all survived uprisings in Paris by fleeing the city; Louis XVI, Charles X and Louis-Philippe however, refusing to abandon the palace, all lost their thrones.

Judicial Palace – Parliament was the kingdom's supreme court of justice. Originally its members were nominated by the king, that is until 1522 when François I sold the rights for money on condition that the position become hereditary; thus the highest dignitaries in the land (the chancellor, peers of the realm, royal princes) secured their position by right or privilege.

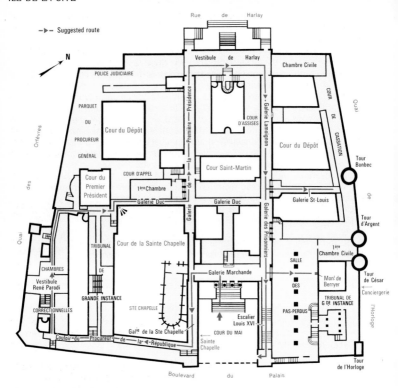

In disputes between the officers of state and the king, matters were settled by courts presided over by the monarch, with offenders being sometimes sentenced to exile or imprisonment. Judges, barristers, clerks and a multitude of others populated the lesser courts in the palace. Bureaucracy proliferated.

Fires were frequent damaging the Grande Salle (1618), Sainte-Chapelle spire (1630), the Cour des Comptes (*Debtors' Court*) (1737), the Gallerie Marchande (1776). In 1788 Parliament demanded the convocation of the States General – not a good idea, because the General Assembly announced its suppression and the Convention sent the members to the guillotine.

The Law Courts – The Revolution overturned the judicial system. New courts were installed in the old buildings which took the name of Palais de Justice. Restoration lasted from 1840 to 1914, interrupted only by the Commune fire; the building was given its present façade overlooking place Dauphine and its extension along the quai des Orfèvres.

Cour du Mai – The Louis XVI wrought-iron grille is especially fine. The name 'cour du Mai' is derived from a very old custom by which the clerks of the court – an important corporation – planted in the courtyard a tree grown from one of the Royal forests each year on 1 May. A similar practice prevailed in England often in honour of a particular person, often festooned in (yellow) ribbons.

The imposing buildings round the courtyard were erected after the fire of 1776. A small yard to the right abuts on the old Conciergerie wicket gate *(see diagram under Conciergerie)* through which the victims of the Terror passed on their way in the tumbrils beneath the watchful eyes of the curious and the *tricoteuses* – the women knitting – perched upon the steps.

From the Galerie Marchande to the Vestibule de Harlay – The Galerie Marchande was once the most animated part of the building, bustling with plaintiffs, lawyers, clerks, court officials, souvenir peddlers and hangers-on. Follow left past the Sainte-Chapelle and then right (along the couloir du Procureur de la République). Through the busy Chambres Correctionnelles (*petty court rooms*). Turn right at the end into the Galerie Duc, taking in the open view★ of the Sainte-Chapelle from the corner. Turn left beyond the ornate Première chambre civile de la Cour d'appel (*Chamber of the Civil Court of Appeal*), into the galerie de la Première Présidence and leave on the left the **Police Judiciaire** (CID) known to all admirers of Inspector Maigret, the detective-superintendent created by Georges Simenon in his famous *Collection Maigret* novels. From the vast and empty Vestibule du Harlay, steps lead to the Cour d'assises (*Assize Court – open only when in session*) on the right. At the end is the Cour de cassation (*Chamber of the Court of Cassation – rarely open*) decorated with frescoes and tapestries.

From the Vestibule de Harlay to the cour du Mai – Turn right along the Galerie Lamoignon (glance down the Galerie St-Louis off to the left) and beyond into the Galerie des Prisonniers (*Prisoners' Gallery*).

Enter the **Salle des Pas-Perdus** (Lobby), formerly the Gothic Grand'Salle of Philip the Fair, twice destroyed, and reconstructed most recently after the Commune of 1871. The two Classical aisles, crowded with plaintiffs, barristers in their gowns (but without the distinctive wig of their British counterparts), clerks and officials, are now the busiest place in the building – Balzac called it "the cathedral of chicanery".

Notice the monument to the 19C barrister, Berryer, on the right, with the tortoise – maligning the delays in the law. At the end on the left is the former apartment of Louis IX, used as Parliamentary Grand Chamber when Louis XII had it decorated with a fine ceiling, and then by the Revolutionary Tribunal under Fouquier-Tinville (1793-94). It is now the **First Civil Court**.

Walk down the grand Louis XVI staircase built by the architect Jacques Antoine, noting the old shop signs.

★★La Conciergerie ⓥ – *1 quai de l'Horloge*. The Conciergerie includes three superb Gothic halls built by Philip the Fair in the 14C, revolutionary prisons and mementoes of its tragic history.

A noble keeper – The name *Conciergerie* was given to a section of the old palace precinct controlled by a person of high degree: the *concierge* or keeper of the king's mansion – a remunerative office involving the licensing of the many shops within the palace walls.

It served as a prison from the 14C; among pre-Revolutionary prisoners were several who had made successful or unsuccessful attempts on successive kings' lives: Montgomery on Henri II; Ravaillac on Henri IV...

The guillotine's antechamber – At the Revolution as many as 1 200 men and women were held at one time in the Conciergerie; during the Terror the building became the antechamber to the Tribunal, which in nine cases out of ten meant the guillotine.

Among those incarcerated here were Queen Marie-Antoinette; Madame Elisabeth, sister to Louis XVI; Charlotte Corday who stabbed Marat; Madame du Barry, the favourite of Louis XV; the poet André Chénier; Philippe-Égalité; the chemist Lavoisier; the 22 Girondins condemned by Danton who, with 15 of his companions, was in turn condemned by Robespierre, who was himself condemned with 20 of his followers by the Thermidor Convention; the public prosecutor Fouquier-Tinville; the judges of the Revolutionary Tribunal.

In all nearly 2 600 prisoners left the Conciergerie between January 1793 and July 1794 for the guillotine under the beady gaze of the "*tricoteuses*" which was erected successively on the place du Carrousel in front of the Louvre, place de la Concorde, place de la Bastille, place de la Nation (where 1 306 heads rolled in 40 days), and lastly place de la Concorde.

La Conciergerie

★Exterior – The best **view** is from Mégisserie Quay on the right bank, with its four towers reflected in the Seine which originally flowed right up to their base. This is the oldest part of the palace built by the Capetian kings. The ground level was raised appreciably at the end of the 16C when quai de l'Horloge was built.

The oldest tower is the crenellated one on the right, la Tour Bonbec which got its name from the babblers being interrogated and tortured within.

The twin towers in the centre of the 19C neo-Gothic façade flanked the palace entrance across the bridge of Charles the Bald. The Tour d'Argent on the right contained the royal treasure; the one on the left, the Tour César, had apartments used during the Terror by the Public Prosecutor, Fouquier-Tinville.

The square **Tour de l'Horloge** has since 1370 housed the first public clock to be installed in Paris, and which has never ceased to mark time. The silver bell, having chimed golden hours for the monarchy, was melted down in 1793. The carvings on the face although much restored, are by Germain Pilon (16C).

★Interior – *Entrance at 1 quai de l'horloge, through the vaulted archway, across the courtyard and down right, into the Guardroom.*

Salle des Gardes – Stout pillars with interesting capitals support the Gothic vaulting in this dark room which now lies some 7m – 23ft below the level of the 16C quay. The first two piers bear the water mark reached by the Seine in 1910.

★★Salle des Gens d'Armes – This magnificent four-aisled Gothic hall covers an area of 1 800m² – 19 375sq ft, on a par with those of the Mont-St-Michel and the Palais des Papes in Avignon.

(Hall of the Men-at-Arms). Buildings erected in the May Courtyard in the 18C unfortunately block out much of the light.

Above used to be the palace's Great Hall and royal apartments. Additional support-piers were added in the 19C by Viollet-le-Duc.

Cuisines – The four huge fireplaces in each corner of the old kitchens fulfilled a specific function: cooking enough meat, spit-roasted or boiled in cauldrons, to feed between 2 000 and 3 000 mouths, including the royal family. The canopies are supported by unusual buttresses.

Prison – The rue de Paris leads into the galerie des Prisonniers, a corridor serving as the main axis of the prison, where penniless prisoners slept on the bare ground while the rich paid for their own cell and better food. It was the busiest part of the building, with a constant flow of prisoners arriving and departing, visitors, lawyers, police and

THE CONCIERGERIE DURING THE TERROR

Existing areas — Areas now disappeared

• • • Route to the scaffold

gaolers. Flanked by police officers, prisoners were ushered from the Grande Chambre du Parlement on the first floor down a spiral staircase hidden in the Bonbec Tower, through the door (now walled up) at the far end of the Gallery. This room gave onto the council room which on one side served as antechamber (parloir) to the men's prison yard (Préau des Hommes) and on the other opened onto a staircase (1) up to the Tribunal. The prisoners were most likely herded into the room now used as the kitchens for the Law Courts restaurant, from where, one by one, they passed into an adjoining room. There, sat on a stool, their last toilet was performed by the executioner's assistants; hands were firmly tied behind the back, collars were cut away and hair was cut short. Batched up, the condemned crossed through the wicket gate *(guichet)* past the clerk of the court (register office – *greffe*) into the May Courtyard – and out to the tumbrils.

The history of the prison and important political prisoners is presented on the first floor. These include the Scots captain of the guard Montgomery who delivered a fatal blow to Henri II's eye during a tourney; Châtel who wounded Henri IV; Ravaillac who killed him; Louvel the assassin of the Duc de Berry and Robespierre.

Chapelle des Girondins – *Ground floor*. The chapel was transformed into a collective prison where prisoners heard mass through the grille on the upper storey. Twenty-two Girondins were held there together in 1793, who it is said, condemned at midnight whiled away the early hours by singing and drinking; one man who managed to commit suicide during his hearing accompanied his fellows to the guillotine.

The chapel was re-consecrated under the Restoration.

From here, one can visit the cell occupied by Marie-Antoinette (2 August to 16 October 1793) and transformed into an expiatory chapel (2) in 1863.

Cour des Femmes – In the centre, as in earlier times, is a pathetic patch of grass and a lonely tree. During the day the women prisoners were allowed out of their cells around the courtyard. The arcaded ground floor and the first floor accommodated different kinds of criminal, additional sections were added in the 19C.

The corridor known as the 'Côté des Douzes' (3) was where prisoners of both sexes could talk through the bars, and from where daily the 12 inmates selected for the guillotine embarked on their final journey.

Back in the prison corridor a door on the right leads to a reconstruction of Marie-Antoinette's cell (4). The furniture consisted of a cot, a chair and a table. A screen separated the queen from watchmen, day and night.

Danton and Robespierre spent time in the adjacent cell, the latter just the one night before his execution.

Tribunal de Commerce – The Commercial Law Courts were built in 1865 on the site of the former St Bartholomew's, the parish church serving the royal household from the 9C to the Revolution. Cross the vestibule for the best view of the dome which rises majestically to a height of 42m – 141ft.

ADDITIONAL SIGHTS

Place Louis-Lépine – A colourful **flower market** animates the administrative offices of the Hôtel-Dieu, the police headquarters and the commercial court which have surrounded the square on three sides since the Second Empire. On Sundays a bird market replaces the flower stalls in the square named after the popular prefect, who instigated great changes in the force – policemen on bicycles, a road traffic system – and gave the Paris police their white truncheons and whistles.

Hôtel-Dieu – The Hôtel-Dieu hospice, founded in the 7C, originally comprised two buildings linked by the pont au Double (*see* les QUAIS), subsidised under the Regency by a tax called the 'poormen's right'. These buildings were replaced in 1880 by the present complex and square overlooked by the statues of Charlemagne and his two valiant knights Roalns and Olivier. The hall and inner court are of architectural interest.

Boulevard du Palais – The construction of this broad thoroughfare by Haussmann eliminated a sinister spot where individuals found guilty by the courts were publicly branded. A tablet further on marks the site of the former St-Michel chapel, a palatine chapel until the reign of St Louis (13C).

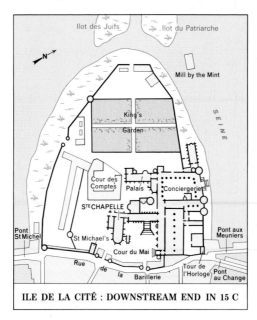

ILE DE LA CITÉ : DOWNSTREAM END IN 15 C

Pont St-Michel – The present bridge (1857) replaced one dating from 1378. Down along the quai du Marché Neuf lived the Huguenot **Theophraste Renaudot**, physician to Louis XIII and founder of the first French periodical, the *Gazette de France.*

Quai des Orfèvres – The properties along the river front were during the 17C and 18C the jewellers' quarter: Strass, inventor of the synthetic diamond, Boehmer and Bassenge who fashioned Marie-Antoinette's celebrated necklace, had their shops in the place Dauphine and along the quay. No **36** is today well known as the head-quarters of the CID (Police Judiciaire).

★**Place Dauphine** – For a long time the western tip of the island gave way to a muddy marshy area broken by the river currents.

In 1314, Philip the Fair had a stake erected on one of the mounds of ground for the Grand Master of the Order of Templars, **Jacques de Molay**, watching him burn from his palace window. The gardens (Jardin du Roi) which extended from the Concier-gerie into the river became the first botanical garden under Marie de' Medici.

At the end of the 16C Henri III decided to re-organise this untidy no man's land: the mud ditches were in-filled consolidating the patches of solid ground, a great earth bank was amassed to support the future Pont Neuf, and the south bank was raised by some 6m – 20ft. By about 1580 the new terrain was ready for the developers. In 1607 Henri IV ceded the land between the Conciergerie and the Pont-Neuf for a triangular square to be built, surrounded by a series of houses constructed of brick, white stone and slate to a uniform design. The square was named after the Dauphin, in honour of the future Louis XIII. Only a few façades such as no **14** retain their original features. The eastern side was razed in 1874 to make way for Viollet-le-Duc's monumental staircase.

In the 18C the square was the scene, each spring, of the Exhibition of Youth, when young painters presented their works in the open air.

★**Pont-Neuf** – The Pont-Neuf is the oldest of the Paris bridges, the first thoroughfare to benefit from pavements that separated the pedestrian from hurtling traffic, and the first highway in France to accommodate an effigy. The original equestrian statue of Henri IV was melted down at the Revolution in 1792 and replaced by the Restoration with the present figure, cast in bronze from the Vendôme Column's first statue *(see* OPÉRA*)* and another from the place des Victoires (*see* GRANDS-BOULEVARDS), by a staunch Bonapartist who is said to have included in the monu-ment a copy of Voltaire's epic poem *La Henriade* (on the League and Henri IV), a statuette of Napoleon and various written articles glorifying the Emperor!

Built in two halves between 1578 and 1604 to the designs of **Androuet Du Cerceau** the bridge is on a broken axis. The 12 rounded arches each have a keystone carved with humorous grotesques. In the olden days, it used to be crowded with stall-holders, tooth drawers, comic characters such as Tabarin and the Italian Pantaloon, Scarlatini, the all-time charlatan and a host of gawpers and pickpockets. Today, one can take in an open view up and down river unobstructed by houses.

Despite having been subjected to restoration at regular intervals, the structure has survived more or less intact – hence the expression "*se porter comme le Pont-Neuf*".

★**Square du Vert-Galant** – Down the steps behind the Henri IV statue, this serene stretch of green below the hum of traffic is at its natural ground level, before the land was built up by Henri III. From the tip is a fine **view**★★ of the Pont-Neuf, the Louvre and the Mint.

Its name derives from the nickname given to Henri IV, alluding to his reputation as an amorous gentleman despite his age!

ILE ST-LOUIS ★★

Michelin plan 11 – fold 32: K 15, K 16
Ⓜ *Pont Marie. Buses: 24, 63, 67, 86, 87, 89*

Calm quays and unpretentious Classical architecture make the Island of St-Louis one of the most attractive places in Paris. The most fulfilling way to explore the island is to wander over the pont St-Louis from Ile de la Cité and follow a circuit along the river and through its streets.

Ile aux Vaches and Ile Notre-Dame – Originally there were two islands where in the Middle Ages judicial duels were held known as the Judgements of God. Early in the reign of Louis XIII, the contractor Marie, together with two financiers, Poulle-tier and Le Regrattier, obtained permission from the king and chapter of Notre-Dame to conjoin the islets and construct two stone bridges for access. In return they were to be allowed to develop the land for resale in lots; work began in 1627 and lasted until 1664, giving the Ile St-Louis, like the nearby Marais, a homogenous Classical style of architecture. What makes the island unique is its atmosphere of old world charm and provincial calm. Bankers, lawyers and nobles accounted for the first residents, now replaced by writers, artists and those who love Old Paris.

On the island there is a 17C house at almost every step: nobly proportioned façades, most with tablets inscribed with historical or anecdotal information, wrought-iron balconies and tall brick chimneys. Behind massive panelled doors, studded with bosses and nails, lurk secluded courtyards where the stone sets and mounting blocks have not changed since the days of horse-drawn carriages.

Quai de Bourbon – From the picturesque tip of the island with chain linked stone posts and canted 18C medallions, there is an altogether delightful **view★** of the church of St-Gervais. A little further on are two magnificent town houses (nos **19** and **15**) which once belonged to parliamentarians – steep mansard roofs, mascarons, spacious stairwells encircled by wrought-iron balusters suggest their former splendour. At no **19** the sculptress Camille Claudel had her studio (ground floor) between 1899 and 1913, devastated by her break with Rodin.

Quai d'Anjou – At no 29, in a former wine-cellar, Ford Madox Ford established his journal *The Transatlantic Review* in collaboration with John Quinn, Ezra Pound and James Joyce. The Marquise de Lambert, hostess of a famous literary salon, lived at no **27** (*Hôtel de Nevers, see* PALAIS ROYAL).

Hôtel de Lauzun – *no 17 (Closed to the public).* The mansion, erected in 1657 by Le Vau for Gruyn, a supplier to the military who was imprisoned shortly afterwards for corruption. It belonged for only three years to the Duke of Lauzun, Saint-Simon's brother-in-law, who nevertheless left it his name. The poet, Théophile Gautier, lived there during the 1840s when he founded his 'Club des Hachischins', experimenting first with Baudelaire and later with Rilke, Sickert and Wagner. The house now belongs to the City of Paris.

Between 1846 and 1863 at no **9** lived the famous painter, sculptor, caricaturist and political satirist **Honoré Daumier**.

Pont de Sully – This bridge, which dates from 1876, rests on the tip of the Ile St-Louis as a pendant to the Pont-Neuf on the Ile de la Cité.
From the first section there is a good **view★** of Notre-Dame, the Cité and the Ile St-Louis. Upstream the river with its ports and quays is more industrial. On the right the quai St-Bernard is bordered by the Pierre and Marie Curie University (*see* JUSSIEU).

Square Barye – This small garden at the tip of the island is the last trace of the terraced estate of a house that once belonged to the financier, Bretonvilliers.
In the 17C there was a beach here for bathing popular with the Court and the aristocracy; even Henri IV and his son are said to have been happy to join in.

★Hôtel Lambert – *2 rue St-Louis-en-l'Ile.* The mansion of President Lambert de Thorigny, known as Lambert the Rich, was built in 1640 by Le Vau and decorated by Le Sueur (sketches now at the Louvre) and Le Brun.
No **16** quai de Béthune, previously known as Quai des Balcons from the number of overhanging balconies, was the house of the Duke of Richelieu (great-nephew of the cardinal).

★Église St-Louis-en-l'Ile Ⓞ – *19bis rue St-Louis-en-l'Ile.* The church is marked outside by an unusual iron clock and its original pierced spire. Designed by Le Vau, who lived on the island, building began in 1664, but was completed only in 1726. The ornate interior, in the Jesuit style, is highly decorated: woodwork, gilding and marble of the Grand Siècle (17C), statuettes and enamels. A plaque presented in 1926 in the north aisle bears the inscription: "In grateful memory of St Louis in whose honour the City of Saint Louis, Missouri, USA is named".

Hôtel de Chenizot – *51 rue St-Louis-en-l'Ile.* A very fine doorway surmounted by a faun mask and a majestic balcony mark this house which, in the middle of the 19C, accommodated the archbishop.

Adam-Mickiewicz Museum Ⓞ – *6 quai d'Orléans.* A 17C building houses the Polish Library. The small museum has portraits, mementoes, manuscripts, documents relating to the poet (1798-1855) and his family. Note the busts by Bourdelle and David d'Angers.
At no **12** a medallion marks the birthplace of the poet Arvers.
From this section of the quai d'Orléans there is a splendid **view★★** of the east end of Notre-Dame and the Left Bank.

Les INVALIDES★★★

This fine neighbourhood elbowing the Faubourg-St-Germain is endowed with elegant buildings that include the most outstanding single monumental group in Paris: the noble Dôme church that houses the tomb of Napoleon and the adjacent Army Museum endowed with its rich and spectacular collections, and the Rodin Museum.

From the **Pont Alexandre III** (see CHAMPS-ÉLYSÉES – Petit and Grand Palais), there is a superb overall view of Libéral Bruant's Classical style buildings and Mansart's crowning dome.

Barracks for 4 000 men – Before Louis XIV's reign, old soldiers, invalided out of the service, were, in theory, looked after in convent hospitals. In reality, most were reduced to beggary.

In 1670 the Sun King founded the Invalides on the edge of what was then the Grenelle Plain. Funds were raised in part by a levy on serving soldiers' pay over a period of five years. Construction of the vast edifice capable of providing quarters for 4 000 stretched over five years (1671-1676) to plans by **Libéral Bruant**. A dome, added to the original complex by Jules Hardouin-Mansart in 1706, lifted the overall effect from the strictly utilitarian to the monumental.

Pillage – On the morning of 14 July 1789 rebels advanced on the Invalides in search of arms. They crossed the moat, disarmed the sentries and entered the underground rifle stores. As further crowds blocked the stairs fierce fighting broke out in the semi-darkness. The mob finally made off with 28 000 rifles towards the Bastille.

Napoleon's return – In 1840, the Dôme accommodated Napoleon's tomb. After seven years of negotiation with the British Government, the French King, Louis-Philippe, was able to dispatch his son, the Prince of Joinville, to St Helena in the frigate, the *Belle Poule (model in the Maritime Museum)* to collect the Emperor's remains. On the prince's arrival on 8 October, the coffin was exhumed and opened for two minutes in the presence of the military generals Gourgaud and Bertrand, the 19C historian Las Cases and Napoleon's valet, Marchand. They found the Emperor's body dressed in his guardsman's uniform in perfect condition despite having been laid to rest 19 years before.

The coffin, after its long sea voyage, was disembarked at Le Havre and brought up the Seine to Paris where it was landed at Courbevoie. The funeral was held on 15 December 1840. A snowstorm enveloped the city as the hearse passed beneath the Arc de Triomphe, down the Champs-Élysées and across place de la Concorde to the Esplanade.

The coffin lay under the cupola and in St Jerome's Chapel until the tomb, designed by Visconti, was completed. The transfer took place on 3 April 1861.

Hôtel des Invalides – Aerial view

The institution's revival – After the two World Wars the institution reverted to its original purpose in providing shelter and care to the war-wounded with modernised hospital facilities.

The buildings today are occupied by military administration and the Army Museum *(see Musée de l'Armée below)*.

★★★HOTEL DES INVALIDES ⓥ

Ⓜ *Invalides. Buses: 28, 49, 63, 69, 72, 83, 93*

Esplanade – The Esplanade, designed and constructed in 1704-20 by Robert de Cotte, Mansart's brother-in-law, affords a spectacular vista 500m – 1/3 mile long and more than 250m – 820ft wide, ending of course in the symmetrical, Classical buildings.

The expanses of green lawn are bordered by avenues of lime trees. On the left before the river is the air terminal, Aérogare des Invalides, with transport links to Orly Airport.

Garden – Fronting the Invalides are a series of gardens, bordered by a wide dry moat, ramparts lined with 17C and 18C bronze cannon and an 18-piece triumphal battery used to fire salutes on such occasions as the Armistice (11 November 1918) and the Victory March (14 July 1919).

The battery, removed by the Germans in 1940 and returned in 1946, now stands on either side of the entrance.

★★**Façade** – The façade is majestic in style and line, in proportion and size – 196m – 645ft long. The central block is dominated by a magnificent doorway, flanked by twin pavilions. Decorative features are restricted to trophies around dormer windows, masks and flaming urns (Antique symbols of military might). An equestrian statue shows Louis XIV supported by Prudence and Justice in the rounded arch above the entrance. The original effigy by Guillaume Coustou (1735), damaged during the Revolution, was replaced by the present figure by Cartelier in 1815.

Restoration of the **lateral walls★** has recovered the noble architecture along boulevard des Invalides and along boulevard de Latour-Maubourg, the fine proportions of Robert de Cotte's Order of Liberation Chancellery and the ditch according to its original design.

★**Cour d'honneur** – Napoleon took great pleasure in reviewing his veterans here, before the perfect proportions of the Classical building with its regimented double tier of superimposed arches.

A central bay projects slightly from each side, its carved pediment breaking the regular architectural lines as do sculptured horses, trampling the attributes of war, at the corner angles of the roof. The dormer windows are decorated, echoing those on the façade, with trophies.

The fifth window to the right of the east central pavilion *(left on entering)* is worthy of note: Louvois, who had been in charge of the construction of the Invalides, inserted his coat of arms in various places; Louis XIV ordered him to have them removed, at which point a stonemason decided to encircle one oval window with the paws of a wolf, thereby making a play on the intendant's name and surveillance; *loup voit* – the wolf sees all.

The most ornate pavilion on the main axis of the complex serves as a frontage to the Church of St-Louis-des-Invalides. At the centre is the Seurre statue of Napoleon, known as the Little Corporal, which stood for some years at the top of the column in place Vendôme.

An impressive series of cannon are laid out along the walls: note the "Catherina" (1487) bearing the name of Sigismund of Austria, the "Württemberg culverin" (16C) with its chiselled breech and its barrel entwined by a snake.

★**Église de St-Louis-des-Invalides** ⊙ – The church, also known as the Soldiers' Church, was designed by Libéral Bruant and built by Mansart, who later added the dome to the group. Its design seems cold and functional, the only relief being the captured enemy banners overhanging the upper galleries.

A window behind the high altar provides a glimpse of the baldaquin in the Dôme Church.

The magnificent 17C organ is enclosed in a loft designed by Hardouin-Mansart. It was here that Berlioz's *Requiem* was first heard in 1837.

The banners were more numerous at the end of the Empire but when the Allies entered Paris in March 1814, the Invalides governor burnt 1 417 of them in the courtyard; the history of each is commemorated on the church pillars.

In the crypt *(not open)* lie former governors of the Invalides, together with 19C and 20C marshals and generals of the field, including Leclerc, Giraud and Juin.

Conserved in an urn is the heart of Mademoiselle de Sombreuil, daughter of the Governor (1789) – who during the massacres of September 1792 moved the murderers to spare her father with her filial love.

★★★Musée de l'Armée ⊙

The galleries of one of the world's richest army museums lie on either side of the main courtyard, on several floors.

Ground floor *(east side)* – These galleries were once part of four refectories situated on either side of the courtyard. They are decorated with frescoes of Louis XIV's campaign in Flanders in 1672.

The **Salle Turenne** contains banners dating from 1619 to 1945. Napoleon's flag of farewell flown at Fontainebleau on his abdication in 1814 is displayed below his portrait in coronation robes by Ingres. In the centre stands a model of the Invalides scaled 1:160.

The **Salle Vauban** is dedicated to the history of the cavalry from 1800 to 1940 and to regulation fire-arms from 1717 to 1979.

2nd floor – These rooms are devoted to **military history** from the Ancienne Monarchie (1618-1782) to the Second Republic. Among the countless souvenirs of French military history are the cannon-ball that killed Turenne (1675) *(Salle Louis XIV)*, mementoes of Napoleon: his coat, hat, sword and medals *(Salle Boulogne)* and charming souvenirs of the King of Rome *(Salle Montmirail)*.

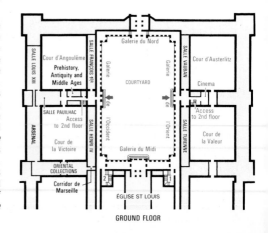

GROUND FLOOR

Musée de l'Armée, Louis XIII-style suit of armour

The **Salle de la Restoration** recalls Napoleon's removal to Elba, the Hundred Days, Waterloo and his exile to St Helena. The Longwood room in which he died is movingly reconstructed. The **Vestibule La Fayette** displays mementoes of général La Fayette, the national guard and the 1830 Revolution. The **Salle Bugeaud** (1830-1852) features the conquest of Algeria.

3rd floor – The **Salle Pelissier** is devoted to the early part of the Second Empire (1852-1860): the Imperial Guard, the Crimean (photographs) and Italian campaigns.
The **Salle Chanzy** deals with the end of the Second Empire (overseas expeditions) and the 1870-1871 Franco-Prussian War: two animated maps show troop movements. The models displayed in these two galleries trace the evolution of regimental uniforms, equipment and arms. The cooks' costumes are unusual.

Ground floor (*west side*) – Diverse arms and armour attractively displayed illustrate the evolution of methods of defence and attack from prehistoric times.
The **Salle François I**, a former refectory, is adorned with paintings depicting Louis XIV's battles and victories in the 1672-78 Dutch war. On display are royal arms and armour.
The **Salle Préhistorique, Antiquité et Moyen Age** contains arms dating from the dawn of history to the reign of Charlemagne (9C).
The **Salle Pauilhac** shows Renaissance swords and daggers, a firearms collection which includes Charles V's pistol, a wheel-lock gun and Philippe V's gun, and fine Spanish armour.
The **Salle Louis XIII** houses splendidly chased royal harnesses and Louis XIII's arms collection.

Arsenal – About 40 complete suits of armour, 1 000 helmets and half suits, 400 pikes and spears, 500 swords and rapiers, 250 projectiles and firearms are on display on shelves and racks.
The **Salle orientale** exhibits arms and armour from Persia, India, Japan: among the helmets are those of the Ottoman sultan Bajazet II and of a Slav ruler (Russia, 16C). In the **Corridor de Marseille** note the 19C saddle cloth.

Salle Henri IV – This former refectory is decorated with frescoes commemorating the taking of Flemish towns during the Dutch war.
Armour for jousting and foot combat, finely decorated helmets and shields.

2nd floor – The **Salle de la guerre de 1914-18** traces three stages in the First World War conflict; maps showing troop movements, model of Verdun, Marshal Foch's military map and 1918 Armistice bugle.
The **Salle de la guerre de 1939-45** (Second World War) contains documents, mementoes, photographs and animated map relating to the military aspect (model of the invasion) as well as civilian life and the Resistance movement.

3rd floor – The **Salle Gribeauval** contains about 200 models tracing the evolution of French artillery from 1550 to 1914.

★**Galerie des Plans Reliefs** – *4th floor*. An audio-visual presentation *(10 min)* traces the history and manufacture of relief-maps and three-dimensional models.

A collection of scale models of towns, harbours and fortresses (1: 600) from the time of Vauban (17C) to the present illustrates the evolution of fortifications in France over the last 300 years. Amongst the most interesting large scale models are those of Perpignan (1686) and of Strasbourg (1836), Trompette Castle in Bordeaux made of separate pieces and the model of Briançon – the highest fortified town in Europe *(son et lumière)*.

The Nîmes Gallery overlooks a courtyard where stone slabs from Napoleon's tomb in St Helena can be seen.

★**Musée de l'Ordre de la Libération** ⊙ – *Pavillon Robert-de-Cotte, 51bis boulevard de la Tour-Maubourg*.

The Order of Liberation, created by général de Gaulle at Brazzaville in 1940, honoured as "companions" those who made an outstanding contribution to the final victory. The list, which was closed in 1946, consists of service personnel and civilians, a few overseas leaders including King George VI, Winston Churchill and General Eisenhower, and several French localities (Paris, Nantes, Grenoble, Vassieux-en-Vercors, Sein Island). The memory is also perpetuated of French heroes from the African campaigns, major operations of the Resistance and the concentration camps: documents, trophies and relics.

★★★Église du Dôme ⊙

From the front courtyard there is a **general view** of the Dôme Church. On the left, behind Mansart's original trench, the Intendant's Garden has been replanted with formal beds.

The church is one of the major masterpieces of the age of Louis XIV. Designed by **Hardouin-Mansart** the French Classical style reaches new heights, perfected from such prototypes as St-Joseph des Carmes *(see FAUBOURG-ST-GERMAIN – Quartier des Carmes)*, St-Paul-St-Louis *(see ILE ST-LOUIS)*, the Sorbonne *(see LATIN QUARTER)* and the Val-de-Grâce *(see PORT-ROYAL)*.

Louis XIV commissioned Hardouin-Mansart to design a church that would complement the Invalides buildings of Libéral Bruant and embody the full splendour of his reign. In 1677, work began on the royal church oriented towards the north and joined to the Soldiers' Church by a common sanctuary. It was completed by Robert de Cotte in 1735. The Dôme Church is perhaps on a par with Versailles in epitomising French 17C or *Grand Siècle* design in religious and secular architecture.

In 1793, the Revolution transformed the two churches, which were still adjoined, into a Temple to Mars, and had the captured enemy standards transferred there from Notre-Dame. When Napoleon had Marshal Turenne (d 1675) interred in the church in 1800, it became a military mausoleum, receiving further countless trophies from the imperial campaigns. These were guarded by the old soldiers, known as the *grognards* or grumblers, billeted in the Invalides barracks. In 1842, two years after the return of Napoleon's body, Visconti enlarged the central altar, replaced the original baldaquin and had the crypt dug to receive the 'Eagle's' sarcophagus. The big window dates from 1873. These alterations disturbed the harmonious proportions of the interior, but its grandeur survives.

ÉGLISE SAINT LOUIS DES INVALIDES

Façade – The central bay projects slightly from the line of the main body of the church, but is equal in height to the lateral projections, thereby eliminating the need for volutes so typical of the Jesuit style. At ground level, in shell niches between Doric columns, are statues of St Louis (Louis IX) by Nicolas Coustou and of Charlemagne by Coysevox; above a projecting entablature free-standing statues of the four Virtues flank the fine shafts of the Corinthian column-supports, emphasising the contrasts in design. The pediment is carved by Coysevox.

Dome – The overall effect is one of graceful dignity. Forty engaged columns articulate the drum, supporting a balustrade that encircles the dome base. At this level, pilasters frame the round-arched windows between consoles, rising to 12 gently arched panels with gilded sections that define the dome. Decorated with trophies, garlands and other ornaments the dome is capped by an elegant gold lantern. Four Virtues seem to anchor the corners of the spire which rises 107m – 351ft into the sky. The dome roof consists of lead sheeting, attached by copper nails to a wood frame. It was first given its golden splendour in 1715.

Interior – The decoration is sumptuous: painted cupolas, walls adorned with columns and pilasters framing low reliefs by the greatest contemporary artists.

1) Tomb of Joseph Bonaparte, elder brother of Napoleon, and King of Spain.

2) Monument to Vauban by Etex. The Emperor himself commanded that the military architect's heart be brought to the Invalides.

3) Marshal Foch's tomb by Landowsky.

4) Ornate high altar surrounded by twisted columns and covered by a baldaquin by Visconti. Vaulting decoration by Coypel.

5) General Duroc's tomb.

6) General Bertrand's tomb.

7) At the back – the heart of La Tour d'Auvergne, first grenadier of the Republic; in the centre, the tomb of Marshal Lyautey.

8) Marshal Turenne's tomb by Tuby.

9) St Jerome's Chapel (carvings by Nicolas Coustou). Against the wall is the tomb of Jerome Bonaparte, Napoleon's younger brother and King of Westphalia.

10) The Emperor's tomb.

Cupola – The cupola is an impressive sight resting on four massive piers of masonry. The corner chapels are visible through openings in the piers. Painted on the pendentives are the four Evangelists by **Charles de la Fosse** and then, in ascending order, the kings of France (in medallions) and the Twelve Apostles by Jouvenet. In the cupola itself a vast composition by La Fosse depicts St Louis presenting Christ with the sword with which he conquered the infidels.

Napoleon's tomb – The majesty of the setting perfectly befits the Emperor's image. In order to preserve the design of the church and a view of the altar, **Visconti** dug a circular crypt for the red porphyry sarcophagus on its base of green granite from the Vosges. Work was completed in 1861.

The Emperor's body is placed in six coffins, one contained inside the other: the innermost is of tin-plate; the second of mahogany; the third and fourth of lead; the fifth of ebony; the last of oak.

"I used to say of him [Napoleon] that his presence on the field made the difference of 40 000 men."
Philip Henry. Earl of Stanhope: Conversations with the Duke of Wellington 1888.

Napoleon's Tomb

Crypt – *Entrance down stairs behind the baldaquin.* Two massive bronze statues stand guard at the crypt entrance, one bearing an orb, the other the Imperial sceptre and crown. Low reliefs around the gallery represent institutions founded by the Emperor.

The sarcophagus stands at the centre of the inlaid marble pavement, designed as a star while, against the pillars circling the crypt, are 12 colossal statues by Pradier symbolising Napoleon's campaigns from the Italian victories of 1797 to Waterloo in 1815. In the *cella*, before a statue of the Emperor in his coronation robes, lies the King of Rome who died in Vienna in 1832 and remained in the crypt of the Hapsburgs before being transferred to Paris on 15 December 1940, exactly one century after his father; he was finally entombed in 1969.

Place Vauban – From here is a fabulous view of the façade of l'Église du Dôme. **Antoine de St-Exupéry** (1900-1944), author of *Le Petit Prince, Courrier Sud* and *Vol de Nuit*, lived on the corner with the avenue de Tourville between 1934 and 1940.

Avenue de Breteuil – To enhance the overall Baroque effect of the Dôme Church, the original plan was to include a colonnaded esplanade like that of St Peter's in Rome by Bernini. Instead, a wide avenue was cut through the then open countryside, creating avenue de Breteuil, thereby achieving a good perspective by more modest means.

Église St François Xavier – This church is a late-19C Renaissance pastiche, and has a fine interior.

Place de Breteuil *(off the map)* – The roundabout is dominated by Falguière's marble monument dedicated to Pasteur, built where there was once an important artesian well. A picturesque view is to be had from here, with the Dôme Church seen framed by grass, trees and sky.

★★MUSÉE RODIN ☉ *77 rue de Varenne.* Ⓜ *Varenne. Buses: 28, 49, 69, 82, 92*

★★**Hôtel Biron** – The house and garden enable one to see Rodin's sculptures in a perfect residential setting.

In 1728, one Abraham Peyrenc, a wigmaker who had accrued a fortune and aggrandised his name to Peyrenc de Moras, commissioned the architect Gabriel the Elder to build him a house in the rue de Varenne. In time the beautiful building passed through the hands of the Duchess of Maine, grand-daughter of the great Condé and wife of the son of Louis XIV, Madame de Montespan, and Marshal Biron, a general in the Revolutionary government who had a passion for flowers and spent 200 000 *livres* a year on tulips alone.

In 1797 the house was used as a dance hall. Under the Empire it was leased as a residence first to the papal legate then to the ambassador of the Tsar. In 1820 it was taken over by the Convent of the Sacred Heart, an educational institution for daughters from large families. It was the Mother-Superior Madame Sophie Barat (canonised: 1925), who had the neo-Gothic chapel constructed (1871) and the greater part of the residence's exquisite wood panelling ripped out which she considered symbols of vanity typical of the age.

After the Congregation Law of 1904, under which many convents were disbanded, the educational buildings and part of the gardens were given to the Lycée Victor-Duruy. The house was made available by the State to artists. Thus Auguste Rodin came to live there until his death in 1917, leaving much of his work to the Nation in lieu of rent.

★★**Musée Rodin** – Rodin's sculpture, primarily figurative in terracotta, bronze and white marble, is immensely striking, vital, lifelike. Creation, in the guise of restless figures emerging from the roughly hewn rock, was a favourite theme **(Hand of God)** although it was his renderings of the nude that demonstrated his true technical genius **(St John the Baptist)** and won him public acclaim in 1879.

The Cathedral by Auguste Rodin

Musée Rodin/B. Jarret © ADA

On the ground floor are some of his most expressive works: **The Cathedral, The Kiss, The Walking Man** and **The Man with a Broken Nose** – which was rejected from the Salon of 1864. At either end of the gallery, in corresponding rotundas which have kept their fine panelling, are **Eve** and the **Age of Bronze** (*see* AUTEUIL). One room is devoted to drawings by the artist which are exhibited in rotation.

At the top of the beautiful 13C staircase, on the first floor, are smaller works: the plaster *maquettes* for the large groups and for the statues of **Balzac** (*see* MONT-PARNASSE – Carrefour Vavin) and **Victor Hugo** (*see* la MUETTE – Musée Marmottan).

It is in the garden, however, that the most famous sculptures which established Rodin's reputation as a grand master during his own lifetime are to be seen: **The Thinker** (right), **The Burghers of Calais** and **The Gates of Hell** (left), and the **Ugolin group** (in the centre of the pool).

Personal artefacts and collections of furniture, pictures and antiquities belonging to the artist are displayed throughout the house and in the former chapel *(temporary exhibitions)*. The latest acquisition to be made by the museum is Camille Claudel's **The Wave**, a composite work in onyx and bronze.

For other fine houses in the rue de Varenne – see FAUBOURG-ST-GERMAIN.

Galerie de la SEITA ⊙ *12 rue Surcouf.* Ⓜ *Invalides*

This modern building stands on the site of France's first cigarette factory (1845). The tiny but fascinating museum traces the history of tobacco through its varied uses, medicinal or other, chewed, snuffed and smoked.

The tobacco trade flourished between the old and new continents with outward cargoes of this American plant being paid for by return loads of manufactured goods. The French Ambassador to Portugal, Jean Nicot introduced Marie de' Medici to snuff-taking (1560s).

The various accoutrements associated with tobacco are displayed in one case and include intricately carved pipes, pouches and pots, snuff boxes, cigarette holders and cases, lighters, matches, cigar cutters...

Le Gros Cailloux – This area, extending north as far as the Seine, was first developed under Louis XIV to accommodate those employed on the construction of the Invalides and access roads use by the military around the Champs-de-Mars (*see* EIFFEL TOWER). It is thought that the name derives from a Druid stone that may have been found on the site and transferred to the Bastille.

Musée-Galerie de la Seita

French tobacconist's tradesign
End 19C

Unusual sculptures

Le Defenseur du Temps, a clock (unfortunately hidden by netting to deter pigeons) created by Monestier in the Horloge District near the Centre Georges-Pompidou, the *Centaur* by César at the corner of the rue du Cherche-Midi and the rue du Four; the orks in the Musée Zadkine (LUXEMBOURG) and by the same sculptor, *Le Messager* (on the quai d'Orsay by the Pont des Invalides), the **Musée des sculptures en plein air** (JUSSIEU), the *Reclining Figure* by Henry Moore (Maison de l'UNESCO), *Listening* by Henri Miller (place René-Cassin, at the entrance to the church St-Eustache – HALLES-BAUBOURG) and all the sculptures on the "promenade" at La Défense.

JUSSIEU *

This area is bordered by the banks of the Seine, the Latin Quarter and the Gare d'Austerlitz. Founded upon Gallo-Roman remains, it boasts contact with the world of Islam and the realms of Science and Natural History. The Salpêtrière Hospital, south of the Gare d'Austerlitz has been appended for reference, despite falling outside the Jussieu neighbourhood.

★★JUSSIEU

M *Jussieu, Cardinal Lemoine. Buses: 63, 67, 86, 87, 89*

Musée de Sculpture en plein air – *Jardin Tino Rossi.* The riverside garden was initiated by Gilioli César in 1980. Amongst the works accommodated are *Chronos 10* by Schoffer, *Bell II* by Kiyomizu, *Development of Form* by Zadkine.

★**Institut du Monde Arabe** ⊙ – *1 rue des Fossés Saint-Bernard.* The aim of the Institute set up by France in conjunction with 20 Arab countries is to promote Islamic culture, cultural exchanges and co-operation. The building enclosed in a mantle of glass and aluminium and cored by a sheath of translucent alabaster, was conceived by the architect Jean Nouvel and the Architecture Studio.

The curved upper north face of the building is etched with a photographic impression of the buildings opposite on the Ile St-Louis; diametrically opposite, a rectilinear **south-facing façade★** winks its 240 mechanical occuli shuttering out unwanted light. The multitude of hexagonal diaphragms recall the patterns in Islamic tiling. On the western side, behind the glass frontage, the cylindrical white marble Book Tower borrows the form of the Samarra mosque minaret.

The Institute houses a museum, library, reference section and audio-visual facilities.

Institut du Monde Arabe – window panel

M. Renaudeau/HOAQUI

Museum – *7th floor.* On display are works of art from the 9C to the 19C from countries ranging from Spain to India illustrating Arab history: cut and over-painted glass, lustre ware, chased bronze, wood and ivory sculpture, geometric or floral carpets. Palace and mosque architecture and scientific achievements in the fields of medicine, astronomy and mathematics are also featured. There is a fine collection of astrolabes the instrument so highly regarded by Arab astronomers.

On the lower level, exhibitions of art from the Arab world since 1950 are held comprising painting, sculpture, calligraphy and the graphic arts, photography...

It is well worth going up to the roof-terrace to admire the view if the restaurant is open.

Hôtel Charles Le Brun' – *49 rue Cardinal-Lemoine.* Now used as offices, this fine building was built by Boffrand in 1700 for Charles Le Brun – nephew of the famous painter at the court of Louis XIV. Watteau lived here in 1718, as did Buffon in 1766; it was here that he completed his treatise on Natural History in several volumes.

Place Jussieu – When the Halles were re-organised *(see les HALLES-BEAUBOURG)* it was here that the former wine market was moved. The site is now lined with the modern high-tech buildings of the Pierre and Marie Curie University (Paris VI and VII). During term-time, this precinct in France's biggest university campus contrasts sharply with the quiet streets in the immediate vicinity.

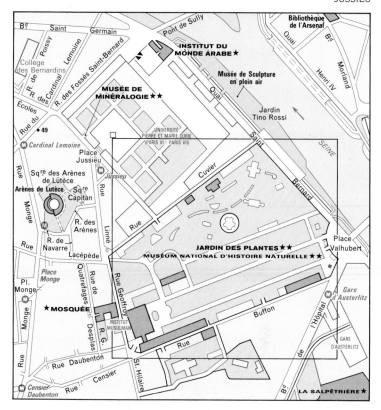

★★Musée de Minéralogie ⊙ – *34 rue de Jussieu*. This geology museum presents its superb study-collections of stones, rocks and dazzling crystals – ranking perhaps amongst the best collections in the world.

Arènes de Lutèce – *off rue de Navarre*. This, and the Cluny public bath house *(see* LATIN QUARTER – *Hôtel de Cluny)* are the only two Parisian monuments to survive from the Gallo-Roman period. The arena, the exact date of whose construction remains unknown, was destroyed in 280 by the Barbarians and lay buried for 1 500 years before being rediscovered by accident when the rue Monge was laid in 1869. The site was methodically excavated and restored only at the beginning of this century.

The arena seems to have been designed for circus and theatrical presentations; although many of its stone tiers have now vanished, the stage and layout of performer changing-rooms survive. Propped against a wall in square Capitan are the engraved stones which indicated the seats reserved for the notables of the period.

★La Mosquée ⊙ – *place du Puits-de-l'Ermite*. It is almost disconcerting to enter this exotic walled compound with its white Hispano-Mooresque buildings overlooked by a minaret, erected between 1922 and 1926. Three holy men oversee the enclave: the *muphti*, a lawyer, administrator and judge; the *imam* who looks after the mosque; and the *muezzin* or cantor who calls the faithful to prayer twice a day from high up in the minaret. This centre functions not only as a religious institution but also as a cultural centre with facilities for learning Arabic and Arab civilisation (library and conference centre).

Most of the interior decoration and courtyard design was entrusted to craftsmen from Mohammedan countries: Persian carpets, North African copper and brass, Lebanese cedar... The courtyard encloses a garden – symbol of Muslim Paradise. At the heart of the religious buildings is a patio surrounded by finely carved arcades, modelled upon the Alhambra in Granada. The prayer chamber is outstanding for its decoration and magnificent carpets.

When planning your evening's entertainment,
be sure to consult the Paris Today section of the INTRODUCTION.

★★MUSEUM NATIONAL D'HISTOIRE NATURELLE

For the Botanical Gardens: Ⓜ/RER *Gare d'Austerlitz*. Buses *24, 57, 61, 63, 65, 89, 91*

For the Grande Galerie de l'Évolution: Ⓜ *Censier-Daubenton, Place Monge. Buses: 67, 89*

Together, the complex encompasses the Botanical Gardens and its menagerie, Natural History Museum, and various other study collections of minerals, fossils etc.

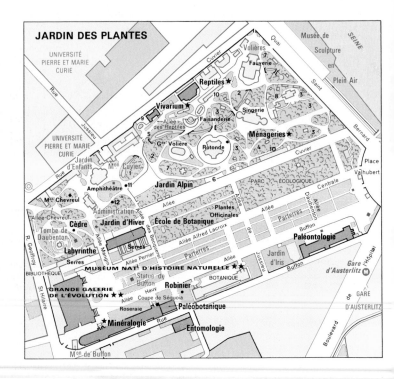

★★**Jardin des Plantes** Ⓥ – *Quai Saint-Bernard*. In 1626 Hérouard and Guy de la Brosse, physicians to Louis XIII, were granted permission to move the Royal Medicinal Herb Garden from the tip of the Ile de la Cité to the St-Victor district. This was to evolve into a school for botany, natural history and pharmacy. In 1640 the garden was opened to the public.

First Fagon, Louis XIV's first physician, then the botanist Tournefort and the three Jussieu brothers journeyed afar to enrich the Paris collection.

It was during the curatorship of Buffon (1739-1788) however, assisted by Daubenton and Antoine-Laurent de Jussieu, nephew of the earlier brothers, that the gardens were at their greatest. Having published his 36 volume *Natural History*, Buffon extended the gardens to the banks of the Seine, planted avenues of lime trees and the maze, built the amphitheatre and galleries... He was so greatly revered that he lived to see a statue erected in his honour.

A national museum for natural history – At the Revolution **Bernardin de Saint-Pierre** was nominated curator of the Royal Botanic Gardens, renamed by the Convention (10 June 1793) the National Museum for Natural History. This body was to be dedicated to investigation, preservation and instruction. The same year a menagerie was instituted with animals from zoos, often privately owned by princes and circus performers. This enabled astounded Parisians to discover such animals as elephants (brought from Holland in 1795), bears (each one to have occupied the pit has been called Martin after the first one), giraffes (1827) etc. In 1870, however, when Paris was under siege, the citizens' hunger exceeded their curiosity and most of the animals were killed for food. With **Géoffroy-Saint-Hilaire, Lamarck, Lacépède, Cuvier, Becquerel** and many other great names, the institute won through its teaching and research in the 19C the international recognition which it maintains today.

Botanic gardens – In the 17C a large accumulation of public waste occupied the site, over which Buffon laid a **maze**; at the heart a small kiosk overlooks the rest of the gardens from the highest point. A column amongst the trees marks the grave of Buffon's collaborator Daubenton, a naturalist.

The famous cedar of Lebanon is one of two planted by Bernard de Jussieu in 1734; these were brought back, so the story goes, in the scientist's hat, from England. (The truth is that Jussieu got the two plants from Kew Gardens; on his way back to the gardens, the pot fell and broke, he therefore scooped the plants up into his hat and presented them thus to the gardener!).

The Ginkgo Biloba and the iron tree from Persia are also worthy of note.

The oldest tree in Paris is a Robinia or false acacia planted here in 1635, near the allée des Becquerel.

Opposite the Winter Garden, the Australian Hothouse contains Mediterranean and Australian species. The cryptogamia laboratories organise an annual mushroom fair here in the autumn.

Jardin d'Hiver, Jardin Alpin, École de Botanique ⊙ – The Winter Garden Glasshouse contains an important collection of tropical plants, beyond which is the Mexican Garden planted with succulents (cacti, euphorbia). The Alpine Garden groups its high-altitude plants by soil type and orientation of the sun: Corsica, Morocco (south face), the Alps and the Himalayas (north face). Note the old pistachio tree (c1700) and the tall deciduous conifer (metasequoia). Over 10 000 species of flora, edible and/or medicinal herbs, are classified by family in the botanical study-beds; the laricio pine was grown from seed brought back from Corsica by Turgot (1774).

★**Ménagerie, Vivarium, Reptiles** ⊙ – Large reptiles, birds and wild animals are presented in a somewhat old-fashioned but serene setting; many appear tame.

The rotunda, the oldest building in this section, houses a **Micro Zoo** ⊙ – Microscopes and special audio-headwear help visitors to discover the world of minute creatures and microcosms that proliferate unseen in our environment.

★★**Grande Galerie de l'Évolution** ⊙ – *36 rue Geoffroy-Saint-Hilaire*. This is one of the world's greatest conservatories in the field of natural science.

"Sleeping Beauty" wakes up – Specimens collected by travelling naturalists or sent by the governors of distant colonies overseas during the 18C and 19C were housed in a new Zoology Gallery built by Jules André in 1889, a robust cast-iron infra-structure clad in stone conforming to the beaux-arts style. The Gallery slowly deteriorated in the 20C – the large glazed roof was shattered by anti-aircraft bombs during World War II and the building was eventually closed in 1965 for safety reasons. For 20 years, it lay abandoned. When an underground zoological gallery was excavated between 1980 and 1985, a large number of dust-impregnated, damaged specimens could be removed. The gallery, excavated to a depth of 10m – 33ft below ground level (thus revealing the majestic millstone-grit foundations on the right-hand side), has recently been revamped by **Paul Chemetov**, an architect from the Ministry of Finances, and **Borja Huidobro** (1990-1994). Running alongside the main area is a reference library – a multi-media documentary extension of the Museum's galleries – a cafeteria and an area reserved for educational activities. Below, there is room for temporary exhibitions and an auditorium.

A sophisticated stage-setting – The architects worked in conjunction with the scenographer **René Allio**, a specialist theatrical designer. The restoration project preserves the cast iron architecture with great attention to detail – glass lifts, oak-framed display cases, metal handrails. The visitor enters the half-light of the great hall where artificial light is projected upon the animals (direct sunlight would in fact damage the exhibits). The light graduates in intensity over a period of 1 hour 40 mins, suggestive of the varying patterns of natural light during a whole day.

In the display cases, thousands of optical fibres focus upon delicate branches of coral and butterfly wings or the hard shell of crustaceans and coleoptera. Noise, a blend of 500 natural sounds and background music enhance the atmosphere. With two films, image banks or interactive games, the public can discover a multitude of animals at first hand – the "fish circle" consisting of fish, turtles, birds and marine mammals; the "African caravan"; marvellous collections of insects, hummingbirds and shells.

The great story of evolution – The theory of evolution is one of the most important in scientific development. It draws together a large number of disciplines which, without it, would have remained isolated. Here, it serves as a constant theme throughout the Gallery presentations.

As an introduction to the great "show" of life, visitors are invited to perceive the diversity of living species according to their environment. Confronted by the two whale skeletons, one example of a land-based mammal which reverted to the ocean, the visitor enters the marine world to encounter the fauna of the great deep (including the impressive cast of a giant squid), hydrothermal springs, coral reefs, the coastline and the high seas. Infinite diversity is most apparent in the realms of the infinitely small, where thousands of micro-organisms live amongst grains of sand – illustrated with a scale model enlarged 800 times.

Grande galerie de l'Évolution

The emphasis then changes from environmental considerations to the relationship between different animals within the same group (crustaceans, for example).

The polar regions are illustrated by polar bears, walruses and an enormous sea elephant; the African savannah by its famous "caravan" of zebras, giraffes, buffalo, lions and antelopes; the rain forest by magnificent display cases of gorgeous insects, and a steel ladder as a perch for monkeys and birds. Around the hall, some of the Museum's fragile illustrations on parchment are exhibited (*orchids, pelargoniums, tobacco, ostriches, monkeys, etc*).

Subdued lighting and sound effects enhance the atmosphere of the place.

The **first floor** shows the effects of human action on evolution: intensive farming or the displacement of species, domestication, changes in habitat and pollution. The most extreme case – hunting and extermination – is illustrated by the magnificent **Galerie des espèces disparues★★★** (Gallery of Extinct Species) which runs the length of the building. Lurking in semi-darkness in fine wooden cases, are the extremely rare and sometimes unique surviving stuffed specimens bathed in subdued light. Note, among the extinct species, the Cape lion with its black mane, turtles from the Seychelles and Rodriguez, the Schomburgh stag, the covagga, the Tasmanian Devil, a black emu skeleton, and the blue hippotragus; plant and animal species threatened with extinction include a wild harpy eagle, the most powerful of all the birds of prey, a tiger from China, the Cry violet and the flower of Saint Louis.

On the **top floor** is the museum's oldest stuffed animal, a rhinoceros from Asia which belonged to Louis XV and Louis XVI. This leads to an "historical display" introducing the scientists who questioned the origin of the diversity of living beings and whose ideas paved the way for the theory of evolution: **Georges Buffon** (1707-1788), who suspected the great age of the earth; **Jean-Baptiste Lamarck** (1744-1829), who believed in the inheritance of acquired characteristics; **Georges Cuvier** (1769-1832), who showed how the knowledge of current species helps us to understand the organisation of fossilised species; **Étienne Geoffroy Saint-Hilaire** (1772-1844); and finally **Charles Darwin** (1809-1882) and his theory of natural selection.

The long adventure of life is retraced from the appearance of the first living beings (bacteria) 3.5 billion years ago, to the development of multi-cellular organisms (670 million years ago) and their diversification in a marine environment. The role of reproduction and natural selection is explained, together with how the **cell** works, that single unit of the living world, the notion of genesis, the nature of DNA and messenger RNA. Recent discoveries put the accent on the **flexibility of the genetic system**, capable of mutating, of producing something new with something old and of generating large effects from small causes. The example given is of the cactus, the plant's adaptation to an arid environment proliferating to many different species, of the changeover from aquatic to terrestrial life, of the amniotic egg, of different types of locomotion, of haemoglobin genes and different growth rates. The stuffed animals in this part of the exhibition include a gavial, or long-nosed crocodile; a coelacanth, or fossil-fish; gorillas and orang-utans and a beautiful display case of birds of paradise.

Natural selection

The appearance and extinction of a species are natural phenomena. In any given environment, certain individuals are better able than others to pass on to their descendants the characteristics which have enabled them to survive – otherwise known as **natural selection**. In this way creatures can overcome a change in habitat or environment as effected by man by adaptation (numerous species of insects have evolved with a resistance to pesticides). Natural selection therefore can lead to the characterisation of a new species if the new strain successfully adapts to and proliferates in its environment.

Other departments – The **Galerie de Minéralogie★** ⊙ possesses exceptional examples of minerals, meteorites and precious stones and a collection of giant crystals, many of which come from Brazil. In the basement are shown the most precious stones, objets d'art and jewels from Louis XIV's collection. The **Galerie de Paléobotanique** ⊙ has one particularly interesting exhibit, a cross-section of the trunk of an American sequoia tree more than 2 000 years old inlaid with tablets describing events contemporary to its growth. Evolutionary trends of flora are here illustrated together with rare specimens of fossilised plants. The **Galerie Entomologique** ⊙ (43 rue Buffon) provides an infantesimal selection from a much larger collection of insects from all over the world. In the ground floor gallery of the **Galerie Paléontologique** ⊙ is presented the comparative anatomy of vertebrates with 36 000 specimens. Fossils are displayed on the first and second floors amongst reproductions of large prehistoric animals and extinct species.

★LA PITIÉ-SALPÊTRIÈRE

47-83 boulevard de l'Hôpital. Ⓜ *St-Marcel. Buses: 57, 91*

★The hospital – *entrance: square Marie-Curie.* The hospital has all the grandeur of the Grand Siècle. During the reign of Louis XIII a small arsenal manufactured gunpowder here, from saltpetre. In 1656 Louis XIV converted the works into a General Hospital for the Poor of Paris in the hope of clearing the capital's streets of beggars and vagrants. In 1660, expansion plans were directed first by Le Vau and then by Le Muet. By 1662, 10 000 pensioners had been taken in, a number exacerbated by the clearance of the Courts of Miracles *(see GRANDS BOULEVARDS)* in 1667. The chapel, designed by **Libéral Bruant** *(see les INVALIDES)*, was added in 1670.

The hospital became home to the mad, the infirm, the orphaned and prostitutes who were indiscriminately incarcerated. One doctor, namely Philippe Pinel (1745-1826) concentrated upon a study of the insane, replacing their harsh treatment with a more humane regime (as so disturbingly depicted by the painter Géricault). Towards the end of the 19C, **Professor Charcot**, whose students included Freud, continued research into neuro-psychiatry and the improvement of conditions at the hospital.

Chapelle St-Louis ⊙ – A formal garden precedes the central bay of the building. At the centre rises the octagonal dome surmounted by a lantern of the chapel.

The Greek cross ground plan is unusual consisting of a rotunda circled by four aisles and four angle chapels; these eight designated areas segregated the inmates.

The ensemble now serves as a cultural centre, with the exception of one of the chapels which is still used by the hospital.

Consult the INTRODUCTION
for background information on History,
Art and Architecture, Music and Literature.

LATIN QUARTER ★★★

Michelin plan 11 – folds 43 and 44: K 14, K 15: L 14, L 15

This part of the Left Bank is built on the Roman – hence Latin – origins of Paris. It is here that the University has grown with its famous schools, the Sorbonne, the Panthéon and St-Étienne-du-Mont Church as the principal landmarks.

★★★LA MONTAGNE STE-GENEVIÈVE Ⓜ/RER: St-Michel. Buses: 84, 89

Gallo-Roman Lutetia – In the 3C Lutetia was a small town of some 6 000 inhabitants: Gauls occupied the Ile de la Cité, while Romans settled around the top and slopes of the rise that was later known as Montagne Ste-Geneviève.

The Romans provided their community with all the usual amenities: an aqueduct stretching 15km – 9 miles brought water to the public baths from the Rungis plain, a network of paved roads was built to serve the first 'Latin' quarter, a temple dedicated to Mercury was constructed on the hill of Montmartre... Thus Lutetia grew up around a major crossroads, bisected north-south by the great Soissons-Orléans road that became so heavily congested that it was made one-way!

The preaching of St Denis on the Ile de la Cité would imply the existence of a Christian church there by AD 250, shortly before invading barbarians ravaged the entire Left Bank with fire (276-280).

The medieval Alma Mater – In the 12C teachers, clerks and scholars threw off the tutelage of the bishops of the Ancien Cloître *(see ILE DE LA CITÉ)* and migrated to the area around the monastic communities of Ste-Geneviève and St-Victor *(see below)* on the Left Bank. With authority from Pope Innocent III (1215) the group was incorporated leading to the founding of the University of Paris, the first in France.

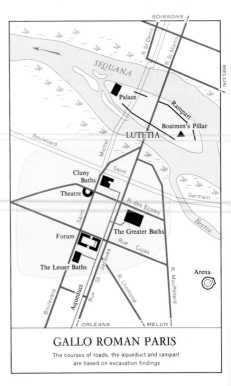

Students were drawn from the provinces and abroad, and registered according to discipline – theology, medicine, the liberal arts, canon law – or by "nationality" into colleges on the hill: the Sorbon College (1253), Harcourt College (1280) built on the ruins of the Lutetia Arena *(see JUSSIEU)* – now the Lycée St-Louis, the Coqueret College *(see below* – Collège de France)*, the Scottish College, Clermont College (1550) which was founded by the Jesuits – now the Louis-le-Grand Lycée, Ste Barbe, Navarre and some 10 others. The restless concentration of youth terrorised the local townspeople – or bourgeois, and held the king in contempt. Indeed, the University had its own jurisdiction of

GALLO ROMAN PARIS

The courses of roads, the aqueduct and rampart are based on excavation findings

which it was extremely protective: in 1407 it compelled the royal marshal, who had hanged several students, to come personally and cut down the corpses from the gibbet before seeking the Sorbonne's pardon.

Meanwhile, the Franciscans (St Bonaventura), Dominicans (St Albert the Great, St Thomas Aquinas), then the Oratorians (Malebranche, Massillon) and the Jesuits attracted thousands of students despite the University's attempts on several occasions, to prevent their institution as centres of learning. Latin as the language of educated men and lingua-franca amongst the different nationalities, continued to be spoken by scholars and teachers in the area until the Revolution in 1789.

From tutelage to autonomy – In 1793 the Convention disbanded all the universities in France. Latin ceased to be the official written language.

In 1806 Napoleon founded the Imperial University of France, with academies being made responsible for education by the State. The traditional autonomy of the university and its enormous influx of students made the system unwelcome and finally unworkable...

New buildings were erected (rue des Saints-Pères, Halle aux Vins, Censier) in order to decentralise the faculties (Orsay, Nanterre, Châtenay-Malabry...) but this did not prevent unrest.

In **May 1968** the tension came to a head, provoked by the forced evacuation of the Sorbonne on 3 May and the closure of the main faculties on 6 May. Demonstrations and street violence left 945 injured as the area was barricaded and the students declared themselves 'independent'. Sympathisers motivated the Unions to go on strike bringing chaos to the national car industry and public transport. On 30 May President de Gaulle was forced to dissolve his government.

October 1970 saw the disappearance of the University of Paris as such and the creation, in its place of 13 autonomous universities in the Paris region, each with a full range of disciplines, its own curricula and examinations; by 1992, these had grown to 17, with a student population of 329 000.

Boulevard St-Michel – The Boul' Mich, as it is known, is the heart of the area with its café terraces, publishing houses and bookshops – some highly specialised (arts, sciences, languages, philosophy). Around the Librairie Gibert bookshops proliferate, selling books, magazines, records, CDs. For more information turn to the INTRODUCTION: Insider's Paris.

★★Le Panthéon ☉

place du Panthéon. Ⓜ/RER: *Luxembourg. Buses: 21, 27, 38, 82, 84, 85, 89*

The Panthéon's situation, intended function and architecture secure its popularity as a national monument and tourist attraction.

A royal vow – Louis XV, when desperately ill in Metz in 1744, vowed that should he recover he would replace the semi-ruined church of the Abbey of Ste-Geneviève *(see below* – Lycée Henri IV*)* with a magnificent edifice built on the highest point on the Left Bank. He entrusted the fulfilment of his vow to his new Surintendant des Bâtiments, the Marquis of Marigny, brother to the Marquise de Pompadour. The project was given to his *protégé,* Jacques Germain **Soufflot** (1713-1780) with whom Marigny had been in Italy. The great neo-Classical architect planned a vast church 110m long by 84m wide by 83m high – 361ft x 276ft x 272ft – with a large crypt, around Ste Geneviève's shrine *(now in the church of St-Etienne-du-Mont)* in the transept crossing, below a huge dome. He intended combining Roman regularity and monumentality with a structural lightness derived from Gothic building for this modern edifice in honour of a medieval saint. The massive scale of such intentions won the architect contempt from all sides.

Foundations were laid in 1758 but a lack of funds, together with major subsidence problems meant that construction was completed only after Soufflot's death (1780) by his pupil Rondelet, in 1789.

The Temple of Fame – In April 1791 its function as a church was suspended by the Constituent Assembly in order to "receive the bodies of great men who died in the period of French liberty" – thus it became a Pantheon, where the gods of Antiquity would have lived. Voltaire and Rousseau are buried here, as were Mirabeau and Marat for a short while.

1) Saint Denis's prediction (Galand).
2) Scenes from the life of Sainte Geneviève (Puvis de Chavannes).
3) Charlemagne crowned Emperor, and protector of the Humanities (H Lévy).
4) Miraculous Cure of Quiblinf and procession of the reliquary of Sainte Geneviève (Maillot).
5) Battle of Tolbiac and Baptism of Clovis (J Blanc).
6) Death and funeral of Sainte Geneviève (J-P Laurens).
7) Towards Glory (Ed. Detaille).
8) Sainte Geneviève watching over Paris and Sainte Geneviève bringing food to the town (Puvis de Chavannes).
9) Story of Joan of Arc (J-E Lenepveu).
10) The Concept of Fatherland, Plenty, Home and Plague (Humbert). Monument to the Unknown Heroes (Landowski).
11) The life of Saint Louis (Cabanel).
12) Sainte Geneviève enrourages and reassures the Parisians (Delaunay).
13) Martyrdom of Saint Denis (Bonnat).

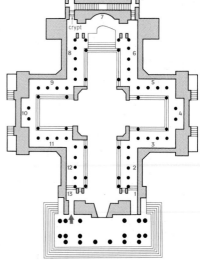

Place du Panthéon

163

Successively the Panthéon has served as a church under the Empire, a necropolis in the reign of Louis-Philippe, a church under Napoleon III, the headquarters of the Commune and finally as a lay temple to receive the ashes of Victor Hugo in 1885.

The building – The edifice as we now know it little resembles Soufflot's original: its bell-towers flanking the apse have lost two storeys; its external elevation has been deadened by not having its intended frieze and garlands, and by having 42 windows bricked-up.

The **dome★★**, strengthened with an iron framework, can be best surveyed from a distance.

Main façade – Eleven steps rise to the peristyle composed of fluted columns supporting a triangular pediment, the first of its kind in Paris. This is inscribed with its dedication 'To the great men, the nation is grateful' in gold letters. Above, sculptured figures (1831) by David d'Angers represent Liberty handing crowns of laurel to the Nation to distribute amongst her great men: civilians on the left, the military led by Napoleon on the right. The central doorway is flanked by marble groups depicting Clovis' Baptism, St Geneviève and Attila.

Interior – Greek-cross in plan, the nave is divided from the aisles by a line of columns supporting a frieze, cornice and balustrade, roofed with flattened domes. Soufflot designed the great central dome as supported on free-standing columns but these have been substituted with heavy piers, thereby reducing the effect of weightlessness.

The upper section has a fresco commissioned from Baron Antoine Jean Gros (1771-1835) by Napoleon in 1811, depicting *St Geneviève's Apotheosis*.

The walls are decorated with **paintings★** dating from 1877 onwards. The most famous are by Puvis de Chavannes and depict scenes from the life of St Geneviève.

Foucault's Pendulum – In 1855 Léon Foucault took advantage of the dome's height to repeat publicly his experiment that proved the rotation of the earth – a discovery he had made in 1849.

His brass pendulum (28kg – 62lb) hung from a steel cable (67m – 220ft), deviated from its axis during oscillation in a circular movement. The direction of this movement was reversed if the experiment was conducted in the northern or southern hemisphere – hence proving his theory of the earth's rotation. The extent of the motion – nil at the Equator, 36 hours at 45° latitude and 24 hours at the pole – proved that the earth was spherical.

The Pendulum can now be seen at the Musée National des Techniques (*see* RÉPUBLIQUE).

Stairs lead up to the dome from where there is a fine **view★★** over Paris.

Crypt – The crypt extends under the full length of the building. A stone urn on the steps down contains the heart of Gambetta placed there since the inhumation of the Unknown Soldier under the Arc de Triomphe (*see* CHAMPS-ÉLYSÉES) on 11 November 1920.

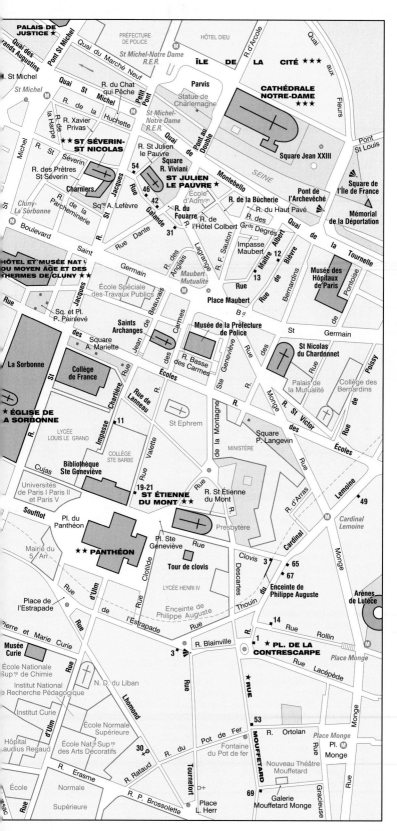

Although strangely eerie and empty, it contains the tombs of great men in all walks of life throughout France's history: La Tour d'Auvergne, Voltaire, Rousseau, Victor Hugo, Émile Zola, Marcelin Berthelot, Louis Braille (inventor of a system of writing for the blind), Jean Jaurès, the explorer Bougainville. The most recent heros to be so honoured are the Nobel Prize winners Pierre and Marie Curie (who is also the first woman).

Bibliothèque Ste-Geneviève *10 place du Panthéon*

The University library was built in the 19C on the site of the Montaigu College, a college that was known for its teaching, its austere discipline and its squalor – its scholars were said to sleep on the ground amidst lice, fleas and cockroaches. Manuscripts, incunabula and 16C-18C works from Ste-Geneviève Abbey were transferred in 1850 to the new building designed by Labrouste, a master of steel architecture, to form the nucleus of the new library (some 2 700 000 volumes).

Behind the library is College Ste Barbe (1460), the last surviving Latin Quarter College. A hexagonal tower (1560), known as **Calvin's Tower**, stands in the courtyard at nos **19-21** rue Valette. It is all that remains of Fortet College where, in 1585, the Duke of Guise founded the Catholic League which was to expel Henri III from Paris.

Bibliothèque Sainte-Geneviève

Rue Soufflot – The rue Soufflot and the semicircular square are lined with the symmetrical block of the former Law Faculty (by Soufflot 1772) – now the offices of Paris I, Paris II and Paris V Universities – and buildings by Hittorff dating from 1844. At no **14** used to stand the **Jacobin Monastery** Church, founded by the first brothers of the Dominican order who arrived in Paris in 1217. Jacques Clément, Henri III's assassin (1589) was a brother in the monastery, as was Humbert II, the last of the Dauphiné princes who, by taking holy orders, brought his province under the French crown.

★★Église St-Étienne-du-Mont ⓥ

place Ste-Geneviève. Ⓜ *Cardinal Lemoine. Buses: 84, 89*

A church for Ste Geneviève – It is in this quite unique church, dedicated to St-Étienne-du-Mont that Ste Geneviève is particularly venerated. Until 1220 the servants of the Abbey of Ste Geneviève attended services in the church crypt, that is until their community grew to such numbers that a parish church, dedicated to St Stephen, was built adjoining the abbey church; by the end of the 15C their number had also outgrown St Stephen's. Rebuilding began with the belfry tower and apse in 1492; in 1610 the foundation stone for the new façade was laid by Queen Margot, first wife of Henri IV, and in 1626 the new church was consecrated.

The façade★★ is highly original. Three superimposed pediments stand at the centre, their lines emphasised by the upward sweep of the belfry; note on the right the considerable height of the south aisle above the chapels. The chancel built in the Flamboyant style has broken arch bays, whilst in the nave, built later, windows are rounded more in keeping with the Renaissance.

St-Étienne-du-Mont, roodscreen.

Interior – Despite its date (16C) the structure is Gothic. Tall aisle walls allow for large windows; an elegant line of balusters cuts the height of the tall pillars.

The Flamboyant vaulting above the transept is most eye-catching with its complex network of ribs and 5.50m – 18ft intricately carved hanging keystone.

The 17C organ loft is highly ornate. Recitals are given regularly on the organ (90 stops). The stained glass, which for the most part dates from the 16C and 17C is particularly unusual in the ambulatory and chancel.

The **roodscreen★★** is the only one in existence in Paris. In the 15C and 16C all the major churches possessed roodscreens from which lessons from the Epistles or the Gospels were read and sermons were delivered. The reason this particular one may have survived is because its broad arch allowed all liturgical ceremony performed in the chancel to be viewed by the faithful in the nave.

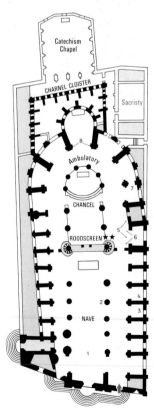

Place Ste Geneviève

The central stone fretwork decoration is typical of the Renaissance; the twin side doors are Classical. Two lovely open spiral staircases lead to the rood loft and the course along the chancel pillars. Delightful feminine figures adorn the arch at either end.

1) Marble slab marking the spot where an archbishop of Paris was stabbed to death by an unfrocked priest (3 January 1857).

2) 1650 **pulpit★** supported by a figure of Samson.

3) **Stained glass window★** of 1586 illustrating the parable of those invited to the feast.

4) 16C Entombment.

5) Over the arch, two ex-votos offered by the City of Paris: on the right, the City giving thanks to St Geneviève, painted by de Troy in 1726; on the left, an earlier painting by Largillière (1696).

6) The epitaphs of Racine (by Boileau) and Pascal.

7) **St Geneviève's shrine** – St Geneviève's relics, originally buried in the crypt of the neighbouring abbey, were exhumed and burnt upon the place de Grève in 1793. When the abbey church was pulled down in 1802, the saint's sarcophagus stone was found and is now encased by the modern gilded copper shrine containing a few small relics.

8) Pascal (1623-1662) and Racine (1639-1699) lie buried near the pillars to the Lady Chapel. Racine was originally interred at Port-Royal-des-Champs and transferred here in 1711.

Cloister – Also known as the Charnel Cloister. At one time the church was bordered to the north and east by two small burial grounds, it was here that the remains of Mirabeau and Marat were brought after they had been removed from the Panthéon. The cloister is built off the right side of the ambulatory at the church's east end, and may at one time have been used as a charnel house. At the beginning of the 17C, the far end of the cloister's main gallery was glazed with **stained glass★**. Surviving sections illustrate the story of the Profane Host, the Holy Grail, the Sending of Manna from Heaven, the Mystical Wine-press – subjects of particular significance at the time of the Counter-Reformation.

The small Catechism Chapel was added by Baltard in 1859.

Lycée Henri-IV – *10 rue Clovis*. It was on this site that Clovis, following his victory over the Visigoths at Vouillé near Poitiers, had a rich basilica erected in 510 in which he and his wife Clotilda were buried, as well as St Geneviève. The widespread devotion to the saint soon led to the foundation of the Abbey of Ste-Geneviève by Augustine canons, which eventually rivalled the Abbey of St-Germain-des-Prés in spiritual, judicial and territorial power. Medieval piety was expressed on all occasions: wars, epidemics, floods and public calamities called for fasting and a great procession of the Saint's shrine through the decorated streets of Paris to the sound of loudly pealing church bells.

The Revolution suppressed such festivities and demolished the abbey precinct of which only the refectory (along rue Clotilde), Gothic cellars and the church belfry, known as the **Tour de Clovis** (Clovis' Tower) survive today. Since 1796 the site has been occupied by the Henri-IV Lycée.

On the corner of rue Descartes is St-Etienne's presbytery erected by the Duke of Orleans when he retired to the Ste-Geneviève Abbey, where he died in 1752.

Further along, a large section of the **Philippe Auguste perimeter wall** can be seen at no **3** rue Clovis. It originally stood 10m – 33ft high and here lacks only its crenellations.

> ### 74 rue du Cardinal-Lemoine
>
> When the aspiring writer Ernest Hemingway came to Paris in early 1922, he and his first wife Hadley moved into a fourth-floor apartment at 74 rue Cardinal-Lemoine, where they remained until the summer of 1923. This early period in Hemingway's multi-faceted Paris experience is nostalgically recounted in *The Moveable Feast*, published posthumously in 1964.

Collège des Escossois ⊙ – *65 rue du Cardinal-Lemoine, opposite rue Clovis*. The **Scottish College**, a building with a noble façade which has belonged to the Roman Catholic Church of Scotland since the 14C now accommodates a hostel for girls, the Foyer Ste-Geneviève. Inside, a magnificent staircase leads to the Classical chapel where the king's brain, a royal relic, was deposited in 1701 on James II's death in exile *(see PORT-ROYAL – Schola Cantorum)*.

Ministère de l'Enseignement Supérieur et de la Recherche – *1 rue Descartes*. Several important academic bodies have been based at this address. First the Navarre College, founded in 1304 by Jeanne de Navarre, wife of Philip the Fair, was originally intended for 70 poor scholars, among whom, at different times, Henri III, Henri IV, Richelieu and Bossuet were numbered. In 1794 the Convention initiated the École Polytechnique to replace a deficit in engineers and trained men as a result of the ongoing war effort. This in turn was transformed into a military college by Napoleon in 1802 providing two years of military discipline and scholarship "for country, science and glory" and ensuring a high standard of technical knowledge among a selected few. From its earliest days, it attracted to its staff the best scientific brains of the 19C. Amongst its erudite students rank many social architects of the Third Republic: the "X", as they are known, Foch, the positivist philosopher Auguste Comte, Joffre, Borotra, André Citroën and the French Presidents, Albert Lebrun and Valéry Giscard d'Estaing. Women were admitted for the first time in 1972.

The college was transferred to Palaiseau on the outskirts of Paris, in 1977.

École Normale Supérieure – *45 rue d'Ulm*. The teachers' training school was created by the Convention in 1794 and moved to these premises in 1847. For many the "Normale" has proved to be the springboard to a brilliant career (Pasteur, Sartre, Pompidou).

> **Samuel Beckett** (1906-1989) was born in Dublin. He went to the ENS as a *lecteur d'Anglais* in 1928, and soon embarked on a long association with his compatriot James Joyce *(see MONTPARNASSE – Boulevard Raspail)* assisting the near-blind author in completing *Ulysses* and its subsequent translation into French.
>
> His reputation, however, was established with the production of *En attendant Godot* (1953) and its translation **Waiting for Godot** (1955). Subsequent works reaffirmed his affiliation with the Theatre of the Absurd, and a growing influence upon Tom Stoppard and Harold Pinter. Regular themes touch upon situations fraught with frustration and impending madness.

Musée Curie ⓥ – *11 rue Pierre-Marie-Curie*. On the ground floor of the Physics and Chemistry Departments of the Curie Institute in the former Radium Institute, this museum collects together the Nobel Prize, papers, documents and photographs relating to the husband-wife Curie team, their daughter Irène and her husband Frédéric Joliot, and the apparatus used in their discovery of naturally occurring radioactivity, and its artificially produced counterpart (1934).

In Marie Curie's office is the lead casket which held one gramme of radium presented to the scientist by women of the United States of America in 1921.

Centre de la Mer et des Eaux ⓥ – *195 rue St-Jacques*. The centre is part of the Oceanographic Institute founded at the beginning of the 20C by Albert I of Monaco. It is devoted to marine biology, the ocean and its role and resources, presented via thematic exhibitions, films, aquaria...

Marie Curie

Église St-Jacques-du-Haut-Pas ⓥ – *252 rue St-Jacques*. The church, built in the Classical style between 1630 and 1685, became a Jansenist centre. The astronomer, Cassini *(see below)*, is buried inside, as is the Abbot of St-Cyran, almoner of Port-Royal-des-Champs.

Institut National de Jeunes Sourds – A hospital to succour pilgrims on their way to Compostela in Spain was established on this site in the 14C by monks from Altopascio near Lucca in Italy.

École Supérieure des Mines – *60 boulevard St-Michel*. The school, founded in 1783, moved to its present site, the former Hôtel de Vendôme, in 1815. Its **mineralogical collection**★★ ⓥ is among the world's richest.

La Sorbonne

47 rue des Ecoles. Ⓜ *Cluny-La Sorbonne. Buses: 21, 27, 38, 63, 82, 84, 86, 87, 89*

In 1253 a college for 16 poor students who wished to study theology was founded by King Louis IX, goaded by his confessor, a Paris canon, Robert of Sorbon (named after his native village of Sorbon in the Ardennes, in accordance with medieval custom). From such a simple beginning was to develop the Sorbonne, the centre of theological study in pre-Revolutionary France and the seat of the University of Paris. In the same buildings three printers summoned from Mainz by Louis XI established the first printing house in France in 1469.

Political and religious struggles – Pressurised by Philip the Fair, an advocate for the Avignon Papacy, the theological faculty condemned the Knights of the Templar which resulted in their dissolution under Clement V in 1314. During the Hundred Years War, the Sorbonne sided with the Burgundians and the English: recognising Henry V of England as King of France, they dispatched one of their most eminent members, Bishop Pierre Cauchon to Rouen as prosecutor in the trial of Joan of Arc. The Sorbonne steadfastly opposed all Protestants and, in the 18C, all philosophers.

University Feast Days – Louis XI instituted the 28 January, dedicated to St Charlemagne as the University's feast day and 11 June (St Barnaby – Lendit Fair – *see* EXCURSIONS: CATHÉDRALE ST-DENIS) as the date all tuition fees had to be paid – hence the timing for its 'rag week' when final attempts to find money are made.

The buildings – Richelieu, elected Chancellor of the Sorbonne, put in hand the first phase of reconstruction by restoring buildings and the church (1624-1642). It was well after Napoleon re-instituted the University, however, that the Sorbonne was rebuilt and expanded to become the most important university in France (between 1885 and 1901). The complex has to accommodate 22 lecture halls, two museums, 16 examination halls, 22 seminar rooms, 37 tutorial rooms for teaching staff, 240 laboratories, a library, a physics tower, an astronomy tower, administration offices, the chancellor's lodge, etc. The most interesting areas to the uninitiated are along the rue des Écoles, the entrance hall, the main staircase and great lecture theatre with Puvis de Chavannes' famous painting, the **Sacred Wood**★. Rooms, halls, corridors are hung with historical or allegorical paintings.

The main courtyard, lined on the left by the library wing, is dominated by the chapel's Classical pediment and cupola. Decorative panels by Weerts beneath the arches illustrate the traditional Lendit Fair held at St-Denis when a huge procession including students and masters made its way north (11 June).

★**Église de la Sorbonne** ⓥ – The church was designed by **Lemercier** between 1635 and 1642 in the Jesuit style of St-Paul-St-Louis *(see* le MARAIS*)*, although here the proportions of the façade do not overwhelm the rest of the building and two, instead of three, orders are superimposed – a format to be used elsewhere.

The **lateral elevation**★ giving onto the main courtyard is completely different: at ground level 10 Corinthian columns frame the main doorway, then the profile of the transept crossing, above which rises the cupola. The full impact is best appreciated from the far end of the courtyard.

Inside, in the chancel is the white marble **tomb**★ of Cardinal Richelieu, designed by Le Brun, and magnificently carved by **Girardon** (1694). The tomb was violated in 1794 when the church became the Temple of Reason; it was not until 1971 that the great churchman was laid to rest once more in the chancel. The cupola pendentives painted with Richelieu's coat of arms, angels and Church Fathers are by Philippe de Champaigne.

The Duke of Richelieu, minister to Louis XVIII, is also buried in the church.

In the crypt are the tombs of faculty members who died for their country.

Collège de France – *11 place Marcelin-Berthelot.* With its great past and an equal present-day reputation, this part of the university stands on the site of large Gallo-Roman baths discovered in 1846 of which nothing remains.

Three Language College – A vulgar form of Latin was spoken throughout the medieval university; the Classical authors were proscribed; Virgil was unknown. In 1530, at the suggestion of the great humanist, Guillaume Budé, François I created a new centre of learning with 12 "king's readers" freed from the constraints of Sorbonne intolerance, scholasticism and disdain of pagan literature. The teachers were paid directly by the king and so could give instruction free.

In the "three language college" students learned to read the greatest Latin, Greek and Hebrew authors. Henri II installed the staff and students in two colleges, Cambrai and Tréguier. It is here that a Royal College of France was instituted in the 17C by Louis XIII. New subjects were added: mathematics, medicine, surgery, philosophy, Arabic, Syriac, botany, astronomy, canon law and, in the reign of Louis XV, French literature.

The college today – In 1778 the building was reconstructed by Chalgrin and, at the Revolution, took its modern name of Collège de France. 19C building reorganisations have been replaced in the 20C by vast additions. The ill-equipped labs, at the corner of rue des Écoles and rue St-Jacques in which Claude Bernard worked on the function of the pancreas from 1847 to 1878, have been replaced by new laboratories – where Frédéric Joliot-Curie produced fission in a uranium particle with his cyclotron. Other outstanding members of the College have been the physicist André-Marie Ampère (1775-1836), the historian Jules Michelet (1798-1874), the Egyptologist Jean-François Champollion (1790-1832) who discovered how to decode hieroglyphics, the philosopher Henri Bergson (1859-1941), the poet Paul Valéry (1871-1946), the physician François Jacob (b1920) winner of the Nobel Prize for medicine (1965) for his work on ARN and ADN.

The college retains complete academic autonomy but has been dependent financially on the state since 1852.

Impasse Chartière – At no 11 stood the **Coqueret College** attended in the 16C under the Hellenist master, Dorat, by the future poets Ronsard, Antoine de Baïf, and later, Rémy Belleau, Jodelle, Pontus de Tyard and du Bellay, who formed the Pléïade literary group.

The former college has been incorporated in St Barbe's.

Rue de Lanneau – *by the entrance to impasse Chartière.* Note the picturesque 16C houses.

★★MUSÉE NATIONAL DU MOYEN ÂGE – THERMES DE CLUNY

6 place Paul-Painlevé. Ⓜ/RER: Saint-Michel, Cluny-La Sorbonne. Buses 21, 27, 38, 63, 85, 86, 87

The old residence of the Abbots of Cluny, the ruins of the Roman baths and the museum's wonderful treasures, make a thoroughly interesting group.

The Roman baths – The present ruins cover about one third of a vast Gallo-Roman public bath house complex from the beginning of the 3C, constructed by the powerful guild of Paris boatmen. It was ransacked and more or less destroyed at the end of the 3C by the barbarians.

Residence of the Abbots of Cluny – About 1330, Pierre of Châlus, Abbot of Cluny-en-Bourgogne, the influential Burgundian Abbey, bought the ruins and the surrounding land to build a residence for abbots visiting Paris and for a college yet to be founded near the Sorbonne. Jacques of Amboise, Bishop of Clermont and Abbot of Jumièges in Normandy, rebuilt the house to its present design between 1485 and 1500.

Hospitality was given to many guests including in 1515 Mary Tudor, eldest daughter of Henry VII, widowed at 16 by the death of Louis XII of France, a man in his 50s who survived the marriage only three months. The 'white queen' – as royal widows endured their period of mourning dressed in white – was closely watched over by Louis' cousin and successor, François I, lest she should bear a child which might cost him his throne. Indeed, when Mary was discovered one night in the company of the young Duke of Suffolk, the king compelled her to marry the Englishman in the chapel there and then before despatching her to England.

In the 17C the house accommodated the papal nuncios, the most illustrious being Mazarin.

Creation of a museum – At the Revolution the residence classed as State property was sold, passing to a variety of owners including a surgeon who used the chapel as a dissecting room, a cooper, a printer and a laundress; the navy installed an observatory in the tower and discovered 21 planets. The baths were covered with six feet of soil so that vegetables and an orchard could be planted. In 1833 Alexandre Du Sommerard came to live in the house, installing his substantial collection of artefacts from the Middle Ages and the Renaissance. At his death in 1842 the mansion and its contents were purchased by the State. The City of Paris having acquired the Baths in 1819 agreed to cede their rights to the land on condition that the whole be opened as a museum (1844); Edmond du Sommerard, son of the former owner was appointed as curator.

The gardens were eventually opened to the public in 1971.

★Hôtel de Cluny – This mansion, together with the Hôtel de Sens and Jacques Cœur's house *(see* le MARAIS), is one of only three large 15C private houses in Paris. Despite much restoration, original medieval details survive in features such as the wall crenellations and turrets, but it is the suggestion of a comfortable lifestyle and refined decoration that is particularly evocative.

In the main courtyard there is a fine 15C well kerb. The left wing is articulated with arches; the central building has mullioned windows; a frieze and Flamboyant balustrade, from which gargoyles spurt, line the base of the roof, ornamented with picturesque dormer windows swagged with coats of arms. A pentagonal tower juts out from the central building to contain a wide spiral staircase. There are other staircases in the corner turrets.

Concerts of Medieval and Baroque music are sometimes held here.

★★Musée National du Moyen Âge ⊙ – The museum's 24 galleries are devoted to the Middle Ages, displaying the richness and skill of the applied arts of the period.

171

The decorative arts of the Middle Ages – Most of the art treasures collected evoke aspects of everyday life, notably in religious communities. These include illuminated manuscripts, furniture, arms and armour, church plate, ironwork, stained glass (29 original 12C-13C medallions from the Sainte-Chapelle, *Room VI*), ceramics, liturgical vestments and embroideries (*Room III*), ivories (11C Byzantine casket, *Room XVII*), alabaster reliefs from Nottingham (*Room V*), stone sculpture (capitals from St-Germain-des-Prés and Ste-Geneviève, statues from the Sainte-Chapelle, *Rooms IX and X*) and wood carvings (stalls from Beauvais, *Room XVIII*).

Room VIII contains fragments of figurative sculpture from the façade of Notre-Dame: notably 21 heads of the Kings of Judah from the Gallery of Kings, vandalised during the Revolution when thought to represent the kings of France. These heads discovered during the restoration of a house in the 9th *arrondissement* date from the mid-12C to mid-13C, and have an air of unexpected freshness and surprising intensity despite their condition. The doorway at the entrance into the room comes from the Lady Chapel of the Abbey of St-Germain-des-Prés.

Some of the finest masterpieces of the late Middle Ages are grouped in Room XIV: the Tarascon Pietà, a tapestry depicting the story of the Prodigal Son; sculptures in stone, marble and wood including two Flemish altarpieces: the Passion and the Averbode retables, a statue of Mary Magdalen thought to be a portrait of Mary of Burgundy... A splendid gold altar frontal from Basel Cathedral is presented in Room XIX; gold plate is displayed in Room XVI: rare votive crowns of the Visigoth kings, gold rose from Basel, reliquaries in *champlevé* and Limosges enamels commissioned by the Avignon Papacy.

The tapestries – A series of 15C and early 16C tapestries of the mille-fleurs or "thousand flower" design, woven in the south of the Netherlands, suggest a love of nature, a taste for harmony and freshness of colour in the grace of the figures and animals portrayed. In Room IV the "Manorial Life" hanging depicts a knight and his lady *c*1500.

★★★ **La Dame à la Licorne** – *(Room XIII rotunda, 1st floor).* **The Lady and the Unicorn** panels are the most exquisite examples of late-15C Belgian weaving. The six tapestries, armor-

ial bearings of the Le Viste family from Lyon, portray the lion (chivalric nobility) and the unicorn (bourgeois nobility) on either side of a richly attired lady. Five are thought to be allegories of the senses with the sixth, 'to my heart's desire', showing the young woman depositing a necklace in a casket, symbolising a renouncement of such earthly, sensual pleasures.

Note the blue-green grass against a plain, flat red background, the lack of any superficial decoration, the detailed observation and sensitive interpretation of the animal and plant kingdoms.

★ **Chapel** – *(Room XX)*. The chapel, on the first floor, was designed as the abbots' oratory. It has an elegant Flamboyant vault supported by a central column. Twelve statues of members of the Ambrose family would have stood in the niches, each with its console and carved canopy. A stone staircase with an open well leads down to the garden.

The Lady and the Unicorn

★ **Les Thermes** – Excavations have determined the plan of these public baths dating from AD 200. The best preserved area, the frigidarium (*Room XII*) measuring 21m x 11m – 69ft x 36ft, 14.5m – 47 1/2ft high with 2m – 6 1/2ft thick walls, was built in layers of small quarry stones divided by courses of red brick. Vault ribs rest on consoles carved as ships' prows – an unusual motif suggesting the idea that the building was constructed by the Paris guild of boatmen. It was this same guild that, in the reign of Tiberius (AD 14-37), dedicated a pillar to Jupiter, discovered beneath the chancel of Notre-Dame: known as **le pilier des nautes**(1) (Boatmen's Pillar), it is Paris' oldest existing sculpture. Excavated in part, a vast underground gallery vaulted in Romanesque brick, extends under the complex.

Rue de l'École-de-Médecine – At no **5** the long-gowned Brotherhood of Surgeons, founded by St Louis in the 13C, performed anatomical operations of every kind until the 17C. Barbers or short-gowned surgeons were allowed to undertake only bleeding and confinements: it was here that **Sarah Bernhardt** was born 25 October 1844. The 1695 candle-lit lecture theatre has been incorporated in the Paris III University. At no **15** stood the **couvent des Cordeliers** – a Franciscan monastery of high repute in the Middle Ages for its teaching. In Louis XVI's reign, the geometrician **Verniquet** worked thereon the first trigonometrical plan of Paris. Shortly afterwards, in 1791, the revolutionary group formed by Danton, Marat, Camille Desmoulins and Hébert, known as the Cordeliers, took over both the monastery and its name; opposite, lived Jean-Paul **Marat** (1743-1793) the pamphleteer who was stabbed in his bath by Charlotte Corday on 13 July 1793. The present buildings, now part of the university (Paris VI), were built between 1877 and 1900 to house the School of Practical Medicine. Of the vast monastic buildings, only the monks' Flamboyant Gothic refectory-dormitory remains, off the courtyard.

The central part of the former Medical School (no 12), now known as the **René Descartes University** (Paris V), dates back to 1775. An Ionic colonnade precedes the large courtyard with a statue by **David d'Angers** of the anatomist Marie-François Bichat (1771-1802), who defined the physiology of human tissue. Students of medicine and surgery who were taught separately before the Revolution were here brought under one roof in 1808.

Musée d'Histoire de la Médecine ⓥ – *Université René-Descartes, 12 rue École-de-Médecine*. This museum houses the College of Surgeons' collections of surgical instruments from Ancient Egyptian to modern times.

Rue Hautefeuille – No 5 with an attractive 16C turret was once a residence of the abbots of Fécamp.

★★QUARTIER ST-SÉVERIN

Ⓜ/RER: St-Michel. Buses: 21, 24, 27, 38, 85, 96

This is perhaps one of the oldest quarters of Paris. **Rue de la Harpe** was the main north-south Gallo-Roman road; **rue de la Parcheminerie** (Parchment Street) was once lined with public scribes, letter-writers and copyists. Today, the bustle continues with local residents, students and tourists attracted by experimental cinemas, undercroft 'dives' and night-clubs, foreign-food restaurants, in search of entertainment late into the night.

★★**Église St-Séverin-St-Nicolas** ⓥ – *1 rue des Prêtres-St-Séverin*. In the 6C there lived in this area of open countryside, a hermit by the name of Séverin who persuaded Clodoald, grandson of King Clovis (future St-Cloud in France), to take holy orders. An oratory, raised to his memory, was burned down by the Normans. It was replaced first by a chapel and later by a church dedicated not to the original Séverin but to a Swiss namesake, St Severinus.

By the end of the 11C, St-Séverin was serving as the parish church for the Left Bank; in the 12C, Foulques, a parish priest from Neuilly-sur-Marne, preached from its pulpit the Fourth Crusade, which was to found the Latin Empire of Constantinople (1204).

Building of the present church began in the first half of the 13C when a master builder, retaining the Romanesque façade, began rebuilding the first three bays of the nave in the Flamboyant Gothic style. Work concluded in 1530.

Holy Communion Chapel

Rue des Prêtres St Séverin

■ 13 C ▨ 14 and 15 C ▨ 16 C

Exterior – The west door, which is 13C, comes from the Church of St-Pierre-aux-Bœufs on the Ile de la Cité which was demolished in 1839. Above, windows, balustrades and rose window are all 15C Flamboyant Gothic. The original porch can be seen on the north side of the tower (the tympanum has been recarved). Still on the north side, in the corner formed by the chapels, is a niche containing a statue of St Severinus. The tower superstructure and *flèche* are 15C.

Chapel and aisle bays are covered by ridge roofs, each gable being ornamented with mouldings and monster gargoyles.

Interior – The width of the building compared to its length, is immediately striking. The extra breadth dates from the 14C and 15C when expansion was possible only laterally. The original hall-church building therefore was flanked by two additional aisles and a double series of chapels. There is no transept. The Communion chapel, on the southeast side, dates from the 17C.

The actual dimensions are: length 50 m, width 34m and height 17m – 164ft x 112ft x 56ft *(For the proportions of Notre-Dame – see* ILE DE LA CITÉ*)*.

Nave – The first three bays of the nave are far superior to the rest. Their short columns are ornamented with capitals, above the broken-arch arcades runs the triforium, a narrow gallery replacing an earlier wide tribune as at Notre-Dame. Tracery is typical of the Late Gothic *style rayonnant*.

In the later bays, columns are reduced to shafts devoid of capitals and the tracery becomes more angular and complicated. Note the capitals on the nave side of the central piers carved with figures of angels, prophets and urchins.

The famous organ has an outstanding Louis XV-style organ loft. The two apostle paintings in the north aisle are 17C.

St-Séverin-St-Nicholas, ambulatory

R. Mazin/TOP

Chancel – The five arches around the apse stand taller than those of the nave, reaching up to the well-articulated Flamboyant vaulting. The double **ambulatory**★★ encircling the chancel is a spectacular further expression of Flamboyant architecture with its bouquets of ribs rising from elegant shafts, faceted with straight or spiralling surfaces. Piers in the chancel are faced with marble and wood – strangely 'modernised' by the architect Le Brun in the 1680s when the capricious Grande Mademoiselle, cousin to Louis XIV, adopted St-Séverin in preference to her parish church St Sulpice, by throwing money from her vast fortune at its embellishment.

★**Windows** – The beautiful stained glass in the upper windows is late 15C; the west end bay partly hidden by the organ illustrates a Tree of Jesse (16C); modern glass in the chevet is by Bazaine.

Charnel House – *(Closed to the public)*. A small garden has been created over the burial ground enclosed by a charnel house *(charniers)*. A section of the galleries, now restored, is the only example of any to survive in Paris from medieval times.

It was in this burial ground that in 1474 the first successful operation to remove gall stones was performed. An archer, who had been condemned to death, was offered his freedom by Louis XI should he survive the experimental operation – in surviving he regained not only his freedom but also his well-being!

★**Église St-Julien-le-Pauvre** ⊙ – *1 rue St-Julien-le-Pauvre*. This small local church in its picturesque setting with an unforgettable view of Notre-Dame, has an appeal all its own. Several chapels dedicated to St Julian have successively occupied this site since the 6C – named after the 3C Martyr, Bishop of Brioude; after Saint Julian the Confessor, the medieval Bishop of Le Mans, also known as the Poor because he gave so much away that his purse was always empty; and finally after the ferry-man Saint Julian Hospitaller. It is the name of the alms-giving bishop however which has stuck.

The present building was constructed at the same time as Notre-Dame by the monks of Longpont, a monastery a few miles outside Paris, between 1165 and 1220.

The University used to hold its assemblies here, including the election of its chancellor, from the 13C until 1524 when students made such a rumpus and damaged the interior so gravely that university proceedings were barred henceforth. In 1655 the priory was suppressed, and the church was attached as a chapel to the Hôtel-Dieu Hospital. Since 1889 it has been a Melchite Chapel.

Church – The courtyard portal was constructed only in 1651 when two bays of the nave and the south aisle were removed. The northern façade and chancel, flanked by twin apsidal chapels, overlook the square René-Viviani *(see* les QUAIS – Quai de Montebello). Inside, the Gothic vaulting of the aisles is original, whereas the nave was re-roofed with cradle vaulting in 1651. The chancel, the most beautiful part of the building, is screened off by a wooden iconostasis hung with icons or holy pictures.

Note the two pillars in the chancel with **capitals**★ carved with acanthus leaves and harpies, and the unusual 15C tombstone in the south aisle.

The **view**★★ of St-Séverin across the entrance to rue Galande is one of the most picturesque of Old Paris, and still a popular subject for painters. An iron well-head, originally from inside the church, now stands against the doorway near two Roman paving stones from the old Orléans-to-Lutétia road (Lutétia being the Roman name for Paris).

Rue St-Julien-le-Pauvre – No 14 dates from the 17C and was at one time the house of the governor of the Petit Châtelet or lesser Barbican.

★QUARTIER MAUBERT

Ⓜ *Maubert-Mutualité /RER St-Michel-Notre Dame. Buses: 21, 24, 27, 38, 85, 96*

This neighbourhood is a fragment of medieval Paris threaded with narrow, winding streets. Its name is probably a corruption of Maître Albert or Albert the Great who taught theology from the square in the 13C. 'La Maube' has recently been subjected to major restoration.

Rue Galande – At nos **54-46** cellars and pointed medieval arches have been unearthed; a carved stone above the door of no **42** shows St Julian the Hospitaller in his boat. Note the 15C façade of No **31**.

Rue du Fouarre – This was one the places where, in the Middle Ages, public lectures were given by the university in the open air attended by students seated on bundles of straw *(fouarre)*. Dante is said to have attended lectures in this street in 1304.

Rue de la Bûcherie – The École d'Administration now occupies the premises of the first Medical School founded in the 15C. The rotunda dates from the 17C.

Impasse Maubert – It was here that the Greek College was founded in 1206 – the first in Paris, and that the infamous Marquise de Brinvilliers *(see* BASTILLE – L'Arsenal*)* concocted her poisons in the 17C.

Rue Maître-Albert – The old houses rise above a network of underground passages down to the banks of the Seine and to the adjoining alleyways that sheltered rogues and conspirators up until the 20C. Mme du Barry's negro attendant, Zamor, who denounced her and caused her to be sent to the guillotine, died in 1820 at no **13**.

Rue de Bièvre – The name is taken from that of a tributary of the Seine. The area around was particularly populated by boatmen and tanners. The entrance of the former St-Michel College at no **12** is surmounted by a statue of St Michael slaying the dragon.

Place Maubert – Since the early Middle Ages, this square has been a traditional rallying point for university students and where barricades have gone up in times of popular uprising. **Rue des Anglais** is named after the English students who lived there in the Middle Ages.

Musée de la Préfecture de Police Ⓥ – *1bis rue des Carmes*. The **Historical Collections of the Police Museum** *(2nd floor)* display the evolution of the Paris police from the time of sentry watchmen in the early Middle Ages to the creation of the Guardians of the Peace Corps in 1870. There are also interesting legal documents on display such as *lettres de cachet* or royal warrants, decrees, prison registers, weapons and souvenirs of famous criminals and conspirators.

Église des Sts-Archanges Ⓥ – *9bis rue Jean-de-Beauvais*. Purchased by the Romanian Orthodox Church in 1882, this much restored chapel is dedicated to the Archangels Michael, Gabriel and Raphael. It was originally built in the 14C as part of the **Beauvais College** founded by Jean Dormous in 1370.

Église St-Nicolas-du-Chardonnet – A chapel was constructed in what was a field of thistles *(chardons)* in the 13C. In 1656 it was replaced by the present building oriented north-south; the façade was completed only in 1934. It is dedicated to St Nicholas, the patron saint of sailors. The **side door**★ on rue des Bernardins has remarkable wood carving designed by Le Brun, a parishioner of the church. The interior is Jesuit in style, liberally decorated with paintings by Restout, Coypel, Claude, Corot and Le Brun (his funeral monument, by Coysevox, stands in an ambulatory chapel on the left near Le Brun's own monument to his mother). Note the interesting funerary monument by Girardon to the right of the chancel. The 18C organ loft is from the former Church of the Innocents.

Rue St-Victor – The St Victor monastery, founded in 1113, with its gardens and church where Bishop Maurice of Sully was buried, once extended beyond the site occupied by the Jussieu University buildings to the Seine.

Rue de Poissy – Constructed in 1772, this street was laid through the gardens of the former **Bernardins College**, which was founded in 1246 to educate monks and taken over by the Cistercians in the 14C. After it was closed down at the Revolution, the building served as a staging-point for prisoners condemned as galley-slaves. Since 1845 the buildings have served as a fire-station (nos 18-24 rue de Poissy). From the road, one can catch a glimpse of the upper part of the refectory with its three ogive-vaulted aisles divided into 17 bays. It is one of the finest Gothic halls in Paris. *Not open to the public.*

Le LOUVRE ★★★

Michelin plan 11 – fold 31, H 13
Ⓜ *Palais Royal-Musée du Louvre*

The Louvre, the largest royal palace in France, now houses one of the richest collections of art and antiquities in the world. Should time allow, it is best to visit a selection of galleries at any one time and return on another occasion for others. The Tuileries gardens, an integral part of the palace's architectural design, provide a pleasant place from which to contemplate the magnificence of the building, the collection it holds or in which to take a break from sightseeing!

★★★THE MUSEUM ⊙ *Note: Closed Tuesdays.*

Product of the Age of Enlightenment and its thirst for universal knowledge, the Louvre has recently celebrated its bicentenary. The new-born French Republic wished to transform the royal collections into a museum for everyone (1793). The inauguration of the Richelieu wing (1993), a major milestone in the "Grand Louvre" development project (1981-97), is entirely in keeping with this aim.

The Pyramide at the Louvre

The collections – **François I** was the first eminent patron of "modern" Italian masters. Twelve paintings from his original collection, including the *Mona Lisa* by Leonardo da Vinci, *La Belle Jardinière* by Raphael and a *Portrait of François I* by Titian, are amongst the most important works presently in State hands. By the time Louis XIV died, over 2 500 paintings hung in the palaces of the Louvre and Versailles.

The idea of making the collection accessible to the public, as envisaged by Marigny under Louis XVI, was finally realised by the Convention on 10 August 1793 when the doors of the Grande Galerie were opened to visitors.

Napoleon subsequently made the museum's collection the richest in the world by exacting a "tribute" in works of art from every country he conquered; many of these were reclaimed by the Allies in 1815.

In turn, Louis XVIII, Charles X and Louis-Philippe all further endowed the collections: scarcely had the *Venus of Milo* been rediscovered when she was brought to France by Dumont d'Urville. Departments for Egyptian and Assyrian art were opened.

Gifts, legacies and acquisitions continue to enrich the collections of the Louvre, with over 300 000 works now catalogued.

PRACTICALITIES

Address – Musée du Louvre, 75058 Paris Cedex 01; recorded information: ☎ 01 40 20 51 51; general enquiries: ☎ 01 40 20 53 17; Minitel access code: 3615 Louvre; Internet: http://www.louvre.fr/

Opening times – The museum opens Wednesday to Monday, from 9am to 6pm (9.45pm Wednesday – all departments, Monday – Richelieu wing only). For detailed information see Times and Charges under PRACTICAL INFORMATION section. Tickets are valid all day and include re-admission.

Parking Carrousel-Louvre *off avenue du Général Lemonnier* – Space for 80 coaches and 620 cars is available; open daily 7am to 11pm. Pedestrian access to museum through shopping mall. ☎ 01 42 44 16 32.

Access – The main museum entrance is via the **Pyramid**; however, there is a direct way from the métro (**Palais-Royal – Musée du Louvre**) through the shopping mall. Other entrances include the **Arc du Carrousel** and 99 rue de Rivoli. The porte des Lions entrance on quai des Tuileries re-opens end-1997.

Public Information – 14 video screens below the Pyramid display daily information on exhibitions and activities. Annual membership of a 'Friends of the Louvre' scheme provides free access to permanent collections and temporary exhibitions.

Temporary Exhibitions – These are held in the Hall Napoléon (*beneath the Pyramid*) or in the Sully and Richelieu wings.

Guided tours – Lecture tours (*1 hour 30 min*) take place daily, except Tuesdays and Sundays. Visitors should buy their ticket on the morning or afternoon of the tour (*details from "Accueil des groupes" beneath the Pyramid*, ☎ 01 40 20 52 09). Groups are requested to book in advance: ☎ 01 40 20 51 77.

Group access – By prior arrangement ☎ 01 40 20 51 77.

Audioguides – Available in six languages from the mezzanine level at the entrances to the Richelieu, Sully and Denon wings.

Disabled visitors – Wheelchairs for use in the galleries and special orientation guides (indicating position of lifts etc) are available from the Information Desk. Information: ☎ 01 40 20 53 17. Exploration by touch of sculpture-casts is possible on the Denon Entresol and Ground floors. Guide dogs for the blind are permitted throughout the museum.

Auditorium du Louvre – Concerts, films, lectures, conferences (420 seats). Information: ☎ 01 40 20 51 86.

Workshop visits (*visites-ateliers*) – Talks on specific works of art are given by artists, teachers and art historians. For quarterly programmes, tickets and meeting point enquire at *Accueil des groupes*. Visitors may sign up for a session on the day itself on a first-come-first-served basis (☎ 01 40 20 52 09).

Books, postcards and posters *Hall Napoléon* – A bookshop opens 0930 to 2200 stocking 17 000 titles (4 000 in foreign languages). Separate shops sell reproductions of works in national collections.

La Galerie Carrousel du Louvre – Michel Macary's **inverted pyramid★** complements the original designed by Ieoh Ming Pei. This enormous crystalline shape provides a well of light in the central area of the arcade; concrete masonry, rows of windows and subdued lighting combine to give the main arcade the appearance of a large entrance hall. On the site of Charles V's moats, the pillars and floor in Burgundy stone exude a certain polished frigidity.

The construction of a shopping arcade of 16 000m² – 172 200sq ft, to house 30 or so shops and conference rooms, virtually under the same roof as the Louvre museum is one of the most original if not controversial aspects of the Grand Louvre development project.

Display areas and retail outlets have been carefully selected to include: **Chalcographie** for traditional engravings and maps (Note *Paris* by Turgot 1734); **Boutique des Musées Nationaux** specialises in reproductions, casts and copies of sculpture and artefacts from national collections, games and books; **Virgin Megastore** for music and books (*1st floor*) on 20C art, cinema, architecture and photography; **Lalique** for crystal and glass ware; **Flammarion** for art books; fashion and jewellery boutiques; bureau de change (near the inverted pyramid) and cashpoint (near the metro) facilities.

The Grand Louvre Project is illustrated with a scale model and panels in the Halle Charles V, Carrousel du Louvre. These show the different phases of construction work and the future layout of the Tuileries gardens.

Refreshments – For gastronomes, the restaurant "**Le Grand Louvre**" beneath the Pyramid offers specialities from the southwest of France, ☎ 01 40 20 53 41. The **Café du Louvre**, the **Café Napoléon** and the **Cafétéria** *(mezzanine)* are self-service. In the museum itself there are the **Café Mollien** *(Denon, 1st floor)* and the **Café Richelieu** *(Richelieu, 1st floor)*. Access to the **Café Marly** is outside the museum, via Cour Napoléon on the side of the Richelieu wing.

In the Carrousel shopping arcade, the **Restorama** (open from 9am to 11pm) has 12 different fast food outlets.

What to see where

The museum collections are displayed in three separate sections: **Denon, Richelieu** and **Sully**, which are located in the two wings and around the Cour Carrée respectively. Plastified information boards are available in most galleries (some translated into as many as five languages) outlining the subject matter of individual works and the contexts in which they were created.

SULLY:	History of the Louvre *Entresol*
	Medieval Louvre *Entresol*
	Egyptian Antiquities *Ground and 1st floors*
	Beistegui Collection *2nd floor*

DENON:	Greek Antiquities *(Salle des Caryatides, Hellenistic Period) Ground floor*
	(Bronzes) 1st floor
	Etruscan Antiquities *Ground floor*
	Roman and Paleo-Christian Antiquities *Ground floor*
	Galerie d'Apollon *(Objets d'art) 1st floor*
	Italian Sculpture *Entresol and ground floor*
	Northern Schools: Sculpture *Entresol and ground floor*
	Italian Painting *1st floor*
	Large Format 19C French Painting *1st floor*
	Spanish Painting *1st floor*

RICHELIEU:	Northern Schools: Painting *2nd floor*
	French Painting (14C-17C) *2nd floor*
	Objets d'art (Medieval Treasure) *1st floor*
	French Sculpture *Ground floor, Cour Marly and Cour Puget*
	Oriental Antiquities *Ground floor*
	Islamic Art *Entresol*
	Special Exhibitions *Entresol*

For each department, the directions given begin from the ticket checkpoint at the entrance to the relevant wing (Sully, Denon or Richelieu).

A museum pass, valid for one, three or five days gives access to the permanent collections of over 65 venues around the capital: check at the Information Desk for details.
Remember to plan your intended visits carefully: some museums close on Mondays, others on Tuesdays.

The ongoing refurbishment of galleries is a disruptive factor to be considered when planning your visit to the Louvre. It may be helpful to note the following:
Egyptian collection (*Sully: ground and 1st floor*) closed until June 1997.
Sections of the Near Eastern Antiquities (*Sully: ground floor*) closed until end 1996, (*Denon: ground floor*) early 1997.
Sections of the Greek, Roman and Etruscan Antiquities (*Sully: 1st floor*) closed until end 1997.
Sections of 19C French and Italian Paintings (*Denon: 1st floor*) closed until end 1996.
Sections of Spanish Painting (*Denon: 1st floor*) closed end 1996 to end 1997.
18-19C British and Northern School paintings are temporarily exhibited on the first floor of the Denon wing.

SULLY WING

★HISTORY OF THE LOUVRE

On the Entresol level. Straight ahead is a rotunda, in the centre of which a round opening in the floor overlooks the pink granite Sphinx in the crypt on the floor below (see below – Egyptian Antiquities).

From the Fortress to the Fulfilment of the "Great Project" – The galleries on each side of the rotunda, decorated with stone reliefs by Jean Goujon, present the architectural and decorative evolution of the Louvre building during its transformation from fortress to royal residence and finally to museum. Numerous documents, paintings and relief models recall the rulers and architects who contributed to the present physiognomy of the palace.

EVOLUTION OF THE LOUVRE PALACE

The Merovingian, Carolingian and Capetian monarchs resisted living in the Louvre, which had been built outside the city of Paris itself. Instead they resided in the palace on the Ile de la Cité (now the Palais de Justice), the Saint-Paul and Tournelles residences (now demolished) in the Marais district, at Vincennes, or in the various châteaux owned by themselves or their richer vassals in the Loire valley.

Philippe Auguste (1180-1223) lived in the Palais de la Cité. In 1200 he had the Louvre fortress built on the north bank of the Seine, at the weakest point in his capital's defences against its English neighbours. A **keep** surrounded by a moat, the symbol of royal power, stood at the centre. This fortress was located on the southwest quarter of the present Cour Carrée. The foundations of the keep and the moat still exist *(see below – Medieval Louvre)*.

Louis IX, also known as Saint Louis (1226-1270), and **Philip the Fair** (1285-1314) both lived in the Palais de la Cité. The former had a great hall and a **lower hall** built; the latter installed his arsenal and the royal treasury in the Louvre, where they were to remain for the next four centuries.

Charles V (1364-1380) withdrew to his mansions in the Marais following the uprising led by Étienne Marcel *(see* ILE DE LA CITÉ – Palais de Justice*)*. The king transformed the old fortress into a comfortable residence, without changing its dimensions. In it, he installed his famous **library** of 973 books, the largest in the kingdom. A miniature in the *Very Rich Hours* of the Duke of Berry depicts this "attractive" Louvre, surrounded by new ramparts which put an end to its military career. After Charles V, the Louvre was not to receive many further guests for the next century and a half.

François I (1515-1547) lived mainly in the Loire valley or the Marais. In 1527, in desperate need of money, he prepared to demand contributions from the Parisian population. To soften them up, he announced his intention to take up residence in the Louvre. Rebuilding began: the keep, a bulky form which cast a shadow over the courtyard, was razed, and the advance defences were demolished; however, orders for a new palace for the King of France to be built on the foundations of the old fortress, were not given to **Pierre Lescot** until 1546. Lescot's designs (**1**) in keeping with the style of the Italian Renaissance which had found such favour on the banks of the Loire, were new to Paris. By 1547, at the death of the king, construction was barely visible above ground level.

Henri II (1547-1559) took up residence in the Louvre and retained Lescot as chief architect. It is from this period that the emblazoned monograms linking C, H and D (Catherine de' Medici, Henri and Diane de Poitiers) date. The old great hall was transformed into the **Salle des Caryatides**; on the first floor, the Salle des Cent-Suisses reserved for the Palace Guard, preceded the royal suite in the south wing (that of the Queen was on the ground floor (**2**). Royalty never occupied the other buildings around the Cour Carrée. The Louvre gateway, 2m – 6.6ft wide opened between two large towers to the east. Visitors arriving on foot were permitted access as long as they were properly dressed; pages and footmen hung about the courtyard and around the gateway, playing dice, arguing and catcalling after passing *bourgeois*.

Catherine de' Medici (1519-1589) withdrew to the Hôtel des Tournelles, her residence in the Marais, after the accidental death of her husband Henri II. Once declared Regent, she decided to take up residence in the Louvre, on the floor since known as the Logis des Reines (Queens' Lodging), but was not at all happy living in the middle of Lescot's building site. In 1564, she ordered **Philibert Delorme** to build her a residence of her own on the site known as "les Tuileries", in which she would have greater freedom of movement.

Between the two palaces, the Queen Mother planned to have a covered passage built to enable people to walk the 500m – 547yds unnoticed, under shelter from inclement weather. The connecting galleries – the **Petite Galerie** and the **Galerie du Bord de l'Eau** (or Grande Galerie), along the banks of the Seine were duly begun, but work was brought to a halt by the Wars of Religion. The Old Louvre was to keep its two Gothic and two Renaissance wings until the reign of Louis XIV.

Henri IV (1589-1610) continued work on the Louvre on his arrival in Paris in 1584. **Louis Métezeau** added an upper floor to the Galerie du Bord de l'Eau; **Jacques II Androuet Du Cerceau** completed the Petite Galerie and built the **Pavillon de Flore**, with another gallery leading off at right angles to link it with the Tuileries palace, whilst seeing to the interior decoration of the Tuileries. The scale of construction on the Louvre site reflected the high status that the monarchy was once again enjoying at this time.

Louis XIII (1610-1643) enjoyed living at the Louvre, but the Court endured severely cramped conditions. Urged by Richelieu, Louis undertook to enlarge the Louvre fourfold. Lemercier built the Clock Pavilion, and the northwest corner of the courtyard, a Classical statement in response to Lescot's design, while continuing work on the Sorbonne and the Palais-Royal. The Royal Mint and the Royal Press were accommodated in the Grande Galerie.

Louis XIV (1643-1715). After the death of Louis XIII, Anne of Austria moved to the Palais-Royal with the under-age Louis. Nine years later, they moved to the Louvre having found the Palais-Royal less than secure, intimidated by the Fronde uprisings. Louis XIV returned to **Le Vau's** extension plans, had him build the **Galerie d'Apollon** and requested a worthy façade be designed to close off the Cour Carrée (the **Colonnade**). In 1682, the king moved his court away from the capital to Versailles. Construction was brought to a halt; Le Vau's and Perrault's buildings were left without roofs.

The Louvre, centre for the arts – The city of Paris gradually engulfed the area around the Louvre site. The abandoned palace apartments were let to a wide variety of people. A Bohemian colony of artists set up camp in the galleries, organising living quarters on the mezzanine level, the floor above was used as a passageway (in which the King touched those afflicted with scrofula on five occasions a year). Resident artists included **Coustou, Bouchardon, Coypel** and **Boucher**; the palace lanterns were tended by **Hubert Robert's** wife. The space along the Colonnade was divided into apartments; rows of stove chimneys pierced the wonderful façade; shacks were erected in the courtyard; cabarets and taverns accommodated lean-tos along the outside façade. The royal apartments became occupied by the *Académies*: the Académie française, having been installed there before Louis XIV moved out of the

Tuileries, attracted other academic bodies dedicated to writing and literature, architecture, science, painting and sculpture. The fine arts academy began organising exhibitions of members' work in 1699, an event held around the feast of St Louis (25 August) which was to become a regular feature in the Salon Carré from 1725, and which lasted until the 1848 Revolution. Diderot, followed by Baudelaire, became critics of these "salons", at which taste in art during the 18C and early 19C was formulated.

18C-19C – By now, the Louvre was so run down as to prompt talk of pulling it down altogether. After the brief interval of the Regency (1715-22), Louis XV lived at Versailles from whence Louis XVI was brought to Paris on 6 October 1789, briefly occupying the Tuileries until his incarceration at the Temple prison.
The Convention used the theatre and the Committee of Public Safety installed itself in the royal apartments of the Tuileries, until appropriated by Bonaparte, the Premier Consul.

Napoleon I (1799-1814) whilst living in the Tuileries, took great interest in the Louvre; his first undertaking was to expel its lodgers. The emperor commissioned the architects **Percier** and **Fontaine** to complete the Cour Carrée, to enlarge the place du Carrousel so that he might review his troops there, and to build the Arc de Triomphe du Carrousel. Work stopped when the emperor fell in 1814.

Napoleon III (1852-1870), also resident in the Tuileries, oversaw the completion of the Louvre. He entrusted first **Visconti**, then **Lefuel** with the task of closing off the Grande Cour (3) to the north. The latter compensated for the difference in levels of the two arms of the Louvre by rebuilding the Pavillon de Flore in an exaggeratedly grandiose style and by modifying the western section of the Galerie du Bord de l'Eau. It was at this time that the Carrousel entrance gates *(guichets)* were inserted.

The Republic – The uprising of the Paris Commune (a week of bloodshed from 21 to 28 May 1871) resulted in the Tuileries palace burning down; its collections however were saved at the last minute. In 1873 the Presidency of the Third Republic installed itself in the Palais de l'Élysée.
In 1875, **Lefuel** undertook the restoration of the Louvre, proposing along with others that the Tuileries be rebuilt. In 1882 the Assembly after due deliberation, had the ruins removed, thereby obliterating any political significance or association with the past regime.

★★★**Medieval Louvre** – Carry on from the rotunda into the Sully crypt. Here, a dark line on the floor indicates the location of one of the 10 towers which made up part of the Old Louvre. Further on, the visitor encounters the impressive surroundings of the **fortress** built by Philippe Auguste in the early 13C.
The wooden walkway follows the line of the north and the east moats. On the left is the counterscarp wall, a simple façade showing visible signs of repair work; on the right is the 2.6m – 7ft thick curtain wall.
On the east side, a trapezoidal construction indicates the location of the foundations of the residence added by Charles V in 1360. In the middle of the ditch, the supporting pier of the drawbridge is framed by the twin towers of the **east gate** of Philippe Auguste's castle. Its rectangular stones are evenly placed and feature putlog holes and heart-shaped engravings carved by the stonemasons.
A modern gallery *(to the right, before the Crypte du Sphinx)* leads to the moat around the circular keep or "**Grosse Tour**" built for Philippe Auguste between 1190 and 1202. The moat, with an average width of 7.5m – 23ft, was once paved with enormous stones.
The tour of the Medieval Louvre ends with two galleries. The first contains the earthenware items discovered during the excavation of the Cour Carrée. The second, the "**Salle Saint-Louis**" with mid-13C vaulting, has a display of royal items found at the bottom of the well in the keep. These include a replica of Charles VI's parade helmet, the "**chapel doré**".

★★★EGYPTIAN ANTIQUITIES

Go through the Medieval Louvre section, which brings you to the Crypte du Sphinx. Take the staircase up on the left. The department of Egyptian Antiquities is being refitted until early 1997. The descriptions given are restricted to the main works of art.
The department of Egyptian Antiquities is the legacy of **Jean-François Champollion**, who drew on the work of the English physicist Thomas Young (1773-1829) for help in unravelling the mysteries of hieroglyphics in 1822, thus founding Egyptology. His department leads visitors along in the wake of famous expeditions. A consistent policy of purchasing, collecting and acquiring excavated material continued until the Second World War, endowing the Louvre with thousands of artefacts. These shed light both on the funerary rituals of a wealthy upper class, which financed sumptuous sarcophagi, and upon the less well-off strata of Ancient Egyptian society.

Sphinx – *In the crypt.* This colossal monolith in pink granite, 4.8m – 16ft long, was found at **Tanis** in the Nile delta, the capital of Egypt during its decline.

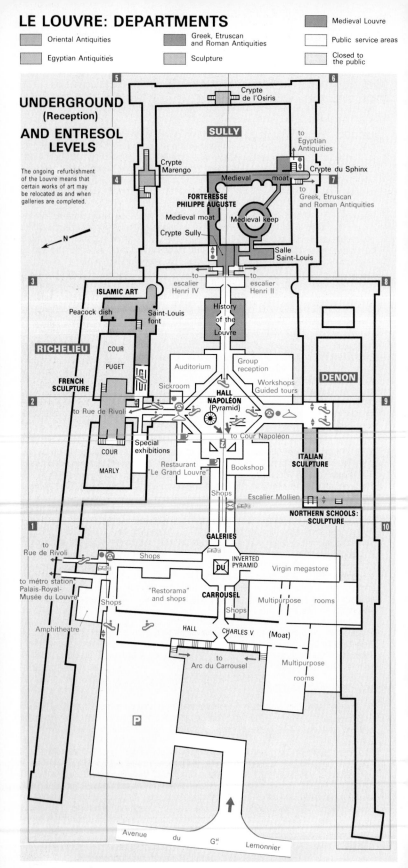

LE LOUVRE: DEPARTMENTS

- Oriental Antiquities
- Egyptian Antiquities
- Greek, Etruscan and Roman Antiquities
- Sculpture
- Medieval Louvre
- Public service areas
- Closed to the public

UNDERGROUND (Reception) AND ENTRESOL LEVELS

The ongoing refurbishment of the Louvre means that certain works of art may be relocated as and when galleries are completed.

N

Crypte de l'Osiris

SULLY

to Egyptian Antiquities

Crypte Marengo

Medieval moat

Crypte du Sphinx

to Greek, Etruscan and Roman Antiquities

FORTERESSE PHILIPPE AUGUSTE

Medieval moat

Medieval keep

Crypte Sully

Salle Saint-Louis

to escalier Henri IV

to escalier Henri II

ISLAMIC ART

Peacock dish

Saint-Louis font

History of the Louvre

RICHELIEU

COUR PUGET

Auditorium

Group reception

Workshops Guided tours

DENON

FRENCH SCULPTURE

Sickroom

HALL NAPOLÉON (Pyramid)

to Rue de Rivoli

COUR MARLY

Special exhibitions

Restaurant "Le Grand Louvre"

to Cour Napoléon

ITALIAN SCULPTURE

Bookshop

Escalier Mollien

Shops

NORTHERN SCHOOLS: SCULPTURE

to Rue de Rivoli

GALERIES

Shops

INVERTED PYRAMID

Virgin megastore

to métro station Palais-Royal-Musée du Louvre

Shops

"Restorama" and shops

CARROUSEL

Multipurpose rooms

Amphitheatre

Shops

HALL

CHARLES V

(Moat)

Shops

to Arc du Carrousel

Multipurpose rooms

P

Avenue du G.al Lemonnier

182

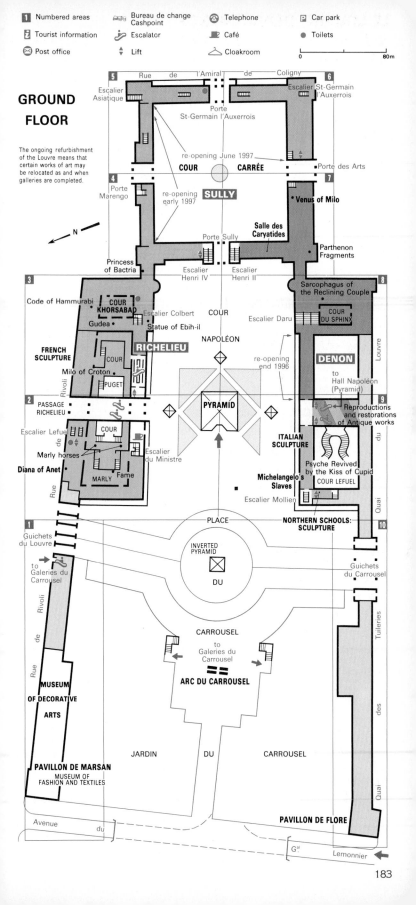

GROUND FLOOR

Numbered areas
Tourist information
Post office
Bureau de change / Cashpoint
Escalator
Lift
Telephone
Café
Cloakroom
Car park
Toilets

0 — 80m

The ongoing refurbishment of the Louvre means that certain works of art may be relocated as and when galleries are completed.

N

5 Rue de l'Amiral de Coligny **6**
Escalier Asiatique
Escalier St-Germain l'Auxerrois
Porte St-Germain l'Auxerrois

re-opening June 1997
COUR CARRÉE
Porte des Arts

4 Porte Marengo
re-opening early 1997
SULLY
7
• Venus of Milo

Salle des Caryatides

Porte Sully
Princess of Bactria
Escalier Henri IV
Escalier Henri II
Parthenon Fragments

3
Code of Hammurabi
COUR KHORSABAD
Gudea •
Escalier Colbert
• Statue of Ebih-il
COUR
NAPOLÉON

Sarcophagus of the Reclining Couple
8
COUR DU SPHINX
Escalier Daru

FRENCH SCULPTURE
COUR
PUGET
Milo of Croton

RICHELIEU

re-opening end 1996
DENON
to Hall Napoléon (Pyramid)

Louvre

2
PASSAGE RICHELIEU
Escalier Lefuel
COUR
Escalier du Ministre
Marly horses
Diana of Anet
MARLY Fame

PYRAMID

9
Reproductions and restorations of Antique works

ITALIAN SCULPTURE
Psyche Revived by the Kiss of Cupid
COUR LEFUEL
Michelangelo's Slaves
Escalier Mollien

Rue de Rivoli

1
Guichets du Louvre
to Galeries du Carrousel

PLACE
INVERTED PYRAMID
DU
NORTHERN SCHOOLS: SCULPTURE
10
Guichets du Carrousel

Quai du Louvre
Tuileries

Rue de Rivoli

CARROUSEL
to Galeries du Carrousel
ARC DU CARROUSEL

MUSEUM OF DECORATIVE ARTS

PAVILLON DE MARSAN
MUSEUM OF FASHION AND TEXTILES

JARDIN DU CARROUSEL

Quai des

Avenue du
G°
PAVILLON DE FLORE
Lemonnier

183

LE LOUVRE: DEPARTMENTS

Egyptian Antiquities

Greek, Etruscan
and Roman Antiquities

Paintings

Graphic arts

Objets d'art

Closed to
the public

1ST FLOOR

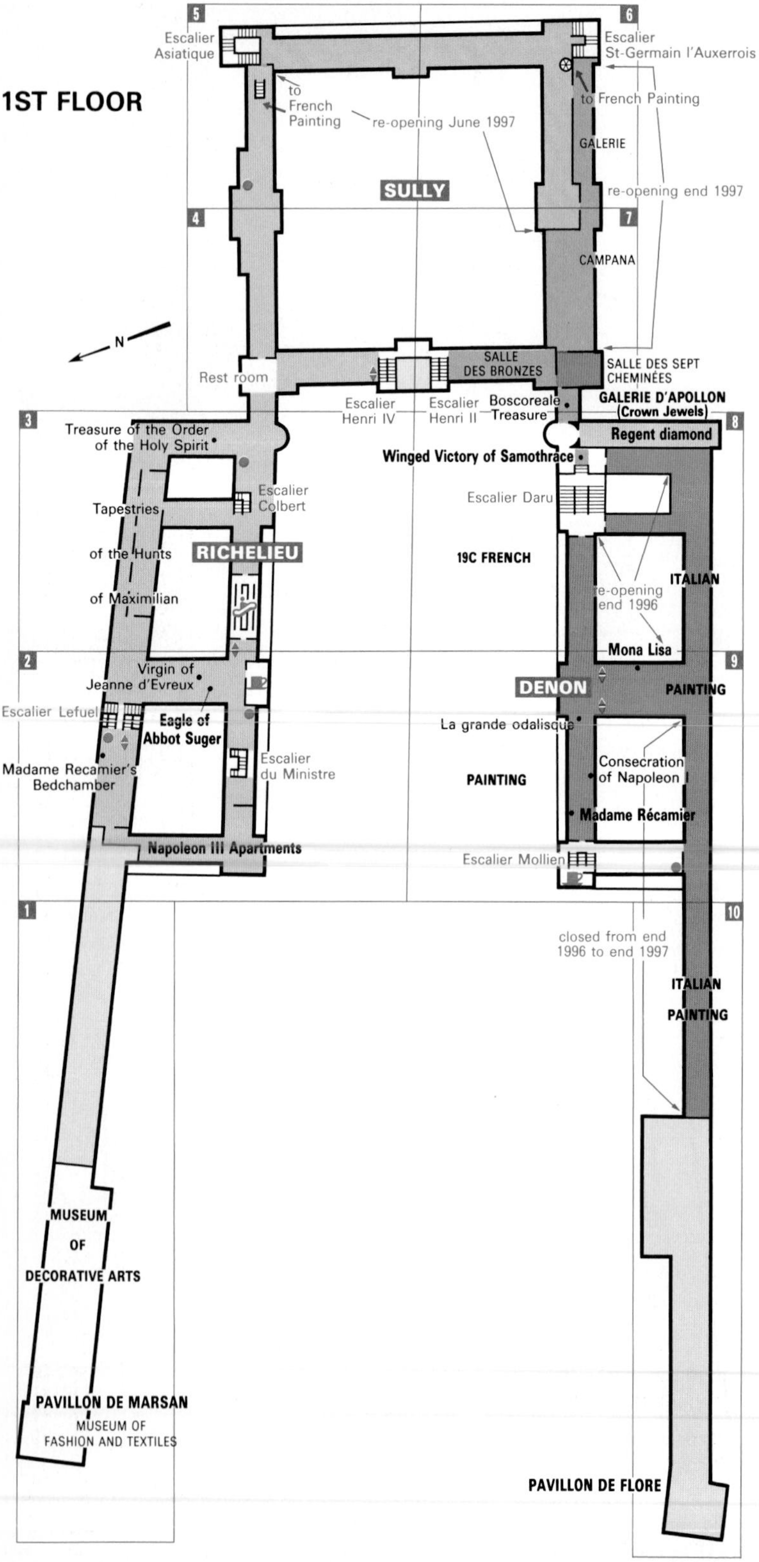

5

Escalier
Asiatique

to
French
Painting

re-opening June 1997

6

Escalier
St-Germain l'Auxerrois

to French Painting

GALERIE

re-opening end 1997

SULLY

4

CAMPANA

7

N

Rest room

SALLE
DES BRONZES

SALLE DES SEPT
CHEMINÉES

Escalier
Henri IV

Escalier
Henri II

Boscoreale
Treasure

GALERIE D'APOLLON
(Crown Jewels)

3

Treasure of the Order
of the Holy Spirit

Regent diamond

8

Tapestries

Escalier
Colbert

Winged Victory of Samothrace

of the Hunts

RICHELIEU

Escalier Daru

19C FRENCH

re-opening
end 1996

ITALIAN

of Maximilian

2

Virgin of
Jeanne d'Evreux

Escalier Lefuel

Eagle of
Abbot Suger

Madame Récamier's
Bedchamber

Escalier
du Ministre

Mona Lisa

9

DENON

PAINTING

La grande odalisque

Consecration
of Napoleon

PAINTING

Madame Récamier

Napoleon III Apartments

Escalier Mollien

1

closed from end
1996 to end 1997

10

ITALIAN

PAINTING

MUSEUM

OF

DECORATIVE ARTS

PAVILLON DE MARSAN

MUSEUM OF
FASHION AND TEXTILES

PAVILLON DE FLORE

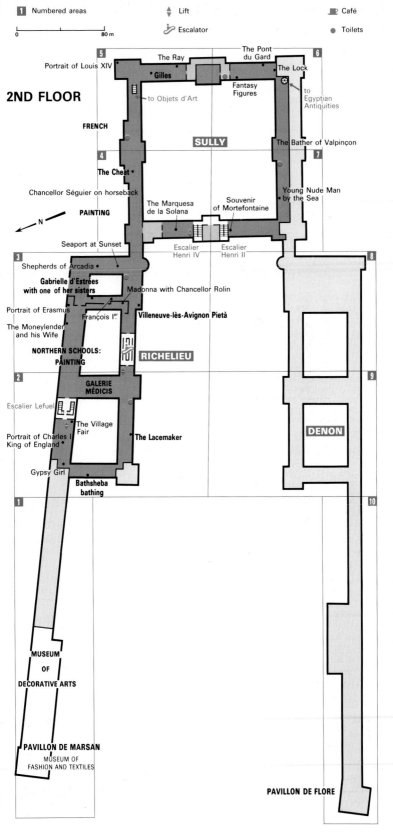

NB Work is still in progress on the Grand Louvre project;
the final location of certain works of art may therefore be subject to variation.

1 Numbered areas   ⇕ Lift   ☕ Café

🛗 Escalator   ● Toilets

0   80 m

2ND FLOOR

5   The Ray   The Pont du Gard   **6**

Portrait of Louis XIV

● Gilles   ● The Lock

to Objets d'Art   Fantasy Figures   to Egyptian Antiquities

FRENCH

SULLY

The Bather of Valpinçon

4   **7**

The Cheat ●

Chancellor Séguier on horseback

Young Nude Man by the Sea

N   **PAINTING**

The Marquesa de la Solana   Souvenir of Mortefontaine

Seaport at Sunset

Escalier Henri IV   Escalier Henri II

3   **8**

Shepherds of Arcadia ●

Gabrielle d'Estrées with one of her sisters

Madonna with Chancellor Rolin

Portrait of Erasmus

François Iᵉʳ   **Villeneuve-lès-Avignon Pietà**

The Moneylender and his Wife

NORTHERN SCHOOLS: PAINTING

RICHELIEU

2   **9**

GALERIE MÉDICIS

Escalier Lefuel

The Village Fair

Portrait of Charles I King of England ●

The Lacemaker

DENON

Gypsy Girl

Bathsheba bathing

1   **10**

MUSEUM

OF

DECORATIVE ARTS

PAVILLON DE MARSAN
MUSEUM OF FASHION AND TEXTILES

PAVILLON DE FLORE

Mastaba of Akhout-Hetep – The upper chamber of a Fifth Dynasty (c2350 BC) civil tomb was used in the cult of the deceased. The inside walls were adorned with carved and painted scenes of the hunt, of banquet preparations and of navigation illustrating the wishes of the deceased to have a beautiful tomb (corridor), to enjoy plenty of good food (bearers of offerings) and to survey by boat the lands which would have yielded such luxuries.

Knife of Gebel-el-Arak – This small exhibit, one of the earliest known to feature low-relief carving dates from the end of the prehistoric era in Egypt (c3200 BC). The engraved rhinoceros-horn handle bears a figure and animals from the sub-desert region of Middle Egypt on one side and, on the other, a river battle scene. One side of the polished flint blade has also been finely worked.

Stele of the Serpent King – This primitive work (Thinite Period) depicts King Djet, one of the first Pharaohs, identified by his symbol the serpent, beneath his protector, a falcon, against the backdrop of the façade of his palace, which frames the whole image.

Sepa and Nesa – These are early examples of civil statuary (Third Dynasty).

Head of King Didoufri – Fourth Dynasty, 2570 BC. This work is a contemporary of the Great Pyramids and one of the first to be adapted to fit a sphinx. It is crowned with the royal headdress.

Seated Scribe – This famous statue in painted limestone from the Fifth Dynasty (c2500 BC) was excavated at Sakkara. Strikingly realistic, the facial expression is alert, the hands poised as if ready to commit to papyrus what he hears, the eyes, inlaid with coloured rock crystal and the eyelids outlined in copper seem to engage the viewer.

Lintel and statues of Sesostris III – Middle Empire. This Twelfth-Dynasty sovereign is depicted at two different stages of life. The expressive portrait of the ageing king is particularly striking.

Bas-relief of King Sethi I and the goddess Hathor – New Empire, c1300 BC. This magnificent bas-relief in colourfully painted limestone comes from the Valley of the Kings. The sumptuously dressed goddess of the Thebes mountain presents the king with a magic collar.

Bust of Amenophis IV – Akhenaton – New Empire, c1375 BC. Amenophis IV changed his name to Akhenaton in deference to the sun god Aton. This sculpture comes from Karnak and was given to France in gratitude for its help in saving the monuments at Nubia. Note the highly developed realism and the inward-looking expression on the face.

Tomb of Chancellor Nakhti – Middle Empire, c2000 BC. The beautiful **statue** in acacia wood depicts the chancellor life-size, dressed in a fringed loincloth. Note also some of the items buried with the chancellor to accompany him in the after-life: models of a granary, of ships, and blue faïence **hippopotami**.

Young woman bearing an offering – Middle Empire, 2000-1800 BC. The body-clinging strapped shift is of the same style as that worn by the goddess Hathor in the bas-relief of Sethi I. The highly stylised female figurine bears offerings of food to the deceased.

Toilet articles – These include spoons used for offerings in the form of women swimming or decorated with delicate floral motifs; jewels and robes suggest the sophisticated lifestyle of New Empire high society.

Busts and statues from the reign of Amenophis III – New Empire, 1403-c1365 BC. Amenophis III is depicted with a child's face (head in diorite). This ideal of preciosity is reflected in the images of his contemporaries: **The lady Touy**, priestess of the god Min; a green enamelled stone statuette of **Queen Tiy**, wife of Amenophis III; the High Dignitary **Nebmertouf**, unrolling a papyrus under the protection of the god Thot.

Royal portraits from the reign of Amenophis IV – New Empire, c1365 – 1349 BC. Note in particular the bust of a princess, a teenage dignitary with the hint of a sulky pout, and the extraordinarily sophisticated features of the **bust of Amenophis IV**.

Rameses II's breast-plate (Sakkara, c1290-1220 BC)

Jewels of Rameses II – New Empire, c1200 BC. Rameses II was the son and heir of Sethi I. The exquisite royal jewellery includes a ring with horses, **Rameses II's great breast-plate**, a gold goblet and a gold cloisonné bracelet decorated with griffins and winged lions. The **Osorkon Triad** regroups Osiris, seated on an altar, his wife and sister Isis and their son Horus, protector of the monarchy.

Queen Karomama – Third Intermediate Period, 870-825 BC. Inlaid bronze work from the Thebes region, depicting the divine consort of Amon.

Blue-glazed funerary servants – Third Intermediate Period, c1000 BC. These figures carry tools and are assembled in squads of 10 under the command of a foreman. Answering to the Egyptian name meaning "here!", they would have been charged with menial duties for the deceased in his or her after-life.

Display case of cats – These bronze statues are ex-votos addressed to the goddess Bastet.

Coptic textiles – Egypt succumbed gradually to the influence of Christianity, increasingly drawing a new iconography from the Hellenist world of the Mediterranean and from Byzantine art. Note the **mummy** dating from the Roman Period with its painted portrait inserted in the swaddling over the face; the large collection of **textiles**, a domain in which Coptic art flourished in the 5C-6C AD, as well as a sculpture fragment of the Annunciation.

Monastery of Bawit – The fragments of the monastery of St Apollo (6C-7C AD) come from the village of Bawit in Middle Egypt. The parts of the basilical chapel arranged as found include panels and friezes in carved limestone or painted wood; the **capitals** are particularly eye-catching. In the chancel, a 7C distemper painting shows Abbot Mena carrying a marvellously embossed book of the Gospels under the protection of Christ.

★**Beistegui Collection**

Take the Escalier d'Henri II to the 2nd floor and turn left (the end of the tour of the galleries of French painting is to the right). Go through the gallery in which the painting of the month ("tableau du mois" – see below) is displayed.
The **Escalier d'Henri II**, built by Pierre Lescot, led to the king's apartments.
The gallery next to the staircase displays a different painting every month – the *"tableau du mois"* – a work which is currently of particular interest (a recent acquisition, restoration, commemorative work, etc).
The entire **collection of Carlos Beistegui** (1863, Mexico-1953, Biarritz) consisting above all of portraits, is displayed in a special gallery.
Note the *Portrait of a young artist* and a scene of dissolute living *(Le feu aux poudres)* by **Fragonard**; David's famous **Unfinished Portrait of Napoleon**; *The Duchess of Chaulnes as Hebe* by Jean-Marc Nattier; *Dido's Suicide* by **Rubens**; and *The Marquesa de la Solana*, one of **Goya**'s best-known works.

DENON WING

★★★GREEK ANTIQUITIES

Via the Salle du Manège (on the ground floor of the Denon wing) which contains reproductions and restorations of Antique works, then turn left through the Galerie Daru (2C-3C AD sarcophagi and 1C-2C AD statues; closed for refitting until mid-1996). At the far end, go round the Escalier Daru (which leads up to the Winged Victory of Samothrace) and carry straight on towards the southwest corner of the Sully wing. Greek Antique sculpture is on the ground floor; the Venus of Milo is at the far end of the series of galleries along the south side of the Sully wing, overlooking the Cour Carrée. The Galerie Campana (vases) and the Salle des Bronzes are on the 1st floor.
Very few great Greek original bronze statues survive, since this material has been melted down and put to other uses over the centuries. However, many copies were made to satisfy the eclectic tastes of the Romans, and it was these that found their way into the extensive art collections of François I, Richelieu, Mazarin and Louis XIV. Over 200 statues were "purchased" by Napoleon I alone from his son-in-law, Prince Camillo Borghese *(see Michelin Green Guide Rome)*.
Starting on the ground floor

Orientalising and Archaic Periods 7C-6C BC: gallery 4 – The **Lady of Auxerre** is one of the earliest examples of Greek sculpture (c630 BC) a gauge for the austere Dorian style, with its rigid, full-frontal pose (the face in line with the body). Although dating from only two generations later, the **Kore of Samos** from the Temple of Hera, is more Ionian in style; it is more sophisticated with its stylised draperies. The **Rampin Horseman** (named after its donor) exemplifies the refined detail of mid-6C BC Attic style, notably in the rendering of hair and beard; the rider's face lit by a slight smile.

Early 5C BC: gallery 5 (originals) – This gallery marks the transition between the Archaic and Classical styles: **Apollo of Piombino**, found in the sea off Tuscany was hewn in the workshops of Magna Graecia that included Sicily and South Italy; the **stele depicting the Exaltation of the Flower** (note the graceful gesture of the hands) is from Pharsalus.

Gallery 6 – The **metopes** from the Temple of Zeus (*c*460 BC) are displayed alongside contemporary bronzes and ceramics of the same period.

Latter half of the 5C and early 4C BC: gallery 7 (originals) – This room contains **sculptural fragments from the Parthenon**, a Doric temple built in honour of Athena on the initiative of Pericles *c*445 BC on the Athens Acropolis at the height of the great period of Hellenistic Classicism. The **fragment of the frieze** (a large part of which is in the British Museum, London) depicts the young girls who embroidered the veil offered to the city's patron goddess during the Panathenaic procession (every four years). The slow, dignified procession, the different expressions and the graceful bearing of the figures testify to the skill of **Phidias**.

5C-4C BC: galleries 14 and 15 (copies) – Several statues recall the "severe" style, notably the *Apollo Citharoedus* and the torso of a discus-thrower. The most important works exhibited here are by **Polyclitus** (*Diadumenus and the Wounded Amazon*, badly restored in the 17C) and **Phidias** (*Apollo* of the "Kassel" type – of which the best copy is the head of *Athena Parthenos*).

Classicism evolved a freer, less severe style: the *Borghese Ares* still conforms to a conventional pose, but the facial expression is more human. The late 5C BC is punctuated by Praxiteles' *Adonis* or *Narcissus (see below)*, his clinging draperies moulding the contours and forms of their female wearers. By the early 4C BC there is a return to realism (*Discus-Bearer of Naucydes*, *Athena Pacifica*).

Red-figure krater (Apulian style, *c*390-380 BC)

4C BC: gallery 16 (copies) – Apart from the muse *Melpomene* from the Theatre of Pompeii (1C BC), these sculptures are replicas of works by the great sculptor **Praxiteles** (active 370-330 BC), who breathed life into the marble he sculpted, his figures having a fluid and careless grace yet charged with spirituality. *Apollo the Lizard-Slayer* poses informally, a youth poised on one leg, his weight carelessly swung on one hip; *Diana of Gabies* embodies all the femininity and modesty of Artemis, the huntress, goddess of the moon, as she fastens her cloak, qualities shared by *Venus of Arles* and the **Cnidian Aphrodite**, the most prized female statue of Antiquity.

2C-1C BC: gallery 13 (originals) – The **"Borghese Gladiator"** (*c*100 BC), a statue of the fighting warrior, exemplifies the standardisation of attitude and expression typical of this period.

2C BC: gallery 12 (originals) – The natural, serene beauty of the **Venus of Milo** (or more properly, the Aphrodite of Milo), twisted in a graceful spiral of movement echoed in the draperies around her body, make this statue one of the masterpieces of Antique statuary. Nearby, a copy of Praxiteles' Cnidian Aphrodite (2C BC), the face of Aphrodite known as the *"Kaufmann Head"* after its former owner, is both alert and serene.

★★**Salle des Caryatides: gallery 17** – This gallery was once the great hall of the Old Louvre palace modified by Pierre Lescot. It is named after the four monumental draped female **statues** by Jean Goujon which support the minstrels' balcony. It was here that Molière first performed before Louis XIV on 24 October 1658.
The sculptures displayed are copies dating from the Hellenistic Period (4C BC), harmonising well with the Renaissance décor. Figures with elongated proportions attributed to be after **Lysippus** are almost Mannerist in style, caught at the point of action: *Hermes tying his sandal*, *Crouching Aphrodite* of Vienna, *Artemis* known as **Diana of Versailles**, *The Three Graces*, and **Sleeping Hermaphrodite** (on a mattress by Bernini). The *Nymph of Fontainebleau* above the minstrels' balcony is by the Florentine, **Benvenuto Cellini** (16C).

The collection continues on the 1st floor, up the Escalier Daru.

***Winged Victory of Samothrace** – Early 2C BC. From its pedestal at the top of the Escalier Daru, designed especially for it, this statue seems on the point of taking flight. This masterpiece of Hellenistic art, the figurehead on a stone ship's prow, commemorates a naval victory at Rhodes. The treatment of draperies sculpted as if blown in a strong wind mould the contours of the winged figure. The suggestion of free movement and powerful action make this work of art particularly impressive. A hand belonging to the statue is displayed separately on the landing.

**Galerie Campana – *Up the Escalier Daru, to the left of the Winged Victory of Samothrace, through the Salle de Boscoreale and Salle des Sept Cheminées. The Galerie Campana is off to the right of the Salle Clarac.*
The collection of the **Marchese Campana**, an enthusiastic antiquarian who excavated the Etruscan necropolises of northern Latium *(see below – Etruscan Antiquities)*, in particular that at Cerveteri (1840s), was bought almost in its entirety in 1861 by Napoleon III. It included numerous Greek vases, which were discovered in the same region.
After the decadence of the Cretan and Mycenaean civilisations, the Geometric Period (10C-8C BC) seems to evolve towards frieze decoration. New **vase** forms develop in Corinth and eastern Greece, decorated with figures (rooms I-III). The same type of ornamentation was used by the Master of the Caere Hydria (room II) and by the painter of Amasis (room III).
The conventions of standard black-figure vase painting seem to have been first contradicted by the potter of Andokides *c*530 BC, who painted-in the background and details of his figures in black, leaving the main profiles in red biscuit (room IV). The technique is perfected in *c*500 BC by **Euphronios** (room IV) and Douris (room V). Contemporary with the building of the Parthenon (447-432 BC), Hellenistic red-figure painting flourished (rooms VI and VII); however, by the 4C BC, compositions had become crowded and cluttered (Apulia and Lucania finds – rooms VIII and Henri II).
Room IX displays the delicate and graceful Myrina and **Tanagra figurines** so full of movement.

**Salle des Bronzes – *Via Salle Henri II with its blue and black ceiling, painted by Braque in 1953 ("The Birds").*
Antique bronzes and jewellery are displayed alongside examples of Archaic pitcher handles with Gorgon head masks. A fascination for apparently unidealised human features, at times even bizarre ones, are most characteristic of this period; portrayals of infancy or old age, stunted growth and deformity are most remarkable: Note: *Eros and Psyche* with the faces of young children; a black adolescent with his hands tied behind his back; a "giant".
The handsome **bust of a young man "from Beneventum"** draws inspiration from the works of Polyclitus.
A flat display case, near the large gilded *Apollo of Lillebonne*, holds an assortment of **Etruscan mirrors** engraved with elegantly delineated figures.
The *Effigy of a kneeling black slave* (2C-3C AD) is Roman.

**ETRUSCAN ANTIQUITIES

Through the Salle du Manège (copies after the Antique) and the Galerie Daru (sarcophagi and statues), pass round to the right of the Escalier Daru; the Etruscan galleries featuring the Cerveteri Sarcophagus of the Married Couple lead off from the Greek Archaic collection.

The origins of the Etruscan people remain uncertain: some claim them to be descended from tribes indigenous to central Italy west of the Apennines, some from Aeneas' men from Troy... What is undisputed is their civilisation drawn in part from Ancient Greece, and absorbed completely by Ancient Rome. In 265 BC Etruria ceded its independence becoming a part of the Roman Empire. Many of the finest artefacts have been recovered from tombs; these include domestic utensils in bronze and terracotta, jewels in gold and precious stones, frescoes, sculpted sarcophagi and funerary urns, bronze toys and devotional objects. Undoubtedly, Etruscan art is most original seeming to exude happiness, humour and sophistication.

Gallery 18 – Villanovian articles made of iron or bronze are inscribed with geometric patterns (throne in laminated bronze); Etruscan terracotta includes the three Campana painted plaques, "impasto" pottery and antefixes (decorative tiles for the ends of roof joints) in the shape of women's heads. The main exhibit, however, is the famous painted terracotta **Sarcophagus of the Marriage Couple** (late 6C BC) found at Cerveteri as was its pair now at the Villa Giulia in Rome. The strikingly life-like sculpture of a couple serenely participating at the Divine Banquet seems moulded directly from a Greek vase painting.

Gallery 19 – "*Bucchero*" black earthenware fashioned to imitate metal is typical of the Orientalising Period (mid-7C). Simple forms with engraved textures gradually ceded in the 6C BC to more complicated designs (deeply grooved lines, details in relief).

Much of this pottery was copied from Greek prototypes, first the black-figure painting (early 6C)
and later the red (5C-4C). The Etruscans were
also highly skilled goldsmiths, here shown in the
sophisticated and elaborate applications of gran-
ulation and filigree, culminating in *repoussé*
work.

Classical and Hellenistic phases: gallery 20 –
The **Gabies head**, an oenochoë (wine pitcher) in the
shape of a human head; alabaster cinerary urns
and terracotta sarcophagi from Volterra and
Chiusi epitomise the artistic originality of this
period. The bronze mirrors with wooden handles
often decorated with scenes from Greek mythology, were produced in large quantities by the
Etruscans.

Gabies head
(Bronze oenochoë, *c*425-400 BC)

★★**ROMAN AND PALEO-CHRISTIAN ANTIQUITIES**

*Through the Salle du Manège (copies after the
Antique) and the Galerie Daru (sarcophagi and
statues), pass round to the right of the Escalier
Daru through to the rotunda and right into the
Appartement d'été d'Anne d'Autriche.*

★★**Appartement d'été d'Anne d'Autriche: galleries 22 to 26** – Anne of Austria's summer suite
with ceilings painted by **Romanelli** displays two of
the most original genres in Roman art: the portrait (a cold and idealised *Marcellus*,
posed in the nude, by Cleomenes the Athenian; four effigies of *Augustus* at different
stages of his life; bust in basalt of *Livia Drusilla*, wife of Augustus); and the relief
carving, whether historical (altar of *Domitius Ahenobarbus*, fragment of the *Ara
Pacis*, the Altar of Peace consecrated by Augustus) or mythological (sarcophagus of
the *Nine Muses*, sarcophagi from Saint-Médard-d'Eyrans in the Galerie Daru).

Galleries 27 to 31 – 3C-4C AD portraits *(Gordian III; Auriga)* surround the *Pillars
of the Incantada* (enchanted palace), the remains of a portico from Thessalonika
(gallery 27).
The opulent residences were adorned with magnificent **mosaics** (**The Phoenix**, *The
Judgement of Paris*, *Preparations for a banquet*), as were the floors of churches
in north Africa and the Middle East (Kabr Hiram, near Tyre in the Lebanon –
gallery 21). Note also the fragments of frescoes from Pompeii *(Winged Spirit)*.
The old Cour du Sphinx contains the great frieze from the Temple of Artemis at
Magnesia on the River Maeander. The marvellous **mosaic floor** depicting the seasons
comes from a villa in Antioch.

★★**Boscoreale Treasure** – *To include the jewellery collection on the 1st floor. Follow
directions above for the Galerie Campana (Greek vases).*
This splendid collection was found at the heart of a vine growing area, in a place
called "Boscoreale", in the ruins of a Roman villa destroyed by the eruption of
Mount Vesuvius in AD 79. The treasure trove consisted of coins, jewellery and **silver
tableware**, all of which had been put into a wine tank for safe-keeping. It gives a good
indication of the sophisticated tastes of the wealthy and cultured social class. The
most beautiful silver items were displayed on special stands for visitors to admire.

★★★**GALERIE D'APOLLON**

*Through the ground floor of the Denon wing (Salle du Manège and Galerie Daru),
go up the Escalier Daru and left of the Winged Victory of Samothrace.*

The dimensions (61m – 200ft long) and decoration of this royal gallery, which was
built under Henri IV and rebuilt after the fire of 1661, make it among the most
magnificent in Europe. **Le Brun** worked on it before painting the Hall of Mirrors
at Versailles. His work was completed by **Delacroix** in 1853 (*Apollo, Slayer of the
Serpent Python*, in the centre of the vault). The wrought-iron **grille** comes from
the château of Maisons-Laffitte. This gallery provides a sumptuous Grand Siècle
context for what remains of the exquisite treasure of the Kings of France.
The **Regent diamond** weighing 140 carats was purchased in 1717. Its exceptional clarity and perfect shape make it one of the most famous precious stones in the world,
it having adorned among other things the coronation crown of Louis XV, the parade
sword of Premier Consul Bonaparte and the diadem of the Empress Eugénie.
Other French Crown Jewels on display include the **Côte de Bretagne** ruby (107 carats),
the pink diamond *Hortensia*, Queen Amélie's **sapphire jewellery set** and Empress
Eugénie's crown and diadem. Other display cases contain Louis XIV's impressive
collection of **semi-precious stone vases**.

★★ITALIAN SCHOOL: SCULPTURE

At Entresol level. The collection continues on the ground floor directly above.

13C Italian sculpture is stylised and static (*Virgin* from Ravenna), produced at a time of instability often coined as the Dark Ages. A century later, artists and sculptors learnt to review Roman reliefs, re-interpreting their subject matter as Christian narrative. From Pisa (graceful *Virgin* by Nino Pisano) to 15C Siena (Jacopo della Quercia *seated Madonna*) and Florence, sculpture evolved to conform with Renaissance aesthetics, towards idealised form and calculated proportion **(Donatello bas-relief of the Virgin and Child, Verrocchio** two delightful little angels). Other fine examples include a **bust** of a young lady in painted and gilded wood and the enchantingly delicate medallion by Desiderio da Settignano.

Francesco Laurana is represented by a bust of the *Princess of Aragon*.

By the close of the 15C Florentine sculpture features a more mannered elegance (Agostino di Duccio bas-relief and the Della Robbia family vitrified lead-glazed terracottas).

Benvenuto Cellini's *Nymph of Fontainebleau* is well placed on the banister of the Mollien staircase.

Michelangelo's two marble **Slaves** (1513-1520) sculpted for the tomb of Pope Julius II, although uncompleted are famous masterpieces as expressions of strength apparently breaking out of the rough stone.

Bernini's distinctive, lively modelling is evident in the modello for the *Angel bearing the Crown of Thorns*, while his bust of *Cardinal Richelieu* is both expressive and monumental.

The neo-Classical **Psyche Revived by the Kiss of Cupid** (1793) is quite exquisite, contrived by **Canova** to blend the Antique with a Rococo lightness of touch.

★★NORTHERN SCHOOLS: SCULPTURE

At Entresol level, beyond the Italian sculptures, and continued on the ground floor above.

The brittle, deeply folded drapery of the **Virgin of Isenheim**, near Colmar, is typical of sculpture of the German School of the late Middle Ages, often executed in polychrome lime-wood. Swabian sculptors imbue their figures with greater serenity (*Mary Magdalen* by Gregor Erhart), while the great Franconian master **Tilman Riemenschneider** produced more delicate pieces such as the marble **Virgin of the Annunciation.**

In the Netherlands, large numbers of polychrome multi-panelled altarpieces composed of small picturesque scenes carved in wood were produced, and exported (*Coligny altarpiece* from Marne).

★★★ITALIAN SCHOOL: PAINTING

Through the ground floor of the Denon wing (Salle du Manège and Galerie Daru), up the Escalier Daru and right at the Winged Victory of Samothrace. Go through the Salles Percier and Fontaine to the Salon Carré, which leads to the Grande Galerie.

The collection of Italian paintings, one of the glories of the Louvre, was carefully acquired as a result of a passion harboured by the Kings of France for the art of that peninsula. Renaissance masterpieces include such key works as the *Mona Lisa*, *The Wedding at Cana* and *The Man with the Glove*, but it is the Baroque pieces, favoured by Louis XIV, that are most especially unique. 19C and 20C bequests and acquisitions have since filled the gaps with works by the Primitives, who were unrepresented in the royal collections, and the Mannerist painters, who had not featured very significantly in them.

The Primitives – The immense cyma of the Grande Galerie displays Trecento (14C) and Quattrocento (15C) works by the precursors of the Renaissance.

The large altarpiece the **Virgin and Angels** by the Tuscan **Cimabue** (*c*1280) shows a move away from Byzantine conventions towards an attempt to portray movement, three-dimensional volume and space. Note the unusually expressive medallion portraits round the frame (busts of saints and prophets).

During the early part of the 14C, it is **Giotto** who maintains the momentum to greater realism. Narrative scenes are reduced to the essentials: in the large portrait of **Saint Francis of Assisi receiving the stigmata**, the saint is depicted in a rugged landscape of monumental proportions. Note the direct appeal in predella scenes of Saint Francis rebuilding the tottering church in *The Dream of Innocent III* and the charming *Saint Francis talking to the birds*.

In Siena, the jewel-like art of **Simone Martini** (small panel of the *Way to Calvary*) recalls the art of illumination.

The Early Renaissance – The Quattrocento was a period of quest and rationalisation: how should space and volume be represented on a two-dimensional plane? how might faith in man's capabilities, as exalted in the art and philosophy of Classical Antiquity, be reconciled with faith in God? At the epicentre of this development is Florence under the patronage of the Medici.

A Dominican monk, **Fra Angelico** "the Blessed", the painter of the convent of San Marco in Florence, evoked life in Paradise as serenely mystical. Saints and angels crowd round in the **Coronation of the Virgin**, painted in 1435 for the church of San Domenico at Fiesole outside Florence. Faces glow with supernatural light, their clothes in celestial hues of pink and blue, the colourful patterns on the stairs leading up the throne. The six predella panels depict scenes from the life of St Dominic.

Subject matter, physiognomy and pose evolve. The *Virgin and Child* provides a constant inspiration explored by Fra Filippo Lippi, Botticelli, Perugino... Portraiture provided an opportunity for detailed observation and sensitive analysis: the medallion portrait in profile of *A Princess of the House of Este* by **Pisanello** *(see also the medallions by this artist in Objets d'art below)* with the two-handled vase of the Este family embroidered on her sleeve; the authoritarian and enigmatic *Sigismondo Malatesta* by **Piero della Francesca; Saint Sebastian** by **Mantegna** is so precisely observed as to be almost sculptural; the sorrowful **Resurrected Christ giving Blessing** by **Giovanni Bellini**. The *Portrait of an Old Man and a Young Boy* by **Ghirlandaio** combines Florentine elegance with Flemish realism, featured also in the strong, proud features of **"Il Condottiere"** and the face of the suffering *Christ at the column* by **Antonello da Messina**.

Intrigued by the problems of portraying perspective, **Paolo Uccello** painted the **Battle of San Romano**, in which the forces of Florence beat those of Siena in 1432 (the other panels, painted for the Medicis, are in Florence (Uffizi) and London (National Gallery): lances articulate the background space into regular stripes; the captain Michelotto Attendoli's black charger suggests depth; the surging crowd of armed warriors in magnificent plumed helmets are depicted ready to advance or retreat, accentuating the theatrical effect of movement and action.

The frescoes from the *Villa Lemmi* by **Botticelli** commemorate the marriage of Lorenzo Tornabuoni (surrounded by allegories of the Liberal Arts) with Giovanna degli Albizzi (offering her bridal veil to Venus and her attendants the three Graces).

The High Renaissance – The fulfilment of objectives and the successful application of ideal principles marked a new phase of the Renaissance, this time concentrated in Rome and nurtured by a reformed Papacy. When the city was sacked in 1527, Venice became the power-base and ultimate patron of the Arts, a possession guarded until the end of the 16C.

Leonardo da Vinci (1452-1519), acclaimed as a universal genius, ranks in pride of place among the artists of this period. It is significant to remember that he died in France in his château at Cloux, given him by the François I. Think of the Louvre, and the da Vinci paintings it houses immediately spring to mind: the portrait of **Mona Lisa**, wife of the Florentine Del Giocondo; **The Virgin of the Rocks**, a mature work in which the play of the hands is particularly remarkable, strengthening the harmonious pyramidal arrangement of the figures against the rather menacing rocky crags of the background landscape; **The Virgin and Child with St Anne**, analysed by Sigmund Freud as suggesting Leonardo's childhood inhibitions: brought up by his grandmother and then his mother, he suffered recurrent nightmares about being attacked by a ravening vulture (seen in the folds of the Virgin's robes).

Raphael (1483-1520), the pupil of Perugino, imbues his paintings with gentleness, his landscapes reflect the soft undulating countryside around his native Urbino. **"La belle Jardinière"** portrays a gentle Virgin watching over the Infants Jesus and John the Baptist, combining humanity and harmony with religious faith. In the **Portrait of Balthazar Castiglione**, the rank and temperament of the author of *Il Cortegiano* (The Courtier), a gentleman who was a close friend of Raphael, is economically portrayed. **Correggio**, who was a keen observer of women's sensibilities, developed in Parma a style combining a delicate and slightly self-conscious sensuality with a romantic elegance that was to influence painting into the 18C: **The Mystical Marriage of St Catherine**, *Antiope Sleeping*.

To the masterful rendering of flesh tones achieved by Leonardo da Vinci's *sfumato* technique (blending in of lines and borders), the Venetians added drama, mystery, a profusion of colour and movement, and an aristocratic elegance: see **The Man with the Glove, Concert Champêtre, The Pardo Venus** and the dramatic **Entombment** by **Titian**.

In the **Wedding at Cana** by **Veronese**, executed in 1563 for the refectory of a convent in Venice, the painter uses the scene from the Gospel as a pretext for painting the Golden Age of Venice "the Serenissima" with its majestic architecture and sumptuous lifestyle in a composition of consummate skill. The 130 figures in this enormous painting (66m^2 – 710sq ft), recently restored, are mainly portraits of contemporary figures (Emperor Charles V, Suleiman the Magnificent, Titian, Bassano, Tintoretto and the artist himself playing the viola).

After 1530, the rest of Italy – Florence, Mantua, Rome – embraced Mannerism, imitating the "style" (It.: *maniera*) of Michelangelo and Raphael (**Giulio Romano**) or creating portraits of an aristocratic and glacial elegance (**Bronzino**). The inimitable **Four Seasons** by **Arcimboldo**, allegorical portraits composed of fruit, flowers and foliage, were later to inspire Surrealist artists.

Late 16C and 17C – Counter-Reformation and the Seicento – This period is dominated by the Bolognese School, following the founding of the Accademia degli Incamminati ("Academy of the Progressives") by the Carracci brothers.

A *Circumcision* is on display by the revivalist **Barocci**. The Grand Manner of the Bolognese and Roman Baroque Schools was to have a significant influence on 17C and 18C French painting. Romanelli, a painter of this period, decorated the summer suite of Anne of Austria *(see* Roman Antiquities*)*.

The canvases of the Aemilian School (from the Emilia Romana region) are eclectic, fusing a tendency towards the academic, a legacy from the study of the masters of the Renaissance (**Domenichino's** *Saints*), with forward-looking realism. This provides for a bold and virtuoso style of composition using varied poses and expressions, magnificent landscape settings and subtle lighting effects. The school's main exponents were: **Annibale Carracci** (who often drew in the country; *Fishing* and *Hunting* might be said to be the best landscapes in the Louvre); **Guido Reni** (who tended more to an aristocratic, decorative style: *Deianeira and the Centaur Nessus*; *David holding the head of Goliath*); **Il Guercino** (painter of marvellously accurate human figures: *The Resurrection of Lazarus*); **Pietro da Cortona**, who practised in Rome *(Romulus and Remus discovered by Faustulus)*; **Domenico Fetti** of Venice (**Melancholy**); and **Luca Giordano** of Naples (*Portraits of Philosophers* dressed in the clothes of ordinary people). This realism was adopted even more forcefully by **Caravaggio**, who modelled his figures upon people drawn from the poorer walks of life (**The Fortune-Teller**). The **Death of the Virgin**, one of his most powerful works, was rejected by the chapter of the Roman church which had commissioned it because of its unorthodox use of an "ordinary" woman as the model for the Virgin.

The Fortune-Teller by Caravaggio

The Settecento (18C) — The opulent lifestyle of the noble classes during the Age of Enlightenment is reflected in the works of Pannini *(Concert given in Rome on the occasion of the marriage of the Dauphin, son of Louis XV)*. **Guardi** captured the atmosphere of the lagoon of Venice in the dazzling series **Ascension Day Ceremonies**, during which the Doge, in a sumptuous state barge, celebrated the marriage of Venice with the Adriatic by throwing a ring into the sea. The luminous religious and mythological compositions of **Giambattista Tiepolo** contrast strongly with the scenes of street life painted by his son, **Giandomenico Tiepolo** *(The Charlatan, Carnival)*. The life of the common man is also portrayed in the work of **Pietro Longhi**, often with a humorous touch *(Presentation)*. *The Flea*, by **Crespi** of Bologna, is reminiscent of Dutch painting.

★★★FRENCH SCHOOL: 19C LARGE-FORMAT PAINTING

Through the ground floor of the Denon wing (Salle du Manège and Galerie Daru), go up the Escalier Daru, before reaching the Winged Victory of Samothrace, take the ramp on the right. The large-format works of the French Revolution, Empire and the early 19C are displayed in the Denon, Daru and Mollien galleries.

The Oath of the Horatii, which **David** despatched from Rome for the Salon of 1785, embodies the main elements of neo-Classicism in painting. As a History painting it tells a story drawn from Classical literature in an uncompromising way, bold in its statement of virtue; masculine strength is contrasted with female sensibility. The overall effect is one of Classical drama. It was immensely well received.

A preliminary sketch for the **Consecration of Napoleon I** shows the new Emperor crowning himself; in the final composition, however, Napoleon is shown in the act of crowning Josephine. The unfinished **Portrait of Madame Récamier**, opposite, depicts Bonaparte's opponent at the age of 23, reclining in the style of Classical Antiquity on a day bed *(see also Objets d'art)*.

Ingres' overwhelming concern with the expressive and sensual use of line can be clearly seen in **La Grande Odalisque** and his *Portrait of Mademoiselle Rivière*, where the aesthetic prevails over anatomical realism.

French art historian Élie Faure saw the art of **Gros** as falling between the statuesque immobility of David and the emotive turbulence of Delacroix, desperately striving to make the transition from one to the other. In *The Plague-stricken of Jaffa*, he portrays the East: unafraid to use realism in depicting anatomical detail he has been likened to Rubens.

Women of Algiers by Delacroix

Théodore Géricault gave artistic expression to current political issues; **The Raft of the Medusa** (1819) drew its subject matter from a recent disastrous shipwreck thought largely to be the result of governmental incompetence. The effects of back-lighting and the positions of the unfortunate victims of the shipwreck of the Medusa, only one of whom is facing the viewer, evoke the wild fluctuations between hope and despair among the ragged survivors, who have just caught sight of the flag of the Argus (the ship which was eventually to rescue them) on the horizon.

Eugène Delacroix, the leading exponent of Romanticism, expressed his support for the cause of Greek independence in **The Massacres at Chios**, inspired by the brutal repression imposed on the inhabitants of that island. His reaction to the days of violence in the 1830 Revolution was **Liberty leading the People**, which he exhibited at the Salon. **The Women of Algiers** was painted in the wake of his trip to Morocco and Algeria, and demonstrates Delacroix' use of contrasting colour (red for foreground, green for depth). In **The Death of Sardanapalus**, the East is portrayed in a mixture of magnificence and barbaric decadence, as the Sultan had ordered that everything and everyone he held dear should be destroyed in front of him, before he himself committed suicide.

★★ SPANISH SCHOOL: PAINTING

The Pavillon de Flore is accessible through the porte Jaujard or from the Grande Galerie.

Spanish painting is characterised by realism and mysticism.

The collection of 15C Spanish Primitives including *The Flagellation of Saint George* by Martorell of Catalonia, *The Flagellation of Christ* by Jaime Huguet and *Man with a Glass of Wine* by a Portuguese master precede the Mannerist Domenikos Theotokopoulos, an icon painter of Cretan origin, pupil of Tintoretto in Venice, better known as **El Greco**. His **Christ on the Cross**, with its stretched figure outlined against a dark, stormy, almost abstract background, appears almost transfigured.

José de Riberac took subjects which were the social antithesis of the Spanish Golden Age, for example the **Club-footed Boy**, depicting the unfortunate cripple armed with his crutch and a note begging for charity (to indicate he was dumb as well), none the less with an open smile. Note also *The Young Beggar* by **Murillo**, unusually lit transversely. The humane realism of such paintings contrasts with the spirituality of **Zurbarán (Funeral Ceremonies of Saint Bonaventura)**, the baroque exuberance of Carreño de Miranda *(Mass for the founding of the Trinitarian Order)* and the stiff court Infanta portraits by **Velasquez**. The delightful Madonnas painted by Murillo in muted colours have the quality of pastels. The **Beistegui Collection** *(Sully wing, 2nd floor, take the Escalier Henri II)* includes the portrait of the **Marquesa de la Solana**, one of Goya's best, along with that of the *La Comtessa de Santa Cruz.*

RICHELIEU WING

Large windows give enticing views into the Richelieu wing providing incentive enough to explore the treasures in this newly opened section of the Louvre museum.

From the Richelieu wing itself, wonderful prospects reach over the heart of Paris and over Parisian rooftops. The lines of the magnificent Second Empire staircases are echoed by dizzying flights designed by Ieoh Ming Pei and the unexpectedly vast expanses of glass designed by **Peter Rice**.

★★★ NORTHERN SCHOOLS: PAINTING

Take the main escalator to the 2nd floor. Turn left off Gallery 3 (French Painting).

This section includes the painting of the German, Flemish and Dutch Schools from the 14C to the 17C. Light in these galleries filters through an overhead structure of cruciform beams, designed by Pei.

Flemish Primitives – The Flemish Primitives paint delicate, oval faces, carefully drawn folds of clothing and exquisite textures whilst paying close attention to domestic detail.

The most famous work on display is the **Madonna with Chancellor Rolin** by **Jan van Eyck**, the artist who, with his brother, pioneered the technique of painting with oils. The serious expressions of the subjects, the detailed observation of the town and landscape in the background are quite remarkable. Nicolas Rolin was the founder of the Hôtel Dieu in Beaune (Burgundy) and an adviser to the Duke of Burgundy, Philip the Good. It may have been this formal portrait that lead to van Eyck's appointment as Court Painter, and to his dispatch to Spain (1427) and Portugal (1428) to negotiate marriage contracts on behalf of the Duke, whose portrait hangs in the next gallery.

The **Braque Family Triptych** is an intensely spiritual work painted by **Roger van der Weyden** in his mature period. The **Annunciation** is depicted against the background of a luxuriously furnished interior.

Hans Memlinc lived in the peaceful surroundings of Bruges with its beguine convents. He formulated a type of woman in his works, serene and beautiful; in the magnificent **Triptych of the Resurrection** and the *Portrait of an Old Woman*, realism is compromised by a mood of gentle meditation.

Hieronymous Bosch's sharp sense of ridicule is well portrayed in **The Ship of Fools**.

German School – The chronological presentation of panels enables a comparison of the Flemish Primitives with those of the German School. The general self-contained harmony of the former is succeeded by the more self-consciously disturbed style of the latter: the colours are harsh; magnificent draperies are as minutely described as are the textures of jewellery and weapons; facial expression is often hard and tormented. Idealisation as portrayed by the Cologne School is sometimes to the detriment of spatial depth.

The *Pietà of Saint-Germain-des-Prés* gives a detailed view of the abbey with its three belltowers and of the Louvre at the time of Charles V. The *Deposition* by the Master of Saint Bartholomew is a sculptural reinterpretation of a work by Rogier van der Weyden (note the headband of the figure at the top of the ladder, the anguish of Mary Magdalen at Christ's feet and of the man carrying him).

In the centre of the gallery, an original **painted table top** by Hans Sebald Beham depicts scenes from the life of David.

The small room adjoining the gallery houses the prize exhibits of the collection: **Portrait of the Humanist Erasmus** by **Hans Holbein the Younger; Portrait assumed to be of Magdalena Luther** by **Lucas Cranach the Elder; Albrecht Dürer**'s **Self-Portrait** with a thistle, the symbol of fidelity, intended for his fiancée; *The Knight, the Young Lady and Death*, a fantastical work by **Hans Baldung Grien**.

16C and 17C Flanders – Flemish Renaissance art retained many medieval features from the International Gothic painting style for some time: *Altarpiece of the Lamentation of Christ* by **Joos van Cleve** (note the predella); interesting portraits by Jan Gossaert, known as **Mabuse** *(Carondelet Diptych)*.

The Moneylender and his Wife is one of the most famous works by **Quentin Metsys**. It depicts the couple absorbed in weighing and counting money – note the exquisite rendering of the hands complete with their shadowy veins; a profusion of minutely observed detail characterises the attributes of their household, a veritable still-life study on the shelves behind including a manuscript and pearls. In the centre of the picture, a convex mirror testifies to the presence of a third character or witness to the scene; a window provides a landscape view of the world outside. To the right of the picture, two more figures confer behind a half-open door.

Brueghel the Elder is represented by the small picture, **The Beggars** (in the room on the side of the Rue de Rivoli) interpreted in several ways to show a parody of royal power (cardboard crown), military power (paper helmet) or ecclesiastical power (bishop's mitre); the fox tails pinned to the beggars' cloaks serve to allude to the poverty-stricken. In the same gallery, *Lot and his daughters*, by an anonymous master, depicts an apocalyptic vision of a city (Sodom) being destroyed by floods. The Flemish Mannerists adopted aesthetic principles for painting the human figure imported from Italy (*David and Bathsheba* by Jan Massys; *Perseus rescues Andromeda* by Joachim Wtewael) but retained their preoccupation with minute detail. The miniaturist tradition continued through the work of Jan Brueghel (son of Brueghel the Elder), known as **Velvet Brueghel** *(Battle of Arbelles)*.

Rubens, master of the Baroque, seems to exalt life itself (*Portrait of Hélène Fourment*, his second wife; **The Village Fair**) with fleshy bodies and sumptuous attire *(Hélène Fourment in great style)*. All these elements abound in the 21-panel cycle celebrating the **Life of Queen Marie de' Medici**, now housed in the new Galerie Médicis designed by Pei. At the entrance to this gallery, on the side of Rue de Rivoli, note the interesting *Standard Bearer* by Victor Boucquet.

Jordaens, a pupil of Rubens, cultivated a highly coloured realism which verged on earthiness: *The King Drinks!*, *Jesus chasing the Merchants from the Temple*, *The Four Evangelists*.

Van Dyck was the portraitist to the Genoese and English aristocracy *par excellence*, catching the refined elegance of both courts: **Charles I, King of England**, *The Marquessa Spinola-Doria*, *The Palatine Princes*.

17C Dutch School – The Netherlands, a maritime republic, fashioned its art to bourgeois taste depicting domestic scenes, portraiture and landscape.

Frans Hals pioneered the "character" portrait with pictures such as the **Gypsy Girl** and the **Lute-player**. His robust style was to influence Fragonard *(see* French Painting*)* and Manet.

Wonderful landscapes are portrayed by **Jacob van Ruisdael** *(Ray of Sunlight)* and **Van Goyen**, his silvery river scenes stretching into far distances.

The Astronomer by Vermeer

Rembrandt gradually forsook *chiaroscuro* in favour of a more limited, but more subtle palette ranging through warm, rich, earthy tones of gold and brown; highlighted detail projects out of the darkness, giving a somewhat unreal but none the less highly emotive effect (**The Philosopher in Meditation**). Frequent exploration of subject-matter drawn from the Bible enabled him to transcend the realms of reality and everyday life (**Pilgrims of Emmaus**) whilst never compromising the very human quality of his figures. Note the rendering of the nude in **Bathsheba bathing**, a portrait of his second wife.; of the problems and loneliness that beset the artist in his old age, painfully etched on the face in his poignant **Self-Portrait before an Easel**.

Other masters of this period include **Ter Borch, Pieter de Hooch, Gerrit Dou** and **Adriaen van Ostade**, who were principally genre painters. **Vermeer van Delft** imbues his contemplative scenes of domestic activity with poetic peace (**The Lacemaker, The Astronomer**) a quality achieved by his use of indirect light and oblique shadows.

★★★FRENCH SCHOOL: PAINTING

Take the main escalator to the 2nd floor. Large-format 19C French Painting is exhibited in the Denon wing as before (see Denon).

It is difficult to define the particular characteristics of the French School of painting, despite the extensive collection of the Louvre spanning the 14C to the 19C. Categorised retrospectively into movements, stylistic development is punctuated by strong individual characters who often sought inspiration from abroad: Italy, Flanders, the Netherlands. A complete tour through 73 galleries is a huge undertaking. The collection is arranged chronologically by *genre*, each serving very well as the focus of a visit in itself (the Primitives, the Fontainebleau School, the "Caravaggisti", 17C religious painting etc). Certain groups of works by particular artists are outstanding: Claude Lorrain, Poussin, Fragonard, Chardin and Corot.

14C: galleries 1 and 2 – **Jean le Bon**, soon to be King of France, posed for a Portrait (1350) at a time when the subjects of painting were almost exclusively religious. The **Narbonne altarcloth**, with its beautiful Gothic decoration on silk, is a typical example of the art of the time.

15C: galleries 3 to 6 – The International Gothic tradition of portraying narrative subjects on a gold background was maintained by the Court of Burgundy (*Altarpiece of Saint Denis* by Henri Bellechose, *gallery 3*). The two Thouzon Altarpiece panels *(gallery 4)* are from a slightly earlier period. Provençal art, with its severe style and strong contrasts in light, is represented by the **Pietà of Villeneuve-lès-Avignon** by **Enguerrand Quarton**, a work of great poignancy: the tragedy of the scene is conveyed in the dislocated body of Christ, scarred by the flagellation, the paralysed rigid attitudes of the other, living figures and the despair of the bowed heads.

In central France, the **Master of Moulins**, trained in Flanders, adds a French predilection for elegance to his meticulous drawings (*Portrait assumed to be of Madeleine of Burgundy with Mary Magdalen*).

In the north, **Jean Fouquet** *(see also Gallery 6: Objets d'art)*, a protégé of Agnès Sorel, created true and realistic portraits: **Charles VII**, on the day after his victory over the English; **Guillaume Jouvenel des Ursins**, Chancellor of France.

16C: galleries 7 to 10 – Renaissance artists were passionately interested in Humanism. Consequently, many works of art of this period focus on the individual, hence the profusion of portraits, such as those by **Jean Clouet (François I)** and his son **François Clouet** *(Pierre Quth)*. Gallery 8 *(to the left)* contains small portraits by the latter, several of which portray protagonists in the Wars of Religion (note in particular that of **Elizabeth of Austria**), and by Corneille de Lyon (*Pierre Aymeric, Clément Marot*).

The Italian artists summoned by François I during the construction of the Château de Fontainebleau introduced Mannerism into French decorative and applied arts. The First and Second Schools of Fontainebleau are represented respectively by *Diana the Huntress*, which has been thought to be the portrait of Diane de Poitiers, Henri II's mistress, and **Gabrielle d'Estrée with one of her sisters**, probably painted to celebrate the birth of one of Henri IV's illegitimate children.

17C: galleries 11 to 34 – This century opened with the "Caravaggisti", painters often patronised by Cardinals who had served in Rome and who encouraged a taste for Caravaggio's distinctive use of *chiaroscuro* and the direct realism of his figures *(see Italian Painting, Denon)*. Next to the magnificent collection of works by **Valentin de Boulogne** *(The Concert, The Judgment of Solomon)* is a charming work by **Claude Vignon**, *Young Singer*, remarkable for the freedom of its execution. During the reign of Louis XIII, the somewhat academic allegories of **Simon Vouet** *(Wealth)* contrast with the austere, controlled style of **Philippe de Champagne**, who emphasises in his **Portrait of Cardinal de Richelieu** the dignity and unbending will of the statesman.

Nicolas Poussin (1594-1665), the artist-philosopher who settled in Rome is represented by a marvellous collection of canvases *(from gallery 12)*. He is regarded as the most Classical of French academic painters, drawing from the formal canons of Beauty and yet remaining sensitive to the sensuality of colour inspired by Titian.

In later life, landscape in his painting becomes increasingly important, as composition is meticulously articulated by near, middle and far distance. Particular canvases to note include **Inspiration of the Poet**; *The Great Bacchanal; The Triumph of Flora*; **Shepherds of Arcadia**. Platonic ideas of Nature as a nourishing force and of the cyclical progression of life and time are expressed in The *Four Seasons*, in landscapes which are cold but harmonious.

Claude Gellée (1600-1682), otherwise known as '**Le Lorrain**' provides another high point. His canvases show land- and seascapes bathed in soft twilight: **Ulysses returning Chryseis to her Father, Cleopatra's Arrival at Tarsus, View of a Seaport at Sunset**. He was perhaps the first painter to attempt to paint the sun as a direct light source, hence his influence upon the English painter Turner and later the Impressionists.

Galleries 25 to 29 – Numerous genre scenes and small-format still-life works were executed by painters inspired by Flemish artists working in Paris, such as **Lubin Baugin** *(behind the screen in gallery 27: Still life with wafers, Still life with chess board)*. Painting becomes a vehicle for portraying social reality in the works of **Le Nain brothers** where sober realism hints at the moderate wealth of a middle-class patron: **Peasant Family at home** (healthy faces, stemmed wine glass).

Eustache Le Sueur (1616-1655) was both a painter of religious subjects *(Life of Saint Bruno, gallery 24)* and a sophisticated decorative artist influenced by Raphael (**The Muses** from the Hôtel Lambert, *gallery 25*).

Georges de la Tour's (1593-1652) paintings are engaging in their portrayal of interacting characters (**Cheat with the ace of diamonds**) and by the play of light which seems to melt the figures into the night thereby concentrating the atmosphere of the scene (**Saint Joseph the Carpenter, Mary Magdalen with a Candle, Saint Sebastian tended by Saint Irene**).

Gallery 31 – **Chancellor Séguier on horseback** is a solemn, official portrait by **Le Brun** of his first patron, shown surrounded by his pages, exuding an awareness of the responsibility conferred on him by Louis XIII. In the same gallery, **Philippe de Champaigne** displays his talent for creating penetrating portraits of his contemporaries *(Portrait of Robert Arnault d'Antilly)*. He also painted the famous **ex-voto of 1662**, a reflection of the Jansenist spiritual ideal, in thanksgiving for the miraculous cure of his daughter, a nun at the convent of Port-Royal-des-Champs.

The Royal Academy of Painting and Sculpture, founded in 1648, regrouped the artists specialising in large compositions on religious themes. Among the paintings executed for Paris churches, the **"Mays"** series *(Sermon of Saint Paul at Ephesus*, May 1649 by Le Sueur) represent an interesting tradition (these works were presented to Notre-Dame cathedral every May from 1630 to 1707 by the goldsmiths' guild).

Gallery 32 – This gallery contains the huge compositions by Le Brun depicting scenes from the life of Alexander.

18C: galleries 34 to 54 – The **Portrait of Louis XIV** by **Rigaud** (1701) was so well received by the monarch that he kept the original for himself despite its having been commissioned as a present for his grandson, Philip V of Spain, who had to be content with a copy. Only a few years separate this image of the Grand Siècle from the dreamy, elegant canvases of **Watteau** (d1721), heralding the spirit of the Age of Enlightenment. In the marvellous **Pilgrimage to Cythera**, the figures preparing to leave the island of Venus are portrayed in a gently curving line against a softly lit landscape.

Theatre was another source of inspiration for painters as demonstrated in works by Watteau's teacher, **Claude Gillot** (**Quarrel of the Cabmen**, inspired by the *Commedia dell'Arte*), and in those of Watteau himself, such as the strange and famous figure of **Gilles.**

Lancret's decorative scenes of light-hearted bantering *(gallery 36: Music Lesson, Innocence)* were intended to be inserted in panelling. The hunting scenes by **Jean-François de Troy** and **Carle van Loo** were painted for the dining room in the Royal Suite at Fontainebleau.

Boucher often drew his subject matter from mythology, allowing him free licence to treat them with a delicacy not untinged with eroticism: **Diana resting after her bath** is painted in fresh, shimmering tones *(Vulcan's Forge) (gallery 47)*.

A more modest realism fashions the works of **Chardin** *(galleries 38 to 40)* in both his still-lifes (**The Ray**, *The Buffet, The Copper Cistern*) and his genre paintings *(Child with Top, The Purveyor, Child saying Grace)*.

Luncheon *(gallery 40)* by **Boucher** was the first during a short period in which the artist was strongly influenced by Dutch masters; in it he depicts his own family at table, thereby providing an insight into the customs and furniture of the period.

Galleries 41 to 45 – The collection of delicate pastels and miniatures in the "Couloir des Poules" and adjacent galleries by **Quentin de la Tour** (**Portrait of the Marquise de Pompadour**), Perronneau *(Madame de Sorquainville)*, Chardin and others surround the great religious and mythological paintings contained in gallery 43: *Pentecost* by **Restout**; *Meal at Simon's House* by **Subleyras** (see also the *Sketch* bought by Louis XVI).

Galleries 46 and 47 – Landscapes, which until now had provided a setting for the main characters in the picture, now become the subject itself in the works of **Joseph Vernet** (*Toulon Roadstead*).

Galleries 48 and 49 – **Fragonard's** light touch and happy sense of movement are combined in **The Bathers** and his **"fantasy figures"** (*Portrait of Abbé de Saint-Non*). **The Lock**, while still light-hearted in spirit, is more formal in composition, succumbing to the neo-Classical influence of Jacques-Louis David.

Shortly before the Revolution, **Hubert Robert** undertook to paint a series of canvases for the apartment of Louis XVI at Fontainebleau, thereby initiating a taste for Romanticised Roman ruins, idealised and juxtaposed irrespective of topographical accuracy (**The Pont du Gard**).

Gallery 51 – Note also, by the same painter, two canvases depicting the **Grande Galerie du Louvre**, one as a construction project, the other as a ruin.

Following Diderot's advice, **Greuze** began painting scenes with moral subjects (comparable perhaps with Hogarth's Harlot/Rake's Progress during the 1730s), thus formulating a new genre that later dwindled into sentimentality. At the time, themes of family tensions in a rustic setting seemed to be ideal for extolling virtue (**The Father's Curse; The Punished Son**).

Neo-Classicism: gallery 54 – Devoted to **David** (*Portrait of Madame Trudaine*) and his pupils: *Portrait of a Negress* by **Marie-Guillaumine Benoist**.

19C: galleries 56 to 63 – Works by **Prudhon**: *Marie-Marguerite Lagnier; Venus Bathing or Innocence*.

Ingres, pupil of David, best epitomises the softer neo-Classical taste of the Empire. Clarity of line and form are the main concerns of this artist who vigorously opposed those of the colourists **Delacroix** and **Géricault**, imposing a different interpretation of exotic subjects beloved to both factions of the Romantic School: **The Turkish Bath**, painted 54 years after **The Valpinçon Bather**, uses the same nude subject seen from behind. The *Portrait of Monsieur Bertin* draws inspiration from Flemish realism.

Géricault regularly painted horses racing (*Epsom Derby*), thrilled by the latent power of the horse, just as his excellent portraits (*The Madwoman obsessed with Gambling – La Monomane du Jeu*) show his fascination with personality through physiognomy.

Delacroix's Romantic passion is apparent through his free and speedy brushwork notably in his *Self-Portrait*; his *Landscape under a wide sky* prefigures the Impressionists.

Ingres was Director of the Académie de France in Rome (Villa Medici) when his pupil **Hippolyte Flandrin** painted his study **Young Nude Man by the Sea** (1837).

Galleries 65 to 73 – Notable works include **Delacroix's Young orphan girl at the cemetery** (*gallery 71*); the reworked study of the head of a young man in the **Massacres at Chios** (*see Large-Format 19C French Painting, Denon wing*).

Corot is recognised by his landscapes, often bathed in nostalgia, vibrant with scintillating light in the fresh, clear air (**Souvenir of Mortefontaine**, *Marissel Church, Bridge at Mantes*). **Douai Belfry** was painted during his stay in northern France; a number of views, notably **Volterra, View of Florence from the Boboli Gardens**, *decorative panels* for a bathroom (*gallery 68*) resulted from three journeys made to Italy. He was also an accomplished portraitist (**The Lady in Blue**, *The Lady with the Pearl*). The final work painted a year before his death is the *View of the Interior of Sens Cathedral*.

★★★ OBJETS D'ART

These are exhibited on the 1st floor; take the corridor on the right, then the escalator designed by Pei.

The galleries in which the 5 500 *objets d'art* of the Richelieu wing are displayed were redesigned in 1993, replacing eight floors of offices conceived during the 1850s when the palace was completed. The department, however, already had a long history dating back to the Revolution when part of the treasure of Saint-Denis was deposited here in 1793. This basic collection was subsequently endowed with the Royal collections of bronzes and vases in precious stones (*see* Galerie d'Apollon, Denon), with furniture from former Royal residences belonging, by the late 19C, to the state, and with many private donations.

Unlike the Museum of Decorative Arts next door, this department of the Louvre holds no copies or reconstructions of period pieces. The beautiful presentation cases are designed by **Jean-Michel Wilmotte**.

★★★ **Medieval treasure of the Louvre** – This is one of the high points of a visit to the Louvre. The most famous exhibits come from the Royal Abbey of Saint-Denis (*see* EXCURSIONS*)* which served the French monarchy as a mausoleum. The gold and silver plate and above all the ivories, some of which are over a thousand years old, are quite astounding.

Gallery 1 – The entrance is flanked by two pink porphyry columns with the bust of an emperor projecting from each just above head level. These columns are supposed to have been part of the atrium of the basilica of Saint Peter in Rome, built by Constantine in the 4C AD.

Byzantium – *Right of the central aisle.* Many western churches have been embellished with the spoils of Constantinople, pillaged by the Crusaders (1204). **Ivories**, luxurious possessions, date mainly from the 10C and 11C, a period when the empire had reached the apogee of its splendour under the Macedonian dynasty.

The central display case holds a lapis-lazuli icon engraved with a Virgin praying and Christ in benediction.

Among the many ivories, note the **Harbaville triptych** (10C), named after the collector who acquired it shortly after its discovery; a casket decorated with rosettes enclosing scenes from mythology; the magnificent "**Barberini ivory**" *(to the left of the central aisle)* depicts a triumphant emperor (6C). Gold and silver plate include **fragments of reliquaries**, some set in mounts much later.

Portable **mosaic** icons of the finest quality include the *Transfiguration of Christ* (13C), *Saint George slaying the dragon* (first half of 14C).

Charlemagne and the High Middle Ages *(to the left of the central aisle)* – Opposite the entrance is displayed a 9C **equestrian statue of Charlemagne** or possibly of **Charles the Bald**, modelled on Antique equestrian statues (the horse has been restored). The ivories are no less splendid than those in the Byzantine section.

The objects discovered in 1959 in the tomb of Queen Arnegonde, wife of Clovis' son Clothair I (511-561), at Saint-Denis testify to the talent of these so-called "barbarian" goldsmiths: large brooch, both parts of an **ornate belt buckle** and a pair of fibulae inlaid with garnets.

The serpentine paten *(central display case)* decorated with little gold fish is Antique, set with precious stones at the court of Charles the Bald (late 9C).

Romanesque and early Gothic art: *(Nearer pair of bays)* – Suger, the Abbot of Saint-Denis (1122-1151), hoped to make his abbey one of the leading churches in Christendom. He experimented with a new type of construction, based on ogive vaulting, and enriched his treasury with liturgical vases. The most famous of these, the "**Eagle of Abbot Suger**", incorporates an Antique porphyry vase *(display case opposite the entrance)*. To the right of the eagle *(same display case)*, note the beautiful "**Aliénor**" **crystal vase** which is thought to be a 6C or 7C Ancient Iranian work, and to the left, a 7C Byzantine **sard ewer**.

In the display cases in the bay to the right of the central aisle, note: ivory oliphants from south Italy and a chess piece from the same region depicting a king and his counsellors; two arms of a cross (Spain) with plant and animal border decoration, a good example of Mozarab art. The display case in the middle of the bay contains a ewer, a Fatimid work, with a wonderfully intricate filigree gold lid made in Italy.

The display cases in the bay to the left of the central aisle contain some marvellous exhibits from Germany *(to the left)*: an **aquamanile** (type of ewer) in the shape of a griffin; quadrifoil *Reliquary of Saint Henri* (the emperor Henri II, beatified in 1152); and the arm-reliquary of *Charlemagne*, from the treasury at Aix-la-Chapelle (Aachen). Ottonian art (Otto the Great founded the Holy Empire in 962) is represented by two interesting little ivory plaques: *The Miracle of the Loaves and Fishes* and *Christ pointing at a child*. Note *(in the display case opposite)* the magnificent **bookbinding** from the treasury of Maastricht Cathedral.

Gallery 2 *(Further pair of bays)* – The central display case contains a **coronation sword** known as "**Charlemagne's**" or the "**Joyeuse**". Next to it are the coronation spurs.

Displayed in the bay to the right is a lovely collection of **reliquary caskets, heads of bishops' croziers**, 12C and 13C Limoges plaques and, in a separate case, the **ciborium by Maître Alpais**. In the bay to the left, note a **double cross** named after Abbot Hugo (north of France, c1200), stained-glass windows from the region of Soissons and the huge reliquary of *Saint Potentin* in copper gilt.

Gothic art: gallery 3 – Objects crafted by Parisian workshops during the 13C and 14C were imitated all over Europe. The increase in royal and princely patronage furthered the evolution of a courtly art, fashioned for elegance of form with costly materials, especially ivory.

Opposite the entrance stands the exquisite ivory statue of the **Virgin and Child** made for the chapel of the palace of Saint Louis (now the Sainte-Chapelle). It follows the Rayonnant Gothic style for large statuary. Note the painstaking detail of the facial expressions – the Virgin's idealised features, the Child's smile – and the deep flowing folds of the Virgin's robes. In a case to the right, note an *Angel* and *Virgin of the Annunciation*, dating from the same period, but parts of different compositions, and displayed in the left case, a famous ivory **Deposition**.

The **polyptych-reliquary of the True Cross** *(in the 1st bay to the left of the central aisle)*, was created for an abbey in the Ardennes. It is a "monument" in itself, complete with porch, pinnacles and ogive arches.

Another display case on the right of the central aisle, holds a *Crown-reliquary* from the Meuse valley.

The striking silver gilt Virgin and Child group *(central aisle between 2nd pair of bays)* known as the "**Virgin of Jeanne d'Evreux**" after its royal donor, Philip the Fair's widow, was given to the abbey of Saint-Denis in 1339. The statuette is unusually large, the Virgin's lily holds a relic.

In the bay to the right of the gallery, cases contain the arm-reliquaries of *Saint Louis of Toulouse* and of *Saint Luke*, a beautiful gilt and inlaid enamel cross from Siena, various **carved ivory mirror frames** (depicting scenes such as the *Siege of Amour's Castle*, or a *Game of Chess*) and some rather endearing tiny gilt and enamel diptychs.

In the bay to the left, the **reliquary of the True Cross of Jaucourt** consists of a Byzantine centre-piece resting on two kneeling angels.

Gallery 4 – At the far side of this gallery, against the magnificent backdrop of the monumental Italian **Embriachi altarpiece** made of wood and ivory, note the **sceptre of Charles V**, made for the coronation of his son; the statuette on top represents Charlemagne.

The display cases to the right of the sceptre of Charles V contain the most famous exhibits from the treasure of Saint-Denis: the large, diamond-shaped **ornamental clasp** decorated with a *fleur-de-lis*, and the beautiful **bookbinding** enclosing a 14C Parisian ivory. Note also the clever little 14C French silver gilt and niello work apple reliquary with slices opened out, and an attractive, early-15C circular ivory and wood marquetry marriage casket from Siena (a lovely hexagonal one may be found in the cabinet on the left side of the gallery).

The left-hand cabinets accommodate four iridescent **enamel medallions** made using an Italian technique, whereby a thin layer of coloured, translucent enamel was applied over a relief in silver or gold to give the finished work its sparkle.

Note also the **hand of justice**, made in 1804 for the consecration of Napoleon I and, like the *"Charlemagne"* crown, decorated with cameos from one of the reliquaries from Saint-Denis; next to this, an **aquamanile** (1400) from Nuremberg in the form of a griffin and a chasuble cross (Bohemia, 1380) embroidered in silk and gold with facial expressions picked out in detail. In the centre is the elaborate **reliquary of the Order of the Holy Spirit** *(see Galleries 27 and 28 below)*, thought to have been made in London before 1412. Each little figure holding tiny identifying symbols (St Peter with his key, etc) is made of gold entirely covered in opaque or translucent enamel (this technique reached its peak in Europe *c*1400).

Griffin aquamanile (Nuremberg, *c*1400)

Gallery 6 – The tapestries were executed in Flanders or in the north of France. The display cases contain masterpieces of the art of gold- or silversmithing: the beautiful **"Saint Louis" chessboard and pieces** (late 15C and 17C) made of rock crystal; a wonderful salt cellar in agate and gold; a Venetian reliquary of the Flagellation; and, perhaps the most interesting exhibit, a copper plaque on which **Jean Fouquet** *(see* French Painting*)* painted his **Self-Portrait** (*c*1450) – a background of black enamel highlighted with a dark grey-brown glaze and gold hatching. This same technique of enamel painting was to flourish in Limoges at the end of the 15C.

Galleries 7 to 17 – This series of galleries encircle the gallery hung with the tapestries of The Hunts of Maximilian *(follow them round in a clockwise direction)*.

Gallery 11 holds painted enamels dating from the reign of Louis XII; particularly fine examples were produced by the workshop of the **Maître aux Grands Fronts** (*Pietà between St Peter and St Paul*, Limoges, *c*1500).

Gallery 12 displays marquetry panels from a church in Padua and a *Self-Portrait of Alberti (1st display case on left)*, the great Renaissance theoretician (15C bronze).

Gallery 13 displays the **Riccio bas-reliefs**, which combine religious themes with the philosophical concepts of scholars at Padua University *(Sacrifice of Asclepius, Hell, Paradise)*.

Gallery 14 exhibits the **Pisanello** medallions *Lionel d'Este; Dante; Aretino; Mehmet II*, conqueror of Constantinople.

Gallery 15 collects together lovely 16C Limoges enamels, many of which are almost monochrome and the beautiful (and colourful) collection by the **Master of the Aeneid** *(The Trojan Horse)*.

Sauvageot Collection: gallery 18 – The art of glass-making in Europe is here shown: compare the delicate Venetian glasses with the interesting 17C German embossed glasses. A painting depicts a view of the collection in 1856.

Tapestries of The Hunts of Maximilian: gallery 19 – This series of sumptuous tapestries woven in silk, wool and gold thread used to belong to the Royal collections. The tapestries depicting 12 hunting scenes set in the forest of Soignes southeast of Brussels, where they were woven c1530, from cartoons by Bernard van Orley. Each scene corresponds to a month of the year and a sign of the zodiac. The figures featured include the Emperor Maximilian's grandchildren: Emperor Charles V-to-be, Ferdinand I-to-be and Maria of Hungary.

In the centre, typical Italian **maiolica** from Urbino is decorated with grotesques, mythological, biblical and religious scenes. Note the strange scene in greens and blues of the *Lovers surprised by death (3rd set of cabinets from entrance)* in which a funereal allegorical figure, poised over the inert body of a young man, is gripping in its teeth the robe of a young woman who is trying to flee. The tiles are from Siena.

Galerie de Scipion: gallery 20 – This series of tapestries, commissioned from the Gobelins workshops by Louis XIV, depict scenes from the life of Scipio Africanus; they are copied from one of the most famous series of tapestries from Renaissance Brussels known as **The Great Scipio** commissioned by François I. In the centre of the room, 16C French enamels *(Earth and Sea, Minerva's Shield)* are displayed.
Carry straight on through gallery 20, into the stairwell, then turn right.

Galleries 21 to 23 – Among the enamel work on display by **Léonard Limousin**, the *Portrait of the Connetable Anne de Montmorency (directly opposite the entrance to gallery 21)* stands out amidst other magnificent altarpieces. A case to the left contains a fine backgammon board in green, white and gold. These galleries also display pieces of delicately decorated faïence from the Saint-Porchaire workshops (in the region of west France once called the Saintonge); note in particular the ewer in gallery 21 (unusual handle). Gallery 23 has an amusing collection of **busts of 12 Caesars**, made in silver and semi-precious stones (labelled), and below these, an elaborate rock crystal ship on wheels.

Gallery 24 *(off gallery 21)* – The walls are hung with splendid 16C Oudenaarde **tapestries** depicting *The Labours of Hercules* against a background of luxurian t foliage. Examples of the virtuoso skill displayed by German Mannerist gold- and silversmiths (the main centres were Nuremberg and Augsburg) include *(in the central display case)* ewers, equestrian statues, a serving dish decorated with little reptiles and shellfish, and goblets in the shape of pine cones.

Gallery 25 – Adolphe de Rothschild's collection is displayed beneath a Renaissance woodwork **ceiling**. Among the 16C Florentine bronzes, note the monkey by Jean Boulogne which once adorned a fountain. A small display case to one side contains a dazzling Spanish cross in rock crystal and gilded silver.

★**Jean Boulogne Rotunda: gallery 26** – This houses a number of bronzes by this master and his pupils. The walls are hung with beautiful tapestries from Ferrara depicting scenes of metamorphosis. Many of the bronzes are on the theme of abduction including Deianeira and the Sabine women. Hercules, wrestling with Antaeus, the Ceryneian hind and the Erymanthian boar, takes pride of place.

★★**Treasure of the Order of the Holy Spirit: galleries 27 and 28** – This, the most prestigious order of the Ancien Régime, was founded by Henri III while the Wars of Religion were raging, to secure the loyalty of the nobility to the crown. The honour's insignia is the blue sash (see that of Louis XVI exhibited, and the *Portrait of Henri III*, in the French Painting collection, *gallery 8*). The monarch's choice of placing the Order under the patronage of the Holy Spirit came about because it was at Pentecost that he had both been crowned King of Poland (1573) and succeeded to the throne of France (1574). Note the marvellous gold- and silverwork: silver-gilt *Kiss of Peace* (north Italy, c1500), a mace and some delightful altar cruets.

In the reconstruction of the **chapel**, the resplendent robes of the knights and officers of the Order are displayed next to 17C gold-embroidered altar cloths. Charles IX's eye-catching **helmet and shield** decorated in gold and brightly coloured enamel is exhibited in gallery 27.

Galleries 29 to 31 – French furniture from the latter half of the 16C shows how designs were influenced by contemporary architecture. The distinctive ceramics embossed with river animals are by Bernard Palissy; the dishes with a metallic sheen are known as lustre ware.

★**Salle d'Effiat: gallery 32** – Louis XIII furniture from the Château d'Effiat in the Puy-de-Dôme (Auvergne) appear somewhat severe in style. The very fine tapestry illustrating *Moses in the Bulrushes* is one of a series on themes from the Old Testament, designed by **Simon Vouet**, and destined for the Louvre.

Galleries 33 and 34 – *Through the Jean Boulogne rotunda, then towards the Cour Carrée.* In the centre of gallery 33 is the ornate **gold "Anne of Austria" casket**. Gallery 34 is a rest room. On the pedestal table that once belonged to Louis XIV, the magnificent **Jupiter hurling thunderbolts at the Titans** is by **Alessandro Algardi** (1598-1654).

The 18C – *Access via gallery 34. Open Mondays, Wednesdays, Fridays and sometimes Saturdays.*

Note in the entrance *(display case on the right)* the sober lines and decoration of Marie-Antoinette's **travelling case**, in sharp contrast with the queen's infamous extravagant taste for ribbons and nosegay ornamentation. The Chinese cabinet contains the queen's elegant writing table, a sophisticated combination of materials (steel and lacquered panels, mother-of-pearl inlay and bronze gilt *or moulu*) by **Adam Weisweiler**. Seats by **Jacob**, one of the pioneers of the Empire style *(see Madame Récamier's Bedchamber below)*, are displayed alongside lacquer furniture by **Carlin**. The cylindrical writing desk by **Riesener**, a new type of furniture in 1770, stands in front of the splendid desk by **Benneman**, at which Napoleon worked when he was at the Tuileries *(see BASTILLE-Faubourg-Saint-Antoine)*.

The recently refurbished Rothschild gallery contains furniture ornamented with Sèvres porcelain plaques and pot-pourri vases, once the property of the Marquise de Pompadour. **Cressent's** monkey commode illustrates the move from Grand Siècle formal design to the more fantastical Rococo, as decoration became more feminine in arrangements of asymmetrical, intertwining plant-like fronds. Louis XV style is represented by **Carel**'s commode in Coromandel lacquer, and by **Bernard Van Risen Burgh** (BVRB).

Boulle was the innovator who, at the end of Louis XIV's reign, opened the way forward to the Golden Age of French cabinet-making by inventing pieces such as the *commode* or the table-desk, although the inlay of pewter in ebony, marquetry in tortoiseshell and copper *(armoires, Elector of Bavaria's desk)* are traditional.

The Gobelins **tapestries** with pink backgrounds *(Loves of the Gods)*, woven to designs by **Boucher**, the candelabra, andirons, wall clocks, console-tables, and cabinets all reflect the degree of artistic imagination of the times, testifying to the delicate tastes of one of the most sophisticated (if not, the most sophisticated) periods in French history.

The Restoration and Louis-Philippe periods (1815-1848) – *To the right off gallery 34.* Note the elegant **dressing table and chair** from the **Escalier de cristal**, a workshop specialising in bronze gilt furniture set with Baccarat crystal, *Charles X's bed* from the Tuileries and the delicately worked **grape harvest goblet** ("coupe des vendanges") in silver gilt, enamel, agate and pearls by **Froment-Meurice** *(display case on the side of the Cour Carrée)*.

Empire style (1798-1815) – The monumental **table centrepiece** in bronze gilt and marble marquetry is by **Valadier** *(gallery 67)*. The sophisticated furniture from **Madame Récamier's Bedchamber** *(gallery 69)* designed by the **Jacob** brothers (1798) epitomises Empire-style design, distinguished by elegant line. The young lady's salon was the hub of opposition to Napoleon *(see also Large-Format 19C French Painting, Denon)*.

The armoire, or "**grand écrin**" ("large casket"), for Empress Josephine's jewellery was designed by **Jacob-Desmalter** *(gallery 73)*; its elegant bronze ornamentation is based on designs by Chaudet *(see French Sculpture)*.

★★★**Napoleon III Apartments** – *These are also accessible via the Cour Marly, up the Escalier du Ministre (towards the Pyramid).*

This majestic carpeted staircase, decorated with a very fine wrought-iron banister, leads the visitor into a stunning world of gold, crimson velvet and crystal. The architect **Lefuel**, having completed the Louvre, went on to design an opulent almost overwhelming décor best seen at night by the light of the chandeliers. In was normal at that time for The Louis XIV style to be applied to the state halls of official palaces. These apartments provide one of the few examples of great Second Empire décors to have survived complete with their original furnishings. They consist of an antechamber, a presentation hall, a "*salon-théâtre*" (used for musical entertainment), a great hall (with a capacity for 265 spectators), a boudoir or "*salon de terrasse*" (with a view of the gardens), a small and a large dining hall. The latter contains an enormous sideboard in ebonised wood. Other characteristic furniture includes circular sofas (three or more upholstered seats joined back to back in a ring) and a few "*indiscrets*" (three armchairs joined like a propeller). Various allegorical paintings include the *Apotheosis of Emperor Napoleon III and Empress Eugénie* by Maréchal junior *(great hall)* where every opportunity to use trompe-l'œil has been exploited: mural paintings imitating Boulle marquetry, sculpted décor in *carton pierre* and imitation polychrome marble. The halls were inaugurated in 1861; 10 years later, they were appropriated by the Ministry of Finance.

★★★**FRENCH SCHOOL: SCULPTURE**

The collection dominates the ground floor of the Richelieu wing: the Cour Marly, Crypte Girardon and Cour Puget together with surrounding galleries.

The inauguration of the Richelieu wing has provoked a re-appraisal of the Louvre sculpture collections. Sheltered by wonderful glass roofs, the sculptural groups which adorned 17C and 18C Royal parks may be surveyed in the Cour Marly and Cour Puget. The Renaissance collection is very comprehensive; any gaps in medieval sculpture may be plugged by a visit to the Cluny Museum *(see LATIN QUARTER)*; neo-Classical sculpture, which had been languishing in storage, is at last enjoying the presentation it deserves.

High Middle Ages and Romanesque: galleries 1 to 3: – The fast evolution of Romanesque architecture enabled sculpture to flourish and develop in tandem, complete with its own regional differences.

Compare the stylised ornamentation of the 12C **Estagel priory doorway** (Gard region) with the three fine double capitals from an abbey in the Languedoc region.

The 12C **"Courajod Christ"**, once part of a Deposition, exemplifies the degree of skill attained in this art form at this time. Other particularly remarkable exhibits include: *Saint Michael vanquishing the dragon*, a marvellous triangular composition from Nevers; a *Virgin in majesty* from Auvergne; **capitals** from Burgundy and Poitiers *(David fights Goliath, Harvest scene)*; and finally, the **Carrières-sur-Seine altarpiece** *(Gallery 3 on the side of Cour Marly)*, which marks the transition from Romanesque to Gothic art.

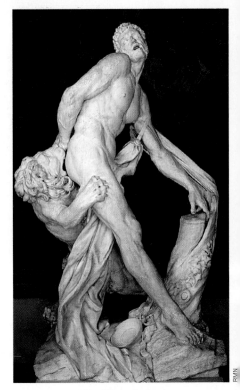

Milo of Croton by Puget

Gothic: galleries 4 to 9 – The "Gothic" Middle Ages, the age of cathedrals, produced figurative sculpture imbued with such grace, poise, sophistication and serene beauty on the one hand and such expressive realism on the other as to bear comparison with the best creations from Antiquity.

The rigid, linear style of the **statue columns** from the old church of Corbeil, Solomon and the Queen of Sheba, reflect the spirituality of nascent Gothic art.

In the 13C and 14C, sculpture progressed towards ever greater regional characteristics: delightful **smiling angels** in northern France; *Saint Matthew being dictated the Gospel by the Angel of God* from the rood screen of Chartres Cathedral; marble altarpiece fragments from the abbey of Maubuisson (Val d'Oise). Displayed in gallery 6 is the Javernant **Virgin of the Annunciation**, tinged with self-consciousness, a fine warrior's head, and a number of representations of the Virgin and Child.

Subsequent galleries accommodate fragments of funerary monuments: small **figures guarding the entrails** (symbolised by little bags) **of King Charles IV the Fair and Queen Jeanne d'Evreux** by Jean de Liège; the statues of *Charles V* and *Jeanne de Bourbon* which were once part of the Louvre's medieval ornamentation.

Late Gothic: galleries 10 to 12 – Funerary monuments become much larger in the 15C: the tomb of *Philippe Pot*, Seneschal of Burgundy, is particularly impressive with its famous hooded mourners; the tomb of *Renée d'Orléans-Longueville* has unusual Italianate decoration; the recumbent figure of *Anne of Burgundy*, resting on a black marble slab, was made in a Paris workshop (note the quality of detail in the facial features of the deceased). In gallery 11, the *Saint George fighting the dragon*, a famous bas-relief by **Michel Colombe**, heralds the Renaissance. Gallery 12 houses the remains of the Commynes chapel, including two painted praying effigies.

Renaissance: galleries 13 to 19 – The *"Mort-Saint-Innocent"* gallery is named after the macabre effigy of death which once stood at the centre of the Parisian cemetery of this name *(see les HALLES-BEAUBOURG)*. To the right of the entrance, note the altarpiece of the *Resurrection of Christ*, a delicately executed work in stone combining Flamboyant Gothic motifs with Renaissance ornamentation.

The influence of Italian art is tempered by ideals of grace and detail: the recumbent figure of *Amiral Philippe de Chabot* resting on its elbow, fashioned by the chisel of **Pierre Bontemps**; the delicate detail of the bas-reliefs by **Jean Goujon**, architect and sculptor of the Old Louvre; the power and masterly skill in the works of Germain Pilon (*Resurrected Christ*, group of the **Three Graces** from the monument of the heart of Henri II, **Mater Dolorosa**). The distant sensuality of **Diana of Anet** echoes the tendencies of the School of Fontainebleau *(see French School: Painting-16C)*.

Mannerism elongates forms and contorts figures into complex poses (*Captives* from the equestrian statue of Henri IV on the Pont Neuf). The works of Jacques Sarazin and Simon Guillain *(Monument of the Pont-au-Change)* point towards Classicism. The *"Longueville pyramid"* in the final gallery is decorated with beautiful reliefs in bronze gilt. Architectural form dominates over sculpture in the funerary monument of *Jacques-Auguste de Thou*.

The staircase, **Escalier Lefuel**, features an impressive array of arcades and banisters *(leading to the Objets d'art Department: medieval treasure, and 17C Flemish Paintings)*.

The 17C – French sculpture evolved little during the reigns of Henri IV and Louis XIII before enjoying a great vogue through the reign of Louis XIV. The new layout of this part of the Louvre into terraced courtyards provides the perfect setting for the magnificent figurative groups that once adorned the parks of royal residences at Marly, Versailles, Sceaux and the Tuileries.

★★**Cour Marly** – The **Château de Marly**, sadly now demolished, was used by Louis XIV as a retreat from the restraints of Court etiquette, to be enjoyed in the company of a few carefully selected courtiers. The grounds were decorated with wonderful sculpture in the late 17C and 18C, only some of which is now here.

The most famous figures adorned the **Abreuvoir**, or horse pond: **Fame** by **Coysevox** comprises *Fame, setting a trumpet to her lips*, and *Mercury, messenger of the Gods*, was replaced in 1745 by the famous rearing **Marly horses** being restrained by horse-tamers, by **Guillaume Coustou**, nephew of Coysevox (*see* CHAMPS ÉLYSÉES – Pont Alexandre III).

Other statues ornamenting the fountains or the park included the charming "running" effigies *(Apollo and Daphne, Atlanta and Hippomenes)* and *Aeneas carrying Anchises* by **Pierre Le Pautre** (1716).

★**Crypte Girardon** – This area between the Marly and Puget courtyards houses an impressive relief by Pierre Puget of the meeting of *Diogenes and Alexander* against a background inspired by the Roman Forum.

Busts on display include **The Grand Condé**, a bronze by Antoine Coysevox, who captures well the ugliness and lean physique of this great soldier and enjoys the display of his aristocratic rank (breast-plate decorated with griffins); the equestrian statue of *Louis XIV* by François Girardon is a smaller version of that which once adorned the place Vendôme.

Hercules wrestling with Achelous in the Cour Puget

★★Cour Puget – The first statues to catch the eye are the **Captives** from the place des Victoires which, like those by the statue of Henri IV on the Pont Neuf, once adorned the pedestal of the equestrian statue of Louis XIV; these were removed during the Revolution, along with all other Royal effigies.

The courtyard is named after the famous self-taught sculptor, painter, decorator and architect from Marseille, **Pierre Puget** (who drew up the designs for the Hôpital de la Vieille-Charité in the city of his birth). Profoundly impressed by Baroque Italy, Puget emerged as a highly individual figure in 17C French sculpture: *Milo of Croton* was displayed at the entrance to the Royal avenue in the gardens of Versailles; **Hercules the Gaul** (or *Hercules resting*) was bought by Colbert for his château at Sceaux. In his series of herms, note those from Colbert's residence *(to the left, rue de Rivoli side)* which include the extraordinary representation of *Winter*, muffled up to the ears and shivering with cold.

The middle level of terraces accommodates the charming *Duchess of Burgundy* by Coysevox and an impressive *Julius Caesar* by Nicolas Coustou. The bas-relief from the Hôtel de Bourbon-Condé *(on the wall)* exemplifies the delicate sculpture of **Clodion**.

The upper level is devoted to neo-Classical sculpture: a lovely replica of the *"Barbe-rini" Faun*, after the statue in Munich; *Oedipus and Phorbas* by **Denis-Antoine Chaudet**; *Roland in a frenzy*, a tormented bound figure in bronze by **Jehan Duseigneur**.

The 18C – *Galleries along the rue de Rivoli*. The smaller sculptures, especially the terracottas, are particularly captivating.

Gallery 22 –The exquisite **Cupid putting a finger to his lips** by **Falconet** was commissioned by Madame de Pompadour to adorn the garden of her mansion, the Hôtel d'Evreux, now the Palais de l'Élysée. In a display case, there is a *Bather* stretching her foot towards the water of a fountain.

Gallery 23 – **Cupid wittling a bow from Hercules' club** by **Bouchardon** was ill-received when presented to the Court in 1750, as Cupid was felt to be too realistic.

Gallery 24 – The **Effigy of Voltaire, nude** by **Jean-Baptiste Pigalle** (1776) is a bold study of the ageing philosopher. Note also the graceful *Bather* (or *Venus*) by **Christophe-Gabriel Allegrain**.

Gallery 25 – This contains fragments of sculpture received by the Académie Royale de peinture et de sculpture: the version of Pigalle's masterpiece **Mercury doing up his sandals** *(display case on the right)* is more sophisticated than that in bronze in the courtyard; *Dying Gladiator (on its own at the far end of the gallery)* by **Pierre Julien**; *Morpheus (display case opposite)* by Houdon.

Gallery 26 – The terracotta bust of *Madame Favart*, the famous comedienne, is by De-fernex; the one in bronze of *Jean-Baptiste Lemoyne* is by his pupil, **Augustin Pajou**, as is the figure of **Mercury** (1780).

Gallery 27 – The bust of the **Comtesse du Barry** by Pajou is a famous representation of the royal favourite; **Psyche abandoned** (because she had just looked on the face of her lover, Cupid, thereby disobeying his request that she should not see him) caused an uproar because of its complete nudity and stark realism.

Gallery 28 – The marble **head of Voltaire** (1778), by **Jean-Anatole Houdon**, was sculpted shortly after the triumphant reception given to the defender of the oppressed on his arrival in Paris; the satirical writer's "hideous smile", at the age of 84, is well rendered, complete with thin, pinched lips. The busts of the **Brongniart children** are wonderfully fresh.

Gallery 29 – The **"gallery of great men"** *(in the centre)* regroups a series of marble effigies between *Diana the Huntress* by Houdon, and *Peace (see below)*.

Gallery 30 – The marvellous **décor** (1782) by **Clodion** for the bathroom of the Hôtel de Bésenval is here preserved.

Gallery 31 – Amongst the neo-Classical sculpture note *Innocence* by Jean-Baptiste Roman; *Cupid* holding a butterfly, symbol of the soul, and a flower, representing earthly pleasure, by **Denis-Antoine Chaudet**; the lovely group of *Zephyr carrying off Psyche (near the window)* arranged around an impressive bronze and silver allegory of *Peace* by Chaudet. In a display case, look out for the silver figurine of *Henri de Navarre* (the future King Henri II) as a child.

Gallery 32 – Mythological figures by **Jean-Jacques Pradier**, the official sculptor, adopt Mannerist poses *(Three Graces)*. *The Genius of Liberty* by Augustin Dumont is a replica of the statue which stands atop the column of the Bastille.

Gallery 33 – The final gallery is devoted to the work of **François Rude**, author of the *Marseillaise* on the Arc de Triomphe (model of face in display case), *Mercury doing up his sandals* and a graceful *Neapolitan Fisherman*; and **Antoine-Louis Barrye** who is famed for his observation of animals, sculpted in minute detail, effectively rendering the morphology of wild creatures: *Lion Hunt*; *Tiger devouring a gavial*.

Consult the Index to find individual monuments or references to famous people.

★★★NEAR-EASTERN ANTIQUITIES (Antiquités Orientales)

Up the main escalator (to the right) to the ground floor: entrance straight ahead.

In 1843, **Paul-Emile Botta**, the French Consul in Mosul (Iraq), excavated the remains of the city built by Sargon II of Assyria – now the site of Khorsabad – thereby discovering a lost civilisation.

The first Assyrian museum opened at the Louvre in 1847. Further digging was actively undertaken by **Victor Place**, until the 1930s when the Oriental Institute of Chicago took charge. The new Louvre galleries house the oldest treaties, laws and representations of historical scenes known to man.

An urban civilisation evolved between 3300 and 2800 BC in the swampy region of the lower reaches of the Rivers Tigris and Euphrates (modern Iraq).

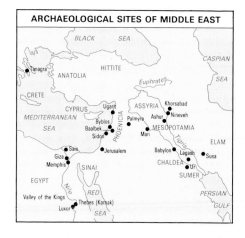

ARCHAEOLOGICAL SITES OF MIDDLE EAST

The land of Sumer was divided among rival cities before the first empires arose.

Archaic Mesopotamia: gallery 1a *(to the left)* – From its earliest evidence to the 3rd millennium BC – The Sumerian site of **Telloh** (ancient Girsu) was home to the famous **vultures stele** (*c*2450 BC – *fragments displayed straight ahead of entrance*), immortalising the victory of the King Eannatum of Lagash over the rival city of Umma. On the side nearest the entrance, the guardian god of the city is seen capturing the enemy in a net; round on the other side, the prince is seen in a war chariot at the head of his foot-soldiers.

On display by the entrance to gallery 1b, note the votive relief of *Ur-Nanshe (to the left)*, the founder of the Lagash dynasty, *(opposite this)* documents in the form of engraved terracotta cones, and the silver and copper vase dedicated by *King Entemena of Lagash to the god Ningirsu (to the right)*.

Gallery 1b – The Sumerian culture spread northwards to what is now Syria (site of **Mari**); one custom was to offer small statues of worshippers intended to perpetuate the prayers of the faithful. The Louvre has an impressive collection of these statuettes dedicated to Ishtar; the most memorable of these being that of the **Intendant of the palace of Ebih-II** (middle of the 3rd millennium BC), with beautiful blue (lapis lazuli) eyes, and clothed in a voluminous, fluffy sheepskin skirt.

Follow the signs to gallery 2.

Mesopotamia and the 3rd millennium BC: gallery 2 – The Semitic dynasty of Akkad (2340-2200 BC) succeeded in uniting Mesopotamia around the ancient Babylonian city of Agade. Wonderful artefacts dating from this dynasty include the marvellous **stele of Naram-Sin** (2250 BC) in pink sandstone *(to the right of the gallery on entering)*, which depicts the victorious king climbing a mountain over the dead bodies of enemy soldiers. To the left of the stele is a display of **cylinder seals**, which were used to indicate ownership by being affixed to contracts, letters and merchandise. Towards 2130 BC, the striking group of about a dozen fairly large **statues of Prince Gudea** and those of his son Ur-Ningirsu were produced in Lagash. This region regained its independence after the decline of the Akkad dynasty. The sovereign, wearing a robe on which there is a long prayer of dedication to the gods, is sometimes represented with an architect's materials.

Hammurabi (1792-1750 BC): gallery 3 *(beyond, left of gallery 2)* – At the beginning of the 2nd millennium BC, Babylon made its first impact on history: the Babylonian king destroyed Mari and conquered Mesopotamia. In the centre of the gallery stands the famous **Code of Hammurabi** (1792-1750 BC), a black basalt stele 2.5m – 8ft high; at the top, the king is depicted receiving from the sun god Shamash (who carries measuring instruments – ruler, surveyor's cord – symbolising justice) 282 laws which are engraved below in the Akkad language. A diorite head (in the display case to the right of the Code) depicts the aged king. The Babylonian Empire was succeeded by the Assyrian Empire in the 8C-7C BC. After the 6C BC, when Babylon reached the height of its power under King Nebuchadnezzar (*Passing Lion*, a relief in green and gold coloured glazed bricks adorned the triumphal route of the palace of Nebuchadnezzar II), the Eastern world, from the Mediterranean to India, was united under the rule of the Persian Empire.

★★Cour Khorsabad: gallery 4 – *To the right of the Passing Lion frieze in gallery 3.*
The large Assyrian reliefs from the palace of Sargon II at Dur-Sharrukin (modern
Khorsabad) greet visitors at the same height as they would have been during the
Assyrian era. Two **winged bulls** with five legs, so that two legs are visible when
viewed from the front and four when in profile, reconstitute part of the decoration
of the third doorway of the Khorsabad palace complex. The wall opposite is a reconstruction of the façade of the throne room (the bull on the left, with its head turned
to look at the viewer, is a cast of the original now in the Oriental Institute, Chicago).
Other wallspace is taken by the frieze of marvellous bas-relief scenes *(Transporting
Lebanese wood; Medes tributaries; (opposite) Bearers of the wheeled throne and
the king's furniture)* interspersed with *Winged Genies giving blessing* and several
images of a *Hero overcoming a lion.*

Anatolia, from earliest evidence to the 1st millennium BC: gallery 5 – The
Hittites, who brought the Hammurabi dynasty of Babylon to ruin, settled on
the Anatolian plateau (at the heart of modern Turkey) in the middle of the
2nd millennium BC. Their hieroglyphic script can be seen on the **stele of Til Barsip**,
which depicts the god of the storm.

Til Barsip: gallery 6 – The palace of this provincial capital was decorated with
frescoes, rather than carving. Here, the fragments have been complemented by
reconstructions of the original works.

Arslan-Tash *(first bay to the left, between two statues of bulls)* – Another provincial
capital provided sites that yielded spoils of war from Phoenician or Armenian cities
including some wonderful **ivories** *(Cow suckling calf, in display case on the right).*

Mesopotamia, Northern Syria and Nimrud *(next bay along on the left)* – Reliefs
from the palace of Ashurnasirpal II depict winged spirits, some with the heads of
birds, giving blessing in front of the sacred tree. Further round the wall to the
right, King Ashurnasirpal II (883-859 BC) is shown with his armour-bearer. The
central display case contains fragments of the bronze door from the palace of King
Salmanasar III at Balawat (9C BC).

Nineveh *(next bay along on the left)* – The reliefs from the palace of Ashurbanipal
are numbered among the masterpieces of world sculpture. The site was excavated
by British archeologists *(see Michelin Green Guide* LONDON: *British Museum).*
Note the stages of the Elamite campaign: the capture of a city; deportation of its
population; view of the city of Arbeles with its many towers. On the far wall,
Ashurbanipal II is shown in his chariot. In the last series of reliefs, note in front
of the guards a marvellously detailed horse's head near the figure of a knight.

Iran – Transhumance between the Fars mountains (to the east, on the mountainous
plateau where Persepolis was later to be built) and the Susa plain perpetuated the
Mesopotamian influence, and gave rise to the first "Iranian" state: Elam.

**The Susa region and the Iranian plateau, 5th to the early 3rd millennia BC: gal-
lery 7** – From the end of the 5th millennium, Elamite potters (the capital of Elam was
Susa) were becoming renowned for their beautiful, highly stylised animal *(large vase
with ibex)* and/or geometric
decoration.

**Susa in the 3rd millen-
nium BC: gallery 8** –
Amongst the furniture from
tombs and temples is the
painted terracotta **"secret-
compartment vase"** *(labelled
"vase à la cachette")* found
containing various objects
including alabaster vases,
weapons and copper tools;
objects for which trade
flourished between central
Asia and the Persian Gulf.

**Iran and Bactria, 3rd and
early 2nd millennia BC:
gallery 9** – The unusual
open-work circular *"standard"* (with little linked
human figures) supported
by two bulls *(display case to
the left, rue de Rivoli side)*
belongs to **Luristan** culture, a
region in the northwest of
Elam widely reputed for its
metalwork.

Princess of Bactria (early 2nd millennium BC)

RMN

Within the bounds of central Asia, a great civilisation was flourishing in **Bactria** (Afghanistan). The figurine known as the **"Princess of Bactria"** *(central display case nearest where you came in)* wears a marvellous blue robe with full sleeves and a crinoline-like skirt, in a fleecy textile reminiscent of that on the statue of the *Intendant Ebih-II (see gallery 1b above).*
Immediately to her right, **"Le Balafré"** ("Scarface" – he has also lost an eye) is the nickname given to the statuette of a mountain spirit.

Susa region during the Middle Elamite era (1500-1100 BC): gallery 10 – The art of bronze reached its apogee during this period: **Statue of Queen Napirasu** in the centre of the gallery (note in particular the embroidery on her robe).
Panels of cast bricks *(along the wall to the right)* depict alternately half-bull-half-man figures protecting a palm tree and Lama goddesses. These would once have adorned a temple.
(*Main works included in the north part of the Cour Carrée.*) From the 6C to the 4C BC Susa reached its apogee under the Achaemenid kings. Gold- and silversmiths produced outstandingly delicate works of art (bracelets and goblets, **winged ibex**). The enormous capital from the palace of Darius at Susa gives some indication of the gigantic scale of the palaces of Persian rulers, which were decorated with enamel brick friezes: note those of the *Archers*, the *Griffins* and the *Lions* with human heads (*c*500 BC).
Among the Phoenician tombs, the sarcophagus in the form of the mummy of *Eshmunazar II*, King of Sidon (5C BC) betrays Egyptian influence in Syria. It is engraved with the text of a curse. Marble sculptures from Sidon evoke the cult of Mithra, and bronzes that of Jupiter from Heliopolis (modern Baalbek) in Syria, during the Roman era.
The colossal *Vase of Amathus* (in fact, a basin) in limestone was made in the 5C BC, probably to collect the water supply necessary for the ceremonies of the city's temple.
The **mosaics** from the palace of Bichapur (3C AD) date from the Sasanian period and mark the transition to Muslim art.

LEVANTINE ART

Palestine and Transjordania from the earliest evidence to the Iron Age: gallery D – The **stele of Mesha**, King of Moab (9C BC), commemorates his victory over the kings of Israel and the Omri dynasty. Its reference to the Hebrew state is the earliest known.

Central Syria from the earliest evidence to the Iron Age: gallery C, B and A – Terracottas (vase bases, models of houses with storeys) and statuette of a seated god *(display case centre left)*.
Excavation of Ugarit (modern Ras Shamra) has uncovered Phoenicia, the crossroads of the Ancient world. For the first time, *c*1300 BC, the cuneiform alphabet is used in place of syllabic script.
Above the figurines of *Baal* brandishing a thunderbolt *(1st display case along wall to left)*, there is a beautiful **patera** depicting a royal hunting scene in repoussé gold (14C-13C BC).
Luxury objects include: ivory **lid of a pyx** (powder box) depicting a goddess feeding some goat-like animals (*c*1250 BC; *1st display case along wall to right*); Egyptian influenced **breast-plate** decorated with the royal falcon (2000-1600 BC; *2nd display case along wall to right*); **stele of Baal with a Thunderbolt** (god of the storm, *centre of the gallery*).
Cult statues from the island of Cyprus (7C-3C BC) and funerary strips in gold leaf *(to the right on entering)*, bowls in electrum (alloy of gold and silver).

★★ISLAMIC ART

On the Entresol level, 1st staircase to the right, then straight on.
Exhibits from Spain, Egypt, Iran, Syria and India *(those from the Maghreb are displayed in the Museum of African and Oceanian Art at Vincennes)* are very effectively displayed beneath the low ceilings of the quiet, environmentally controlled galleries of the Entresol. The department despite being fairly small, none the less gives a taste of the Louvre's rich collection of Muslim art. Each exquisite exhibit displays the height of sophistication and refined stylisation.

The dawn of Islam – From Iran, seek out the dish inscribed with a partridge (Sasanian silverwork, 7C-9C), and the stone relief panel bearing two ibex face to face (7C-8C), a recurrent decorative motif, and the strange zoomorphic vase, made of blue and white glass *(on display to the left of the entrance)*.

Abassidian world (8C-10C): gallery 2 – The intricate fragment of cenotaph or chest (Egypt, late 9C-early 10C) is a rare early example of marquetry, an art-form that was to become popular from the 12C: wooden door panel with plant ornamentation from the palace of Djawsaq al-Khaqani (Iraq, 836).

Islam in the West (10C-15C): gallery 3 – The contribution made by the civilisations of Islam to Western philosophy, art and science is considerable. The kingdom of Granada in Spain flourished until 1492. Note the *Peacock aquamanile* (Spain, 12C), the work of a Muslim craftsman in the service of a Christian prince; marvellous caskets and ivory pyxes (sculpted cylindrical boxes) from Spain and Sicily, in particular the **pyx called after Al-Mughira** (10C, with a domed lid); the *Lion with an articulated tail* (Spain, 12C-13C) with a very large, wide-open mouth, possibly once part of a fountain.
In the display cases to the left, note the tiny bottles in rock crystal, parts of a necklace and pendants decorated with cloisonné enamel and a beautiful gold bracelet (Syria?, 11C-12C).

East Iran (10C-12C): gallery 4 – The 11C-12C dish decorated with an epigraphic inscription *(at the top of the display case by the entrance)* reads: "The taste of knowledge is bitter at first, but is ultimately sweeter than honey. Health to him who possesses it."

Seljuq Iran (11C-13C): gallery 5 – Ceramics include a ewer with an animal's head *(in the centre of the 1st display case)*. Scientific and technological instruments comprise astrolabes, celestial spheres, pestle and mortar, "magic mirrors", a scale pan with beautifully intricate engraving (signs of the zodiac etc) and a **goldsmith's box of tools**. The glass-case at the far end of the gallery displays writing tools (a knife with a coral handle was used to carve the calami). **Gallery 6** *off to the left halfway down gallery 5* accommodates a chandelier with ducks from Khurasan (12C-13C, *in the centre of far display case opposite entrance*) with decoration symbolising the idea of light and an open-work ceramic ewer with a cock's head *(to the right in the same display case)*. **Gallery 7** *left at the far end of gallery 5* has funerary stele and carved stones displayed in an alcove with subdued, "atmospheric" lighting.

Egypt, the Middle East and Anatolia (12-13C): gallery 8 – This gallery houses some really marvellous exhibits in copper inlaid with gold and silver, carved with intricate patterns. The **Saint-Louis font**, a masterpiece of Mameluke art (1300), was used to baptise French children (decorated with *fleur-de-lis*, a frieze of knights and animals).

The Mamelukes (1250-1517): gallery 9 – Blue-glazed ceramics, lamps in blown glass, a *Koran desk*. Near the entrance, hanging from the wall, is the salver named after a Sultan of Yemen, a 14C work from Cairo.

Mongol Iran (13C-14C): gallery 10 – The large dish with rings of fish *(at the far end of the display case along the left wall)* recall Chinese celadon ware (pale grey-green porcelain or earthenware) which was exported in large quantities during the Song and Yuan dynasties.

The Timurids (1370-1506): gallery 11 – Fragments of frieze, an earthenware star with different blue glazes ("cuerda seca" technique). Further along the same wall, the tapestry called *"Siege of Vienna"* (Iran or India, 17C) came from the tent of Kara Mustafa, the Grand Vizier of the Ottoman troops during the second siege of the Austrian capital (1683).

Safavid Iran (1501-1736) – This was a period of magnificence for Iran, during which the capital, Ispahan, was one of the greatest cities in the world: decorative wall panel in painted tiles and, in the display case beyond it, a bookbinding decorated with scenes of royal entertainment out of doors.

Qajar Iran (1779-1924) – The portrait of the second sovereign of the dynasty was offered to Napoleon I's ambassador to Persia. In the display case next to it, note two 19C cat figurines inlaid with gold and silver.

Mughal India (1526-1858) – Collection of weapons *(daggers)* and armour *(15C Iranian helmets)*; hookah bases (water pipes) – note the delicate inlaid work; dagger with a horse's head (with a rock crystal handle) and its sheath; early 18C floral stand.
In the centre of the gallery, the **"Mantes" carpet** (so-called as it once adorned the floor of a church in this town) is a splendid late 16C Iranian work.

The Ottoman world (14C-19C): gallery 12 – It was in the Imperial workshops, especially in **Iznik**, a suburb of Istanbul, that painters and draughtsmen produced the distinctive motifs that adorn these ceramics and tiles.
Various colours, including the famous Iznik red, were added to under-glaze blue and white during the 16C. Note the **"saz"** style of long, flowing flowers with frilly edges (saz), amongst the open leaves and real flowers (tulips, carnations and hyacinths). The masterpiece of this style is the **peacock dish** with its original bird motif *(in the middle display case on the right on entering)*.
The red and midnight blue carpet with the central medallion (18C, Turkey, Ushak) belongs to a type that was destined for the Court or for mosques.

To the left of the entrance, note the beautiful **scribe's table** (a little chest with legs) in wood, mother-of-pearl and tortoiseshell marquetry (Istanbul, 16C-17C). In the little bay tucked behind this display case, jade and rock crystal **cupels** (assay dishes) inlaid with gold wire and precious stones are displayed with two archer's rings designed to protect the archer's thumb from the rubbing of the bowstring. Two ceramic plaques in an alcove on the wall to the right depict the holy mosques of Mecca (Ka' ba veiled in black) and Medina.

RMN

Peacock dish (Iznik, 16C)

The Art of the Book: gallery 13 – Bookbindings and miniatures (note the marvellously subtle use of colour on those from Mughal India).

THE LOUVRE PALACE EXTERIOR

★★**Pyramid** – The pyramid, 21m – 69ft high and 33m – 105ft wide at the base, was designed by the architect **Ieoh Ming Pei**; it is built of sheet glass supported on a framework of stainless-steel tubes. The extravagantly decorated façades overlooking the Cour Napoléon make a majestic backdrop to the sharply contrasting, rigidly geometric form of the glass pyramid at the centre of the courtyard.

It is from directly below the pyramid, in the museum reception area over which it forms a huge vault, that one can fully appreciate the originality of design and materials used. An **equestrian statue of Louis XIV**, a copy of a marble statue by Bernini, stands on the axis leading to the Champs-Élysées, slightly at an angle with the Old Louvre.

★★★**Cour Carrée** – At night, a new system of illuminations sets off the most impressive remnant of the Old Louvre to full effect. The fine elegant Renaissance façade between the Clock Pavilion, in the centre of the west wing, and the south wing is the work of **Pierre Lescot**. The graceful, expressive sculpture of the three avant-corps (projecting bay) and the upper storey are by the master **Jean Goujon**, depicting allegorical scenes in high-relief, animated figures in niches, friezes of children and garlands. The Clock Pavilion was built during the reign of Louis XIII by **Lemercier**, who was also responsible for the northwest wing, a replica of Lescot's façade. The three other wings, while harmonising with the west wing, are more Classical in style.

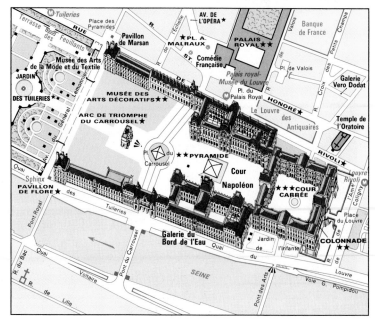

★★Colonnade – In 1662, Louis XIV decided that the palace exterior on the side facing Paris was still not quite grand enough for a royal residence. He therefore summoned the Italians Rainaldi, Pietro da Cortona and above all **Bernini**, the great master of the Italian Baroque, to design plans for a new one.

Bernini arrived in France and suggested demolishing the existing palace: work on his third proposal was begun on 17 October 1665, and suspended by Louis XIV a year later, with full support from Colbert, in favour of plans by three French architects: **Perrault, Le Vau** and **D'Orbray**.

The Colonnade is attributed to Claude Perrault, however François d'Orbay, Le Vau's draughtsman, appears also to have played a decisive role in its design. This splendid, original work, finally completed in 1811, has sometimes been criticised for having little in common with the rest of the Louvre. It features the cipher of Louis XIV – two L's back to back. The central pediment, carved during the Empire, featured a bust of Napoleon I, which was replaced at the time of the Restoration by one of the Sun-King, who is thus crowned rather inappropriately by a Minerva in imperial dress.

The true height and Classical harmony of the structure can be fully admired now that moats have been cleared to a depth of 7m – 23ft around the rusticated base, in accordance with the original 17C plans.

★Embankment façade – From the south side of the Louvre, there is an attractive view of the Pont des Arts and the dome of the Institut de France. The first floor of the gallery overlooking the river, the Galerie du Bord-de-l'Eau, features a charming **frieze of cherubs** riding on the backs of sea-monsters.

★Pavillon de Flore – The corner of the quai des Tuileries and the Pont Royal is a good vantage point for appreciating the high relief by **Carpeaux, The Triumph of Flora★**, which adorns the corner pavilion beneath the great allegorical scene on the south pediment. In front of the Pavillon de Flore, where avenue du Général-Lemonnier meets the quay, two sphinxes, brought back after the capture of Sebastopol in 1855, stand guard.

★Arc de Triomphe du Carrousel – This delightful pastiche, inspired by the Roman triumphal arch of Septimus Severus, was built from 1806-08, according to designs by **Percier** and **Fontaine**. The six bas-reliefs commemorate the Napoleonic victories of 1805. The pink marble columns, retrieved from the old Château de Meudon *(see Michelin Green Guide* FLANDERS, PICARDY AND THE PARIS REGION*)*, are surmounted by statues of soldiers wearing various types of uniform. On the platform, where Napoleon placed the four horses removed from the basilica of San Marco in Venice (until they were returned there in 1815), **Bosio** sculpted an allegorical goddess, representing the Restoration of the Bourbons, accompanied by Victories and driving a quadriga.

From directly beneath the arch there is a magnificent **view★★★** along the axis that runs from the Louvre through the Tuileries, place de la Concorde, the Champs-Élysées, the Arc de Triomphe and avenue de la Grande Armée, as far as the Grande Arche at La Défense. The square takes its name from the lavish equestrian and theatrical tournament held there in honour of the birth of the Dauphin in 1662.

Arc de Triomphe du Carrousel

★LES TUILERIES

see plan under CHAMPS-ÉLYSÉES. Ⓜ *Concorde, Tuileries*

Stretching between the Louvre and the place de la Concorde, the Arc de Triomphe and the Grande Arche at La Défense, the Tuileries Gardens were envisaged by Colbert as the first section of the road from the Royal palace to the forest of Saint Germain.

The lost château – For 10 centuries the area fell outside the city walls. In the 15C it was used as a rubbish tip by butchers and tanners of the Châtelet district. The local clay was dug for making tiles – *tuiles* – hence the name: Tuileries. In 1563, Catherine de' Medici decided to have a château built next to the Louvre, a project she entrusted to **Philibert Delorme** in 1564. Work was abruptly halted when the Queen Mother learnt that her horoscope predicted that she would die 'near to Saint-Germain', and that the Tuileries depended upon Saint-Germain-l'Auxerrois. A house was therefore built in the lee of Saint-Eustache (the prediction nevertheless came true as 22 years later, Monsignor de Saint-Germain gave her the last rights).

Twenty-two years later, shortly after his arrival in Paris, Henri IV orders work to proceed and the Pavillon de Flore was built. The riverside gallery designed to link the Louvre with the Tuileries followed, raised by a second storey.

Louis XIV extended the complex to accommodate a theatre (1659-1661), named after the complicated scene-changing equipment, Salle des Machines. In 1664, the king moved to the Tuileries while building progressed on the Louvre. **Le Vau** revamped the exterior and constructed the Pavillon de Marsan. Parties, ballets and masques punctuated the three winters spent by the king at the Tuileries.

The 18C – In 1715, on the death of the Sun King, the Regency installed the young Louis XV in the Tuileries. In 1722, he moved the court back to Versailles, and the palace was more or less abandoned as a residence.

Instead, Paris' first public concert-hall is set up in the salle des Suisses, open on religious holidays. It drew many major composers and musicians, from home and other European courts, including **Mozart** (1778). Important performances of religious works lasted until 1789.

Simultaneously, when fire devastated the Opéra theatre in April 1763, the Company moved into the salles des Machines, refurbished by Gabriel and Soufflot. The Comédie Française took over in 1770, staging Beaumarchais' *Barber of Seville* and Voltaire's *Irène* before 1782.

Troubled times – 17 October 1789 and the royal family were forced back to Paris by the angry mob; the queen and her children took flight on 20 June 1791. A year later, to the day, the palace was invaded by rioters who seized the king; two months later, on 10 August, the palace was attacked: 600 of the defending 900 Swiss guards were slaughtered and the palace was ransacked.

During the Convention, the buildings served as ministry offices.

Final decline – First Consul Bonaparte took up residence on 20 February 1800. In 1810, the Emperor Napoleon I celebrated his marriage to Marie-Louise in the Salon Carré of the Louvre. A year later, the King of Rome was born at the Tuileries which continued to serve as the Royal household to subsequent kings. Under Napoleon III the architects **Visconti** and **Lefuel** completed the galerie Rivoli, thereby completing the union of the Tuileries and the Louvre.

During the week of Commune uprisings (1871), the Tuileries palace was burnt down. In 1883, the stone ruins were purchased by a Corsican family who went on to use the stones to build a replica palace in Ajaccio (this too was burnt down in 1978).

The gardens – Catherine de' Medici envisaged an Italian-style park, complete with fountains, a maze, a grotto, populated with terracotta figures by **Bernard Palissy**, and a menagerie for her palace next to the Louvre. East of the octagonal basin stood a semicircular screen of trees famous for its echo. Henri II later added an orangery and a silkworm farm. The park became a fashionable place for an outdoor stroll thereby breaking new ground, for hitherto fashion and elegance had always been displayed indoors.

Le Nôtre French Garden – By 1664 the gardens required attention: Colbert delegated the work to Le Nôtre, born near the Marsan Pavilion and a gardener at the Tuileries, like his father and grandfather before him. He raised two terraces lengthways and of unequal height to level the sloping ground thereby creating the magnificent central axis; he hollowed out the pools and designed formal flowerbeds, quincunxes and slopes.

Colbert was so delighted that he intended the gardens to be kept for the royal family, but was subsequently persuaded by the author, Charles Perrault, to allow access to the public. In the 18C the gardens became ever more attractive with chairs available for hire and toilets installed. Louis-Philippe reserved a part of the gardens for the royal family. In 1783 the physicist, Charles, and the engineer, Robert, made an early balloon flight from the gardens.

The Revolution – On 10 August 1792, Louis XVI and his family fled the Tuileries Palace, crossed the gardens and sought refuge with the Legislative Assembly. When the Swiss Guards attempted to follow, two-thirds were slaughtered by the mob.

The Festival of the Supreme Being, organised by the painter David on 8 June 1794, opened in the gardens before proceeding to the Champ-de-Mars.

The Tuileries today – The gardens have recently undergone a substantial restoration programme. Parts designed by Le Nôtre remain unaltered, although some sculptures have been moved and others added, including the fine collection of **nudes★** (Pomona, Action in Chains, Venus...) by Maillol donated by the Dina Vierny Foundation (see FAUBOURG-ST-GERMAIN).

The riverside terrace – From here there is a splendid **view★★** over the gardens, the Seine and, in the background, the Louvre. This was the playground of the royal princes including the sons of Napoleon I and III. The bronze group The Sons of Cain is by Landowski. Below, an underground passage running the length of the terrace to place de la Concorde enabled Louis-Philippe to escape from the palace in 1848.

The parterres – The small grille, marked by a ditch, formerly divided the royal garden from the public area. The paths are lined with copies of statues from Antiquity and decorative vases. Towards the eastern end are works by Le Pautre, Auguste Cain and Rodin.

Quinconces (Quincunxes) – The central alley affords a magnificent **vista★★★** between the greenery lined with 19C and 20C statues: Autumn, Winter and Night.

The octagonal fountain and terraces – Around the huge octagonal basin are arranged statues, terraces, slopes and stairways in one single architectural whole (Numbers correspond with numbers on the plan under Champs-Élysées).

1) The Seasons (N Coustou and Van Clève)

2) Arcade from the Tuileries Palace

3) Bust of Le Nôtre (Coysevox). The original is in St-Roch (see PALAIS-ROYAL)

4) The Tiber copied from the Antique

5) The Seine and the Marne (G Coustou)

6) The Nile copied from the Antique

7) The Loire and the Loiret (Van Clève)

8) Commemorative tablet of the balloon ascent of Robert and Charles in 1783

9) Fame on a winged horse (after Coysevox)

10) Mercury on a winged horse (after Coysevox). Originals in the Louvre.

Until 1716 there was no exit from this end of the Tuileries, the moat at the foot of the Louis XIII wall cutting it off from the Esplanade or future place de la Concorde. A swing bridge was constructed over the moat and ornamented in 1719 by Coysevox' Winged Horses which were brought for the purpose from Marly (see CHAMPS-ÉLYSÉES – Place de la Concorde). The bridge disappeared when Louis-Philippe had Place de la Concorde redesigned.

Steps and ramps afford access at several points to the terraces (the Feuillants on the north side, the Bord de l'Eau on the south, which run the length of the gardens and culminate in the Jeu de Paume and Orangery Museums.

The two pavilions, the **Orangerie** and the **Jeu de Paume** were built during the Second Empire and have served as art galleries since the beginning of the 20C. The latter, now known as the **Galerie National du Jeu de Paume** ⊙, has been soberly refurbished to display to best advantage the most advanced elements in contemporary art.

★★**Musée de l'Orangerie** ⊙ – The horseshoe staircase with wrought ironwork by Raymond Subes leads to the first-floor galleries that accommodate the Walter-Guillaume Collection (Impressionists to 1930).

This famous collection includes the work of many artists including **Soutine** (1894-1943) the painter of anguished portraits and haunted still-lifes (The young pastry cook), who like **Picasso** (Nude against a red background) and **Modigliani** (Antonia) were members of the group of foreign artists drawn to Paris from abroad. **Cézanne** explored still-life compositions (Apples and biscuits). **Renoir** repeatedly returned to portraiture (Bather with long hair, Woman with a letter). **Derain** (1880-1954) structured his bleak compositions in brown tones (A blond model). **Matisse** (1869-1954) experimented with colour (Three sisters). **Henri Rousseau** (le Douanier, 1844-1910) lit his naive compositions with special effects (Old Junier's cart).

The two oval rooms on the ground floor are hung with panels from the water-lily series painted by **Monet** of his garden at Giverny, in Normandy known as the **Nymphéas★★★**.

'Paris is devine. I mean Dorothy and I got to Paris yesterday, and it really is devine. Because the French are devine.'

Anita Loos – Gentlemen Prefer Blondes

LUXEMBOURG★★

Michelin plan 11 – folds 31 and 43: J 13, J 14, K 13, K 14, L 13

This area extends from the Latin Quarter across to the Church of Saint Sulpice, to include the Odéon area. Its main feature, undoubtedly, is the magnificent gardens of the Luxembourg Palace, which attract people of all ages, from all walks of life. It was here that the hungry and impecunious Hemingway used to come and catch pigeons to eat. Today, the area's proximity to the Senate and to various University faculties (Law School, Art History and Archeology...), children's play areas and puppet theatre, philately fairs and such like, the neighbourhood is a popular place in which to stay and absorb the atmosphere of Paris.

Religious beginnings – The site in Gallo-Roman times was occupied by an encampment and villas. The area was left deserted by the ravages of invading barbarians, until a ghostly highwayman named Vauvert created his lair in an old ruin nicknamed the 'château de Vauvert'; he terrorised the neighbourhood until 1257 when some Carthusians, installed by St Louis at Gentilly, suggested to the king that they eliminated the outlaw. Having succeeded, they lay claim to the area and built a vast monastery with extensive grounds. Their fabulous vegetable garden and orchards became legendary in the capital.

Marie de' Medici's palace – After the death of Henri IV, his queen, Marie de' Medici, disliking living at the Louvre, decided to build her own palace modelled on the Palazzo Pitti in Florence where she had spent her childhood. In 1612 she bought the mansion of Duke François of Luxembourg together with various properties around: in 1615 her architect, **Salomon de Brosse** began construction; in 1621 **Rubens** was commissioned to paint a series of 24 large allegorical pictures representing the queen's life – these now hang in the Galerie Médicis in the Louvre.

The day of deceit – In 1625 the queen installed herself in the palace but her joy was short-lived. As head of a religious faction she opposed Richelieu's policies; during a heated discussion held in her private apartments on 10 November 1630 she extracted a promise from her son, Louis XIII to dismiss the Cardinal. Twenty-four hours later, back at Versailles, he revoked on his undertaking and confirmed the minister's authority. The conspirators were apprehended and Marie de' Medici was banished to Cologne where she died penniless in 1642. The palace reverted to its original Luxembourg title and, although abandoned, remained Crown property until the Revolution.

The palace as parliament – In 1790 when the monastery was suppressed, the gardens were enlarged and the palace vista extended to the far end of the avenue de l'Observatoire. Under the Terror the palace was used as a prison. The building successively became home to a Parliamentary assembly for the Directory, the Consulate, the Senate and its successor the Peers' Chamber. Chalgrin, architect of the Arc de Triomphe and the Odéon, completely transformed the interior. Between 1836 and 1841 Alphonse de Gisors enlarged the complex on the garden side, by the addition of a new front to the main building and two lateral pavilions in keeping with the original style.
At various dates Marshal Ney, the conspirator Louis-Napoleon Bonaparte (and future Napoleon III) and other reactionary members of the Commune were all tried in the palace.

Luxembourg Palace

★★LUXEMBOURG PALACE ⊙

15 rue de Vaugirard. Ⓜ *Odéon /RER: Luxembourg. Buses: 21, 27, 38, 82, 84, 85, 89*

The building was occupied during the Second World War by the Germans. On 25 August 1944 it was freed by Leclerc's Division and the French Resistance.

The palace is now the seat of the **Sénat** (the French Upper House) composed of 319 members chosen by an electoral college. This consists of deputies, departmental and municipal councillors. In the event of the Presidency of the Republic becoming vacant, the Senate President exercises the functions of Head of State. The Senate itself interacts with l'Assemblée nationale in matters of Constitutional changes and legislation, it also may act as adjudicator between the Assemblée nationale and the Government. Sessions are open to the public when ministers are requested to reply to questions in debate from the floor.

Most of the monastic grounds have been pared away by road building schemes and urban development.

★★Palace

Exterior – To give a Florentine quality to his design for the palace, Salomon de Brosse used bosses, ringed columns and Tuscan capitals, whilst keeping the typically French ground plan of a central block built around an arcaded courtyard, with a central domed gateway-pavilion. The Doric order, applied throughout the symmetrical ground floor lends the design a robust elegance.

Rooms in the basement are flooded with natural light permitted by the two inner courtyards below the level of the allée de l'Odéon, laid with French *parterre* gardens.

The **Petit Luxembourg**, now the residence of the president of the Senate, comprises the original Hôtel de Luxembourg presented to Richelieu by Marie de' Medici and also the cloister and chapel of a convent founded by the queen.

The **musée du Luxembourg** houses temporary exhibitions during the summer months.

Interior – The library is decorated with **paintings★** by Delacroix *(Dante and Virgil walking in Limbo, Alexander placing Homer's poems in Darius' gold casket).* The ceiling of the library annexe is decorated with a painting of the *Signs of the Zodiac* by Jordaens. In the Golden Book Room are the 17C panelling and paintings which once adorned Marie de' Medici's apartments.

The **Senate council chamber**, the state gallery and most of the salons were furnished during the reign of Louis-Philippe. The main staircase by Chalgrin leading to the gallery used to be hung with the Rubens paintings.

★★Gardens

The Luxembourg Gardens exert a great draw on Parisians probably ever since Napoleon decreed that they should be dedicated to children. They attract students and young mothers or nannies with children who stop to watch the tennis or *boules*, to see the *marionette* puppet shows or listen to the free concerts, to sail boats on the *grand bassin*, or play on the pedal-car circuit.

Overall they conform to a formal layout, the only serpentine lines of the more English-style garden being along rue Guynemer and rue Auguste-Comte. The spirit of the monks lives on in the serious tending of trees and bees.

The **fontaine de Medici★** (Medici Fountain) (1624) in its leafy setting at the far end of a long pool shaded by plane trees, shows obvious Italian influence in its embossed decoration and overall design. In a niche the jealous Cyclops, Polyphemus, waits to crush Acis and Galatea (by Ottin, 1863) while on the rue de Médicis side is a low relief of Leda and the Swan (1807).

Statues began to invade the lawns under Louis-Philippe and today have reached such numbers that they seem to stand around every corner. The Queens of France and other illustrious women line the terraces. Perhaps the best of all is the Delacroix monument by Dalou.

The Senate has extended its premises to a series of buildings across rue de Vaugirard. In the ground-floor galleries can be seen exhibitions of Coins and Medals and Sèvres Porcelain. Incorporated in the new building at no **36** is the doorway of a mansion built by Boffrand for the Palatine princess Anne of Bavaria (1716), and round the corner at no **17** rue Garancière, the façade of another mansion adorned with mascarons representing the Seasons.

For the Observatory and Val-de-Grâce – see PORT-ROYAL

'If you are lucky enough to have lived in Paris as a young man, then wherever you go for the rest of your life, it stays with you, for Paris is a moveable feast'
Ernest Hemingway to a friend, 1950.

★ODÉON Ⓜ *Odéon. Buses: 58, 63, 70, 86, 87, 96*

Bordering upon the Latin Quarter and the St Germain-des-Prés neighbourhood, this area is permanently animated by young students, university staff, publishers at work and at play.

Place de l'Odéon – This semicircular square has remained essentially unchanged since its creation in 1779.

At no **1**, the Café Voltaire was frequented by the Encyclopedists and, at the turn of the 20C, by famous writers and poets: Barrès, Bourget, Mallarmé and Verlaine.

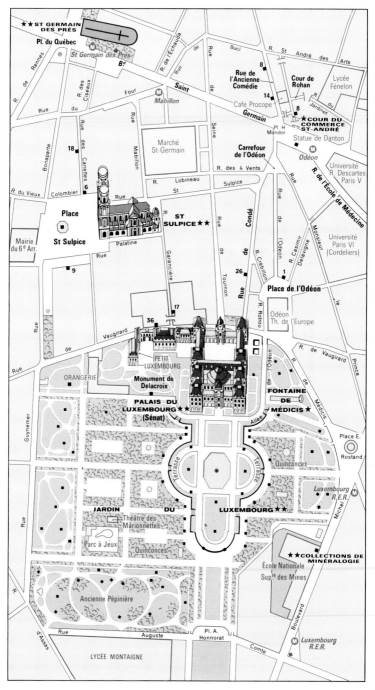

Théâtre de l'Odéon – In 1782 a theatre was built in the gardens of the former Condé mansion to accommodate the French Comedians who for the past 12 years had been confined to the Tuileries Palace Theatre. The new theatre, built in the popular 'Antique' style of the day, was given the name Théâtre Français.
Beaumarchais' *Le Mariage de Figaro* was particularly well received in 1784.
With the advent of the Revolution, the actors split between Royalists and Republicans disbanded in 1792. Talma and a group of the most fool-hardy headed for the theatre in rue de Richelieu to found the present Comédie-Française *(see* PALAIS-ROYAL)*.* Those loyal to the Crown soon ended up in prison.
In 1797 the theatre was taken over and renamed the Odéon, after the building used by the Greeks to hold musical competitions. Concerts and dances were generally popular before works began to be staged with disastrous results. In 1807 the building was rebuilt to its original plans after a fire. In spite of the great success of Alphonse Daudet's play, *L'Arlésienne*, set to music by Bizet, the theatre's audience dwindled, migrating to theatres on the Right Bank.
Between 1946 and 1959, known first as the salle Luxembourg and then as the Théâtre de France, it began to specialise in 20C plays, achieving pre-eminence in 1968 under Jean-Louis Barrault and Madeleine Renaud.
Inside, the ceiling is painted by André Masson (1963).
All around in what were the grounds of the Condé townhouse, unpretentious houses were built with uniform frontages; the roads between them are named after famous writers: Corneille, Racine, Voltaire (now renamed Casimir-Delavigne), Molière (Rotrou), Crébillon, Regnard.

Richard Wright: a writer in exile

American writer and intellectual Richard Wright lived at 14 rue Monsieur-le-Prince with his wife and two daughters from 1948 to 1959. Wright's novels *Black Boy*, *Native Son* and *American Hunger* and essays forcefully exposed racism in American society. Discontented with the racial and political climate in post-WWII America, Wright was finally granted an American passport thanks to the intervention of Gertrude Stein, who arranged to have the French Government extend him an official invitation. Among the haunts frequented by Wright and other members of the black intelligentsia was the nearby Café Tournon, *20 rue de Tournon*. Martin Luther King visited the writer in his rue Monsieur-le-Prince apartment in 1959. Richard Wright died in Paris in 1960. His ashes are preserved in Père Lachaise cemetery (*see* PERE-LACHAISE).

Rue de Condé is lined with old houses; at no 26, Beaumarchais wrote *Le Barbier de Séville* in 1773.

Carrefour de l'Odéon – This great junction marked by place Henri-Mondor is dominated by a bronze statue of Danton (1759-1794). Full of movement, it was erected at the end of the 19C on the site of the famous Revolutionary leader's house.

★**Cour du Commerce-St-André** – *entrance via 130 boulevard St-Germain, opposite Danton's statue*. This courtyard was opened in 1776 on the site of a 'real' tennis court *(jeu de paume)*. It was here in a loft in 1790 that Dr Guillotin perfected his "philanthropic decapitating machine" using sheep. At no **8**, Marat printed his paper L'Ami du Peuple *(the People's Friend)*. In the first alleyway (gated) to the right, one of the towers of the Philippe Auguste city wall can be seen on the corner.

Cour de Rohan – A series of three courtyards once (15C) formed part of a mansion owned by the Archbishops of Rouen (Rohan is a corruption of Rouen). The middle one is overlooked by a fine Renaissance house belonging to Diane de Poitiers.
The peaceful rue du Jardinet, built on the site of former gardens, runs into rue de l'Éperon where the Lycée Fénelon stands, the first girls'school to be opened in Paris (1893).

Rue de l'Ancienne-Comédie – Formerly the rue des Fossés-St-Germain, this street was renamed in 1770, the date the Comédie-Française moved out. When the Four Nations College (*see* les QUAIS – Institut de France) opened in 1688, the austere and stuffy Sorbonne directors disapproving of the proximity of the Comédie-Française forced the company to leave the rue Mazarine. The players, who included Molière's widow, Armande Béjart, eventually settled in another real tennis court at no **14** – note between the 2nd and 3rd floors the reclining figure of *Minerva* by Le Hongre. The painters David, Gros and Horace Vernet also lived there, having studios overlooking the courtyard.

The theatre was inaugurated in 1689 with *Phèdre* by Racine and Molière's *Le Médecin malgré lui*. At ground level, the unkempt mob would stand and jeer, above in the tiers of boxes fashionable society would take their seats and revel at each other rather than the stage!

In 1770, the company on the brink of financial ruin went to the Tuileries Palace Theatre before finally moving to the Odéon.

At no 8, stood the **restaurant d'Agneau** frequented by Henri Murger, the author of *Scènes de la Vie de Bohème* (1848) – which provided Puccini with a story for his opera *La Bohème* – Victor Hugo, Théophile Gautier, George Sand and Coping.

At no **13**, the **Café Procope** was founded in 1686 by the Sicilian Procopio dei Coltelli who was well-known in 18C and 19C literary circles as a philosopher. It has been a regular meeting place through the ages for successive generations of writers and thinkers: La Fontaine, Voltaire, the Encyclopedists, Jean-Jacques Rousseau, Beaumarchais, Marat, Danton, Robespierre, Bonaparte, Musset, George Sand, Gambetta, Verlaine...

QUARTIER ST-SULPICE Ⓜ *Mabillon. Buses 63, 70, 84, 86, 87, 96*

★★Église de St-Sulpice ⊙ – *place St-Sulpice*. The church, dedicated to the 6C Archbishop of Bourges, St Sulpicius, was founded by the abbey of St-Germain-des-Prés as a parish church for peasants living in its domain. Rebuilding began in 1646 with the chancel. A succession of six architects took charge over a period of 134 years. In 1732 a competition was held for the design of the façade and won by a Florentine, Servandoni, who proposed a fine façade in the style of the Antique, in contrast to the rest of the edifice. Of the 20 artists who worked on the internal paintings, Delacroix's genius dominates.

Exterior – The final façade differs considerably from Servandoni's original concept. The colossal pediment has been abandoned; the belfries are crowned not by Renaissance pinnacles but by balustrades; the towers are dissimilar, the left one being taller and more ornate than the other which was never completed.

Walk back along the south side of the church, down rue Palatine. The transept façade is in the Jesuit style with two superimposed orders and heavy ornaments. Seen from the corner of rue Palatine and rue Garancière, St-Sulpice is a building of some size, shouldered by massive buttresses designed as inverted consoles and ending in the dome and corbelled apse of the Lady Chapel.

Interior – The interior, which measures 113m long by 58m wide by 34m high – 371ft x 190ft x 112ft – is extremely impressive.

In the transept, a copper band inlaid in the floor stretches from a plaque in the southern (right) transept to a marble obelisk in the northern (left) arm. At noon at the winter solstice, a ray of sunlight, passing through a small hole in the upper window in the south transept, strikes marked points on the obelisk in the far transept. At the spring and autumn equinoxes the ray is caught by the metal plaque. This 1744 meridian *(see* PORT ROYAL – Observatoire*)* registers midday every day.

The sculpted *Christ*, *Mater Dolorosa* and *Apostles* beside the chancel columns are by Bouchardon.

The **Lady Chapel★** in the apse was painted under the personal supervision of Servandoni. The *Virgin and Child* group behind the altar is by Pigalle; the walls are hung with paintings by Van Loo and the dome is frescoed by Lemoyne.

The **organ loft★** was designed by Chalgrin in 1776. The organ, rebuilt in 1862, is the largest in France and considered one of the finest. The post of church organist has been held by such eminent musicians as Widor and Dupré (until 1971).

Delacroix's **murals★** in the first chapel on the right, were painted between 1849 and 1861. Full of Romanticism in colour, composition, movement and temperament, they illustrate *St Michael killing the demon* (ceiling), *Heliodorus being driven from the Temple* (Heliodorus, a minister of the King of Syria, coveting the treasures of the Temple was struck down by three avenging angels, one of whom is riding a horse – right wall), *Jacob wrestling with the Angel* (left wall).

Two stoups abutting the second pillars of the nave are made from giant shells given to François I by the Venetian Republic and by Louis XV to the church of St-Sulpice in 1745. Their 'rock' supports were carved by Pigalle.

Place St-Sulpice – Initiated in 1754, the square was designed as a semi circular space defined by uniform façades of the type at no **6** (at the corner of rue des Canettes), designed by Servandoni. But this did not materialise.

The central fountain was erected by Visconti in 1844 and is known as the Fontaine des Quatre Points Cardinaux after the sculpted portraits of Bossuet, Fénelon, Massillon and Fléchier, facing the cardinal points of the compass. The name, Fountain of the Cardinal Points or the Four Cardinals Who Never Were, is a play on words as none of the four churchmen ever was made a cardinal (*point* in French means both point and never).

No **9** was the site of a former seminary.

Rue des Canettes – 'Duckling Street' takes its name from the low relief at no **18**. **Rue des Ciseaux** has many old picturesque houses.

Le MARAIS★★★

The Marais district stretches between place de la Bastille and Hôtel de Ville, the Seine and the quartier du Temple. Business built up traditionally around tailoring: the rag trade and leather work have been in part revived by internationally successful young fashion designers.

The quartier du Temple is notable for jewellers and goldsmiths.

It is unusual for its fine pre-Revolution residential architecure, now restored and converted into museums and municipal offices. Visitors should tour the area on a weekday when access to buildings is possible.

The order given provides a rough itinerary facilitating exploration on foot...

Historical Notes – In the 13C marshland surrounding the raised rue St-Antoine, a highway since Roman times, was drained and converted into arable land.

Philippe Auguste's defensive wall, which also served as a dike, and the Charles V wall ending in the powerful Bastille fortress in the east, brought the Marais within the city limits. Royal patronage began after the flight of Charles V *(see* ILE DE LA CITÉ – Palais de Justice*)* from the royal palace to the **Hôtel St-Paul**. Charles VI also took up residence there and the royal menagerie and park are recalled in the rue des Lions-St-Paul and rue Beautreillis.

By the beginning of the 17C the then place Royale, now place des Vosges, built by Henri IV, had become the focal point of the Marais.

The Jesuits were the first to settle along the rue St-Antoine, with members of the nobility and royal courtiers following after; splendid mansions were erected and decorated by the best contemporary artists. The *hôtel*, a discreet Classically designed private residence, standing between entrance court and garden, developed as a distinctive feature in French architecture. Women of the world attracted free-thinkers and philosophers through their *salons* – the brilliant conversational groups who frequented their houses. Two churches, St-Paul and St-Gervais, attracted famous preachers and musicians.

Then, gradually, the nobility began to move west to Ile St-Louis, then Faubourg St-Germain and Faubourg St-Honoré. After the taking of the Bastille, the quarter was virtually abandoned.

In the 20C, the derelict quarter was essentially saved from complete destruction by André Malraux, Charles de Gaulle's Arts Minister.

★★★Place des Vosges Ⓜ *Chemin-Vert. Buses: 20, 29, 69, 76, 96*

This is Paris' oldest square.

Hôtel des Tournelles – The house, acquired by the Crown in 1407 on the assassination of the Duke of Orléans *(see below),* was the residence of Charles VII where Louis XII ended his days and Henri II died; it was subsequently pulled down by Catherine de' Medici.

Place des Vosges

A. Ell/MICHELIN

Place Royale – In 1605, Henri IV determined to transform the Marais into a splendid quarter with a vast square at its centre in which all the houses would be "built to a like symmetry". On its completion in 1612, the Royal Square became the centre of elegance, courtly parades and festivities. Duels were also fought there in spite of Cardinal Richelieu's ban. At the Revolution the square lost its central statue of Louis XIII (replaced in 1818) and was named place de l'Indivisibilité.

From 1800 it took the name of place des Vosges after the Vosges *departement*, the first to pay its taxes.

The square today – The 36 houses retain their original symmetrical appearance: two storeys with alternate stone and brick facings are built over the ground-level arcade rising to steeply pitched slate roofs pierced by dormer windows.

Pavillon du Roi – The soberly decorated King's Pavilion on the south side and the largest house in the square, is balanced by the Queen's Pavilion (Pavillon de la Reine) to the north. Also of interest around the square are no **1bis** where Madame de Sevigné was born; no 9, the **Hôtel de Chaulnes**, home to the Academy of Architecture *(not open)*; no **11** which was occupied by the courtesan Marion Delorme in 1639-1648; no **17** where Bossuet lived; no **21** where Richelieu lived (1615-1627); no **14** Hôtel de la Rivière, whose ceilings by Le Brun are in the Carnavalet Museum.

★**Maison de Victor Hugo** ⊙ – *6 place des Vosges*. A museum opened in 1903 in the former Hôtel de Rohan-Guéménée (early 17C) which was the home of the writer from 1832 to 1848. Drawings by Hugo himself are shown in rotation as part of temporary exhibitions on the first floor. On the second floor the displays evoke Hugo's various residences (the Chinese salon and the furniture from his house on Guernsey illustrate his talent as a decorator). There are also portraits, busts, photographs and mementoes of the poet and his family.

Exploring the neighbourhood

★**Hôtel de Sully** ⊙ – *no 62*. This fine mansion was built in 1625 by Du Cerceau and bought 10 years later by the ageing Sully, former minister of Henri IV. Part of the building is presently given over to the **Caisse Nationale des Monuments Historiques et des Sites** (Ancient Monuments and Historic Buildings Commission).

The main gate, between massive pavilions, has been restored and opens once more into the inner **courtyard**★★, an outstanding Louis XIII architectural composition with ordered decoration, carved pediments and dormer windows; allegorical figures represent the Elements and the Seasons.

The main building retains its original painted ceilings (restored); especially noteworthy is the painted decoration of the Duchess of Sully's rooms, in the garden wing.

Temporary exhibitions are held in the main building and garden wing (ground floor and basement).

At the far end of the garden, the Orangery (1625) opens onto place des Vosges.

Rue St-Antoine – Ⓜ *St-Paul*. From the 14C this unusually wide street became a popular setting for gatherings and celebrations. The area in front of the church was turned into a tilt-yard after the cobbles had been removed and the ground covered with sand. It was here that in 1559 **Henri II** received a fatal blow to his eye in a tourney with his Scots captain of the guard, Montgomery. The king died in the Hôtel des Tournelles. Montgomery fled but was executed in 1574.

In the 17C the rue St-Antoine was the city's most elegant thoroughfare. At the corner of rues St-Antoine and des Tournelles, a bronze statue of Beaumarchais commemorates the fact that the famous writer and popular playwright (1732-1799) lived nearby at no 2 boulevard Beaumarchais; it is by Louis de Clousade (1895).

Hôtel Colbert-de-Villacerf – *23 rue de Turenne*. Its fine salon decorated with painted panelling is now in the Carnavalet Museum.

★★Hôtel Carnavalet ⊙ *23 rue de Sévigné*. Ⓜ *St-Paul. Buses: 29, 69, 76, 96*

Construction was started in 1548 for Jacques des Ligneris, president of Parliament; the house was given its present appearance by **François Mansart** in 1655. The buildings surrounding the three garden courts are 19C.

Marie de Rabutin, the **Marquise de Sévigné**, who wrote the famous *Letters* which, with a light touch and quick wit give a lucid picture of day-to-day events, lived in the house from 1677 to 1696.

Exterior – **Jean Goujon** carved the lions at the main entrance which is 16C, and the keystone cornucopia. The supporting globe was later recarved into a carnival mask in allusion to the mansion's name.

The **statue**★ of Louis XIV in the courtyard by **Coysevox** was originally at the Hôtel de Ville. The building at the end is Gothic; only the four statues of the Seasons are Renaissance in style. The large figures on the wings are 17C; the cherubs with torches decorating the end of the wing are again by Jean Goujon.

The Nazarene arch in rue des Francs-Bourgeois is 16C.

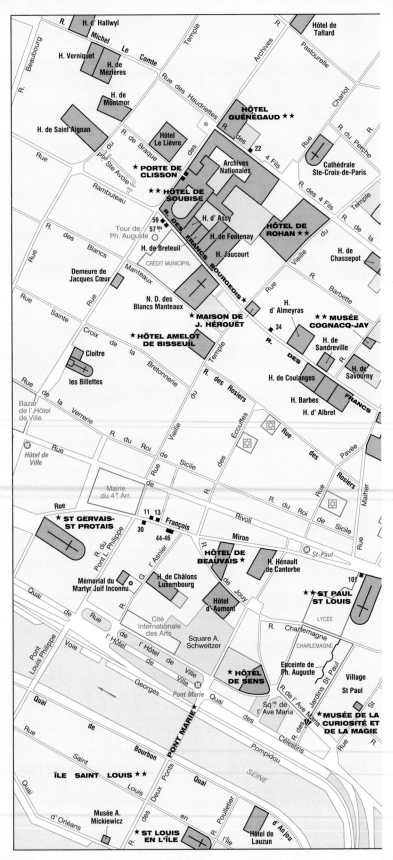

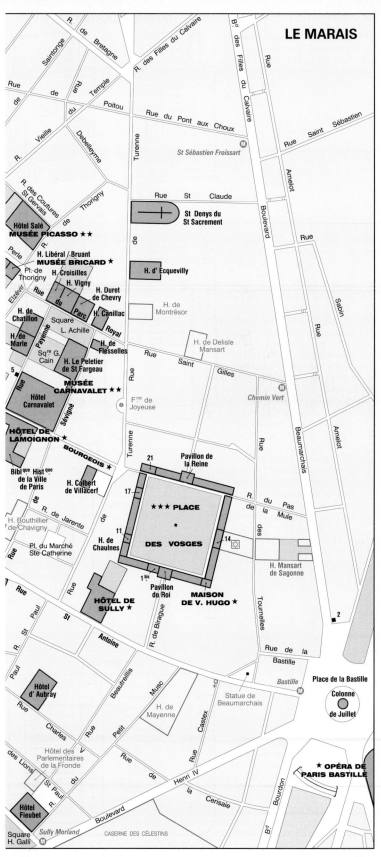

LE MARAIS

- R. Saintonge
- Rue de Bretagne
- R. de
- Rue des Filles du Calvaire
- B.d des Filles du Calvaire
- Rue
- Rue du
- Rue de Poitou
- Vieille
- Rue du Temple
- Debelleyme
- R.
- R. de Thorigny
- Rue du Pont aux Choux
- Turenne
- St Sébastien Froissart
- Rue Saint Sébastien
- Amelot
- R. des Coutures de St Gervais
- Rue St Claude
- St Denys du St Sacrement
- Boulevard
- Rue
- Hôtel Salé
- **MUSÉE PICASSO ★★**
- Perle
- H. Libéral / Bruant
- **MUSÉE BRICARD ★**
- Pl. de Thorigny
- H. Croisilles
- H. d' Ecquevilly
- Elzévir
- Rue du Parc
- H. Vigny
- H. Duret de Chevry
- H. de Chatillon
- Rue
- H. Canillac
- H. de Montrésor
- Sabin
- Rue
- Square L. Achille
- Royal
- Payenne
- H. de Marle
- Sq.re G. Cain
- H. de Flesselles
- H. de Delisle Mansart
- H. Le Peletier de St Fargeau
- Rue
- Saint
- Gilles
- 5
- **MUSÉE CARNAVALET ★★**
- Rue Sévigné
- Chemin Vert
- Amelot
- Hôtel Carnavalet
- F.ne de Joyeuse
- **HÔTEL DE LAMOIGNON ★**
- Turenne
- **BOURGEOIS ★**
- Rue
- Beaumarchais
- Bibl.que Hist.que de la Ville de Paris
- H. Colbert de Villacerf
- 21
- Pavillon de la Reine
- de
- R. de Jarente
- 17
- **★★★ PLACE**
- R. du Pas de la Mule
- des
- H. Bouthillier de Chavigny
- Rue
- 11
- H. de Chaulnes
- **DES VOSGES**
- 14
- Pl. du Marché Ste Catherine
- Rue
- H. Mansart de Sagonne
- Rue
- 1 bis
- Pavillon du Roi
- **MAISON DE V. HUGO ★**
- 2
- St Paul
- St
- **HÔTEL DE SULLY ★**
- R. de Biraque
- Tournelles
- Antoine
- Beautreillis
- Rue de la
- Paul
- Musc
- Bastille
- Rue
- Hôtel d' Aubray
- H. de Mayenne
- Castex
- Place de la Bastille
- Bastille
- Colonne
- de Juillet
- Rue
- Charles
- Petit
- Statue de Beaumarchais
- Rue
- des Lions
- Hôtel des Parlementaires de la Fronde
- St Paul
- Rue
- du
- Henri IV
- ★ **OPÉRA DE PARIS BASTILLE**
- Hôtel Fieubet
- la
- Cerisaie
- Bourdon
- Square H. Galli
- Sully Morland
- Boulevard
- CASERNE DES CÉLESTINS
- B.d

MUSÉE CARNAVALET

★★**Museum** – The collections illustrating the history of Paris are presented chronologically in two separate mansions, linked by a first-floor gallery. The Hôtel Carnavalet covers the period up to 1789, while the Hôtel Le-Peletier-St-Fargeau continues the story from the Revolution to the present. The Hôtel Carnavalet is currently being refurbished and rearranged.

The three rooms on the ground floor with monumental chimneypieces are typical of a Renaissance dwelling. One of the rooms (**21**) presents mementos of **Mme de Sévigné**, who lived in the house for almost 20 years. The staircase (**32**) leading to the first-floor is decorated with paintings by Brunetti, a trompe l'œil specialist active during the reign of Louis XV. The paintings originally came from a staircase in the now-demolished Hôtel de Luynes in boulevard St-Germain.

The delicately worked panelling from other Parisian _hôtels_ provide attractive settings for fine pieces of period furniture of Louis XIV, Régence, Louis XV and Louis XVI styles.

On the second floor of the **Hôtel Le-Peletier-de-St-Fargeau**, the Revolution and its best known personalities are depicted in paintings, sculptures, engravings, and other varied objects by such artists as Hubert Robert, David, Boilly and Chinard. Note the large painting by Charles Thévenin depicting the _Festival of Federation_ (see CHAMP-DE-MARS) (**103**), the furniture of the royal family during their captivity in the Temple (**106**) and a selection of watercolours by Le Sueur (**112**).

The larger rooms on the ground and first floors present the successive political regimes and some of their most notable events: the Empire, the Restoration, the Three Glorious Days or Trois Glorieuses of 1830 (a model shows the Duke of Orléans' arrival at the Hôtel de Ville) (**119**), the July Monarchy, the events of February and June 1848, the Second Empire and the

Commune of 1871. Paintings and mementoes illustrate how the artistic life in the capital flourished during this period. Look for the portrait of Mme Récamier by François Gérard (**115**), one of the composer Franz Liszt by Henri Lehmann (**122**), as well as numerous street scenes including those by Béraud depicting Paris during the Belle Époque. The bedchambers of both Marcel Proust and Anna de Noailles (**147**) have been recreated. Beyond are the salon from the Café de Paris by the architect Sauvage (**141**), the workshop of the goldsmith Fouquet by Mucha (**142**) and the ballroom decorated by Sert (**146**) from the Hôtel de Wendel.

In the connecting gallery are some very personal visions of Paris by 20C artists (Signac, Marquet, Utrillo, Foujita).

Rue de Sévigné – Beyond the Hôtel Carnavalet is the **Hôtel Le-Peletier-de-Saint-Fargeau** (no **29**) built by Pierre Bullet 1686-90 and named after its owner who was responsible for Louis XVI's death sentence. No **52**, the much-restored **Hôtel de Flesselles**, bears the name of Paris' last provost.

Rue du Parc-Royal – The 17C mansions lining the street opposite Léopold-Achille Square form a remarkable architectural group notwithstanding remodelling: **Canillac** (no **4**), **Duret-de-Chevry** (no **8**, extensively restored), **Vigny** (no **10**, a National Documentation Centre) and **Croisilles** (no **12**) which houses the library and archives of France's historic buildings commission.

Rue de Turenne – The **Hôtel d'Ecquevilly** (or du Grand Veneur) at no **60** has a fine façade decorated with emblems of the chase and a magnificent **great staircase★** adorned with hunting trophies and a wrought-iron balustrade. The **Église St-Denys-du-St-Sacrement** ⊙ no **68bis**, built in the form of a Roman basilica at the time of the Restoration, contains a remarkable **Deposition★** by Delacroix (1844) at the back of the chapel to the right of the entrance *(light switch)*, a painting by Pujol in grisaille depicting *St Denis preaching* in the chancel, and *the Pilgrims of Emmaüs* a wax painting (1840) by Picot.

Hôtel Salé *5 rue de Thorigny.* Ⓜ *St-Sébastien-Froissart. Buses: 29, 96*

The house was built from 1656 to 1659 for a salt tax collector, hence its name; it passed in the 18C to the de Juigné family, before becoming the École Centrale (1829-84) and subsequently the École des Métiers d'Art (1944-69). Recently restored and refurbished, the mansion now houses the Picasso Museum. Inside, the main **staircase★** with its spacious stairwell and splendid wrought-ironwork rises majestically to the first floor and a profusely sculptured ceiling.

★★**Musée Picasso** ⊙ – One of the dominant figures of 20C art, Pablo Ruiz Picasso (1881-1973) was born in Malaga. The young Picasso took courses in art at both Barcelona, where his father was a teacher, and Madrid. Aged only 23 he left his native country to settle in France, where he pursued his long and active career. Between 1936 and 1955, during his stay in Paris, Picasso lived at 7 rue des Grands Augustins (the 17C Hôtel d'Hercule) where he painted *Guernica* (1937).

Following his death at Mougins in 1973, Picasso's heirs donated an outstanding collection of the artist's works in lieu of estate duties. The collection comprises over 200 paintings, an excellent group of sculptures, collages, more than 3 000 drawings and engravings, 88 ceramics as well as illustrated books and manuscripts.

To follow the chronological order of the different phases *(explanatory notices)* of Picasso's prodigiously productive and long painting career, start on the first floor with his *Self Portrait* from the Blue Period. All the artist's styles and techniques are represented in his sketches for *Les Demoiselles d'Avignon, Still Life with Cane Chair* and *Pipes of Pan* and other favourite subjects such as female nudes, travelling acrobats and portraits of couples and of his own family (his son, *Paul as Harlequin*).

Also exhibited is Picasso's private collection of works by his friends and contemporaries (the Picasso Donation – *1st and 2nd floors*) such as Braque, Cézanne, Rousseau...

Films on the artist, his life and work are shown on the third floor.

The **rue des Coutures-St-Gervais** and **rue Vieille-du-Temple** skirt the gardens and afford glimpses of the imposing garden front. There is an unusual fountain by Simounet in the formal public garden beyond the museum's garden.

Rue de la Perle – Nos **3-5** are occupied by the **Hôtel de Chassepot**. At no **1**, the **Hôtel Libéral Bruant** was built in 1685 by the architect of the Invalides for himself. This elegant mansion has been restored to its original appearance and now houses a lock museum.

★**Musée de la Serrurerie Bricard** ⊙ – In five well-lit rooms the art of the locksmith is traced from the Roman era to the Empire: collections of iron and bronze keys, wrought-iron Gothic locks; Venetian door knockers; gilded bronze locks from the Tuileries and Palais-Royal, combination lock, etc. as well as 20C ironwork and pieces from the Bricard workshops. To the right of the courtyard is a reconstruction of a locksmith's workshop.

★★Hôtel de Rohan ⓘ
87 rue Vieille-du-Temple.

In 1705 Delamair started work on the mansion simultaneously with the Hôtel de Soubise *(see below)*, for the Soubise's son, the Bishop of Strasbourg who later became Cardinal de Rohan. It was successively the residence of four cardinals of the Rohan family, all of whom were Bishops of Strasbourg. The last one lived there in grand style until his disgrace in the affair of the queen's necklace (1785). It was occupied by the state press (Imprimerie Nationale) under Napoleon and later in 1927 by the national archives.

Hôtel de Rohan – Horses of Apollo

Ph. Gajic/MICHELIN

The Necklace Affair

The Countess de la Motte, having lost favour with Marie-Antoinette, persuaded Cardinal de Rohan to acquire an expensive necklace with which to win the Queen's favour on her behalf. When the Countess failed to complete payment for the jewels, the Cardinal decided to disclose the identity of the usurper. The Cardinal was imprisoned but later absolved, despite which the case was instrumental in signalling his ultimate downfall.

The courtyard differs from that of the Soubise mansion as the main façade gives onto the garden which serves both properties.

On the right the former stables are crowned by the wonderful **Horses of Apollo★★** by Robert Le Lorrain. The excited horses are depicted at a drinking trough.

A staircase leads to the Cardinals' **apartments★**. Gobelin tapestries hang in the entrance hall. The first salons are adorned with Beauvais tapestries after cartoons attributed to Boucher. Also of interest are the Gold Salon and the amusing small Monkey Room with animal decorations by Christophe Huet, and the delicate panelling and wall hangings of the smaller rooms (Fable Room).

Cathédrale Ste-Croix-de-Paris – This much-restored church was erected in 1624 as a Capuchin monastery chapel and was attended by Mme de Sévigné. It is now the Armenian church.

The chancel is adorned with 18C gilded panelling from the former Billettes church. To the left stands a remarkable **statue★** of St Francis of Assisi by Germain Pilon (16C), and to the right a *St Denis* by J Sarazin.

★★Hôtel de Guénégaud
60 rue des Archives. Ⓜ *Rambuteau. Buses: 29, 47, 75*

This mansion, built *c*1650 by **Mansart**, was minimally remodelled in the 18C and has been beautifully restored in the 20C. With its plain harmonious lines, its majestic staircase and its small formal garden, it is one of the finest houses of the Marais.

★★**Musée de la Chasse et de la Nature** ⓘ – The collection includes arms from prehistory to the 19C *(1st floor)* and trophies and souvenirs from Mr Sommer's (who restored the Hôtel) own big game expeditions *(2nd floor)*. On the stairs and in the red, green and blue salons are pictures by Desportes, Oudry, Chardin and Carle Vernet. Tapestries, ceramics and sculptures on the theme of the hunt are also on view.

Walk left in rue des Quatre-Fils to see the garden and rear façade of the mansion. At no **22** Mme du Deffand held a famous salon in the 18C.

Hôtel de Tallard – *78 rue des Archives*. Having been recently restored to Bullet's designs, this house has regained its Classical splendour, including its medallions on the garden side.

Rue Michel-le-Comte – In this street are the ruined **Hôtel de Mézières** (no 19) and the **Hôtel Verniquet** (no 21), named after the geometrician who at the end of the 18C completed the first detailed maps of Paris. The **Hôtel d'Hallwyl** (no 28), where the writer Mme de Staël was born in 1766, was built in the late 17C and remodelled by Ledoux, architect to Louis XVI.

Rue du Temple – The **Hôtel de Montmor**, *no 79*, was built in the reign of Louis XIII for his treasurer Montmor, and remodelled in the 18C. It was here that Montmor's son instigated regular meetings of the great physicians and doctors of the day around Abbot Gassendi. A practise that was to herald the founding of the Academy of Science (1666).

A fine balcony with a carved pediment adorns the façade pierced with tall windows overlooking the first courtyard. The wrought-iron banister of the stairway is particularly fine.

Hôtel de Saint-Aignan – *nos 71-73*. This house completed in 1650 by Le Muet was acquired in 1680 by the Duke of Saint-Aignan, Colbert's son-in-law and joint tutor (with Fénelon) of Louis XIV's three grandsons. A monumental gateway decorated with fantastic masks precedes the main façade with its colossal order. The left side of the courtyard is painted with trompe-l'œil windows, applied by Le Muet to the Philippe Auguste wall.

The house was greatly disfigured during the Revolution when it was used by the municipal administration (1795-1823). The outbuildings house a section of the Paris Archives' reading room. The stables *(no 75)* have attractive pointed vaulting. The house is to accommodate the Jewish Museum *(see MONTMARTRE)*.

Hôtel Le Lièvre – *4-6 rue de Braque*. It was built in 1663 and has interesting twin doorways and balconies. There is a formal grand staircase at no 4.

★★Hôtel de Soubise

60 rue des Francs-Bourgeois. Ⓜ *Rambuteau, Saint-Paul.*

In about 1375 the Constable of France, Olivier de Clisson, companion in arms of the great French hero Du Guesclin, began to build a manor house on the site of the present buildings. Only the **gateway★** remains, flanked by a pair of corbelled turrets *(58 rue des Archives)*. Known as the "porte Clisson"; this is a unique example of 14C domestic building design.

In 1553 the manor passed into the Guise family, who made it their headquarters during the Wars of Religion.

In 1700 François de Rohan, Prince of Soubise, acquired the house thanks to generous gifts from Louis XIV to the prince's wife in return for illicit favours rendered. From 1705 to 1709 the mansion was remodelled into an elegant palace. The plans were entrusted to an unknown architect, Delamair, who retained the existing Guise mansion, but built the main façade at right angles to it, and created a majestic horseshoe-shaped **courtyard★★**.

★★**The apartments** – Delamair's Classical architectural style, typical of Louis XIV's reign (simple façade, vast courtyard and suite of rooms), contrasts with Boffrand's extravagant Rococo decoration under Louis XV, when formal décor gave way to more intimate interiors. Between 1735 and 1740 the most gifted painters (Boucher, Natoire, Van Loo) and sculptors of the period worked under Boffrand, a pupil of Mansart, to decorate with all the delicacy and flourish of the Rococo style as was fashionable at Versailles.

Archives de France

Hôtel de Soubise, Salon ovale de la Princesse

On the first floor, beside the Guise chapel is the Salle des Gardes (*guardroom*) which served as the League headquarters during the Wars of Religion. Note the two 17C Gobelin tapestries copied from 16C Belgian hangings woven for Charles V depicting Maximilian out hunting, together with the collection acquired from the Parlement de Paris archives (1847). This room is part of the circuit extended from the medieval display in the reading room that progresses through history to the present day. The Assembly rooms, decorated with painted panels by Carl Van Loo (*Venus bathing*) and Boucher (*Venus at her toilet*), are reserved for temporary exhibitions.

★★**Chambre de la Princesse** – This spectacular, dazzling interior has survived intact. A large bed with baldaquin furnishes this splendid room fitted with white and gold panelling. Note the fine corner medallions in brushed gold depicting the Loves of Jupiter. On either side of the bed hang superb paintings by Boucher: *The Cage* or *Obliging Shepherd* and *The Garland* or *Gallant Shepherd*.

★**Salon ovale de la Princesse** – Masterful display of Rococo at its most refined, the sky-blue ceiling contrasts well with Nattier's feminine hues in his depiction of the *Story of Psyche*.

Petite chambre de la princesse – Fine roundels illustrate the Elements, and panels by Van Loo, Restout, Trémolières and Boucher are set over the doors.

The next room, called "salle du dais" is dedicated to 'Patriotism... Nationalism in France from 1789 to 1945'.

★**Musée de l'Histoire de France** ☉ – Since 1990 the CARAN occupies the top two floors, open only to National Archive readers.

On the ground floor, the former reading room complete with its benches displays medieval documents from the mid 7C to the 15C. Laid out chronologically, historical events, the unification of the kingdom and the development of important royal institutions are outlined against a presentation of contemporary social order: religion and the Church, learning and the Univerisity, war and the army; nobility, rural society and husbandry; the third estate; urbanisation and trade.

Among the most interesting exhibits are an Edict written in Latin on papyrus signed by Clovis II, an early rare text in *langue d'oc* (c1103), two statements made by Philippe Auguste – the earliest surviving by a French king – and a moving letter written by Joan of Arc to the people of Reims (6 August 1429) rallying them to defend their city. The collection rationalises major events in French history (Crusades, Hundred Years War) as well as appealing to students of graphology, medieval French and seals.

★**Rue des Francs-Bourgeois** – This old street was originally known as rue des Poulies after the pulleys *(poulies)* on the looms of the local weavers' shops. It took its present name in 1334 when almshouses were built in it for the poor who were known as "the men who pay no tax" or *francs bourgeois*.

At no **59**, against the wall, is a fragment of the façade of a 1638 hôtel. Behind the gateway of no **57bis** rises one of the towers of Philippe Auguste's perimeter wall. Opposite the Crédit Municipal Bank, a former pawnbroker's, are the Hôtels **d'Assy** (no 58bis), **de Breteuil** (no 58), **de Fontenay** (no 56), and **de Jaucourt** (no 54), annexes to the French Archives.

Rue Vieille du Temple – The **Maison de Jean Hérouet**★ *no 54*, belonged to the treasurer to Louis XII; it was built around 1510, and still has its mullioned windows and an elegant corbelled turret.

Nearby stood in the 15C the **Hôtel Barbette**, the discreet residence of Queen Isabella of Bavaria who began the fashion for masked balls, while the king, Charles VI, resided at the Hôtel St-Paul.

★**Hôtel Amelot-de-Bisseuil** (or **Hôtel des Ambassadeurs de Hollande**) – *no 47*. The present mansion dating from 1655 replaced the medieval residence of the Marshals de Rieux, companions in arms of Du Guesclin and Joan of Arc. In 1407, Duke Louis d'Orléans, after visiting Queen Isabella at the Hôtel Barbette, was assassinated nearby by the supporters of John the Fearless. This led to civil war during which Paris was occupied by the English (1420-1435) and besieged by Charles VII and Joan of Arc.

Hôtel Amelot-de-Bisseuil, door panel

The 17C house, which has been remodelled at various periods, was at one time let to the Dutch ambassador's chaplain, hence its name.

By 1776 the house, by now the home of the playwright Beaumarchais and author of the *Marriage of Figaro*, had become a depot for arms destined for the American rebels; it was later a home for destitute mothers.

The **gateway★**, decorated with masks and allegories, is one of the Marais' most outstanding. *(Ring to see the courtyard – the house is not open to the public.)* Note the house's ornamental carvings and four monochrome sundials.

Église de Notre-Dame-des-Blancs-Manteaux ⊙ – *12 rue des Blancs-Manteaux*. The Crédit Municipal bank stands on the site of a monastery founded by Louis IX for a mendicant order, the Serfs of the Virgin, whose members wore white cloaks *(blancs manteaux)*. It was first remodelled in 1695, when the Benedictines of St William, the Guillemites, who had replaced the earlier order at the end of the 13C, rebuilt the old monastery chapel; then, at the time of Baron Haussmann's transformation of Paris, during the Second Empire, the architect Baltard incorporated the 18C façade of the Church of St-Éloi into the building.

The interior has remarkable woodwork – an inner door, organ loft, communion table and a magnificent Flemish **pulpit★** with marquetry panels inlaid with ivory and pewter, framed in gilded and fretted woodwork, typical of the period's Rococo style (1749). Concerts of organ music are held in the church, especially during the Marais Festival.

Demeure de Jacques Cœur – *40 rue des Archives*. Resurfacing work on a building in 1971 uncovered a façade decorated with brick panels in a red and black lattice pattern. This led to its identification as the 15C house of Jacques Cœur, Chancellor of the Exchequer to Charles VII. It is one of the oldest buildings in Paris.

Église des Billettes ⊙ – *22 rue des Archives*. It is here, according to legend, that the miracle of the "boiled God" occurred in 1290: a usurer, Jonathan, cut a host and threw the pieces into a cooking pot; the water turned to blood and ran into the street, implicating the moneylender who was burned alive. In the 14C a monastery was erected on the site by the Brothers of Charity known as the Billettes on account of the heraldic billet on their habits. Carmelites built the present sanctuary in 1756, which in turn became a Lutheran church in 1812.

Cloître des Billettes – *1st door to the left after the Church*. The only remaining medieval cloister in Paris gives onto a small courtyard. Note the simplicity of its architectural elements: rib-vaulted galleries with corner bays resting on pendentives that abut the pillars.

★Rue des Francs-Bourgeois – *Between rue Vieille du Temple and rue Payenne*. The **Hôtel Poussepin**, *no 34*, now serves as the Swiss Cultural Centre. At **Hôtel d'Almeyras**, *no 30*, the brick and stone façade is hidden behind a gateway featuring curious rams' heads. **Hôtel de Sandreville** *no 26* dating from 1586, has been converted into flats. **Hôtel de Coulanges** *nos 35-37* now Europe House, is 18C. **Hôtel Barbes**, *no 33*, with its fine courtyard, was built around 1634. **Hôtel d'Albret** *nos 29bis and 31*, was built in the 16C for the Duke of Montmorency, Constable of France, and remodelled in the 17C. It was in this house that the widow of the playwright Scarron, the future Marquise de Maintenon, became acquainted with Mme de Montespan to whose children Louis XIV appointed her governess in 1669; she later became the king's mistress. The unusual façade was altered in the 18C. The restored mansion houses the city's Cultural Affairs Department.

★★Cognacq-Jay Museum ⊙ *8 rue Elzévir*. Ⓜ *St-Paul*.

This collection of 18C European art was bequeathed to the city of Paris by Ernest Cognacq (1839-1928), founder of the Samaritaine department store *(see* les QUAIS-Quai de la Mégisserie*)*.

The **Hôtel Donon** has been refurbished to provide a worthy setting for the collection. The late-16C main part of the building with its tall roof is typical of Philibert Delorme's syle. The harmony and taste of both the mansion and the collection it houses give a good impression of the gallant and sophisticated lifestyle of the Age of Enlightenment.

In the panelled ground-floor rooms is a selection of drawings by Watteau and paintings by Rembrandt, Ruisdael, Largillière and Chardin. Portraits bring to life some of the personalities of Louis XV's court: his Queen, Marie Leczinska (1703-1768), their daughter Madame Adélaïde, and Alexandrine, the daughter of Madame de Pompadour, Louis XV's mistress.

On the second floor, watercolours by Mallet illustrate the Spartan but elegant life of the Bourgeoisie under Louis XVI (1774-1792). In the Oval Room Fragonard's portrayals of children and Rococo pastoral pictures contrast with terracottas by Lemoyen and paintings by Greuze. The sculpture gallery groups together works showing a strong Italian influence (Falconet, Houdon and Clodion) alongside paintings by Hubert Robert and Boucher.

The third floor is dedicated to Mme Vigée-Lebrun and her period, pastels including a self-portrait by La Tour, and British School paintings. In the carved oak-panelled salon are an oval table and *commode* signed RVLC by Roger Vandercruse, better known as Lacroix *(see* BASTILLE – Faubourg St-Antoine*)*; and a pair of *commodes* by Martin Carlin. The study is hung with Venetian paintings, including Guardi's *St Mark's Square*. Showcases display Meissen and Sèvres porcelain, snuffboxes and bonbonnieres.

Hôtel de Savourny at 4 rue Elzevir has an attractive courtyard.

Rue Payenne – The architect François Mansart died at no **5**. The old gateway was uncovered during restoration.

The square Georges-Cain, lined by the orangery and the façade of the Hôtel St-Fargeau, has a paved garden.

The **Hôtel de Marle** or **de Polastron-Polignac** (*no 11*) has a fine mask above the entrance and a keel-shaped roof attributed to Philibert Delorme; once owned by the Countess of Polignac, the governess of Marie-Antoinette's children, this house now accommodates a Swedish Cultural Centre.

The neighbouring **Hôtel de Châtillon** (*no 13*) has a paved courtyard and an interesting staircase.

★Hôtel de Lamoignon 24 *rue Pavée*.

The Hôtel d'Angoulême, which was built around 1585 for Diane of France, the legitimised daughter of Henri II, was bought in 1658 by Lamoignon, president of the first Parliament to sit in Paris. There he entertained Racine, Mme de Sévigné, the Jesuit preacher Bourdaloue, and the poet and critic Boileau. Malesherbes, the jurist and royal administrator who conducted Louis XVI's defence before the Convention, another Lamoignon, was also born here. In the 19C, Alphonse Daudet resided in the house.

An unusual square turret overlooks the street. On the far side of the courtyard the majestic building is divided by six Corinthian pilasters which rise unbroken to the cornice – the first example in Paris of the colossal order designed by J-B Androuet Du Cerceau (1584). Two rudimentary wings are crowned with curved pediments adorned with attributes of the hunt and crescent moons (allusions to the goddess Diana).

Bibliothèque Historique de la Ville de Paris Ⓥ – Founded in 1763, the library is rich in French Revolution documents and has valuable collections of books, journals, manuscripts, maps, posters, photographs, cuttings, etc. The **reading room** with its painted ceiling is one of the finest in Paris.

Rue des Rosiers – This street, together with the adjoining rue des Écouffes, which derives its name from a pawnbroker's shop sign, is the main axis of the **Jewish quarter** which has grown up in Paris' 4th *arrondissement* (*see* INTRODUCTION-Ethnic enclaves).

Synagogues

In the Middle Ages, there were two main synagogues in rue de la Cité and rue de la Tâcherie (behind the Hôtel de Ville). By the 18C numbers had grown with settlers from Alsace and Lorraine moving to the Réamur Sébastopol area, especially around Hôtel du Chariot d'Or in rue de Turbigo. Confidence was high when all Jews were granted French nationality during the Revolution. Haussmann included two synagogues in his plans for urban development: rue de la Victoire founded in 1874 and rue des Tournelles founded in 1876. The latter was built with an iron substructure that was manufactured in Normandy, most probably under the auspices of Gustav Eiffel! The façade of the synagogue at 8 rue Pavée was designed by Guimard.

★★Église St-Paul-St-Louis Ⓥ 99 *rue Saint-Antoine*.

In 1580 the Jesuits established a community for ordained members. Louis XIII donated them land to build a new church (1627-1641): this was modelled on the Gesù church in Rome, but dedicated to St-Louis in the king's honour.

The Jesuits were expelled in 1763 since when its buildings have been used by a school.

After the demolition of an old church dedicated to St-Paul, the edifice in rue St-Antoine accommodated a larger parish, thereby becoming known as the Church of St-Paul-St-Louis (1796).

Façade – The tall Classical orders of superimposed columns screen the dome, a feature favoured by the Jesuits (*see* FAUBOURG ST-GERMAIN – Quartier des Carmes*)*, and one which was subsequently adapted at the Sorbonne, Val-de-Grâce, the Invalides.

Interior – It has a single aisle and inter-communicating barrel-vaulted chapels, a cupola with a lantern hovers above the transept crossing and tall Corinthian pilasters line the walls.

This well-lit, spacious church with its ornate decoration and sculptures, drew an elegant congregation attracted by musical excellence (directed by Marc-Antoine Charpentier) and eloquent preaching. Many of its rich furnishings were lost at the Revolution. (Reliquaries holding the hearts of Louis XIII and Louis XIV were melted down, while the hearts were purchased by the painter Saint-Martin who ground the organs to mix with oil to varnish his paintings. Having used only a small part of Louis XIV's heart, the larger of the two, he gave the remainder to Louis XVIII, who rewarded the painter with a gold tobacco box.) The twin shell-shaped stoups at the entrance were given by Victor Hugo who lived locally in place des Vosges. In the transept three 17C paintings illustrate scenes from the life of St Louis. A fourth having disappeared, has been replaced by a painting of Christ on the Mount of Olives by Delacroix (1826). In the chapel to the left of the high altar there is a **Mater Dolorosa** in marble by Germain Pilon (1586) – the terracotta version is now in the Louvre.

Opposite the church, François Raspail (1794-1878), specialist in parasitology and advocate for universal suffrage, used to treat the sick between 1840 and 1848.

Lycée Charlemagne ⊙ *no 101 (courtyard left of the church)* occupies the site of a former Jesuit convent. There is a fine **stairwell** crowned by a dome in trompe-l'œil depicting the Apotheosis of St Louis.

Rue François-Miron – This road, once a Roman highway through the marshes, still bears the name of a local magistrate of the time of Henri IV. In the Middle Ages it started from what is now the church of St-Gervais *(see* les QUAIS*)* and was lined with the town houses of several abbots of Ile-de-France. The **Hôtel Hénault-de-Cantorbe** *(no 82)* has attractive balconies and a pleasant inner courtyard.

★**Hôtel de Beauvais** – *no 68.* In 1654 Catherine Bellier, known as One-Eyed Kate, first woman of the bedchamber to Anne of Austria, bestowed her favours on the 16 year-old Louis XIV and was rewarded with a fortune. In addition, for her services, her husband Pierre Beauvais and she were ennobled and acquired the site of the former (13C) town house of the Abbots of Chaalis. They commissioned the architect Lepautre, to build them a splendid mansion from the balcony of which Anne of Austria, the Queen of England, Cardinal Mazarin and dignitaries watched the triumphal entry of Louis XIV and Marie-Thérèse into Paris in 1660.

In 1763, when Mozart aged seven, came to Paris accompanied by his father and sister, he stayed in this house by courtesy of the Bavarian ambassador, for whom he gave several concerts.

The association for the preservation of Paris' historic buildings has uncovered in the basements of nos **44-46** fine Gothic **cellars**★ from the town house belonging to the Abbey of Ourscamp ⊙, north of Compiègne.

The half-timbered and much restored nos **13** and **11** date back to the reign of Louis XI (15C).

The beautiful Marie Touchet, mistress of Charles IX, is said to have lived at no **30**.

For the church of St-Gervais-St-Protais see les QUAIS.

Rue Geoffroy-l'Asnier – Hôtel de Châlons-Luxembourg *(no 26)*, built in 1610, has a carved main gate and an interesting stone and brick façade.

In the **Mémorial du Martyr Juif Inconnu** ⊙ *(no 17)* burns an eternal flame in memory of the Jewish victims of National Socialism. There is also a museum devoted to the Jewish struggle against Hitlerism.

Hôtel d'Aumont – *7 rue de Jouy.* Built in the early 17C by Le Vau, it was later re-modelled and enlarged by Mansart, and decorated by Le Brun and Simon Vouet. The formal garden is attributed to Le Nôtre. The inner courtyard and façades are almost severe in line. Four successive Dukes of Aumont lived there until 1742, accumulating large collections of objects and entertaining lavishly. A large garden has since been created between the house and the river. It presently is occupied by the Paris administrative court.

★**Hôtel de Sens** – *1 rue du Figuier.* The Hôtel de Sens, Hôtel de Cluny and Jacques Cœur's house are the only great surviving medieval private residences in Paris.

The mansion was constructed between 1475 and 1507 as a residence for the archbishops of Sens of which Paris was a dependency until 1622. During the period of the Catholic League in the 16C it became a centre of intrigue conducted by the Cardinal of Guise. In 1594 Monsignor de Pellevé died of apoplexy within its walls while a *Te Deum* was being sung in Notre-Dame to celebrate Henri IV's entry into Paris. In 1605 Queen Margot, Henri IV's first wife, came to live in the mansion having been exiled from Auvergne. Upset by an incident outside the house, she later moved to the Pré aux Clercs *(see FAUBOURG ST-GERMAIN)*. At the age of 53, the former queen continued to enjoy a busy social-life, when a man rode up to her carriage and shot dead a rival suitor out of jealousy. Margot had him beheaded on the spot, outside the gates of her house.

From 1689 to 1743 the house was occupied by the Lyons Stage Coach Company which made a journey reputed to be so unsafe that passengers made their wills before setting out.

The old houses which originally surrounded the mansion have been pulled down. Its façade has corner turrets and a tall dormer window with a stone finial. A large and a small door each with basket-handle arches are surmounted by pointed arches.

The Flamboyant Gothic porch leads into the courtyard with a square battlemented tower enclosing a spiral staircase. Turrets and beautiful dormer windows adorn the external walls. The **Forney Library** ⊙ is devoted to the Decorative and Fine Arts, and industrial techniques. It has a large collection of posters and wall papers.

Village St-Paul – The area bordered by the rues des Jardins-St-Paul, Charlemagne, St-Paul and Ave-Maria has been restored; houses and antique shops crowd around the inner courtyards.

A long section of the **Philippe Auguste City Wall** (Enceinte de Philippe Auguste), intersected by two towers, can still be seen in the rue des Jardins-St-Paul. It linked the **Barbeau Tower** at 32 quai des Célestins to the St-Paul postern and is the largest surviving fragment.

It was in rue St-Paul that Rabelais died in 1553.

At the far end there is a view of the east end and dome of the St-Paul-St-Louis Church.

★**Musée de la Curiosité et de la Magie** ⊙ – *11 rue Saint-Paul.* A few steps down into a series of vaulted cellars, the visitor is welcomed by the **Pigalle Clairvoyant**, an automaton that bleats "bonjour!". The collection of ingenious accessories dispels some of the mystery from the art of magic, conjuring, legerdemain, prestidigitation and sleight-of-hand; a fascination that has been with us since Ancient Egyptian times when special effects were engineered in their temples with the use of clever hydraulic mechanisms. Midway through the museum, a stage, a few seats and a number of tiers provide the setting for regular magic shows *(time: about 1/2 hour; included in the entry fee).* Amongst the exhibits, the gold box containing a woman sawn in half and a thousand and one props that deceive the audience's eye by making objects 'disappear'. Note the beautiful turned objects, so often made of boxwood in Nuremberg and fundamental to the magic boxes given to children in the last century: the **secret box** or **nest** (the piece of jewellery which disappeared was naturally found in the smallest box); **automatons**; objects fashioned in soft metal (brass, tin) made in Dinand (Belgium) whence their name "dinanderie"; a bottomless vase; a saucepan producing doves; balls full of scarves...

In the automaton room, above the door and display cases, are several **optical illusions**: one, a fairly long hollow box, appears to be a solid volume. A few metal bolts and a hollow bust of **Robert Houdini** (1805-1871) that diplomat and ingenious clockmaker who elevated conjuring to the rank of an art in 19C *(see PALAIS-ROYAL)*, are used to produce the same effect. Additional rooms contain further optical illusions and mirror games. Plates decorated with fairground scenes, street pedlars and charlatans decorate the last room, in which a video film describes people's infatuation with magic and the irrational during the Age of Enlightenment.

Hôtel d'Aubray (or de la Brinvilliers), *12 rue Charles-V*, has a fine wrought-iron banister in the left wing *(closed to the public).* In the 17C it belonged to the notorious poisoner, the Marquise de Brinvilliers *(see BASTILLE – l'Arsenal).*

Hôtel Fieubet – *Square Henri-Galli.* Ⓜ *Sully-Morland.* The house was built by Jules Hardouin-Mansart in 1680 for Gaspard Fieubet, Queen Anne of Austria's chancellor. An ornate decoration was added to the plain façade around 1850. Since 1877 the buildings have been used by a school.

The Michelin Paris Index-Plan no 11:
A practical aid for exploring in Paris
A complete street index
A complete plan of the city:
> *one-way streets, administrative boundaries, public buildings, car parks, underground (métro) stations and taxi ranks*
> *Useful addresses:*
> *Public Services: government organisations, embassies and consulates,*
> *General: business, religion, education, health, shows, sports, tourism, transport...*

The most important telephone numbers
Plan of the underground, the urban rail network (RER) and the bus routes
The following detailed maps:
> *La Défense*
> *Bois de Boulogne*
> *Bois de Vincennes*
> *Orly Airport and Charles-de-Gaulle Airport*

MONTMARTRE ★★★

Michelin plan 11 – folds 6 – 7 and 19: C 12 – D 14
Ⓜ Abbesses, Blanche, Barbes-Rochechouart. Buses: 30, 54, 67, 80, 95, Montmartrobus

The "Butte", as it is known locally, meaning the hillock or mound, is the part of Paris most full of contrasts – anonymous boulevards run close to delightful village streets and courts, steep stone steps lead to open terraces, Sacré-Cœur pilgrims tread the streets beside nightclub revellers. To explore the area, a provisional circuit is suggested with sights listed in geographical order rather than by merit.

Martyrs' Mound – The name Montmartre derives in part from its Roman hill-top temple dedicated to Mercury or Mars, in part from a local legend dating from the 8C ascribing its dedication to the local martyrs, St Denis, first Bishop of Lutetia, the priest Rusticus, and the deacon Eleutherius. Having undergone torture by the grill in the Cité in about AD 250, they were brought here to be decapitated, after which, it is said, St Denis picked up his gory head and walked north to the place now known as St-Denis.

A powerful abbey – Rue des Abbesses commemorates 43 Benedictine nuns at the convent which flourished on the hill in the 12C. This was used by the King of Navarre, the future Henri IV, as his headquarters four centuries later when he laid siege to Paris in 1589; before succeeding in taking the city he set off on his next campaign, his only conquest having been the 17-year-old abbess, Claude de Beauvilliers.

During the reign of Louis XIV the ruined "upper" convent at the top of the hill and its chapel, were abandoned in favour of the "lower" convent on the lower slopes. In 1794 the last abbess was guillotined, the convent buildings were razed, and the area provisionally became known as Mont-Marat.

Shortly afterwards the gypsum quarries were abandoned when miles of tunnelling threatened to collapse, and the 30 flint and grain mills were closed.

The Sacré-Cœur by Suzanne Valadon

RMN © SPADEM

The early days of the Commune – In 1871, after the fall of Paris, the people of Montmartre collected 171 cannon on the hill to prevent their capture by the Prussians. The battery was declared government property, and on 18 March the military were sent to seize the weapons but were unable to remove them, whereupon the crowd seized the generals and shot them – a bloody episode which was to mark the beginning of the Commune. Montmartre remained under Federal control until 23 May.

Bohemian life – Throughout the 19C, artists and men of letters were drawn to the free-and-easy way of life as lived on the Butte.

The composer Berlioz and the writers and poets Nerval, Murger and Heine, were the precursors of the great 1871-1914 generation; young painters sought inspiration on place Pigalle, artists' models and seamstresses led a Bohemian existence. In the early days, groups of poets (le Chat Noir) congregated in cafés enlivened with songs by **Aristide Bruant**, poems by Charles Cros and Jehan Rictus, humour, drawings by Caran d'Ache, André Gill, Toulouse-Lautrec. These evolved into the *caf' conc'* (café-concert) with programmed entertainment: the Moulin-Rouge opened in 1889 with Yvette Guilbert, Valentin le Désossé, Jane Avril and Louise Weber nicknamed *La Goulue*. The Butte, thanks to the **Lapin Agile** café and **Bateau-Lavoir** studios, remained until the outbreak of the Great War the capital's literary and artistic centre.

As the successive generation of artists and émigrés congregated in Montparnasse, Montmartre abandoned itself to its nocturnal entertainments. Today, although still run-down, Montmartre draws tourists from far afield in search of the spirit of la Belle Époque, or more simply to enjoy the view over the city.

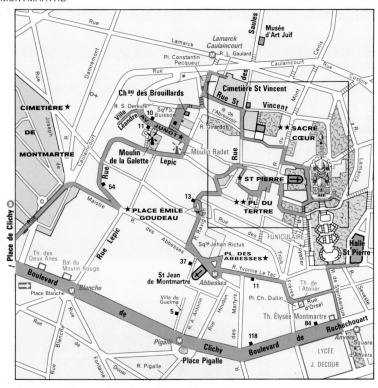

From place de Clichy to square d'Anvers

Ⓜ *Place de Clichy, Pigalle, Anvers. Buses: 30, 54, 68, 74, 80, 81, 85, 95, Montmartrobus*

Place de Clichy – The bustling square was the site of one of Ledoux's toll-houses *(see* INTRODUCTION), where in March 1814 Marshal Moncey's troops put up a spirited defence against the Allied army.

Boulevard de Clichy – The boulevard runs along the line of the Farmers General wall. Restaurants, cinemas, theatres and nightclubs make it a centre of Paris night life. The **Deux-Anes Theatre** at no 100 maintains the Parisian cabaret tradition whilst beyond, the sails of the **Moulin Rouge** identify the famous music-hall which was the cult of Paris at the time of the Belle Époque and renowned for the French cancan as immortalised in Toulouse-Lautrec's posters. **Place Blanche** owes its name to the former chalk quarries; **Raoul Dufy** lived at 5 villa Guelma between 1911 and 1953 at the peak of his painting career.

Place Pigalle – The sculptor Jean-Baptiste Pigalle (1714-1785), admired in his own lifetime for the tomb of Marshal Saxe and the nude figure of Voltaire (in the Louvre) is here honoured in name. The square and its adjoining streets were at the end of the 19C lined with artists' studios and literary cafés, of which the most famous was the Nouvelle Athènes *(see* ST-LAZARE). Today the quarter is as brilliantly lit and populous as ever, frequented by a rich mix of residents, tourists and artistic types. It is well depicted in the **Georges Simenon** detective novels.

Boulevard de Rochechouart – One-time infamous places of entertainment survive: at no **118** the former Belle-en-Cuisses cabaret; at no **84**, Rodolphe Salis opened the Chat-Noir cabaret night-club made famous in a song by Aristide Bruant:

> *Je cherche fortune*
> *Autour du Chat Noir*
> *Au clair de la lune*
> *A Montmartre le soir.*

At no **72**, all that remains of the former Élysée-Montmartre music-hall is its Belle Époque façade.

Night owls...
The introductory chapter of this guide lists some of the city's nightspots and "hip" bars.
But beware! The metro system shuts down at 12.30am.
Consult the PRACTICAL INFORMATION section for details.

The Abbesses Quarter

Ⓜ *Abbesse, Barbès-Rochechouart. Buses: 30, 31, 54, 56, 67, 80, 85, 95, Montmartrobus*

Halle St-Pierre Ⓘ *2 rue Ronsard* – Part way up the hill and off to the right stands a fine 19C cast-iron textile market that has been transformed into an exhibit hall. The ground floor hosts temporary year-long exhibitions. On the first floor, the **Musée d'Art naïf Max Fourny** displays paintings and sculpture by contemporary artists from some 30 countries.

Théâtre de l'Atelier *place Charles-Dullin* – The small theatre nestling among the trees was founded in the early 19C; it grew to fame between the wars.

Martyrium Ⓘ – *11 rue Yvonne-Le-Tac*. A chapel has replaced the medieval sanctuary built to mark the site where St Denis and his companions are presumed to have been decapitated. It was here in the former crypt on 15 August 1534, that Ignatius Loyola, Francis Xavier and their six companions undertook apostolic vows in the service of the Church thereby instituting the Society of Jesus. Six years later the order was recognised by Pope Paul III, subsequently known as the Jesuit Order.

★**Place des Abbesses** – This animated little square is the very heart of the community, with its distinctive original **Hector Guimard** Art-Nouveau entrance to the Metro (the only other is at Porte Dauphine), which leads down 280 spiralling steps past a continuous mural painted by 20 local artists!.

Église St-Jean-l'Évangéliste – *119 rue des Abbesses*. This unusual church designed by Baudot was the first to be built of reinforced concrete (1897-1904); it continues to impress structural engineers on account of its audacious use of the material, especially given the slenderness of supporting beams and piers. Fraught with controversy, building work was interrupted several times; the brick facing and interior decoration are therefore later in date than the main structure, as is its nickname St John of Brick.
To the right of the façade, steps lead up to rue André Antoine. At the bottom of the steps, at no **37** a modest hall, of which nothing survives, saw the amateur beginnings of the Antoine free theatre *(now the Théâtre Antoine-Simone-Berriau, 14 boulevard de Strasbourg)*.

Le Bateau-Lavoir – This high point in artistic and literary realms, burnt down in 1970 just as it was to be restored, superseded the no less famous Ruche *(see MONTPARNASSE)*. Located at 13 **place Émile-Goudeau**★, the rickety wooden building harboured from 1900 the pioneers of modern painting and poetry: **Picasso**, Van Dongen, Braque, and Juan Gris, evolved Cubism – with Picasso's famous *Demoiselles d'Avignon*, whilst Max Jacob, **Apollinaire** and Mac Orlan broke away from traditional poetic form and expression. Now rebuilt, the block continues to provide artists' studios and apartments.
Continue up rue Ravignan to place Jean-Baptiste Clément and along rue Norvins past a former water tower.

The 'Butte' Ⓜ *Abbesses. Buses: 80, Monmartrobus*

Auberge de la Bonne-Franquette – The **crossroads**★ with rues Norvins, des Saules and St-Rustique was often painted by Utrillo, son of the artist Suzanne Valadon, and it is his renderings that best evoke the spirit of Old Montmartre for us today.
During the latter half of the 19C, this haunt was frequented by Pissarro, Sisley, Cézanne, Toulouse-Lautrec, Renoir, Monet, Émile Zola... *La Guinguette*, the painting by Van Gogh was in fact inspired by its garden.

The narrow and often deserted rue St-Rustique rises to the highest poin – in Paris (129.37m – 427ft).

Espace Montmartre – Salvador Dalí Ⓥ – *9-11 rue Poulbot*. This enclosed area displays the more unusual sculptures, lithographs and engravings by the Catalan Surrealist (1904-89).

The minute place du Calvaire commands an exceptional view over Paris.

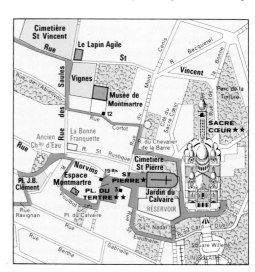

★★Place du Tertre – This simple, shaded square fronted with small houses retains in the early morning a village atmosphere; later, invaded by sight seers, it becomes a veritable tourist trap animated by cafés, restaurants, art-galleries, the bustle of street artists offering their second-rate canvases, a personalised charcoal portrait or paper cut-outs.

No 21 (formerly no **19 bis**) is the seat of the Free Commune founded in 1920 by Jules Dépaquit to preserve the imaginative and humorous traditions of the Butte; it also houses the tourist information centre.

No **3**, once the local town hall, is now Poulbot House to commemorate local children (P'tits Poulbots), popularised in the artist's delightful line drawings and illustrations from the early 20C.

The first petrol-powered motor-car to have reached the top of the Butte was driven by its designer Louis Renault on 24 December 1898.

★Église St Pierre-de-Montmartre ⊙ – *2 rue du Mont-Cenis.* The Church of Saint Peter is the last surviving vestige of the great Abbey of Montmartre and one of the oldest churches in the capital (with St-Germain-des-Prés and St-Martin-des-Champs). The first stones were laid in 1134 on the site of an earlier Merovingian church and consecrated in 1147 by Pope Eugenius III in the presence of the convent's founder Queen Adelaïde of Savoy and her son the future Louis VII. The nave was revaulted in the 15C; the west front dates from the 18C. The three bronze doors showing St Denis, St Peter and the Virgin, are by the Italian sculptor, **Gismondi** (1980).

Interior – In the north aisle is the tombstone of Louis VI the Big's widow, who founded the abbey in 1133.

Four Roman marble column-shafts with 7C capitals are thought to come from the former temple and later church on the site; two have been placed against the west wall in line with the nave columns and two in the chancel, where the oldest pointed arches in Paris (1147) meet in the single bay of the apse. In places, the worn Romanesque capitals have been replaced. The apse and aisles are lit by modern stained glass designed by Max Ingrand (1953).

The high altar is adorned with enamelled panels depicting the Butte Montmartre with its vineyard, the Virgin, St Peter and St Dominic by Froidevaux (1977). The Way of the Cross is by Gismondi.

Jardin du Calvaire – *Closed to the public.* The Calvary Garden occupies the site of the old Benedictine abbey. In 1794 the Convention installed Chappe's new telegraphic invention in the church apse relaying Paris with Lille.

Cimetière St-Pierre ⊙ – To the north of the church lies this very old and minute cemetery. Amongst those interred here are the sculptor Pigalle (1714-1785), the heart of the explorer Bougainville (1729-1811), members of the Fitz-James family, the brothers Debray, the original owners of the Moulin de la Galette, and Montmartre's first Mayor, Félix Desportes. Gismondi's bronze door features the Resurrection.

★★La Basilique du Sacré-Cœur ⊙ – *Place du Parvis du Sacré-Cœur.* After the disastrous Franco-Prussian War of 1870, a group of Catholics vowed to raise money by public subscription to erect a church to the Sacred Heart on Montmartre hill. The proposal was declared a state undertaking by the National Assembly in 1873.

Paul Abadie (1812-1884) – The man associated with the restoration of St-Front Cathedral in Périgueux *(see Michelin Green Guide to Dordogne)*, based his designs for a neo-Romano-Byzantine basilica on the old church. Building began in 1876 and concluded in 1914 at a cost 40 million francs (Abadie died in 1884, when only the foundations had been laid); the church was consecrated in 1919 and has attracted countless pilgrims ever since.

The edifice – The tall white silhouette is a feature of the Paris skyline, with its pointed cupolas dominated by the 80m – 262ft campanile.

Internally, this pilgrim church is decorated with mosaic; the chancel vault designed by Luc-Olivier Merson depicts France's devotion to the Sacred Heart. The stained-glass windows, shattered during 1944, are new.

The dome ⊙ – From inside there is a bird's-eye view down into the church whilst from the external gallery a **panorama★★★** extending for over 30km – 18 1/2 miles may be glimpsed on a clear day.

La Savoyarde hanging in the belfry is one of the heaviest bells in the world (19 tons). It was cast in 1895 at Annecy, and offered as a gift from the dioceses of Savoy.

The church plate is visible in the crypt, as is an audio-visual display on the history and cult of the basilica.

The terrace – From the church steps there is a remarkable **view★★** over the capital. Immediately below is the square Willette laid out in 1929 (a funicular train shuttles up the steep hill thereby saving a steep climb for the price of a metro ticket!).

From Sacré-Cœur to Montmartre Cemetery

Follow rue Chevalier-de-La-Barre and turn right into rue du Mont-Cenis.

Rue Cortot – No **12** boasts of having put up Renoir, Othon Friesz, Utter, Dufy, Émile Bernard, Suzanne Valadon and her son Utrillo, and the radical poet Paul Reverdy over the years. It is now the entrance to the Montmartre Museum.

Musée de Montmartre ⊙ – The house itself was the country residence of the actor Rosimond who like Molière *(see* PORT-ROYAL) died on stage (*d*1686). It now houses the museum's rich collection of mementoes evoking the quarter's Bohemian life, its nightclubs and personalities, and hosts interesting temporary exhibitions. Besides the many topographical paintings there are reconstructions of the Café de l'Abreuvoir where Utrillo was a frequent visitor, and of the composer Charpentier's studio; documents relating to the statesman Clemenceau who was the local mayor in 1870; a collection of porcelain made in 1870 for the Count of Provence by the Clignancourt factory.

The vineyard – On the first Saturday in October, the grapes are harvested – always a most festive event.

Butte Montmartre – Au Lapin Agile

R. Besse/MICHELIN

Rue St-Vincent – The junction★ with rue des Saules is one of the most delightful corners of the Butte: flights of steps drop away mysteriously straight ahead while another road rises steeply beside the cemetery...the picturesque charm is further enhanced by the famous **Lapin Agile**, half-hidden by an acacia. First known as the 'Cabaret des Assassins', then as 'A ma compagne' under new ownership before taking the name of its new sign painted by André Gill: it attracted between 1900 and 1914 a host of often penniless writers and artists (Francis Carco, Roland Dorgelès, Pierre Mac Orlan, Picasso, Vlaminck...). Literary evenings are still held daily *(9pm, except Mondays)*.
On the corner with rue du Mont-Cenis once lived Hector Berlioz, in the house where he composed *Harold in Italy* and *Benvenuto Cellini*.

Cimetière St-Vincent – This modest cemetery is the resting place of the musician Honegger, the painter Utrillo, the writer Marcel Aymé, and Émile Goudeau the founder of the Club des Hydropathes.

Château des Brouillards – This was built in the 18C as a folly; it was later used as a dance hall; Gerard de Nerval lived there for a time. Its grounds have become square Suzanne-Buisson (a statue of St Denis stands on the spot where he is said to have washed his decapitated head).

★**Avenue Junot** – Opened in 1910, this wide peaceful thoroughfare gave onto the Montmartre *maquis*, an open space of ill repute where mills still turned their sails to the wind. Among the artists' studios and private houses is the Hameau des Artistes (no **11**) and the **Villa Léandre** (no 25). There is a view of the windmill from no 10.

Moulin de la Galette – The dance-hall which enjoyed such a rage at the turn of the century, inspired many painters including **Renoir** *(see* ORSAY*)*, Van Gogh, Willette... The windmill which has topped the hill for more than six centuries is the old *Blute-fin* which was defended against the Cossacks in 1814 by the heroic mill-owner Debray whose corpse was finally crucified upon the sails. Nearby stands the 1736 Paris bearing for North *(see* PORT-ROYAL – plan under l'Observatoire*)*. The Radet mill stands at the corner with rue Lepic.

Rue Lepic – The old quarry road that winds gently down the steep hill is the scene each autumn of a veteran car rally. Van Gogh lived with his brother at no **54**.

★**Cimetière de Montmartre** Ⓥ – Access to the cemetery by the stairs on the left.

1) Lucien and Sacha Guitry (playwrights and actors).
2) The Cavaignac family (statue by Rude).
3) Émile Zola (novelist).
4) E Labiche (playwright).
5) Hector Berlioz (composer).
6) Greuze (painter).
7) Heinrich Heine (poet and writer).
8) François Truffaut (film producer).
9) Théophile Gautier (poet and critic).
10) Henri Murger (novelist).
11) Hittorff (architect).
12) Edgar Degas (painter).
13) Leo Delibes (composer).
14) Poulbot (illustrator).
15) Jacques Offenbach (composer).
16) Nijinsky (dancer).
17) Ernest Renan and Ary Scheffer (philosopher; painter).
18) Alexandre Dumas the Younger (novelist).
19) Edmond and Jules de Goncourt (novelists).
20) Charcot (explorer).
21) Stendhal (H Beyle) (novelist).
22) Alfred de Vigny (poet).
23) Louis Jouvet (actor).
24) Alphonsine Plessis, the Lady of the Camelias.
25) La « Goulue » (cabaret dancer).
26) Dalida (singer).

MONTPARNASSE★★

Michelin plan 11 – folds 41 and 42: L 11, L 12 – M 11, M 12

This crowded quarter, which traditionally belonged to artists and the working class, has these past 20 years been subject to major redevelopment.

Mount Parnassus – The debris from age-old quarries formed a deserted rough-grass-covered mound. For students, chased away from the Pré-aux-Clercs by Queen Margue-rite *(see* FAUBOURG ST-GERMAIN*)*, it became a favourite haunt where they could freely declaim poetry. They named this wild place Mount Parnassus after the sacred mountain where Apollo entertained his Muses.
In the 18C the ground was flattened, but this section of the boulevard, a fragment of the Farmers General perimeter wall, complete with toll-booths, kept the name alive.

A pleasure ground – At the time of the Revolution, cafés and cabarets mushroomed on the city's outskirts. Revellers congregated at the Montagnes-Suisses and Élysée-Montparnasse gardens, the Arc-en-Ciel and Grande Chaumière dance-halls. It was from here that the polka and the cancan began to pervade Paris. At the Observatory crossroads where the Closerie des Lilas *(see* PORT-ROYAL – l'Observatoire*)* now stands, there used to be the Bullier Dance Hall; crowds gathered at the Constant Dance Hall and in the drinking dens of the village of Plaisance to dance the mazurka between sips of rough Suresnes wine.
As the sprawl continued, Haussmann intervened, ordering the area into confined neighbourhoods around the villages Plaisance, Vaugirard and Montrouge, accessed by the rue de Rennes, boulevards Arago and d'Enfer (now boulevard Raspail).

Bohemian Montparnasse – At the turn of the century avant-garde artists, poets and writers, moved to the Left Bank and to Montparnasse in particular, following a lead set by Alfred Jarry and Douanier Rousseau (who worked locally at a customs-house), Henri Murger who had already described the Bohemian lifestyle in his *Scenes of Bohemian Life*. The newcomers included Apollinaire, Max Jacob, Jean Moréas...

The former Wine Pavilion from the 1900 Exhibition – designed by Eiffel – was reconstructed at no 52 rue de Dantzig, alongside the Vaugirard slaughterhouse. The main pavilion, circular in shape, with a cubist roof, accommodated 24 painters in narrow cells or 'coffins' on two floors thereby earning its name **La Ruche** meaning Beehive. Flanking pavillions tended to have bigger studio spaces designated for sculptors. Run by the benevolent Père Boucher, himself an unsuccessful academic sculptor, the rabbit warren replaced the Bateau-Lavoir *(see* MONTMARTRE – Abbesses Quarter*)* by providing lodging and studios to impoverished, often foreign, artists, notably Modigliani, Soutine, Chagall, Zadkine and Léger. It was from such cramped quarters that the Expressionist movement emerged.

Discussion and debate was the food of these men, animated by the Russian political exiles (Lenin, Trotsky), composers (Stravinsky, Satie and "the Six"), foreign artists and writers (Hemingway, Foujita, Picasso, Eisenstein, Blasco Ibañez, Man Ray, Cendrars, Fargué, André Breton, Cocteau)... This was the golden age of the **Paris School** *(see* HALLES-BEAUBOURG – Centre G-Pompidou*)* lasting into the mid-1930s, and ending with the outbreak of war in Spain and Western Europe.

This former international Bohemian quarter became entirely Parisian; in the frenzy of materialism and exhibitionism prevalent after the war which drove the pace of fashion (as observed by Fernand Léger), the Vavin crossroads (*see below*) became the 'navel of the world': it came to be frequented by the trendy set, sporty 'stylish' hatchback cars cruised the streets, and outlandish, provocative outfits walked the pavements jostling the locals. At the Dingo, the Viking, the Caméléon bars, crazy concoctions and cocktails began to replace the old-time cafés-crèmes, late-night opening stretched ever further into the morning: such was the American influence of the 1950s.

During the 60s, the pace became too much; Aragon, Cocteau, Braque, Sartre, de Beauvoir continued to be glimpsed, but already the likes of Foujita, Picasso, Chagall had moved on.

Montparnasse today – Since redevelopment the Maine-Montparnasse complex has become the nucleus of a business area while the Vandamme-Nord section has a mixture of offices, housing, sporting facilities and hotel accommodation. Beyond the old village of Plaisance, part of Paris for less than a century, is transformed by the presence of modern high-rise blocks.

Along the Boulevard du Montparnasse, anonymous crowds of revellers and artists continue to be attracted by the cafés, cinemas and nightclubs, ever rubbing shoulders with the local population of workers, shopkeepers and artisans.

★The Maine-Montparnasse Complex

Ⓜ *Montparnasse-Bienvenüe. Buses: 28, 48, 58, 82, 89, 91, 92, 94, 95, 96*

Dating from 1934, the original plan for this area was revised in 1958 when it became a major urban renewal project with the aim of creating a high-density business area on the Left Bank. Work began in 1961 and the tower was completed in 1973.

Place du 18-Juin-1940 – Until 1967 this site, lined by cafés, was occupied in the 19C by the old railway station, the Gare Montparnasse, which will be remembered as General Leclerc's headquarters at the time of the liberation of Paris. It was also where, on 25 August 1944, the German military governor signed his garrison's surrender. A mural plaque at the entrance to the commercial centre *(left side)* commemorates this event.

At the corner of boulevard du Montparnasse and rue de l'Arrivée stands the cube-shaped building of the **International Textile Centre** (CIT), which houses over 200 companies on 12 floors.

Centre Commercial – The podium extending from place du 18-Juin-1940 to the foot of the tower has eight levels, six of which are underground. The uppermost three floors are leased to department stores (Galerie Lafayette, Habitat, C & A), and luxury shops selling the latest in fashion, cafés and restaurants. The subterranean floors accommodate parking, installation equipment and a sports centre *(entrance rue du Départ)* with swimming pool.

★★Tour Montparnasse ⊙ – This 209m – 688ft high tower dominates the whole quarter – adding a modern landmark to the Paris skyline. It is perhaps the most spectacular and controversial feature of the complex as a whole. The strictly geometric lines of the façades are softened by their gently curved surfaces.

The foundations are sunk to a depth of 70m – 230ft – bearing 120 000 tons of masonry and shafts. The weight load of the building is distributed between two different structures: a central reinforced-concrete core, of the same shape as the building, and the outer "walls" of closely spaced vertical columns. These are linked by horizontal beams. The curtain walls are covered with bronze-tinted glass.

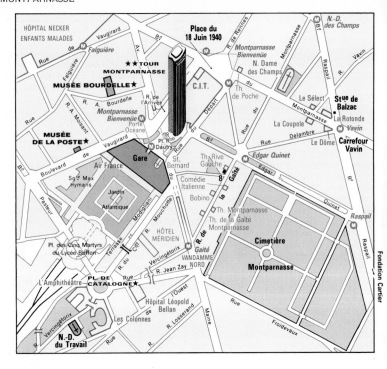

The building is separated from the new railway station, by a parvis paved with pink Sardinian granite under which passes the Avenue du Maine.

Ascent – It takes 40 seconds to reach the 56th floor air-conditioned observatory which affords a magnificent **panorama★★★** of Paris and its suburbs. Viewing tables help to pick out the main landmarks: the Eiffel Tower with the skyscrapers of the new Défense quarter in the distance, the Louvre, the Sacré-Cœur, Notre-Dame, the Bois de Vincennes, Orly Airport and the Bois de Boulogne. By night Paris becomes a fairy-tale wonderland. There is also a bar and panoramic restaurant at this level. From the open roof terrace (59th floor) the view can extend as far as 49km – 30 miles.

Railway station – Traditionally, this station was the link with Brittany and Maine – from which many street names are taken. Today, trains run south-westwards from a U-shaped terminus surrounded on three sides by immense 18 storey glass, steel and concrete blocks. The station proper, on five levels, occupies the central area – a vast concourse connects with the metro and supplies every amenity, even a small chapel to St Bernard *(entrance at no 34)* – the lectern was carved from a railway sleeper.

The station has been redeveloped to cater for the French high-speed train on the southwest line (TGV Atlantique) and to absorb some of the traffic from Austerlitz Station. Porte Océane, the main entrance, is a vast glass-clad arch linking the city to the station. A massive concrete slab suspended over the tracks has been laid with a large expanse of garden and tennis courts. The **Jardin Atlantique** is typical of Paris' modern green oases, appealing to all the senses, with textured walkways, fountains, colourful flowers, rustling and odoriferous plants.

Around Montparnasse

Musée Jean Moulin – Mémorial du Maréchal Leclerc – This exhibition area is presently dedicated to documents, photographs and artefacts commemorating two French heroes of the Second World War.

★Musée Bourdelle ⊘ – *16 rue Antoine-Bourdelle.* **Antoine Bourdelle**'s (1861-1929) house, garden and studio have been converted to display the artist's sculptures, paintings and drawings. Having studied under Rodin, his work evolved from an animated naturalistic figurative style to a more stylised and archaic one modelled on Romanesque, Byzantine and Gothic examples. It remained monumental throughout. In the great hall are the original plaster prototypes for his huge sculptures cast in bronze – the Champs-Élysées Theatre panels *France*, *Heracles the Archer★★*, *Monument to General Alvear*, flanked by the four virtues (*Victory, Eloquence, Liberty and Strength*). This monument, erected to the glory of one of the leaders of Argentine independence, was inaugurated in Buenos Aires in 1926.

The most outstanding items among his immense output are the huge bronzes, now in the garden, his portrait busts of his contemporaries (Rodin, Anatole France) and the **portraits of Beethoven★** of whom he made 21 different studies.

The extension to the museum, designed by Christian de Portzamparc and completed in 1992, presents all the studies and fragments relating to the *Monument to Adam Mickiewicz*, erected in Cours Albert 1er(*see* ALMA) and the 1870 *War Monument* in Montauban (including *Howling Figures* and the *Roland Column*).

Le Monde building – *15 rue Falguière*. A streamlined profile distinguishes this modernist building (1990) on the site of a former garage. Striking yet Classical in line, the design is intended to reflect the serious yet uncontroversial stance of the national newspaper's political leanings.

Maison de la Poste et de la Philatélie
⊙ – *34 boulevard de Vaugirard*. The unusual façade has five decorative panels of light-reflecting prisms to break the monotony of the windowless walls of the five exhibition floors.

★**Musée de la Poste** – The museum presents an attractive account of the postal services through the ages (incised clay tablets from 2500BC, medieval manuscripts on parchment). The development of the postal communication network in France encompasses changes from the early relay posts for mounted carriers, via carrier pigeons, to the 18 000 post offices of today and the minitel.

Of particular note are the stamp printing and franking machines displayed, a complete collection of French stamps since the first issue in 1849 and displays of other national collections, shown in rotation.

Stamps may also be bought in virgin state from the specialist philatelic counters.

Motorised postmen, 1899

Musée de la Poste

Plaisance – *West of the Maine-Montparnasse complex.* In the mid-19C Plaisance was one of the villages surrounding Paris. Now as the developers encroach upon the old houses beyond the Cinq-Martyrs-du-Lycée-Buffon Bridge, the area is undergoing radical change.

★**Place de Catalogne** – The two six-storey strikingly modern yet neo-Classical buildings were designed by Ricardo Bofill around oval 'squares'. The continuous semicircular façades of the stone Amphithéâtre provide an effective design around a vast sunken disc-shaped fountain in the centre, which in turn leads into the Les Colonnes residential development (1986), where glass surfaces ripple with reflections around an open green space.

M. Renaudeau/HOAQUI

Les Colonnes designed by Ricardo Bofill

Église Notre-Dame-du-Travail – *59 rue Vercingétorix*. This unusual church appears uninteresting from the outside. Internally, however, it shows an audacious use (1900) of metal structures at a time when industrial techniques were radically changing building methods. Here the bare iron girders are meant to honour the combined simple notions of work and worship.

Méridien-Montparnasse Hotel – This elegant white building, designed by architect Pierre Dufau, who was also responsible for two of the towers at La Défense (the Septentrion and Assur towers) contrasts with its surroundings. The hotel with its 1 000 rooms and conference hall is part of a larger complex comprising office and housing space, a commercial centre and a bowling alley. Two overhead passageways link the Vandamme-Nord centre to the Modigliani Terrace.

Rue de la Gaîté – This old country road has, since the 18C, been lined with cabarets, dance-halls, restaurants and other pleasure spots – hence its name. The street's reputation began with the Mère Cadet, the Veau qui Tète and the Gigoteurs Dance Halls, and is maintained today by the Grand Edgar Theatre (no **8**) and the Montparnasse Theatre (no **31**) whose reputation for popular drama was revived in the 1930s. The pink candy-floss façade of the Comédie Italienne (no **17**) belies a small but special theatre dedicated to the Italian Commedia dell'Arte genre.

At no 20 stands the famous **Bobino** Music Hall, now alas defunct where Piaf and George Brassens amongst many others used to sing.

Cimetière Montparnasse ⓥ *entrance in boulevard Edgar-Quinet.*

Ⓜ *Edgar Quinet, Raspail. Buses: 320, 54, 80, 95*

This is a tranquil spot cut by shaded avenues of lime trees (the benches can be sticky). Here is a selection of the most famous graves among many others worthy of note (Man Ray, Maréshal Pétain, Mr and Mrs Max Rosenberg of the Ballet Rambert).

Cimetière Montparnasse :

1) J-P Sartre, philosopher, and Simone de Beauvoir, writer.
2) Soutine, painter.
3) Baudelaire, poet.
4) Laurens, sculptor.
5) Bourdelle (no inscription), sculptor.
6) Dumont d'Urville, admiral.
7) Tristan Tzara, Romanian Dadaist poet.
8) Zadkine, sculptor.
9) Mounet-Sully, actor.
10) Houdon, sculptor.
11) Jussieu, botanist.
12) Rude, sculptor.
13) Serge Gainsbourg, singer-composer.
14) Le Verrier, astronomer.
15) Baudelaire's Cenotaph.
16) Henri Poincaré, mathematician.
17) César Franck, composer.
18) Guy de Maupassant, writer.
19) Bartholdi, sculptor.
20) Kessel, writer.
21) André Citroën, engineer and industrialist.
22) Pigeon, sculptor.
23) The Kiss by Brancusi, Romanian sculptor.
24) Sainte-Beuve, writer-critic.
25) Saint-Saëns, composer.
26) Vincent d'Indy, composer.
27) H Langlois, film specialist.
28) Leon-Paul Fargue, poet.
29) Boucicaut, businessman.

> **James Joyce** (1882-1941) was the archetypal impoverished artist in Paris. He came for a two-week visit at the request of Ezra Pound and stayed for 20 years. Shortly after his arrival, the Irishman managed to live rent-free in rue de l'Assomption, but it was at a small abode on the boulevard Raspail and during his subsequent stay at 71 rue Cardinal Lemoine, that he completed his masterpiece *Ulysses* with the help and support of **Samuel Beckett**.

Boulevard Raspail Ⓜ *Vavin, Raspail. Bus: 68*

Carrefour Vavin – *place Pablo Picasso*. This crossroads, originally the summit of the Parnassus Mound, continues to bustle with life at the heart of the old quarter. All around, the famous café-restaurants Le Dôme, La Rotonde, Le Sélect, La Coupole still serve a mean plate of oysters well into the early hours!

In 1939 the famous statue of **Balzac** by Rodin was placed on its island site.

Rue Campagne Première

Man Ray arrived from New York to photograph the haute couture of Paul Poiret and Schiaparelli in July 1921. In 1923, he fell in love – at first sight – with Kiki, who worked locally at Le Jockey, an American-style nightclub. She moved in with him at 31 rue Campagne Première almost immediately, where she posed for many of his most original plates (*the Mask, Violon d'Ingres...*).

The **Hôtel Istria**, nearby, accommodated other strangers to the area: Picabia, Marcel Duchamp, Kisling, Rilke, Tzara...

More recently, the street was used in the closing sequence in the film *A Bout de Souffle* with Jean-Paul Belmondo...

Rue Delambre – This bustling street running through the heart of the Montparnasse quarter counted among its numerous watering holes the legendary Dingo Bar (no 10), where Hemingway first met F Scott Fitzgerald. Nearby at no 9, lived Isadora Duncan.

École Spéciale d'Architecture – *no 254*. In a prime position between traditional solid buildings, this compact, modern structure maximises on space and natural light. The internal area is completely open-plan uncluttered by stairways or lift shafts which have been accommodated externally. The contrast between old and new is particularly apparent from the cemetery behind.

Fondation Cartier ⊙ – *no 231*. From the outside this building appears to float behind a larger panel of glass, sandwiched between street life and a garden with trees beyond. Designed by Jean Nouvel in 1994, it provides an airy, light and spacious venue for temporary exhibitions of contemporary art. The upper floors are reserved for the Foundation's administration.

MOUFFETARD ★

Michelin plan 11 – fold 44: L 15 – M 15
Ⓜ *Place Monge. Bus 47*

This area on the fringe of the Latin Quarter is dotted with small restaurants and clothes shops catering for the many students that permanently throng the neighbourhood.

★**Place de la Contrescarpe** – An inscription at no **1** recalls the Pinecone cabaret – La Pomme-de-Pin – described by Rabelais.

★**Rue Mouffetard** – The '*Mouffe*' as it is known winds downhill to Saint Médard, lined with old houses and crowded most mornings with market shoppers in search of a bargain, on Sundays, street musicians play jazz adding further touches of colour to the area. Picturesque painted signs are a reminder of past times, like that at no **69** where a carved oak tree once topped the sign for *Le Vieux Chêne* and "At the Clear Spring" at no **122**.

Nos **104** and **101** mark the entrances to the Passages des Postes and des Patriarches.

The **Pot-de-Fer Fountain** like others in the district, runs with surplus water from the Arcueil Aqueduct which Marie de' Medici had constructed to bring water to the Luxembourg Palace. Its Italian-style bosses recall the Medici Fountain *(see* PORT ROYAL*)*. Almost opposite, at no **53** a cache of 3 350 gold coins bearing the head of Louis XV was discovered when the house was demolishd (1938), placed there by Louis Nivelle, the king's bearer and counsellor.

Other streets in the vicinity – During the Middle Ages the area abounded in student colleges. One of the rare examples is the **Scottish College** *(see* LATIN QUARTER*)*.

René Descartes lived at **14** rue Rollin during his stay in Paris (1644-1648).

Denis Diderot (1713-1784) lived at **13** rue de l'Estrapade between 1747 and 1754 whilst overseeing the publication of his famous Encyclopedia. There is a striking view to be caught over the dome of the Panthéon.

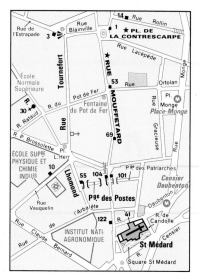

Rue Lhomond is lined with flights of steps – an indication of the former height of the hill. At no **30** stands the chapel serving the Séminaire du Saint-Esprit built in 1780 by Chalgrin. The passage des Postes starts level with no 55.

At **10 rue Vauquelin** Pierre and Marie Curie isolated radium in October 1898 and discovered the principles of radio-activity.

Église St-Médard ⓥ – *141 rue Mouffetard*. St Medard's was once the parish church of a small market town overlooking the River Bièvre. Its patron, Saint Medard, counsellor to the Merovingian kings of the 6C, was also the author of the delightful custom of giving a wreath of roses to maidens of virtuous conduct. The church, started in the mid-15C, was completed in 1655.

A gate and passage lead from **41** rue Daubenton to a small side entrance to the church.The Flamboyant Gothic nave has modern stained glass; the unusually wide chancel is Renaissance-influenced with asymmetrical semicircular arches and rounded windows. In 1784 the pillars were transformed into fluted Doric columns. There are paintings of the French school, a remarkable 16C triptych *(behind the pulpit)* and, in the second chapel to the right of the chancel, a *Dead Christ* attributed to Philippe de Champaigne.

Its famous cemetery surrounds the apse.

The "Convulsionnaries"

In 1727 a Jansenist deacon with a saintly reputation died at the age of 36 of mortification of the flesh and was buried in the churchyard beneath a raised black marble stone. Sick Jansenists came to pray before the tomb, to lie upon and underneath it giving rise to a belief in miraculous cures which led to massive scenes of collective hysteria.

In 1732, Louis XV decreed an end to the demonstrations; the cemetery was closed. The inscription nailed to the gate meant:

> *By order of the King, let God*
> *No miracle perform in this place!*

La MUETTE

Michelin plan 11 – folds 26 and 27: H 4, H 5 – J 4, J 5
Ⓜ/RER: Boulainvilliers-La Muette. Buses: 22, 32, 52

The original Muette Estate was developed as an elegant quarter. Today it enjoys the green open space of the Ranelagh Gardens and the attraction of the Marmottan Museum with its rich collection of art.

Historical notes – It was here that Charles IX (1550-1574) had a hunting lodge where he kept his falcons when in moult (french *en mue* hence Muette). The name was preserved when Philibert Delorme built a château set in a park extending to the Bois de Boulogne.

The château had many royal residents: Marguerite de Valois, first wife of Henri of Navarre (Queen Margot); Louis XIII; Duchesse de Berry – whose stay until she died aged 24, was 'short and sweet' as per her motto; Louis XV used the château as a clandestine meeting place during his affair with the Marquise de Pompadour; the future Louis XVI and Marie-Antoinette spent the first years of their married life here.

At the Revolution the estate was divided up.

In 1820 the piano maker Sébastien Erard purchased the château and part of the park bordering on the Ranelagh. A century later the property was sold off in lots for development.

★★Musée Marmottan ⓥ – *2 rue Louis-Boilly*. In 1932 the art historian **Paul Marmottan** bequeathed his private house and collections of Renaissance tapestries and sculpture, Consular and First Empire portraits (26 of Boilly), medallions, paintings (Vernet) and furniture (Desmalter *commode*) to the Académie des Beaux-Arts. In 1950 Mme Donop de Monchy donated a part of her father's collection, including works by the Impressionists befriended and treated by Dr de Bellio (*Impression – Sunrise* which gave the Impressionist Movement its name). In 1971, Michel Monet left 65 of his father's painted canvases to the museum which has been further endowed by the Wildenstein legacy of 228 13C-16C illuminated manuscripts from various European schools.

The collection of Claude Monet paintings, probably the most important known body of work by the Master of Impressionism, is accommodated by a special purpose-built underground gallery; many of the works were painted at the artist's Normandy home at Giverny, depicting his beloved water-lilies, wistaria, iris, rose-garden, weeping willows and Japanese bridge. Other panels show the painter's pre-occupation with light (*The Houses of Parliament – London, The Europe Bridge, Rouen Cathedral*).

The Duhem Bequest of about 60 paintings, drawings and watercolours includes Gauguin's splendid *Bouquet of Flowers* painted in Tahiti and an interesting pastel by Renoir: *Seated Girl in a White Hat*.

Exceptional pictures by Albrecht Bonts *Christ on the Cross* (16C), Fragonard and Renoir provide interesting points of comparison.

Jardin du Ranelagh – *Avenue Raphael*. Originally, Parisians came to the area to dance in the open air. In 1774 a Café was built, extended to accommodate a dance-hall-cum-stage. At the time, during a period of Anglomania, the locality was named the 'Petit Ranelagh' after Lord Ranelagh's most fashionable pleasure gardens outside London.

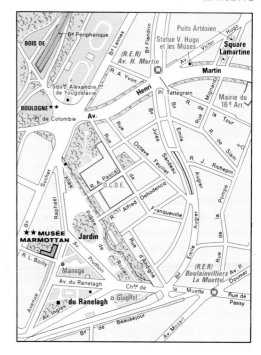

The present gardens were laid out by Haussmann in 1860.

Allée Pilâtre-de-Rozier – On 21 November 1783, the famous aeronaut accomplished the first 'free flight' in a hot-air balloon.

The marble relief at the end of the avenue honouring Victor Hugo is entitled *The Poet's Vision*.

Rue André-Pascal – André Pascal was the pen-name used by Baron Henri de Rothschild to publish his writings; it was for this same banker that the adjacent sumptuous mansion was built. Since 1948 the mansion has been classed as international territory the seat of the Organisation for European Cooperation and Development (in French the OCDE *closed to the public*).

Place de Colombie is overlooked by the statue of Peter I of Serbia and his son Alexander I of Yugoslavia.

Square Lamartine – Ⓜ/RER: *Avenue-Henri-Martin. Buses: 52, 63, PC*. This peaceful district grew up around the Passy artesian wells dug in 1855. Residents collect their supply of sulphur-rich water at a temperature of 28 °C – 82 °F from a depth of 600m – 1 970ft.

At the point where the elegant avenue Henri-Martin (formerly the avenue de l'Empereur) cuts the avenue Victor-Hugo has been placed **Rodin's** statue *Victor Hugo and the Muses*. The monumental bronze sculpture was cast after the Occupation from a plaster prototype.

For a good view of the city:
Arc de Triomphe (Platform)
Montparnasse (Tower)
Notre-Dame (Towers)
Basilique du Sacré-Cœur (Dome)
Eiffel Tower (3rd platform)
Georges Pompidou Centre (5th floor)
Consult the PARIS AT LEISURE for additional viewpoints.

OPÉRA★★

This district, encompassing the distinctive Opera House with its long avenue stretching down to the Palais-Royal and the splendid place Vendôme is at the hub of theatre land. Home to many of the more classic contemporary fashion designers, the streets are thronged with elegantly attired people day and night.

Quartier de l'Opéra
Ⓜ *Opéra. Buses: 20, 21, 22, 27, 29, 42, 52, 53, 66, 68, 81, 95*

★★**L'Opéra-Garnier** Ⓥ – *Place de l'Opéra*. The celebrity of France's first home of opera, the prestige of its ballet company, the architectural magnificence of the great staircase and foyer, the sumptuous decoration of the auditorium, incite its guest to treat himself to an enjoyable evening.

The Opéra Company – The Paris Opéra has successively been based at the Palais-Royal theatre (1673), at the salle des Machines in the Tuileries palace (1764), then back at the Palais-Royal for the great perfomances of Rameau (*Zoroastre*) and Gluck (*Orphée*), the salle Favart (1820) – home of the Opéra-Comique – and the salle Le Peletier (1821). It was transferred to the Opéra-Bastille in 1990 *(see BASTILLE)*.

The Opera House – The site of Garnier's Opera House was determined by Haussmann's town planning schemes. In 1820 the idea for a purpose-built opera house was born. It took 40 years before a competition was held to find an architect: 171 submitted plans. **Charles Garnier**, a 35-year-old unknown architect, winner of the Rome prize in 1848, was awarded the contract. Within a year Garnier had solved the problem posed by flooding from an underground spring – building started but progressed slowly; it was finally opened in 1875. Garnier dreamed of creating a 'Napoleon III style' of architecture, opposed to the mundane Classical pastiches which were the order of the day, but the new building was not to have a great following. It is nevertheless perhaps the most successful monument of the Second Empire.

J. Moatti/EXPLORER

Opéra-Garnier, the Great Staircase

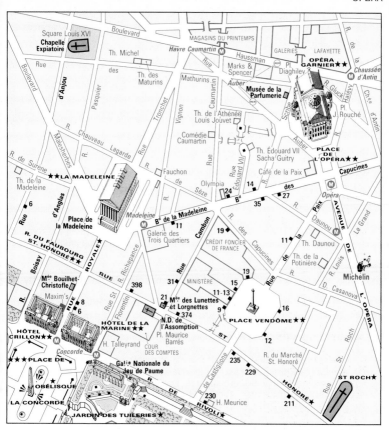

It is a large theatre with a total area of over 11 000m^2 – 118 404sq ft with a vast stage that will hold up to 450 performers, and a central chandelier that weighs eight tons: but given the huge space allowed in the wings for stage changes etc, the auditorium seats only 2 200.

Ballet – The ballet company repertoire is extensive, with programmes that include contemporary music and dance as well as Classical pieces. Recent modifications have equipped it with 20C high-tech facilities.

The building – The main façade overlooks place de l'Opéra. At raised ground level, between the arched entrances into the theatre are a series of sculpted figures that Garnier wished to commission exclusively from Carpeaux. His allegorical group **Dance** has been replaced by a Paul Belmondo copy (the weathered original is now in the Orsay Museum – *see* ORSAY). On the first floor, the foyer opens out onto a broad balcony, with a giant order of twin columns supporting a monumental frieze. Beyond extends the flattened green dome over the auditorium, a raised roof level over the stage area, framed by a grandiose pediment. The full impact of these superimposed foreshortened forms is best appreciated from the avenue de l'Opéra. A walk around the back from the right emphasises the sheer scale of the building. A projecting bay and side entrance were originally reserved for subscribers, who were able to drive their carriages into the courtyard lit by lanterns borne by statues of women by Cartier-Belleuse. The so-called Emperor's Pavilion, on rue Scribe, has a double ramp for the sovereign's carriage, facilitating direct access to the royal box. The pavilion has housed the Opéra Library and Museum since 1882.

★★★**Interior** – A feature of the building's originality is Garnier's use of multi-coloured marbles quarried in different parts of France: white, blue, pink, red and green. The magnificent **Great Staircase** and the **Grand Foyer** are conceived for sumptuous occasions. The ceiling in the **auditorium**, which may be visited outside rehearsals, is painted with figures taken from the realms of opera and ballet by Marc Chagall (1964).

Bibliothèque-Musée (*Tickets from ticket office in left hall, access on first floor, Baignoires / Orchestre level*) – The library was started in 1866. Documenting living memories of the house and its companies since 18C, it contains every score performed since 1669 and over 80 000 books and prints relating to dance, the singing voice, music and the theatrical arts. All exhibitions are presented in the stripped stone rotunda.

Garnier's architectural drawings hang up the stairs to the second-floor library with its fine period wooden furnishings, the models gallery (three-dimensional stage set designs), and painting collection (Hubert Robert, Renoir, Van Dongen, Perroneau...).

★★**Place de l'Opéra** – Haussmann envisaged place de l'Opéra not simply as a setting for the National Music Academy but also as a circus from which a number of roads should radiate. This vision was criticised for being too grandiose: the square seemed enormous at that time, whereas today, choked with traffic, it barely seems big enough! The square is presently lined with luxurious shop-windows proffering elegant leather goods (Lancel) and jewellery (Clerc) while the Café de la Paix terraces provide an enticing break to the foot-weary.

Le Grand-Hôtel – *2 rue Scribe*. This is a grand vestige from the era of Napoleon III (1862), with its once-fashionable domed 'Opera' room, converted now into a restaurant. It was here that the Grand Duke Dimitri, Offenbach, Winston Churchill, Eisenhower... stayed on their sojourns in Paris.

Musée de la Parfumerie Fragonard Ⓥ – *9 rue Scribe*. All kinds of paraphernalia relating to perfume making are collected together in this museum: distillation equipment to extract essences and oils, bottles and pots – some from Ancient Egypt, tickets and labels, the famous 'organ' used by early 'noses' in the creation of Fragonard perfumes, *vinaigrettes* to hold smelling salts that might revive a woman from her swoon... and a shop selling Fragonard products at factory prices.

★**Avenue de l'Opéra** – This luxurious thoroughfare was begun simultaneously at either end by Haussmann in 1854 and completed in 1878. The most serious obstacle in the road's path was the butte St-Roch, which would have been level with rues Thérèse and des Pyramides. It was here that Joan of Arc positioned her culverins (long-barrelled cannon) to reinforce troops preparing to attack the St Honoré Gate (*see* PALAIS-ROYAL – Rue St-Honoré). An attempt to level the mound was made in 1615 but squalid conditions subsisted until the end of the 17C when the slums were finally demolished. Vast amounts of rubble were used to infill excavations around the Champ-de-Mars. The avenue quickly became one of Paris' prestige streets and most animated thoroughfares. For the tourist the avenue is the ideal shopping centre for perfumes, scarves, gifts and *articles de Paris* (fancy goods). It is also a thriving commercial centre with many large banks (money-changers), the head offices of the advertising and travel industries, with the Havas Travel Agency at no **26**.

At no **27**, in the entrance of the National Centre for the Visual Arts is a trompe-l'œil representation of the Palais-Royal.

For place Gaillon – see PALAIS-ROYAL.

Rue de la Paix – Napoleon, on his column in the square, turns his back on this street laid in 1806 through the site of a former Capuchin monastery and originally called rue Napoléon. Jewellers and goldsmiths, **Cartier** (no **11**) amongst others, have brought it international fame making its name synonymous with elegance and luxury.

The Michelin Tourist Guides

In 1900 there were 3 000 vehicles on France's roads – a phenomenon which threw country folk into a panic. Car owners bought petrol at the local grocer and it was for these car owners and drivers that André Michelin, brother of Édouard, who manufactured tyres, compiled a little red book: the **Guide Michelin**. This, with its selection of hotels and restaurants and pages of practical information, has grown in size and fame until it is now known to seasoned travellers the world over, complete with its star rating system for restaurants. The young André Michelin next created in Paris, in 1908, a Car Travellers' Information Bureau which provided enquirers with itineraries and road information. He went on to supply the local authorities with name plates for towns and villages; to undertake, in 1910, the mapping of France to a scale of 1: 200 000 – 1 inch: 3 miles; the numbering of all roads (1913) and the production, from locally quarried pumice-stone near Clermont-Ferrand, of large square milestones covered in distinctive vitreous enamel. After the 1914-1918 War, guides were published to the Battlefields and in 1926, the Regional Guide Brittany, the first tourist guide in the series now known as the Michelin Green Tourist Guides. Today Michelin publishes a full range of guides and maps: 150 Green Guides, 12 Red Guides, and over 160 maps, at the last count!

Boutique Michelin at 32 avenue de l'Opéra 75002.

★★Place Vendôme Ⓜ *Opéra-Tuileries. Bus: 72*

Place Vendôme epitomises the full majesty of 17C French design.

In *c*1680, on land north of rue St-Honoré earmarked for development, Louvois, Superintendent of Buildings, conceived the idea of designing a square lined with buildings that would be suitable for the Academies, the National Library, the Mint and the Residence for Ambassadors Extraordinary, around a monumental statue of Louis XIV. It should even surpass place des Victoires *(see* GRANDS BOULEVARDS*)* in splendour. In 1685, the Duke of Vendôme's mansion and the neighbouring Capuchin convent were purchased.

Jules Hardouin-Mansart was commissioned to design the square, which was originally called place des Conquêtes but soon renamed place de Vendôme or Louis-le-Grand. In 1699 the equestrian statue of the king by Girardon was unveiled in the square defined by a mere painted semblance of beautiful façades. Only gradually were the plots of land purchased by speculators between 1702 and 1720.

During the Revolution the royal statue was destroyed and the square temporarily renamed place des Piques, and in 1810 Napoleon erected the Austerlitz column at its centre.

The layout – A continuous line of arches rings the square at ground level supporting a giant order of pilasters up to a steeply pitched roof with dormer windows. The slightly projecting, pedimented façades of the principal buildings and of those standing obliquely at each corner of the rectangle (224m x 213m – 245yds x 233yds) break the uniformity of line.

Each house around the square evokes a memory or a name: no **19** is the former Hôtel d'Évreux (1710) owned by the governor of the Crédit foncier de France; no **15** now houses the **Ritz Hotel**; nos **13** and **11**, occupied by the Ministry of Justice, were formerly the Royal Chancellery – the official measure for the metre was inlaid in the façade in 1848; no **9** was the house of the military governor of Paris at the end

Place Vendôme

of the 19C; Chopin died at no **12** in 1849; no **16** was the home of the German, Dr Mesmer, founder of the theory of Mesmerism.

The square and its surrounding area collect together all the great names in jewellery design: Van Cleef & Arpels, Boucheron, Mauboussin...

The column – The column's stone core, 44m – 132ft high, is enfolded in a bronze spiral cast from 1 250 cannon captured at the Battle of Austerlitz (1805), and decorated with military scenes in imitation of Trajan's column in Rome.

The original statue mounted on the column was of Napoleon as Caesar; in 1814 it was replaced by one of Henri IV, removed for the 100 Days (1815) when Napoleon attempted to regain power. Louis XVIII then had a colossal fleur-de-lis hoisted there; Louis-Philippe re-established Napoleon, this time in military uniform, and Napoleon III substituted a replica of the original. The Commune tore down the column in 1871 – an incident for which the painter Gustave Courbet was blamed and exiled; the Third Republic restored it with a replica of the original statue.

Handbags, costume jewellery, scarves and perfume...
consult the Paris at Leisure section in the INTRODUCTION...
chocolates, cheese, canaries, chop-sticks,
books and tapes, bread and cakes, food and flea-markets..

★Rue St-Honoré Ⓜ Concorde

The windows of the section of rue St-Honoré between rue Royale end rue de Castiglione are a window-shopper's paradise.

Under the Ancien Régime, before rue de Rivoli was laid, this road was the main route out of Paris towards the west. Its reputation goes back many years to the pre-Revolution era when members of the royal court, nobility and financiers, all came to do their shopping.

Hôtel de Mme Geoffrin *no 374* – Mme Geoffrin, married at 14 to an industrialist and widowed at 17, here held her literary salon frequented by all the great European names from the Age of the Enlightenment under Louis XV. Known as the Realm of rue St-Honoré, she entertained the philosopher Jean Le Rond d'Alembert (1717-1783) and the early advocate of Materialism Claude-Adrien Helvétius (1715-1771). She also had a subscription to Diderot's Encyclopedia

Musée des Lunettes et Lorgnettes ☉ – *no 380.* In this museum, founded by the optician Pierre Marly, the history of spectacles, lorgnettes, field and opera glasses and other aids to vision unfolds from the very earliest pair of spectacles (dating from the 13C, these had to be held manually in place on the bridge of the nose). The collection includes lorgnettes incorporated into walking sticks, *pince-nez*, monocles, telescopes, sun shields for field glasses, magnifying glasses.... Among the many rare and valuable exhibits, note the exquisite carved box-wood spectacles case and Sarah Bernhardt's gold lorgnettes.

At a stone's throw, in rue Cambon, is the house from which **Coco Chanel** reigned over the fashion world for half a century, while living at the Ritz Hotel nearby.

"Coco" Chanel's headquarters

At the end of 1910, Gabrielle Chanel (1883-1971), the descendant of a family of stall holders from the Cévennes, and well versed in financial dealings and horse racing, set up shop as a milliner in a basement at no 21 rue Cambon. Ten years later she moved to no 31.

Her essential talent was in fabric-cutting and dress-making, applied with skill in the use of 'humble' fabrics such as jersey, tweed and plaid. She had an expert eye for colour and designed clothes that relied on line rather than ornament for effect, austere but graceful. Her tailored outfits were often based on the British Sporty Look designed for comfort and ease of movement, popular amongst modern, independent and career-minded women after the First World War. It is to Chanel that we owe the 'little black number' – that prerequisite element of the female wardrobe, versatile enough to be dressed 'down' if worn with flat court shoes or 'up' with stilettos and large imitation jewels, and the tailored suit. Survival of Chanel's business during the war was ensured by the launch of the famous "Number 5" perfume (1920), a stable, indefinable scent blending animal and vegetable extracts with artificial stabilisers. Naturally thin, Coco wore her hair short, often under simple hats. Impressed and forever interested in the Ballet and the Theatre, Chanel shaped the trends in fashion – she even made the sun-tan fashionable!

Église Notre-Dame de l'Assomption – *Place Maurice-Barres.* This was the former chapel of the Convent of the Sisters of the Assumption (now the Polish Church in Paris). The circular building capped by a disproportionately large dome dates from the 17C. Above the main altar is an *Annunciation* by Vien (18C) and to its right an *Adoration of the Magi* by Van Loo. In the dome is a fresco of the Assumption by Charles de la Fosse (17C).

The modern buildings in the square are occupied by the Cour des Comptes (Auditor General's Office, 1912). No **398** is the site of the house in which Robespierre lived until the eve of his execution on 9 Thermidor (27 July 1794).

Rue de Castiglione – This street was known formerly as the Passage des Feuillants after the Benedictine monastery which it skirted. The crossroads of rue de Castiglione and rue St-Honoré affords a view of the place and Colonne Vendôme. *For section beyond rue de Castiglione – see* PALAIS-ROYAL.

Hotel X

George Orwell (1903-1950) in his novel *Down and Out in Paris and London* (1933) describes the sordid conditions below stairs in a grand hotel on the rue Castiglione; a job he managed to scrounge through the intervention of his street-wise Russian companion Boris. During his 20-month stay in Paris '*to escape... from every form of man's dominion over man*', Orwell lived in the Latin quarter at Chez Georgette, 6 rue du Pot de Fer (renamed rue du Coq d'Or in the novel).

ORSAY ★★★

From rail station to museum – At the end of the 19C the Orléans rail company acquired the site of the ruined Orsay Palace, formerly occupied by the Auditors' Office and the State Council and set ablaze in 1871 during the Commune, on which to build a new rail terminus. The company commissioned Victor Laloux (1850-1937), the winner of the Prix de Rome in 1878 and professor of architecture at the École des Beaux Arts, to design a station which would harmonise in style with the buildings of this elegant quarter facing the Louvre and the Tuileries across the Seine. He designed an iron and glass structure screened on the outside by a monumental façade modelled on the Louvre and on the inside by a coffered ceiling with stucco decoration. He also planned an adjoining hotel. Two years later the building was inaugurated, on 14 July 1900.

For nearly 40 years Orsay station, the terminus for the southwest region and the first to be purpose-built for electric traction, handled about 200 trains daily. As electrification spread to the rest of the network, longer trains came into service and the platforms at Orsay station soon proved inadequate. In 1939 progress outpaced the building's capabilities; the main-line station functioned briefly for suburban traffic before succumbing to closure. It was put to a number of uses: as reception centre for prisoners at the Liberation, a film-set for Kafka's *The Trial* filmed by Orson Welles in 1962, a theatre for the Renaud-Barrault Company in 1973, temporary auction-rooms during the refurbishment of the Hôtel Drouot in 1974...

The hotel closed on 1 January 1973.

Shortly after the station closed, a plan was mooted to convert Orsay, which had been saved from demolition, into a museum for 19C art. A conclusive decision was taken in 1977 by President V Giscard d'Estaing; the architects P Colboc, R Bardou and J-P Philippon were selected by competition to remodel the building. Gae Aulenti, the architect who had carried out the renovation of the National Museum of Modern Art in Paris and of the Palazzo Grassi in Venice, was entrusted with the museum's interior design and decoration. Six years on the museum was inaugurated by President F Mitterrand on 1 December 1986.

Permanent exhibitions – Extensive collections drawn from the period 1848 to 1914 include all the fine, decorative and applied arts (painting, sculpture, architecture, furniture, ceramics, jewellery, cinema, photography, printed graphics, music, literature, history...); these are presented in chronological order on three floors (ground floor, middle and upper levels).The Orsay museum bridges the gap between the Louvre collections and that at the museum of modern art at the Pompidou Centre *(see HALLES-BEAUBOURG).*

Outside the main entrance, stand six large statues of the continents (America is split in two), to the left a horse and a rhino and further on is a young elephant caught in a trap by Frémiet.

The galleries – The ground floor is dedicated to the period 1840 to 1870. This leads into the Impressionist movement, the Post-Impressionist, the Pont-Aven School and the Nabis, shown on the uppermost level. The middle floor features works from the late 19C and early 20C (Art Nouveau and sculpture, 1870 to 1914).

The Great Clock with *David* by Antonin Mercie (1845-1916)

● ● ● ● ● ● ● ● ● ● ● ● ● ● ● **PRACTICALITIES** ● ● ● ● ● ● ● ● ● ● ● ● ● ●

Guided Tours – Guided tours daily at 11am and 1pm and at 7pm on Thursday. A single work of art "A work to see" is presented every day at 12.30pm.

The meeting point is at the accueil des groupes 15 min before the start.

Short guides on a particular theme enable the visitor to do a quick tour of the museum.

Facilities: Wheelchairs are available for disabled visitors from the cloakroom *(vestiaire)*, and staff are on hand to assist with lifts.

Bookshop, telephones, bureau de change, audioguides. Special facilities and activities for young visitors (5-15 years old).

Refreshments: Coffee-shop and snack-bar are located on the top floor. Restaurant facilities are open daily for lunch, and on Thursdays for dinner.

Lectures and Conferences: Free lectures are programmed in the Auditorium – see listing in free bi-monthly *Nouvelles du Musée d'Orsay*, available at the information desk.

★★★MUSÉE D'ORSAY ⊙

1 rue de Bellechasse. Ⓜ Solférino /RER: Musée-d'Orsay. Buses: 24, 63, 68, 69, 73, 83, 84, 94. Note: Closed Mondays – Late opening to 9.45pm on Thursdays.

1848 – 1870

The expressive *Spirit of the Fatherland* (1), a fragment of the high relief of the Arc de Triomphe, by Rude (1784-1855) is a fitting introduction to the museum.

The central gallery is devoted to sculpture; the side galleries feature *(right)* Classicism, Romanticism and Academism and *(left)* Realism, the Barbizon School and pre-Impressionism.

Sculpture

The Lion (2) is a realistic composition by **Antoine-Louis Barye** (1796-1875), who followed courses under Cuvier at the Botanic Gardens *(see* JUSSIEU – Museum National d'Histoire Naturelle*)*. Note also the allegorical sculptures (3).

The period between 1850 and 1870 is perhaps dominated by Romanticism, a movement that emerged in the 1830s inspired by Antiquity and the Renaissance.

Pradier (1790-1852) – His style, although Classical in essence, is animated by Romanticism.   *Sappho* (4)

The large canvas *Romans in the Period of Decadence* (7) is by **Thomas Couture** (1815-1879) a 'history' painter on the grand-scale.

Carpeaux (1827-1875) – A follower of Rude and inspired by Michelangelo, he was known for his fine busts and important official commissions.   *Ugolin* (5)
    Four corners of the World (6)

For the Observatory Fountain – see PORT-ROYAL.

La Danse (8) – The original stone group by Carpeaux used to adorn the Opera House façade. It has been replaced by a Paul Belmondo copy *(see OPÉRA)*.

Second Empire (1852-1870) architecture

At the far end of the central gallery is the scale model (1:100) of the Opera quarter. The neo-Baroque design for the Opera House by **Charles Garnier** (1825-1898) integrates well into its urban context. Marble, bronze, copper, porphyry are used with sculpted figures and balustrades to grand effect. The cross-section reveals the foyer, stage, auditorium, machines as well as the grandiose internal decoration.

Viollet-le-Duc (1814-1879) – *First floor of the Pavillon Amont*. The architecture and writer, Viollet-le-Duc, is particularly known for his work as restorer of great Gothic monuments; he was keenly interested in decorative painting (murals of Notre-Dame's chapels).

The decorative and applied arts (1850-1880)

Access to this section at the far right of the central gallery is from the far end or middle of the gallery behind Couture's painting.

The key quality inherent in the exhibits of this period from 1850 to 1880 is versatility, as fashion and taste succumbed to the influence of colonisation, foreign travel, the universal exhibitions, in particular that of 1867 which revealed Japanese art (fine Japanese-style **porcelain service** (9) made by the painter-engraver Bracquemont for E Rousseau). New industrial businesses employed artists who combined good design with practicality, able to produce the one-off (dressing table from the house of Froment Meurice 11) as well as the mass-produced. **Christofle** radically changed their orientation as electro-plating processes enabled mass production of silver-plate without losing the fine art of crafting quality in solid silver. Certain pieces like the **Vase depicting the Education of Achilles** (12) were made for the universal exhibitions. The cabinet-maker **Diehl**, famous for his boxes fashioned in different styles and materials, and for occasional furniture, also made ornate show-pieces. The **medal cabinet** (13), regarded as one of the most original pieces of the 1867 exhibition, is decorated with scenes from Merovingian history (low-relief in silver-plated bronze by Frémiet). **Jules Desfossé** commissioned artists to paint landscapes applied to wall-paper: **Armide's garden** (14) is the central panel of a décor by Müller.

Painting (1848-1880)

Classicism, Romanticism and Academism – *Right gallery near decorative arts. Walk down some steps.*

Painting during the 1850s is dominated by **Ingres** and **Delacroix** who have come to represent the two main currents of the time, Classicism and Romanticism. A majority of their works remain in the Louvre.

Classicism: Ingres (1780-1867) has a distinctively linear style of composition.	*The Spring* (15) *(1856)* *Jupiter and Antiope* (16)
Romanticism: Delacroix (1798-1863) worked expressively with colour and strong light effects.	*The lion hunt* (17)
Academism: **Chassériau** (1819-1856) combines draughtsmanship with colour according to prescribed formulae.	*Tepidarium* (18)

Cabanel (1808-1879) won great acclaim at the Salon of 1863.	*The Birth of Venus* (19)

Winterhalter (1806-1873) was essentially a society painter and official portraitist of Napoleon III. (*Portrait of Mme Rimski-Korsakov* – 21)

The dawn of Symbolism – *Right gallery.* **Puvis de Chavannes** (1824-1898) recognised for his fresco wall paintings of Biblical subjects, used the same pale, flat colours for his oil palette (*The Poor Fisherman* – 22). The serenity and nobility of his figures embody such inherent expressions of sensitivity as to set him well apart from Impressionism. By contrast, **Gustave Moreau** (1826-1898), influenced by Chassériau, painted colourful mythological and allegorical fantasies with delicate detail. His poetic mysterious vision is suffused with languid sensuality (*Orpheus* – 23, *Jason and Medea* – 24). **Edgar Degas** (1834-1917) even in the early years before 1870, used pure pigment for effective clear and vibrant colour harmonies. His rigorously designed compositions and bold use of perspective is articulated by his masterful ability to draw. The psychological intensity of his portraits is particularly powerful (*Bellelli Family portrait* – 25, *Portrait of a young woman* – 26).

Realism and the Barbizon School – *First section of left gallery (Chauchard Collection).* Some artists, aware of their observations of everyday life and of nature, painted their figures life-size. The development of industrial towns prompted some to rediscover the countryside. Corot moved to Barbizon in 1830. Others followed him there to found the Barbizon School favouring dark earthy hues of colour, muted tones of twilight, inspired by the wooded landscapes around Fontainebleau.

Daumier (1808-1879) chiefly a lithographer and illustrator, he portrayed a satirical view of the social and political life of the period.	*Busts of Parliamentarians* (27) *The Republic* (28) *The laundress* (29)
Théodore Rousseau (1812-1867) is considered as the leader of the Barbizon School of painters, skilfully catching the effect of fleeting light.	*An avenue in the forest of l'Isle Adam* (31)

GROUND FLOOR

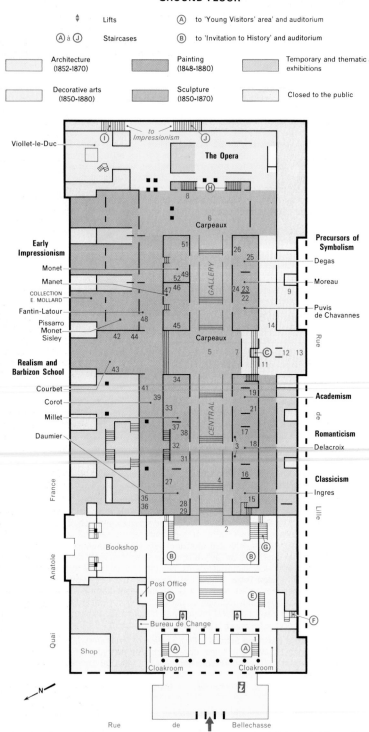

| | Lifts | Ⓐ to 'Young Visitors' area and auditorium |
| Ⓐ à Ⓙ | Staircases | Ⓑ to 'Invitation to History' and auditorium |

| | Architecture (1852-1870) | | Painting (1848-1880) | | Temporary and thematic exhibitions |
| | Decorative arts (1850-1880) | | Sculpture (1850-1870) | | Closed to the public |

Viollet-le-Duc

to Impressionism

The Opera

8

6
Carpeaux

Early Impressionism

51

26
25

Precursors of Symbolism

Monet
Manet
COLLECTION E. MOLLARD

52 49
47 46
48

Degas
Moreau

24 23
22

Fantin-Latour
Pissarro
Monet
Sisley

45
42 44

GALLERY

14

9

Puvis de Chavannes

Carpeaux

Rue

Realism and Barbizon School

43

5 7
C 12 13
11

Courbet
Corot
Millet

34
41
39
33
37
38
32
31

19
21
17
3 18

Academism

de

Romanticism
Delacroix

Daumier

CENTRAL

35
36
27
28
29

4
16
15

Classicism
Ingres

France

2

Lille

Bookshop

Ⓑ Ⓑ Ⓖ

Anatole

Post Office

Ⓓ Ⓔ

Ⓕ

Bureau de Change

Quai

Shop

Ⓐ Ⓐ

Cloakroom Cloakroom

N

ℹ

Rue de Bellechasse

Carte musées et monuments – *The Paris museum pass, valid for one, three or five consecutive days, provides direct access to the permanent collections (no temporary exhibitions) of over 65 different venues.*
But remember that several museums are free to children (under 18 years), special concessions apply to students (18-25 years) and to senior citizens (over 60s).

Jean-François Millet (1814-1875) was born into a peasant family, and spent his life portraying the land and the ways of the country.

The Angelus (**32**)
The Gleaners (**33**)
Spring (**34**)

The Angelus earned Millet much scorn from the contemporary critics who saw the work as condescendingly moralising. In fact, the painter was merely expressing his personal understanding of country people and rural life, in this case the importance of work and faith.

Constant Troyon (1810-1865) specialised in scenes with cattle.

Oxen driven to the fields (**35**)

Rosa Bonheur (1822-1899) painted rustic scenes and animals.

Ploughing in the Nivernais (**36**)

Camille Corot (1796-1875) captured the play of light through trees and in ponds.

The glade (**37**)
The Windmill at St-Nicolas-lès-Arras (**38**)
The catalpa (**39**)

Daubigny (1817-1878) was attracted to simple things, the shimmering waters of rivers and the silence of forests.

The harvest (**41**)

Gustave Courbet (1819-1877) was greatly inspired by the landscape and people of his native Ornans.

Burial at Ornans (**42**)
Painter in his studio (**43**)
Self-portrait (**44**)

The *Burial at Ornans* (1849) is perhaps the first real expression of Realism. Likened to his contemporary Émile Zola who developed the Realist novel, Courbet here depicts the real life of ordinary people from his home village, full of dignity and reverence whilst attending the funeral of a working man. The scale of the figures, standing upright against the horizontal elements of the composition, makes a bold statement to the glory of common people, 13 years before Victor Hugo was to do the same in literature.

Early Impressionism – *Second section of left gallery*. The new generation of artists, in reacting against the sombre shades used by their predecessors, set out to render the vibrations of light and to capture impressions of colour; hence their choice of subjects: sunlit gardens, snow, mist and flesh tones. Despite remaining susceptible to the charm of the forest of Fontainebleau, they chose to settle at Chailly, open to the advice proffered by the Barbizon group, yet independent of them.

Édouard Manet (1832-1883) was influenced by Spanish painting, experimenting boldly with composition and colour.

Olympia (**45**)
The balcony (**46**)
The fife player (**47**)

Le déjeuner sur l'herbe was shown at the 1863 Salon des Refusés. Despite having been inspired by Raphael's *Judgement of Paris* and recalling Giorgione's *Concert Champêtre* in the Louvre, Manet's naked Bourgeois figures depicted in a harsh uncompromising light scandalised contemporary audiences. Two years later, Manet was further to affront his public with *Olympia* who unlike her idealised nude Renaissance counterparts is depicted with realism, unashamedly naked.

Fantin-Latour (1836-1904) admired Manet and was on good terms with the Batignolles group. His portraits and flower compositions are particularly fine.

The corner of the table (**48**)

Frédéric Bazille (1841-1871) was fascinated by contrasting light effects.

A family reunion (**49**)

Claude Monet (1840-1926) was the true founder of the Impressionist movement *(see below)*.

The magpie (**51**)
Le déjeuner sur l'herbe (**52**)

Monet was once described by Cézanne as "only an eye, but my God what an eye!" a description that is apt when considering Monet's tendency to sacrifice form for atmosphere.

In 1870, Monet escaped the Franco-Prussian War by going to London, where he met up with Pissarro and saw works by John Constable (V & A) and J M W Turner (National Gallery) – he is said to have been unimpressed by either master. A year later he painted his celebrated canvas entitled *Impression-Sunrise* (on view in he musée Marmottan – *see* la MUETTE).

UPPER LEVEL

Impressionism
Access from the tower or by the escalator behind the tower.

The **Moreau-Nélaton Collection** includes such masterpieces as *Le déjeuner sur l'herbe* (53) by Manet, *Hommage à Delacroix* (54) by Fantin Latour, the *Foot-bridge at Argenteuil* (55), the *Poppy-field* and the *Railway ay Argenteuil* (56) by Monet.

The 1870 war prompted artists to disperse and to regroup in the Ile-de-France region: Pontoise, Auvers-sur-Oise... As the official Salons repeatedly rejected their paintings, they decided to show their work independently: the first exhibition was held in 1874 at the studio of the photographer **Nadar** where the term "impressionists" was first coined after Monet's *Impression-Sunrise*.

The Nabis (Bonnard, Vuillard and Maillol) rallied to Maurice Denis' directive: "*Remember that a picture, before being a horse, a nude, or some kind of anecdote, is essentially a flat surface covered with colours assembled in a certain order*".

UPPER LEVEL

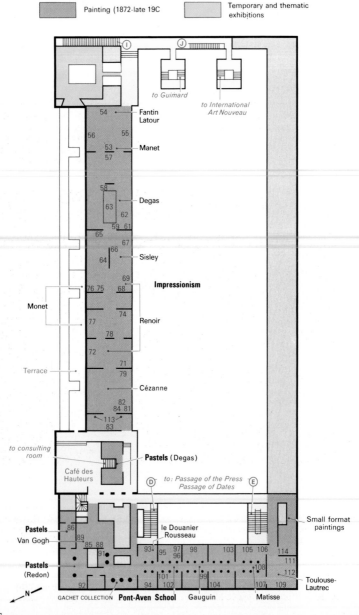

Caillebotte (1848-1894) showed canvases at several Impressionist exhibitions but he is better known as a patron of the arts: the Caillebotte bequest is part of the museum's Impressionist collections.

Planing the floor (**57**)

Edgar Degas (1834-1917) was a follower of Ingres. He remained aloof from the group until the end of the Second Empire, capturing the movement of racing horses or the world of theatre and dance under artificial lights rather than that of sunlight outdoors. His compositions betray his keen interest in photography and Japanese prints.

The dancing class (**58**)
The Laundresses (**59**)
Blue dancers (**61**)
The absinthe drinker (**62**)
Sculptures (**63**)

The real subject-matter of the *Blue Dancers* is the effort and exhaustion of dancers at work, and the apparent ease and grace they portray to mask the muscle-control and pain of their art.

The bronze sculptures, executed late in life, are cast from wax maquettes.

Pissarro (1830-1903) endlessly painted fields, hills, streets, hamlets peopled with idealised peasant women.

Red roofs (**64**)

Alfred Sisley (1839-1899) was of English descent but lived the last 20 years of his life at Moret-sur-Loing; fascinated by the light of the Paris region he painted landscapes with flowing water and scudding clouds.

Flooding at Port-Marly (**65**)
Snow scene at Louveciennes (**66**)

Auguste Renoir (1841-1919) was directed towards Impressionism by Monet in 1875. His art celebrates the joys of life, imbuing his bathing female nudes with sensual charm.

Le Moulin de la Galette (**68**)
Nude study (**69**)
Young girls at the piano (**71**)
Dance in the City and Dance in the Country (**72**)

Bal du Moulin de la Galette by Auguste Renoir

Musée d'Orsay, Paris/RMN

Claude Monet (1840-1926) was the leading exponent of Impressionism. His paintings seem to capture the very atmosphere of landscapes he visited. In 1883 he settled at Giverny where he explored the subject of his Nympheas.

The Houses of Parliament, London in the mist (**73**)
Women with a parasol (**74**)
Saint-Lazare station (**75**)
Rue Montorgueil (**76**)
Rouen Cathedral (**77**)
Blue water-lilies (**78**)

Paul Cézanne (1839-1906) returned to Aix-en-Provence after spending several years with Pissarro at Auvers. His portrayals of landscape tend to be constructed around simplified geometrical volumes (cone, sphere, cylinder) shaded with tones of colour.

L'Oncle Dominique (**79**)
Still-Life apples and oranges (**81**)
The card-players (**82**)
Woman with a coffee pot (**83**)

L'Estaque, view of the gulf of Marseilles, 1878 (**84**) shows one of Cézanne's favourite subjects worked as a study of light, colour, form and space on a flat ground: concepts to be explored subsequently by Gauguin and the Cubists. Note also *The house of the hanged man.*

Vincent van Gogh (1853-1890) was Dutch. He only took up painting in 1880 after visiting the Borinage countryside. Influenced by Impressionism, he lightened his palette and discovered the luminosity of Provence. His disturbed mind led him to suicide at Auvers-sur-Oise *(see the Michelin Green Guide to Flanders, Picardy and the Paris Region)* despite the friendship of Dr Gachet and his intense correspondence with his brother Theo. *Self-portrait* (**85**), *A woman of Arles* (**86**), *The church at Auvers-sur-Oise* (**88**), *La Meridienne after Millet* (**89**), *Portrait of Dr Gachet* (**91**).

The *Self-portrait* betrays the mental anguish of the 30-year-old artist in the bold lines and almost violent colour contrasts. Note also *A room at Arles* and *Woman with a coffee-pot.*

Musée d'Orsay/EDIMEDIA

Church at Auvers by Van Gogh

Late-19C post-Impressionist painting

Pastels – Chalks and crayons became popular with several artists namely Degas, Redon, Manet, as a means of drawing with pure colour; it is best suited to sketching landscape, portraiture, still-life and genre scenes.

Redon (1840-1916) portrays his fantastical world of Symbolism.

The Buddha (**92**)

Henri Rousseau (1844-1910) – 'Le Douanier' occupies a singular place in the history of art with his distinctively naïve allegorical paintings.

War (**93**)
The snake charmer (**94**)

The Pont-Aven School – The charming Breton village of Pont-Aven attracted the likes of Gauguin, Émile Bernard, Sérusier and Lacombe who together formulated a new style by eliminating detail, simplifying forms and using flat, bright colours.

Gauguin (1848-1903), after making several visits to Pont-Aven, travelled to the South Seas where he was captivated by the beauty of the landscape and the charm of the people.

Les Alyscamps (**95**)
La belle Angèle (**96**)
Self-portrait with the yellow Christ (**97**)
Tahitian women (**98**)
The white horse (**99**)

Aréaréa, Joyeusetés – Mystical names and traditional block-printed fabrics complement the stylised representaion of the native women of Tahiti that so charmed Gauguin.

Émile Bernard (1868-1941) abandoned detail for the sake of form.

Madeleine au Bois d'Amour (**101**)
Breton ladies with parasols (**102**)

Neo-Impressionism – Divisionism or Pointillism merely shares with Impressionism a concern for suggesting light by means of dabs of pigment. Here small dots of pure colour are painstakingly juxtaposed to evoke shimmering light.

Seurat (1859-1891) evolved the theory of Divisionism.

Circus (**103**)

The *Circus* was left incomplete at Seurat's death in 1891. It clearly demonstrates the scientific use of spectrum colours to achieve luminosity and movement. Note the contrasts between the texture of the swinging acrobats and that of the mesmerised spectators.

Paul Signac (1863-1935) concentrated on intensifying luminosity.

The red buoy (**104**)
The Papal palace (**105**)

Maximilien Luce (1858-1941) paints cityscapes, the working classes engaged in menial tasks.

Notre Dame de Paris (**106**)

H E Cross (1856-1910) developed an assured and vigorous technique.

Evening (**107**)

Matisse (1869-1954) stands between the neo-Impressionists and Fauves.

Luxe, calme et volupté (**108**)

Toulouse-Lautrec (1864-1901) was a keen observer of Montmartre's night life whose spirit he captured in sketches of people.

Jane Avril dancing (**109**)
The clown Cha-U-kao (**111**)
The bed (**112**)
The La Goulue panels (**113**)

Note in passing *The Talisman* (**114**) by Sérusier, the painting that formulated the Nabis painting style *(see below)*.

Passage of the Press – The selection of contemporary newspapers shows the move towards a more democratic press, the introduction of advertising and broadsheets; slowly articles were introduced with features on sport and gastronomy as were serialisation of novels and more illustrations.

Passage of Dates – *Below the Passage of the Press.*
Panels trace the historical events arising from a particular date, event or painting.

Photography and cinema – About 13 000 photographs testify to the wealth of talented photographers at home in France and abroad from the invention of the daguerotype in 1839 to the First World War. The early days of the cinema are represented by the praxinoscope, the photochronograph, Edison's praxinoscope and public film shows.

MIDDLE LEVEL

Painting and sculpture
from the proclamation of the Third Republic to 1914
Left wing, first half beyond the reception hall.

The hotel's reception hall and dining room now used as the museum's restaurant have retained their decorative paintings, sculpture and gilding.

Naturalism, History painting and Symbolism – The official style favoured by the **Third Republic** tended to sentimental depictions of events or episodes from contemporary life. This genre evolved out of Pre-Raphaelite painting in England and pedestrian Academy painting. In reaction to this naturalism and to Impressionism evolved Symbolism, in which the realms of fantasy, poetry, religion and opium-induced dreams take on the attributes of reality.

Jules Lefebvre (1836-1912) won great acclaim for his idealised female nudes.

The Truth (**116**)

Bouguereau (1825-1905), inspired by Raphael, sought to define his allegorical and mythological subjects with pure line and clear forms.

Birth of Venus (**117**)

Gérôme (1824-1904) was primarily an Academic painter turning to sculpture only at the end of his life.

Tanagra (**118**)

MIDDLE LEVEL

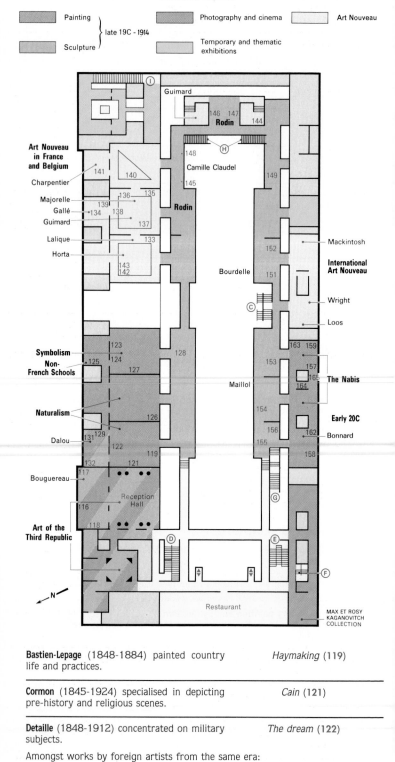

Painting ⎫
Sculpture ⎬ late 19C - 1914
Photography and cinema
Temporary and thematic exhibitions
Art Nouveau

Guimard

146 147 144
Rodin

Art Nouveau in France and Belgium

Charpentier — 141   140

Majorelle — 136   135
Gallé — 139   138
Guimard — 134

Lalique — 133

Horta — 143 142

148
Camille Claudel
145
Rodin
149

152 **Mackintosh**

International Art Nouveau

Bourdelle 151

Wright

Loos

Symbolism
Non-French Schools — 125 123 124 127

128

163 159
153   157   165
164   **The Nabis**

Maillol

Naturalism

154   **Early 20C**

Dalou — 131 129   126   156 162 — **Bonnard**

122 119 155

132 121 158

117
Bouguereau

Reception Hall

116

118

Art of the Third Republic

N

Restaurant

MAX ET ROSY KAGANOVITCH COLLECTION

Bastien-Lepage (1848-1884) painted country life and practices.   *Haymaking* (119)

Cormon (1845-1924) specialised in depicting pre-history and religious scenes.   *Cain* (121)

Detaille (1848-1912) concentrated on military subjects.   *The dream* (122)

Amongst works by foreign artists from the same era:

Böcklin (1827-1901), from Switzerland, suggests his love of Italy in his mythological paintings.   *Diana the huntress* (123)

Burne-Jones (1833-1898), from England, greatly admired Botticelli and Michelangelo; his subjects are taken from medieval legends.

The Wheel of Fortune (**124**)

Klimt (1892-1918), from Austria, developed a style that is perhaps more decorative than pictorial, stylising forms that are lost in flattened space.

The rosetrees (**125**)

Breitner (1857-1923) painted history pictures and scenes of Old Amsterdam.

Two white horses drawing a load in Amsterdam (**126**)

Homer (1836-1910) was American. This naturalist painter was famous for his country scenes and for his colourful and powerful paintings of the sea.

Summer evening (**127**)

Monumental sculpture – Following the proclamation of the Third Republic on 4 September 1870, commissions for the decoration of new buildings, commemorative busts and statues proliferated. Some artists turned to history and mythology while others found inspiration in daily life. Exaggerated gesture and expression mark a revival of the Baroque style.

Frémiet (1824-1910) pays attention to historical detail.

St Michael (**128**)

Meunier (1831-1905) portrays life at work at sea, in factories and down the mines.

Harvest (**129**)

Dalou (1838-1902) was one of the great 19C naturalist sculptors.

Peasant (**131**)
Bacchanal (**132**)

Art Nouveau – *left wing, 2nd half and part of right wing.* A desire for change and for a new form of expression away from the past swept through Europe in around 1890, most notably affecting architecture and the applied arts, namely Art Nouveau or the Modern Style. This movement associated with industrial progress is characterised by serpentine lines and organic decoration. 'Art in everything', a fundamental concept to the style, broke down distinctions between artist and craftsman, painter and decorator, to achieve the most complete design.

In France Art Nouveau was launched by the Nancy School, an association of artists and craftsmen founded by Emile Gallé.

Lalique (1860-1945) after studying sculpture and painted wall-papers, turned his hand to moulded glass and jewellery. His distinctive designs drawn from plants, fuse gold with silver, ivory, enamel, polished stone and glass in combinations of colour and surface texture.

Pendant and chain (**133**)

Gallé (1846-1904) started as a master glazier before working in ceramics and wood intarsia.

Vases
Cabinet with dragonflies (**134**)
Ornamental platter (**135**)

Majorelle (1859-1926) decorated his mahogany furniture with gilded bronze orchids and water-lilies.

Writing desk and bookcase (**136**)
Bed (**137**)

Gruber (1870-1930) worked in various fields before specialising in stained glass.

Door of Nancy's fitting-room (**138**)

Carabin (1862-1932) fantastical furniture is purely sculptural.

Bookcase (**139**)

Charpentier (1856-1909) was a sculptor and medal maker.

Dining-room (**141**)

Guimard (1867-1942) is most often associated with iron street furniture and the métro station entrances.

Cast-iron motifs

Van de Velde (1863-1957) designed functional houses and furniture in Belgium, while remaining true to line continuity and design. His chairs exhibit a particularly clean elegance.	*Writing desk and armchair* (**142**)

Horta (1861-1947), both architect and decorator, demonstrate a sober yet fantastical style.	*Panelling* *(Hotel Aubecq, Brussels)* (**143**)

International Art Nouveau – From 1880 the first examples of Art Nouveau appeared in England and soon spread to other parts of Europe (Glasgow, Vienna) and to the United States.

Michael Thonet (1796-1871) manufactured furniture in stained beech in Vienna.	*Bentwood furniture* *(in the tower)* (**144**)

C R Mackintosh (1868-1928) was both architect and designer famous for his complete schemes for domestic and public interiors (Argyle Street, Glasgow).	*Table, bed, chest of drawers and mirror*

F L Wright (1867-1959) reinstated detached housing with his "prairie" houses. Seating plays an important role in room layouts (Chicago).	*Chairs*

Loos (1870-1933) favoured straight lines and stark volumes.	*Bedroom suite*

Rodin and his followers – *2nd part of terrace.*

Rodin (1840-1917) – The closing years of the 19C were marked by Rodin's strong personality as suggested through the works displayed. During the 1880s he undertook a series of portrait busts *(Laurens, Victor Hugo)* including one allegory modelled on Camille Claudel (*Thought* **145**). *The Gates of Hell* (**146**) comprises several pieces, worked as individual units as well as part of a whole: *The Thinker, the Kiss, Fugit Amor* and *Ugolin and his children*, a moving composition full of anguish. *Balzac* (**147**) Rodin felt was a true expression of his own art, representing the great novelist in an abstracted pose that contrasts with the brilliance of his creative genius. Of his pupils, Desbois remained faithful to the master's style while Bartholomé and Bourdelle turned back towards the monumentality of the Antique.

Camille Claudel (1864-1943) was Rodin's collaborator and Muse.	*Old age* (**148**)

Medardo Rosso (1858-1928), sensitive to Impressionism, experimented with texture and the vibration of light, preferring to model in wax thereby capturing fleeting impressions of movement and agility.	*Ecce Puer* (**149**)

Antoine Bourdelle (1861-1929) was greatly inspired by Antiquity and Romanesque sculpture.	*Hercules with a bow* (**151**) *Apollo* (**152**)

Aristide Maillol (1861-1944) moulded strong, rounded, young female figures.	*The Mediterranean* (**153**) *Monument to Cézanne* (**154**)

Joseph Bernard (1866-1931) returned to more primitive forms, hewing carvings from blocks of wood and stone.	*Dancing woman and child* (**155**) *Dance* (**156**)

The Nabis – This group of painters whose name is derived from the Hebrew for prophet, rallied around Paul Sérusier (1864-1927) who painted *The Talisman* (*see above*), the Nabis pictorial manifesto under the direction of Gauguin in October 1888 at Pont-Aven. All the artists involved were concerned as much with easel paintings as with large decorative panels, book illustration, prints, stage sets... Post 1900 the group tended towards softer colours and more complex composition on a larger scale.

Maurice Denis (1870-1943) published pamphlets outlining the group's aspirations; his paintings tend to represent a mystical view of everyday life.	*The Muses* (**157**)

Pierre Bonnard (1867-1947) used sinuous line, unusual perspective and patterning, often affiliated to the influence of Japanese wood-block prints.

In a boat (**158**)
A game of croquet (**159**)
Women in a garden (**140**)
The balcony (**162**)

Edouard Vuillard (1868-1940) dispels a certain charm in his depiction of domestic or street scenes.

Public gardens (**163**)

Félix Vallotton (1865-1925) discarded his dark naturalistic painting style for wood-block printing, with simplified forms and a paler palette largely in reaction to the 1890 exhibition of Japanese art.

The balloon (**164**)
In bed (**165**)

PALAIS-ROYAL★★

Michelin plan 11 – folds 19, 30 and 31: G 12, G 13 – H 13

In this part of Paris the Palais-Royal, the Bibliothèque Nationale and St-Roch Church remind one vividly of the city's past, in contrast to the rue de Rivoli which seems to epitomize the present.

★★PALAIS-ROYAL

place du Palais-Royal. Ⓜ *Palais-Royal-Musée du Louvre. Buses: 21, 27, 39, 48, 67, 69, 72, 81, 85, 95*

The Cardinal's Palace – In 1624, Richelieu, having just become Prime Minister, acquired a mansion near the Louvre with grounds extending to the Charles V perimeter wall. In 1632 he commissioned the architect Jacques Lemercier to build the huge edifice known as the Cardinal's Palace.

The Royal Palace – The Cardinal on his deathbed in 1642 left his mansion to Louis XIII who soon followed him to the grave. His widow, Anne of Austria, with her young son, the future Louis XIV, then quit the Louvre for the smaller and more comfortable, beautiful mansion which henceforth became known as the Royal Palace. The Fronde in 1648 forced their hasty departure. When Louis XIV returned to Paris he settled back in the Louvre, lodging Queen Henrietta Maria of France, widow of Charles I of England, and then her daughter, Henrietta, in the Palais-Royal.

The Orléans – After a sudden fatal illness had struck Henrietta, the palace was given in apanage to her husband Philippe of Orléans, brother of Louis XIV. He was followed by his son, Philippe II of Orléans, Regent during the minority of Louis XV, a highly gifted but also highly dissolute man whose palace suppers were notorious.
In 1780 the palace passed to Louis-Philippe of Orléans, who being forever short of money undertook to redevelop the site: around three sides of the garden he commissioned **Victor Louis** to build uniformly fronted blocks of apartments over arcades of shops at ground level. Three new streets were called after the younger Orléans brothers: Valois, Montpensier and Beaujolais. The palace precinct became the favourite idling place for Parisians. Between 1786 and 1790 the same architect, Victor Louis, was commissioned by Philippe-Égalité to build the Théâtre-Français (now the Comédie-Française) and the Palais-Royal Theatre at the corner of rues de Montpensier and Beaujolais (now a vaudeville theatre).
After the Revolution, the palace became a gambling house until, in 1801, Napoleon converted it into offices, and in 1807 into the Exchange and Commercial Court.
Louis XVIII returned the mansion to the Orléans family and it was from there that Louis-Philippe set out for the Hôtel de Ville, in 1830, to be proclaimed king.

The garden formerly – In the 18C it was the setting for cafés which attracted a varied clientele: a circus, a riding school, a dance hall, a theatre until this went up in flames, a wax museum, funfair attractions and gambling houses.
During the Revolution, the garden became a popular meeting-place. It was here that **Camille Desmoulins** distributed to the rabble chestnut leaves for their hats, as symbols of hope for the new era; that Charlotte Corday purchased the dagger that was to kill Marat; that Bonaparte was to engage upon his first conquest...
The July monarchy closed the gaming houses in 1838 and the popularity of the arcade shops began to decline. The Commune eventually set the buildings on fire, which were later restored (1872-1876).

The palace – Richelieu's palace now accommodates the Ministry of Culture and the Council of State *(closed to the public)*. The quiet garden has retained its 18C atmosphere. The façade overlooking the square consists of a central block with two recessed lateral wings, the whole decorated with restrained, 18C carvings of military trophies and allegorical figures by Pajou.

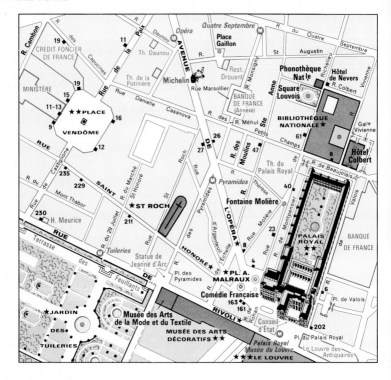

The east wing accommodated Richelieu's theatre, for which Molière created several of his major plays. Indeed, he was engaged in a performance here of *Le Malade Imaginaire* when he collapsed, dying in 1673. It later became an opera house staging works by Lulli until it was burnt down in 1763.

Another theatre was subsequently constructed at **202** rue St-Honoré, but that too was destroyed by fire in 1781, forcing the Opéra Company to move to boulevard St-Martin *(see GRANDS-BOULEVARDS)*.

At no **6**, rue de Valois with its fine balcony, Richelieu conducted the early sessions of his new foundation, the French Academy (1638). Nearby is the quiet place de Valois on the site of the palace's former outbuildings.

Main courtyard – Enter by the covered passage. Enclosed within a continuous arcaded gallery, it is dominated by an impressive central façade, surmounted by allegorical statues. A monumental modern composition (280 black and white columns of unequal height) by **Daniel Buren** fills the central space. Separating the courtyard from the garden is a double colonnade, the Orléans Gallery, built at the time of the Restoration (1814-1830) and formerly covered by an iron and glass roof. It presently accommodates two sculpture-fountains by Pol Bury.

The Valois side gallery is known as the Prow Gallery because of its nautical decoration (Richelieu was minister for the navy).

★★The garden – It is overlooked by the elegant façades designed by the architect Victor Louis. There are specialist shops in the arcade: soft furnishings, coins and medals, porcelain, postage stamps...

On the grass by the palace, on a pedestal behind a statue, stands a toy cannon, known as the Palais-Royal cannon. From 1786 until 1914 it used to go off at midday provided the sun, when reflected through a magnifying glass, was hot enough to ignite the charge. It was restored to working order in 1990.

★Place André-Malraux – From this altogether Parisian crossroads – formerly known as the place du Théâtre-Français – created in the time of Napoleon III and ornamented with modern fountains, there is a splendid view up the avenue de l'Opéra.

Comédie-Française – *2 rue de Richelieu*. In 1680 Louis XIV combined the former Molière company with that at the Hôtel de Bourgogne *(see les HALLES-BEAUBOURG – St-Eustache)* and granted it the sole right of performance in the capital. The new company took the name Comédie-Française.

The company, however, found itself the object of hostility simultaneously from the Sorbonne and the orthodox, compelling it to move home frequently – from the Guénégaud *(see ST-GERMAIN DES PRÉS – Institut de France)* to the rue de l'Ancienne-Comédie *(see LUXEMBOURG – Odéon)*, the Tuileries Palace and the Odéon.

At the Revolution a dispute broke out in the company between players who supported the Republicans and those favouring the Royalists. In 1792 the former, led by Talma, took over this theatre. Napoleon showed a great interest in the Comé-die-Française, in the tragedian Talma – and also in the leading lady, Mlle Mars. In 1812 he decreed that the company should consist of an association of actors, active associates, apprentice players and retired players on pension. Today the theatre continues to be managed by a director nominated by the State. On 21 February 1830 the company, playing *Hernani*, was involved in the famous battle – a battle of taste – which marked Victor Hugo's triumphal *début* as a playwright.

The repertoire of the Comédie-Française has, by tradition, been Classical, with set rules in style of acting and in interpretation – Molière, Corneille, Racine, Marivaux, Musset, Beaumarchais. Recently, however, works by foreign and 20C French authors have been admitted – Pirandello, Claudel, Giraudoux, Anouilh...

In the foyer are Houdon's famous bust of **Voltaire★★** and the chair in which Molière was sitting when taken fatally ill on stage.

Rue de Richelieu – At no **23bis** lived and died Pierre Mignard (1612-1695), painter to Anne of Austria. The 19C **Molière** fountain by Visconti with statues by Pradier stands just before no **40**, the site of Molière's house, to which he was taken after collapsing on stage on 17 February 1673 at the age of 51. No **61** served as home to Henri Beyle (1783-1842), more commonly known as **Stendhal**, where he wrote his novels *Le Rouge et le Noir* and *Promenades dans Rome*.

Note at no **8**, rue des Petits-Champs, through the grille the courtyard and sombre brick and stone façade of the Tubeuf mansion built by Le Muet in 1633. Opposite stands Colbert's mansion (1665) now an annexe of the National Library. At street level the charming 19C **Colbert Arcade** illustrates by means of window displays the various activities of the National Library.

★**Bibliothèque Nationale de France** – *58 rue de Richelieu*. In the Middle Ages the kings of France accumulated manuscripts in their palaces; Charles V mustered nearly 1 000 volumes in the Louvre Library, dispersed at his death; Charles VIII and Louis XII built their libraries at Blois.

The present national collection was founded upon François I's library from Fontainebleau, endowed with a copy of every book subsequently printed in France, as decreed in 1537. Today it includes records and photographs.

In the 17C the Hôtel Tubeuf was enlarged by Mansart and named after Cardinal Mazarin whose 500 pictures and personal decorative art collection it housed. Opposite, Colbert installed the Royal Library's 200 000 volumes (1666) in his own mansion in the rue Vivienne. In 1720, this collection was moved in with the Mazarin collection. The Nevers and Chivry mansions were taken over in the 19C.

The Library today

The Bibliothèque Nationale, pending its transfer to its new purpose-built location in Tolbiac, is divided into the following departments:

Printed Books: About 12 million volumes dating from the 15C and including two Gutenberg bibles, first editions of Villon, Rabelais, Pascal... The central store-room comprises 11 levels and 240km – 149 miles of shelving. The reading room designed by Labrouste is an architectural masterpiece (19C).

Manuscripts: papyri, Dead Sea scrolls, illuminated manuscripts including Char-lemagne's Gospel, Charles the Bald's Bible and St Louis' Psalter; parchments, letters, MSS of Hugo, Proust, Pasteur and Marie Curie...

Engravings and Photographs: This is the richest collection in the world counting over 12 million engravings and 2 million photographs.

Maps and Plans: 13C-20C atlases, *mappa mundi*...

Coins, Medals and Antiques: Cameos, bronzes and objets d'art. This department is also responsible for research into treasure troves discovered in France.

Music and Record Library: Records, tapes and talking machines.

The east side of the main courtyard is by the 18C architect, Robert de Cotte. The reading room (1868) – *reader card-holders only* – can be seen through a window. At the end of the hall on the right is the Mansart Gallery *(free access during exhibitions)* – an interim home for the Stock Exchange after the collapse of John Law's bank *(see* les HALLES-BEAUBOURG – la Bourse*)* – and opposite, the State Room with the plaster *maquette* for the marble bust of Voltaire by Houdon at the Comédie-Française (the philosopher's heart is enclosed in the base).

The great staircase leads to the **Medals and Antiques Museum★** ☉ *(mezzanine level)*: exhibiting amongst others, *objets d'art* requisitioned or confiscated from royal collections at the time of the Revolution. Note the ivory chess-sets, Dagobert's legendary throne, the Sainte-Chapelle Cameo and coins. On the floor above is the magnificent **Mazarin Gallery★** by Mansart *(access during temporary exhibitions)*.

Square Louvois – Presently the square accommodates a fine fountain by Visconti (1884). In 1793, the Opéra Company moved into the Hôtel Louvois; it remained there until 1820, when the premises were burnt down following the murder of the duc de Berry at the hands of a certain Louvel; it subsequently moved to rue Le Peletier.

The former **Hôtel de Nevers**, on the corner, was designed by Mansart and has served to accommodate in turn Mazarin's personal library, Mme de Lambert's literary salon (18C), and the royal medal collection.

Rue Ste-Anne – no **47** is the house the composer Lulli had built in 1671, borrowing 11 000 *livres* from Molière to do so. Note the music masks and motifs ornamenting the façade.

Rue des Moulins gets its name from the windmills which stood high upon the mound of public waste like the neighbouring Butte St-Roch. The ground was cleared in 1668, and the Radet mill *(see MONTMARTRE)* was moved to Montmartre.

The short **rue Méhul** leads to what was the old Ventadour Theatre, inaugurated in 1838 with a melodrama, *Ruy Blas*, written for the occasion by Victor Hugo in 30 days! It is now an annexe of the Banque de France.

Place Gaillon – The original fountain was erected in 1707 but remodelled by Visconti in 1827. The **Restaurant Drouant** is probably best known as the place from which the winners of the much acclaimed Goncourt Literary Prize are announced each autumn.

★RUE ST-HONORÉ Ⓜ *Tuileries, Pyramides*

The **Feuillants Monastery**, which had grounds extending to the Tuileries riding school, augmented its income by building an apartment house which can still be seen between nos **235** and **229**. It was here that the short-lived Feuillants Club of moderates who, in line with La Fayette, Bailly, Sieyès and Talleyrand, dissociated themselves from the extremist Jacobin group, met in 1791.

No **211** is the former **Hôtel de Noailles** where General La Fayette married one of the daughters of the house in 1774. It is now the St James and Albany Hotel. On the left there used to be a **Jacobin Monastery** (a Dominican order of St James), taken over in 1789 by a club that took its name; this became famous during the Revolution under the leadership of Robespierre, who lived nearby at no 398 in the Duplay household.

The rue du Marché St-Honoré now cuts across the site of the monastery church; a covered market, dating back to 1810 and now being renovated by Ricardo Bofill, occupies the ground on which the monastery once stood.

★**Église St Roch** – *no 269*. St-Roch was the scene on 13 Vendémiaire – 5 October 1795 – of bloody fighting. A column of royalists leading an attack on the Convention, then in the Tuileries, aimed to march through the rue St-Roch. Bonaparte, who was in charge of the defence, however, mowed down the men massed on the church steps and perched on its façade with gunfire. The bullet holes can still be seen.

Some idea of the scale of Baron Haussmann's earth-moving undertakings can be gained from the fact that to enter the church nowadays you have to walk up 13 steps, whereas before the construction of the Opera Avenue, you had to go down seven.

The foundation stone of the church dedicated to Saint Roch or Rocco (c1350-c1380), the patron saint of the plague-stricken often represented with the dog that tended his sores, was laid by Louis XIV in 1653. The elevated Moulins site compelled the architect, Lemercier, to orientate the church on a north-south axis rather than the more usual east-west.

Funds quickly ran dry but work was able to continue as a result of a lottery organised in 1705. Instead of completing the nave however, a series of chapels was constructed beyond the apse, extending the church from the planned 80m to 125m – 262ft to 410ft (5m – 16ft shorter than Notre-Dame) thereby destroying any unity of design.

The **Lady Chapel**★ by Jules Hardouin-Mansart, with its tall, richly decorated dome, leads into a Communion Chapel with a flat dome and finally a Calvary Chapel, *(closed for restoration)* rebuilt in the 19C.

In 1719 a gift of 100 000 *livres* from John Law *(see les HALLES – BEAUBOURG)*, who had recently converted to Catholicism, enabled the nave to be completed. Robert de Cotte's Jesuit-style façade dates from 1736.

Among those buried in St-Roch in the Lady Chapel and side chapels are the playwright Corneille, the garden designer Le Nôtre, the Abbot de l'Épée, the philosophers Diderot and d'Holbach, and Mme Geoffrin, hostess of a famous 18C *salon*. The 17C mariner, Duguay-Trouin, has been transferred to Saint-Malo.

Works of Art:

1) Tomb of Henri of Lorraine, Count d'Harcourt by Renard (17C) and bust of the 17C Marshal de Créqui by **Coysevox** (17C).

2) Funeral monument of the astronomer Maupertuis by d'Huez, and statue of Cardinal Dubois by **Guillaume Coustou**.

3) Tomb of Duke Charles de Créqui.

4) Godefroy de Bouillon Victorious by **Claude Vignon** (17C). Funerary plaque to Duguay-Trouin.

5) *The Triumph of the Virgin* painted by J B Pierre on the dome *(illumination: apply to the sacristan)*. The **Nativity★** at the altar by the Anguier brothers, was brought from the Val-de-Grâce.

6) *Resurrection of the Son of the Widow of Naïm* by *Le Sueur* (17C).

7) Le Nôtre bust by Coysevox and funerary inscription.

8) Monument to the Abbot de l'Épée (19C).

9) Bust of the painter Mignard and statue of his daughter by **Lemoyne** (18C).

10) *Baptism of Christ* by Lemoyne. Medallion by Falconet.

11) Baptismal Chapel: frescoes by Chassériau (19C).

Porte St-Honoré – Level with no **163** rue St-Honoré, stood a gate in the Charles V perimeter wall. It was here that **Joan of Arc** was wounded on 8 September 1429 when leading her attack on the capital.

She had already freed Orléans *(see Michelin Green Guide* CHÂTEAUX OF THE LOIRE) and accompanied the King to Reims for his coronation, but her task, as she saw it, was far from complete. Paris was still in the hands of the English under the Regent Bedford, who wished not only to retain the city but to make it safe enough to bring over the young Henry VI and crown him King of England and France in Notre-Dame.

The girl soldier paused to pray at the small St-Denis-de-la-Chapelle (the church, now remodelled, is at no 16, rue de la Chapelle, 18th *arr.*), before undertaking her attack on the fortified gate across a moat. Realising this would have to be filled in, she moved to measure the water's depth with her lance when she was wounded in the thigh by an arrow. She was taken to what is now **4** place André-Malraux while her men beat a hasty retreat. Henry VI was crowned nevertheless in Notre-Dame (1431).

Although this is the only episode linking *la Pucelle* with the capital there are, in addition to the medallion by Réal del Sarte on the Café de la Régence façade, four statues of her in the city (place des Pyramides, 16 rue de la Chapelle, place St-Augustin, 41 boulevard St-Marcel). For the most avid fans, it may be worth checking out a local café that celebrates her cult with kitsch!

The **Café de la Régence**, now at **161** rue St-Honoré, was founded in 1681 in the place du Palais-Royal; it was forced to move in 1854 when the square was enlarged.

★RUE DE RIVOLI

Ⓜ *Concorde, Louvre-Rivoli. Buses: 21, 67, 72, 74, 75, 76, 81, 85*

Between rue de Castiglione and place des Pyramides – The rue de Rivoli crosses the site of the former Tuileries **Riding School**. In 1789 the school was hastily converted into a meeting place for the Constituent Assembly. Sessions were subsequently held there by the Legislative Assembly and the Convention, until on 21 September 1792, the day following the French victory over the Prussians at Valmy (commemorative tablet on a pillar in the Tuileries railings opposite no **230**), it became the setting for the proclamation of the Republic and the trial of Louis XVI (1792).

It was Napoleon who, in 1811, had this part of the avenue constructed, although it was not to be completed until nearly the middle of the century. The houses facing the Tuileries are of uniform design above arcades lined with both luxury and souvenir shops.

Calvary Chapel

Holy Communion Chapel

Lady Chapel

5

Sacristy

CHANCEL

NAVE

Rue St-Honoré

17 C   18 C   19 C

In 1944 the German General von Choltitz, Commandant of Paris, who had his headquarters at the **hôtel Meurice** (no **228**), took a momentous decision in the capital's own history by refusing to follow Hitler's orders to blow up the capital's bridges and principal buildings when the tanks of General Leclerc's division and the Resistance were known to be approaching. He surrendered on 25 August and Paris was liberated intact. At the far end by the place de la Concorde several commemorative plaques record the heroism of those who fell during the Liberation.

Place des Pyramides – Just off rue des Pyramides in rue d'Argenteuil was where Corneille died in 1684; continue to the square. The equestrian statue of Joan of Arc is by the 19C sculptor, Frémiet.

On the right is the **Pavillon de Marsan**, which, with the Pavillon de Flore (reconstructed), is all that remains of the Tuileries Palace built by Philibert Delorme and Jean Bullant in the 16C for Catherine de' Medici and burnt down in 1871.

Musée des Arts de la Mode et du Textile ⊙ – *Pavillon de Marsan, 109 rue de Rivoli.* The collection encompasses over 12 500 outfits and 100 000 fabric samples dating from the 18C to the present day, displayed in changing exhibitions.

The **rue de l'Échelle** is so called after the ladder or flight of steps leading to a scaffold which stood on the site during the Ancien Régime. The ecclesiastical courts then sent polygamists, perjurers and blasphemers to the steps where they were exposed in shame before the public.

★★**Musée des Arts Décoratifs** ⊙ – *no 107*. The numerous exhibits provide a broad cross-section of the evolution of design and taste in the decorative and applied arts in France: sculpture, painting, furniture, soft furnishings, glass, tableware...

First floor: home décor from 1950 to the present, including a reconstruction of **Jeanne Lanvin**'s flat; Dubuffet Bequest including paintings, drawings and sculpture by the artist.

Second floor: furnishings from the Middle Ages to the Renaissance.

Third and fourth floors: fashionable domestic interiors from the reign of Louis XIV to the Second Empire.

Fifth floor: specialist departments (wallpaper, drawings...) and reference departments: fashion, textiles, glass, toys, crafts, toys, advertising...

Out of the museum and on the right, note the last section of the Louvre façade (remodelled during the Third Republic) to have been built, with its line of generals of the First Empire.

Rue de Rohan – The street runs over the original site of the Quinze-Vingts Hospital *(see* BASTILLE*)* for the blind which in the reign of Louis XVI was transferred by Cardinal de Rohan, the institution's administrator, to barracks in rue de Charenton where it remains to this day.

*Explore Paris with **Michelin Paris Transport Map** no 9 (bus, underground, urban rail network (RER), taxis, the main traffic routes...)*

*The **Michelin Paris Atlas** no 11 provides numbers for radio-taxis*
It also provides the telephone numbers of the taxi ranks in each arrondissement

---

PARC DES BUTTES-CHAUMONT★

Michelin plan 11 – fold 22: D 19, D 20 – E 19, E 20
Ⓜ *Buttes Chaumont. Buses: 26, 60, 75*

Le mont chauve – The denuded (literally *shaven*) rise of Chaumont, riddled with open quarrying and full of dumped rubbish, used to be a sinister place until Haussmann and Napoleon transformed the area with the very first park on the northern edge of Paris between 1864 and 1867.
A lake was created, fed by water from the canal St-Martin *(see* RÉPUBLIQUE*)* and landscaped with an island – built with huge rocks 50m – 150ft high half natural, half artificial. Access was provided by two bridges: one in brick – nicknamed the suicide bridge, the other a footbridge. A little temple on the island commands a good view over Montmartre and St-Denis. Additional 'folly' features include a waterfall and cave encrusted with stalactites.
It was here that the invading Prussian armies were halted in 1814.

A-de-Rothschild Ophthalmic Foundation – The home of the French eye bank stands at the corner of rue Manin and avenue Mathurin-Moreau.
Steps lead up to the streets that overlook the hospital and provide an attractive perspective towards Montmartre.

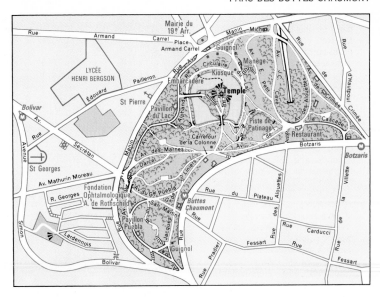

*For other gardens and green spaces,
consult INTRODUCTION – A different perspective over Paris.*

PARC MONCEAU ★

Michelin plan 11 – fold 17: E 9 – E 10
Ⓜ Monceau. Buses 30, 84, 94

Parc Monceau – In 1778 the Duke of Chartres, the future Philippe-Egalité, commissioned the painter-writer Carmontelle to design a garden on the Monceau Plain,
then rich in game.

The artist created a land of dreams, scattered with follies in keeping with English and German landscaped gardens of the period. A pyramid and a pagoda, a Roman Temple, medieval ruins, Dutch windmills, a Swiss farm, naumachia and mounds, linked by a network of
paths are set amongst ornamental ponds and copses in the undulating landscape.

At the Revolution, the Monceau park – in which Garnerin, the world's first para-
chutist, was to land on 22 October 1797 – passed to the lawyer and statesman
Cambacérès before reverting to the Orléans family (who had shed their title for
political reasons). Major changes were involved in 1852 when the financier, Pereire,
sold part of the park for the building of luxurious houses; 10 years later, the engineer Alphand further transformed a section into an English-style garden.

The rotunda, with its fine wrought-iron gates at the entrance, known as the
Chartres Pavilion, is what remains of one of Ledoux's toll-houses built in the Farm-
ers-General perimeter wall (*see* INTRODUCTION – Urban development). Many statues nestle amongst the greenery and mature trees with varied foliage.

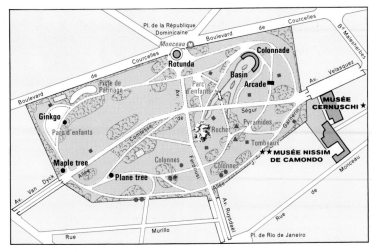

The oval **naumachia basin** is modelled on the Roman pools constructed for the simulation of naval battles, its decorative colonnade borrowed from the never-completed mausoleum of Henri II at St-Denis. Nearby is a Renaissance arcade that once stood in front of the Hôtel de Ville.

★★**Musée Nissim de Camondo** ⊙ – *63 rue de Monceau*. In 1936 Count de Camondo presented his house and 18C art collection to the nation in memory of his son Nissim, killed in the First World War. The house built in 1910 overlooks the adjoining Monceau Park at the rear.

The mansion preserves an elegant Louis XVI interior with panelled salons, furniture made by the greatest cabinet-makers (Riesener and Weisweiler), Savonnerie carpets and Beauvais tapestries, paintings by Guardi and Hubert Robert, gold and silver ornaments by the royal goldsmith, Roettiers and a se-

Riesener sideboard

lection of porcelain from the most famous factories (Vincennes, Meissen, Chantilly). Among the outstanding pieces are tapestries of the *Fables* of La Fontaine after cartoons by Oudry, a roll-top desk by Oeben and a splendid Sèvres porcelain service, known as the Buffon service, in which every piece is decorated with a naturalistic depiction of a different bird.

Although packed with exquisite furniture, the rooms appear quite uncluttered and retain much of the elegant yet intimate aura of a private house. Individual objects are poorly labelled, but an illustrated catalogue is available.

★**Musée Cernuschi** ⊙ – *7 avenue Vélasquez*. The banker Henri Cernuschi bequeathed his house and extensive collection of Oriental art to the City of Paris in 1896.

Devoted to ancient Chinese art the collection includes Neolithic terracottas, bronzes (the famous *Tigress* – wine flask in the shape of an animal crouching protectively over the clan patriarch) and archaic jades, ceramics, some fine funerary statuettes and pen and ink drawings. Note the 5C stone Bodhisattva and 8C Tang silk scroll painting illustrating *Horses and their Grooms*.

On the first floor, temporary exhibitions alternate with displays of traditional Chinese painting.

Musée Henner ⊙ – *43 avenue de Villiers*. Collected together in the Alsatian artist Jean-Jacques Henner's (1829-1905) house are paintings, drawings and sketches. Several portraits of members of his family and friends are real-

Horseman, Han dynasty

istically rendered. Landscapes full of clear, warm light evoke an early trip he made to Italy where he studied the works of Titian and Correggio. His larger canvases characterised by simple compositions and rigorous brushstokes, often depict languorous Romantic figures of nymphs.

An audio-visual display describes the artist's work and its development.

This guide, which is revised regularly,
is based on tourist information provided at the time of going to press
Changes are however inevitable owing to improved facilities and fluctuations
in the cost of living

PARC MONTSOURIS ★

Michelin plan 11 – fold 55: R 13 – S 13, S 14
Ⓜ *Porte d'Orléans /RER: Cité Universitaire*

The Montsouris Park and the Paris University Residential Campus form a large green open space to the south of the city.

★PARC MONTSOURIS

The park – Haussmann began work on this area undermined by quarries and capped by dozens of windmills, in 1868. By 1878 he had turned it into a park: the 16ha – 50 acres were landscaped 'English-style' with paths snaking up the mounds and circling the cascades, and a large artificial lake (the engineer specifically involved in the construction committed suicide, when the lake suddenly dried out on opening day).

The park is dominated by the **South bearing** (mire du Sud *on plan*) of the old Paris meridian (*see* PORT-ROYAL – l'Observatoire). The municipal meteorological observatory is housed in a building nearby.

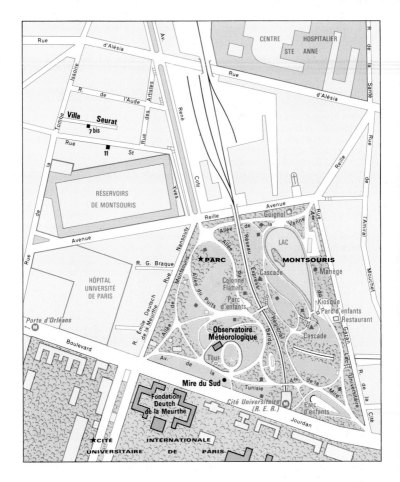

Beyond the park – Several of the smaller streets, some still cobbled, retain the peaceful air of past eras (rue des Artistes and rue St-Yves bordered by **Cité du Souvenir** at no 11).

At the turn of the century, painters attracted by the park's peace and its proximity to Montparnasse came to live here, notably Douanier Rousseau and Georges Braque, who had a studio (west of the park) in a street which now carries his name. During the inter-war period famous residents of the **Villa Seurat** included the artist Gromaire, Lurçat, Orloff the sculptor, Henry Miller (installed in Artaud's studio at no 18 by Anaïs Nin), Dalì and Soutine. No **7bis** was designed by Auguste Perret.

The avenues Reille and René Coty are overlooked by the Montsouris reservoirs with grass-covered sides and roofs. Collected here in these 100-year-old reservoirs are the waters of the Vanne, Loing and Lunain. Trout in aquaria vouch for the purity of the water which provides for half the city of Paris' supply.

271

> ### Villa Seurat
>
> In the 1930s American novelist **Henry Miller** immortalized this tranquil cul-de-sac (fictionalised as the Villa Borghese) in his controversial novel *Tropic of Cancer* (published in Paris in 1934 and banned in the USA and England until the 1960s). *…The whole street is given up to quiet, joyous work. Every house contains a writer, painter, musician, sculptor, dancer or actor. It is such a quiet street and yet there is such activity going on, silently…*

★CITÉ INTERNATIONALE UNIVERSITAIRE DE PARIS

Main entrance: 19-21 Boulevard Jourdan.

Since the Revolution when many of the student colleges in the Latin Quarter were swept away, accommodation has been a problem for undergraduates. This situation was further exaggerated by the reform of the Sorbonne into the University of France (*see* LATIN QUARTER).

Just before the 1914-1948 War, a French financier M Deutsch de la Meurthe allocated large funds for the institution of a "hall" on the lines of a British college, where students might live cheaply but comfortably and enjoy various shared amenities.

Paris University Residential Campus – The "city" on the edge of Montsouris Park spreads over an area of 40ha – 100 acres, housing over 5 500 students from 120 different countries in its 37 halls of residence. Each hall forms an independent community, its architecture and individual character frequently inspired by the country which founded it.

E-and-L-Deutsch-de-la-Meurthe Foundation – This was the very first hall to be built, inaugurated in 1925.

Maison Internationale (1936) with a swimming pool, theatre and vast rooms was sponsored by John D Rockefeller Jr.

The **Fondation Suisse** and **Fondation Franco-Brézilienne** were designed by Le Corbusier.

The **Fondation Avicienne** (Persian Foundation) is constructed to an interesting modern design (1968).

Église Sacré-Cœur – Built between 1931 and 1936 on the edge of the city parish boundary, it now stands on the far side of the boulevard périphérique in Gentilly, and is reached by a footbridge. Its façade has a relief by Saupique, dominated by a great belltower. Inside, its sober interior is striking, lit by a predominance of blue stained-glass windows.

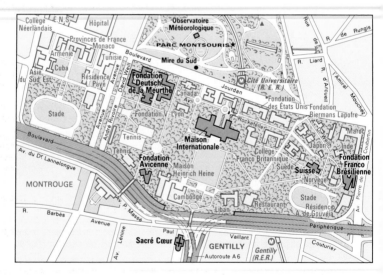

Keep us informed!

Send us your comments and suggestions
MICHELIN TYRE
Public Company Limited
Tourism Department – The Edward Hyde Building –
38 Clarendon Road – WATFORD –
Herts WD1 1SX

PASSY

Michelin plan 11 – fold 27: H 5, H 6 – J 5, J 6
Ⓜ *Trocadéro, Passy*

In the 13C Passy was a woodcutters' hamlet; in the 18C it became known for its ferruginous waters and in 1859 it was incorporated into the city of Paris.

The "Fellows of Chaillot" or bonshommes was the familiar name by which the Minim Friars, whose monastery stood on the hill until the Revolution, were known, presumably because of the red wine produced by the community and still recalled in the names of the rue Vineuse and rue des Vignes.

Today the houses in their own gardens that used to make up the peaceful residential quarter are being replaced by large blocks of flats.

Cimetière de Passy Ⓘ – *2 rue du Commandant-Schloesing*. Passy Cemetery, above place du Trocadéro, contains the graves of many famous figures, deceased since 1850, from the worlds of literature (Croisset, T Bernard, Giraudoux), painting (Manet, Berthe Morisot), music (Debussy, Fauré), aviation (Henry Farman) and film (Fernandel). In the chapel is the tomb of a 24-year-old Russian painter-cum-poet, Marie Bashkirtseff.

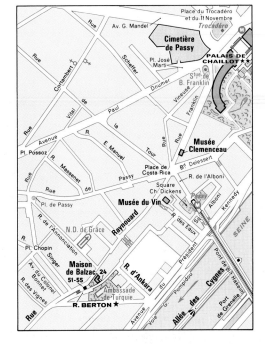

Musée Clemenceau Ⓘ – *8 rue Franklin*. The great man's apartment is as it was on the day of his death in 1929. Mementoes in a gallery on the first floor recall Georges Clemenceau's career as a journalist and statesman: the Montmartre mayoralty, the Treaty of Versailles and the premiership.

Allée des Cygnes – From halfway across the Bir-Hakeim Bridge there is access down to the man-made islet in the Seine. The Allée des Cygnes, or Swans' Walk, built at the time of the Restoration, provides a good view of the Maison Radio-France (*see* AUTEUIL) on the right and of the Front de Seine (*see* AUTEUIL) on the left with the Beaugrenelle mall. The figure of *France Renaissante* looking upstream is by the Danish sculptor, Wederkinch (1930) whilst a bronze replica of the Statue of Liberty faces downstream, rising tall above weeping willows (*see* AUTEUIL).

Musée du vin – Caveau des Échansons Ⓘ – *5-7 square Charles-Dickens*. No 5 rue des Eaux marks the original entrance to the former quarries. Under the Empire they were converted into France's first sugar beet refinery. The underground galleries now house a wine museum with waxwork figures and implements recalling the days when monks produced wine there.

Rue d'Ankara – The former château and grounds of Marie-Antoinette's devoted friend, the Princess of Lamballe, at the end on the left, is now occupied by the Turkish Embassy and private houses. In the 19C it belonged to Doctor Blanche, a specialist in mental illness who converted it into a home for the insane, and whose patients included the writers Maupassant and Nerval.

★**Rue Berton** – The rue Berton, on the left, is one of the most unusual in Paris, its ivy-clad walls and gas-light brackets giving it an old country town atmosphere. No 24 was the back entrance to Balzac's house.

Rue Raynouard – This street is full of historical interest. Many famous people have lived in this street named after an obscure academician of the Restoration, including Louis XIV's powerful financier Samuel Bernard, the Duke of Lauzun, Jean-Jacques Rousseau, the song-writer Béranger. It was at no 66 that Benjamin Franklin resided during his visit to France to negotiate an alliance with Louis XVI on behalf of the new Republic of the United States; he erected over his house the first lightning conductor in France!

The modern blocks of flats in reinforced concrete at nos 51 to 55 show a confident application of the new material by Auguste Perret who lived here from 1932 to his death in 1954.

Maison de Balzac ⓥ – *no 47.* Down its original metal stairway, half-hidden in a garden, is the house occupied illicitly by Honoré de Balzac, under the pseudonym of his governess Mme de Breugnol between 1840 and 1847; on the run from his creditors, the back route out of the house provided him with some security. Manuscripts, caricatures and engravings pertaining to the author of La Condition Humaine (the Human Comedy) described in his novels complement an adjoining library.

Cimetière du PÈRE-LACHAISE★★

Michelin plan 11 – folds 34, 35; H 20 – H 22
Boulevard de Ménilmontant. Ⓜ *Père-Lachaise. Buses: 26, 61, 69*

Cemetery – The Père Lachaise Cemetery ⓥ has become a popular place of pilgrimage, with visitors to Paris mingling with Parisians in the laying of flowers on the tombs of their loved ones. It is rarely completely deserted, especially since security has had to be implemented by the authorities to protect the grave of Jim Morrison from vandals and graffiti artists.

In 1626 the Jesuits bought a piece of land in the open countryside to build a retreat for retired priests. One frequent visitor to the place was Louis XIV's confessor, Father La Chaise, who gave generously to the house's reconstruction in 1682. The Jesuits were expelled in 1763. Forty years later, the city acquired the property for conversion to a cemetery.

On the evening of 27 May 1871 the last insurgents of the Paris Commune, having shot their hostages in Belleville, rallied in the cemetery. It was there among the tombstones that bitter fighting ensued with the

Cimetière du Père-Lachaise.

arrival of the men of Versailles. At dawn on 28 May, the 147 survivors were stood against the wall in the southeast corner – the **Federalists' Wall** (Mur des Fédérés) – and shot. They were buried where they fell in a communal grave – a place of pilgrimage for many ever since.

Paris' largest cemetery, designed by Brongniart, spreads over the sloping ground, the final resting place of many famous figures. A selection are pin-pointed here, but many including the likes of Maria Callas, Gertrude Stein and Alice B Toklas, Isadora Duncan, Richard Wright… have been left unmarked. A sculpture by Paul Landowski in the basement of the **Columbarium** is noteworthy.

An 'Américaine' in Paris

"Paris was where the twentieth century was"

American expatriates Gertrude Stein and Alice B Toklas lived just minutes from the Luxembourg Gardens at no 27 rue de Fleurus.

From 1903 to 1937, their courtyard apartment and atelier with its famed collection of paintings by contemporary masters hosted Paris' most avant-garde expatriate salon; their guest list reads like a Who's Who of the early 20C art and literary world: Picasso, Juan Gris, Matisse, Erik Satie, Hemingway, Pound, Sherwood Anderson… Although Gertrude Stein significantly influenced numerous expatriate writers (the term "*Lost Generation*" is attributed to her), international recognition for her own experimental works came only in 1933 with the publication of *The Autobiography of Alice B Toklas*.

In 1938 the two women moved nearby to no 5 rue Christine (in the Odéon quarter). Gertrude died in 1946 and was buried in Père Lachaise Cemetery. Alice joined her in 1967.

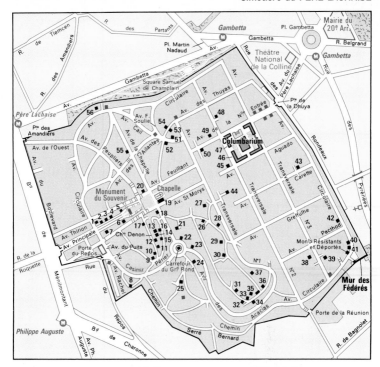

1 Colette.
2 Rossini (cenotaph).
3 A de Musset (in the shade of a willow, as he requested).
4 Baron Haussmann.
5 Generals Lecomte and Thomas.
6 Félix Faure.
7 Arago.
8 Abélard and Héloïse.
9 Miguel Ángel Asturias.
10 Gustave Charpentier.
11 Chopin.
12 Cherubini.
13 Boïeldieu (cenotaph).
14 Bernardin de Saint-Pierre.
15 Gréty.
16 Bellini.
17 Branly.
18 Géricault.
19 Thiers.

20 David.
21 C Bernard.
22 Monge.
23 Champollion.
24 Auguste Comte.
25 Jim Morrison.
26 Gay-Lussac.
27 Corot.
28 Molière and La Fontaine.
29 Alphonse Daudet.
30 Hugo family.
31 Bibesco family (Anna de Noailles).
32 Marshal Ney.
33 Beaumarchais.
34 Larrey.
35 Marshals Davout, Masséna, Lefebvre.
36 Murat and Caroline Bonaparte.
37 David d'Angers.

38 Modigliani.
39 Édith Piaf.
40 Henri Barbusse.
41 Paul Éluard, Maurice Thorez.
42 Gertrude Stein, Alice B Toklas.
43 Oscar Wilde.
44 Sarah Bernhardt.
45 Simone Signoret, Yves Montand.
46 Richard Wright.
47 Isadora Duncan.
48 Marcel Proust.
49 Guillaume Apollinaire.
50 Allan Kardec (founder of the Spiritualist movement).
51 Delacroix.
52 Michelet.
53 G de Nerval.
54 Balzac and the Countess Hanska.
55 Georges Bizet.
56 Georges Méliès.

★Église St-Germain-de-Charonne – *4 place St-Blaise (off the map, beyond the Mur des Fédérés)*. The church and square were once surrounded by vineyards, the focal point of the village of Charonne. The stunted bell tower dates from the 13C and has interesting carved capitals.
It was here that St-Germain-d'Auxerre met Geneviève, the future saint, in 429.

PORT-ROYAL

Michelin plan 11 – fold 43: L 13, L 14 – M 13, M 14
Michelin plan 11 – fold 42: N 12

The Port-Royal area extends from the Luxembourg gardens to the edge of the city. It once comprised various religious institutions which over the years have ceded to the expansion of the university *(see LATIN QUARTER)* and such academic bodies as the Observatory. The area was particularly refashioned by Haussmann as the city encroached upon disused quarries turned catacombs.

★★Quartier Val-de-Grâce Ⓜ/RER: Port-Royal. Buses 21, 27, 38, 83, 91

The "Valley of Grace" – This area is now devoted to medicine and higher education. The first half of the 17C saw the establishment of religious communities: in 1605, the **Carmelites** (no 284 rue St-Jacques) – amongst whom Louise de la Vallière retreated when no longer favoured by Louis XIV; in 1612, the **Ursulines;** in 1622, the **Feuillantines** founded by Anne of Austria; in 1626, the **Visitandines.** The same year, Mother Angélique Arnauld ordered the construction of **Port-Royal,** the dependency of the Jansenist Port-Royal-des-Champs.

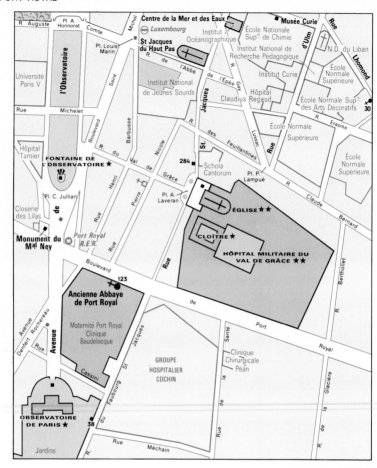

Ancienne abbaye de Port-Royal ⊙ – *123 boulevard de Port-Royal*. The cloisters have survived intact, as has the period woodwork in the chapter-house. In the church, built in 1646 rests the abbey's founder.

Val-de-Grâce – A few years after the foundation of the new Oratory congregation in rue St-Jacques in 1611, Anne of Austria bought the mansion to establish in it a Benedictine community which took the same name as its provincial convent, Val-de-Grâce. Anne visited the community frequently to pray and discreetly to intrigue against Richelieu. At 37, Anne, who had been married 23 years, was still childless; she promised the gift of a magnificent church if her prayers were answered, and kept her vow on the birth of Louis XIV in 1638. The plans for the Val-de-Grâce Church were drawn by **François Mansart**.

The foundation stone was laid by the young king himself in 1645. Anne, finding Mansart too slow, employed **Lemercier** to oversee the execution of his predecessor's designs, until his death. The building was at last completed by Le Muet in 1667 and consecrated in 1710 (Louis XIV was 72).

★★**Hôpital militaire du Val-de-Grâce** – All the 17C buildings of the former abbey remain. The Val-de-Grâce became a military hospital in 1795 and a medical school in 1850.

★★**L'église** ⊙ – The church, probably the most Roman-looking in France, was erected in the Jesuit style after the Sorbonne and before the Invalides. Its façade framed between consoles is articulated by pilasters supporting a double triangular pediment. Note the effective interplay of light on surfaces, alcoves and sculpture. The dome, shouldered by 16 pilasters is encrusted with carved elements (garlands, statues, composite capitals). Inside, the Baroque influence is apparent in the polychrome floor, the bold entablature between arcade and deeply coffered vault, the altar baldaquin with its six twisted barley-sugar columns. The **dome**★★ is frescoed by Mignard with 200 figures three times life-size. The sculpture is by Michel Anguier and Philippe Buyster.

The St-Louis Chapel (*right*) was originally the chancel used by the Benedictines. From 1662 the hearts of members of the royal and Orléans families were deposited in the St-Anne Chapel (*left*). When the caskets were desecrated at the Revolution there were 45, including those of Queen Marie-Thérèse, "Monsieur" (Philippe, Duke of Orleans), the Regent, Philippe of Orleans and Marie Leczinska. Most have disappeared.

Former convent – Beyond the porch (right of the church) is the Classical **cloister★**, with two superimposed tiers of bay and a *mansard* roof. The gardens, through the courtyard's second arch, are overlooked by the convent's majestic rear façade. The pavilion used by Anne of Austria is distinguished by its porch with ringed columns.

Museum – Displays include documents and mementoes of the great military physicians (Parmentier, premier pharmacist during the Empire; Villemin, Roussin, Broussais, Vincent, Laveran-Nobel Prizewinner, 1907) and the French Health Service. Models and equipment indicate treatment meted out to the wounded during the Empire and the First World War.

Schola Cantorum – *269 rue St-Jacques.* The conservatory was founded privately in 1896 by Charles Bordes, Guilmant and the composer Vincent d'Indy, to

Val-de-Grâce, the dome

restore church music. The buildings formerly belonged to a community of English Benedictines who sought refuge in Paris after the Anglican Schism of 1531; the body of James II, who died in exile at St-Germain-en-Laye in 1701, rested in the chapel (now secularised) until the Revolution when the building was desecrated. It is now a music, dance and drama school.

★L'Observatoire

61 avenue de l'Observatoire. Ⓜ*/RER: Port-Royal, Denfert Rochereau. Buses: 38, 83, 91*

The observatory Ⓥ – The construction, on orders from Colbert and to plans by **Claude Perrault**, was begun at the summer solstice, on 21 June 1667, and completed in 1672 – the dome and wings were added under Louis-Philippe.

Important milestones in the history of the Observatory include the calculation of the true dimensions of the solar system (1672), the exact determination of longitudinal meridians (Louis XIV remarked that the Academician's calculations had considerably reduced the extent of his kingdom!), a calculation of the speed of light, the production of a large map of the moon (1679), the discovery by mathematical deduction of the planet Neptune by **Le Verrier** (1846), the invention of new instruments (astrolabe, electronic camera), etc...

The building – The four walls are oriented towards the cardinal points of the compass, the south side of the building determines the capital's latitude, and its median plan is bisected by the Paris Meridian, calculated in 1667. This determined 0° Longitude until 1884 when Greenwich Mean Time was adopted generally, with the exception of France and Ireland, they only followed suit in 1911 (the meridian is marked by 135 bronze discs laid into the street and into the floor of buildings as a memorial to **François Arago** (1786-1853). Midday bearings are to be found elsewhere in Paris (south bearing appears as Mire du Sud) besides on the actual meridian *(see diagram)*.

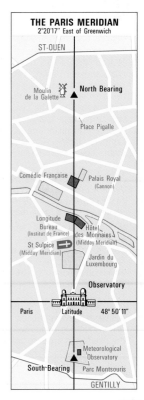

THE PARIS MERIDIAN
2°20'17" East of Greenwich

ST-OUEN

Moulin de la Galette — **North Bearing**

Place Pigalle

Comédie-Française — Palais Royal (Cannon)

Longitude Bureau (Institut de France) — Hôtel des Monnaies (Midday Meridian)
St Sulpice (Midday Meridian)

Jardin du Luxembourg

Observatory

Paris — Latitude — 48° 50' 11"

Meteorological Observatory

South-Bearing — Parc Montsouris

GENTILLY

The Observatory has been the seat of the **International Time Bureau** which since its inauguration (1919) sets Coordinated Universal Time (UTC), based upon International Atomic Time (IAT). The speaking clock (☎ *36 99*) gives Coordinated Universal Time accurate to one millionth of a second.

Avenue de l'Observatoire – The wide avenue with its central flower borders runs on an axis with the Luxembourg Palace (*see* LUXEMBOURG). It is lined with buildings belonging to the Paris V University (note the unusual red brick lateral façade of the Institute of Art and Archeology with its Antique-style frieze).

The **Observatory Fountain★** (1873) by Davioud is known for its famous four quarters of the globe by Carpeaux (Oceania was omitted for reasons of symmetry!).

There is a fine view across the Luxembourg gardens towards Montmartre.

La Clôserie des Lilas –
171 boulevard St-Germain.
This café, so famous in the 1920s, was haunted by such literary lights as Baudelaire, Verlaine, Gide, Jarry, Apollinaire, Hemingway, Fitzgerald and Paul Fort who once held 'poetry evenings' each Tuesday there... It retains much of its period decoration, although restored.

> **Hemingway's haunt**
>
> This landmark café-restaurant on the eastern fringe of the Montparnasse quarter was well frequented by Ernest Hemingway in the 1920s. The novelist often wrote in various Left Bank cafes, and in La Clôserie he penned much of *The Sun Also Rises*. It was also here that fellow expatriate F Scott Fitzgerald asked Hemingway to peruse the manuscript that would be published as *The Great Gasby*.

Monument of Maréchal Ney – This vigorous statue by François Rude was regarded by Rodin as the best in Paris. It marks the spot where the officer was executed by firing squad in 1815 for his support of Napoleon.

Musée Zadkine ⊘ – *100bis rue d'Assas (off the map.* Ⓜ *Vavin /RER: Port-Royal. Buses 58, 68, 82, 83)* – Russian by birth and French by adoption, the sculptor Ossip Zadkine (1890-1967) came to Paris in 1909, after a stay in London. His works in wood and stone began to express anguish and anxiety. This house, now presented as a museum, was his home from 1928 to his death. Amongst the works on display the *Woman with a Fan*, from his Cubist period, the elm-wood sculpture of *Prometheus* and the model of his memorial to the destruction of Rotterdam (*The Destroyed City*). The last room exhibits works from the last years of the artist's life, several busts and portraits of Van Gogh, including a plaster cast of his statue now in Auvers-sur-Oise.

Bronze figures.

Photothèque des Musées de la Ville de Paris

★Les Catacombes ⊘

1 place Denfert-Rochereau. Ⓜ *Denfert-Rochereau. Buses: 38, 68. For access underground, a torch may be useful.*

In the middle of place Denfert-Rochereau is a reduced bronze version of Bartholdi's Lion in commemoration of Colonel Denfert-Rochereau's successful defence of Belfort in 1870-71. The two elegantly-proportioned buildings adorned by sculpted friezes are examples of Ledoux' city gates (*see* INTRODUCTION) and toll-houses, which punctuated "the Hellish wall".

The three "mountains" – Montparnasse, Montrouge and Montsouris were quarried from Gallo-Roman times.

In 1785 it was decided that the abandoned excavations should be transformed into ossuaries. Several million skeletons from the cemetery of the Innocents and other parish burial grounds were transferred to Montrouge. Stacked against the walls, the skulls and crossed tibias formed a macabre decoration.

At the liberation of Paris in August 1944 it was found that the Resistance Movement had established its headquarters within the catacombs.

Substantial sums have recently (1995) been allocated for the installation of air conditioning, dehumidifiers and improved lighting.

Les QUAIS★★★

A tour of the Ile de la Cité and Ile St-Louis along the quays and bridges over the Seine affords the most magnificent **views**★★★ that Paris has to offer. Tree-shaded in parts, the banks of the river remain, even today, Paris' busiest thoroughfare; 14 bridges span its course of a little over a mile through the capital; *bouquinistes* garnish the parapets and offer early editions and etchings, comics and phone cards, but bargains are rare.

LEFT BANK

Quai de Conti Ⓜ *Pont-Neuf, Odéon; Buses: 24, 27, 39, 48, 58, 70, 72, 95*

It begins level with the rue Dauphine and extends past the Mint and the Institut de France.

For Institut de France see ST-GERMAIN-DES-PRÉS

★**Hôtel des Monnaies** – *11 quai Conti*. In the 13C the Nesle Mansion occupied the site of the rue Dauphine and the Philippe Auguste wall. The house was rebuilt in 1572 by Luigi di Gonzaga, Prince de Nevers, and remodelled as the Hôtel de Guénégaud in 1641. In 1670 the Princesse de Conti settled in the house which was renamed after her.

In the 18C Louis XV installed the Mint there, selecting the architect, **Antoine**, to design the workshops which were built between 1768 and 1775. The simplicity of line, sober rustication and restrained decoration was praised by the contemporary public, tired of excessive Classical orders and colonnades. Antoine's immediate success seconded him to the Academy of Architecture.

Before being transferred to Pessac (Gironde), the Mint together with the Ministry of Finance used to have all France's and other foreign currencies struck in the workshops. These still cast editions of collection pieces, dies for the Assay and Weights and Measures offices; medals and decorations are still produced here.

In the second courtyard on the left is a Meridian marker (*see* PORT-ROYAL – l'Observatoire).

Interior – A staircase rising from the beautiful coffered entrance hall, circles twice before reaching the suite of panelled rooms overlooking the Seine, which are used for temporary exhibitions.

The **Coin Museum** ⊙ (*back of main courtyard*) occupies the refurbished minting and milling halls. Exhibits retrace the history of French coin-making and minting from 300BC and includes the art of medal-making which developed in the 16C under Italian influence. A fine collection of coins, medals, banking documentation, paintings, engravings and drawings illustrate various political, social and financial developments. In the laminating section, note the different weighing scales and the 1807 Uhlhorn steam-driven press.

Guided tours are restricted to areas where official medals and decorations are fashioned.

Medals, jewellery and collection pieces are available for sale at no 2 rue Guénégaud.

The junction with the Pont-Neuf was where the scientist Pierre Curie was crushed to death by a horse-drawn carriage in 1906.

A. Nadeau/EXPLORER

Booksellers' stalls

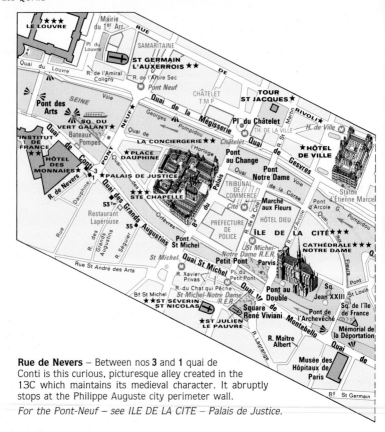

Rue de Nevers – Between nos **3** and **1** quai de Conti is this curious, picturesque alley created in the 13C which maintains its medieval character. It abruptly stops at the Philippe Auguste city perimeter wall.

For the Pont-Neuf – see ILE DE LA CITE – Palais de Justice.

The bouquinistes

Their distinctive dark green boxes have changed little over the years, but their pitches have. They began selling their wares on the riverside, when they were little more than travelling salesmen specialising in books of alchemy, but later they congregated on the Pont-Neuf where they began to set up collapsible stalls. In the 18C, they were chased off the bridge and returned to the quaysides. No stroll along the Seine would be complete without a quick scan of the *bouquiniste* stalls because they are an integral part of the Paris scene. Gone are the days though, when the erudite Montval, librarian at the Comédie-Française at the turn of the century, discovered an autographed manuscript of Diderot's *Le neveu de Rameau*, or Parison the "King of the Readers" found a copy of Plantin's *Julius Caesar* with a portrait of the dictator sketched in by Montaigne.

Quai des Grands Augustins Ⓜ *St-Michel. Buses: 24, 27, 58, 70*

The oldest quay in Paris dates from 1313, and derives its name from the Great Augustine Monastery established by St Louis in the 13C on a nearby site which extended across the waterfront between rue des Grands-Augustins and rue Dauphine, as opposed to the Petits Augustins *(see ST-GERMAIN-DES-PRÉS – École des Beaux-Arts)* beyond. No 53 used to be the Paris Omnibus Co headquarters – Note, as you pass, two 17C mansions, no 51 now the famous Lapérouse Restaurant, and no **35**.

Quai St-Michel Ⓜ *St-Michel. Buses: 21, 24, 27, 38, 58, 70, 85, 96*

Bookshops line the quay, broken only by two old and narrow streets, rues Xavier Privas and du Chat-qui-Pêche.

Place St-Michel – The present square and bridge of the same name date from the reign of Napoleon III. It owes its name to a former chapel in the precincts of the Palais de Justice *(see ILE DE LA CITE)*. In August 1944 a number of violent scuffles broke out when students allied to the Resistance confronted German soldiers. Since the B line of the RER (regional express railway) was built as a link line with the suburbs, place St-Michel has become a popular meeting point for students and young people.

Le Petit Pont – This bridge (1853) stands on the site of the oldest river crossing in Paris – the Romans built a wooden bridge there as a terminal to the road south to Orléans (now the rue St-Jacques). It was first built in stone in 1185 by Bishop Maurice of Sully, architect of Notre-Dame, and was the only bridge which minstrels were allowed to cross toll-free. It has been destroyed 11 times by floods and fire.

Quai de Montebello

In the Middle Ages, wood for building and heating was floated on rafts down to Paris and stored at the Port-aux-Bûches between the Petit Pont and the pont au Double.

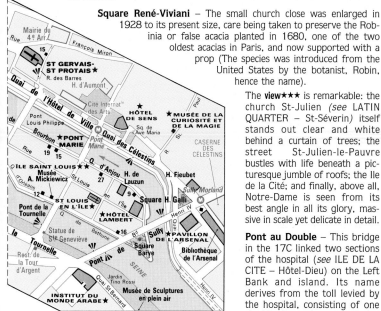

Square René-Viviani – The small church close was enlarged in 1928 to its present size, care being taken to preserve the Robinia or false acacia planted in 1680, one of the two oldest acacias in Paris, and now supported with a prop (The species was introduced from the United States by the botanist, Robin, hence the name).

The **view**★★★ is remarkable: the church St-Julien (see LATIN QUARTER – St-Séverin) itself stands out clear and white behind a curtain of trees; the street St-Julien-le-Pauvre bustles with life beneath a picturesque jumble of roofs; the Ile de la Cité; and finally, above all, Notre-Dame is seen from its best angle in all its glory, massive in scale yet delicate in detail.

Pont au Double – This bridge in the 17C linked two sections of the hospital (see ILE DE LA CITE – Hôtel-Dieu) on the Left Bank and island. Its name derives from the toll levied by the hospital, consisting of one double tournois, a particular doubloon minted in Tours until the 13C, which had only 75% of the value of the coin minted in Paris). The present bridge was built in 1885.

Shakespeare and Company

The famed English-language bookshop Shakespeare and Company was located at no 12 rue de l'Odéon from 1921 to 1941. Its American founder, Sylvia Beach, is perhaps best known as the audacious publisher of James Joyce's masterpiece *Ulysses*, which was banned in the US until the 1930s. Beach's congenial bookshop and lending library immediately became a centre of Paris' vibrant expatriate literary scene. Regulars included Hemingway, Pound, Ford Madox Ford, Sherwood Anderson, Gertrude Stein, T S Eliot and George Antheil. Hemingway described it as "*a warm, cheerful place with a big stove in winter, tables and shelves of books in the window and photographs on the wall of famous writers both dead and living*". Shakespeare and Company closed its doors in 1941 during the German occupation.

The present Shakespeare and Company located off Quai de Montebello at 37 rue de la Bûcherie has no direct affiliation with Beach's establishment. Founded by American George Whitman in 1956, the bookstore attracted prominent black expatriates (Wright, Baldwin, Himes) and Beat writers Burroughs and Ginsberg.

Quai de la Tournelle
Closest Ⓜ *Maubert-Mutualité. Buses: 24, 63, 67, 86, 87*

Just before the pont de l'Archevêché (1828) are a line of old houses with a splendid view over Notre-Dame.

Musée de l'Assistance Publique – Hôpitaux de Paris ⓥ – *47 quai de la Tournelle*. The Hôtel Martin (1630) has variously served as a private residence, a hostel for young girls employed in good works, a bayonet forge (during the Revolution), a General Dispensary turned museum.

The museum traces the evolution of the public health service in Paris from the Hôtel-Dieu (650), and its relationship with Church charity. On display are documents, paintings, engravings, drug jars, vaccination equipment and artefacts...

No 15, opposite the bridge, is the very old Tour d'Argent restaurant where Henri IV is said to have discovered the use of a fork *(a small museum is open to restaurant patrons)*.

Pont de la Tournelle – The first bridge on this site was built of wood (1370); the present one was widened between 1923 and 1928. A striking statue of St Geneviève by Landowski makes the bridge particularly unusual. At this point in the Philippe Auguste perimeter wall stood the St-Bernard gate – of which no trace remains. In the Middle Ages a chain curtain was suspended from a square tower in the 14C **Tournelle Castle** (destroyed 1787) across the Seine to the Barbeau Tower *(see* le MARAIS*)* on the right bank to defend against attacks from the river. The castle, meantime, was used by men condemned to the gallows pending being shipped from Marseille, twice a year.

There is a splendid **view★★★** of Notre-Dame from the bridge. The modern building on the right houses the Institute of the Arab World *(see* JUSSIEU*)*.

For Pont de Sully and square Barye – see ILE SAINT-LOUIS.

The **view** from the bridge's second section is delightful – the quai d'Anjou and Hôtel Lambert, quai des Célestins, pont Marie and St-Gervais belfry.

RIGHT BANK

Quai des Célestins M *Pont-Marie. Buses: 67, 86, 87*

From the quai des Célestins there is an attractive **view★** of the Ile St-Louis and the Marie Bridge. By the square de l'Ave Maria on the right you can catch a glimpse of the Hôtel de Sens *(see* le MARAIS*)*.

★**Pont Marie** – This bridge was first completed in 1635 and named after its builder: it was rebuilt in 1850.

Quai de l'Hôtel de Ville M *Pont-Marie. Buses: 67, 86, 87*

Cité Internationale des Arts – *18, rue de l'Hotel de Ville.* Built in 1965, this complex provides painters, composers, architects, sculptors and film makers with lodgings and studios for a period of up to one year.

In line with the **Louis-Philippe Bridge** on the left, which replaced a suspension bridge during the reign of Louis-Philippe, can be spotted the Panthéon and the church of St-Etienne-du-Mont *(see* LATIN QUARTER*)*.

Take rue des Barres for a clear view of the east end of St-Gervais church and its original buttresses. At no 15 is the fine balcony of a former charnel-house.

Walk down rue François-Miron on the left. In the **St-Gervais precincts**, note the uniform façades of the 18C houses with wrought-iron balconies featuring an elm.

★**Église St-Gervais-St-Protais** – *Place St-Gervais.* The church stands on a low mound emphasised by steps leading up to the façade. A basilica dedicated to the brothers Gervase and Protase, Roman officers martyred by Nero, has stood on the site since the 6C. The main part of the present building, in Flamboyant Gothic, was completed in 1657. On Good Friday (29 March) 1918, a German bomb was dropped on the church, wounding and killing 160 of the congregation. The elm in the square was, according to medieval custom, a place where justice was dispensed as well as a place for wheeling and dealing, employment and *rendezvous*.

Exterior – The imposing façade (1616-1621) with superimposed Doric, Ionic and Corinthian orders was the first expression of the Classical style in Paris, attributed to Métezeau or Salomon de Brosse.

Interior – There remain from the original building the Flamboyant vaulting, 16C windows and 16C to 17C fine stalls carved with misericords representing various trades. The organ built in 1601 and enlarged in the 18C is the oldest in Paris. The position of organ-master was held successively by members of eight generations of Couperins between 1656 and 1826.

In the north aisle, near the font, is a model of the church façade carved by du Hancy who executed the large panels in the main door. In the third chapel a 13C low relief altar-front depicts the *Death of the Virgin*. In the left transept hangs a beautiful 16C Flemish oil panel on wood of the Passion. At the crossing, against a pillar, stands a Gothic *Virgin and Child* in stone. A wooden Christ by Préault (1840) and a fine 17C wrought-iron grille adorn the sacristy exterior. In the Lady Chapel there is a remarkable Flamboyant keystone, hanging 1.5m – 5ft below the vault and forming a circlet 2.5m – 8ft in diameter. The adjoining chapel contains the tomb of Chancellor Michel Le Tellier (d 1685).

★Hôtel de Ville ⓥ – *Place de l'Hôtel de Ville*. The Hôtel de Ville is Paris' official reception and city government building.

Maison aux Piliers – Paris was administered by a representative of the king until the 13C when Municipal government was introduced. The powerful watermen's guild held the monopoly over traffic on the rivers Seine, Oise, Marne and Yonne, and regulated levies thereof. In 1260, **Louis IX** appointed leading men of the guild to administer the township.

Étienne Marcel

This rich draper, a merchant provost, became leader of the States General in 1357 and came out in open revolt against royal power (*see* ILE DE LA CITE – *Palais de la Justice*). In holding Paris, he tried to rally the whole of France to arms, allied himself with the peasants in revolt and allowed the English into the city. But Charles V who had taken refuge in the Hôtel St-Paul (*see* le MARAIS) resisted victoriously, leaving Marcel to die a miserable death at the hands of the Parisians in 1358, just as he was about to open the city gates to Charles the Bad, King of Navarre.

The municipal assembly was headed by a merchant provost and four aldermen who were elected by notables, who in turn nominated the town councillors. It moved from place du Châtelet to the Pillared House on place de Grève (*see below*) in 1357, at the instigation of Étienne Marcel.

The Hôtel de Ville – Under François I, the Pillared House fell into ruin. The king had plans drawn up by Domenico Bernabei (*Il Boccadoro* on account of his abundant golden moustache), and the first stone was laid in 1533. Building however continued until the early 17C. The central section of the present façade reproduces the original.

Until the Revolution the municipal authority was weak, the king making his own appointments – Pierre Lescaut, Guillaume Budet, François Miron, Etienne Turgot (who drew up the first maps of Paris) on condition they be citizens of Paris.

July 1789 – After the fall of the Bastille, the rioters marched on to the town hall for arms. On 17 July 1789 Louis XVI appeared in the hall to kiss the newly adopted tricolour cockade. Between red and blue, the city colours since the provostship of Etienne Marcel in the 14C, La Fayette introduced the royal white.

The Commune – Throughout the Revolution the town hall was controlled by the Commune. The popular insurrection of 10 August 1792, which was led by Danton, Robespierre and Marat, forced the king to flee the Tuileries Palace and take refuge with the Legislative Assembly. The Montagnard faction, or deputies of the extreme left, was an offshoot of the Commune and dominated the National Convention (1793-1794).

On 9 Thermidor (27 July 1794) the National Convention tired of Robespierre's tyrannical behaviour, had him imprisoned at the Luxembourg palace. Released by the Commune he was given refuge in the town hall where as a result of a suicide attempt or of disciplinary action he had his jaw shattered by a pistol shot. He was guillotined the following day.

In 1848, when Louis-Philippe was dismissed, it was in the Hôtel de Ville that the provisional government (led by Lamartine, Arago, Ledru-Rollin) was set up and from there that the Second Republic was proclaimed on 24 February 1848.

The Second Empire and Commune of 1871 – Napoleon proclaimed himself emperor in 1851 and charged his Prefect of the Seine, Baron Haussmann, with replanning the area around the Hôtel de Ville. He razed the adjoining streets, enlarged the square and built the two barracks in rue de Lobau.

On 4 September 1870, after the defeat of the French Army at the Battle of Sedan, Gambetta, Jules Favre and Jules Ferry proclaimed the Third Republic from the Hôtel de Ville and instituted a National Defence Government. The capitulation of Paris on 28 January 1871, however, roused the citizens to revolt against the government, installing in its place the Paris Commune. In May during its final overthrow, the Hôtel de Ville, the Tuileries and several other buildings were set on fire by the Federalists.

25 August 1944 – It was from here that General de Gaulle made his famous speech "Paris! Paris outragé! Paris brisé! Paris martyrisé! mais Paris libéré! libéré par lui-même! libéré par son peuple avec le concours des armées de la France..."

The building – The Hôtel de Ville was entirely rebuilt between 1874 and 1882 in the neo-Renaissance style by Ballu and Deperthes, complete with 146 statues of the illustrious and of French towns to adorn the building's façades.

Inside, the sumptuous main staircase leads to a ballroom and reception rooms. Ornate decoration, part Renaissance, part Belle Époque, reveals the official style in the early years of the Third Republic. Amid the caryatids and rostra, coffered ceilings and crystal chandeliers are panels by Laurens depicting Louis XVI's reception at the Hôtel de Ville and mural paintings by Puvis de Chavannes (*The Seasons*). Note the unusual architecture of the triple chambers of the Arcade Room (salon des Arcades).

Place de l'Hôtel de Ville – The **place de Grève**, as it was known until 1830, shelves gently down to the Seine. In the Middle Ages, the foreshore or *grève*, became a meeting place for those out of work, hence the expression *"faire la grève"* meaning 'not working' or 'on strike'.

It was the place for popular fairs, where a huge bonfire was lit in midsummer for the feast day of St-John-the Baptist (24 June).

During the Ancien Régime, it was where *bourgeois* and commoners were hanged and where gentlemen were beheaded by the axe or the sword; witches and heretics were burnt at the stake; murderers were condemned to the wheel and punishment for treason consisted of being drawn and quartered.

Paved in granite, the square boasts modern rectangular fountains on either side of a boat-like form, representing the coat of arms of the 13C watermen's guild *(illustration see* INTRODUCTION: Paris today).

Quai de Gesvres

Ⓜ/RER: *Châtelet. Buses: 21, 38, 58, 67, 69, 70, 72, 74, 75, 76, 81, 85, 96*

This quay stretches from the Arcole Bridge (rebuilt 1888). Several of Haussmann's monumental creations – the Hôtel-Dieu, police headquarters, commercial courts, and Law Courts – can be admired on the Ile de la Cité.

Pont Notre-Dame – (1913) This was the Great Bridge in Roman times, as opposed to the Small Bridge (Petit Pont) on the far side of the island. Burnt down by the Normans and rebuilt on piles in 1413, it was the first to be given an official name, and the houses built on it were the first to be numbered in Paris. It fell down in Louis XII's reign (1499), but was rebuilt and lined with identical houses with richly decorated façades, since it was on the royal route of solemn entries into Paris. One of the houses belonged to the art collector Gersaint who befriended Watteau, figuring in Watteau's famous picture *L'Enseigne de Gersaint* (it now hangs in the Charlottenburg Museum in Berlin).

★Tour St-Jacques – The tower is the former belfry of the church of St-Jacques-la-Boucherie, built in the 16C and one of the starting points for pilgrims journeying up the rue St-Jacques and on to Santiago de Compostela in Spain. The church was pulled down in 1802. When rue de Rivoli was laid the tower had to be built up as the natural rise in the land was flattened.

The statue of Pascal, recalls the physicist-cum-philosopher's experiments into the weight of air carried out first in the Puy-de-Dôme, then on this spot in 1648.

Place du Châtelet – The area gets its name from the Grand Châtelet, a great fortress which defended the northern entrance into the city, over the Pont au Change. This in turn accommodated the city notaries, surrounded by the halls of powerful guilds (butchers, sausage-makers, skinners and tanners). The Châtelet or Palm Fountain (1808) commemorates Napoleon's victories; the base was decorated with sphinxes in 1858.

The two theatres on either side were built by the architect Davioud in 1862. The Châtelet, after extensive renovation, is now the Théâtre Musical de Paris (West side). Opposite, the Théâtre de la Ville, formerly the Sarah Bernhardt Theatre, is a centre of popular culture (east side).

Pont au Change – The Money Changers' Bridge was established in the 9C by Charles the Bald. It was so tightly lined with workshops and houses all through the Middle Ages that one could cross the river without glimpsing it! These were cleared in 1788. Louis VII instituted a money changer here in 1141, since when all foreigners and visitors to Paris had to barter for the best rate of exchange. The present bridge dates from 1860.

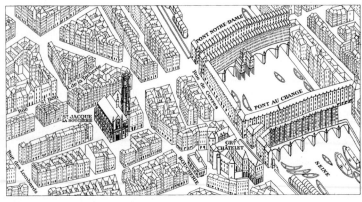

Châtelet in 1734

Quai de la Mégisserie

Ⓜ Pont-Neuf /RER: Châtelet. Buses: 21, 38, 47, 58, 67, 69, 70, 72, 74, 75, 76, 81, 85, 96

The Mégisserie Quay gets its name from the stinking public slaughterhouse (*mégisserie:* tawing) that lined the river until the Revolution. Now there are rows of pet-shops and seed merchants selling exotic birds in cages and fish in tanks. It was hereabouts that press-gangs operated collecting 'volunteers' for the armed forces. An attractive view★★ extends over the Law Courts, Conciergerie, and the old houses along quai de l'Horloge on Ile de la Cité and Pont-Neuf.

Overlooking the bridge is the **La Samaritaine** department store, named after a pump under the Pont-Neuf that drew water from the river to supply the Louvre until 1813 and which being decorated with a figure of the woman of Samaria giving Jesus water at the well became known as the *Samaritaine*. From the terrace of shop no 2 there is an excellent view★★ over the whole of Paris (*see* INTRODUCTION – A different perspective), and around the back in rue de l'Arbre Sec, there is a good view of the Gothic chevet of St-Germain-l'Auxerrois rippling across the rectilinear glass lateral 'deco' façade of the shop depository.

★★**Église St-Germain-L'Auxerrois** – *2 place du Louvre*. On the northern side there is the neo-Renaissance townhall designed by Hittorff and a neo-Gothic belltower erected by Ballu, with a peal of 38 bells.

The church is named after St Germanus, Bishop of Auxerre in the 5C, who recognised the beatification of Ste Geneviève of Nanterre not to be confused with the patron of St-Germain-des Prés. A sanctuary in the 8C was first replaced by a Norman construction, then by a church built by Robert the Pious. The complex spans five centuries of architectural development from the Romanesque (belfry) via High Gothic (chancel) and Flamboyant (porch and nave) to the Renaissance (doorway). Substantial restoration in the hands of Ballard and Lassus (1838-1855) emphasise its composite nature further.

When the Valois moved into the Louvre in the 14C, St-Germain became the king's parish church and thereby subject to embellishments and endowment. On the night of 24 August 1572 the bells rang for matins giving the signal for the **St Bartholomew's Day Massacre** when thousands of Huguenots, invited to celebrate the marriage of Henri of Navarre to his cousin, Marguerite of Valois, were slaughtered according to a plan hatched by the Cardinal Duke of Guise, Catherine de' Medici, Charles IX and the future Henri III.

Many poets (Jodelle, Malherbe), painters (Coypel, Boucher, Nattier, Chardin, Van Loo), sculptors (Coysevox, the two Coustous), architects (Le Vau, Robert de Cotte, Gabriel the Elder, Soufflot) and others associated with the court and living at the Louvre are buried in the church.

Since 1926, following a vow by the painter and illustrator Adolphe Willette (1857-1926), artists come to St-Germain on the first Sunday in Lent to receive ashes and to pray for those artists who will die in the year.

Exterior – From the side of La Samaritaine there is a good view of the east end and the Romanesque belfry which abuts the transept.

Below the roof line along the chancel aisles are a series of small attic-like spaces in which were heaped the bones from tombs in the cloisters, which at one time surrounded the church. The apsidal chapel endowed by the Tronson family is decorated with a frieze of carp.

Porch – The porch is the building's most original feature dating from between 1435 and 1439. The column-statues are modern. The outermost, lowest, bays accommodate small chambers, covered with slate, in which the chapter placed the church archives and treasure.

The three middle bays have multi-ribbed Flamboyant vaults, flanked by a plain Gothic bay. The most interesting, central doorway is 13C. The figure in the right embrasure represents St Geneviève holding a candle which a small devil tries to snuff out, whilst an angel nearby, stands ready with a taper to rekindle it.

Interior – The restored 17C organ (**1**) comes from the Sainte-Chapelle (see ILE DE LA CITE – Palais de Justice). The **churchwarden's pew** (**2**), dating from 1684, is thought to have been used by successive kings and their families. In the fourth chapel is a fine early 16C, Flemish **altarpiece** (**3**-light switch).

The **stained glass** in the transept and the two rose windows are late 15C. The multi-lierne vault in the south arm of the transept is typical of the Flamboyant style.
The chancel is surrounded by an 18C grille before which stand 15C polychrome statues of St Germanus (**4**) and St Vincent (**5**). In the 18C the fine Renaissance roodscreen carved by Jean Goujon and Pierre Lescot was removed to allow for processions (the rescued low-relief panels are in the Louvre).

The **Chapel of the Holy Sacrament** contains a 14C polychrome stone statue of the Virgin (**6**); a 14C Crucifixion (**7**); one of the original statues from the main doorway, St Mary the Egyptian (**8**); a Last Supper (**9**) by Theo Van Elsen (1954) and a 13C statue of St Germanus (**10**).

★**Place du Louvre** – In what is now the place du Louvre, the Roman Labienus pitched his camp when he crushed the Parisii in 52 BC, as did the Normans when they besieged Paris in 885. Until the Second Empire, fine mansions stood between the Louvre and the church, including the Petit Bourbon (demolished 1660) where the States General met in 1614, Molière performed his plays in 1658 and the young Louis XIV danced before the court.
In 1854 Haussmann transformed the narrow rue des Poulies into the wide rue du Louvre (this part is now rue de l'Amiral-de-Coligny), demolishing in the process the last of the 17C houses. These were replaced by a neo-Renaissance building by Hittorff and a neo-Gothic belfry by Ballu with a 38-bell carillon.
From the quai du Louvre, the view extends over the weeping willows at the tip of the square du Vert-Galant, the Hôtel des Monnaies and the Institut de France (see ST-GERMAIN-DES-PRES).

Pont des Arts – The "academic" bridge dating from 1803 was the first to be built of iron and the first to be exclusively for pedestrians. Chairs were made available between orange trees in pots for people to use to pause and watch the river. Access was subject to a toll of one sou as for most of the Paris bridges, levied until 1849. Its success was immediate: 65 000 Parisians paid to walk over it the day it opened. The present construction is of steel and has only seven arches instead of the original eight.
The **view**★★★ is outstanding, encompassing the full length of the Pont-Neuf, the square du Vert-Galant, the Law Courts, the Sainte-Chapelle flèche and finally the towers and flèche of Notre-Dame; visible beyond a screen of plane trees are the two theatres on place du Châtelet, the top of the St-Jacques Tower, the Hôtel de Ville and the St-Gervais belfry; downstream the Louvre, the Grand Palais and the Carrousel Bridge.

QUARTIER LATIN★★★

See LATIN QUARTER

RÉPUBLIQUE

Michelin plan 11 – folds 32 – 33, 21: G 15 – G 17, D 17 – G 17
M République. Buses: 20, 54, 56, 65, 75

This neighbourhood encompasses three quite distinctive districts extending from place de la République, on the periphery of the Marais and Beaubourg: Arts et Métiers, the Temple quarter and the St-Martin Canal that branches off towards la Villette.

Place de la République – When originally named place du Château-d'Eau, it was here that Alexandre Dumas founded the Théâtre Historique in 1847, as a venue for his historical dramas – it opened with his Queen Margot for which crowds queued for seats for two days and nights. It later became the Théâtre Lyrique where Gounod's Faust was first performed (1859).
In 1854 **Haussmann** incorporated the small square into his grand anti-revolutionary urban scheme, demolishing the diorama built in 1822 by Daguerre, and replacing it with barracks for 2 000 soldiers and sweeping broad avenues – the boulevard Magenta, avenue de la République, boulevard Voltaire and rue de Turbigo. The boulevard du Crime was razed.
The square was completed by 1862 and the **Statue to the Republic** by Morice erected in 1883. This work was favoured over Dalou's bolder composition, now at place de la Nation (see BASTILLE), who also designed the bronze low reliefs around the base, representing the great events in the history of the Republic from its inception to 1880 to the first 14 July commemoration celebration.

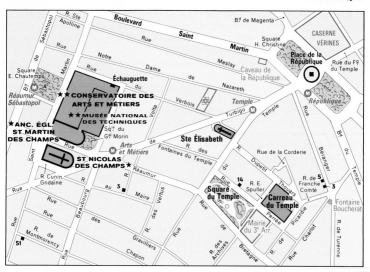

★Quartier du Temple Ⓜ *République, Temple. Buses: 20, 75*

This quarter was once the domain of the Knights Templar and the Benedictines from St Martin-in-the-Fields. Today, it is the main centre for the rag trade and technical training schools.

The Former Templar Domain – In 1140 the religious and military order, founded in 1118 in the Holy Land by nine knights to protect pilgrims and known as the Order of Knights Templar, established a house in Paris. By the 13C the order, dressed in their distinctive white habits emblazoned with a red cross, had achieved great power with 9 000 *commanderies* throughout Europe. Independent of any ruling monarch, they were soon entrusted with great wealth, underpinning a substantial and unrivalled international banking system. Their property investments counted almost one quarter of the land area of Paris – including all the Marais neighbourhood. The Templars fortified their domain and its keep providing refuge to local peasants and those fleeing royal jurisdiction; craftsmen congregated, exempt from guild taxes: soon 4 000 souls were living within the walls where even kings were known to have sought shelter.

Philip the Fair decided to suppress this 'state within a state'. On 13 October 1307, all the Templars in France were arrested, amongst whom the leader, Jacques de Molay and 140 knights were imprisoned in Paris. Having been granted authority by the Pope, the king dissolved the order and had Molay together with 54 knights burnt at the stake. Two-thirds of the estates were confiscated by the Crown, the rest was given to the Knights of St John of Jerusalem, later known as the Knights of Malta.

The Templar Prison – At the time of the Revolution, the Knights of Malta were suppressed in their turn and their prior, the Duke of Angoulême, nephew of Louis XVI, put to flight. On 13 August 1792, the King, Marie-Antoinette, Madame Elisabeth (the King's sister), the young Dauphin aged seven and his sister were all imprisoned in the Temple Tower *(see le MARAIS – Musée Carnavalet)*. Their trial begins on 11 December; 20 January 1793, Louis XVI is condemned by the Convention and sent to the guillotine.

The following July the Dauphin was separated from his mother and moved to the fourth floor; she meanwhile was transferred with her sister-in-law to the Conciergerie *(see ILE DE LA CITE)* on 2 August, which she was to leave only to go to the guillotine on 16 October. Two years later, on 8 June 1795, a young man died in the Temple Tower and was buried at the Church of St Margaret *(see BASTILLE – Faubourg St-Antoine)*, although it is not certain whether he was indeed Louis XVII, the son of Louis XVI, or not. Madame Royale was freed on 18 December 1795.

In 1808 the tower was razed to prevent Royalist pilgrimages and the area converted into an open-air second-hand clothes market known as the Carreau du Temple after the square flagstones. In 1857 Haussmann designed the covered market, the town hall opposite, and the present square.

Square and Carreau du Temple Ⓥ – To the north of the square at **14** rue Perrée is the Paris Assay Office, **Hôtel de la Garantie** for endorsing precious metals. At the far end, left of the town hall, is the Carreau, still lined, like the surrounding Picardie, Corderie and Dupetit-Thouars streets, with clothes, costume and fancy clothes shops and stalls.

287

Rue de Franche-Comté – rue de Turenne crossroads – In the south corner is the Boucherat Fountain dated 1699, whilst at 3-5 rue Béranger, there is an 18C *hôtel* now used as a school, where the poet and writer of popular songs, Béranger, died in 1857.

Église Ste-Elisabeth – *195 rue du Temple*. This former monastic chapel (1628-1646) dedicated to St Elisabeth of Hungary is now the church of the Knights of Malta. Of particular interest are the 100 early 16C Flemish **low reliefs★** depicting biblical scenes around the ambulatory. These would have come from the former abbey of St Vaast in Arras. Turn left in rue de Turbigo to approach the former **St-Martin-des-Champs★** with its Romanesque east end (1130 – restored), fine capitals, belfry, and Gothic nave.

★★Around the Conservatoire National des Arts et Métiers

Ⓜ *Réaumur-Sébastopol, Arts et Métiers. Buses: 20, 38, 47, 75*

Rue Volta – At no **3** is a **timber-framed house**, dating from the 17C (gable now gone).

House of the alchemist Nicolas Flamel – *51 rue de Montmorency*. This writer, sworn member of the university and bookseller, made his fortune copying and selling manuscripts. He invested the proceeds in charity, setting up an "almshouse" above his shop (now a restaurant) in which the high rent charged for the lower floors allowed the upper rooms to be used rent-free by the poor. These were asked to say a prayer for their benefactor.

★**Église St-Nicolas-des-Champs** – *252bis rue St-Martin*. The church, built in the 12C by the priory of St Martin in the Fields for the monastery servants and neighbouring peasants, is dedicated to one of the most popular medieval saints, Nicholas, 4C Bishop of Myra in Asia Minor and patron saint of young boys, sailors and travellers. It was rebuilt in the 15C and enlarged in the 16C and 17C. The Revolution re-dedicated it to Hymen (Marriage) and Fidelity.

The façade and belfry are Flamboyant Gothic, the south **door★** is Renaissance (1581). Inside, the nave is divided into five by a double line of piers; the first five bays are 15C; in the chancel and chapels hang a considerable number of 17C, 18C and 19C paintings; on the double-sided altar is a retable by Simon Vouet (16C) and four angels by the 17C sculptor, Sarrazin. The best view of the many piers around the double ambulatory is to be had from the Lady Chapel. (Note the *Adoration of the Shepherds* by Coypel). The fine Paris-made organ was rebuilt in the 18C, looked after for a time by Louis Braille.

★★**Conservatoire national des Arts et Métiers** ⊙ – *292 rue St-Martin*. An institution for technical instruction, a considerable industrial museum and a laboratory for industrial experiment have incorporated in the present buildings the old church and refectory of the **St Martin-des-Champs** priory which once stood on the site.

This Benedictine priory grew around a chapel dedicated to St Martin, Bishop of Tours in the 4C. In 1273 the precincts were fortified with walls. The Conservatoire, created by the Convention in 1794, was installed in the priory in 1799.

On the corner of rue du Vertbois, once stood a main watchtower (*échauguette*), replaced in 1882; fragments of the 1273 masonry survive further down the road. In the courtyard, on the right, the present library, once the monastery **refectory★★**, was designed by Pierre of Montreuil (13C). Inside, seven slender columns run down the centre bisecting the space, articulated into perfect proportions with elegant Gothic lines. The doorway halfway down the right side has delightful carvings on the outside.

★★**Musée National des Techniques** – The museum illustrates technical progress in industry and science. Extensive collections of period pieces include full-scale machines and reduced scale models.

On the **ground floor**, there is the former **Church of St-Martin-des-Champs★**; its early 12C ambulatory vaulting clearly shows the transitional phase in building from Romanesque to Gothic.

Exhibits focus upon locomotion – cycles, cars, aircraft (including Blériot's with which he crossed the channel) and 19C railways; early mathematical and scientific instruments – astrolabes, globes, sundials, pendulums (including Foucault's (*see* LATIN QUARTER – le Panthéon), chronometers (Pascal's arithmetic machine), clocks and automata (Marie-Antoinette's clockwork dulcimer-playing puppet of 1784).

The Echo Room (as whispers are distinctly audible across the domed room), shows apparatus and mementoes of the 18C chemist, Lavoisier.

Other thematic collections touch upon collective working environments (late-18C workshops); energy – mills, model of the Marly machine (1678-1655), turbines, boilers; early scientific instruments (physics, optics, mechanics); industrially-produced glass from the greatest European glassworks; acoustics and music-making (early instruments, Edison's phonograph). Electronic technology shows developments with radio, television, telecommunications (Chappe telegraph, Morse telegraph), radar, laser and satellite – photography, cinema, (cameras of Niepce, Daguerre and Edison, the magic lantern used by the Lumière brothers in 1895) and the graphic arts (printing, duplicators, typing machines).

St Martin's Canal

J.-P. Bourret/PITCH

★Canal St-Martin M *République, Jaurès*

The waterway – The peaceful, old-fashioned reaches of the 4.5km – 2 3/4 mile canal, dug at the time of the Restoration to link the Ourcq Canal at la Villette with the Seine via l'Arsenal *(see* BASTILLE*)*, are still navigated by numerous barges. The raised level of the watercourse straddled with iron walkways, its nine locks and rows of trees, make for an unusual, serene Paris landscape.

The canal disappears into an underpass beyond the quai Valmy from Frédéric-Lemaître square, resurfacing beyond place de la Bastille as the Arsenal Basin. The basin followed the line of the moat skirting Charles V's ramparts and has been developed as a pleasure boat harbour, the **Arsenal Marina** (Port de Plaisance de Paris-Arsenal),

Boat trips

The boat passes through nine locks including four double locks. The finest is the Récollets named after a Franciscan convent which stood nearby. The tunnel built by Baron Haussmann in 1860, is 1 854m – 6 082ft long, lit and ventilated by openings at street level (*see* PRACTICAL INFORMATION for details).

to accommodate over 200 boats. The quaysides have been landscaped as terraced gardens.

St-Louis Hospital – *Entrance: Rue Bichat.* One of the oldest Parisian hospitals, St-Louis pioneered the science of dermatology. The brick and stone buildings, reminiscent of the places des Vosges and Dauphine with their steeply pitched roofs and dormer windows, are separated by flowered courtyards. A historic study **collection of mouldings** ⊙, illustrating various skin conditions before the advent of photography is available for consultation – for all save the most squeamish.

Montfaucon Gallows – The canal, rues Louis-Blanc, de la Grange-aux-Belles and des Écluses-St-Martin delimit an area once dominated by gallows that might have hanged up to 60 condemned people at any one time. Various finance ministers died by it, notably Marigny, who built the gibbet during the reign of Philip the Fair, Montaigu, who repaired it, and the unlucky Semblançay who had nothing whatsoever to do with it. After the assassination (1572) of Admiral Coligny, his body was displayed here. Although already in disuse during the 17C it was 1760 before the gallows were dismantled.

Rotonde de la Villette – *Place de Stalingrad.* The rotunda, one of the ring of tollhouses designed by Ledoux serves as a storehouse for archeological finds.

'When good Americans die they go to Paris.'
OSCAR WILDE – Portrait of Dorian Gray

This old quarter on the Left Bank is known for its beautiful church as well as for its narrow streets, antique shops, restaurants, cafés and cellars. The church, the oldest in Paris, and the abbatial palace are all that remain of the famous Benedictine abbey.

★★Abbaye St-Germain-des-Prés ① boulevard St-Germain

Ⓜ St-Germain-des-Prés. Buses: 39, 48, 63, 70, 86, 87, 95, 96

A powerful abbey – In 542 King Childebert, son of Clovis, returned from Spain with a piece of the True Cross and St Vincent's tunic, and set to building a monastery in the open fields (*prés*) around the relics. He was subsequently buried in the church as were other Merovingian Kings until King Dagobert (639), buried at St-Denis (*see* EXCURSIONS – St Denis). St Germanus, Bishop of Paris, after whom the church was named, is also interred here (576).

St-Germain-des-Prés was from the 8C, a link in the prodigious chain across Europe of

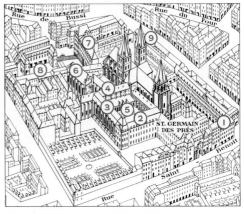

Abbey of Saint-Germain-des-Prés in 1734

① Annexe.
② Guest rooms.
③ Refectory.
④ Chapter-house.
⑤ Main cloister.
⑥ Lady Chapel.
⑦ Abbatial palace.
⑧ Stables.
⑨ Prison.

17 000 Benedictine abbeys and priories, an order which provided 24 popes, 200 cardinals, 1 560 recognised saints, 43 emperors, 44 kings... In its own right it became sovereign ruler of a domain of some 17 000ha – 42 000 acres, answerable in spiritual matters to the pope alone.

The monastery was sacked four times in 40 years by the Normans and the present church is, therefore, a rebuilding dating in its earliest parts from 990 to 1021 – the oldest in Paris. Accruing numbers necessitated a larger chancel, consecrated in person by Pope Alexander III in 1163. Maurice de Sully, having just laid the foundation stone of Notre-Dame (*see* ILE DE LA CITE), chose to absent himself from the service to safeguard his independence as Bishop of Paris. The abbey's design was based upon Cluniac aesthetics, extended later with Gothic cloisters, refectory, and a Lady Chapel in the 13C by Pierre of Montreuil. The surviving complex is one of the finest Medieval groups.

In the 14C, whilst Charles V enclosed the city, the abbey fortified itself with crenellated walls, towers and a moat linked to the Seine. These were demolished at the end of the 17C to be replaced by houses, so creating the "noble faubourg" around the boulevard St-Germain (*see* FAUBOURG SAINT-GERMAIN) extending westwards.

A centre of learning – The Cluniac rule imposed between the 11C and the 16C declined to decadence under commendatory abbots, often lay princes and cardinals appointed by the King. Major reforms were implemented in 1515 and 1631, becoming subject to the austere Congregation of St Maur which slowly reinstated its reputation for holiness and learning until 1789. The Benedictines devoted themselves to the study of inscriptions (epigraphy), ancient writing (paleography), the Church Fathers, archeology, archives and medieval documents – specialised studies that survive today at the Academy of Inscriptions and Literature at the Institut de France *(see below)*.

Decadence – At the Revolution the abbey was suppressed: the rich library was confiscated, the church, from which the royal tombs disappeared, was turned into saltpetre works, whilst other buildings were sold, demolished or burnt. Under the Restoration the nave was eventually saved, but the twin transept towers had already gone.

Exterior – Given its history, the 11C Romanesque church has altered considerably in appearance: the chancel flying buttresses are contemporary with Notre-Dame; of the three original belltowers there remains only one towering over the façade – the top arcaded storey, rebuilt in the 12C was restored by the architect Baltard in the 19C when it was crowned with its present pitched roof; the original porch is hidden by an outer doorway added in 1607; the presbytery is an 18C addition;the twin square towers at the end of the chancel were truncated in 1822. The small square along the south side replaces the monks' cemetery where in September 1792 318 priests and monks incarcerated in the Abbey-turned-prison were massacred.

The glazed stoneware portico placed against the far wall was executed by the Sèvres factory for its pavilion at the 1900 Universal Exhibition.

Interior – St-Germain, built as a monastery chapel and not as a parish church, is not so vast – 65m x 21m x 19m – 213ft x 69ft x 62ft high. 19C restoration on a grand scale has left vaults, walls and capitals painted in garish colours.

Off to the right of the cradle vaulted porch, is the Merovingian sanctuary with the tomb of St Germanus, known as **St Symphorian's Chapel** ⊙. Excavations in the chapel have uncovered several decorated stone and plaster sarcophagi and some foundations which could date from the 6C – 7C or from the 11C.

The nave and transept would originally have been roofed in wood, replaced in 1646 with Gothic vaulting on the lines of that in the chancel; the capitals are copies of the 11C originals now in the Cluny Museum (see LATIN QUARTER).

The academic, rather wooden frescoes (1841-1863) above the arches are by Flandrin, a student of Ingres, and depict scenes from the life of Christ together with its complement episode foretold in the Old Testament (*The Resurrection* and *Jonah and the whale*).

The chancel and ambulatory survive more or less from the 12C. the arcading – round arched in places – would have supported a tribune as at Notre-Dame, but this was transformed into a purely decorative triforium in 1646. The 6C slender marble shafts came from Childebert's original building, these with the St Symphorian Chapel and finds made at Notre-Dame are the sum of Paris' Merovingian remains.

The **chancel capitals** are typically Romanesque depicting foliage, birds, monsters.

1) Modern wrought-iron grille by Raymond Subes.
2) Our Lady of Consolation (1340).
3) Tomb by Girardon (17C).
4) Mausoleum of James Douglas, a 17C Scottish nobleman attached to the court of Louis XIII.
5) Descartes' and the learned Benedictines, Mabillon's and Montfaucon's tombstones.
6) Boileau, the poet and critic's tombstone.
7) Tomb of William Douglas, a Scottish nobleman attached to the court of Henri IV.
8) Statue of St Francis Xavier by N Coustou.
9) Tomb of John Casimir, King of Poland, who died in 1672, Abbot of St-Germain-des-Prés.
10) St Symphorian Chapel.

Place St-Germain des Prés

11 C   12 C   17 C

★The 'quartier'

Rue de l'Abbaye – A Picasso sculpture, *Homage to Apollinaire*, has been placed in a small square on the corner of Place St-Germain-des-Prés and Rue de l'Abbaye among fragments of the Lady Chapel demolished in 1802 (the portal is in the Cluny Museum, see LATIN QUARTER).

Abbatial Palace nos 1-5 – The impressive brick and stone former abbatial palace was built in 1586 by the Cardinal-Abbot Charles of Bourbon who was subsequently proclaimed King of France during the League (1589), his reign as Charles X however, was short-lived since he died the following year, a prisoner of his nephew Henri IV, at Fontainebleau.

The palace was remodelled in 1699 by the Cardinal de Fürstemberg and sold in 1797 as State property.

The angle pavilion and the Renaissance façade have been restored to the original. The severity of the façade is tempered by the twin-casement windows with alternate round and triangular pediments.

At nos 12-14 stood the refectory designed in 1239 by Pierre of Montreuil and burnt down in 1794. The chapter-house was at no 11.

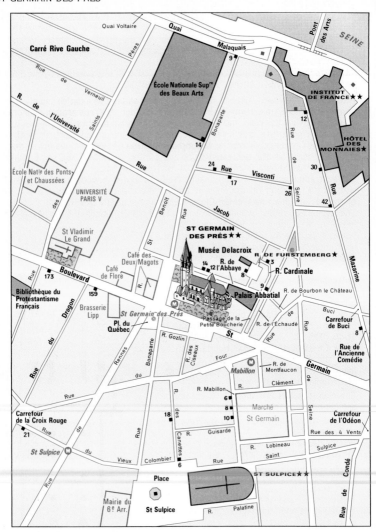

> *A deserted spot, bleak, spectral. In the middle four black trees that have not yet begun to blossom. Intellectual trees. Like T S Eliot's verse.*
> Description of the intimate Fürstemberg square at night by **Henry Miller** in *Tropic of Cancer*.

★Rue de Fürstemberg – This old-fashioned street with its charming square shaded by paulownia and white-globed street-lights was built in 1699 by the cardinal of the same name, through the former monastery stableyard. The nos **6** and **8** are the remains of the outbuildings.

Musée Eugène Delacroix Ⓥ – *no 6*. A museum dedicated to Delacroix, leader of the Romantic painters, has been made of the colourist's last studio-home where he died in 1863.

Rue Cardinale – Twisting and turning, it was opened in 1700 by Fürstemberg, across the long monastery tennis court. Still partially lined by old houses (nos **3** to **9**) it extends to a picturesque crossroads with rue de l'Échaudé (1388) and rue Bourbon-le-Château.

Rue de l'Échaudé – The construction of the boulevard St-Germain in about 1870, razed the meeting point of several small roads which had served as the abbey's place of public chastisement. Justice was meted out to thieves, counterfeiters, pimps, who were punished by gibbet and pillory – a penalty suppressed by Louis XII in 1636.

The old St-Germain Fair – Across the boulevard in rue de Montfaucon one gained access to the St-Germain fairground. The fair, founded in 1482 by Louis XI for the benefit of the abbey, had until the Revolution (1790) a considerable effect on Paris' economy: a forerunner of International Exhibitions and world-trade fairs today. The ground level has been considerably raised as the 'gangways' outside nos **6, 8** and **10** rue Mabillon show. In 1818 the covered St-Germain market was built on part of the site, and local streets were named after Benedictine luminaries. The main University Examination Hall accommodates the upper floor (since 1900) and the basement is being fitted out as a gym and fitness centre.

Rue Guisarde – Built in the 17C, it derives its name from the secret meetings of the League formed by the Duke of Guise's supporters.

Place du Québec – Charles Daudelin's fountain reproduces the effect of the snow-melt breaking up great layers of ice.

Boulevard St-Germain – Just off place St-Germain-des-Prés are the Café des Deux-Magots and the Café de Flore, the famous meeting spots for Right Bank intellectuals and artists. Opposite, the Brasserie Lipp (*no 151*) is a popular venue with politicians, writers and celebrities. Further on, the odd 18C mansion survives (nos **159** and **173**).

The antiquarian quarter – The numerous art galleries and antique shops in the streets (rues des Saints-Pères, Jacob, Bonaparte, de Seine) between the boulevard and the river attract *connoisseurs* and collectors. The **Carré Rive Gauche** (between rues des Saints-Pères, de l'Université, du Bac and quai Voltaire, *see* INTRODUCTION – Shopping) holds a five-day antiques fair in May when each dealer presents one particular object remarkable for its beauty, rarity, or craftsmanship.

Rue Jacob

From 1909 to 1972, the courtyard town house at no 20 was home to **Natalie Clifford Barney**, a wealthy American heiress who settled in Paris to escape the strictures of puritanical America. Known more as a libertine Sapphist and a patroness of the arts than for her own literary accomplishments, Miss Barney hosted a reputed salon frequented by a circle of female companions and literary giants such as Joyce, Proust, Gide and Pound.

Rue des Sts-Pères – The name is a distortion of St-Pierre to whom a chapel (*no 51*) belonging to a Charity hospital was dedicated in the 17C. It is now the Ukrainian Catholic church of St Vladimir the Great. The Engineering School is housed in the 18C mansions at no **28**. Opposite belonging to the Paris V University is a fine bronze door by Paul Landowski.

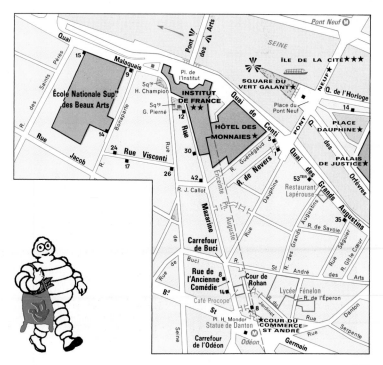

École Nationale des Beaux-Arts – *17 quai Malaquais*. This site was once occupied by a monastery founded in 1608 by Marguerite of Valois, first wife of Henri IV. **La Reine Margot** when imprisoned, made a vow that should she regain her freedom she would have a monastery built in honour of the Patriarch Jacob; on being released she kept her word and entrusted the buildings to the Augustinian order (nicknamed the *Petits Augustins*).

When religious institutions began to be disbanded in 1791, the complex was used to store works of art from other deconsecrated or demolished buildings.

The archeologist **Lenoir** founded the Museum of French Monuments where 1 200 small busts, statues, etc were displayed. Some treasures from St-Denis, the Louvre, Versailles and many churches were thus saved.

The museum was closed in 1816 and replaced by the School of Fine Arts; only the church and cloister of the monastery were kept. In 1860, the school acquired the **Hôtel de Conti** *(11 quai Malaquais)* followed, in 1885, by the Hôtel de Chimay *(nos 15-17)*.

The courtyard and some monuments are open to visit at no **14** rue Bonaparte; these include the doorway from the Château d'Anet – the retreat of Diane de Poitiers, fragments from the Hôtel Legendre, demolished in 1841 and low-reliefs from the Louvre's south wing. There are casts and copies in the courtyards and galleries.

Quai Malaquais – On the corner with rue Bonaparte at no **9** stands a 17C stone and brick house.

The writer Anatole France (1844-1924) was born in a house at no **19** (plaque on no **15**), which also served George Sand between 1832 and 1836, when she wrote *Lélia*.

Rue Bonaparte follows the course of the canal which fed water from the Seine to the moat surrounding the abbey of St-Germain-des-Prés *(see above)*.

Rue Visconti – This narrow alleyway was known in the 16C as "Little Geneva" because many Protestants, including the distinguished ceramist Bernard Palissy (*c*1510-1590), lived in its vicinity. The playwright **Racine** died at no **24** in 1699. Two hundred years later, Balzac founded a printing-house at no **17** (1826) which soon went bankrupt. Later still, **Delacroix** had his studio here from 1836 to 1844.

At **26** rue de Seine amongst the art galleries, note the sign for the famous 17C nightclub, Le Petit Maure.

★★Institut de France ⊙

23 quai de Conti Ⓜ *Pont-Neuf, Odéon. Buses: 24, 27, 39, 48, 58, 70, 72, 95*

A magnificent dome distinguishes the building from afar. Long before the existence of the present building, the Philippe Auguste perimeter wall defended by the **Nesle Tower**, extended to what is now the left wing of the Institute (the Mint side). The tower's history was popularised by Alexandre Dumas' play.

Institut de France from the Pont des Arts

In 1661, three days before he died, Cardinal Mazarin made final bequests from his immense wealth: he left 2 million *livres* for the foundation of a college for 60 scholars from the four provinces (Piedmont, Alsace, Artois and Roussillon) acquired by France under his ministry. The College of Four Nations built in 1663, was opened in 1688: it was closed in 1790 and used as a prison and an art college.

The Institute was a body founded by the Convention, transferred from the Louvre by Napoleon in 1805. It consists of five academies: the Académie Française, founded by Richelieu in 1635 and the Académies des Inscriptions et Belles Lettres (1663), Sciences (1666), Beaux-Arts (1803) and Sciences morales et Politiques (1832).

Académie Française – This is perhaps the most famous academy, best known by linguists for safeguarding the French language from '*franglais*'. It is presently working on the ninth revised edition of the definitive Dictionary of the French Language, of which five out of ten volumes has been published. Forty members are drawn from the worlds of literature, the Church, diplomatic service, medicine, journalism; an elected member holds this position of honour for life.

Exterior – A circular central unit – the Jesuit-styled chapel – flanked by two square pavilions were designed by **Le Vau**, architect of the Louvre across the river. The drum of dome bears the Mazarin coat of arms: a lictor's fasces and a leather strap (his father was a saddler).

In the courtyard, to the left of the dome, is the **Mazarin Library**★.

Interior – The former chapel is now the formal audience chamber where members are sworn in. The Mazarin commemorative monument is by **Coysevox**.

For Hôtel des Monnaies – see les QUAIS.

Rue Mazarine – At no **12**, beyond the square G-Pierné stood a theatre where **Molière** made his first appearance as an actor. The company included the Béjart family of two brothers and two sisters who lived at no 10. In 1643, on inheriting some money from his mother, the 21 year-old changed his name from Poquelin to Molière and gladly abandoned his legal career chosen by his father, a tapestry-maker to the king.

The troupe leased the real tennis court and transformed it into a theatre which they named the Illustrious Theatre. But the venture failed and a year later, the company was forced to move to quai des Célestins.

At no **30**, the first Paris **fire station** was home to the capital's first fire brigade created in 1722 by François Dumouriez du Perrier (one-time valet to Molière, and later member of the Comédie-Française).

No **42**, again an indoor real tennis court converted into the **Guénégaud Theatre**, was where in 1671, opera was presented for the first time in France. The work, *Pomone* by Perrin and Cambert, played for eight months before a rival composer, Lulli, jealous of its success, had the theatre closed. After Molière's death in 1673, his company, evicted from the Palais-Royal by Lulli again, made the theatre their home until 1689.

Carrefour de Buci – In the 18C the Buci crossroads was the focal point of the Left Bank. It boasted a sedan chair rank, a corps of 20 sentries, a gibbet and a pillar to which miscreants were attached by an iron collar.

Jeux de Paume – There were a number of **real tennis courts** in the area, three in the rue de Buci alone. This archaic form of tennis as we know it was a very popular game: until the 15C the ball was thrown by hand, then a glove was used and finally the racket was introduced. In 1687, the best players received a fee for appearing in public – an early example of sport being played professionally!

'With the fishermen and the life on the river, the beautiful barges with their own life on board, the tugs with their smoke-stacks that folded back to pass under the bridges, pulling a tow of barges, the great elms on the stone banks of the river, the plane trees and in some places the poplars, I could never be lonely along the river. With so many trees in the city, you could see the spring coming each day until a night of warm wind would bring it suddenly in one morning...

You expected to be sad in the fall. Part of you died each year when the leaves fell from the trees and their branches were bare against the wind and the cold, wintry light. But you knew there would always be the spring, as you knew the river would flow again after it was frozen...

ERNEST HEMINGWAY – A Moveable Feast

Quartier St-Lazare

Ⓜ *St-Lazare, St-Augustin. Buses: 20, 21, 22, 24, 26, 27, 28, 29, 32, 43, 49, 53, 66, 80, 81, 84, 94, 95*

The neighbourhood – The St Lazare main-line railway station links northwest France (Dieppe, Caen, Le Havre...) with Paris, shuttling people from the suburbs to town or out to the coast and seaside. The exciting development of the railway was especially well captured by the Impressionist painter Claude Monet. The area around was developed in the 19C to accommodate a middle-class society in standardised, comfortable apartment blocks served by convenient large department stores.

La Gare St-Lazare by Claude Monet

Le Printemps – *64 boulevard Haussmann*. This store was founded in 1865 and owed its immediate success to its proximity to the station. It was the first to install lifts, and boasts fine window displays for children at Christmas!

Galeries Lafayette – *40 boulevard Haussmann*. A tiny haberdasher's founded in 1895 by Alphonse Khan is the origin of this modern-day chain. Its dome and balustrades were designed by Ferdinand Chanut in 1910. On 19 January 1919, the aviator Védrines landed his Caudron G3 on the shop's roof terrace.

★Église St Augustin ⓥ – *Place St-Augustin*. The church was designed by Baltard (*see* les HALLES-BEAUBOURG) between 1860 and 1871 and was the first ecclesiastical building to consist of a metal infra-structure clad in stone. The innovative means of construction meant that the traditional Gothic design could be retained without any need for external buttressing. The triangular site dictated the church's unusual form, broadening out from the porch to the domed chancel. It was here that Charles de Foucault was converted in October 1886.

A replica in bronze of the equestrian statue of Joan of Arc by Paul Dubois in Reims (1896) stands before the church and the imposing 1927 building of the Cercle Militaire.

Chapelle Expiatoire ⓥ – *Square Louis XVI (entrance: 29 rue Pasquier)*. The cemetery, opened in 1722, was used as a burial ground for the Swiss Guards killed at the Tuileries on 10 August 1792, and for the victims of the guillotine which stood in place de la Concorde (*see* CHAMPS-ÉLYSÉES). These last numbered 1 343 and included Louis XVI and Marie-Antoinette.

Hector Berlioz died dejected and alone at 4 rue de Calais. His first great success was in 1854 with *L'Enfance du Christ*, which gained him nomination to the Académie des Beaux Arts (*see* ST-GERMAIN-DES-PRÉS). The final years, however were fraught with tragedy: the death of his second wife (1862), the failure of his *Les Troyens* (1863), the death of his son Louis and the onset of a nervous disorder.

Immediately on his return to Paris, Louis XVIII had the remains of his brother and sister-in-law disinterred and transported to the royal necropolis at St-Denis (21 January 1815). Between 1816 and 1821 the chapel was built to Fontaine's plans.

The cloister occupies the site of the old burial ground. The tombs of Charlotte Corday (who stabbed Marat in his bath to avenge the Girondins) and Philippe-Égalité are on either side of the steps leading into the chapel; inside, two marble groups show Louis XVI with an angel (by Bosio) and Marie-Antoinette supported by an allegory of Religion with the features of Madame Elisabeth, the king's sister (by Cortot). The crypt altar marks the place where Louis XVI's and Marie-Antoinette's bodies were found.

Quartier de L'Europe M *Europe, Liège, Rome. Buses: 53, 66, 80, 95*

Place de l'Europe – The major intersection of six important roads straddles the railway lines north of St Lazare; the bridge was last rebuilt in 1930. It also marks the boundary between the *bourgeois* neighbourhood to the west and a more popular quarter to the east, as defined at the time of the Restoration and the Second Empire.

The radiating axes were named after the grand European metropolises: London, Madrid, Amsterdam, Vienna, Stockholm, Milan, Moscow to attract the right kind of residents.

Towards the close of the 19C, the symbolist poet Stéphane Mallarmé (1842-1898) lived at 89 rue de Rome, where he entertained Verlaine and Rimbaud.

> Émile Zola lived until his death on 28 September 1902 from asphyxiation at 21bis rue de Bruxelles.

La Nouvelle Athènes

M *Trinité, Saint-Georges, Pigalle. Buses: 32, 43, 49, 68, 81*

The 'Nouvelle Athènes' and quartier Saint-Georges were developed in the 1820s for a moneyed professional middle-class of 'modest' means that was fast replacing the aristocracy of the Ancien Régime. Buildings were designed in sober blocks, five or six storeys high. Modern industrial processes meant that large glass windows could be manufactured more cheaply than before, as could sculpted mouldings and friezes, cast-iron balcony railings, staircase banisters and door grilles: all features that proliferate in this new residential style. Travel to England

> Georges Bizet, composer of the operas *l'Arlésienne* (1872) and *Carmen* (1874) lived his final years at 22 rue de Douai.

during the aftermath of the Revolution introduced the French refugees to the urban style of John Nash (1752-1835) who designed long terraces of houses in Bath (Royal Crescent) and London (Regent's Park 1811-1825) (*see Michelin Green Guide* GREAT BRITAIN) as part of a greater urban scheme.

Avenue Frochot – This gated private compound has counted amongst its residents Alexandre Dumas, Baudelaire's muse Mme Sabatier, the painter Renoir and his film director son, and Toulouse-Lautrec who had his last studio there.

Place Saint-Georges – None of the original buildings from 1824 survive. The neo-Renaissance pastiche that dominates this pleasant square dates from the 1840s, complete with griffins, grotesques, busts of Diana and Apollo, allegories of Architecture and Sculpture, Wisdom and Plenty. The centrepiece of the square was once a fountain that watered horses, drained, alas when the metro was built. The central column bears in delicate relief several comic characters often drawn by the illustrator and cartoonist Gavarni who lived locally.

The Théâtre Saint-Georges was used for filming Truffaut's film '**Le Dernier Métro**' in 1980.

Square d'Orléans – *80 rue Taitbout*. The private square is a miniature fragment of England, built 1829-1845 by Edward Creasy to accommodate 46 apartments and six artist's studios. Its success was immediate attracting sculptors (Dantan), painters (Dubufe), dancers, singers and musicians. The pianist Zimmerman received Rossini, Berlioz, his future son-in-law Gounod and Chopin, his neighbour at no 9. Meanwhile, George Sand lived on the first floor of no 5; she recalls in her memoirs the pleasures of living in such proximity to the composer before his death in 1849.

> Impressionist painters Bonnard and Vuillard shared a studio with Lugné-Poe at 28 rue la Bruyère (1891); at no 45 once lived the composer Hector Berlioz and then the family of Jean Cocteau. At 9 rue Henner lived the Surrealist poet Guillaume Apollinaire with the painter Marie Laurencin.

★Musée Gustave Moreau

– *14 rue de La Rochefou-cauld*. Gustave Moreau (1826-1898) bequeathed to the French nation with specific instructions that it should remain intact, his house and collection from a life's work: 850 paintings, 7 000 drawings, 350 watercolours and wax sculptures. Moreau was greatly influenced by the Colourist techniques of Delacroix and the neo-Mannerist Chassériau; he delighted in the fantastical, biblical and mythological subjects, reworking such figures as Sappho, Salome, Orpheus, Leda... throughout his life. Among his students rank Roualt, Matisse and Desvallière.

Musée Gustave Moreau

An especially designed cabinet with wings holds many of his drawings, while another curious piece of furniture contains watercolours.

The cramped and cluttered living quarters were situated on the first floor: note a working sketch by Poussin and a photograph of the pre-Raphaelite work by Burne-Jones in the corridor.

Other personal possessions on view include Bernard Palissy and Moustiers ceramics (dining room), furniture, a rare portrait of the artist by Degas, the effects of Alexandrine Dureux, his close and intimate friend for 25 years who died in 1890.

The second and third floors of the family house were considerably altered by the artist to accommodate his paintings, in a large, airy space.

> **Rue Notre-Dame-de-Lorette** was home to Delacroix from 1844 to 1857 *(no 50)*; where Paul Gauguin was born *(no 56)*; immortalises Abelard and Héloïse *(no 54)*; accommodated Pissarro *(no 49)* around the corner from Theo Van Gogh *(8 Cité Pigalle off 41 rue Pigalle)*.

Musée de la Vie Romantique – *Maison Renan-Scheffer, 16 rue Chaptal*. The charming house set back from the street with its garden was where **Ary Scheffer** (1795-1858) lived and worked for nearly 30 years. This artist of Dutch origin was influenced by the Romantics and greatly admired by Louis-Philippe. On Friday evenings his home was the meeting-place for a group of painter and literary friends (Delacroix, Ingres, Liszt, Chopin, George Sand and Ernest Renan who married Ary's niece).

Aurore Lauth-Sand's bequest of paintings, jewellery and drawings evokes memories of her grandmother **George Sand**, her family and friends. Exhibitions dedicated to the 19C French Romantic movement are held on the first floor of the house. In the studio-annexe are exhibited canvases by Ary Scheffer together with a collection of his furniture, easel, photographs...

> **Marcel Proust** (1871-1922), perhaps the most famous of the French Romantic novelists, spent 12 years at 102 Boulevard Haussmann. The second floor bedroom has recently (1996) been restored and opened, by appointment, to the public. The author of *A la recherche du temps perdu (Remembrance of things past)* chose to live in his aunt's flat for the macabre reason that he had witnessed his uncle die there, and this memory might provide inspiration for his writing.
>
> Being very susceptible to noise, Proust tended to work at night and struggled to sleep by day through the noise of the boulevard below; to this end he had the bedroom muffled with cork tiles and heavy curtains. There he would spend days on end shut-up in bed, brewing various vapours to help his chronic asthma.
>
> His main distraction, other than occasionally venturing out to socialise with the upper classes at the Ritz, was the "*théâtrephone*" which relayed live performances of opera down an early version of the telephone, at some exorbitant expense.
>
> When *Du côté de chez Swann*, the first volume of the collection was submitted to the Gallimard publishers, it was turned down by André Gide who subsequently admitted that his decision had been the "gravest mistake ever made".

TROCADÉRO ★★

Michelin plan 11 – fold 28: H 7
See street maps under EIFFEL TOWER *and* PASSY.
Ⓜ *Trocadéro. Buses: 22, 30, 32, 63*

The Chaillot Palace with its broad terrace and powerful fountains set in the Trocadero Gardens provides a raised view over the Seine, Champ-de-Mars and Eiffel Tower. It is this view, coupled with the rich and diverse museum collections that draws the visitor to this imposing architectural monument of the early 20C.

The Bassompierre Mansion – In the latter half of the 16C, Catherine de' Medici built a country house on the Chaillot Hill, then a rural area some distance from the city. This was bought, in due course, by Marshal Bassompierre, a companion in arms of Henri IV. Handsome, witty, valiant in the field, he lived life to the full; he was also a reckless gambler. Having offended Cardinal Richelieu he was sent to the Bastille in 1631 – careful to burn 6 000 love-letters before he went.

The Convent of the Visitation – At the demise of Bassompierre, Queen Henrietta of England, wife of Philip of Orleans, acquired the mansion and founded a Convent of the Visitation of Holy Mary – Parisians innocently referred to the nuns as the Daughters of Bassompierre!
The convent became renowned for its great preachers: Bossuet, Bourdaloue and Massillon, and as a retreat for royal and ennobled ladies of the court, including Marie Mancini, Cardinal Mazarin's niece, and Mlle de La Vallière – for both of whom it seemed politic to withdraw from the attentions of Louis XIV.

Grandiose projects – Napoleon chose Chaillot as the site for a palace for his son, the King of Rome. Stupendous plans were drawn up by Percier and Fontaine; the convent was razed; the top of the hill levelled; the slope reduced; the léna Bridge built: then the Empire fell. Marshal Blücher demanded that the bridge that commemorated a Prussian defeat be destroyed but Louis XVIII interposed, proposing to sit in his sedan mid-way across and be blown up with it.

Trocadéro – The name Trocadero was given to the area in 1827 after a military tournament on the site had re-enacted the French capture four years previously of Fort Trocadero, near Cadiz.
The square, place du Trocadéro, was laid out in 1858. A Moorish-inspired edifice was then built for the 1878 Exhibition which in 1937 made way for the present Chaillot Palace. Today, the semicircular square, dominated by an equestrian statue of Marshal Foch, is a centre point from which major roads radiate to the Alma Bridge, the Étoile, the Bois de Boulogne and the Passy quarter; the wall at the corner of avenue Georges-Mandel encloses the Passy cemetery *(see PASSY)*.
Opposite the Passy wing of the Palais de Chaillot stands a statue of **Benjamin Franklin** (1706-1790), the statesman who during his stay in Paris (1777-1785), successfully negotiated financial and military support from the French that permitted the 13 States of America to secure independence from British Rule.

★★PALAIS DE CHAILLOT

The spectacular, low-lying palace of white stone, consisting of twin pavilions linked by a portico and extended by wings curving to frame the wide terrace, was the design of architects Carlu, Boileau and Azéma. The palace's horizontal lines along the brow of the hill make a splendid foil to the vertical sweep of the Eiffel Tower across the river. The pavilion copings, back and front, bear inscriptions in letters of gold by the poet Paul Valéry.

★★★**Terrace** – Looking across to the Champ-de-Mars, you get a wonderful **view★★★**, in the foreground, of the Seine and the Left Bank, and beyond dominating all, the Eiffel Tower; in the far distance is the École Militaire, a handsome reminder of the 18C.
8 gilded figures line the terrace along the wings – *Flora* by Marcel Gimont being the most famous. Before the left pavilion stands a monumental bronze of *Apollo* by H **Bouchard** *(see* MONTPARNASSE*)* balanced on the Passy side, with *America* by Jacques Zwoboda. Set into the actual pavement is a plaque citing the words of Father Wrésinszki, the founder of the ATD Third World movement.

R. Besse/MICHELIN

Palais de Chaillot
Art Déco statue

Théâtre National de Chaillot – Beneath the palace terrace is one of the capital's largest theatres *(access through the hall in the left pavilion)*. Under skilled directors and talented actors, it became the home of the People's National Theatre – Théâtre National Populaire (TNP). Since modernised, this theatre serves as a multi-purpose cultural centre, seating 1 200. On the left, below the steps to the gardens, is the small **Salle Gémier**, erected in 1966 as an experimental playhouse.

★**Jardins du Trocadéro** – *avenue de New York*. These were designed for the 1937 Exhibition. Beyond the walls on either side of the long rectangular pool on an axis with the Iéna Bridge, the final slopes of Chaillot Hill lead down, beneath flowering trees, to the banks of the Seine.

The pool, bordered by stone and bronze gilt statues, is at its most spectacular at night when the powerful fountains are floodlit.

Right wing

★★**Musée de la Marine** ⓥ – *first on right*. The Maritime Museum was founded in 1827 by order of Charles X to display scale models and important artefacts from the naval dockyards; figureheads, pictures, dioramas, and mementoes of naval heroes enhance the original collections.

The great hall is devoted to naval art and maritime history from the 17C. The side gallery overlooking the Trocadero gardens deals with the scientific, technical and traditional aspects of the evolution of navigation.

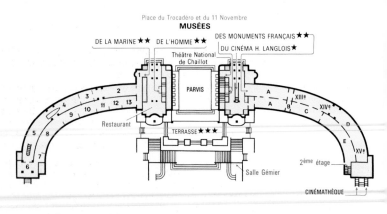

Place du Trocadéro et du 11 Novembre
MUSÉES

1) The **Océan**, a late 18C vessel.

2) 17C and 18C ships: The **Louis XV** (an educational toy for the young king), The **Royale** and the **Louis le Grand**. Fine group of galleys dominated by **The Réale** (with decoration attributed to Puget).

3) The **Ports of France★**, a series of canvases by the 18C artist, Joseph Vernet. The **Royal Louis**, a rare model from the Louis XV period; remains of the vessel, **Le Juste**, lost in 1759. Stern and bow of Marie-Antoinette's barge at Versailles.

4) The Revolution and the First Empire. The **Emperor's Barge** (1811). The **Belle Poule** in which Napoleon's body was returned from St Helena in 1840.

5) The Restoration, the Second Empire and the Third Republic. **The Valmy**, modelled in ebony, ivory and silver, the Navy's last sailing ship. **The Gloire**, the first armourplated vessel in the world (1859). Dioramas of the dismantling, transportation and erection of the Luxor obelisk (1831). Mementoes of great naval heroes: F de Lesseps, Brazza, Charcot.

6) The modern navy. Reconstruction of a gun-boat bridge.

7) Underwater exploration, hydrography and diving.

8) Fishing and maritime traditions.

9) Model of an early steamship (Jouffroy d'Abbans). Model restoration workshops.

10) History of merchant shipping.

11) Wooden boats (18-19C). The great expeditions. The **Astrolabe**, the sloop of the 19C navigator and Antarctic explorer, Dumont d'Urville. Wreckage from the ships of the 18C navigator La Pérouse.

12) Marine charts and navigation instruments.

13) Temporary exhibitions.

★★**Musée de l'Homme** ⓥ – *Straight ahead*. The Museum of Mankind maps out the evolution of mankind, its different races and ways of life.

On the first floor is the anthropological gallery explaining the origin of species, the palaeontological gallery where human characteristics are compared by means of fossils (examples include the mammoth ivory Lespugue Venus and the neolithic Grossgartach burial from the Yonne Valley).

The African collections include prehistoric artefacts (frescoes from the Ahaggar area in the Sahara), ethnographic displays (costumes, tools, arms) and art (medieval Abyssinian art, Central African sculpture). The European Gallery is at the far end of the first floor.

On the second floor are presentations of the Arctic regions (Eskimo crafts, masks from Greenland), the Near and Far East and the Pacific (Easter Island, New Guinea). The Continental America galleries are particularly rich in pre-Columbian, Maya and Aztec art, much of which come from the Royal collections (painted ceramics, bark paintings, beautiful rock crystal skull and statues of the god Quetzalcóatl).

The Music Room groups together a broad range of wind, string and percussion instruments from prehistoric times (Vietnamese Lithophone) to the present day.

Left wing

★★Musée des National Monuments Français ⊙ – This museum of France's monumental art and mural painting, comprising casts and replicas, was the brainchild of the Gothic Revival architect and restorer of medieval monuments Viollet-le-Duc. It was opened in 1880.

The exhibits are grouped by geographical region, by school and by period, making evolutions of style, themes, geographical and other influences, easy to follow.

Sculpture – *(left) double gallery on the ground floor: Rooms 2 to 6.* (**A**) Romanesque sculpture and tympana from Moissac, Vézelay, Autun – *Room 7* (**B**) Military Crusader architecture: fortified castles in Syria. – *Rooms 8 to 11* (**C**) Gothic cathedral statuary (Chartres, Amiens, Reims, Notre-Dame). – *Rooms 12 to 18* (**D**) 13C, 14C and 15C sculpture (tomb effigies from St-Denis and other churches; palace ornaments, fountains, calvaries). *Rooms 19 to 21* (**E**) The Renaissance (tombs from Tours and Nantes).

2nd floor: Rooms 22 to 24: works by Jean Goujon, Ligier Richier, Germain Pilon. *Room 25:* Sculpture from the gardens at Versailles. *Rooms 26 to 29:* an introduction to architecture, models and temporary exhibitions.

Mural painting – *(right; pavilion's upper floors)* Replicas of the most famous Romanesque and Gothic frescoes are applied to full-scale architectural reproductions: the crypt of St-Germain at Auxerre (featuring the oldest frescoes in France), the vault, porch and gallery of St-Savin-sur-Gartempe, the chancel of St Martin's at Vic, the apse of Berzé-la-Ville, the dome of Cahors Cathedral, The Dance of Death of La Chaise-Dieu Abbey-Church, etc. Note the vivid colour and expression of the figures.

★Musée du Cinéma Henri Langlois ⊙ – The history of motion pictures, from the very beginning of photography, is traced through 60 galleries. Reynaud's *théâtre optique* (1888), Marey's photographic rifle, Edison's *kinétoscope* (1894); the Lumière brothers' kinematograph and photorama, posters, models (some of them completed by the Russian director Eisenstein), film sets (the robot of Fritz Lang's *Metropolis*), film studios (Méliès, Pathé), costumes and dresses worn by film stars (Rudolph Valentino, Greta Garbo) illustrate the film world.

Over 5 000 objects show the evolution of the technical aspects of filming: shooting, staging, projection, and evoke the magical world of cinema.

Cinémathèque – *Jardins du Trocadéro, avenue Albert-de-Mun side.* The film library is one of the richest in the world. As many as three or four films are shown daily. It is a meeting place for the professionals and amateurs of the film world.

VAUGIRARD

Michelin plan 11, folds 40 – 41: M 8 – M 9, N 7 – N 9
Michelin plan 11, fold 39: M 5
Ⓜ *Pasteur, Vaugirard, Volontaires, Convention. Buses: 39, 49, 80*

Located between the Farmers General Wall and the Thiers Fortifications (*see* INTRODUCTION – History), the faubourg de Vaugirard used to be a rural dependency of the Abbey of St-Germain-des-Prés, where a retreat was built in 1256; in the 18C it consisted of a village of 700 people. In 1860 Vaugirard – a corruption of the names Vauboitron and Val Gérard, became a district of Paris with a population of 40 000 inhabitants. It is bisected by two principle streets: rue de Vaugirard and rue Lecourbe.

Rue de Vaugirard is Paris' longest street, running between the Latin Quarter and Porte de Versailles, once lined with inns up to the late 19C, and Rue Lecourbe, the old main road out of Paris to Sèvres and Meudon.

The 15th *arrondissement* is off the usual tourist track. It is a lively district where traditional tenement blocks are dotted amongst open spaces and modern, faceless residential developments. Shops tend to centre around intersections of rue de la Convention and rue de Vaugirard, rue Lecourbe, rue du Commerce and rue St-Charles. Although night life is probably non-existent, the neighbourhood has some redeeming features like the

Georges-Brassens Park, la Ruche which was a large artists' residence in the years around 1910 (passage de Dantzig), the **Santos-Dumont villa**, the 21C gardens in the **André-Citroën Park**, a building designed like a "passenger liner" (3 boulevard Victor, Ⓜ Balard), magnificent council housing built in 1913 (5 rue Saïda, Ⓜ Porte-de-Versailles) and the headquarters of the Canal+ Television channel. For those who enjoy water sports, the **Aquaboulevard** is worth a visit.

Pasteur Institute Ⓥ – *25 rue du Docteur-Roux*. A scientific foundation of international repute, the Pasteur Institute mainly comprises centres of basic and applied research, of teaching and documentation, of inoculation and screening with laboratories producing serums, vaccines and diagnostic tests, and a hospital specialising in infectious diseases.

The Institute has branches in Lille and Lyon, and 22 others worldwide, continuing pioneering research into such infectious diseases as Hepatitis and AIDS with international support. It was to this cause that Wallace Simpson bequeathed her famous jewellery collection when she died in 1993.

Émile Roux had studied the toxins of diphtheria and discovered its antidote in the late 19C, when he was appointed director of the Pasteur Institute. He subsequently summoned from Lille his researchers Albert Calmette and Camille Guérin who, in 1915, isolated tuberculosis and developed its vaccine (BCG).

Louis Pasteur's living quarters may be visited, together with scientific memorabilia, as can the neo-Byzantine **crypt★** with his tomb.

Louis Pasteur (1822-1895) is one of the greatest scientists ever to have lived. At the age of 25, in his laboratory at the École Normale Supérieure (*see* LATIN QUARTER), he established the principle of molecular dissymmetry; at 35, that of fermentation; at 40, he laid the foundations for asepsis thus refuting preconceived ideas about spontaneous generations, he studied the ruinous diseases affecting beer and wine production and of the silkworm; at 58, he studied viruses and vaccines. He isolated the rabies virus, researching its prevention, delivering an antidote for the first time on 7 July 1885.

★Parc Georges-Brassens – *Rue des Morillons*. This is one of the largest parks created in Paris since the last century. It occupies the site of the old Vaugirard abattoirs, of which a few vestiges survive – the horse hall, two bronze bulls by the animal sculptor Cain at the main entrance, and the auction belfry reflected in the central basin.

A wooded hill dominates the park with its children's play areas, a belvedere, a climbing rock and a vineyard harvested in early October accompanied with great celebrations.

An olfactory garden has been created for the blind, containing over 80 species of odoriferous plants.

La Ruche – Passage Dantzig

The three-storey wine pavilion designed by Eiffel for the Exposition Universelle of 1900 was salvaged from scrap by the socially successful sculptor Boucher, with the intention of adapting it for use as artists' bedsits-cum-studios. The gate was rescued from the Pavillon de la Femme.

Amongst its most famous lodgers were Fernand Leger (1905), Chagall (1910), Soutine, Modigliani and the Swiss novelist Blaise Cendras. The second generation included the sculptors Archipenko, Idenbaum, Lipchitz, Zadkine, Brancusi, Kisling...

★★Parc André-Citroën

Main entrance: rue Balard Ⓜ *Balard or Javel. Bus: 42*

The park – A Citroën manufacturing plant was closed down in the mid-70s, leaving a vast 14ha – 35 acre site for a futuristic park where vegetation merges with stone, glass and above all water, which is omnipresent. The symbolism of each thematic garden – the white and black gardens, the 'restless' garden and the "serial" gardens in which each of the six senses is associated with a metal and a colour.

The park draws upon traditional French formal garden design for its inorganic features, dark colours, right angles and symmetry (canal, water-lilies), upon English garden design for the glasshouses and the 'restless' garden, while the smaller enclaves (serial and black and white gardens) recall Japanese prototypes.

Parc André-Citroën

The white garden – *On the other side of rue Balard, at the entrance to the actual park.* High walls enclose a small square planted with white-flowering perennials. To the north, water tumbles over a series of striated granite blocks.

★**The black garden** – Here, connoisseurs will recognise spirea, reeds, bear's breech, rhododendrons, poppies, irises… amongst the bushy, dark-leafed vegetation. Magnificent clipped conifers recall bonsai. A circuitous path leads into an open space with 64 fountains.

The main lawn is a pleasant spot to stop and rest. The striking mirrored forms of the Ponant complex contrast with the rhythm of the fountains, the water-lilies in the still stretches of water; solid granite towers provide two raised look-out points, while the huge transparent glasshouses appear weightless. The orangery houses exhibitions during the summer; another contains native shrubs from the Australian sub-continent. Between the two extends a "water peristyle" where a hundred water fountains enact their synchronised dance, showering the more intrepid. Behind the glasshouses, a regiment of clipped magnolias stand to attention.

★**The serial gardens** – A series of six beds is bisected by stretches of cascading water. Ramps and walkways provide a bird's-eye view over the whole area including its most secret nooks. Each garden is a conceit – yellow is associated with gold and the sixth sense, silver with sight, red with bauxite and taste, orange with rust and touch, green with oxidised copper and hearing, blue with mercury and smell. Paths paved in stone or over wooden ramps thread their way through open space or dense foliage, under a pergola or through the air.

The restless garden – Clumps of rustling bamboo and random trees punctuate this man-made wilderness where apparently wind-sown plants are left to grow in the uncut grass, ever changing with the seasons.

Exit by the railway line and up-river towards the Eiffel Tower to reach Javel Ⓜ*/RER.*

★**Aquaboulevard** – *place Balard.* Ⓜ *Balard. Buses: 42, PC, 169.* This semi-indoor water-world complex comprises a swimming pool with jacuzzi, wave-machine and giant slide, set amongst plants and trees. Additional activities provided include minigolf, bowls, tennis and squash, billiards, exercise gym and body-building, restaurant and shops. Aquaboulevard is designed rather for recreation and leisure than for serious sport.

La VILLETTE ★★

Michelin plan 11 – folds 10 and 11: B 20, B 21, C 20, C 21
Ⓜ *Porte de la Villette (north – Cité des Sciences et de L'Industrie) and Porte de Pantin (south – Grande Halle)*

The city's largest park extends between the Portes de la Villette and de Pantin, comprising one large complex dedicated to science and industry, one to music with its independent concert venue (le Zénith), and a series of peripheral buildings for screening films, temporary exhibitions and other seasonal attractions. Today, it plays an important role in presenting and encouraging popular culture at all levels.

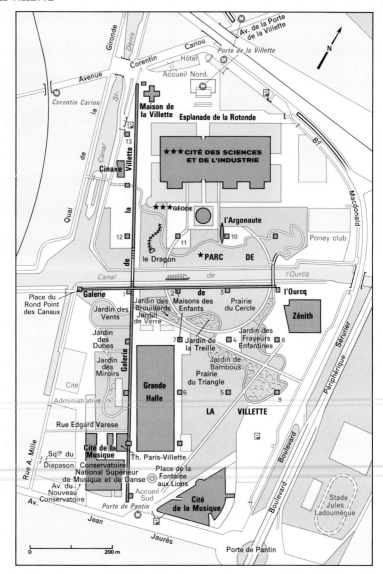

LES FOLIES :

1 - Brasserie
2 - Video workshop
3 - Crèche

4 - View point
5 - La Ville café
6 - First Aid post
7 - Sculpture workshop
8 - Zénith Reception

9 - Jazz club
10 - Submarine folly
11 - Observatory
12 - Band stand
13 - Refreshments

★★★ Cité des Sciences et de L'Industrie ⊙

30 avenue Corentin-Cariou.

The interactive complex devised by Maurice Lévy was opened in 1986 in the shell of the former cattle-market auction-hall, converted by the prize-winning architect Adrien Fainsilber.

The building – Three elements mould the building's inception:

Water – in the moat encircles the main building.

Vegetation – penetrating the building within three large temperature-controlled conservatories.

Light – 'source of energy for the living world' floods through two rotating domes (17m – 56ft) into the exhibition space. A number of contemporary works inspired by technology and the Scientific world are her displayed: *Souvenirs* by Jacques Monory near the Planetarium, *Invent the Earth* by Jeffrey Shaw invites the visitor to glimpse synthesised images through a periscope.

Facilities – Information desks at either end of the complex provide floor plans and event programmes.

Three upper floors of the main museum area are reserved for permanent displays and interactive terminals dedicated to the ergonomic exploration of science and technology.

Explora houses various departments structured on the concept of the **Universe** (space age, geological evolution of the planet Earth, the oceans and their forces); **Life** (biological make-up, living matter, evolution of man and his future); **Matter** (elemental structures and their workings, robotics, energy and its applications); **Communication** (sound, light, computers simulating flight by means of images in real time).

Infra-red head-sets pick-up commentary in a choice of four languages from receptors throughout the gallery, designed thereby to allow for free movement between the departments.

The **Aquarium** recreates a 'typical' environment for flora and fauna found at a depth of between 5 and 40 metres in the Mediterranean.

The solar system can be explored in the **Planétarium** (*2nd floor*) – one of the prime visitor attractions. Astronomical phenomena are described with projections of actual real-life images, a simulator and triphonic sound.

The **Salle Sciences-Actualités** serves as a kind of press-room with multimedia facilities for accessing published articles and research findings, sometimes sponsored by the centre.

The **Cité des Enfants** (*Inventorium*) is a hands-on interactive section reserved for 3 to 12 year-olds.

The **Cinéma Louis-Lumière** screens film-documentaries and organises scientific demonstrations, film seasons and thematic programmes in conjunction with the teaching of the school curriculum.

The **Médiathèque** (*1st floor basement*) is a library that provides not only books and printed data, but also access to externally held computerised published information in the form of video, CD-ROM and other educational material.

The **Salle Louis-Braille** consists of a specially designed facility for those with impaired sight. Other additional professional research amenities are available on request.

★★★**La Géode** – The shining steel globe, 36m – 118ft in diameter, designed by Adrien Fainsilber, seems to hover over a sheet of water: a brilliant feat of engineering in terms both of structure and technology. The weight of the auditorium seating (6 000 tons) is diffused via a fine web of supports to a single pillar, completely independent of the external globe designed separately by Chamayou. The geodesic mesh frame, assembled to a tolerance of 0.1mm, is enclosed in a a mantle comprising 6 433 triangular stainless-steel panels. Inside, the **auditorium** is equipped with 357 reclining seats set at an angle of 30°. The hemispherical aluminium 1 000m^2 (11 000sq ft) screen is perforated for sound. The distortion caused by the 26m – 85ft curved screen, is unusual but somehow effective for panoramic views. The wide-angle lens encompasses a 180° field of vision, exceeding that of the human eye (140°), but similar to that of a bird's. The multimedia system which consists of an Omnimax projector (70mm film running horizontally to project a picture nine times bigger than the 35mm film) has a sound capacity of 21 000W reproduced by 12 quadraphonic amplifiers and 6 low-frequency modules.

La Géode, Cité des Sciences et de l'Industrie

L'argonaute – This submarine was launched on 29 June 1957 at Cherbourg; it has covered 210 000 miles, the equivalent of four times the circumference of the earth, and was submerged a total of 32 700 hours before finally coming to rest beside the Géode. It now serves as an additional exhibition space dedicated to the submersible's technology.

Le Cinaxe ⓘ – *Located on the west side of la Géode, near St Denis canal.* The Cinaxe simulator enables up to 60 people to 'physically' experience a particular film action – a flight through outer space, driving round a motor-racing track, etc during a 4-5 minute 'ride'. This sensation is in part achieved by the capsule's actual hydraulic motion in any direction to a degree of between $+30°$ or $-30°$ tilt.

★Parc

The park has been designed by **Bernard Tschumi** around three principle sets of features: follies, galleries and 'play' areas. It can be particularly pleasurable to spend a summer evening in the park watching films projected in the open air. Chairs and mats are available for hire.

Nine red pavilions built of enamelled iron over a concrete frame, punctuate the park every 120m – 394ft on a grid pattern. '**Follies**', more usually denoting 18C fanciful pavilions, are here designed with a particular function be it a slide, weather vane or viewing platform.

Jardin de l'Energie

This garden has been laid out in a 6m – 19ft pit to create a micro-climate and encourage the growth of bamboo. Alternate bands of black and white pebbles, black and green bamboo extend to the energy wall which dispenses heat and humidity through a system of superimposed gargoyles. At the far end, the sound cylinder experiments with the perception of sound in space.

The '*circulations*' comprise two perpendicular galleries running north/south, **Galerie de la Villette**, and east/west, **Galerie de l'Ourcq**, and a walkway through the gardens planted with willow, hornbeam, golden and Pennsylvania ash. These gardens in turn have been arranged to accommodate various recreational areas around contemporary sculptures. Chemetoff's bamboo garden provides a context for a piece by Daniel Buren and Bernhard Leitner's pillar of sound. Vexlard's trellis garden angles its perspectives through Jean-Max Albert's sculptural compositions, whilst Alain Pélissier merges his water-garden with Fujiko Nakaya's artistic concepts. In between, great grassy spaces provide open play areas or '**surfaces**'.

The great hall – The Grande Halle once served as the cattle auction hall. Built in 1867 by J de Merindol, it typically for a building of its kind combines cast-iron columns, an iron frame and a lead roof. In 1983, it was converted into a multi-function venue with movable partitions with a capacity of over 15 000. Various artistic events are held here ranging from exhibitions, trade fairs, concerts (classical, rock, jazz), dance, theatre...

Le Zénith – Inaugurated in 1984, this hall is used mainly for variety and rock concerts. Its light modular structure and canopy mark a turning-point in the design of modern concert-halls.

Hire a deck-chair and watch a film on a summer's evening...
For details of exhibitions, concert seasons, film screenings and open-air festivals Consult the weekly programme (Le Pariscope *or* Officiel des Spectacles) *published on Wednesdays.*

Cité de la Musique

Located at the southern entrance to the park, near Porte de Pantin, and on either side of the Lion Fountain, Music City, designed by Christian de Portzamparc, houses all the facilities needed to study dance and music in France today. The western part contains the **Conservatoire National Supérieur de Musique et de Danse de Paris** (Paris National Conservatory of Music and Dance), formerly in rue de Madrid.

The **Conservatoire** owes its existence to the initiative of Sarrette, intended as a training ground for the newly constituted National Guard, officially founded in 1795 under the Convention; it came to be called the National Institute of Music.

Musée de la Musique ⓘ – The east wing contains a concert-hall (1 200 people) and a music museum which today, contains over 4 500 musical instruments from the 16C to the present time. An audio-visual tour, taking the visitor through the history of western music, includes Stradivarius and Amati violins, some 50 spinets, harpsichords, and pianos, a 100 or so guitars, recorders, bass viols and lutes. Also on display are tools used by stringed-instrument and piano makers, and instruments once owned by famous musicians (Berlioz, Chopin and Fauré, Adolphe Sax).

Paris... captured on film

Whether seeking inspiration for planning your trip,
or a memento of your actual visit,
you can now sample the delights of Paris
from the comfort of your own home
with the Michelin video "Paris".
This fifty-minute film, one of six in Michelin's brand
new "Vidéo Découvertes" series on regions of France,
provides the perfect complement to the Michelin Green Guide,
focusing on Parisian sights and sounds
to evoke the atmosphere of the city itself.
Get a close-up look at some of Paris' most famous monuments,
unimpeded by other visitors,
or a private viewing of some of the treasures in its museums.
Discover the more intimate side of the city
by strolling along the banks of the Seine,
browsing in one or two book stalls,
before stopping off at a Paris café.
Check out Parisian night-life
with a ringside seat at one of the famous cabarets,
or bop the night away at a club.
Whatever the aspects of Paris that charm you the most,
trust Michelin to give you a taste of "la gaieté parisienne".

Excursions

In 1840 the locality of St-Denis numbered a few thousand inhabitants; the industrial revolution brought this number to 100 000 and made the town one of the main manufacturing centres of the northern suburbs.

The Gérard-Philipe Theatre and summer music festivals staged every year provide a wide range of intellectual and artistic activities. The most interesting sight in St-Denis, however, is its cathedral which houses the mausoleum of the Kings of France. *For a quick visit allow 1 hour.*

Effigies of Louis XVI and Marie-Antoinette

'Monsieur saint Denis' – Legend has it that after being beheaded in Montmartre (*see* MONTMARTRE), the evangelist St Denis, the first bishop of Lutetia, got to his feet, picked up his head and walked north out of the city. He is said to have been buried where he was found by a passing woman. An abbey was built on the site of his tomb, which soon attracted streams of pilgrims. In fact, vestiges of the Roman city Catolacus have been found to date from the 1C AD where it would have commanded views of the river and the main road out of Paris to Beauvais. It is believed that the man known as Monsieur (Monseigneur) St Denis was secretly buried in one of the fields around the city after his martyrdom.

In 475 a large village church was erected on the site. Dagobert I had it rebuilt and offered it to a Benedictine community who took charge of the pilgrimage. This abbey was to become the most wealthy and the most celebrated in France. Towards 750 the church was dismantled a second time and rebuilt by Pepin the Short, who set up a shrine under the chancel to receive the sacred remains of saints. The building as it stands today is principally the work of Abbot Suger (12C) and Pierre de Montreuil (13C).

Abbot Suger – The abbot's formidable personality dominates the history of the cathedral. He was born of a peasant family and was given to the abbey at the age of 10. His remarkable gifts caused him to gain ascendancy over one of his fellow novices, a young boy whose destiny it was to become Louis VII. The King made friends with the monk, invited him to court and consulted him on numerous matters.

Elected Abbot of St-Denis in 1122, Suger personally drew up the plans for the abbey church. The minister of Louis VII, he was made Regent of France when the King took part in the Second Crusade. His wisdom and concern for public well-being were so great that when Louis VII returned, he gave him the name Father of the Homeland.

The Lendit Fair – Lendit was an important trade fair founded by the abbot in 1109. It was held on St-Denis plain, on the site presently occupied by the Landy gasometers. It remained a major European event for over 600 years. A total of 1 200 booths were placed at the disposal of the participants. Every year the University of Paris would travel to Lendit to buy the parchment used in the Montagne Ste-Geneviève faculties (*see* LATIN QUARTER – la Sorbonne).

Mausoleum for the Kings of France – Most of the kings of France from Dagobert I to Louis XVIII over a remarkable span of 12 centuries, were buried at St-Denis. In 1793 Barrère asked the Convention for permission to destroy the tombs. They were opened and the remains thrown into unmarked graves. Alexandre Lenoir salvaged the most precious tombs and moved them to Paris, entrusted to the Petits-Augustins (*see* ST-GERMAIN-DES-PRÉS – École des Beaux-Arts), later to become the Museum of French Monuments (*see* TROCADÉRO-Musée des Monuments Français).
In 1816 Louis XVIII returned the tombs to the basilica.

Construction of St-Denis – This cathedral marks a turning-point in the development of French architecture: it was the first large church to feature a unity of design in plan and style. This, combined with its significance as a centre of pilgrimage proved to be the spring-board for subsequent late 12C cathedrals and the evolution towards Gothic (Chartres, Senlis and Meaux).
Suger supervised the construction of the west front and the first two bays of the nave from 1136 to 1140, the chancel and crypt between 1140 and 1144. The Carolingian nave was provisionally preserved and remodelled between 1145 and 1147. The amazing rapidity of the whole operation was due to Suger's dedication and to the help he received from his parishioners: they all teamed up to pull the wagons of stone from the limestone quarries of Pontoise.
In the early 13C the north tower was crowned by a magnificent stone spire. Work on the chancel was resumed and the transept, then the nave, were entirely restored. In 1247 **Pierre de Montreuil** was appointed master mason by St Louis: he remained in charge of the work until his death in 1267.

Decline – The basilica subsequently fell into disrepair. The French Revolution caused further ravages and in his *Genius of Christianity*, Chateaubriand lamented the sorry state of the church. Napoleon gave orders to repair the damage and reinstated public worship in 1806.

Restoration – Debret the architect who took over in 1813 aroused a wave of public indignation on account of his poor knowledge of medieval methods. For the spire, he used heavy materials which disrupted its gentle harmony. It collapsed in 1846 and had to be dismantled.
In 1847 Debret was succeeded by **Viollet-le-Duc**, who studied a number of original documents which guided him in his work. From 1858 up to his death (1879), he toiled relentlessly and produced the cathedral that stands today. Essentially, the choir and west front (although much restored) provide some idea of the original. The rest must be gleaned from contemporary buildings (Chartres, Sens). Archeological excavation of the crypt has revealed sections of the Carolingian martyrium and the remains of a Merovingian mausoleum (late-6C tomb of Princess Aregunde, the wife of Clotaire I, magnificent sarcophagi, splendid jewels). Foundations of earlier sanctuaries have also been uncovered.

Exterior

The absence of the north tower mars the harmony of the west front. In the Middle Ages the building would have been fortified from which some crenellation survives at the base of the towers.
The tympanum on the central doorway represents the Last Judgement, that on the right doorway depicts the Last Communion of St Denis and on the left the Death of St Denis and his companions Rusticus and Eleutherus.

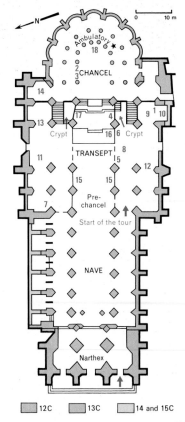

All three doorways have been restored. The columnar figures of the doorways feature the Wise and Foolish Virgins (*centre*), the labours of the months (*right*) and the signs of the Zodiac (*left*).

On the north side of the cathedral, the nave is supported by double flying buttresses. The transept, which presents a wonderful rose window, was initially to have had two towers but work stopped after the first floor. If the original plans had been carried out, the church would have had six towers altogether.

Interior ⓥ

The cathedral is marginally smaller than Notre-Dame (*see* ILE DE LA CITÉ) 108m – 354ft long, 38m – 125ft wide in the transept and 29m – 95ft high.

The narthex, designed by Suger, in the two bays beneath the towers, would have had pointed vaulting throughout. The elegant nave is attributed to Pierre de Montreuil. The triforium elevation, open onto the exterior, was also innovative. The stained-glass windows in the nave are modern.

Recumbent figure of Jeanne de Bourbon, St-Denis Cathedral

★★★**Tombs** – St-Denis Cathedral houses the remains of kings, queens and royal children, as well as those of leading personalities who served the French court, such as Bertrand du Gueslin (**1**). It is possible to date most monuments simply from their appearance, thus they serve as a chronological chart of French funeral art through the Middle Ages and into the Renaissance (79 recumbent figures). All tombs have been empty since the Revolution.

During the 14C it was customary to remove the heart and viscera from the bodies of French kings before embalming them. The inner organs, the heart and the body were all buried in different places. The bodies were taken to St-Denis.

Up to the Renaissance, the only sculpture to adorn tombs was in the form of recumbent figures. Note the 12C funeral slab of **Clovis** (**2**) and **Fredegonde** (**3**), worked in mosaic and copper, from the abbey of St-Germain-des-Prés.

Around 1260 St Louis commissioned a series of effigies of all the rulers who had preceded him since the 7C. The figures were mere allegories but they provide a telling example of how royalty was portrayed towards the mid-13C. They include the imposing tomb of **Dagobert** (**4**), with its lively, spirited scenes, the recumbent statues of Charles Martel (**5**) and Pepin the Short (**6**), and the female effigy carved in Tournai marble (**7**). The statue of **Philippe III the Bold** (**8**), who died in 1285, shows an early concern for accurate portraiture imbued with a strong sense of personality. Towards the middle of the 14C, the wealthy oversaw the building of their tomb in their own lifetime. The effigies of Charles V by Beauneveu (**9**), Charles VI and Isabella of Bavaria (**10**) are therefore extremely lifelike.

During the Renaissance, these mausoleums took on monumental proportions and were lavishly decorated. They had two tiers, representing life and death, each contrasting sharply with the other. On the upper level the king and his wife are featured kneeling in full regalia; on the lower level, the deceased were pictured lying down as naked cadavers. Admire the twin monument built for **Louis XII** and Anne of Brittany (**11**), and that of François I and Claude de France (**12**), executed by Philibert Delorme and Pierre Bontemps.

After commissioning the royal tomb, Catherine de' Medici, who survived her husband Henri II by 30 years, actually fainted in horror on seeing herself portrayed dead according to the standard convention; she therefore ordered a new effigy to be made showing her asleep. Both, by **Primaticcio** (**13**), and Germain Pilon (**14**), are here displayed.

Chancel – The beautiful pre-Renaissance stalls (**15**), in the pre-chancel were taken from the Norman Château at Gaillon. The splendid Romanesque **Virgin★** in painted wood (**16**) was brought from St-Martin-des-Champs. The episcopal throne opposite (**17**) is a replica of Dagobert's royal seat (the original lies in the Medals and Antiquities Gallery at the Bibliothèque Nationale in Paris – see PALAIS-ROYAL). At the far end, the modern reliquary of Saints Denis, Rusticus and Eleutherius (**18**) stands at the edge of Suger's **ambulatory★**, with its wide arches and slim columns. The radiating chapels are decorated with several altarpieces and fragments of stained glass dating from the Gothic period.

★★Crypt – The lower ambulatory was built in the Romanesque style by Suger (12C) and restored by Viollet-le-Duc (acanthus capitals). In the centre stands a vaulted chapel known as Hilduin's Chapel (after the abbot who had it built in the 9C). Beneath its marble slab lies the burial vault of the Bourbon family, including the remains, among others, of Louis XVI, Marie-Antoinette and Louis XVIII. The communal grave in the north transept received in 1817 the bones of around 800 kings and queens, royal highnesses, princes of the blood, Merovingians, Capetians and members of the Orléans and Valois dynasty.

Ancienne Abbaye – *Private*. The former Abbey that adjoins the cathedral was once the abbey church. The present monastic buildings date from the 18C and are the work of Robert de Cotte. In 1809 Napoleon I made the abbey the seat of a college for the daughters of holders of the French order of merit, the Légion d'Honneur.

Musée d'Art et d'Histoire ⊙ – *22bis rue Gabriel-Péri*. The museum is set up in the former Carmelite convent, part of which has been restored. The convent was founded by Cardinal de Bérulle in 1625 and occupied by Louis XV's daughter Madame Louise de France between 1770 and 1787. The refectory and kitchen contain archeological finds from St-Denis (medieval potsherds) or from the old hospital (17C and 18C ceramic apothecary phials and jars).
Other artefacts are displayed in the cells on the first and second floors.
The former Carmelite chapel has a splendid Louis XVI dome. It was here that the prioress Louise de France died in 1787.

CHÂTEAU DE VERSAILLES★★★

Michelin map 106 folds 17 and 18
Michelin map 101 folds 22 and 23, Michelin plan 20

Access – RER: (line C) Versailles Rive Gauche – Château de Versailles. Rail: commuter trains from Montparnasse rail station. By car: from the Porte de St-Cloud, take Motorway A13 to exit 14 and follow signs to Château de Versailles (16 km). Average travel time: 30-45 min.
Symbol of absolute monarchy and the apogee of the arts in France under the reign of the Sun King, Versailles became the residence of the court and seat of government on 6 May 1682 and remained so without interruption until the Revolution.

Small beginnings – In 1624 **Louis XIII** gave orders to build a small hunting lodge around the present Marble Court. Philibert le Roy reconstructed the château in brick and stone in 1631. **Louis XIV** retained his father's château; from 1661 he had the gardens embellished for his splendid festivals. In 1668 the King's architect **Louis Le Vau** constructed a stone "envelope", around the small château, building façades which concealed the old façades on the garden side of the château. Le Nôtre laid out the flower beds and park while Le Brun designed the sculptures for the park, notably, for the important order of 1674.

Grand schemes – **Jules Hardouin-Mansart** succeeded Le Vau and modified the palace with the Galerie des Glaces (Hall of Mirrors) and two wings in the south (1682) and the north (1689).
Under Colbert and Le Brun, the Gobelins factory and the artists of the Académie Royale designed the main furniture and decoration with the remarkable stylistic unity which defines Versailles Classicism.
Through a complex system of etiquette and magnificent feasts, Louis XIV managed to control the ever-dangerous nobility, thwarting their political ambitions.
Under **Louis XV** changes were limited mostly to the interior which J A Gabriel restructured to create the "Petits Cabinets".
When the **Revolution** drove Louis XVI from Versailles, a century of royal occupation came to a close. In the 19C, **Louis-Philippe** transformed part of the palace into a museum dedicated to French history. Since 1914 the State, supported by private patronage, has carried out important restoration work and refurbished the palace.

★★★LE CHATEAU

A complete tour of the palace, park and the Grand and Petit Trianons takes two days. If you have only one day it is recommended that you begin with the interior of the château, where the most magnificent apartments are to be found.
The park and gardens are best enjoyed at leisure.

Exterior *for a brief visit allow about 1 hour*

Set back from the château on the Place d'Armes are the **Écuries Royales★** (Royal Stables) by Jules Hardouin-Mansart.

Courtyards – Beyond the palace's wrought-iron railings, created under Louis XVIII, lie three courtyards. In the centre of the forecourt, the **Cour des Ministres** (Ministers' Court) is a statue of Louis XIV commissioned by Louis-Philippe. Next is the **Cour Royale** (Royal Court) which only persons of high rank were permitted to cross in horse-drawn carriages. The two bordering wings were furnished with a colonnade under Louis XV. Finally there is the **Cour de Marbre★★** (Marble Court) with its black and white marble pavement, the heart of Louis XIII's château.

★★★Garden front – *Go through the north arcade, skirt the central part of the palace and step back for a good view.* Designed by Le Vau in 1669, the façade is lined with pillars and Ionic columns rising from a bossaged base. The balustrade crowning the façade bears trophies and vases and conceals the flat Italian-style roof. Le Vau created a terrace in the space in front of the building, but in 1678, Jules Hardouin-Mansart covered the space, and it became the Hall of Mirrors. This he extended with two wings.

Along the façade four metal casts of ancient statues are perched on the pedestals; these are the first works of the Keller brothers. Two giant Medici **vases★** representing War (by Coysevox) and Peace (by Tuby) stand under the windows of the War Salon and the Peace Salon located at either end of the Hall of Mirrors.

Statues of Apollo and Diana, surrounded by the Months of the Year, top the central building of the palace where the royal family lived.

Interior ⊙ – *From the visitors' entrance go though the vestibule which houses the ticket office and up by the circular staircase to the Chapel Room (**a**) on the first floor.*

Château de Versailles

★★★**Chapelle Royale** – The two-storey palatine chapel with a royal gallery is dedicated to St Louis. It was constructed by Jules Hardouin-Mansart, and finished in 1710 by his brother-in-law Robert de Cotte. The ceiling is the work of the painters Jouvent, Coypel and La Fosse. The marble altar sculpted by Van Clève is decorated in front with a gilded bronze low relief representing a Pietà by Vassé.

★★★**Grands Appartements** – The State apartments consist of the reception rooms – the Salon d'Hercule, the Grand Appartement and the Galerie des Glaces – and the living quarters, of which the most interesting are the royal bedrooms.

Salon d'Hercule – Known as Hercules' Salon, this room, begun in 1712 and completed in 1736, owes its name to the ceiling painted by Lemoyne. The artist needed three arduous years to cover the 315sq m – 3 390sq ft ceiling with a painting of Hercules entering the Kingdom of the Gods. The artist committed suicide in 1737 shortly after finishing it. Two Veronese canvases occupy their original places: **Christ at the House of Simon the Pharisee★**, *Eliezer and Rebecca.*

★★★**Grand Appartement** – The six-room suite with decoration by Le Brun was the King's apartment from 1673 to 1682. Then Louis XIV took up residence definitively at Versailles and had a new apartment designed around the Marble Court. Three times a week on Mondays, Wednesdays and Thursdays from 6pm to 10pm the king held court in the Grand Apartment.

One entered the rooms through the Royal Court by the Ambassadors' Staircase, sumptuously designed to impress visitors, but which was torn down by Louis XV in 1752.

Salon de l'Abondance (b) – When the king held court during the time of Louis XIV there were three buffets, one for hot drinks and two for cold. The ceiling painted by Houasse portrays all the royal magnificence and the gold ware collections of Louis XIV in trompe-l'œil.

Salon de Vénus (c) – The ceiling was painted by Houasse and like the ceilings of the following rooms it features decorated panels with gilt stucco borders.

Salon de Diane (d) – Billiard room under Louis XIV. Notice the bust of Louis XIV by Bernini (1665), a stunning example of Baroque workmanship. Paintings by La Fosse and Blanchard.

D. Hée/MICHELIN

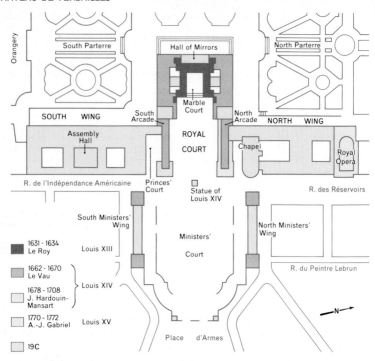

Salon de Mars (**e**) – Guard room before 1682, this room was later used by Louis XIV for balls, games and music.

Two paintings have been restored to their 18C places: *Darius' Tent* by Le Brun and *The Pilgrims of Emmaüs* after Veronese. On the side walls, *Louis XV* by Rigaud and *Maria Leczczynska* by Van Loo occupy their original places. The ceiling with its martial scenes is by Audran, Jouvenet and Houasse. Above the fireplace hangs one of Louis XIV's favourite paintings, *King David* by Domenichino in which he is pictured playing the harp. It originally hung in the king's bedchamber.

Salon de Mercure (**f**) – Formerly the antechamber, it occasionally served as a place where kings were laid in state. In 1715 Louis XIV in his coffin was kept here a whole week, with 72 ecclesiastics keeping vigil to ensure that four masses could be said simultaneously every day from five in the morning until noon without interruption. The ceiling is by J B de Champaigne.

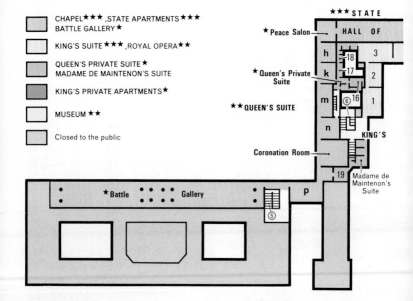

Salon d'Apollon or **Salle du Trône** (**g**) – The throne stood on a central platform beneath a large canopy. The three hooks would have supported a canopy. It was here that ambassadors were received, that dances and concerts were put on when the king held court. The ceiling features *Apollo in a Sun Chariot* by La Fosse.

The entire width along the front of the palace overlooking the gardens is occupied by the Hall of Mirrors and its two wings, the Salons de Guerre et de la Paix.

Crossing the **Salon de Guerre★** (War Salon), which links the Grand Apartment and the Hall of Mirrors, notice the large oval low-relief by Coysevox representing Louis XIV triumphing over his enemies.

★★★**Galerie des Glaces** – Designed by Jules Hardouin-Mansart in 1687, the **Hall of Mirrors** was the showpiece under Louis XIV where court celebrations and elaborate receptions for foreign potentates took place.

The hall is 75m – 246ft long, 10m – 33ft wide, and 12m – 40ft high, and it is illuminated by 17 large windows echoing 17 glass panels on the opposite wall. The 578 mirrors of glass which compose these panels are the largest that could be manufactured at that time. The hall enjoys the last rays of the setting sun.

On the ceiling **Le Brun** executed the most important cycle of his career as the King's chief painter. The cycle illustrates the life of Louis XIV and his military victories until the Treaty of Nijmegen in 1678.

The Hall of Mirrors was abundantly decorated with solid-silver furniture cast under Louis XIV.

The German Empire was proclaimed in this room on 18 January 1871 and the **Treaty of Versailles** was signed on 28 June 1919.

From the central windows one has a good **view★★★** of the Grand Perspective.

Entrance to the Queen's Suite is through the **Salon de la Paix★** which is decorated with a canvas by Lemoyne of Louis XV presenting peace to Europe.

★★★**Appartement de la Reine** – The Queen's suite was constructed for Louis XIV's wife Queen Marie-Thérèse who died here in 1683.

Chambre de la Reine (**h**) – Le Brun's original decoration for Marie-Thérèse was redone for Queen Maria Leczczynska between 1729 and 1735. The white and gold woodwork, the greyish tones of the ceiling by Boucher, and the doors decorated by Natoire and de Troy demonstrate the inclination towards the Rococo under Louis XV. Marie-Antoinette had other renovations made in 1770: the two-headed eagle and the portraits of the house of Austria recall the Queen's origins. The floral wall hangings were re-woven to the original pattern in Lyon, matching exactly the original hanging of the Queen's summer furnishings of 1786.

In France, royal births were public events: in this room 19 children of France were born, among them Louis XV and Philip V of Spain.

Salon des Nobles de la Reine (Peers' Salon) (**k**) – In this one-time antechamber presentations to the Queen took place. This room was also where queens and dauphins of France lay in state. The room has been restored to the way it looked in 1789.

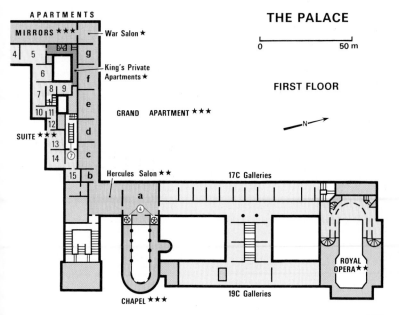

In the **antechamber** (**m**) note the painting by Madame Vigée-Lebrun of Marie-Antoinette and her children (1787). The **Salle de gardes de la Reine** (Queen's Guardsroom) (**n**) protected her against intrusions such as that which occurred on the morning of 6 October 1789, when a rioting mob tried to invade the Queen's Suite and had to be fought off by the royal guard in a prolonged and bloody scuffle.

Salle du sacre – The Coronation room was initially used as a chapel from 1676 to 1682; otherwise this large guardroom housed the sessions of Parliament which passed laws here. Louis-Philippe had the room altered to accommodate three enormous paintings: *Murat at the Battle of Aboukir* by Gros, *Champ de Mars Eagles* and *The Consecration of Napoleon* by David.

When it is open the visitor may see the **Galerie des Batailles★** (Battle Gallery) which occupies the south wing. Designed in 1836 for Louis-Philippe by the architects Fontaine and Nepveu, it created a sensation. The 33 vast pictures evoke France's greatest military victories and include works by **Horace Vernet**, **Eugène Delacroix** and **Baron Gérard**.

★★★**Appartement du Roi** or **Appartement de Louis XIV**

The king's suite stretches around the Marble Court. Designed between 1682 and 1701 by Mansart in Louis XIII's château, the decoration marks a clear break in the evolution of Louis XIV style. The ceilings are not coffered but painted white; the white and gold panelling replaces the marble tiling; large mirrors adorn the fireplaces.

Escalier de la Reine – ⑥ The Queen's Staircase was the normal entrance to this apartment at the end of the Ancien Régime.

After the guard room (**1**), an antechamber (**2**) leads to the **Salon de l'Œil de bœuf** (**3**). Here gentlemen attended the ceremonious King's rising (*le lever*) and retiring (*le coucher*). The decoration marks the first flowering of Louis XV style.

Chambre du Roi (**4**) – This was the bedroom of Louis XIV from 1701 and it was here that he died.

Above the bed, the alcove decoration represents "France watching over the sleeping King" and was sculpted by Coustou. The wall hangings are faithful reproductions of the summer furnishings of 1705. The paintings belonged to the King's personal collection.

Grand Cabinet du Roi or **du Conseil** (**5**) – Characteristic of Rococo, the Council Chamber was created under Louis XV by uniting two rooms. In this room decisions were made that involved the destiny of France, among them the decision to participate in the American War of Independence.

★★★**Appartement Privé du Roi**

The King's Private Suite served as private apartments to Louis XV, reserved for those closest to him. Here the king removed himself from the constraints of the Court. The rooms were designed by Gabriel and are decorated with carvings by Verberckt: shells, foliated scrolls and Rococo flower motifs are scattered everywhere.

Chambre à coucher (**6**) – Louis XV, and then Louis XVI, retired to this bedroom after they had "performed" the rising and retiring ceremonies which took place in the Grand Apartment. It was here that Louis XV died of smallpox on 10 May 1774.

Cabinet de la Pendule (**7**) – The Clock room served as a gaming room when the king held court. Until 1769 it owed its name to the astronomical clock whose works were built by Passemant and Dauthiau with bronze embellishments by Caffiéri.

When crossing the **Antichambre des chiens** (Dogs' Antechamber) (**8**) note the Louis XIV panelling. In the dining room called **Retours de chasse** (Hunters' Dining Hall) (**9**) Louis XV gave private dinners on hunting days.

Cabinet intérieur du Roi (**10**) – The Corner Room became a workroom in 1753. As an example of Verberckt's Rococo style, the furniture is remarkable; the medal cabinet is by Gaudreaux (1739), corner cupboards by Joubert (1755), a roll-top **desk★** by Oeben and Riesener (1769).

Salles neuves – The 'new rooms' were designed under Louis XV in the place of the Ambassadors' Staircase. In the **Cabinet de Mme Adélaïde** (**12**), the child **Mozart** played the harpsichord. The medal cabinet by Benneman is a masterpiece. The following rooms, Louis XVI's **Library** (**13**) and the **Porcelain Salon** (**14**), show the evolution of Versailles style towards the sober under neo-Classicism. The most notable is the **Salon des Jeux** (Louis XVI's Gaming Room) (**15**) as it appeared in 1775; corner cupboards by Riesener (1774), chairs by Boulard, gouache landscapes by Van Blarenberghe.

Go down the Louis-Philippe staircase ⑦ *to leave via the north gallery.*

★★★**Opéra Royal**

The opera house begun by Gabriel in 1768 was inaugurated in 1770 for the marriage celebrations of the dauphin, the future Louis XVI, and Marie-Antoinette.

The first oval hall in France, it received other exceptional technical touches from the engineer Arnoult: for festivals the floor of the stalls and circle could be raised to the level of the stage.

The balconies' low-reliefs, executed by **Pajou**, represent the gods of Olympus (*dress circle*) and the children and their signs of the zodiac (*upper circle*).

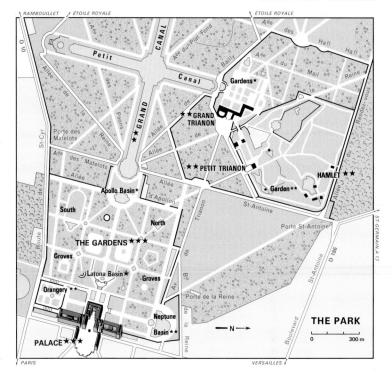

The map shows THE PARK of Versailles with labels including: RAMBOUILLET, ÉTOILE ROYALE, Petit Canal, GRAND CANAL, Porte des Matelots, Allée des Matelots, Apollo Basin★, South, North, THE GARDENS★★★, Groves, Latona Basin★, Orangery★★, Neptune Basin★★, PALACE★★★, PARIS, Gardens★, ★★GRAND TRIANON, ★★PETIT TRIANON, Garden★★, HAMLET★★, St-Antoine, Porte St-Antoine, Porte de la Reine, ST-GERMAIN A 13, VERSAILLES, N, 0 300 m

Initially reserved for the court, the opera hosted sumptuous receptions on the occasion of visits from the King of Sweden in 1784, of Emperor Joseph II in 1777 and 1781, and of **Queen Victoria** in 1855. The National Assembly held session here from 1871 until 1875. On 30 January 1875 the adoption of the Wallon Amendment here laid the foundation of the Third Republic. A reception for **Queen Elizabeth II of England** in 1957 coincided with completion of the final restoration.

★★★PARK AND GARDENS

Laid out principally by Le Nôtre during the years 1660 to 1670, the park and gardens are masterpieces of the art of French landscape gardening, in which nature is ordered geometrically according to the principles of Classicism.
The basins, fountains and statues are perfectly integrated with nature. The grand perspective or east-west axis symbolically retraces the path of the sun, from the **Latona Basin★** and fountain to the **Apollo Basin★**, continuing along the **Grand Canal★★**. On both sides of the axis, flower beds, hedgerows and sculptures are to be found.

The Boutique Michelin stocks the full range of National, Regional and City Guides, as well as that Epicure's companion to good living the Michelin Red Guide.

> Boutique Michelin
> 32 avenue de l'Opéra
> Paris 75002

DISNEYLAND PARIS ★★★

Michelin map 106 fold 22 – Michelin Green Guide Disneyland Paris

Access – *RER: (line A) Marne-la-Vallée – Chessy. By car: Motorway A4 direction Metz; exit at junction 14 and follow signs to Disneyland.*
Standing on the Brie plain about 30km – 18 miles east of Paris is a unique development in Europe: Disneyland Paris.

Disneyland Paris theme park – The enormous site, which was conceived as a complete holiday resort and will continue to develop until the year 2017, already comprises the theme park and a resort complex offering accommodation and other recreational facilities.
The **Disneyland Hotel**, built in the style of a turn-of-the-century American mansion from a seaside resort, stands at the entrance to the theme park. Five other hotels stand beside Lake Disney or along the Rio Grande, each bringing to life a different American theme: the **Hotel New York** (Manhattan), the **Newport Bay Club** (a 19C New England beach resort), **Sequoia Lodge** (the National Parks), **Hotel Santa Fe** (New Mexico) and the **Hotel Cheyenne** (a small western town).
Not far from the hotels, the main entertainment centre, **Festival Disney**, recreates the American way of life with shops, restaurants and a nightclub. An evening spectacular, **Buffalo Bill's Wild West Show★★** complete with horses, bison, cowboys and Indians evokes the epic days of the Wild West. At a slight distance from the complex lies **Golf Disneyland Paris** with its 27-hole course. The **Davy Crockett Ranch** is a caravan and camp site in the woods 4.5km – 3 miles away, with wooden cabins recalling the life of the trappers.

A magician called Walt Disney – Walt Disney's name is linked to innumerable cartoon strips and animated cartoons which have entertained children throughout the world, and the heroes of his creations Mickey Mouse, Minnie, Donald, Pluto, Pinocchio, Snow White, etc no one can forget.
He was born Walter Elias Disney in Chicago in 1901, the fourth child of Flora and Elias Disney. Walt soon showed great ability in drawing. After the First World War, in which he served as an ambulance driver in France, he returned to the United States where he met a young Dutchman called Ub Iwerks, who was also passionate about drawing. In 1923 the pair produced in Hollywood a series of short films called **Alice Comedies**. In 1928 Mickey Mouse, the future international star, was created. There next followed the era of the Oscar-winning, full-length animated cartoon films: **The Three Little Pigs** (1933), **Snow White and the Seven Dwarfs** (1937), **Dumbo** (1941). Disney productions also developed to include films starring real people, such as **Treasure Island** (1950) and **20 000 Leagues Under the Sea** (1954), and some mixing of the two, for instance **Mary Poppins** (1964) which won six Oscars.
On 15 December 1966 the man who had spent his life trying to bring dreams to life died; the Walt Disney Studios continued to make films, however, remaining faithful to Walt's ideas: **The Aristocats, Who Killed Roger Rabbit?** (which won four Oscars), **The Little Mermaid** (two Oscars), **Beauty and the Beast** (1991), **Aladdin** (1992) and **The Lion King** (1994).

★★★DISNEYLAND PARIS THEME PARK ⊙

This theme park, like those in the United States (opened in California in 1955 and in Florida in 1971) and Japan (Tokyo, 1983), is a realisation of Walt Disney's dream of creating a small, enchanted park where children and adults can enjoy themselves together.
The large Disneyland Paris site (over 55ha – 135 acres) is surrounded by trees and comprises five territories or lands, each with a different theme. As well as the spectacular shows featuring amazing automatons (Audio-Animatronics), each region has shops, bars, restaurants and food stalls.
Every day, the **Disney Parade★★**, a procession of floats carrying all the favourite Disney cartoon characters, takes place. On some evenings and throughout the summer the **Main Street Electrical Parade★★** adds extra illuminations to the fairytale setting. The **Fantasy in the Sky★** firework display spectacularly rounds off an eventful day.
Listed below are descriptions of the main attractions only; for more detailed information and plans refer to the Michelin Green Guide DISNEYLAND PARIS.

Main Street USA

The main street of an American town at the turn of the 20C, bordered by shops with Victorian-style fronts, is brought to life as though by magic. Horse-drawn street cars, double-decker buses, limousines, fire engines and Black Marias transport visitors from Town Square to Central Plaza (the hub of the park) while colourful musicians play favourite ragtime, jazz and Dixieland tunes. On each side of the road are **Discovery Arcade** and **Liberty Arcade** (exhibition on the famous Statue of Liberty at the entrance to New York harbour).
From Main Street station a small steam train, the **Euro Disneyland Railroad★**, travels across the park and through the **Grand Canyon Diorama**.

Main Street Motors – Enthusiasts of classic cars can peruse the cars exhibited here, and even have their photo taken in front of one of them.

Frontierland

The conquest of the West, the gold trail and the Far West with its legends and folk-lore are brought together in Thunder Mesa, a typical western town, and Big Thunder Mountain which rises on an island washed by the Rivers of the Far West. The waters here are plied by two handsome **steamboats★**, the *Mark Twain* and the *Molly Brown*.

★★★**Big Thunder Mountain** – In the bowels of this arid mountain lies an old gold mine which is visited via the mine train: this turns out to be a runaway train which hurtles 'out of control' to provide a thrilling ride.

★★★**Phantom Manor** – A dilapidated house stands not far from Thunder Mesa, over-looking the Rivers of the Far West. Inside, a strange atmosphere hangs in the air: a spine-chilling tour of the house reveals hundreds of mischievous ghosts...

★**The Lucky Nugget Saloon** – This horseshoe-shaped saloon – every western town had its saloon – is richly decorated. Dinner show: **Lilly's Follies.**

Adventureland

This is the land of exotic adventure: waterfalls, an oriental bazaar, African drum-beats, a treasure island, swashbuckling pirates... Access is from Central Plaza, through Adventureland Bazaar.

★★★**Pirates of the Caribbean** – In the tropical Caribbean seas, marauding pirates attack and loot a coastal fort and village in this famous action-packed encounter.

★★**Indiana Jones et le Temple du Péril** – In the jungle lies a ruined temple; courageous arche-ologists in wagons enter it and defy the laws of gravity. This is not for the faint-hearted.

★★**La Cabane des Robinson** – A giant tree (27m – 89ft high) offering panoramic views serves as the ingeniously-furnished home of the shipwrecked Swiss family Robinson from J D Wyss' novel.

Fantasyland

This area, based around Walt Disney's familiar trademark, Sleeping Beauty's castle, recalls favourite fairytales by authors such as Charles Perrault, Lewis Carroll and the Brothers Grimm. Here familiar figures – Mickey Mouse, Pinocchio, Captain Hook – will happily pose for photographs.

★★**Le Château de la Belle au Bois Dormant** – The fairytale castle with its blue and gold turrets crowned with pennants is at the very heart of Disneyland. Inside, Aubusson tapestries recount episodes from this famous story. Below, in the depths of the castle, a huge scaly dragon appears to be sleeping...

★★**It's a Small World** – The delightful musical cruise is a celebration of the innocence and joy of children throughout the world.

★**Blanche-Neige et les Sept Nains** – Enjoyable tours lead through the mysterious forest in mining cars from the dwarfs' mine – just watch out for the wicked witch...

★**Les Voyages de Pinocchio** – Lively scenes based on Carlo Collodi's enduring tale present the lovable puppet Pinocchio and his friends.

★★**Peter Pan's Flight** – Fly in a boat through the skies above London and in Never-Never Land reliving the adventures of Peter Pan and the sinister Captain Hook who is relentlessly pursued by a hungry crocodile.

★**Alice's Curious Labyrinth** – At the end of this maze guarded by playing cards stands the Queen of Hearts' Castle where the queen from Lewis Carroll's classic story awaits those brave enough to visit...

★**Le Carrousel de Lancelot** – This is an enchanting merry-go-round of brightly-painted horses.

Discoveryland

This is the world of past discoveries and dreams of the future with great visionaries such as Leonardo da Vinci, Jules Verne and H G Wells and their wonderful inventions.

★★★**Star Tours** – This is a breathtaking inter-planetary experience full of special effects inspired by the film *Star Wars*: voyage into space, piloted by a robot!

★★★**Space Mountain** – Fantastic journey through space, based on Jules Verne's novel *From the Earth to the Moon* (1873).

★★**Cinémagique** – Enjoy rhythm, music and dance in a three-dimensional film about the adventures of Captain EO, played by Michael Jackson.

★★**Le Visionarium** – A 360° screen reveals the wonders of Europe.

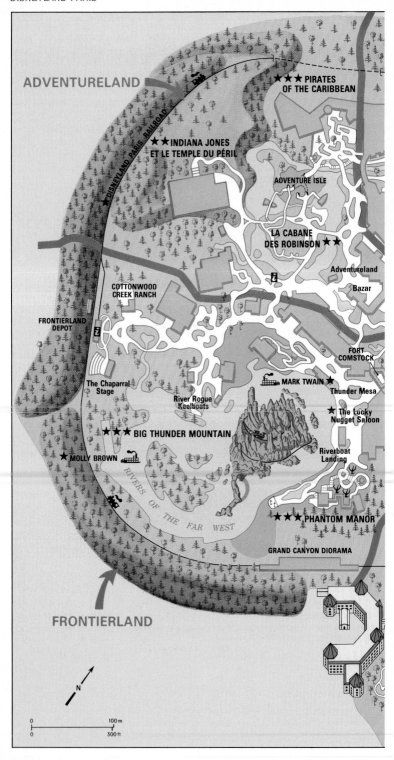

ADVENTURELAND

★★★ PIRATES
OF THE CARIBBEAN

DISNEYLAND PARIS RAILROAD

★★ INDIANA JONES
ET LE TEMPLE DU PÉRIL

ADVENTURE ISLE

LA CABANE
DES ROBINSON ★★

Adventureland
Bazar

COTTONWOOD
CREEK RANCH

FRONTIERLAND
DEPOT

FORT
COMSTOCK

The Chaparral
Stage

MARK TWAIN ★
Thunder Mesa

River Rogue
Keelboats

★ The Lucky
Nugget Saloon

★★★ BIG THUNDER MOUNTAIN

★ MOLLY BROWN

Riverboat
Landing

RIVERS OF THE FAR WEST

★★★ PHANTOM MANOR

GRAND CANYON DIORAMA

FRONTIERLAND

N

0   100 m
0   300 ft

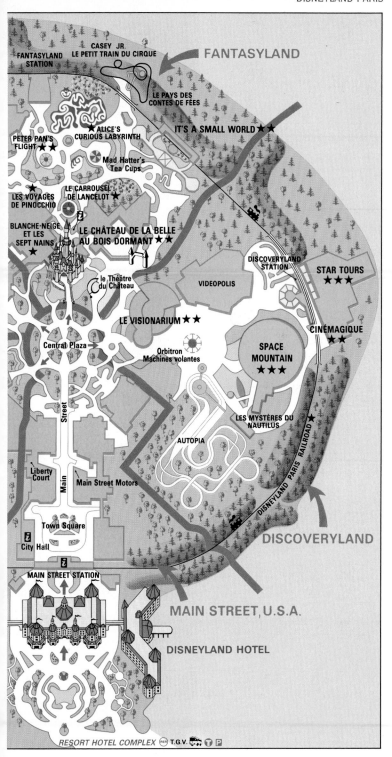

FANTASYLAND STATION

CASEY JR.
LE PETIT TRAIN DU CIRQUE

FANTASYLAND

LE PAYS DES
CONTES DE FÉES

★ALICE'S
CURIOUS LABYRINTH

IT'S A SMALL WORLD ★★

PETER PAN'S
FLIGHT ★★

Mad Hatter's
Tea Cups

LES VOYAGES
DE PINOCCHIO
★

LE CARROUSEL
DE LANCELOT ★

BLANCHE-NEIGE
ET LES
SEPT NAINS
★

LE CHÂTEAU DE LA BELLE
AU BOIS DORMANT ★★

DISCOVERYLAND
STATION

STAR TOURS
★★★

le Théâtre
du Château

VIDEOPOLIS

CINÉMAGIQUE
★★

LE VISIONARIUM ★★

Central Plaza →

Orbitron
Machines volantes

SPACE
MOUNTAIN
★★★

LES MYSTÈRES DU
NAUTILUS ★

AUTOPIA

Street

Liberty
Court

Main Street Motors

Main

Town Square

City Hall

DISCOVERYLAND

MAIN STREET STATION

MAIN STREET, U.S.A.

DISNEYLAND HOTEL

RESORT HOTEL COMPLEX (RER) T.G.V. 🚌 🚇 P

The Michelin Man...

*Known as "Bibendum", he is represented in all his various metamorphoses
from the early 20C to the present.*

From the Pont Alexandre III

Practical
Information

Planning your trip

Passport – Visitors travelling to France must be in possession of a valid national passport (this includes the British Visitor's Passport). Citizens of other European Union countries need only a national identity card. In case of loss or theft report to the embassy or consulate and the local police.

Visas – Entry visas are required by Australian, New Zealand, and Canadian and US citizens (if their intended stay exceeds three months). Apply to the French Consulate (visa issued same day; delay if submitted by mail). US citizens may find the booklet **Your Trip Abroad** (US$1.25) useful for information on visa requirements, customs regulations, medical care, etc. when travelling in Europe available from the Superintendent of Documents, PO Box 371954, Pittsburgh, PA 15250-7954, ☏ (202) 512-1800.

Remember to take some passport-size photos with you if you want to purchase a public transport and museum pass on arrival.

Customs – **A Guide for Travellers** outlines British customs regulations and duty-free allowances; it is available from the HM Customs Office (UK). The US Customs Service, PO Box 7407, Washington, DC 20044, ☏ (202) 927-5580, offers a free publication **Know Before You Go** for US citizens.

Refunded VAT – In France a sales tax (TVA or Value Added Tax ranging from 5.5 % to 20.6 %) is added to almost all retail goods. Non-Europeans may reclaim this tax from accumulated purchases exceeding 3 000F.

When to go – In winter the streets are bright with Christmas illuminations, the shop windows brilliant; in summer you can sit beneath the trees or an awning with a long cold drink between seeing the sights or idle away an evening on a café terrace, or go on an open boat on the Seine; in the autumn Parisians are back from their own holidays and there is an air of energy and bustle; and Paris in the spring...

		Mean Temperatures			
	January	February	March	April	May	June
Min/max °F	21/59	23/59	30/70	34/75	41/81	46/88
Min/max °C	-6/15	-5/15	-1/21	1/24	5/27	8/31
	July	August	September	October	November	December
	52/91	50/88	45/84	34/75	28/63	25/55
	11/33	10/31	7/29	1/24	-2/17	-4/13

Where to stay – There are hundreds of hotels and restaurants in Paris. Hotels range from the sumptuous to modest family *pensions*; restaurants equally can provide luxurious fare at frightening prices and very good food at reasonable cost: the great advantage with French restaurants is that the menu, with prices, is displayed outside. For a comprehensive list including prices of hotels and restaurants, look in the Michelin Booklet *Paris and Environs* (an extract from the Michelin Red Guide France). There are several youth and student organisations – apply to the French Government Tourist Office *(address below)*, the French Consulate General, 21-23 Cromwell Road, London SW7, ☏ 0171 581 5292 or the Central Bureau for Educational Visits and Exchanges, Seymour Mews House, Seymour Mews, London W1H 9PE, ☏ 0171 486 5101.

Youth Hostels – There are two main youth hostel associations (auberges de la jeunesse) in France: **Ligue Française pour les Auberges de la Jeunesse**, 38 boulevard Raspail, 75007 ☏ 01 45 48 69 84, Fax 01 45 44 57 47 and the **Fédération Unie des Auberges de Jeunesse**, 27 rue Pajol, 75018 ☏ 01 44 89 87 27, Fax 01 44 89 87 10, Minitel 3615 code FUAJ (1.01FF/min).
Holders of an International Youth Hostel Federation card should contact the **International Federation or the French Youth Hostels Association** to book a bed.
Hostelling International / American Youth Hostel Association in the US (☏ 202-783-6161) offers a publication *International Hostel Guide for Europe* (US$13.95) – also available to non-members.

French Tourist Offices – Information, brochures, maps and assistance in planning a trip to France are provided by the official tourist office in each country:

Australia-New Zealand – BNP Building, 12 Castlereagh Street, Sydney, New South Wales 2000. ☏ (61) 2-231-5244; Fax (61) 2-221-86-82

Canada – *Either:* 30 St Patrick's St, Suite 700, Toronto, ONT M5T 3A3. ☏ (416) 593-4723. *Or:* 1981 av McGill College, Suite 490, Montreal, PQ H3A 2W9. ☏ (514) 288-4264; Fax (514) 845-48-68

Republic of Ireland – 35 Lower Abbey St, Dublin 1. ☏ (1) 703-40-46; Fax (1) 874-73-24.

United Kingdom – 178 Piccadilly, London W1. ☎ (0891) 244-123; Fax (0171) 493-6594

United States – France On Call Hotline: 900-990-0040 (US$0.50/min). **East Coast:** 444 Madison Avenue, NY 10022. ☎ (212) 838-7800; Fax (212) 838-7855. **Mid-West:** 676 North Michigan Avenue, Suite 3360, Chicago, IL 60611-2819. ☎ (312) 751-7800; Fax (312) 337-6339. **West Coast:** 9454 Wilshire Boulevard, Suite 715, Beverly Hills, CA 90212-2967. ☎ (310) 271-2693; Fax (310) 276-2835.

Embassies and Consulates

Australia: 4 rue Jean-Rey, 75015 ☎ 01 40 59 33 00; Fax 01 40 59 33 10.

Canada: 35 avenue Montaigne, 75008 ☎ 01 44 43 29 00; Fax 01 44 43 29 99.

Republic of Ireland: 4 rue Rude, 75016 ☎ 01 45 00 20 87; Fax 01 45 00 84 17.

New Zealand: 7ter rue Léonard de Vinci, 75016 ☎ 01 45 00 24 11; Fax 01 45 01 26 39.

South Africa: 59 Quai d'Orsay, 75007 ☎ 01 45 55 92 37.

United Kingdom: Embassy – 35 rue du Faubourg-St-Honoré, 75008 ☎ 01 42 66 91 42; Fax 01 42 66 95 90. **Visa section** – 16 rue d'Anjou, 75008 Paris. ☎ 01 42 66 06 68.

> *It is important to take out medical insurance prior to departure as treatment in France may be extremely expensive.*

United States: Embassy – 2 avenue Gabriel, 75008 ☎ 01 42 96 12 02; Fax 01 42 66 97 83. **Consulate** – 2 rue St-Florentin, 75001 ☎ 01 42 96 14 88.

Fontaine Wallace

Parlez-vous anglais?

If your French is rusty or non-existent, where can you turn for current information about what's on in Paris?

The weekly *Pariscope* guide, offering comprehensive listings of the city's myriad cultural happenings, includes a "Paris in English" section *(available wherever newspapers are sold)*. The monthly newspaper *The Paris Free Voice* features general-interest articles and reviews written from the expatriate point of view and contains listings of the month's cultural events. It is available at various English-American haunts throughout the city (bookstores, cafés, restaurants – see our listings in the PARIS AT LEISURE section).

Getting there

By air

Paris is served by two major international airports: **Roissy-Charles de Gaulle** 27km – 14 miles to the north of Paris on the A1, and **Orly** 16km – 10 miles to the south along the A6. Internal flights are handled by Orly. Public services giving access to and from the city include Air France coach shuttles, public transport (RATP) buses, private minibuses, RER trains and taxis.

Check whether the train or bus is running before buying your ticket from an automatic ticket machine – these are not refundable!

From Roissy-Charles de Gaulle – Autocars Air France run every 15 minutes from 5am to 11pm to Gare Montparnasse *(boulevard Vaugirard)*, via Terminal Maillot *(place de la Porte-Maillot)* and place Charles-de-Gaulle-Étoile *(corner with avenue Carnot)*. Approximate journey time to Montparnasse one hour. ☎ 01 48 64 14 24. Cost 48F.

Bus RATP run the ROISSYBUS to rue Scribe *(corner with rue Auber)* between Roissy and Paris from 6am to 11pm and from Paris to Roissy from 5.45am to 11pm. Departures every 15 minutes. Approximate journey time 45 minutes. ☎ 01 48 04 18 24. Cost 30F.

Underground trains RER line B run every 15 minutes between Roissy-CDG and Paris from 4.30am to 11.40pm, and between Paris and Roissy-CDG from 5.30am to 00.15am. Average journey time to Gare du Nord 35 minutes. Cost 53F in first class, 35F in second class.

Taxis are subject to road traffic conditions; it is best to allow one hour journey time at an approximate cost of 200F.

Paris Aéroport Service (PAS) provide a private shuttle service to the main line railway stations, Eurodisney, hotels or homes in the city and the suburbs around the clock. ☎ 01 49 62 78 78 or 01 09 14 16 93 for emergency reservations (lead-time two hours). Approximate cost per person 120F to the capital, 200F to the suburbs.

Useful numbers – Airport Information ☎ 01 48 62 22 80. Tourist Information for hotel reservations etc *(7am-11pm)* ☎ 01 48 62 27 29.

From Orly – Autocars Air France run every 12 minutes from 5.50am to 11.10pm to Gare Montparnasse *(36 avenue du Maine)*, via Aérogare des Invalides *(2 rue Esnault-Pelterie)*. Approximate journey time to Montparnasse 30 minutes. ☎ 01 41 75 44 40. Cost 32F.

Bus RATP run the ORLYBUS to place Denfert-Rochereau *(outside RER station)* between Orly Sud and Orly Ouest terminals and Paris from 6.30am to 11.30pm and from Paris to Orly Sud and Orly Ouest from 6am to 11pm. Departures every 15 minutes. Approximate journey time 25 minutes. ☎ 01 43 46 14 14. Cost 30F.

Underground trains RER line C run from Pont-de-Rungis. Connection with the air-terminals is by separate bus. Trains run every 15 minutes to Paris from 5.35am to 23.15pm, and from Paris between 5.50am and 10.50pm. Average journey time to Gare d'Austerlitz 35 minutes. Cost 41F in first class, 27F in second class.

Underground trains RER line B run as far as Antony and connect with ORLY VAL. Scheduled departures in either direction from Orly Sud or Antony, every 4 to 8 minutes, between 6.30am and 9.15pm (7am and 10.55pm Sunday). Average journey time between Châtelet and Orly 30 minutes. Cost 45F.

Taxis are subject to traffic conditions. Allow 30 minutes journey time at an approximate cost of 130F.

Paris Aéroport Service (PAS) provide a private shuttle service to the main line railway stations, Disneyland Paris, hotels or homes in the city and the suburbs around the clock. ☎ 01 49 62 78 78 or 01 09 14 16 93 for emergency reservations (lead-time two hours). Approximate cost per person 110F to the capital, 200F to the suburbs.

Useful numbers – Airport information ☎ 01 49 75 77 48. 24hr emergency line Orly Sud ☎ 01 49 75 77 48; Orly Ouest ☎ 01 49 75 78 48.

Airline Offices – Air France: 119 avenue des Champs-Élysées, 75008 ☎ 01 42 99 23 64.

Air Canada – 31 rue Falguière, 75015 ☎ 01 42 18 19 20.

Aer Lingus – 47 avenue de l'Opéra, 75002 ☎ 01 47 42 12 50.

British Airways – 12 rue Castiglione, 75001 ☎ 01 47 78 14 14.

Quantas – 7 rue Scribe, 75009 ☎ 01 44 94 52 00.

TWA – 6 rue Christophe-Colomb, 75008 ☎ 01 49 19 20 00.

By rail

Paris has six mainline stations: **Gare du Nord** ☎ 01 45 26 94 82 (for northern France, Belgium, Denmark, Germany, Holland, Scandinavia, UK); **Gare de l'Est** ☎ 01 46 07 17 73 (for eastern France, Austria, Germany, Luxembourg); **Gare de Lyon** ☎ 01 43 43 33 24 (for Eastern and southern France, the Alps, Greece, Italy, Switzerland); **Gare d'Austerlitz** ☎ 01 45 84 91 70 (for southwest France, Portugal, Spain); **Gare Montparnasse** ☎ 01 43 22 19 19 (for western France); **Gare St-Lazare** (for regional lines to northwest France). For general information ☎ 01 45 82 50 50; Minitel 3615 SNCF. It is important for disabled travellers to check procedures and facilities before undertaking their journey.

All tickets must be validated (composter) prior to boarding a French train, on the day of travel, by using the orange automatic date-stamping machines on proceeding onto the platform. For a place on the TGV (Train à Grande Vitesse) seats must be pre-booked.

All stations have tourist information facilities that will assist in finding overnight accommodation.

Eurostar runs regular departures from London (Waterloo International Station ☎ 0345 881 881) and Brussels (☎ 02 224 58 90) to Paris (Gare du Nord ☎ 05 12 21 22 [0800 12 21 22]; Minitel 3615 / 3616 SNCF).

Rail passes – Special deals are available for the over 60's, unlimited travel or group travel in Europe: check with travel agents, contact French Railways, 179 Piccadilly, London, W1.☎ (0891) 515 477; or call in the US ☎ (212) 308-3103 (information) and 1-800-223-636 (reservations).

By car

Nationals of the European Union require a valid **national driving licence**. Nationals of non-EU countries should obtain an **international driving licence** (obtainable in the US from the American Automobile Association, cost for members: US$10, for non-members US$22).

Remember!

Traffic drives on the RIGHT.

The **minimum driving age** is 18 years.

Seat belts are required to be worn by passengers in the front of vehicles at all times; they are also compulsory for back-seat passengers when the car is fitted with them at the back.

Full or dipped **headlights** must be switched on in poor visibility and at night; use side-lights only when the vehicle is stationary.

In the case of a **break down** a red warning triangle or hazard warning lights are obligatory.

In built-up areas **priority** must be ceded to vehicles coming from the right (junctions and roundabouts). Outside built-up areas (indicated by a yellow diamond sign), priority is given to traffic on the more major road and on a roundabout.

Vehicles must stop when the **traffic-lights** turn red at road junctions and may filter to the right only where indicated by a flashing amber arrow.

The regulations on **drinking and driving** (limited to 0.50 g/litre) and speeding are strictly enforced – usually by an on-the-spot fine and/or confiscation of the vehicle.

Speed limits on motorways (toll-paying) maximum 130kph – 80mph (110kph – 68mph when raining) and minimum in outside lane during daylight, on level ground and with good visibility 80kph – 50mph; on dual carriageways and motorways without tolls 110kph – 68mph (100kph – 62mph when raining); other roads 90kph – 56mph (80kph – 50mph when raining); in towns 50kph – 31mph.

Parking in urban areas tends to be zoned for restricted use by residents or subject to a fee: timed tickets should be obtained from machines (horodateurs) with coins and displayed inside the windscreen on the driver's side; failure to do so may result in a fine or the car being removed.

Zone bleue: In some areas blue parking zones marked by a blue line on the pavement or a blue signpost with a P and a small square underneath require use of a "time disc" (a cardboard disc with different times) which allow a stay of 1 1/2 hours (2 1/2 hours over lunchtime) free. "Time discs" may be purchased from supermarkets or petrol stations.

Petrol – Four types of petrol (US:gas) are sold in France: super leaded (super), super unleaded 98 (sans plomb 98); super unleaded 95 (sans plomb 95); diesel (diesel/gazole).

For the vehicle it is necessary to have the **registration papers** (log-book), **nationality plates** of the approved size, and a valid certificate of insurance. Certain UK motoring organisations (AA, RAC) offer **accident insurance** and **breakdown service** schemes for members. Europ-Assistance (252 High St, Croydon CRO 1NF) has special policies for motorists. Members of the American Automobile Association should obtain the free brochure *Offices To Serve You Abroad.*

There are no customs formalities for holiday-makers bringing caravans into France for a stay of less than six months.

Car Rental – There are car rental agencies at airports, air terminals, railway stations and on the main streets. European cars usually have manual transmission but automatic cars are available. An international driving licence is required for non-EU nationals.

Getting around

Public transport

In the mid 17C, on the initiative of the philosopher Pascal, there operated in Paris a network of carriages known as *fiacres* for which the fare charged was 5 sols or a few pence. The system worked well but eventually died out, only returning in 1828 under the Restoration. In 1855 carriages known as *Joséphines*, *Gazelles*, *Dames Réunies*, *Carolines*, *Hirondelles* or *Sylphides*, and seen in all parts of Paris speeding along the streets, were united to form the General Omnibus Company. Horses were replaced in time by trams and buses. After 1918 all the road companies combined and in 1942 this joint company amalgamated with the underground. The present **RATP** – Independent Paris Transport Authority – came into being in 1949, and is responsible for running the underground metro system, the RER (Regional Express Rail network) and the buses.

Tickets – Standard metro and bus tickets are sold singly on buses or in books of ten *(carnets)* for 46F from metro stations, tobacconists, shops with the RATP sign outside and on certain buses. These are not however, valid for the RER outside the central Paris area which requires a separate ticket relative to journey destination from station ticket machines.

Multi-journey **passes** are more economical for a stay in the capital. These include the **Carte hébdomadaire** – week pass. **Formule 1** – day pass for unlimited travel. The **Carte Orange** comprises a coupon that is valid for travel on the metro, RER and bus for one calendar month for any given number of zones. **Paris-Visite** provides unlimited travel for 3 or 5 consecutive days and can be bought on production of a passport, in larger metro stations, at Services Touristiques de la RATP, 55, Quai des Grands Augustins; at the Paris Tourist Office, 127 avenue des Champs-Élysées and in London, SNCF (Bureau officiel); price varies according to number of zones covered by ticket and number of days for which it is valid. Telephone RATP, ☎ 01 43 46 14 14, for further details.

Metro – Most journeys, excluding those on the RER, require the **flat rate** of one ticket. Insert your ticket in the machine and keep it with you until you have left the metro. Inspectors do spot check them so do not throw them away before your journey's end. **Last trains** leave the end of their lines at approximately 11.45pm. **The Metro Map is located after the Index.**

Avoid changing lines at Châtelet and Montparnasse: the interchange involves a long walk!

Porte-Dauphine – metro station

Construction – Parisians first took the metro on 19 July 1900. The first Paris line was on the Right Bank, from Porte de Vincennes to Porte Maillot.

The engineer responsible was Fulgence Bienvenüe and the architect for what became the standard metro entrance, that master of the "noodle" style, Guimard.

Facts and figures – There are over 200km – 124 miles of track for the 15 lines, apart from the RER, and 370 stations of which 87 are interchanges. No point in the capital is more than 500 m – 550 yds from a metro station.

RER – The Regional Express Network includes four lines: **line A** runs from St-Germain-en-Laye to Boissy-St-Léger and Torcy; **line B** from Robinson and St-Rémy-lès-Chevreuse to Roissy and Mitry-Claye; **line C** links Versailles (south bank) and St-Quentin-en-Yvelines to Dourdan and Etampes; **line D** Le Châtelet with Villiers-le-Bel. **The Metro Map is located after the Index.**

Regular services run between 5.30am and 12.30am. Metro tickets may be used for RER trains within the Metro system – outside these special fares and tickets apply (including to airports, Versailles and Disneyland – Paris).

Buses – References in the main text will help you to find the stop to look for on the bus itineraries. Bus-routes are displayed in bus shelters as well as inside the buses themselves – this helps in locating the stops as required; note that most bus-stop shelters bear the name of the stop, but if in doubt ask a passenger: they are usually delighted to help!

Journeys are divided into stages – 1 ticket takes you the whole length of the bus line. If you hold a pass, show this to the driver on entering the bus – do not punch it into the machine. All buses run from 7am to 8.30pm. Service on some lines is extended to midnight and may be reduced or suspended on Sunday and public holidays.

Classic routes include numbers **20** (Gare St-Lazare – Gare de Lyon); **21** and **27** from Gare St-Lazare via Opéra, Palais-Royal, the Louvre, the Quais, Latin Quarter and Luxembourg gardens; **52** from Opéra passes via la Madeleine, place de la Concorde, Champs-Élysées, the Faubourg-St-Honoré and on to Auteuil; **72** follows the river from Pont de St-Cloud to the Hôtel de Ville via Alma, the Grand Palais, place de la Concorde, the Palais-Royal, the Louvre and place du Châtelet; **73** runs between la Défense down the main axis of the Arc de Triomphe, the Champs-Élysées, place de la Concorde and over the Seine to the Musée d'Orsay...

Taxis – There are some 14 300 **taxis** in Paris, cruising the streets day and night and parked in ranks alongside the kerb close to road junctions and other frequented points beneath the signs labelled Tête de Station. Taxis may also be hailed in the street when showing the illuminated sign. The rate varies according to the zone and time of day (nocturnal rate between 8pm and 6.30am). The white, orange or blue lights correspond to the three different rates A, B and C and these appear on the meter inside the cab. A supplementary charge is made for taxis from station forecourts, air terminals, and for heavy baggage or unwieldy parcels as well as for a fourth person and domestic animals.

Radio-taxis – Taxis Bleus ☎ 01 49 36 10 10; Alpha Taxi ☎ 01 45 85 85 85; Artaxi ☎ 01 42 41 50 50; Taxi G7 ☎ 01 47 39 47 39; Taxi-radio Étoile ☎ 01 42 70 41 41.

Private cars – Paris is served by a six-lane outer ring-road, the **boulevard périphérique** (35 km – 22 miles) built in 1919 along the line of the Thiers fortifications. Traffic from the motorways into Paris all merges onto the *périphérique* before filtering into the inner city via the 'Porte'. As traffic can move at considerable speed during off-peak periods, it is advisable to have pin-pointed which exit you require before getting into the ring-road system. Once on the *périphérique*, cross into the central lanes allowing traffic to join from the right-hand side, and cross back into the outside lane before leaving the ring road. This may be particularly hazardous for left-hand drive vehicles. If in doubt, try to avoid tackling the *périphérique* during rush hour! Parking sites have been built near the outlying stations to promote the use of public transport.

Once inside Paris, a west-to-east expressway (**Georges Pompidou expressway**, 13 km – 8 miles) runs along the Right Bank speeding up the flow of cars through the capital. Beware of '*axe rouge*' or red routes along main thoroughfares where parking is prohibited in order to maintain free flow of traffic (between Gare de Lyon and Gare de l'Est, via Bastille, République, quais des Célestins and de la Rapée). NEVER – even in congested traffic – use the lanes reserved for buses and taxis. Severe fines are enforced.

Useful numbers – SOS Dépannage (**24hr Breakdown service**) ☎ 01 47 07 99 99; Pré-Fourrière (**car pound**) ☎ 01 42 60 33 22; États des Routes (**road traffic conditions**) ☎ 01 48 58 33 33.

Do not leave anything of value in unattended vehicles at any time!

Explore Paris with **Michelin Maps:**

Conversion tables

Weights and measures

1 kilogram (kg)	2.2 pounds (lb)	2.2 pounds
1 ton (tn)	2.2 tons	2.2 tons

to convert kilograms to pounds, multiply by 2.2

1 litre (l)	1.7 pints (pt)	2.1 pints
1 litre	0.22 gallon (gal)	0.26 gallon

to convert litres to gallons, multiply by 0.26 (US) or 0.22 (UK)

1 hectare (ha)	2.47 acres (a)	2.47 acres
1 square kilometre (km²)	0.39 square miles (sq mi)	0.39 square miles

to convert hectares to acres, multiply by 2.4

1centimetre (cm)	0.3937 inches (in)	0.3937 inches
1 metre (m)	3.2 feet (ft) - 39.3 inches - 1.09 yards (yd)	
1 kilometre (km)	0.6214 miles (mi)	0.6214 miles

to convert metres to feet, multiply by 3.28 . kilometres to miles, multiply by 0.6

Clothing

Women	🇪🇺	🇺🇸	🇬🇧		🇪🇺	🇺🇸	🇬🇧	Men
	35	4	2½		40	7½	7	
	36	5	3½		41	8½	8	
	37	6	4½		42	9½	9	
Shoes	38	7	5½		43	10½	10	Shoes
	39	8	6½		44	11½	11	
	40	9	7½		45	12½	12	
	41	10	8½		46	13½	13	
	36	4	8		46	36	36	
	38	6	10		48	38	38	
Dresses &	40	8	12		50	40	40	Suits
Suits	42	12	14		52	42	42	
	44	14	16		54	44	44	
	46	16	18		56	46	48	
	36	08	30		37	14½	14,5	
	38	10	32		38	15	15	
Blouses &	40	12	14		39	15½	15½	Shirts
sweaters	42	14	36		40	15¾	15¾	
	44	16	38		41	16	16	
	46	18	40		42	16½	16½	

As sizes often vary depending on the designer, it is best to try on the articles before purchasing.

Speed

kph	10	30	50	70	80	90	100	110	120	130
mph	6	19	31	43	50	56	62	69	75	80

Temperature

Celsius (°C)	0°	5°	10°	15°	20°	25°	30°	40°	60°	80°	100°
Fahrenheit (°F)	32°	40°	50°	60°	70°	75°	85°	105°	140°	175°	212°

to convert: °F = (°C × 1.8) + 32   °C = 0.55 × (°F -32)

Coins and notes

500 Francs featuring
the scientists
Pierre and Marie Curie
(1858-1906), (1867-1934)

200 Francs featuring
the philosopher
Ch. de Montesquieu
(1689-1755)

100 Francs featuring
the Romantic painter
Eugène Delacroix
(1798-1863)

50 Francs featuring
the pilot and writer
Antoine de Saint-Exupéry
(1900-1944)

20 Francs

10 Francs

5 Francs

2 Francs

1 Franc

50 Centimes

20 Centimes

10 Centimes

5 Centimes

General information

Medical emergencies

It is advisable for non-EU visitors to France to take out comprehensive medical insurance to cover any medical treatment by a doctor or emergency intervention in hospital as all costs must be borne by the individual. Reimbursement of fees is negotiated with the insurance company according to the policy held. Nationals of EU countries are subject to reciprocal agreements between France and their own countries: British and Irish citizens should apply to the Department of Health and Social Security before leaving home for **Form E111**, which entitles the holder to urgent treatment for accident or unexpected illness in EU countries. If stationed in France, a refund of part of the costs of treatment can be obtained on application in person or by post to the local Social Security offices (Caisse Primaire d'Assurance Maladie).

Do not hesitate to ask for a photocopy of any prescription. This may be important if follow-on treatment is required back home.

To contact a doctor for **first aid**, **emergency medical advice** and **chemist's night service**, consult the rota displayed in the nearest chemist/drugstore (ask for *la pharmacie* identified by a green cross sign).

Useful numbers – **SOS Medecins** ☏ 01 47 07 77 77.

Pharmacie Dhéry – 84 avenue des Champs-Élysées (Galerie des Champs-Élysées) Metro George-V. Open around the clock, seven days a week.

Pharmacie Européenne de la place de Clichy – 6 place de Clichy. Open around the clock, seven days a week.

American Hospital – 63 Bd Victor-Hugo, 93 Neuilly-sur-Seine (7.5km – 5 miles from central Paris) ☏ 01 46 41 25 25.

British Hospital – 3 rue Barbès, 92 Levallois-Perret (7.5km – 5 miles) ☏ 01 46 39 22 22.

American Express offers its cardholders its service "Global Assist", for any medical, legal or personal emergency ☏ 01 47 16 25 29.

Money

Currency – There are no restrictions on the amount of currency visitors can take into France. To facilitate the export of currency in foreign bank notes in excess of the given allocation, visitors are advised to complete a currency declaration form on arrival.

Notes and coins – The unit of currency in France is the French Franc (FF), subdivided into 100 centimes. French coins come in 5, 10, 20, 50 centimes pieces (brass-coloured except the 50 centimes coin which is silver) and 1, 2, 5, 10, 20 franc pieces (silver except the 10 and 20 franc coins which are bimetallic). Notes come with the following denominations: 50, 100, 200 and 500 francs (the old 20 franc note is being phased out).

Banks – Open for the most part from 9am to 4.30pm weekdays *(except public holidays)*. Most have **cash dispensers** (ATM) that accept international credit cards and transact Euro-cheque withdrawals with PINs. These are easily recognisable by the CB logo. You will require ID (passport) for cashing cheques (travellers' or ordinary) in banks, which on the whole levy a smaller commission than that taken by hotels.

Bureaux de Change – Those open seven days a week include the **Banco Central** at the Gare d'Austerlitz; **Thomas Cook** at Gare de l'Est, Gare St-Lazare, Gare Montparnasse; **CIC** at Gare de Lyon; **UBP** at 154 avenue des Champs-Élysées; **Société Général** at 27 boulevard Haussmann; **Change de Paris** at 2 rue de l'Amiral-de-Coligny, 2 place St-Michel, 2 place Vendôme.

Credit cards – American Express, Visa, Mastercard-Eurocard and Diners Club are widely accepted in shops, hotels, restaurants and petrol stations.

American Express cards can be used only in dispensers operated by the Credit Lyonnais bank or by American Express.

Should your card get lost or stolen, report it to the following 24-hour hot-lines: **American Express** ☎ 01 47 77 72 00. **Visa** ☎ 01 42 77 11 90. **Mastercard/Eurocard** ☎ 01 45 67 84 84. **Diners Club** ☎ 01 47 62 75 50.
The loss should also be reported to the Police who will issue a crime certificate for insurance or credit card company.

Lost property office – Préfecture de Police *36 rue des Morillons; Metro Convention.* ☎ 01 45 31 14 80. 8.30am to 5pm Monday and Wednesday, to 5.30pm Friday and to 8pm Tuesday and Thursday.

Telephone

Public pay-phones – Most public phones in France use pre-paid phone cards *(télécartes* with 50 or 120 units); some accept credit cards (Visa, Mastercard/Eurocard). Phone cards can be bought in post offices, branches of France Télécom, bureaux de tabac (authorised cigarette sellers) and newsagents. Pay-phones may be used to make calls both within France and abroad, and may receive calls if bearing a blue bell sign.

Internal calls – Until October 1996 – When calling within either of the two main zones (French provinces and Greater Paris) dial only the last 8 digit correspondent's number (ie omit the 01 given here). From Paris to the provinces dial 16 + 8 digit number. From the provinces to Paris dial 16 + 1 + 8 digit number. After a few initial short pips, the French ringing tone is a series of long tones; the engaged (busy) tone is a series of short beeps.

After October 1996 – Dial the 10 digit number starting 01 given here, whether calling from the provinces or from within the Paris catchment area, without prefix.

All French toll-free numbers beginning with 05 will be amended to 0800 in October 1996.

International calls – To call the Paris region from abroad, dial the country code (33) + 1 + last 8 digit number. For the provinces, the country code (33) + 1 digit area code + 8 digits. When calling abroad from France dial 19 (00 after October 1996), wait for the continuous tone, then dial the country code, followed by the area code and number of your correspondent. For international enquiries dial 19 33 12 + country code (00 33 12 + country code after October 1996) and be prepared to wait for up to an hour.

International dialling codes: Australia: 61. United Kingdom: 44. Eire: 353. United States: 1

For **personal calling card** dial: AT&T: 19-0011. MCI: 19-0019. BT: 19-0044.

Be aware that calling from France is very expensive – more so from hotels where a commission is charged per unit.

Reduced rates to the UK: from 9.30pm to 8am Monday to Friday; from 2pm Saturday; all day Sunday and public holidays.

Reduced rates to the US and Canada: the lowest rates apply from 2am to noon all week.

Reduced rates to Australia: from 9.30pm to 8am from Monday to Saturday and all day Sunday.

For information in English dial 05 (0800 post October 96) 201 202.
Directory enquiries in English on Minitel: 3614 ED (0.37/min).

Minitel – The French Telecom videotext service offers a wide variety of information at your fingertips (fee charged). Minitel terminals are installed in hotel chains, post offices and certain petrol stations. Listed below are some of the telematic services offered:
3614 ED – electronic service in English
3615 TCAMP – camping information
3615 METEO – weather report
3615 or 3616 HORAV – general airline information and flight schedules
3615 BBC – BBC news
3615 LIBE – USA TODAY
3615 MICHELIN – Michelin tourist and route information.

Other useful information

Emergency numbers: Police: 17. Fire: 18.

Time – In France the 24-hour clock is used to denote opening hours, train times etc. rather than "am" / "pm" (1.30pm is equivalent to 13.30, 7pm to 19 h).
France is normally one hour ahead of Greenwich Mean Time (GMT). There may be a short overlap between the end of September and the end of October, when it is the same.
When it is 12 noon in France, it is: 11am in London; 11am in Dublin; 6am in New York; 3am in Los Angeles; 7pm in Perth; 9pm in Sydney; 11pm in Auckland.

Electricity – The electric current is 220 volts. Circular two-pin plugs are the rule. You should buy adaptors before leaving home. They are on sale at most airports.

Post-offices – The Bureaux de Poste are open Monday to Friday 8am to 7pm, Saturday 8am to 12noon. Paris Louvre at 52 rue du Louvre is open 24 hrs-a-day; Paris Champs-Élysées at 71 avenue des Champs-Élysées is open 8am to 10pm weekdays, and 10am to 12noon, 2pm to 8pm Sunday and public holidays.
Stamps are also available from newsagents and tobacconists. Stamp collectors should ask for *timbres de collection* in any post office, or go to the Musée de la Poste in Montparnasse.
Poste Restante mail should be addressed as follows: Name, Poste Restante, Paris and an *arrondissement* number. When no *arrondissement* number is given the mail may be collected from the post office at 52 rue du Louvre, Paris 75001, ☎ 01 40 28 20 00. Take your passport as identification when collecting your mail.

Postage – Airmail to UK: letter/postcard (20 g) 3.00FF; North America: letter/postcard (20 g) 4.40FF; Australia and NZ: letter/postcard (20 g) 5.20FF.

Shops – The big stores and larger shops are open Monday to Saturday from 9am to 6.30-7.30pm; some are open late one day a week. Smaller, individual shops may close during the lunch hour. Food shops – grocers, wine merchants and bakeries – are open from 7am to 6.30pm; many close local market-day afternoons; some open on Sunday mornings and are closed on Monday.

Tipping – Since a service charge is automatically included in the price of meals and accommodation in France, it is not necessary to tip in restaurants and hotels; taxi drivers, bellboys, doormen, hairdressers, filling station attendants or anybody who has been of assistance are usually tipped at the customer's discretion. Most French people give an extra tip in restaurants and cafés (about 50 centimes for a drink and several francs for a meal). There is no tipping in theatres.

Sightseeing in Paris

To get the "feel", the atmosphere of Paris, besides seeing the sights described in the Guide you will want to sit at a café table on the pavement to sip a drink, or go in one of the boats on the Seine, which enables you to see many of the major buildings from an unusual angle and rest at the same time, or go, one week-end, to the Flea Market.

Riverboats – Many of the boats have glass roofs and provide a spectacular way of sight-seeing in a thunderstorm. The evening trips provide a more enchanting view of the capital's riverside buildings as floodlighting highlights the architectural details.
Bateaux-mouches – ☎ 01 42 25 96 10; Embarkation: pont de l'Alma (Right Bank) Ⓜ *Alma-Marceau*. **Bateaux Parisiens Notre-Dame** – ☎ 01 43 26 92 55; Embarkation: quai de Montebello, opposite Notre-Dame Ⓜ/*RER: Saint-Michel*. **Bateaux Parisiens Tour Eiffel** – ☎ 01 43 11 33 44: Port de la Bourdonnais Ⓜ *Trocadéro*. **Vedettes du Pont-Neuf** – ☎ 01 46 33 98 38. Embarkation: square du Vert-Galant Ⓜ *Pont-Neuf*. **Vedette de Paris Ile-de-France** – ☎ 01 45 50 23 79. Embarkation: port de Suffren.
Batobus – A service operates from April to September from the Eiffel Tower (porte de la Bourdonnais) to the Hôtel de Ville (quai de l'Hôtel de Ville), stopping at port de Suffren, quai Malaquais and quai de Montebello, **Bateaux Parisiens** ☎ 01 47 05 50 00.

Barge trips on the Canal St-Martin and Canal d'Ourcq – Canal boats start from the Villette Basin *5 quai de la Loire*, a vast stretch of water on the east side of Paris Ⓜ *Jaurès*.
Coaches shuttle between the Rotonde de la Villette and the Cité des Sciences et de l'Industrie (15min).
Canauxrama *13 quai de la Loire* – ☎ 01 42 39 15 00 Ⓜ *Jaurès*. **Paris Canal** *11 quai de la Loire* ☎ 01 42 40 96 97. Cruise "Discovering the parc de la Villette" (1h 15min).

Bateau-mouche

By bus – **Cityrama Excursions** *147 rue St-Honoré.* ☏ 01 44 55 61 00. **Paris Vision** *214 rue de Rivoli.* ☏ 01 42 60 31 25.

By helicopter – Apply to 4 avenue de la Porte de Sèvres or Hélicap ☏ 01 45 57 75 51. Hélifrance ☏ 01 45 57 53 67.

Paristoric – *Espace Hébertot, 78bis boulevard des Batignolles.* ☏ 01 42 66 62 06. This lively and interesting multi-media show presents the capital's important monuments from Lutetia's earliest ruins to the modern landmarks of today, such as the Grande Arche at La Défense. It makes an ideal introduction to a visit to the city as it places the main sights in their historical context. Daily on the hour from 9am to 6pm (9pm Friday and Saturday); price: 50F (children 30F).

Museums, art galleries and exhibitions

Some 100 museums, 200 art galleries and numerous temporary exhibitions keep up Paris' international reputation as a cultural and artistic centre. All national museums and art galleries are closed on Tuesday, and all those belonging to the City of Paris on Monday. A special Museums and Monuments Pass *(Carte Musées et monuments)* gives access to 65 museums and monuments in the capital. It may be purchased in the museums themselves, in *métro* stations or from travel agents before leaving home. *Price: 60F, 120F or 170F for 1, 3 and 5 days respectively.*

R. Mazin/TOP

Montmartre

Public holidays

The following are days when museums and other monuments may be closed or may vary their hours of admission:

1 January – New Year's Day
Easter Sunday and Monday
1 May – May Day
8 May – V E Day
14 July – France's National Day
Whit Sunday and Monday

15 August – Assumption
1 November – All Saints' Day
11 November – Armistice Day
25 December – Christmas Day

In addition to the usual school holidays at Christmas, Easter and summer there are long mid-term breaks (10 days to a fortnight) in February and early November.

> *Cinemas offer reduced tickets on Wednesday, but be prepared to queue!*

Office du Tourisme de Paris – *127 avenue des Champs-Élysées.* Ⓜ *Charles-de-Gaulle-Étoile.* Open daily from 9am to 8pm. Closed 1 January, 1 May, 25 december. ☏ 01 49 52 53 54.

Telephone codes...
As from mid-October 1996,
all French telephone numbers must have ten digits.
Before the old 8-digit number insert:

        01 for Paris and the Paris region.
        02 for northwest France.
        03 for northeast France.
        04 for southeast France.
        05 for southwest France.

Calender of events

January

Paris – Dakar car rally . . . . start from the esplanade de Vincennes (New Year's Day).

Prix d'Amérique horse race . . . . Hippodrome de Vincennes (last Sunday).

February

Salon mondial du Tourisme
(Paris Travel Fair) . . . . CNIT-Paris-La Défense ☎ 01 46 92 46 92.

February – March

Tournoi des Cinq Nations
(5 Nation Rugby Trophy) . . . . Parc des Princes.

March

Salon du Livre (Paris Bookfair) . . . . Parc des Expositions, Porte de Versailles.

April

Paris Marathon . . . . Through the capital.

Musicora (International Music Festival)   Grand Palais ☎ 01 43 59 39 14.

Martial Arts Festival . . . . Palais Omnisport de Bercy.

Prix du Président de la République . . .   Hippodrome d'Auteuil (Sunday in the first fortnight).

Azalea Flower Show . . . . Bagatelle and Serres d'Auteuil.

Tulip Flower Show . . . . Parc Floral de Paris-Vincennes ☎ 01 43 43 92 95.

May

Cinq jours des objets extraordinaires   Carré Rive Gauche (mid-May).

Spring Stamp Fair . . . . Carré Marigny (end May).

Classic car race . . . . in Montmartre (4th Sunday)

Rhododendron Flower Show . . . . Parc Floral de Paris-Vincennes ☎ 01 43 43 92 95.

End May – early June

French Open Tennis . . . . championships at Roland Garros.

June

Nuit de Saint Jean . . . . fireworks at the Sacré-Cœur in Montmartre.

Fête de la Musique . . . . ☎ 01 42 20 12 34 (21 June).

French Football Cup final . . . . Parc des Princes.

Festival de Paris . . . . ☎ 01 40 27 99 07.

Best waiter / waitress' race . . . . Champs-Élysées to Bastille.

Grand Steeple-chase . . . . Hippodrome d'Auteuil (3rd Sunday in June).

Grand Prix de Paris Louis-Vuitton . . . . Hippodrome de Longchamp (last Sunday in June).

July

Défilé militaire . . . . Champs-Élysées (14 July).

Fireworks . . . . Trocadéro (14 July).

Tour de France . . . . last lap up the Champs-Élysées.

Mid-September to mid-December

Festival d'automne .... ☎ 01 42 96 12 27

Dahlia Flower Show .... Parc Floral de Paris-Vincennes ☎ 01 43 43 92 95.

Biennale des Antiquaires
(mid-September/early October) .... Grand Palais

Journées du Patrimoine .... ☎ 01 44 61 21 50 (last weekend in September).

October

Fête des vendanges .... Montmartre (1st Saturday).

Prix de l'Arc de Triomphe .... Hippodrome de Longchamp (1st Sunday).

Paris Motor Show .... Parc des Expositions, Porte de Versailles (alternate 'even' years).

FIAC (International Contemporay Art Fair) Grand Palais ☎ 01 49 53 27 00.

Festival d'Art sacré .... ☎ 01 49 27 06 62 or 3615 CAPITALE.

Festival de Jazz .... ☎ 01 47 83 33 58.

November

Military march-past .... Arc de Triomphe (11 November).

December

Salon nautique (Boat Show) .... Parc des Expositions, Porte de Versailles ☎ 01 43 95 37 00.

Living nativity play .... Place de l'Hôtel de Ville.

Champs-Élysées at night

Keep us informed!
Send us your comments and suggestions
MICHELIN TYRE
Public Company Limited
Tourism Department – The Edward Hyde Building –
38 Clarendon Road – WATFORD –
Herts WD1 1SX

Admission times and charges

The visiting times marked in the text with the **clock-face symbol** ⊙ indicate the normal hours of opening and closing. These are listed here in the same order as they appear in the main text. Admission times and charges are liable to alteration without prior notice and so the information given here should serve merely as a guide-line. Museums, churches, etc may refuse admittance during private functions, religious services or special occasions, and may stop issuing tickets up to an hour before the actual closing time.

When **guided tours** are indicated, the departure time for the last tour of the morning or afternoon will once again be prior to the given closing time.

Most tours are conducted by French-speaking guides but in some cases the term 'guided tour' may cover group visiting with recorded commentaries. Some of the larger and more frequented museums and monuments offer guided tours in other languages. Enquire at the ticket or book stalls.

The **admission prices** indicated are for single adults benefiting from no special concession; reductions for children, students, the over 60s and parties should be requested on site and be endorsed with proof of ID. In some cases, admission is free (notably Wednesday, Sunday and public holidays).

Churches and chapels are usually open from 8am to 12noon and from 2pm to dusk. Visitors are not admitted during services and so tourists should avoid visiting at that time. As it is the norm for all churches to be open daily, only exceptional conditions are here listed. Although no fee is charged, donations towards upkeep are welcome.

Tourism for the disabled – Some of the sights described in this guide are accessible to disabled people (marked &.). They are listed in the publication Touristes quand même! Most places may be accessible to wheelchair users, but have steps or stairways to contend with. Venues can provide assistance in giving wheelchair access to temporary exhibitions; it may be helpful therefore to check for recommended procedures, designated parking facilities and best times for by-passing long queues, before setting out.

Detailed information is available from the Comité National Français de Liaison pour la Réadaptation des Handicappés 38 boulevard Raspail ☎ 01 45 48 90 13.

Access in Paris is a guide for the disabled and those who have problems getting around. This carefully researched guide (see PARIS AT LEISURE – Further Reading) gives information about travel, accommodation and tourist attractions in Paris and is cross-referenced to Michelin maps and guides.

PARIS AT LEISURE

Louvre des Antiquaires – &. Open 11am to 7pm. Closed Monday; 1 January; 1 and 8 May; Sunday and public holidays in July and August; 25 December. ☎ 01 42 97 27 00.

Village Suisse – Open 10.30am to 7pm. Closed Tuesday; Wednesday; and throughout August.

Musée des Arts Forains – Open weekends only from 2pm to 7pm. 42F adult, 25F child. Recorded information ☎ 01 45 58 31 76.

La Samaritaine – Access to the terrace is free of charge (lift). Shop opening hours 9.30am to 7pm Monday to Saturday (10pm Thursday).

Musée d'Art Juif – Open from 3pm to 8pm. Closed Friday; Saturday; for Jewish festivals and throughout August. 30F. ☎ 01 42 57 84 15.

ALMA

Palais de Tokyo: Musée d'Art moderne de la Ville de Paris – &. Open 10am to 5.30pm (8.30pm on Wednesday; 7pm Saturday and Sunday). Closed Monday. 40F. ☎ 01 53 67 40 00.

Musée National des Arts Asiatiques-Guimet: Buddhist Panthéon – Closed for refurbishment. February 1996-1998. ☎ 01 47 23 61 65.

Palais Galliera: Musée de la Mode et du Costume – Open 10am to 5.40pm. Closed Monday and four months during which temporary exhibitions are held. 35F. ☎ 01 47 20 85 23.

Les Égouts – &. Entrance: corner of Quai d'Orsay and Pont de l'Alma. Open 11am to 5pm (4pm between 1 October and 30 April). Closed Thursday and Friday; the last three weeks in January. 25F. ☎ 01 47 05 10 29. 20 min audio-visual presentation; no tour during storms, after heavy rainfall or when the Seine is in flood.

AUTEUIL

Maison de Radio-France – Guided tours (1hr) at 10.30am, 11.30am, 2.30pm, 3.30pm and 4.30pm. Closed Sunday and public holidays. 15F. ☎ 01 42 30 33 83.

Fondation Le Corbusier – Open 10am to 12.30pm, and from 1.30pm to 6pm (5pm Friday). Closed weekends and all public holidays; throughout August and between 25 December and 1 January. 15F. ☎ 01 42 88 41 53.

Musée Bourdelle – &. Open 2pm to 7pm Wednesday and Saturday. Closed last fortnight of every quarter. 25F. ☎ 01 46 27 63 46. Special concession for those with impaired sight.

Cimetière d'Auteuil – Open from 8am (8.30 Saturday; 9am Sunday) to 6pm (5.30 in winter). ☎ 01 44 10 86 50.

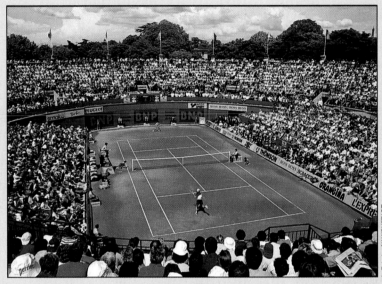

Stadium Roland-Garros

BASTILLE

Arsenal: Bibliothèque (Library) – Open for group visits (1hr 30min) by prior arrangement only. ☎ 01 42 77 44 21 (six months lead-time). **Pavillon** – Open 10.30am to 6.30pm Tuesday to Saturday, 11am to 7pm Sunday. Closed 1 January. No charge. ☎ 01 42 76 33 97.

Église Ste-Marguerite – Open weekdays 3pm to 6pm. Closed Sunday.

Musée de l'Argenterie Insolite – Museum and workshops are open weekdays between 10am to 12noon and 2pm and 5pm (4pm Friday). Only the museum is open on Saturday. Closed Sunday and certain bank public holidays. 35F. ☎ 01 43 40 20 20.

Cimetière Picpus – & Guided tour (1hr 30min) between 2pm and 6pm (4pm between 15 October and 15 April). Closed Monday; Sunday during winter months; bank public holidays; throughout August and during one week in winter. ☎ 01 43 44 18 54.

BOIS DE BOULOGNE

A miniature train links the park entrance and Porte Maillot on Wednesday, Saturday, Sunday and public holidays (daily during school holidays) from 1.30pm to 6pm. 4.50F.

Jardin d'Acclimatation – Entrance: Carrefour des Sablons. &. Open 10am to 6pm. 10F. ☎ 01 40 67 90 82. Special attractions on Wednesday, Saturday, Sunday and school holidays from 1.30pm. ☎ 01 40 67 90 80.

Musée en Herbe – Open 10am to 6pm (2pm to 6pm Saturday outside school holidays); closed 1 January and 25 December. 13F. ☎ 01 40 67 97 66. **Boats** – 30F an hour are available for hire between 15 April and 16 October. Boat trips on the lac inférieur: 51F for 1 – 5 people.

Lac inférieur – 10am to 8pm. Closed 1 November to 28 February. 44F. ☎ 01 45 25 44 01.

Musée National des Arts et Traditions Populaires – &. Open 9.45am to 5.15pm (last admissions 4.30pm). Closed Tuesday; 1 January; 1 May; 1 November and 25 December. 20F. ☎ 01 44 17 60 00.

BOIS DE BOULOGNE

Parc de Bagatelle – &. Open 8.30am to 6.30pm between 16 March and 30 September (7.30pm between May and July), 9am to 5.30pm October to 15 March (4.30pm during December and January). 6F. ☏ 01 40 67 97 00.

Jardin des Serres d'Auteuil – &. Open 10am to 6pm (5pm 1 October to 31 March). Certain greenhouses close between 11.30am and 1pm and again at 4pm. 3F. ☏ 01 40 71 75 23.

Musée National du Sport – 24 rue du Commandant Guilbaud. Open 9.30am to 12.30pm and 2pm to 5pm; closed Wednesday, Saturday and public holidays. 20F. ☏ 01 40 45 99 12.

Shakespeare garden – Guided tours 3pm to 3.30pm and 4 to 4.30pm. 3F. ☏ 01 40 71 75 23.

Hotel Concorde-La Fayette Panoramic bar – Open 11am to 2am, patrons only.

Musée Arménien – Open Thursday and Sunday 2pm to 6pm. Closed certain public holidays and throughout August. ☏ 01 45 56 15 88.

Musée d'Ennery – Open 2pm to 6pm Thursday, Sunday and some public holidays. Closed throughout August. ☏ 01 47 53 57 96.

Musée de la Contrefaçon – Open Monday and Wednesday between 2pm and 4.30pm; between 9.30am and 12noon on Friday. ☏ 01 45 01 51 11.

Musée Dapper – Open daily between 11am and 7pm. Closed between exhibitions. 20F, free on Wednesday. ☏ 01 45 00 01 50.

BOIS DE VINCENNES

Château – Guided tours of the keep and chapel daily between 10am and 6pm (time: 45min); closed 1 January, 1 May, 1 and 11 November and 25 December. 28F. ☏ 01 43 28 15 48. **Musée des Chasseurs** – & Open Wednesday 10am to 12noon, 2pm to 5pm and Saturday afternoons only (except during July and August). ☏ 01 49 57 32 00, extension (*poste*) 2383. **Musée de la Symbolique Militaire** – Open Wednesday 10am to 12noon and 2pm to 5pm. ☏ 01 49 57 33 60.

Foire du Trône – From 2pm to 12midnight for eight weeks from the last weekend in March.

Parc Floral de Paris – Open from 9.30am to 8pm during the summer (6pm from last Saturday in September, 5pm from October). 10F (5F in winter). ☏ 01 43 43 92 95.

École du Breuil: arboretum – Weekdays 8am to 4.30pm. Weekends 10am to 7pm (6pm in March and October, 5pm from November to February). Closed 1 January and 25 December. 5F weekends. ☏ 01 43 28 28 94.

Centre boudhique – Access to the Temple during Cambodian festivals in April to October. ☏ 01 43 51 54 48.

Lac Daumesnil – Bicycles for hire from end June to early September between 10am (11am weekdays) and 7pm. 20F for 30mins, 30F for 1hr. ☏ 01 47 47 76 50.

Zoo de Vincennes – &. Open 9am to 6-6.30pm during the summer (5-5.30pm winter). 40F. ☏ 01 44 75 20 10.

Musée des Arts d'Afrique et de l'Océanie – Open 10am to 12noon, and 1.30pm to 5.30pm weekdays, 12.30pm to 6pm weekends and public holidays, 10am to 6pm during exhibitions. Closed Tuesday; 1 May. 27F. ☏ 01 44 74 84 80.

CHAMPS-ÉLYSÉES

Arc de Triomphe – Open 9.30am to 6.30pm between 1 April and 30 September, between 10am and 5pm from 1October to 31 March. 32F. ☏ 01 43 80 31 31.

Musée du Petit-Palais – Open 10am to 5.40pm. Closed Monday and public holidays. 27F. ☏ 01 42 65 12 73.

Palais de la Découverte – &. Open 9.30 to 6pm, 10am to 7pm Sunday and public holidays. Closed Monday. 22F. ☏ 01 40 74 80 00. Minitel 3615 DÉCOUVERTE.

La DÉFENSE

La Grande Arche – &. Open daily 9am to 7pm (6pm 1 October to 31 March). 40F. ☏ 01 49 07 27 57.

Colline de la Défense – &. Open 12noon to 6pm Tuesday, Thursday, Sunday and public holidays; 12noon to 7pm Monday, Wednesday, Friday; 12noon to 10pm Saturday. 35F. ☏ 01 36 67 06 06.

Dôme Imax – Screenings at 12noon to 6pm on Tuesday, Thursday and Sunday; 12noon to 7pm Monday, Wednesday and Friday; double bill at 8pm on Saturday. 55F. ☏ 01 36 67 06 06.

EIFFEL TOWER

Tour Eiffel – &. Access to third level from 9am to 12midnight between 1 July and 30 September; 9.30am to 11pm the rest of the year. Lift to first level: 20F, second level: 38F, third level: 55F. On foot to first and second levels: 12F. ☏ 01 44 11 23 23.

Maison de l'UNESCO – Open 9am to 12.30pm and 2.30pm to 6pm. ☏ 01 45 68 03 59.

FAUBOURG ST-GERMAIN

Palais Bourbon: Assemblée Nationale – Open to the public at 10am, 2pm and 3pm on Saturday only unless Parliament is in session. ☏ 01 40 63 77 77. Entrance at 33 quai d'Orsay. Proof of ID required.

Musée de la Légion d'Honneur et des Ordres de la Chevalerie – Open from 2pm to 5pm. Closed Monday and public holidays. 20F. ☏ 01 40 62 84 25.

Hôtel de Tavannes – Guided tour (15min) between 10am and 12noon, 2.30pm and 6pm from 20 August to 30 September.

Fondation Dina Vierny – Musée Maillol – Open from 11am to 6pm. Closed Tuesday. 40F (enquire about concessions for under 18s and over 60s). ☏ 01 42 22 59 58. Fax 01 42 84 14 44.

Musée Hébert – Open from 12.30pm (2pm weekends and public holidays) to 6pm. Closed Tuesday. 15F. ☏ 01 42 22 23 82.

Ancien Couvent des Carmes – Guided tour (1hr 30min) of church, convent buildings, gardens and crypt each Saturday at 3pm. 10F. Telephone to confirm ☏ 01 44 39 52 00, extension (*poste*) 405.

FAUBOURG ST-HONORÉ

La Madeleine – Closed from 12.30pm to 3.30pm Sunday and public holidays. ☏ 01 42 65 52 17.

Musée Bouilhet-Christofle – Guided tour (1hr) between 2pm and 6pm. Closed weekends and public holidays. 40F. ☏ 01 49 33 43 00.

Musée Jacquemart-André – Open daily, 10am to 6pm. 45F. ☏ 01 42 89 04 91.

Cathédrale St-Alexandre-Newski – Open 3pm to 5pm, Tuesday and Friday. ☏ 01 42 27 37 34.

Les GOBELINS

Manufactures nationales des Gobelins – &. Guided tour (1hr 30min) of workshops on Tuesday, Wednesday and Thursday between 2pm and 2.45pm. 37F.

GRANDS-BOULEVARDS

Hôtel des Ventes Drouot-Richelieu – Open 11am to 6pm. Closed Sunday, public holidays and from end July to early September unless under exceptional circumstances. ☏ 01 48 00 20 20.

Musée Grévin – Open from 1pm (10am during school holidays) to 7pm. 50F adults, 34F child. ☏ 01 47 70 85 05.

Musée de l'Éventail – Open Tuesday from 2pm to 5pm. Closed throughout August. 30F. ☏ 01 42 08 19 89.

La Bourse (The Stock-Exchange) – Galerie des visiteurs open Monday to Friday from 1.30pm to 4pm.. 30F. ☏ 01 40 41 62 20.

Notre-Dame-de-Bonne-Nouvelle – Closed 12noon to 4pm on Sunday. ☏ 01 42 33 65 74.

Musée Baccarat – Open from 10am to 6pm. Closed Sunday and certain public holidays. 15F. ☏ 01 47 70 64 30.

Hôtel Bourrienne – &. Guided tour (45 min) Saturday and Sunday between 2pm and 4pm. 25F. ☏ 01 47 70 51 14.

Église St-Laurent – Open 9am to 12noon and 4pm to 6pm.

Musée du Grand Orient de France – &. Open from 2pm to 6pm. Closed Sunday and first two weeks of September. ☏ 01 45 23 20 92, extension (*poste*) 303.

HALLES-BEAUBOURG

Espace Grévin du Forum des Halles – ♿. Guided tour (45min) weekdays between 10.30 and 6.45pm, 1pm and 6.30pm Sunday and public holidays. 42F. ☎ 01 40 26 28 50.

Bourse du Commerce (Commodities-market) – Open from 9am to 6pm. Closed weekends and public holidays.

Temple de l'Oratoire – Open Sunday mornings between services or by appointment. ☎ 01 42 60 21 64.

Église St-Leu-St-Gilles – Open 3pm to 6pm Tuesday to Saturday (from 5pm in August). ☎ 01 42 33 50 22.

Centre Georges-Pompidou – ♿. Open from 12noon (10am weekends and public holidays) to 10pm. Closed Tuesday and 1 May.

Musée national d'art moderne – 35F.

Grande Galerie – 45F. Day pass 60F. All tickets available on ground floor. ☎ 01 44 78 12 33.

ILE DE LA CITÉ

Notre-Dame Crypte Archéologique – Open from 10am to 6pm (5pm from 1 October to 31 March). Closed most holiday. 27F. ☎ 01 43 29 83 51.

Notre-Dame North Tower – Ascent (386 steps) from 9.30am (10am depending on time of year) to 6pm (or 4pm depending on time of year). Closed certain public holidays. 27F. ☎ 01 43 29 50 40.

Notre-Dame Treasury – Open from 9.30am to 12noon, 12.30pm (2pm Saturday) to 5.30pm. Closed Sunday and at Easter, 15 August, 1 November and 25 December. 15F. ☎ 01 42 34 56 10.

Musée Notre-Dame – Open Wednesday and weekends from 2.30pm to 6pm. Closed certain public holidays. 12F. ☎ 01 40 27 61 51.

Mémorial de la Déportation – Open 10am to 12noon and from 2pm to 7pm (5pm between 1 October and 31 March).

Sainte-Chapelle – Open from 9.30 to 1pm, 2pm to 6pm 1 April to 30 September; from 10am to 1pm and 2pm to 5pm during October, February and March; from 10am to 1pm and 2pm to 4pm during November to January. Closed certain public holidays. ☎ 01 42 65 35 80.

Palais de Justice – Open from 8am to 6pm. Closed Sunday and public holidays. Free access in principle, to civil or criminal cases. The galerie des Bustes and Children's Court are closed to the public. ☎ 01 44 32 67 19.

La Conciergerie – Open from 9.30am to 6pm between 1 April and 30 September; from 10am to 5pm between 1 October and 31 March. 26F. ☎ 01 43 54 30 06, fax: 01 44 61 20 36.

ILE ST-LOUIS

Église St-Louis-en-l'Ile – Closed Monday.

Adam Mickiewicz Museum – Guided tour (45min) at 2pm, 3pm, 4pm, 5pm on Thursday only. Closed bank public holidays, 10 days over Easter and 15 days over Christmas. ☎ 01 43 54 35 61.

Les INVALIDES

Église St-Louis-des-Invalides – Open daily from 10am to 6pm (5pm in winter).

Musée de l'Armée – Open from 10am to 5.30pm (4.30pm from 1 October to 31 March). Closed public holidays. 35F. ☎ 01 44 42 37 67. The ticket is valid two days to allow for a complete visit of the museum, documentary films and slide projections, and the Dome church.

Musée de l'Ordre de la Libération – Open 10am to 6pm (5pm between 1 October and 31 March). Closed 1 January, 1 May, 17 June, 25 December. No charge. ☎ 01 47 05 04 10.

Église du Dôme – see Army Museum above. The church remains open until 7pm between 1 June and 31 August. ☎ 01 44 42 38 42.

Musée Rodin – ♿. Open from 9.30 to 5.15pm between 1 April and 30 September; from 9.30am to 4.15 1 October to 31 March. Closed Monday; 1 January, 1 May and 25 December. 27F. ☎ 01 44 18 61 10. Special concession for those with impaired sight.

Musée-Galerie de la SEITA – ♿. Open from 11am to 7pm. Closed Sunday and public holidays. Free access to permanent collection, fee for temporary exhibitions. ☎ 01 45 56 60 17.

Institut du Monde Arabe – &. Open from 10am to 6pm. Closed Monday; 1 May. 25F.
☏ 01 40 51 38 38.

Musée de Minéralogie – *Université Pierre-et-Marie-Curie.* Open from 1pm to 6pm.
Closed Tuesday; 1 January, Easter weekend; 14 July; 25 December. 25F.
☏ 01 44 27 52 88.

La Mosquée – &. *Entrance on place du Puits-de-l'Ermite.* Guided tour (30min) from
9am to 12noon, from 2pm to 6pm. Closed Friday and Muslim holy days. 15F.
☏ 01 45 35 97 33.

Le Jardin des Plantes: Jardin alpin – Open 8am to 11.45am and from 1pm to 4.45pm
from 1 April to 30 September. Closed Tuesday, weekends and public holidays.
☏ 01 40 79 30 00.

Jardin d'hiver – Open 1pm to 5pm weekdays and 10am to 6pm (5pm during winter)
weekends. Closed Tuesday; 1May; 15 August. 12F. ☏ 01 40 79 30 00.

École de Botanique – Open from 8am to 11am and from 1.30pm to 5pm. Closed Tuesday;
weekends; 1May and 15 August. ☏ 01 40 79 30 00.

Ménagerie – Open from 9am to 6pm (5pm in winter). 25F. ☏ 01 40 79 37 94.

Microzoo – Open 10am to 12noon, 1.30pm to 4.45pm from 1 April to 30 September;
10am to 12noon and 2pm to 3.15pm weekdays, 10am to 12noon and 2.30pm to
5.45pm weekends the rest of the year. 25F. ☏ 01 40 79 37 88.

Muséum National d'Histoire Naturelle: Grande Galerie de l'Évolution – &. Open from
10am to 6pm (10pm Thursday). Closed Tuesday; 1 May; 15 August. 40F.
☏ 01 40 79 30 00.

Galerie de Paléontologie, Galerie de Minéralogie, Galerie de Paléobotanique – Open from 10am to
6pm (5pm weekends between 1 October and 31 March) Closed Tuesday; 1 May;
15 August. 25F. ☏ 01 40 79 30 00.

Galerie d'Entomologie – Open from 1pm to 4.30pm weekdays 10am to 6pm weekends
between 1 April and 30 September (1pm to 5pm in winter). Closed Tuesday, 1 May,
15 August. 12F. ☏ 01 40 79 34 00.

La Salpêtrière: Chapelle St-Louis – Open from 8.30am to 6.30pm.

Panthéon – Open from 9.30am to 5.45pm from 1 April to 30 September (from 10am
to 4.45pm 1 October to 31 March). Closed public holidays. 26F. ☏ 01 43 54 34 51,
fax: 01 44 61 20 36.

Église St-Étienne-du-Mont – Closed Monday throughout July and August.

Collège des Escossois – Apply in writing to the Mother Superior: Madame la Supérieure,
65 rue du Cardinal Lemoine, 75005 Paris. ☏ 01 43 54 11 41.

Musée Curie – Guided tour (1hr) from 1.30pm to 5pm. Closed weekends; public holidays and throughout August. ☏ 01 40 51 67 49.

Centre de la Mer et des Eaux – &. Open from 10am to 12.30pm and from 1.15pm to
5.30pm weekdays, 10am to 5.30pm weekends and public holidays. Closed Monday;
1 January, 1May, 14 July, 15 August and 25 December. 25F. ☏ 01 46 33 08 61.

École nationale supérieure des Mines: Mineralogical collection – Open from 1.30pm
to 6pm weekdays, from 10am to 12.30pm, and from 2pm to 5pm Saturday. Closed
Monday; Sunday and public holidays. 20F. ☏ 01 40 51 91 45.

La Sorbonne: Église – Open during temporary exhibitions and cultural programmes only.

Hôtel de Cluny: Musée national du Moyen Âge et des Thermes de Cluny – Open
from 9.15am to 5.45pm (last admission 5.15pm). Closed Tuesday; 1 January, 1 May,
1 November and 25 December. 27F. ☏ 01 46 34 45 17.

Musée d'Histoire de la Médecine – Open from 2pm to 5.30pm. Closed Sunday and
public holidays; Saturday between 1 July and 15 September. 20F. ☏ 01 40 46 16 93.

Musée de la Préfecture de Police – Open from 9am (10am Saturday) to 5pm. Closed
Sunday and public holidays. ☏ 01 44 41 52 50.

Église des Sts-Archanges – Open from 10am to 1pm on Sunday only. ☏ 01 43 54 67 47.

See Practical Information in text. &. Open from 9am to 6pm (10pm Wednesday, aile
Richelieu only Monday). Last admissions at 5.15pm (9.15pm). Closed Tuesday.
The historical section is open from 9am to 10pm. Bookshops and restaurants from
9.30am to 10pm. Temporary exhibitions under the pyramid from 10am to 10pm. 40F,
20F after 3pm and all day Sunday. No charge for under 18s. Tickets are valid all day
and allow for re-entry into the museum. General recorded information
☏ 01 40 20 51 51; enquiries ☏ 01 40 20 53 17; Minitel 36 15 LOUVRE. Special concession for those with impaired sight.

Musée National de l'Orangerie – Open from 9.45am to 5.15pm. Closed Tuesday;
1 January; 1 May and 25 December. 27F. ☏ 01 42 97 48 16.

LUXEMBOURG

Luxembourg palace – &. Guide tour (1hr 30min) from 9.30am to 4.30pm. Closed Sunday and public holidays; from 2 April to 30 June; from 2 October to 20 December for Parliamentary sessions). Enquire 3 months ahead ☎ 01 42 34 20 60.

Le MARAIS

Maison de Victor-Hugo – Open from 10am to 5.40pm. Closed Monday and public holidays. 17,50F. ☎ 01 42 72 10 16.

Hôtel de Sully – Tour of the exterior from 8.30am to 7pm.

Musée Carnavalet – Open from 10am to 5.40pm. Closed Monday and public holidays. 27F. ☎ 01 42 72 21 13. Special concession for those with impaired sight.

Musée Picasso: Hôtel Salé – &. Open from 9.30am to 5.15pm (5pm in winter). Closed Tuesday; 1 January, 25 December. 27F. ☎ 01 42 71 63 15.

Musée de la Serrurerie-Bricard – Open from 10am to 12noon and from 2pm to 5pm. Closed Monday; weekends and public holidays. 30F. ☎ 01 42 77 79 62.

Hôtel de Rohan – Open only during temporary winter exhibitions.

Cathédrale Ste-Croix-de-Paris – Open 3pm to 7pm Monday; Wednesday and Friday; 10am to 11am Sunday. Ring the bell at 13 rue du perche. ☎ 01 42 78 31 93.

Musée de la Chasse et de la Nature – Open from 10am to 12.30pm and from 1.30pm to 5.30pm. Closed Tuesday and public holidays. 25F. ☎ 01 42 72 86 43.

Hôtel de Soubise: Musée de l'Histoire de France – Open from 1.45pm to 5.45pm. Closed Tuesday. 15F. ☎ 01 40 27 62 18.

Église Notre-Dame-des-Blancs-Manteaux – Open from 10am to 12.45pm and from 4pm to 7pm. Closed Monday.

Église des Billettes – Open 12.15pm to 1.30pm Wednesday; 6.15pm to 7.30pm Thursday; 9.45am to 12noon Sunday. ☎ 01 42 72 38 79

Cloister – Open from 11am to 7pm.

Musée Cognacq-Jay – Open from 10am to 5.40pm. Closed Monday and public holidays. 17,50F. ☎ 01 40 27 07 21.

Hôtel de Lamoignon: Bibliothèque historique de la Ville de Paris – The actual library is closed, however an exhibition area at 22 rue Mahler is open from 10am to 6pm. Closed Monday. ☎ 01 44 59 29 40.

Lycée Charlemagne – Open to the public only on the National Heritage Days in September.

Maison de l'Abbaye d'Ourscamp: cellars – Guided tours (30min) from 2pm to 6pm (check for August). Closed public holidays. 40F. ☎ 01 48 87 74 31.

Mémorial du Martyr Juif Inconnu – Open from 10am to 1pm and from 2pm to 6pm (4.30pm Friday). Closed Saturday and for all Jewish festivals. 15F. ☎ 01 42 77 44 72.

Hôtel de Sens: Forney Library – Open from 1.30pm (10am Saturday) to 8pm. Closed Monday; Sunday and public holidays. 20F for temporary exhibitions. ☎ 01 42 78 14 60.

Musée de la Curiosité et de la Magie – Open from 2pm to 6pm Wednesday and weekends. 45F. ☎ 01 42 72 13 26.

MONTMARTRE

Halle St-Pierre: Musée d'Art naïf Max-Fourny – &. Open from 10am to 6pm. Closed 1 January; 1 May and 25 December. 25F. ☎ 01 42 58 72 89.

Espace Dalì – Open from 10am to 6pm. 35F. ☎ 01 42 64 40 10.

St Pierre de Montmartre Cemetery – Open 1 November only.

Basilique du Sacré-Cœur: Dome – Open from 9am to 7pm (6pm from 1 October to 31 March). 15F. (300 steps). **Crypt** – Open from 9am to 8pm 1 July to 30 September; 9am (1pm Sunday) to 6pm from 1 October to 30 June. 10F or 25F for combined ticket dome and crypt.

Musée de Montmartre – Open from 11am to 5.30pm. Closed Monday; 1 January; 1 May. 25F. ☎ 01 46 06 61 11.

Cimetière de Montmartre – Open from 8am (8.30am Saturday; 9am Sunday) to 6pm (5.30pm from 6 November to 14 March). General enquiries ☎ 01 43 87 64 24.

MONTPARNASSE

Tour Montparnasse – (56th floor only). ♿. Open from 9.30am to 11.30pm (11pm Friday and Saturday; and 10.30pm Sunday to Thursday from 1 October to 31 March). 42F. ☎ 01 45 38 52 56.

Musée Bourdelle – Open from 10am to 5.45pm. Closed Monday and public holidays. 27F. ☎ 01 45 48 67 27.

Musée de la Poste – ♿. Open 10am to 6pm Monday to Saturday, 12noon to 7pm Sunday. Closed public holidays. 18F. ☎ 01 42 79 23 45.

Cimetière de Monparnasse – Open from 8am (8.30am Saturday; 9am Sunday) to 6pm (5.30pm from 6 November to 14 March). General enquiries ☎ 01 44 10 86 50

Fondation Cartier – ♿. Open from 12noon to 8pm (10pm Thursday). Closed Monday and occasionally between exhibitions. 30F. ☎ 01 42 18 56 50.

MOUFFETARD

Église St-Médard – Closed Monday.

La MUETTE

Musée Marmottan – ♿. Open from 10am to 5pm. Closed Monday; 1 May and 25 December. 35F. ☎ 01 42 24 07 02.

OPÉRA

Opéra-Garnier: Bibliothèque-Musée – Open from 10am to 4.30pm. Closed 1 January; 1 May. 30F. ☎ 01 40 01 22 63.

Musée de la Parfumerie Fragonard – Open 9am to 5.30pm Monday to Saturday, 10am to 2pm Sunday and public holidays. ☎ 01 47 42 04 56.

Musée des Lunettes et Lorgnettes – Open from 10am to 12noon, from 3pm to 6pm. Closed Monday; Sunday, public holidays and throughout August. 20F. ☎ 01 40 20 06 98.

ORSAY

Musée d'Orsay – ♿. See Practical Information in text. Open from 10am (9am Sunday and between 20 June and 20 September) to 6pm (9.45pm Thursday) Last admissions 5.15pm (9.15pm). Closed Monday; 1 January; 1 May; 25 December. 35F. General recorded information ☎ 01 45 49 11 11.

PALAIS-ROYAL

Bibliothèque Nationale de France: Cabinet des Médailles et Antiques – Open from 1pm to 5pm; 12noon to 6pm Sunday and public holidays. 22F. ☎ 01 47 03 83 40.

Musée de la Mode et du Textile – Reopening December 1996. ☎ 01 44 55 57 50.

Musée des Arts Décoratifs – Closed for refitting. Partial reopening in Spring 1997. ☎ 01 44 55 57 50.

PARC MONCEAU

Musée Nissim de Camondo – Open 10am to 5pm Wednesday to Sunday. Closed 1 January, I May, 25 December. 27F. ☎ 01 45 63 26 32.

Musée Cernuschi – Open 10am to 5.40pm Tuesday to Sunday. Closed public holidays. 17,50F. ☎ 01 45 63 50 75.

Musée Henner – Open from 10am to 12noon and from 2pm to 5pm. Closed Monday; 1 May and certain other public holidays. 20F. ☎ 01 47 63 42 73.

PASSY

Cimetière de Passy – Open from 8am (8.30am Saturday; 9am Sunday) to 6pm (5.30pm from 6 November to 14 March). General enquiries ☎ 01 44 10 86 50.

Musée Clemenceau – Open from 2pm to 5pm Tuesday, Thursday and weekends. Closed 1 January; throughout August; 1 November; 24, 25 December. 20F. ☎ 01 45 20 53 41.

Musée du Vin-Caveau des Échansons – ♿. Open 10am to 6pm. Closed 1 January; Monday during July and August; 24, 25 and 31 December. 30F. ☎ 01 45 25 63 26.

Maison de Balzac – Open from 10am to 5.40pm. Closed Monday and public holidays. 17,50F. ☎ 01 42 24 56 38.

Cimetière PÈRE-LACHAISE

Open from 8am (8.30am Saturday; 9am Sunday) to 6pm (5.30pm from 6 November to 14 March). General enquiries ☎ 01 43 70 03 70.
Guided tours (2hr) at 2.30pm Saturday all year around and on Wednesday from March to December. Collection point by main gate on boulevard de Ménilmontant. 35F. ☎ 01 43 70 70 33.

PORT-ROYAL

Ancienne abbaye de Port-Royal – Contact the CNMHS (Caisse National des Monuments Historiques et Sites) at the Hôtel de Sully (*see* MARAIS) for conditions of opening.

Le Val-de-Grâce: Musée – Scheduled to re-open end 1996.
Église – Open from 10am to 6pm.

Observatoire – Guided tour (1hr 30min) first Saturday of each month at 2.30pm, or on written application to l'Observatoire de Paris, service des visites, 61 avenue de l'observatoire, 75014 Paris. Closed between 15 July and 31 August. 30F. ☎ 01 40 51 21 74.

Musée Zadkine – Open 10am to 5.30pm Tuesday to Sunday. Closed public holidays. 17,50F. ☎ 01 43 26 91 90. Special concession for those with impaired sight.

Les Catacombes – Open 2pm to 4pm Tuesday to Friday, 9am to 11am and 2pm to 4pm Saturday and Sunday. Closed public holidays. 27F. ☎ 01 43 22 47 63.

Les QUAIS

Hôtel des Monnaies: Musée de la Monnaie (*Coin Museum*) – Open 1pm to 6pm Tuesday to Sunday (9pm Wednesday). Closed public holidays except 8 May, 1 and 11 November. 25F. ☎ 01 40 46 55 35. **Ateliers de frappe** (*workshops*) – ᶑ. Open 2pm to 3pm Tuesday and Thursday, guided tour (1hr). Closed from end July to early September. ☎ 01 40 46 55 35. **Galerie de vente** (*shop*) – Open 9am to 5.45pm, Monday to Friday, 10am to 1pm and 2pm to 5.30pm Saturday. Closed public holidays and Saturday between 15 July and 1 September.

Musée de l'Assistance Publique – Hôpitaux de Paris – Open Tuesday to Saturday, 10am to 5pm. Closed public holidays and throughout August. 20F. ☎ 01 46 33 01 43.

Hôtel de Ville – Guided tours (1hr) of the interior Monday at 10.30am from the north porch, rue Lobau. ☎ 01 42 76 50 49 or 01 42 76 59 27.

RÉPUBLIQUE

Carreau du Temple – Open from 9am to 12noon (12.30pm weekends). Closed Monday; 14 July; 15 August.

Conservatoire National des Arts et Métiers – Closed for refurbishment until 1998. Information and sales desks are open Tuesday to Sunday from 10am to 5.30pm. Closed public holidays. ☎ 01 40 27 23 31.

Hôpital St-Louis: Musée des Moulages – Guided tours (2hr) third Thursday of each month at 2pm (*sharp!*). 20F. Telephone to confirm 15 days ahead: Melle Durand ☎ 01 42 49 99 15.

Cirque d'Hiver

ST-GERMAIN-DES-PRÉS

Église de St-Germain-des-Prés: Chapelle St-Symphorien – Guided tour from 1pm to 5pm Tuesday and Thursday (subject to confirmation during school holidays), and the third Sunday each month at 3pm. ☎ 01 43 25 41 71.

Musée Eugène Delacroix – Open 9.45am to 5.15pm. Closed Tuesday. ☎ 01 43 54 36 70.

Institut de France – Guided tour (1hr 45mins) at weekends at 10.30am and 3pm on request. 20F. ☎ 01 44 41 43 35.

ST-LAZARE

Église St-Augustin – Closed Sunday afternoon; national holidays; throughout the school holidays and the first fortnight in July.

Chapelle Expiatoire – Open Wednesday from 10am (9.30am from 1 April to 30 September) to 1pm and from 2pm to 4pm, 5pm or 6pm depending the time of year. ☎ 01 48 09 83 54.

Musée Gustave-Moreau – Open 11am to 5.15pm Monday and Wednesday; 10am to 12.45pm Thursday to Sunday and from 2pm to 5.15pm. Closed Tuesday; 1 January and 25 December. 20F. ☎ 01 48 74 38 50.

Musée de la Vie Romantique – Open 10am to 5.45pm Tuesday to Sunday. Closed public holidays. 17,50F. ☎ 01 48 74 95 38.

TROCADÉRO

Musée de la Marine – Open from 10am to 6pm. Closed Tuesday; 1 May. 31F. ☎ 01 45 53 31 70.

Musée de l'Homme – Open from 9.45am to 5.15pm. Closed Tuesday and holidays. 25F. ☎ 01 44 05 72 72.

Musée National des Monuments Français – &. Open from 10am to 6pm. Closed Tuesday. 21F. ☎ 01 44 05 39 05.

Musée du Cinéma-Henri-Langlois – Guided tour (1hr 30min) Wednesday to Sunday at 10am, 11am, 2pm, 3pm, 4pm and 5pm. Closed holidays. 25F. ☎ 01 45 53 74 39.

VAUGIRARD

Pasteur Institute: museum – Guided tour (1hr) between 2pm and 5.30pm. Closed weekends; holidays and throughout August. 15F. ☎ 01 45 68 82 82.

LA VILLETTE

Cité des Sciences et de l'Industrie – &. Open from 10am to 8pm. 45F for a 'Cité-Pass' including access to the **Argonaute** submarine. Recorded information ☎ 01 36 68 29 30; enquiries 01 40 05 70 00; fax 01 40 05 82 35; Minitel 3615 VILLETTE.

Cité des enfants – 20F.

Médiathèque – 10am – 8pm, no charge.

Cité-Géode – Combined ticket 85F. Other combinations (Cité-Cinaxe/Cité-Géode-Cinaxe) available enquire on site. Closed Monday; 1 May; 25 December.

La Géode – Screenings every hour between 10am and 9pm. Closed Monday except holidays – subject to confirmation. 55F. General information ☎ 01 40 03 75 03; Ticket office ☎ 01 36 68 29 30.

Cinaxe – Sessions every 15min between 11am and 6pm. Closed Monday. 33F. ☎ 01 36 68 29 30.

Musée de la Musique – Open 12noon to 6pm (9.30pm Thursday); 10am to 6pm Sunday. Closed Monday. *Fee to be confirmed.* General information ☎ 01 44 84 46 00; advanced group visits ☎ 01 44 84 46 46.

EXCURSIONS

Cathédrale St-Denis – Open daily, 10am (12noon Sunday) to 6.30pm (4.30 from October to March). Closed 1 January, 1 May, 11 November, 25 December. 26F. ☎ 01 48 09 83 54.

Château de Versailles – &. Tour of the Grands Appartements and the Chapelle Royale from 9am to 6.30pm (5.30pm from 1 October to 30 April); 40F. Guided tours of the Appartements du Roi and the Opéra Royal from 9.30am to 4pm. 25F.

Parks and gardens – The fountains play to background music every Sunday from early May to early October at 3.30pm. ☎ 01 39 50 36 22.

Disneyland Paris – &. Open daily July to August 9am to 11pm. Rest of the year daily from 9am or 10am to 6pm or 8pm depending on season. Disneyland passes (prices vary with the season): One day: 195-150F (adult), 150-120F (3-11yrs). Two days (not necessarily consecutive): 370-285F (adult), 285-230F (child). Three days (not necessarily consecutive): 505-390F (adult), 390-310F (child). Free for children under 3 years. Parking 40F. ☎ 01 60 30 60 30.

Glossary

Basic vocabulary

oui/non	yes/no	grand	big
s'il vous plaît	please	quand?	when?
merci	thank you	pourquoi?	why?
bonjour	hello/good morning	avec	with
au revoir	goodbye	sans	without
excusez-moi	excuse-me	aéroport	airport
pardon, excusez-moi	I am sorry, excuse-me	la gare	the station
petit	small	un billet (d'avion, de train, d'entrée)	a ticket (aeroplane, train, entrance)

Numbers

1	un	13	treize	70	soixante-dix
2	deux	14	quatorze	80	quatre-vingt
3	trois	15	quinze	90	quatre-vingt-dix
4	quatre	16	seize	100	cent
5	cinq	17	dix-sept	200	deux cents
6	six	18	dix-huit	1000	mille
7	sept	19	dix-neuf	premier	first
8	huit	20	vingt	deuxième	second
9	neuf	30	trente	troisième	third
10	dix	40	quarante	quatrième	fourth
11	onze	50	cinquante	cinquième	fifth
12	douze	60	soixante	sixième	sixth

Time, days of the week and seasons

1.15		1.45	
une heure et quart	one fifteen	deux heure moins le quart	a quarter to two
1.30			
une heure et demie	one thirty		
matin	morning	Mercredi	Wednesday
aprés-midi	afternoon	Jeudi	Thursday
soir	evening	Vendredi	Friday
hier	yesterday	Samedi	Saturday
aujourd'hui	today	Dimanche	Sunday
demain	tomorrow	hiver	winter
une semaine	a week	printemps	spring
Lundi	Monday	été	summer
Mardi	Tuesday	automne	autumn/fall

Sightseeing and orientation

fermé	closed	Ouest	west	vestiaire	cloakroom, coats and bags depositary
ouvert	open	une vue	a view		
droite	right	étage	floor		
gauche	left	tirer	pull	ascenseur	lift
Nord	north	pousser	push	fauteuil-	
Sud	south	lumière	light	roulant	wheel-chair
Est	east	escalier	stairway	les toilette	WC facilities

Food and drink

une assiette	a plate	du jambon cru	ham cured
un couteau	a knife	(cuit / de Paris)	(cooked/roasted)
une fourchette	a fork	du poulet	chicken
une cuillère	a spoon	du poisson	fish
la nourriture	food	des œufs	eggs
un plat végétarien	a vegetarian dish	des légumes	vegetables
un verre	a glass	du beurre	butter
de l'eau	water	du fromage	cheese
du vin rouge	red wine	un dessert	a dessert
du vin blanc	white wine	des fruits	fruit
une bière	a beer	un yaourt	a yoghurt
de la viande	meat	le / du sucre	the / some sugar
du bœuf	beef	le sel	salt
du porc	pork	le poivre	pepper
de l'agneau	lamb	la moutarde	mustard

Shopping

un magasin	a shop	un bouquet	a bunch
la poste	a post office	une boulangerie	a baker's
des timbres	stamps	du pain	bread
une boucherie	a butcher's	un pain complet	wholemeal (brown) bread
une pharmacie	a chemist's		
sirop pour la toux	cough mixture	un supermarché	a supermaket
cachets pour la gorge	sore throat tablets	un libraire	a bookseller
		le journal	a newspaper
un marchand de fleurs	a flower seller, florist	une poissonnerie	a fishmonger

Urban sites

une église	a church	un beffroi	a belfry
la mairie, l'hôtel de ville	the townhall	une place	a square
un hôtel	a town house or mansion	un jardin	a garden
		un parc	a park
une banque	a bank	un marché	a market
une maison	a house	une rue	a street
un château	a castle	une statue	a statue
une chapelle	a chapel	un pont	a bridge
une abbaye	an abbey	un quai	a quay
une cour	a courtyard	un port	a port/harbour
un moulin	a windmill	un cimetière	a cemetery
un musée	a museum	un passage clouté	pedestrian or zebra crossing
une tour	a tower		

Natural sites

une rivière	a river	le bois	the wood
un lac	a lake	une forêt	a forest
un belvédère	a viewpoint	un barrage	a dam
une cascade	a waterfall		

On the road

un péage	a toll	un phare	headlight
une autoroute	a motorway/highway	le parebrise	the windscreen
		le moteur	the engine
un permis de conduire	driving licence	sens unique	one way street
un garage	a garage (for repairs)	le carrefour	the cross roads
		les feux	(traffic) lights
au parking	in the car-park	le centre-ville	the city centre
essence	petrol/gas	la banlieue	the suburbs
station essence	petrol station	parking souterrain	underground parking
un pneu	a tyre		

Useful phrases

Parlez-vous anglais?	Do you speak English?
Je ne comprends pas.	I do not understand.
Parlez lentement.	speak slowly.
Où sont les toilettes?	Where are the toilets?
Où est....?	Where's....?
A quelle heure part...?	At what time does the...leave?
A quelle heure arrive...?	At what time does the... arrive?
Combien cela coûte?	What does it cost?
Où puis-je acheter un journal en anglais?	Where can I buy a newspaper in English?
Où se trouve la station essence la plus proche?	Where is the nearest petrol station?
Où puis-je échanger des traveller's cheques?	Where can I change traveller's cheques?
Entrez!	Come in!
Est-ce que vous acceptez les cartes de credits?	Do you accept credit cards?
Est-ce que ce bus / train va à (Montmartre)?	Does this bus / train go to (Montmartre)?
Tarif réduit enfant / troisième âge.	Reduced rate, child / over 60s
Avez-vous une chambre pour la nuit?	Do you have a room for the night?
Une chambre simple / double / à deux lits ?	A single / double / twin room?
Avec baignoire / douche?	With bath / shower?

351

Index

354

MANUFACTURE FRANÇAISE DES PNEUMATIQUES MICHELIN
Société en commandite par actions au capital de 2 000 000 000 de francs
Place des Carmes-Déchaux – 63 Clermont-Ferrand (France)
R.C.S. Clermont-Fd B 855 200 507
© Michelin et Cie, Propriétaires-Éditeurs 1996
Dépôt légal mai 1996 - ISBN 2-06-135503-X - ISSN 0763-1383

Printed in the EC 05-96

Photocomposition : EURONUMÉRIQUE, Montrouge
Impression et brochage : CASTERMAN, Tournai (Belgique)

Illustration de la couverture par Alain SAGUEZ/Grégoire CIRADE

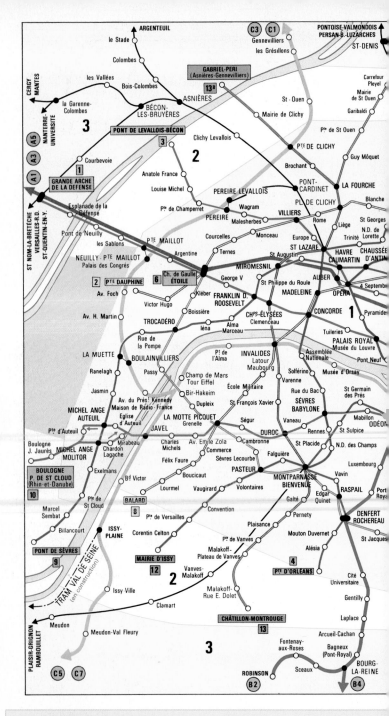

The Michelin Paris Index-Plan n° 11:

A practical aid for exploring in Paris

A complete street index

A complete plan of the city:
    one-way streets, administrative boundaries, public buildings, car parks,
    underground (métro) stations and taxi ranks

Useful addresses:
    Public Services: government organisations, embassies and consulates,
    General: business, religion, education, health, shows, sports, tourism,
    transport...

The most important telephone numbers

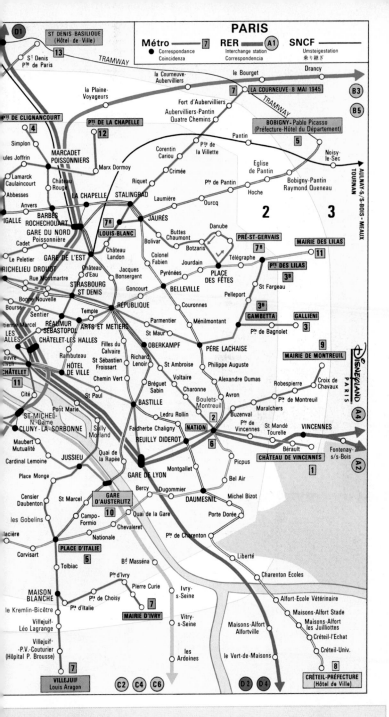

Plan of the underground, the urban rail network (RER) and the bus routes

The following detailed maps:

> La Défense
> Bois de Boulogne
> Bois de Vincennes
> Orly airport and Charles-de-Gaulle airport
> Rungis Market
> Garonor
> Genevilliers port

For an explanation of how the public transport system works, see pp. 330-331.

MICHELIN®

32, avenue de l'Opéra
75002 Paris

Open
Tuesday to Saturday
from 10 am to 7 pm
and Monday from noon to 7 pm

Bibendum by Michelin
Tel: 42 68 05 00

The Map and Guide Boutique
Tel: 42 68 05 20

Fax: 47 42 10 50

Metro station: Opéra